AGING

AGING

Volume I
Abandonment — Injuries among the elderly

Editor
Pamela Roberts, Ph.D.
California State University, Long Beach

Project Editor
Tracy Irons-Georges

SALEM PRESS, INC.
Pasadena, California   Hackensack, New Jersey

Editor in Chief: Dawn P. Dawson
Copy Editor: Douglas Long
Research Supervisor: Jeffry Jensen
Acquisitions/Photograph Editor: Mark Rehn
Production Editor: Joyce I. Buchea

Project Editor: Tracy Irons-Georges
Assistant Editor: Andrea E. Miller
Research Assistant: Jun Ohnuki
Assistant Photograph Editor: Philip Bader
Layout: William Zimmerman

Note to Readers

The medical material presented in *Aging* is intended for broad informational and educational purposes. Readers who suspect that they suffer from any of the physical or psychological disorders, diseases, or conditions described in this set should contact a physician without delay; this work should not be used as a substitute for professional diagnosis or treatment. This set is not to be considered definitive on the medical topics covered, and readers should remember that the field of health care is characterized by a diversity of opinions and constant expansion in knowledge and understanding.

Library of Congress Cataloging-in-Publication Data

Aging / editor, Pamela Roberts.
    p. cm.
    Includes bibliographical references and index.
    ISBN 0-89356-265-3 (set : alk. paper) — ISBN 0-89356-266-1 (v. 1 : alk. paper) —
ISBN 0-89356-267-x (v. 2 : alk. paper)
    1. Aged—Encyclopedias. 2. Aging—Encyclopedias. I. Roberts, Pamela, 1952-

HQ1061 .A42453 2000
305.26'03—dc21   99-088984

First Printing

PRINTED IN THE UNITED STATES OF AMERICA

PUBLISHER'S NOTE

In 1997, the oldest members of the baby-boom generation turned fifty. As the "graying of America" continues to shift demographics, increasing attention has been focused on what it means to grow older in the United States, both for society and for individuals. What is the impact on politics and the workforce? What is the effect on families, health care decisions, and housing options? Can the aging process be slowed or even stopped? Who decides what is considered "old"? How does someone come to grips with the myriad changes that accompany advancing years?

Aging approaches these questions from multiple perspectives, providing coverage of sociocultural issues, physical changes, health concerns, medical procedures, family dynamics, financial and employment issues, legislation and court cases, organizations and programs, the media, and prominent people. Its interdisciplinary approach will attract wide interest among the general public and students or teachers in the fields of gerontology, biology, medicine, family studies, human development, sociology, and psychology. Although aging is a phenomenon that occurs throughout the life span, for the purposes of this encyclopedia it is narrowed to the range from "middle age" to "old age"—even as its essays seek to define these terms. The broad array of topics charts the experience of aging in the United States. The set is illustrated with more than 225 photographs, medical drawings, tables, and graphs.

The 319 entries in *Aging*, ranging in length from 300 to 4,000 words, are presented in an alphabetical format for ease of access. Thirty-three articles address important social issues that arise in the last half of life, from "Senior citizen centers" and "Vacations and travel" to "Nursing and convalescent homes" and "Elder abuse." Seventeen entries cover cultural attitudes and groups, such as the experience of older "African Americans" or the changing definition of "Beauty" with age. Twelve articles discuss such crucial employment issues as "Age discrimination," "Retirement," and "Volunteering." Twenty-four entries examine aging from the perspective of the family with such topics as the "Cohabitation" of elders, the impact of "Death of parents" on those in midlife, and the struggles of "Widows and widowers." Fourteen essays explain the importance of such financial issues as "Discounts," "Fraud against the elderly," "Life insurance," and "Pensions."

In 112 entries, the physical changes that occur with the aging process, and the health concerns that follow, are addressed. Diseases and disorders that often strike in middle age or later, such as "Arthritis," "Cataracts," and "Emphysema," are discussed, as are natural conditions such as "Gray hair" and "Wrinkles." Some of the therapies and procedures used to counteract or hide the effects of increasing age are also examined. Such end-of-life issues as "Hospice," "Euthanasia," and "Living wills" receive attention. Also addressed are nineteen crucial psychological issues, including "Alzheimer's disease," "Memory changes and loss," "Midlife crisis," and "Wisdom."

Ten articles cover significant legislation and court cases pertaining to elders, and twenty-one programs and organizations devoted to the rights and well-being of older people are profiled, such as the "American Association of Retired Persons (AARP)" and "Social Security." Fifty-one articles examine the image of aging in literature, advertising, and other forms of media through overviews and descriptions of books, plays, films, and television shows. Finally, six entries provide information about such people as Erik Erikson and Elisabeth Kübler-Ross.

The encyclopedic format of *Aging* enables readers to find information about subjects both large and small. For example, readers seeking information about the living conditions of older people may begin with the overview article "Housing" and then turn to articles on more specific issues, including "Home ownership," "Independent living," "Relocation," and "Retirement communities." They will also find essays on related programs such as "Home services" and "Meals-on-wheels programs" and legislation such as the "Older Americans Act of 1965."

Each article begins with easily accessible ready-reference listings of important information such as authors, directors, cast members, and dates, where appropriate. Every article identifies the issues relevant to the topic and then defines the significance of the entry to aging in general. Every entry carries an author byline, and each article lists cross-references to other articles in the set. Finally, articles of 1,500 words or more conclude with a bibliography, and those of 2,500 words or more include annotations.

In the front of each volume appears an Alphabetical List of Entries for all topics in the encyclopedia, and a List of Entries by Category can be found in the back of both volumes. Volume 2 contains four appendices: a general Bibliography of nonfiction works, divided into subject categories; a Mediagraphy of novels, short stories, plays, films, television shows, and songs that address the experience of aging; a select listing of Resources, organizations and programs designed to help older people and those who care for and about them; and Notable People in the Study or Image of Aging, individuals who researched the sociological and physical aspects of aging or who achieved success later in life or as representatives of the elder population. A comprehensive Index of concepts, organizations, names, and events, with cross-references, concludes the encyclopedia.

We would like to thank the many authors who devoted their time and talents to this project; a complete list of writers and their affiliations appears in the front of Volume 1. We particularly wish to acknowledge the expertise and advice of the Editor, Pamela Roberts of California State University, Long Beach. The generous contributions of these individuals made this encyclopedia possible.

INTRODUCTION

In 1976, when I decided to study aging in graduate school, the most common reaction was "Why?" which was frequently followed by "How depressing." At that time, the field was in its infancy—most of the original researchers in gerontology were still alive, there were only a handful of professional journals, media coverage of aging issues was rare, and discussions of aging inevitably led to stories of nursing homes and dementia. How things have changed. Now, a seventy-seven-year-old has traveled in space to the delight of an adoring nation, aging is a frequent topic in news reports and other media, there are over one hundred professional journals, and students who decide to study aging are rarely asked to defend their choice; it seems that aging is everywhere.

There are many reasons for the increased interest in aging, but two of the driving forces have been the graying of the population and advancements in medicine and health sciences.

In June, 1999, the mean age of Americans was at a historical peak of 36.4, and with the aging of the baby boomers (the largest generation in the population), the mean age is predicted to rise for several years. As it has throughout its history, the baby-boom generation continues to affect the economy and sensibilities of the nation; as they pass through midlife into old age, there is a greater demand for aging-related goods and services and more dialogue about aging issues.

A second reason for the heightened interest in aging stems from advances in medicine and an increased understanding of nutrition, exercise, and lifestyle which have created a healthier and more productive midlife and old age for many adults. These advancements have made the declines once associated with aging less predictable, and have given the individual more control over the aging process. Correspondingly, the presentation of aging has changed dramatically; for example, at the time of this writing, the entire issue of *Modern Maturity* (the magazine of the American Association of Retired Persons) is devoted to sex, with featured articles entitled "Great Sex" and "Who's Sexy Now?" The cover pictures the attractive actress Susan Sarandon in an alluring pose and promises to name the fifty sexiest people over the age of fifty. Throughout the media, images of middle-aged and older adults in athletic events, starring in rock concerts, climbing mountains, and excelling in most professions are becoming common. In short, advances in medicine and health science have increased the number of active, positive role models for middle and late life, and the increased age of the population has heightened the demand for coverage of these models. This encyclopedia is another reflection of how things have changed in the past few decades. Now there is extensive research on a variety of aging issues and tremendous interest in the findings of those studies. Clearly, the time has come for volumes such as these.

Aging should be an important topic to all adults because it is one process that is shared—we all age at the same rate and, provided that we live long enough, all of us will become middle aged and eventually old. Despite progress in research on life extension, the simple dictum remains true—the only way to avoid old age is to die young. However, advancements in medicine and the health sciences have provided more control over how one ages, and it is clear that the decisions made throughout the life span concerning nutrition, exercise, lifestyle, and medical care affect the personal experience of aging. The fact that choices made in adolescence and young adulthood affect the aging process is one of the most significant reasons that not only middle-aged and older adults will be drawn to this encyclopedia, but so should those entering young adulthood. The earlier people understand aging, the more impact they can have on the quality of their own aging experience. Another important reason that aging should be studied by the young is that it enhances understanding of family dynamics and dispels myths about older adults. For example, the depth of grief experienced by one's father upon the death of his elderly, bedridden mother may be difficult to comprehend without some knowledge of the complex relationships between older parents and their middle-aged children. Similarly, most people have more sympathy for older adult drivers when they understand that vision and reaction time change with age.

Aging is complicated. Not only does hair turn gray, weight redistribute itself, and years of wear and tear transform themselves into disability or disease, but the individual interprets these physical changes in the context of cultural, social, and personal experiences. No two people age in exactly the same way. Because of its complexity, the study of aging is conducted by a wide variety of professionals, including anthropologists, psychologists, sociologists, economists, demographers, social workers, historians, and geographers as well as the medical researchers, physiologists, biologists, and nutritionists whose research most often appears on the evening news.

In aging, as in most new fields, the majority of early studies have been descriptive, in this case, describing the conditions and processes that change with age. Much of this research has focused on changes in physical condition and health. Correspondingly, the majority of entries in the current volumes cover health and medical conditions that become more prevalent with age, ranging from strokes to bunions to menopause to specific diseases. These volumes are an excellent first resource for understanding common medical conditions that accompany aging. However, not all age-related changes are physical; other transitions can include a variety of social and personal changes such as remarriage, death of parents, the responsibility for raising grandchildren, age discrimination, and memory change. Because personal and social changes can be as transforming as any medical condition, their inclusion in these volumes is crucial.

Although a preponderance of the research has studied changes that accompany aging, those transitions do not take place in a vacuum—actions, services, and remedies that improve the lives of middle-aged and older adults are positive aspects of aging in this society. Accordingly, entries discuss existing legislation, political activities like advocacy and voting, government programs such as Social Security and Medicare, and community resources including senior centers. Furthermore, factors that affect quality of life are covered also, including such diverse topics as prosthetic devices (for example, hearing aids and canes), immunizations, home services, and friendship. The importance of resources that lessen the impact of age-related changes cannot be overstated; in the midst of difficult life changes, solace comes from the awareness that there are support groups for caregivers of Alzheimer's patients, the homebound

can make friends on the Internet, transportation services are available for the visually impaired, and living wills allow the dying control over their last moments.

Aging is a uniquely personal experience which is influenced by the individual, social, cultural, and societal conditions in which one finds oneself. Research indicates that factors such as ethnicity, gender, income, and family circumstances affect various aspects of the aging experience. One aspect is psychological, in which differing circumstances color the perception of events and their contributions to feelings of well-being. For example, the paunch of middle age has a different meaning to the individual who has struggled to achieve goals of prosperity than to the athlete sidelined with a broken bone. Similarly, widowhood is a more enriching experience for those whose cultures dictate clear roles for the grieving spouse and provide a supportive community than for those from cultures where death and grief are hidden. Other aspects are physical and social; for example, health, life expectancy, and social support vary by culture, ethnicity, gender, income, and family circumstances. Because of their importance to the experience of aging, detailed entries on various ethnic groups, family styles, income levels, and the influence of gender are integral parts of this encyclopedia.

The aging experience is not only influenced by unique individual, social, and cultural circumstances but also affected by the shared images of aging portrayed in popular culture. Books, films, television programs, advertising, and humor not only provide factual information on aging but also present role models for and stereotypes about aging which inform personal expectations and provide the backdrop for aging experiences. Most active, healthy, older adults have to contend with birthday cards about being "over the hill," while individuals experiencing health problems often are flooded with books on healthy lifestyles, inspirational videos, and advertisements selling the newest cure for their disease. Popular culture provides a context for aging in society, therefore descriptions of books, films, and television programs as well as discussions of advertising, humor, and greeting cards are included in these volumes.

Thus far, aging has been presented as it is today, including the changes, available resources, and variables that affect the aging experience. Another area of interest, however, is in the future of aging, especially in how aging can be improved. This topic has been addressed in several ways; some suggest that to improve aging, we first must understand why we age. Theories on the causes of aging affect research on prevention and repair and often prescribe behaviors for greater control of aging processes. Consequently, current theories on why we age are covered in these volumes. Another viewpoint suggests that aging can be improved simply by adopting a lifestyle that promotes health and well-being. Behaviors that improve the aging experience are discussed in many entries, including those on nutrition, exercise, continuing education, and retirement planning. Coverage of these and other lifestyle issues allows readers of all ages to consider the impact of their current behaviors and to plan for their future aging.

Creating an encyclopedia of aging is a difficult task. The field is broad; aging is studied from a variety of perspectives by numerous disciplines, each with its own theories, heroes, and villains. In addition, knowledge of aging continues to change rapidly; every day there are new research findings, new legislation, and new feats accomplished by older members of society. Despite these challenges, the authors present a detailed, thorough account of aging as we now know it—with all its complexity and variations. Although not every work on aging, famed gerontologist, or role model is covered here, the most widely researched topics within the field and a good representation of works about aging and the individuals associated with aging are discussed in these volumes. No work of similar size could do more. Because of the increasing importance of aging to individuals and society, it is essential to be informed about aging processes. These volumes are an excellent resource for information on specific aging topics and a good starting point for an aging education.

Pamela Roberts, Ph.D.
Associate Professor of Human Development
California State University, Long Beach

CONTRIBUTOR LIST

Steven Abell
The University of Detroit Mercy

Richard Adler
University of Michigan, Dearborn

Oluwatoyin O. Akinwunmi
Muskingum College

Sara Alemán
Northern Arizona University

Mary E. Allen
University of Oklahoma

Ola Allen
University of Mississippi Medical Center

Emily Alward
Independent Scholar

Margaret Anderson
Smith College

P. Michele Arduengo
Morningside College

Bryan C. Auday
Gordon College

Ann Stewart Balakier
University of South Dakota

Carl L. Bankston III
Tulane University

Amanda Smith Barusch
University of Utah

Janet C. Benavente
University of Guam

Mary L. Bender
University of Nebraska at Omaha

Bezaleel S. Benjamin
University of Kansas

Alvin K. Benson
Brigham Young University

Milton Berman
University of Rochester

R. L. Bernstein
San Francisco State University

Matthew Berria
Independent Scholar

Sue Binkley
Temple University

Margaret Boe Birns
New York University

Barbara R. Bjorklund
Florida Atlantic University

Virginiae Blackmon
Independent Scholar

Elizabeth Ann Bokelman
Southside Regional Medical Center

Prodromos G. Borboroglu
Navy Medical Center, San Diego

Anne L. Botsford
Marist College

Gayle Brosnan-Watters
Vanguard University of Southern California

Lillian Bee Brown
New Mexico State University

Mitzie L. Bryant
St. Louis Board of Education

Fred Buchstein
Dix & Eaton and John Carroll University

James J. Campanella
Montclair State University

Edmund J. Campion
University of Tennessee

Richard K. Caputo
Yeshiva University

Jack Carter
University of New Orleans

Matilda E. Casler
Eastern Nazarene College

Christine R. Catron
St. Mary's University

Ranès C. Chakravorty
University of Virginia

Karen Chapman-Novakofski
University of Illinois

Paul J. Chara, Jr.
Loras College

Francis P. Chinard
New Jersey Medical School

Robert Christenson
California Polytechnic State University

Gail Clark
Louisiana Tech University

Clifford Cockerham
Independent Scholar

Maureen C. Creegan
Dominican College of Blauvelt

Margaret Cruikshank
University of Maine

Sherry Cummings
University of Tennessee

Bruno J. D'Alonzo
New Mexico State University

Brian de Vries
San Francisco State University

Shawkat Dhanani
West Los Angeles VAMC

Linda M. Dougherty
Piedmont Geriatric Hospital

Kristen L. Easton
Valparaiso University

John W. Engel
University of Hawaii

Meika A. Fang
VA Medical Center West Los Angeles

Cathleen Jo Faruque
Winona State University, Rochester Center

Mary C. Fields
Medical University of South Carolina

Kimberly Y. Z. Forrest
Slippery Rock University

Roxanne Friedenfels
Drew University

Gloria Fulton
Humboldt State University

Roger G. Gaddis
Gardner-Webb University

Colleen Galambos
University of Tennessee

Soraya Ghayourmanesh
Nassau Community College

Karl Giberson
Eastern Nazarene College

Irene N. Gillum
Maine Hospice Council

Daniel G. Graetzer
University of Washington Medical Center

Hans G. Graetzer
South Dakota State University

Gregory D. Gross
The College of Saint Rose

Michael Haas
California State University at Fullerton

Ronald C. Hamdy
East Tennessee State University

Susan E. Hamilton
Independent Scholar

Mazharul Haque
University of Southern Mississippi

Roger D. Hardaway
Northwestern Oklahoma State University

Linda Hart
Independent Scholar

Joan Hashimi
University of Missouri, St. Louis

Robert M. Hawthorne, Jr.
Independent Scholar

Celia Ray Hayhoe
University of Kentucky

Carol A. Heintzelman
Millersville University

Thomas E. Heinzen
William Paterson University

Peter B. Heller
Manhattan College

Patricia I. Hogan
Northern Michigan University

Mary Ann Holbein-Jenny
Slippery Rock University

Beverley E. Holland
Bellarmine College

David Wason Hollar, Jr.
Rockingham Community College

Betsy B. Holli
Dominican University

Howard L. Hosick
Washington State University

Jennifer J. Hostutler
University of Akron

Mary Hurd
East Tennessee State University

Raymond Pierre Hylton
Virginia Union University

Robert Jacobs
Central Washington University

Kristine Kleptach Jamieson
Ashland University

Albert C. Jensen
Central Florida Community College

Virginia W. Junk
University of Idaho

Manjit S. Kang
Louisiana State University

Laurence M. Katz
University of North Carolina at Chapel Hill

Mara Kelly-Zukowski
Felician College

Stephen T. Kilpatrick
University of Pittsburgh at Johnstown

Terry J. Knapp
University of Nevada, Las Vegas

Karen Kopera-Frye
University of Akron

Nancy P. Kropf
University of Georgia

Philip E. Lampe
University of the Incarnate Word

Robert Landolfi
Fairleigh Dickinson University

Naomi J. Larsen
Union University

Calvin J. Larson
University of Massachusetts at Boston

Thomas T. Lewis
Mount Senario College

Samuel Liebman
University of Detroit Mercy

Martha Oehmke Loustaunau
New Mexico State University

Joe E. Lunceford
Georgetown College

Courtney H. Lyder
Yale University School of Nursing

Maxine M. McCue
College of Eastern Utah-San Juan Campus

Scott Magnuson-Martinson
South Dakota State University

Janet Mahoney
Monmouth University

Nancy Farm Mannikko
Independent Scholar

Bonita L. Marks
University of North Carolina at Chapel Hill

Charles E. Marske
St. Louis University

Lee Anne Martínez
University of Southern Colorado

Sherri Ward Massey
University of Central Oklahoma

Steve J. Mazurana
University of Northern Colorado

Paul Moglia
St. Joseph's Family Medicine at Clifton

John Monopoli
Slippery Rock University

Robin Kamienny Montvilo
Rhode Island College

Penny Wolfe Moore
Southwestern Adventist University

Rodney C. Mowbray
University of Wisconsin, La Crosse

Donald J. Nash
Colorado State University

Shirley Rhodes Nealy
Texas Southern University

Byron Nelson
West Virginia University

Elizabeth McGhee Nelson
Christian Brothers University

Bryan Ness
Pacific Union College

Jane Cross Norman
Tennessee State University

Gary L. Oden
Sam Houston State University

Cynthia A. Padula
University of Rhode Island

William G. Pagano
St. Joseph's Occupational Health Services

Robert J. Paradowski
Rochester Institute of Technology

Robert L. Patterson
Armstrong Atlantic State University

Paul M. Paulman
University of Nebraska Medical Center

Cheryl Pawlowski
University of Northern Colorado

Linda L. Pierce
Medical College of Ohio

Thomas W. Pierce
Radford University

Nancy A. Piotrowski
University of California, Berkeley

Enid J. Portnoy
Independent Scholar

Frank J. Prerost
Midwestern University

Thomas A. Ramunda
St. Joseph's Hospital and Medical Center

Lillian M. Range
University of Southern Mississippi

David Redburn
Furman University

Phyllis J. Reeder
Olivet Nazarene University

William L. Reinshagen
Independent Scholar

Wendy E. S. Repovich
Eastern Washington University

Betty Richardson
Southern Illinois University, Edwardsville

Pamela Roberts
California State University, Long Beach

Rosellen M. Rosich
University of Alaska—Anchorage

William J. Ryan
Slippery Rock University

Susan L. Sandel
MidState Behavioral Health System

Tulsi B. Saral
University of Houston, Clear Lake

Lisa M. Sardinia
Pacific University

Elizabeth D. Schafer
Independent Scholar

Carolyn L. Scholz
University of Connecticut

Kathleen Schongar
May School

Catherine Schuster
Western Kentucky University

Rebecca Lovell Scott
College of Health Sciences

Rose Secrest
Independent Scholar

Kevin S. Seybold
Grove City College

Peggy Shifflett
Radford University

Jay S. Shivers
University of Connecticut

R. Baird Shuman
University of Illinois at Urbana-Champaign

George F. Shuster
University of New Mexico

Bobbie Siler
Medical College of Ohio

Donald C. Simmons, Jr.
Mississippi Humanities Council

Virginia L. Smerglia
University of Akron

H. David Smith
University of Michigan

Barbara C. Stanley
Independent Scholar

Sharon W. Stark
Monmouth University

C. Turner Steckline
Northeast Louisiana University

Glenn Ellen Starr Stilling
Appalachian State University

Irene Struthers-Rush
Independent Scholar

Wendy L. Stuhldreher
Slippery Rock University

Steven R. Talbot
Independent Scholar

Billie M. Taylor
Independent Scholar

Charlotte Templin
University of Indianapolis

Roberta Tierney
Indiana University-Purdue University

Paul B. Trescott
Southern Illinois University

CONTENTS

ALPHABETICAL LIST OF ENTRIES

AGING

AARP. *See* **AMERICAN ASSOCIATION OF RETIRED PERSONS (AARP).**

ABANDONMENT

RELEVANT ISSUES: Family, psychology, race and ethnicity, sociology

SIGNIFICANCE: Abandonment of elders by family members is a growing problem with complex causes

Elder abandonment, much like the wider category of elder abuse of which it is a part, has been defined in many ways. To achieve some uniformity of definition, in 1985 the American Medical Association defined elder abuse, in part, as a failure to provide care or to perform some act, in either case resulting in harm to a dependent elder. Neglect may be considered a more temporary form of these acts of omission, while abandonment may be considered a more permanent form.

Abandonment is often physically and emotionally disastrous to an elder. Case studies show that dependent elders are often so fearful of abandonment that they may tolerate abusive relationships because of an underlying fear that they will be abandoned if they do not. Yet the effects of abandonment do not stop with the elder, who may be left in a rest home or in varying degrees of isolation, but extend to the abandoning family members, who frequently have to cope with extreme feelings of guilt.

Although the status of elders varies in different racial and ethnic groups within American society, a strong taboo exists against abandonment in nearly all groups. Despite this taboo, researchers have found significant differences among ethnic groups as to the quality and amount of support provided to the elderly by their families. There are also significant differences among these groups as to how much their elderly utilize, or are aware of, available support services in their respective communities. Utilization of services is helpful in reducing the impact of isolation that comes from lessened involvement or complete abandonment by family members.

To help understand the complex factors that lead to abandonment, experts often focus on understanding the nature of dependency in elders. Many causes of dependency have been proposed. Some experts highlight social causes and maintain

that because American culture emphasizes youth, there is often a loss of status and self-esteem that accompanies aging in American society. To counteract these feelings of inadequacy, elders may become overly attached to a strong figure to meet their needs for self-esteem. Critics of this approach have called it a way of "blaming the victim" and, instead, have focused on understanding the perpetrator. This research has revealed that perpetrators frequently find caring for an elder to be a source of great stress.

A typical scenario of abandonment begins when an elder becomes dependent on an adult family member following a stroke or accident. The stress on this family member may become intolerable as the demands of the elder increase with the physical decline. In fact, the elder may view even brief absences of this protective figure as an abandonment. The caretaker must often choose between unpleasant options at this point; meeting personal needs and the needs of other family members must be considered in a decision to distance oneself or continue to care for the elder. Experts have suggested that family counseling or family meetings may be helpful in spreading the burden of care among family members.

—Robert Landolfi

See also Caregiving; Depression; Elder abuse; Family relationships; Loneliness; Multigenerational households; Neglect; Nursing and convalescent homes; Sandwich generation.

ABSENTEEISM

RELEVANT ISSUES: Economics, family, health and medicine, work

SIGNIFICANCE: The aging of the workforce has many different effects on employment. Workers in their fifties and sixties must assist relatives in their seventies and eighties while taking time off for their own health needs

Beginning in the 1990's, American society faced the challenge of providing elder care, a crisis that was likely to intensify when the baby boomers reached their eighth decade in 2025 and beyond. The fastest growing segment of the population was among those eighty-five years and older, the group requiring the most assistance to remain independent. In the late 1990's, only 25 percent of these elderly people were in nursing homes. The other 75 percent were living at home and frequently depended on relatives for help.

TIME OFF FOR ELDER CARE

Family members provide about 80 percent of the care given to the elderly in the United States. Most caregivers are women, and 33 percent of these caregivers work outside the home. Many people do not realize the impact that caring for elderly relatives has on one's career. The "sandwich" generation are those adults who find themselves caught between caring for children and caring for elderly relatives. The impact of these demanding family obligations on employment can be considerable.

It is easy to understand how the demands of work, children, and care of elderly relatives can be overwhelming. These stressors can result in an increase in absenteeism, which can adversely affect productivity. Employees who are frequently distracted by family concerns will not be productive workers. Caregivers may call in sick when they need to take days off to help elderly relatives. Sick days are much more difficult for an employer to manage than planned days off. These effects on the quality and quantity of work only serve to increase the stress that employees feel. Caregivers may also miss opportunities for advancement and training, which will have a negative impact on their careers.

Caregivers may respond to all these forces with increased stress and guilt. They may feel guilty for not performing to their potential at work as well as not being able to care for their elderly relatives as they would like to. It feels like a lose-lose situation.

What is the impact of this problem on the American economy? A large manufacturer with 87,000 employees conducted a survey of its workforce to get an idea of the impact of elder care on absenteeism. It was estimated that 2 percent of the workforce called in sick per year as a result of family needs such as elder care, which meant 1,740 employees called in sick when they were not actually ill. It was estimated that these additional days cost the company $5.5 million annually. A survey in Australia was even more striking on the effect of work and life stress on attendance. It found that 12.5 percent of sick calls were related to family stress and obligations such as elder care, costing the Australian economy an estimated $2.56 billion annually in lost production and replacement work-

ers. Many companies have seen an increase in unscheduled time off, lateness, or leaving early in order to care for elderly relatives.

The cost to the employer is great, but so is the cost on a personal level for many of these caregivers. Workers who experience considerable stress because of elder care are not as productive as they could be. Lack of sleep and family obligations may cause caregivers to get to work late and perform below standard. Morale may suffer as these individuals try to balance the demands of family, work, and elderly relatives. This excessive stress can lead to feelings of inadequacy, anxiety, and depression. Many of these workers will sacrifice their careers in order to care for elderly family members, which can lead to anger about perceived missed opportunities.

TIME OFF FOR HEALTH CARE

In addition to the demands of caring for elderly relatives, the aging worker has personal health problems as well. As larger numbers of workers reach their fifties and sixties, more time off will be needed for their own health needs. Beginning in the fifth decade of life, there is an increased prevalence of chronic diseases such as diabetes mellitus, hypertension, heart disease, chronic lung disease, and malignancies. Many older workers need time off for doctors' appointments, diagnostic tests, therapy, and hospitalization. The result can be negative effects on attendance and job performance.

The association in the U.S. health care system of health benefits with maintaining one's job compounds these problems. Workers who lose their jobs not only lose a source of income and other positive social benefits of work but also lose their health insurance.

THE SEARCH FOR A SOLUTION

Employers are looking for ways to keep down the costs of lost time and to increase productivity. Workers are searching for methods to cope with the many demands placed on them by family and work. As the workforce ages, the demands of family and personal health needs will continue to increase. How can these two seemingly conflicting goals of increasing productivity and increasing family demands be resolved? Two major forces in the workplace are driving a resolution to this problem: the Family and Medical Leave Act of 1993 and competition for skilled workers.

The Family and Medical Leave Act requires that companies with fifty or more employees provide up to twelve weeks of unpaid leave per year for employees. This time can be used either to care for newborn or adopted children or first-degree family members who have serious medical problems or to address the employee's own serious health problems. There is a mechanism to verify the seriousness of the medical condition. The law also requires employees to notify their employers in advance of needed time off, if possible, to minimize disruption of business.

An equally important factor changing the American workplace is the need to attract and retain qualified employees with the high-tech skills necessary in a competitive economic environment. A flexible work schedule that permits an employee to address both personal and professional needs is a benefit for which an increasing number of workers are looking.

The introduction of flexible work practices can result in benefits for both the employer and the employee, including reduced absenteeism, lateness, and stress; expanded employee availability for overtime, travel, shift work, and training; and increased employee motivation and commitment to work. The result will be increased productivity, decreased absenteeism, decreased cost, and retention of valued employees.

The key factors necessary to create a family-friendly work environment are flexibility on the part of the employer and cooperation on the part of the employee. Several strategies have been found to be effective in developing a workplace that is more family-friendly. Flexible work hours permit a worker to accrue time that can be used to meet family needs. Letting an employee work part time on a temporary basis during a time of need can allow the employee to meet the demands of both family and work. Job sharing permits two employees to share a full-time position on a permanent basis. Personal leave permits an employee to take unpaid leave under the Family and Medical Leave Act during a time of need. Telecommuting permits an employee to work from home through technology, allowing greater availability for family needs while meeting the needs of the employer.

Market forces, legislation, and the changing demographics of the workforce all have an impact on employment in ways that will change the work-place. The aging of the workforce will require employers to develop a more flexible and family-friendly work environment in the twenty-first century.
—William G. Pagano

See also Baby boomers; Caregiving; Elder care; Employment; Family relationships; Filial responsibility; Health care; Job loss; Long-term care for the elderly; Medical insurance; Middle age; Midlife crisis; Sandwich generation; Senior citizen centers; Stress and coping skills.

FOR FURTHER INFORMATION:
American Association of Retired Persons. *Working Options: How to Plan Your Job Search, Your Work Life.* Washington, D.C.: Author, 1994.
Barling, Julian, et al. "Predictors and Outcomes of Elder-Care-Based Interrole Conflict." *Psychology and Aging* 9, no. 3 (September, 1994): 391-397.
Hoskins, Irene, ed. *Combining Work and Elder Care: A Challenge for Now and the Future.* Geneva, Switzerland: International Labour Office, 1996.
Marosy, John Paul. *A Manager's Guide to Elder Care and Work.* Westport, Conn.: Quorum Books, 1999.
National Eldercare Institute on Business and Aging, Washington Business Group on Health. *Eldercare in the Workplace: An Annotated Bibliography.* Washington, D.C.: Author, 1993.
Sheley, Elizabeth. "Flexible Work Options: Beyond Nine to Five." *HRMagazine* 41, no. 2 (February, 1996): 52.
Walter, Kate. "Elder Care Obligations: Challenge the Next Generation." *HRMagazine* 41, no. 7 (July, 1996): 98.

ABUSE. *See* **ELDER ABUSE.**

ACQUIRED IMMUNODEFICIENCY SYNDROME (AIDS)

RELEVANT ISSUES: Death, health and medicine, marriage and dating
SIGNIFICANCE: Data from the Centers for Disease Control (CDC) in the 1990's indicated that AIDS was increasing at a significant level in persons over the age of fifty

Acquired immunodeficiency syndrome (AIDS) is the clinical manifestation of the human immunodeficiency virus (HIV). HIV infection is a communicable disease that may be transmitted through sexual contact, blood or blood products, or child-birth. HIV has been found in high concentrations in blood, semen, and female genital secretions and in smaller concentrations in spinal fluid, tears, urine, breast milk, and saliva. To become infected, an individual must come in contact with a body fluid from an infected person.

While the impact of HIV has been widely discussed in gay men and intravenous (IV) drug users, little attention has been given to HIV in older persons. In 1992, the CDC reported a significant increase in the number of older adults who are HIV-positive. The most common mode of transmission of HIV in older adults is blood transfusions; however, sexual contact cannot be overlooked.

MODES OF TRANSMISSION

Transmission of HIV though the blood is accomplished through receipt of blood products or IV drug use. Almost one-fourth of the reported cases of HIV infections occurs in intravenous drug users. In such cases, syringes and needles contaminated with HIV-infected blood are shared by a second person without being cleaned properly. After an infected user injects drugs, any blood left in the syringe may be injected into a second individual. Only a small percentage of older adults, however, contract HIV through intravenous drug use.

Prior to 1985, there was no testing of blood products for HIV antibodies. Many people who received blood products developed HIV infections from contaminated blood products, and some of these people transmitted the virus to others. Since 1985, blood donors have been tested for HIV antibodies prior to the acceptance of blood. This testing has greatly decreased the chance of HIV transmission through blood transfusions.

Another mode of transmission is through the skin. Any time that blood from an HIV-positive person comes in contact with a break in the skin, there is a portal of entry for the virus. Contamination may occur as a result of using surgical or dental instruments that have not been properly sterilized. Accidental puncture of the skin with an HIV-contaminated instrument can also expose an individual to the virus.

Sexual transmission of HIV is through the exchange of body fluids such as semen or vaginal secretions. In homosexual and bisexual men, transmission is generally the result of anal-receptive sexual intercourse and multiple sexual partners. HIV infections, however, are transmitted primarily through heterosexual intercourse. Data from the CDC in the 1990's indicated an 18 percent increase in the incidence of AIDS in persons over the age of forty. Over 10 percent of AIDS cases in the United States are reported as occurring in the fifty and older age group. Not only was there an increase in the number of

AIDS Deaths in the United States, by Age, 1982-1995

305,843 Deaths

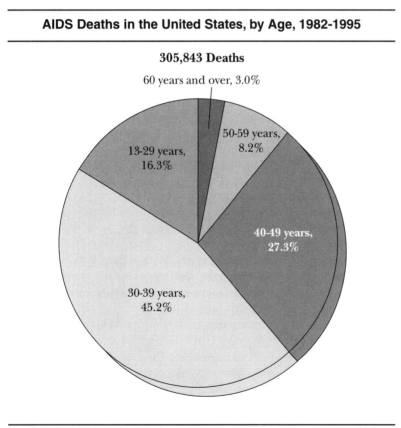

Source: U.S. Bureau of the Census, *Statistical Abstract of the United States: 1997.* Washington, D.C.: GPO, 1997.

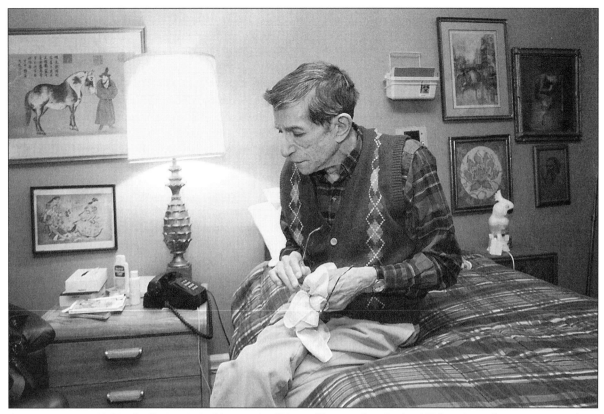

Seventy-six-year-old Charles Borin sits in his room in Chicago House, a hospice for AIDS patients. Better treatments have resulted in more older individuals living with this disease. (AP Photo/Beth A. Keiser)

older adults with HIV but there was a dramatic increase in older women as well. In 1990, the number of women reported to have contracted HIV increased by 34 percent. In 1992, 25 percent of HIV-positive people age sixty or older were women. Epidemiologists at the CDC suggested that the number of older adults may be significantly higher, however, as a result of underreporting, particularly in older women who may not seem at risk.

STAGES

During all stages of HIV infection, whether a diagnosis is known or unknown, the virus can be transmitted to others. A 1992 article by S. Ferro and I. Salit suggested that the transmission of HIV is more rapid in adults who are middle aged or older and that death following the diagnosis of AIDS is also more rapid in these individuals.

During the initial infection phase, the individual feels well and symptoms may be subtle. Flulike symptoms such as fatigue, headache, fever, and sweating may occur. A blood test containing HIV antibodies is the only way to determine the diagnosis during the initial phase.

During the intermediate stage, the symptoms continue to be vague or may be more serious. The individual may complain of diarrhea, fatigue, or swollen lymph nodes. Visual deficits and confusion may also occur. The individual may continue to feel healthy during this stage.

During the AIDS stage, the individual develops dementia as a result of the virus. In older adults, the dementia may be mistakenly diagnosed as Alzheimer's disease. Immune system compromise during this stage may lead to a multitude of opportunistic fungal, bacterial, and viral infections. Abnormal blood conditions are also reported. Another manifestation of AIDS in the elderly is tumors. The most prevalent tumors are Kaposi's sarcoma and non-Hodgkin's lymphoma. The individual during this stage may look and feel unhealthy and may require extensive caretaking and health care service. Reaching the AIDS stage does not indicate imminent death, however, although death may occur during any of the stages.

PREVENTION STRATEGIES

Prior to March, 1985, the blood products in the United States could be contaminated with HIV. Individuals who received blood products and their sexual partners could be at risk for contracting the virus. Today, strict restrictions are placed on blood products and blood donors, virtually eradicating the risk of transmission via blood products.

Risk reduction strategies must now focus on portals of entry for the HIV organism. Portals of entry include the mucosal linings, skin, vagina, cervix, penis, rectum, mouth, and throat. With the exception of the skin, these portals of entry involve risky sexual behaviors. Few older persons, particularly postmenopausal women, consider condom use because they are no longer concerned with birth control. Older adults, particularly women, need educational programs that openly address the transmission and occurrence of HIV and protective measures that can be used to prevent spread of the infection.

Failure to use a condom may be safe in a monogamous relationship provided that both partners remain monogamous. Older individuals, however, often face lifestyle changes such as the death of a spouse that increase the chance of a new sexual relationship. Older homosexual, bisexual, or heterosexual men during the middle adult years may become sexually involved with younger individuals. Heterosexual men who have lost a spouse may turn to a younger woman or may have multiple sexual partners. Older women, particularly those who have gone through the menopause and no longer fear becoming pregnant, may choose to become sexually active following the loss of a spouse. All these relationships may place the older adult at risk for HIV infection through sexual activity.

Lifestyle changes mandate a modification of sexual behavior. Abstinence, safe alternate sexual practices (such as mutual masturbation or sensual massage), and safe sexual practices (including latex condom use and restricting the number of sexual partners) are effective methods to decrease the potential for contracting HIV. —Ola Allen

See also Death and dying; Gay men and lesbians; Illnesses among the elderly; Sexuality; Terminal illness; Widows and widowers.

FOR FURTHER INFORMATION:
Adler, W., and J. Nagel. "Acquired Immunodeficiency Syndrome in the Elderly." *Drugs and Aging* 4, no. 5 (May, 1994): 410-416.
Blaxhult, A., F. Granath, K. Lindman, and J. Giesecke. "The Influence of Age on the Latency Period of AIDS in People Infected by HIV Through Blood Transfusions." *AIDS* 4, no. 2 (February, 1990): 125-129.
Centers for Disease Control: HIV/AIDS Surveillance Report. Atlanta: Department of Health and Human Services, 1992.
Ferro, S., and I. Salit. "HIV Infection in Patients over Fifty-five Years of Age." *Journal of Acquired Immune Deficiency Syndrome* 5, no. 4 (April, 1992): 348-355.
Ship, J., A. Wolff, and R. Selik. "Epidemiology of Acquired Immune Deficiency Syndrome in Persons Aged Fifty Years or Older." *Journal of Acquired Immune Deficiency Syndrome* 4, no. 1 (January, 1991): 84-88.
Tichy, A., and M. Talashek. "Older Women: Sexually Transmitted Disease and Acquired Immunodeficiency Syndrome." *Nursing Clinics of North America* 27, no. 4 (December, 1992).
Wallace, J., D. Paauw, and D. Spach. "HIV Infections in Older Patients: When to Expect the Unexpected." *Geriatrics* 48, no. 6 (June, 1993): 61-70.

ADA. *See* **AGE DISCRIMINATION ACT OF 1975; AMERICANS WITH DISABILITIES ACT.**

ADEA. *See* **AGE DISCRIMINATION IN EMPLOYMENT ACT OF 1967.**

ADOPTED GRANDPARENTS

RELEVANT ISSUES: Culture, family, values
SIGNIFICANCE: Adopted grandparents are individuals who have been selected to enter into caring relationships with children to whom they are not related by birth or marriage. Such relationships are valuable both to the parents and children and to the adopted grandparent

Some children "adopt" grandparents in nursing homes. Both the older and the younger generation benefit from such interaction. (James L. Shaffer)

The role of adopted grandparent can be a paid position or a voluntary one. These individuals are selected because of their nurturing abilities or for other stable qualities that come from previous experience with parenthood. Parents may seek out adopted grandparents for their children for several reasons. Some families want children to have a relationship with adopted grandparents because the family's own grandparents are deceased or not available. Many younger families want older individuals with parental experience to help care for their children. Others want children to become acquainted with members of an older generation who may also be from a different cultural group. Some parents are looking for a housesitter when the family is away. Adopted grandparents who are middle aged are especially valuable because of their mature outlook but generally better health compared to elder caregivers.

A major advantage of the adopted grandparent relationship is that both parents and adopted grandparents have a choice about whether to accept the relationship and responsibility for the children. Single or working parents have the security of knowing that they have quality child care. The adopted grandparent, who may have been lonely and depressed or simply missing what it is like to play with children, can spend time with young people who care about them too.

—*Lillian Bee Brown*

See also Caregiving; Family relationships; Grandparenthood; Great-grandparenthood; Loneliness; Multigenerational households; Parenthood; Single parenthood; Wisdom.

ADULT EDUCATION

RELEVANT ISSUES: Culture, recreation, values

SIGNIFICANCE: Adults differ from children in their ways of learning and reasons for learning as well as in their ages and physical characteristics

Adult education, as its name suggests, offers learning opportunities to adults. It differs from children's education in at least three respects. First, the age of the students is higher than that of typical students. Second, the participants learn somewhat differently from children and young people. Third, and perhaps most significant, the motivation for learning is typically different in adult students.

AGE AND THE ADULT LEARNER

Aside from age, there are certain characteristics that set apart the older learner. The average person over sixty-five years of age has at least one chronic condition, which may or may not be a limiting factor in lifestyle options. Certain physiologic changes occur with aging. Although these changes do not represent disease states, they can cause the person of later years to modify certain activities. Among the normal changes are decreased elasticity and resilience, slower cell replacement, decreased stamina, altered renal function, and decreased cardiac output. In addition, certain other changes occur in body systems. Along with certain expected changes in physical appearance (such as graying hair, wrinkles, and redistribution of fat), older persons experience changes in reaction time and eye-hand coordination. With age, most persons experience some changes in flexibility and muscle mass, along with joint stiffness caused by connective tissue changes. Most persons over forty require more light for reading and brighter lighting for many tasks. Bladder capacity may change with age. Diseases common in the older population include heart disease, hypertension, arthritis, diabetes, osteoporosis, and depression.

These changes have implications for adult education because they can affect the adult student's participation. However, if adult education programs are properly planned, most older adults can participate. A number of factors should be considered in planning adult education programs for comfort and safety. Classrooms should be easily accessible, with few or no stairs leading to them.

Throw rugs or highly polished floors should not be present, as these present a hazard for falls. Classrooms should be at comfortable temperatures, since most older persons do not accommodate quickly to fluctuations in temperature. Class periods should be no longer than two hours, with breaks scheduled to allow for restroom visits and refreshments. Bathrooms and snack areas should be well marked and easily accessible. Consideration should also be given to presenting programs during daylight hours, as many elders prefer not to drive after dark.

LEARNING AND THE OLDER PERSON

Many ideas exist about the ability of persons to learn in later years. Some people subscribe to the idea that "you can't teach an old dog new tricks." Such notions are often shared by both learners and instructors. Older persons sometimes lack the confidence to attempt a program or course of study because they believe that they are the "old dogs" who cannot learn new tricks. This societal attitude is so pervasive that it affects the self-image of individuals. Some program planners or instructors who believe that it is difficult to teach "new tricks" to the "old dogs" alter their offerings accordingly. The truth is that research has not shown that persons lose intelligence as they age. While the measurement of intelligence is sometimes controversial, the concept that intelligence has many facets is well accepted. The characteristics of older learners may or may not change in some or all facets of intelligence. J. L. Bischof, an adult psychologist, noted that in regard to intelligence, those who start out as clever young people usually end up as wise adults.

Another area of concern regarding older adults and learning is memory. Many persons worry about losing their memory as they get older. Concerns about Alzheimer's disease and senility reinforce these fears. Most studies of memory deal either with short-term or long-term memory. Although myriad studies of memory have been conducted, many have involved settings in which participants were tested by their ability to recall strings of numbers or nonsense words. Studies that test subjects' ability to remember in more realistic scenarios have demonstrated little difference in short-term memory between younger and older subjects. When the memory tasks are related to speed or become more complex, older persons may perform less well than younger persons. Most adults find that their short-term memory occasionally fails them; typically, though, the stresses of daily life, not age, are the cause of such failures.

Long-term memory also is frequently discussed in relation to aging. When information is stored in the long-term memory, it must be encoded much like information entered in a computer. Similarly, for the information to be remembered, it must be retrieved, much as a file is retrieved by a computer. One of the differences shown in research is that it takes older persons longer to store and retrieve information in the long-term memory. An analogy might be made to the differences between older, slower computers and newer, faster models. Older persons may have a slower "processor," hence the reduced speed of storing and retrieving information. They also have years of memory and experience, so that their "hard drives" may be quite full. The speed at which memories can be entered and recalled thus diminishes; however, just as with a slow computer, eventually the information can be processed. It has been shown that older adults who engage in formal memory training can improve their memory skills, and the use of mnemonics and other memory aids is useful not only for high school and college students but for older learners as well.

MOTIVATION AND THE ADULT LEARNER

When asked why they participate in adult learning activities, participants give a variety of answers. Most, however, participate in learning activities simply because they want to do so—unlike younger students, many of whom participate in educational programs under varying degrees of compulsion.

Educational scholar Cyril Houle has identified three types of learners based on their motivation for learning. The first type is the goal-oriented learner who sees education as a means to achieve a goal. An individual who studies to become licensed as a pilot is an example of this type of learner. Sec-

Many older adults find that the challenge of learning new information and skills keeps them in touch with both young people and a changing job market. (James L. Shaffer)

ond are activity-oriented learners. These individuals participate in learning activities for social purposes and for the sake of the activity itself. For example, a recently widowed person who is lonely might enroll in a dancing course to meet other people and to participate in an enjoyable activity. The third type is the learning-oriented learner. These learners seek knowledge for its own sake, for the pure pleasure of learning and acquiring knowledge. For example, retired persons who take courses in art or music appreciation may do so for no other reason than that they have always wished to know more about the subjects. The three types can overlap, as a learner's motivation may be primarily in one area with some lesser degree of one or both of the other motivations.

Adults differ in their motivation also because they seek learning opportunities as needs arise in their lives. As they experience needs and interests that learning will satisfy, they look for appropriate programs or courses.

TYPES OF ADULT LEARNING ACTIVITIES

Adult learners may choose from a wide variety of programs and courses to meet their expressed needs. One of the best-known programs is Elderhostel, a nonprofit organization founded in 1975. Elderhostel annually serves hundreds of thousands of older adult students who travel to programs throughout the world. Adhering to the premise that learning is a lifelong process, Elderhostel programs offer a wide range of experiences. A representative sampling of Elderhostel programs includes courses studying the literature of Jane Austen in the White Mountains of New Hampshire, exploring art and architecture of ancient civilizations in Greece, and conducting field research in Belize to save the endangered dolphin population. Elderhostel programs are offered to people fifty-five and over.

Although somewhat different from Elderhostels, programs for older adults have been developed in many universities. At Ohio State University and the University of Virginia, for example, older adults are invited to take classes for free and to participate in the academic and cultural life of the university. Not only do the older participants benefit from these experiences, but the students also benefit. College-age students have the opportunity to discuss classroom topics with persons who have much more life experience than they and who perhaps have experienced some of the topics being discussed. From the realities of World War II to the struggles of the Civil Rights movement to the difficulties involved in synthesizing antibiotics, older participants bring life and career experiences along with them to the classroom.

Many less formal but equally enriching programs for older learners are offered through community colleges, civic groups, retirement centers, parks and recreation departments, and adult education divisions of public school systems. Localities sponsor lecture series, music appreciation courses, art history programs, and a wealth of courses on other topics for interested adults.

Moreover, learning opportunities for adults have been broadened by the advent of the Internet. Discussion groups, bulletin boards, chat rooms, self-paced learning programs, and distance-learning courses are all available to anyone with access to a computer and on-line service. Older adults are among the fastest-growing groups of computer users. The Internet offers knowledge and information to individuals at their convenience, an important consideration to many older adults with infirmities or other age-related conditions that may otherwise restrict their access to educational services.

SUMMARY

Older learners differ from younger students not only in their age and physical characteristics but also in their styles of learning and their motivation to learn. Adult education offers opportunities not only for formal learning but for informal learning as well. Programs such as Elderhostel, university courses for older adults, and community-based offerings provide the opportunity for any individual to be a lifelong learner.

—Elizabeth Ann Bokelman

See also Communication; Leisure activities; Memory changes and loss; Mentoring; Senior citizen centers; Social ties; Wisdom.

FOR FURTHER INFORMATION:

Brookfield, Stephen D. *Understanding and Facilitating Adult Learning: A Comprehensive Analysis of Principles and Effective Practices.* San Francisco: Jossey-Bass, 1991. An authoritative discussion of issues essential to adult education.

Knowles, Malcolm. *The Adult Learner: A Neglected Species.* 4th ed. Houston: Gulf, 1990. A classic in adult education. Discusses general theories of learning and andragogy, a theory of adult learning.

_____, et al. *The Adult Learner: The Definitive Classic in Adult Education and Human Resource Development.* Houston: Gulf, 1998. Discusses current thinking in adult education and human resource development.

_____. *The Modern Practice of Adult Education: From Pedagogy to Andragogy.* Rev. ed. Englewood Cliffs, N.J.: Prentice Hall Regents, 1988. A complete and practical guide to the theory and practice of adult education.

Merriam, Sharan B., and Rosemary S. Caffarella. *Learning in Adulthood: A Comprehensive Guide.* 2d ed. San Francisco: Jossey-Bass, 1998. A comprehensive overview of adult learning, research, and theories, including the writings of many well-known authorities in the field of adult education.

ADULT PROTECTIVE SERVICES

RELEVANT ISSUES: Family, health and medicine, law, violence

SIGNIFICANCE: Adult Protective Services may be necessary for adults who are unable to provide care for themselves or who do not have a significant other who might provide it

Adult Protective Services (APS) are human services funded by the U.S. government that often include social, medical, legal, and custodial care. People requiring APS are vulnerable to being harmed by or to inflicting harm on others. Such people are often incapable of acting appropriately on their own behalf.

A social agency or other care facility provides the relevant service, after a legal decision has been made, until the service is no longer viewed as necessary. Guardians are made responsible for the care, comfort, and maintenance of a ward, and conservators are appointed to manage the ward's estate and to ensure oversight and accountability. Power of attorney is typically given to authorize a guardian to manage the ward's affairs, including the power to sign documents and conduct transactions on the ward's behalf. A durable power of attorney is not affected by a ward's subsequent incapacity. When wards receive Social Security benefits

or other income, representative payees must be identified.

The Social Services Block Grant Act of 1981 and the Older Americans Act of 1965 authorized and funded APS at the federal level. Most service activities are handled through state or county service systems. In addition, the 1975 Title XX legislation mandated that APS be provided without regard to a person's financial or residential eligibility.

—*Carol A. Heintzelman*

See also Abandonment; Alzheimer's disease; Caregiving; Dementia; Disabilities; Durable power of attorney; Elder abuse; Estates and inheritance; Family relationships; Fraud against the elderly; Home services; Homelessness; Long-term care for the elderly; Mental impairment; Neglect; Nursing and convalescent homes; Older Americans Act of 1965; Poverty; Psychiatry, geriatric; Violent crime against the elderly.

ADVERTISING

RELEVANT ISSUES: Culture, economics, media, psychology

SIGNIFICANCE: In the late 1990's, people aged fifty-five and older represented one-third of households in the United States and constituted a significant and influential segment of the consumer market

In 1987, while it was projected that the total U.S. population would grow only 19 percent by 2015, the mature market (those aged fifty-five and older) was expected to grow by 62 percent. Even though the average income of households headed by those fifty-five or older was somewhat less than that of average U.S. households, these households owned a far greater share of financial assets and discretionary income. Discretionary income is defined as money that consumers have left after paying taxes, grocery bills, mortgages, and other essentials. In the late 1990's, the poverty rate among the older Americans was low, with only 14 percent living below the poverty level. Households headed by persons aged seventy-five or older accounted for more than 17 percent of total discretionary income in the country, even though this group accounted for only 6 percent of the population. Half of the nation's total discretionary income accrued to households of those aged fifty and older, while only a fifth was held by those under thirty-five.

It is, therefore, important to examine how advertisers have traditionally attempted to attract this sizable and increasing segment of the population and what images they have projected of the elderly in their advertisements. It has been suggested that advertising has the ability to play an important role in the socialization of the elderly and influencing younger audiences' view of them. Socialization to old age involves learning to behave in new roles in the context of loss of old familiar ones and the loss of reference groups.

According to a 1987 article by W. Lazer and E. H. Shaw entitled "How Older Americans Spend Their Money," some marketing specialists divide the older consumer market into four segments: the "older" population (fifty-five to sixty-four), the "elderly" (sixty-five to seventy-four), the "aged" (seventy-five to eighty-four), and the "very old" (eighty-five and older). According to J. J. Burnett's 1991 article "Examining the Media Habits of the Affluent Elderly," others segment older Americans by labeling the same categories as the "young-old," the "middle-old," the "senior sector," and the "very old." Age-based segmentation in advertising is regarded by some people as an unsatisfactory approach. Instead, they suggest that income, education, personality types, values, and lifestyles should be taken into account by advertisers. Many believe that cognitive age—how one feels or thinks about oneself—is more important than chronological age because purchase and consumption behavior is often driven by perceptions of age and value-sensitivity of products. D. B. Wolfe notes in his 1987 article "The Ageless Market" that most older respondents to surveys claim to feel 20 to 25 percent younger than their chronological age.

OLDER INDIVIDUALS IN TELEVISION COMMERCIALS

In the 1970's, the number and proportion of older characters on television did not correspond to that in the population. A study of network prime-time television dramas sampled between 1969 and 1971 found only 4.9 percent of the characters to be older, about half of their share of the real population. Moreover, aging in prime-time dramas was associated with evil, failure, and unhappiness. In 1977, Al Harris and J. F. Feinberg examined not only prime-time shows but also news, game shows, children's programs, and commer-

cials. Their analysis of commercials indicated that about 11 percent of characters were older, a figure close to the proportion in the real population, but there was a preponderance of men. Close to 70 percent of characters in advertisements giving advice were older men in the sixty-to-seventy age group.

In the 1980's, a noteworthy change in the image of the elderly on television began. In a study of popular television shows in the early 1990's with older central characters, including *Murder, She Wrote, The Golden Girls, Matlock, Jake and the Fatman,* and *In the Heat of the Night,* J. Bell found that many of these characters held powerful and authoritative positions—murder investigator, police chief, lawyer, schoolteacher—and contributed to the well-being of the community. They were healthy, active, quick-witted, and humorous, and they commanded respect and admiration. Commercials, however, continued to reveal negative patterns in their portrayal of the elderly. In a 1983 article, R. Hiemstra and colleagues analyzed commercials on network television and concluded that only 3.1 percent contained characters over the age of sixty and that older women accounted for less than 1 percent of the characters. In addition, the elderly were presented as "young-old" with no noticeable physical characteristics of aging, such as baldness or wrinkled skin. There were very few older African Americans in the commercials. Commercial messages directed toward older people were related to health products, food, consumer services, and household products.

The main target audience for television is viewers aged eighteen to forty-nine. However, the proportion of advertisements that target the older market is greater than that of this segment of the population. The older market is targeted through general-interest media advertising, with most products related to health (85 percent). Researchers have found that most viewing by older viewers occurs during prime time and that commercials are especially helpful in purchase decisions of the older segment of the audience. In 1995, T. E. Robinson, R. Duet, and T. V. Smith examined prime-time commercials on the American Broadcasting Company (ABC), Columbia Broadcasting System (CBS), National Broadcasting Company (NBC), and Fox networks and found that almost 12 percent of the commercials had older persons in them (aged sixty-five or older). They also found that commercials with older men outnumbered those with older women, that older men appeared more frequently in major roles than older women did, and that as a group, older individuals were frequently part of the background or were neutral characters. About 30 percent of the older characters played the role of advisers, with a few being assigned humorous roles (13 percent). A small number (4 percent) were portrayed as feeble or confused. The researchers also noticed a transgenerational approach in commercials. Advertisers believe that the presence of multiple age groups enhances the appeal of the commercial messages to different segments of the population. A significant finding indicates that more than 90 percent of older characters were presented in a positive manner, without negative stereotyping. Stereotyping is defined by the Gray Panthers, an activist group for the elderly, as oversimplified opinions, unethical judgment, and exaggerated beliefs about a group based on misconception or overcategorization.

A subsequent study of portrayals of older people by Robinson found that older persons accounted for only 5.4 percent of the total number of people in television commercials in 1996. However, 16 percent of the commercials had at least one older individual in them. The representation was somewhat different in the print media, at 9 and 8 percent for magazines and newspapers, respectively. The overall percentage for media was 12 percent, a figure close to the proportion of older people in the U.S. population at the time.

A closer look at the advertisements indicated that only 16 percent of television commercials targeted the older market, as compared to 23 percent for magazines and 17 percent for newspapers. Robinson's 1996 study found that 73 percent of older characters in magazines and 72 percent in newspaper advertisements were male; in television commercials, the percentage of older men was 67 percent. This gender difference is noteworthy, especially in view of the fact that women, on average, live six to seven years longer than men. The inability or unwillingness of advertisers to represent older women may suggest a lack of understanding of the older market, although it may also reflect the lower discretionary incomes of many elderly women.

OLDER INDIVIDUALS IN PRINT ADVERTISING

Print media advertisements tend to follow similar patterns of portrayal as television. A study conducted by Smith in 1976 examined advertisements in journals in the medical field, such as *Medical Economics* and *Geriatrics*. It found that characters were almost always white, more often male (58 percent), and active at leisure and home (36 percent). Only a few inactive or disabled characters were shown. Nevertheless, 70 percent of the assertions made about age were negative.

Researchers W. Gantz, H. M. Gartenberg, and C. K. Rainbow examined advertisements in a variety of major magazines published in 1977, including general interest, news, sports, women's, and men's categories. They found that only 6 percent of the advertisements contained an older person, a clear underrepresentation. There was also a preponderance of men over women. A longitudinal study of advertisements in nine categories of magazines from 1950 to 1980 by the Ursic family found that only 9 percent of the advertisements had older persons. This thirty-year period showed an increase in the representation of older individuals, but the increase in numbers was not statistically significant. More than half of the characters were shown in prestigious jobs. Men far outnumbered women; they also appeared more frequently in work situations, while women appeared more often in social and family settings. In 1992, a study of magazine advertisements found that 82 percent contained individuals younger than forty-five, but when a product was targeted to the older market, 79 percent of the advertisements contained models over forty-five years of age. The researcher also found that many older characters were presented in a manner that was both undesirable and negatively stereotyped.

ADVERTISING USE BY THE ELDERLY

Some researchers hold that aging has two faces, an optimistic one and one that is pessimistic. The pessimistic view of aging suggests a disadvantaged population of older Americans who are poor, unhealthy, and lonely and who have multiple social and psychological problems. The optimistic view, on the other hand, points to the existence of millions of older Americans who are competent and independent and who enjoy a high quality of life. The elderly market is not homogeneous; it is composed of segments that are different because of the differences in attitudes and values of the elderly, their consumption behaviors, and financial resources. Researchers L. E. Swayne and A. J. Greco suggest that media use and exposure to advertisements can have a significant effect on the socialization process of older individuals.

Researchers have claimed that media seem to serve some basic functions for the elderly. For example, media use tends to supplement or substitute for interpersonal interactions, and it helps them gather content for interpersonal interaction. Media use also helps them form or reinforce self-perceptions and gather information about others' perception of various groups of people. Media can stimulate and challenge the elderly and can help them in networking for mutual support. Media can also help the elderly learn age-appropriate behavior. By providing particular symbolic role models, advertisements can have an impact on the self-perceptions of the elderly and can affect their behavior.

CONCLUSION

In the 1988 article "The Elderly as Communication: The Perceptions of Advertising Practitioners," Greco summarizes the research on the use of elderly persons in advertising by pointing to three perspectives. The first suggests that the elderly have been underrepresented and negatively stereotyped in advertising. This trend changed during the 1980's when the advertisers began to increase the number of the elderly in advertisements and to provide more positive portrayals. The second perspective focuses on the reaction of the elderly to age-based advertising. Since many elderly individuals see themselves as younger than their chronological age, it would seem likely that they would not respond positively to elderly models or spokespersons for advertised products. R. E. Milliman and R. C. Erffmeyer found, however, that even though there was no significant difference in the favorability ratings of young, middle-aged, and old-aged models, there were significant differences in the credibility ratings of younger and older models. The older models were found to be more credible than the younger ones by elderly consumers. The third type of research involved the socialization effects of advertising on the elderly.

Researchers have tried to understand various dimensions of the effectiveness of advertising messages in the mature market. A basic question that needs to be asked is how useful older Americans find commercial messages in making consumer decisions. E. S. Schreiber and D. A. Boyd's survey indicated that 69 percent of elderly respondents saw advertisements in a positive light and believed them to be useful in decision making. Yet, a majority (64 percent) also found them confusing, and 28 percent found them totally useless. Evidently, advertisers need to improve their performance significantly. —*Mazharul Haque*

See also Ageism; Communication; Consumer issues; Fraud against the elderly; Greeting cards; Scams and con artists; Stereotypes; Television.

FOR FURTHER INFORMATION:

Bell, J. "In Search of a Discourse on Aging: The Elderly on Television." *The Gerontologist* 32, no. 3 (1992): 305-311.

Burnett, J. J. "Examining the Media Habits of the Affluent Elderly." *Journal of Advertising Research* 31, no. 5 (October/November, 1991): 33-41.

Gantz, W., H. M. Gartenberg, and C. K. Rainbow. "Approaching Invisibility: The Portrayal of the Elderly in Magazine Advertisements." *Journal of Communication* 30 (1980): 56-60.

Greco, A. J. "The Elderly as Communication: The Perceptions of Advertising Practitioners." *Journal of Advertising Research* 28, no. 3 (1988): 39-46.

Harris, Al, and J. F. Feinberg. "Television and Aging: Is What You See What You Get?" *The Gerontologist* 17, no. 5 (1977): 464-468.

Hiemstra, R., M. Goodman, M. A. Middlemiss, R. Vosco, and N. Ziegler. "How Older Persons Are Portrayed in Television Advertising: Implications for Educators." *Educational Gerontology* 9, nos. 2-3 (1983): 111-122.

Lazer, W., and E. H. Shaw. "How Older Americans Spend Their Money." *American Demographics* 7, no. 3 (1987): 36-41.

Milliman, R. E., and R. C. Erffmeyer. "Improved Advertising Aimed at Seniors." *Journal of Advertising Research* 29, no. 6 (1990): 31-36.

Robinson, T. E., II, R. Duet, and T. V. Smith. "The Elderly in Advertising: A Content Analysis of Prime-Time Television Commercials." In *Proceedings of the 1995 Conference of the American Academy of Advertising*. Waco, Tex.: Baylor University, 1995.

Schreiber, E. S., and D. A. Boyd. "How the Elderly Perceive Television Commercials." *Journal of Communication* 30, no. 1 (1980): 61-70.

Swayne, L. E., and A. J. Greco. "The Portrayal of Old Americans in Television Commercials." *Journal of Advertising* 16, no. 1 (1987): 48-54.

Wolfe, D. B. "The Ageless Market." *American Demographics* 9, no. 7 (July, 1987): 26-29, 55-56.

ADVOCACY

RELEVANT ISSUES: Demographics, economics, health and medicine, law

SIGNIFICANCE: Advocacy helps frame public debate over equal rights for senior citizens by defining priorities, devising solutions to problems of old-age injustices and needs, and arousing and mobilizing government, media, and public support

Advocacy on behalf of the elderly means championing and orchestrating change to benefit the aging and aged. Advocates focus on gaining equal access to society's decisions, benefits, power, and responsibilities. Where institutional abuses, barriers, or obstacles exist, advocates act as agents for change. Governments at all levels have institutionalized advocacy for the elderly through a variety of laws and administrative rules and regulations.

Senior citizen advocates possess certain advantages not enjoyed by other minority groups. For example, since most people will eventually become old, it is easier to gain support. Disadvantages include the realities of death, disabling injury, illness, and limited mobility. Advocacy in the interest of the elderly reflects the diversity of the aging and aged. Not all senior citizens are poor, alone, disabled, and living from one Social Security check to another. Demographers distinguish between the mentally and physically frail elderly and the young-old, the population roughly between sixty-five and seventy-five years old who are still reasonably healthy. Some seniors are "slightly privileged," while others are rich. Many of the "oldest-old" are women who may need supportive services to remain independent. No one leader, group of leaders, or organization speaks for all seniors.

ADVOCACY CAMPAIGNS

A successful advocacy campaign achieves the goals of the advocate and benefits the aging and aged. It delivers the right appeal, message, or story to the right audience at the right time in the right way in the right place. An advocacy campaign consists of two phases: analysis of the problem and development of a resolution strategy.

During the first phase, the advocate determines whether the problem is advocable. Is a large enough number of people affected? Are the dollars involved significant? What groups or opinion leaders will ally themselves with righting the injustice? What is the time frame for achieving the goal? Will the public ignore, resist, or support the solution? Can the advocate win in time? What message will rouse the news media, elected and public officials, and special interest groups? Who would lose the most power, influence, or money, and thus oppose the proposed solution?

The second, or resolution, phase involves targeting individuals or organizations with the power to solve the problem. Tactics are formulated to win over the undecided or opponents. Pressure tactics may include speaking at public hearings and proactively seeking media exposure and editorial support. Other tools in an advocacy group's arsenal include public rallies, petition and letter-writing campaigns, and voter drives. On occasion, advocates picket to dramatize injustices, such as the abuse of seniors in long-term nursing homes. The successful execution of whatever strategy is chosen is equally important.

DEVELOPMENT OF ADVOCACY FOR THE AGING

The idea and practice of old-age pensions dates to 1792, when Thomas Paine argued for creation of a pension system to prevent impoverishment in old age. The first pension system provided half pay to disabled veterans of the Revolutionary War. In 1862, lawmakers created a pension system for Civil War soldiers.

Where possible, the state stayed out of family matters. The common expectation was that families would care for their dependent elderly. In the 1870's, churches in large, industrial cities established homes or almshouses for the indigent elderly. By 1900, a number of counties and states had passed laws requiring families to support dependent family members. In the twentieth century, disgruntled citizens began lobbying for old-age pensions and reform of the social problems afflicting the aged.

Signs at a "Senior Rally" in Indiana demand better living conditions for older Americans. (AP Photo/Tom Strattman)

Activism on behalf of the aging truly began during the 1920's and 1930's. Advocates successfully legitimized the idea of old-age pensions in the public's mind. For example, the Fraternal Order of the Eagles succeeded in establishing the principles of governmental responsibility for old-age security and for offering model legislation to solve problems. The Eagles and other advocacy groups employed publicity, a large and vocal membership, and lobbying to plead their cases. Abraham Epstein, an advocate who founded the American Association for Old-Age Security, coined the term "social security."

No senior citizens' organization had the membership and money to engage in a national-level advocacy movement before the mid-1930's. The economic hardships and dislocations of the Great Depression dramatically demonstrated the need for more favorable federal policies and private pensions for the elderly.

THE 1930'S THROUGH THE 1950'S

The landmark Social Security Act of 1935 established the first-federal agency to serve the elderly and made old-age assistance a right. The act's passage represents the beginning of the federal government's involvement in the lives of senior citizens. A social insurance program, Social Security provides retirement benefits for the elderly. It is probably the most important source of income for older people. Taxes paid by both the worker and the employer generate revenues for the program. Social Security benefits did not begin until 1940 and lagged behind increases in the cost of living. Social Security also had an unintended effect: pushing workers out of the workforce by setting an arbitrary retirement age of sixty-five years.

With the exception of Social Security, advocacy on behalf of the elderly is primarily a post-World War II phenomenon. During the postwar years, major political parties and news media in the United States began to view elderly voters as a separate and distinct constituency with special needs. To represent the rights and interests of the elderly, federal, state, and local governments established such agencies as the Administration on Aging (AoA), a federal program that provides community-based services to senior citizens. Advocacy also intensified as more professionals—attorneys, physicians, and social workers—offered solutions to the problems faced by the elderly.

The decades of the 1940's and 1950's witnessed the development of several organizations, such as the American Association of Retired Persons (AARP), founded by Ethel Percy Andrus. Andrus founded the AARP in 1947 to provide low-cost insurance to the elderly, many of whom were frightened by not knowing what would happen to them in case of accident or illness. The AARP became the largest interest group that emerged during the period. In 1945, the Gerontological Society of America began advocating for the elderly through research. Its members fought for development of a national policy to protect and benefit the elderly. The organization made the problems of the elderly part of the public agenda when it convinced the Social Security Administration to hold the National Conference on Aging in 1950.

THE 1960'S AND 1970'S

By the early 1960's, a nationwide network of senior rights organizations coalesced into a powerful lobby. Intensive lobbying by senior rights organizations paved the way for the legislative victories of the decade—Medicare, the Older Americans Act (OAA), and cost-of-living amendments to the Social Security Act. In 1960, the Democratic Party created a campaign organization called Senior Citizens for Kennedy. The group's creation symbolized the development of elderly voters into a major electoral force worthy of the attention of both Democrats and Republicans. In 1961, labor union leaders and Senior Citizens for Kennedy cofounded the National Council of Senior Citizens to to lobby for passage of Medicare. The 1961 White House Conference on Aging paved the way for the establishment of Medicare and passage of the Older Americans Act.

In 1965, after a long and bitter struggle between the American Medical Association and the AFL-CIO, Medicare became law. Medicare provides a basic health insurance for most Americans aged sixty-five and older. The Older Americans Act was also enacted that year to provide a comprehensive system of community- and home-based care for the elderly. The struggles to enact Medicare and the Older Americans Act helped legitimize senior citizen involvement in the legislative process.

The legislative victories of 1965 encouraged the AARP, the National Council of Senior Citizens, and labor organizations such as the United Auto Workers retirees' organization to leverage even further their large memberships and financial power. On behalf of its tens of millions of members, for example, AARP lobbyists opposed compulsory retirement and advocated higher Social Security benefits. The National Council of Senior Citizens was instrumental in the passage of Medi-

care in the 1960's and in amending Social Security in 1972. During the early 1970's, the Gray Panthers united the aged and youth to foster a new public consciousness of the potentials of elderly people and to offer the elderly greater dignity. The Gray Panthers also advocated elimination of mandatory retirement. A new kind of advocacy group emerged with the creation of the AoA and the National Institute on Aging. These organizations represented the elderly from within the executive branch of government.

The struggle for senior citizen rights—variously called "senior rights," the "senior movement," and the "gray lobby"—reached full stride by the early 1970's. During this period, a coordinated national network of senior advocacy organizations with large memberships proliferated. By joining forces, advocates increased their political influence and their ability to pressure elected officials to vote for legislation benefiting seniors. The 1971 White House Conference on Aging marked another significant event in the struggle for senior citizen rights; advocates could air their grievances and introduce reform proposals with legislators and policymakers listening.

Starting in the mid-1970's, senior rights advocates faced a new challenge: fending off efforts by conservatives such as Presidents Ronald Reagan and George Bush to trim federal old-age entitlements. Many conservatives believed that a Social Security crisis would occur in the near future. Unless reformed, Social Security would drift into bankruptcy. Ways to stem the financial hemorrhaging included privatizing Social Security and reducing benefits. Many people worried that young workers were contributing to a system that would be bankrupt by the time they reached retirement age. Older people were blamed for consuming an increasingly burdensome portion of the federal budget. When President Reagan proposed cutting Social Security benefits, senior rights advocates warned that any elected official who supported cutbacks would lose the support of senior citizen voters. Democratic congressman Claude Pepper, a leading advocate for the aging, described the proposed cuts as a breach of faith against senior citizens.

Starting in the mid-1970's, senior rights advocates emphasized society's obligation to care for the elderly. Advocates positioned Social Security as a sacred, inviolable "contract" between government and the elderly. Social Security payments were an "earned" right. After all, retirees had been paying taxes on their wages throughout their working lives. Senior rights advocates argued that seniors and younger workers must cooperate to preserve the stability and financial future of Social Security.

THE 1990'S

During the 1990's, programs for the elderly were vulnerable for the first time in decades. They were no longer viewed as sacred and untouchable. Some conservative economists and policymakers supported the notion that the aged and their families must bear greater responsibility for their own retirement. They argued that unless workers saved more during their working lives, they could become a burden to government, taxpayers, and even their own families. Many conservatives called for reducing Social Security benefits and Supplemental Security Income, as well as Medicare and Medicaid. Fiscal responsibility meant requiring retires to fund more of the services and benefits they received. The debate over the 1996 federal budget hinged on the extent of cuts in Medicare. The political impasse between President Bill Clinton and Congress over how to balance the budget and put Medicare on a sound financial footing led to a government shutdown. When Clinton won election in November, 1992, he received a majority of the senior citizen vote.

The struggle for senior rights intensified in the late 1990's as the approximately 76 million Americans born between 1946 and 1964, the baby boomers, prepared to join the ranks of the aging in the twenty-first century. Advocates worked to dispel the view that the elderly were consuming an unfair share of society's scarce resources. Rather, they championed cooperation between generations to solve the complex structural problems that foster inequality. The struggle shifted from construction of the safety net to figuring out how to do more for the aging in need with fewer federal resources. The alternatives included asking the elderly to take on more responsibility in the form of cost-sharing and private-market alternatives. Advocates shifted their attention to framing the public debate over the justice of old-age policies and rights. They positioned themselves as a political force with which to be reckoned.

Much of the struggle over finding solutions to the problems of supporting citizens in old age proceeded as a battle over the perception of what is fair and equitable for the young, aging, relatively healthy aged, and frail elderly. During this ongoing struggle, advocates have served as a vital force in alerting and educating the public and policymakers to the needs and value of the aging and aged. A benefit of their achievement has been to restore the sense of dignity to the elderly—their feeling wanted, useful, important, and contributing members of society.   —*Fred Buchstein*

See also Age discrimination; Age Discrimination Act of 1975; Age Discrimination in Employment Act of 1967; American Association of Retired Persons (AARP); Baby boomers; Employment; Forced retirement; Gray Panthers; Health care; Income sources; Job loss; Kuhn, Maggie; Laguna Woods, California: Medical insurance; Medicare; National Council of Senior Citizens; Older Americans Act of 1965; Older Workers Benefit Protection Act; Pensions; Politics; Poverty; Retirement; Social Security; Townsend movement; Voting patterns; White House Conference on Aging.

FOR FURTHER INFORMATION:

Hardcastle, David A., Stanley Wenocur, and Patricia R. Powers. *Community Practice: Theories and Skills for Social Workers.* New York: Oxford University Press, 1997. This text includes a comprehensive and integrated overview of practices that promote the welfare of community groups, including the elderly. The chapter on using various advocacy tools and techniques is especially strong.

Hess, Clinton W., and Paul A. Kerschner. *The Silver Lobby: A Guide to Advocacy for Older Persons.* Los Angeles: The University of Southern California Press, 1978. Readers learn how to create and execute a lobbying campaign to promote the quality of life for the elderly. A series of questions guides the reader through the advocacy planning stage.

Morgan, Leslie, and Suzanne Kunkel. *Aging: The Social Context.* Thousand Oaks, Calif.: Pine Forge Press, 1998. The authors analyze age-based government policies and practices.

Morris, Charles R. *The AARP: America's Most Powerful Lobby and the Clash of Generations.* New York: Times Books, 1996. This work chronicles the rise and development of the AARP and provides insight into the workings of the organization.

Powell, Lawrence Alfred, John B. Williamson, and Kenneth J. Branco. *The Senior Rights Movement: Framing the Policy Debate in America*. Twayne, 1996. The authors chronicle the history of the struggle for old-aged justice in America.

Pratt, Henry J. *The Gray Lobby*. Chicago: The University of Chicago Press, 1976. Pratt tells the story of the development of federal policies toward the aged.

Van Tassel, David D., and Jimmy Elaine Wilkinson Meyer, eds. *U.S. Aging Policy Interest Groups*. Westport, Conn.: Greenwood Press, 1992. Although dated, this book is a handy reference guide to organizations advocating for changes in public policy regarding the aging and aged.

AFRICAN AMERICANS

RELEVANT ISSUES: Culture, demographics, family, race and ethnicity, religion, sociology

SIGNIFICANCE: According to the *Statistical Abstract of the United States* for 1994, African Americans made up approximately 12 percent of the population of the United States and 7.9 percent of those over age sixty-five

Aging is similar in many ways for all racial and ethnic groups, but there are differences as well. African Americans are the largest minority group, and the history and heritage of black people in America make their aging experience unique.

African American aging may be summed up in seemingly contradictory statements. First, economic hardships from prejudice and discrimination in the younger years may follow into old age. Second, in spite of hardships, African Americans often age well. What is aging like for African American elders? How might their experience differ from that of the majority culture? What special challenges do they face? What are the positive aspects of growing old in this culture? Research is sparse about African Americans in general, and few studies address cultural and ethnic differences in African American aging. Studies that have been done, however, provide some understanding of the African American experience.

African Americans continue to suffer from faulty stereotypes—for example, that all African Americans are lower class, that all African American families are headed by women, and that their African American elders die much sooner than their white counterparts. As with all elders, life expectancy actually improves for African Americans once they reach the later years. In *Social Forces and Aging* (8th ed., 1997), Robert Atchley reported a robustness among older African Americans and called attention to the fact that the difference in life expectancy between blacks and whites decreases after age fifty-four. Many husbands and fathers in African American communities, often unnoticed, quietly tend to their responsibilities at home and at work. Moreover, African Americans are a highly diverse group; they are not all poor, by any means, and approximately one-third of African Americans are members of the middle or upper classes. Differences, however, between those who are poor and those who are better off make a difference in later years, regardless of one's ethnic group.

MIDDLE AGE

Relatively little is written about middle age and even less about cultural differences that may exist. Middle age, roughly ages forty to sixty-five, is a good time for many people, with some of the challenges of youth behind them, children grown, and job earnings at their peak. Most have discovered their priorities and a few coping strategies.

For many African Americans, activities during these years are influenced by family responsibilities since, according to *Aging for the Twenty-first Century* (1996), edited by Jill Quadagno and Debra Street, black children are much more likely than white children to be cared for by a grandparent. While grandparents may be accepting of this situation, continued family involvement in child rearing influences their lifestyle and helps determine daily activities. Economics affect the middle years as well. Therefore, middle age, like other stages, is influenced by a number of factors, including finances, family and individual situations, and opportunities afforded or denied for various reasons.

CHALLENGES AND OPPORTUNITIES

Challenges for older African Americans include racial inequality at any age, the cumulative effects, for many, of lifelong prejudice and discrimination, and the dramatic effects of social inequality. Even if difficulties with discrimination ease in later years, their effects may continue to be manifested in reduced income and lost opportunities throughout life, including in retirement.

Practically speaking, old age should be especially difficult for African Americans because of the accumulated disadvantages of prejudice and discrimination throughout life. Yet, there are positive aspects as well for African American aging, and studies indicate that many elders enjoy old age.

Positive aspects of aging in the African American community include the social supports of community and family, the importance of religion and the church, a respect for old age, possible buffers against suicide, and the awarding of a special "survivor" status. Old age may even become a leveler of social and racial differences, making life somewhat easier for African Americans in old age.

Essays in *Aging for the Twenty-first Century* suggest that gender may be less important in old age for blacks than for whites because African Americans and women tend to have had more similar work lives. Both groups are inclined to be lifetime workers without continuous work patterns. In 1996, the average life expectancy of African American women still exceeded that of African American men, and women, more than men, tended to live without a spouse.

Despite hardships along the way, there may be advantages to growing old for African Americans. Studies suggest positive aspects of aging and possible buffers to protect them from some of the problems faced by elders in other groups. Support systems and kinship networks may be greater among blacks, and these networks, along with coping abilities learned early in life, may contribute to more positive lifestyles and emotional states and better care of their ill elderly, according to researcher Colleen Johnson. Elders often expressed a high level of contentment in the African American family, community, and church and enjoyed their survivor status.

Older women often hold an important place in an African American family as caregivers and the keepers of tradition. (Unicorn/Tom McCarthy)

ECONOMIC REALITIES

African American comedian Pearl Bailey once said, "I've been rich and I've been poor. Rich is better." Understanding the economic situation of older African Americans requires an understanding of the effects of successive disadvantage in the job market and the consequences in old age. The average net worth of black families is a fraction of that for white families, with home ownership lagging behind as well. In *Surviving Dependence: Voices of African American Elders* (1995), Mary Ball and Frank Whittington discuss how group concentration in low-paying jobs earlier in life results in lower Social Security benefits, fewer pensions, and less savings later in life.

In the late 1990's, the median household income for African Americans sixty-five and older was about two-thirds that of whites. Chronic disability was common in the older population, especially among African Americans. With the combination of a reduced income and the added expenses of disease and disability that often accompany poverty, life clearly becomes more difficult for some African American elders.

RETIREMENT

Atchley reports that long-term patterns of disadvantage in income and employment result in decreased opportunities throughout life, and freedom of choice is afforded to some groups more than others. According to Rose Gibson in *Aging for the Twenty-first Century*, retirement differences between whites and blacks may be seen in the timing of retirement, reasons for retirement, and retirement activities.

Gibson reports that the main reason that African Americans retire is poor health, followed by job-related considerations, with financial readiness and new interests last on the list. Age of retirement was the same for black men and women, with 15 percent of Gibson's sample working until seventy or later, supporting the theory that the role of the working older African American may be one of economic necessity. While reasons for retirement did not vary greatly by gender, activities did somewhat. Black women listed housekeeping and black men listed gardening as the major activity in retirement, along with sitting, resting, sports, hobbies, church, reading, and television. Gibson's research did not differentiate between those of lower and higher incomes.

ELDER ABUSE

Linner Griffin's 1999 research on elder abuse found few studies involving older people themselves and fewer addressing African American elders. Numbers are difficult to determine because of the very nature of such behavior and the secrets that families keep. Elder abuse is believed to exist among African Americans as well as in other groups, but perhaps in a somewhat different form. Griffin's research found physical abuse of elders especially unacceptable among African Americans. Abuse among that group tended to be emotional or financial in nature, findings backed by social service records. In her studies, Griffin often heard the response, "You just don't hit your momma!"

Historically, and unique to African Americans, is the idea and existence of the matriarch, the strong mother who keeps the family together, often working at another job as well. Intense loyalty and protectiveness were seen by Griffin, and what some may perceive as exploitation of elder women could also be family support or intergenerational help.

LONG-TERM CARE

In the late 1990's, only an estimated 5 percent of older people in the United States were in nursing homes at any one time, and the rates were even lower for African Americans, as reported by James Thorson in *Aging in a Changing Society* (1995). In a 1996 study, Carole Cox and Abraham Monk found unique strengths among African American caregivers, with duties and obligations viewed differently by blacks and whites. African American families were less inclined to institutionalize elders with cognitive and other impairments, and dementia was less problematic for them.

With the high costs of institutional care, home-based care has been welcomed by professionals, families, and elders, and both formal and informal support services can meet needs that either type of care would find difficult to provide alone. According to a 1992 study by Sharon Bryant and William Rakowski, African Americans faced barriers when seeking formal services, and many found it difficult to trust those providing them. If this attitude leads African Americans to take care of their own, however, elders can stay integrated in their own communities.

SUICIDE RATES

Suicide is a serious problem for some groups, but less so for older African Americans, especially older women. For people aged sixty-five and older, suicide rates are highest for white men, lower for black men and white women, and so low for older black women that, in some tables, rates cannot be calculated.

Although the reasons for such figures are not well understood, research suggests some differences between the black and white experience. Most suicide research has been directed toward the white population, but suicide predictors and explanations that are possibly true for whites may not hold true for blacks. If negative events become suicide risk factors, then protective factors may also exist.

Johnson believed that older African Americans learn to adapt to predictable difficulties while maintaining optimism for the future. Their expectation matches reality, and their optimism comes from contentment and security in the African American family, church, and community.

In 1994, Jeffrey Levin, Robert Taylor, and Linda Chatters reported a rich diversity in black religiosity, reflecting the diversity of African Americans overall. In their studies, blacks indicated a greater level of religiosity than did whites, and women appeared more religious than men. This greater religiosity emerged regardless of demographic factors such as age, education, health, income, or marital status. Religion, within the tradition of African Americans, is a dynamic resource for managing life's stressors, personally and socially. It provides resiliency for confronting hardships and offers alternative ways to meet them.

In a 1998 study comparing older black and white women's attitudes toward suicide, blacks reported less acceptance of suicide as normal behavior. Some said, "Commit suicide? Black people just don't. It's a white thing." Others said, "The Lord gives me purpose" or "You're prepared for the hard with the easy." Still others said, "These are our harvesting years" or "We've had enough hell; we don't need anymore." Reasons for these attitudes about suicide are not well understood, but many African Americans simply would not kill themselves, even in the toughest times. Johnson believed that the religiosity of many older African Americans provides a buffer in difficult times, with the church helping to offset prejudicial attitudes by offering self-esteem and social support.

THE DREAM LIVES ON

With hardships to make them strong; the social supports of family, church, and community; strong faith; and an optimism for the future, it is no wonder that most African Americans enter old age with dignity and courage. For many African Americans, life has been a difficult journey—a lesser people might have given up. From the words of James Weldon and J. Rosamond Johnson's Black National Anthem, "Lift Ev'ry Voice and Sing" (written in 1921 and still sung today), struggle and hope unite, offering encouragement and strength even into old age: "Sing a song full of the faith that the dark past has taught us; Sing a song full of the hope that the present has brought us; Facing the rising sun of our new day begun. Let us march on till victory is won."
                                          —*Mary L. Bender*

See also Aging: Biological, psychological, and sociocultural perspectives; *Autobiography of Miss Jane Pittman, The*; Caregiving; Cultural views of aging; Demographics; *Driving Miss Daisy*; Elder abuse; Family relationships; Grandparenthood; *Having Our Say: The Delany Sisters' First One Hundred Years*; Long-term care for the elderly; Men and aging; Multigenerational households; National Caucus and Center on Black Aged; Parenthood; Poverty; Religion; Single parenthood; Skipped-generation parenting; Stereotypes; Suicide; Women and aging; *Worn Path, A*.

FOR FURTHER INFORMATION:

Atchley, Robert C. *Social Forces and Aging: An Introduction to Social Gerontology*. 9th ed. Belmont, Calif.: Wadsworth, 1999. This textbook discusses, in detail, many aspects of individual aging.

Ball, Mary, and Frank Whittington. *Surviving Dependence: Voices of African American Elders*. Amityville, N.Y.: Baywood, 1995. Offers individual case studies of older African Americans.

Bender, Mary. *African Americans and Suicide*. Lincoln: University of Nebraska Press, 1997. Dissertation research comparing older African American and Caucasian women's attitudes toward suicide.

Bryant, Sharon, and William Rakowski. "Predictors of Mortality Among Elderly African Americans." *Research on Aging* 14, no. 1 (March, 1992).

Argues that African Americans face barriers when seeking formal support services but that informal services provide for many needs.

Cox, Carole, and Abraham Monk. "Strain Among Caregivers: Comparing the Experience of African American and Hispanic Caregivers of Alzheimer's Relatives." *International Journal of Aging and Human Development* 43, no. 2 (September, 1996). This article looks at the role of culture and informal helping, and why African Americans report less stress in caregiving.

Gibson, Rose. "The Black American Retirement Experience." In *Aging for the Twenty-first Century*, edited by Jill Quadagno and Debra Street. New York: St. Martin's Press, 1996. Readings on a number of social issues that affect older African Americans, especially in retirement.

Griffin, Linner. "Elder Maltreatment in the African American Community: You Just Don't Hit Your Momma!!!" In *Understanding Elder Abuse in Minority Populations*, edited by Toshio Tatara. Philadelphia: Brunner/Mazel, 1999. An essay on the causes and nature of elder abuse in minority populations.

Johnson, Colleen. "Determinants of Adaptation of Oldest Old Black Americans." *Journal of Aging Studies* 9, no. 3 (Fall, 1995). A discussion of the ways in which oldest African Americans adapt to aging.

Johnson, James Weldon, and J. Rosamond Johnson. "Lift Ev'ry Voice and Sing." In *Lift Every Voice and Sing*. New York: Walker, 1993. The words of the Black National Anthem, written in 1921, make up the complete text of this illustrated book. Illustrations by Elizabeth Catlett, with an introduction by Jim Haskins.

Levin, Jeffrey, Robert Taylor, and Linda Chatters. "Race and Gender Differences in Religiosity Among Older Adults: Findings from Four National Surveys." *Journal of Gerontology: Social Sciences* 49, no. 3 (May, 1994). In these four studies, significant racial and gender differences were found, regardless of sociodemographic factors.

Quadagno, Jill, and Debra Street, eds. *Aging for the Twenty-first Century*. New York: St. Martin's Press, 1996. Readings about the various facets of aging by researchers and scholars.

Statistical Abstract of the United States: The National Data Book. Washington D.C.: U.S. Government Printing Office, 1994. Published since 1878, this is the standard summary of statistics on the social, political, and economic organization of the United States. A convenient volume for statistical reference on both government and private data.

Thorson, James. *Aging in a Changing Society*. Belmont, Calif.: Wadsworth, 1995. Students love this textbook. It is academic and informative, yet readable and interesting.

AGE DISCRIMINATION

RELEVANT ISSUES: Economics, law, work

SIGNIFICANCE: Although older persons seeking equal opportunities under the law are often frustrated by employers and others who subject them to unequal treatment because of their age, there are legal remedies for discrimination

Before the industrial age, elderly persons lived in relatively stable families, commanding respect in rural communities because they could perfect their economic skills during a lifetime while assisting their offspring in learning a trade. With the advent of factories in towns, where artisanship was replaced by a division of work into small duplicated tasks, worker productivity became valued more than craftsmanship quality. Employers in factories especially came to value unmarried younger workers for their good health, high output, and ability to adapt to new technologies; in contrast, employers came to regard older workers as more prone to accidents and illnesses, slower in motor skills, more rigid in outlook, and desirous of higher wages to support dependents. To maximize profits, the captains of industry preferred younger workers, who moved to the towns to take advantage of new employment opportunities, thus serving to separate older from younger family members.

CAUSES OF AGE DISCRIMINATION

Age discrimination is also called "ageism," as distinct from racism, sexism, and other forms of discrimination in which members of one subgroup are treated unequally. There are several social psychological reasons for age discrimination. First, stereotypes applying to older persons have emerged because some—but not all—older persons are less productive and more resistant to learning new technologies than younger people are. Second, with the advent of public schools aimed at imparting new skills not likely to be found at home, modern society became increasingly sex-segregated, resulting in competition between cohorts of the same age for power, whether in politics or in the workplace. Third, much of modern culture glorifies youth, giving rise to gerontophobia and intergenerational hostility. Fourth, the emphasis on early independence f children in competitive industrial society has meant that older persons are often abandoned by their children and are left to care for themselves in years of declining income and physical vitality.

As the postindustrial society began to replace the industrial age, however, an increasing proportion of jobs came to involve the provision of services rather than manufacturing. Quality of work and specialized knowledge have thus in many cases become more important than quantity of output. As life expectancy has increased, moreover, older persons have come to constitute an increasing proportion of the population. Nevertheless, many employers and younger persons continue to treat older persons on the basis of rivalries and stereotypes. Discrimination based on age is not merely tragic for well-qualified individuals but also deprives society of some of its best talent.

SOCIAL SECURITY

During the Great Depression of the 1930's, many older workers were unemployed and, as a result of pervasive age discrimination, had no prospect of reemployment. Dr. Francis Everett Townsend then launched a campaign to have the federal government provide all workers with pensions of $200 per month starting at age sixty. Known as the Townsend movement, the campaign's goal was to ensure more jobs for younger workers by providing older workers with a comfortable paycheck in retirement.

In 1935, President Franklin D. Roosevelt succeeded in having Congress pass the Social Security Act, which provided for government pensions for U.S. citizens sixty-five and older who lacked earned income. Many employers responded by establishing mandatory retirement policies for workers at age sixty-five. Although the reform provided a safety net for workers who were unemployed or so fatigued that they wanted to spend the rest of their lives without the stress of daily labor, the law

encouraged more age discrimination than before by legitimating different treatment of workers on the basis of age. If a worker wanted to retire at age sixty-one, no Social Security benefits would be available; if a worker wanted to stay on the job until age seventy, employers could point to a federally sanctioned policy and demand retirement at sixty-five. Moreover, according to law, Social Security obenefits could be withheld from anyone who worked part-time between the ages of sixty-five and seventy-five (the upper exempt age was lowered to seventy in 1982).

As a supplement to Social Security, Congress in 1965 passed the Older Americans Act, one of President Lyndon Johnson's Great Society programs. The act defines "older persons" as those age sixty and over; it established an Administration on Aging (AoA), which later became part of the Department of Health and Human Services headed by an assistant secretary. AoA provides funds to state governments for two types of grants: research and development projects (which make needs assessments, develop new approaches such as legal-assistance clinics and multipurpose activity centers, develop new methods to coordinate programs and services, and evaluate the various programs) and training projects (for personnel to run the programs). States, however, differ substantially in the quality of services provided under the act, and AoA has done little to establish minimum standards. Instead, AoA offers technical assistance to assist in upgrading programs. An amendment established a means test to ensure that the beneficiaries are needy.

Even before Social Security legislation existed, many employers offered company retirement plans to provide incomes to employees who were subject to mandatory retirement upon reaching a certain age. Some of these plans, however, proved to be scams. In 1974, Congress passed the Employee Retirement Income Security Act (ERISA) to provide minimum standards for these plans.

In the 1980's, corporate and university downsizing seemed imperative as personnel costs mounted. Accordingly, employers offered "golden handshake" plans with early-retirement incentives. In so doing, they asked employees to waive various rights, including the right to sue in case these incentives benefited some employees more than others. Congress responded to these abuses by passing the Older Workers Benefit Protection Act of 1990, which provides many specific procedural protections, including ample time to consider an early retirement plan and an interval of time to cancel a decision to accept a plan.

PROVING DISCRIMINATION

Standards of legal proof for the existence of discrimination have changed over time. Clearly, discrimination is most obvious when one person formulates an intention to discriminate and then carries out that intention. Thus, there are two factors involved, intentionality and disparate treatment.

In order for a plaintiff to prove intentionality in court, the person engaging in discrimination must be shown to have confessed a bias against a class of persons, either verbally or in writing; in the former case, there must be credible witnesses, whereas documentary proof is necessary to establish written intentionality. Disparate treatment can be proved by showing that the person alleged to discriminate has treated one class of persons quite differently from another class, such as when an employer asks older applicants for the position of police officer to perform an agility test but younger applicants are not asked to take the same test.

The Fourteenth Amendment to the U.S. Constitution states that all persons are entitled to "due process of law" and "equal justice under the law." Although this language was intended to prohibit discrimination on the basis of race, the amendment's provisions have been interpreted to apply to any class of persons. Therefore, age discrimination is prohibited by the Fourteenth Amendment in principle, though many types of "reasonable" age-related practices—for example, the segregation of students by age—are not prohibited. Proving illegal age discrimination under the amendment requires evidence of both intentionality and disparate treatment and must rebut reasonableness arguments; the burden of proof rests with those suffering discrimination. Although disparate treatment is a matter of fact that often can be demonstrated by the existence of records or by empirical research, many bigots in authority are careful not to provide verbal or documentary evidence of intentionality. Accordingly, age discrimination cases were rarely pursued under the Fourteenth Amendment.

The civil rights legislation of the 1960's dramatically changed legal standards for proving discrimination. The Civil Rights Act of 1964 dropped the intentionality requirement, and disparate treatment became one of the two major legal standards for proving employment discrimination. According to the 1964 act as it was later interpreted by the Supreme Court, those alleging discrimination could win a case if they had evidence of disparate treatment alone; thus, the burden of proof shifted to the employer if objective evidence showed the existence of disparate treatment. To rebut an allegation of disparate treatment, an employer had to show that such disparity resulted from the application of a factor related to job performance that was uniformly applied to all employees or applicants for employment. A second doctrine for proving discrimination under the 1964 law, known as "adverse impact," was established in order to handle cases in which employers screened employees or applicants for employment by using criteria unrelated to job performance. These changes in standards of proof, however, applied largely to cases of race discrimination. For the changes to apply to age discrimination, new laws had to be adopted by Congress.

THE AGE DISCRIMINATION IN EMPLOYMENT ACT (ADEA)

In 1964, while Congress was debating the proposed law to ban employment discrimination based on race, opponents of the legislation proposed to add age discrimination provisions to the bill. Their aim was to kill the proposed law by diverting attention away from the primary concern of the moment, discrimination against African Americans. In the event, age discrimination was not addressed in the Civil Rights Act of 1964; Congress, though, asked the secretary of labor to study the question and to make a report on the parameters of age discrimination in employment by June 30, 1965.

According to the report, presented to Congress on schedule, about half of all jobs in the private sector were closed to persons aged fifty-five and above, and a quarter of these jobs were not being offered to persons over forty-five. Moreover, about 40 percent of all those suffering long-term unemployment were over forty-five. After receiving the report on age discrimination, Congress asked the secretary of labor to make recommendations regarding an age discrimination law. Upon receiving these recommendations, Congress passed the Age Discrimination in Employment Act (ADEA) of 1967 after a short debate.

Initially, the ADEA covered employment discrimination in the private sector on the basis of age for those aged forty to sixty; thus, only middle-aged persons were covered. Rather than forcing aggrieved parties to engage expensive lawyers to sue and try discrimination cases in court to enforce the law, ADEA provided the option of filing administrative complaints against employers with the Department of Labor, which could investigate, issue rulings, and negotiate with errant employers on behalf of victims of discrimination.

As originally written, the ADEA had many exceptions. Employers with fewer than twenty-five employees were exempt, as were elected officials and their personal staff, policy-making appointees, legal advisers on specific cases, firefighters and law enforcement officials, and corporate executives eligible for pensions of $27,000 or more (a figure raised to $44,000 by 1985).

Passage of the ADEA did much to strengthen lobbying organizations on behalf of the elderly, notably the American Association of Retired Persons (AARP). As a result of AARP pressure, the ADEA has been amended on several occasions, often after court decisions made unwelcome rulings based on loopholes in the law. The amendments have tended to plug loopholes and to expand coverage.

In 1974, the ADEA was extended to cover employees of federal, state, and local governments, and the minimum number of employees was dropped to twenty for firms in the private sector. In 1978, mandatory retirement was abolished for federal workers, the highest age covered by the statute was raised to seventy, administration of the law was transferred from the Department of Labor to the Equal Employment Opportunity Commission (EEOC), and jury trials were guaranteed for litigants. Under the latter provision, the number of court cases increased considerably. By the late 1990's, approximately 85 percent of the plaintiffs suing under the ADEA were older white male professionals, who often won large settlements, although the original intention of the act was to protect more those with much lower incomes.

In 1982, the health benefits guarantee was extended to age seventy, and mandatory retirement for tenured teachers was repealed. In 1984 and 1985, the health benefits guarantee was extended to spouses of employees up to the age of seventy, coverage was extended to overseas employees of U.S. corporations, and mandatory retirement of corporate executives was disallowed unless company pensions were at least $44,000 per year.

In 1986, amendments eliminated mandatory retirement for private-sector workers and required employers to extend health insurance benefits to workers beyond the age of seventy. In 1987, Congress banned any denial of accrued pension benefits for those still working after the age of sixty-five. In 1988, an amendment extended the time limit for filing complaints with the EEOC; in 1990, the Older Workers Benefit Protection Act amended the ADEA to subject employer retirement benefits plans to certain procedural guarantees.

Loopholes in the law still provide paradoxes. Employers can offer lesser life insurance benefits to older workers than to younger workers if the cost of such benefits is higher. Early retirement incentives can offer more to younger workers if these plans are Social Security supplement plans or if they eliminate all or part of actuarial reduction. Older workers terminated through staff reductions may have no recourse under the law if younger persons are hired in their positions after the statutory time limit for filing complaints has expired.

Still, the ADEA has brought about major changes in employment practices. Compulsory retirement has been abolished for all but a few professions. Fringe benefits of older workers are now available on the same basis as for younger workers, with the exception of life insurance. Older persons find that employers are much more likely to hire them than before the law was passed. The high likelihood of success in court deters employers from discriminating against employees on the basis of age.

In the late 1990's, approximately 75 percent of all age discrimination cases filed with the EEOC were for termination thought to have been based on age, and only about 10 percent were for refusal to hire. The average cash settlement for age discrimination cases was approximately $450,000, though the original purpose of the act was to stop long-term age-related unemployment among less-affluent older workers.

THE AGE DISCRIMINATION ACT (ADA)

The Civil Rights Act of 1964 banned not only employment discrimination but also discrimination in the distribution of benefits from federally funded programs on the basis of race. Age discrimination was not covered. Congress plugged this loophole by passing the Age Discrimination Act (ADA) of 1975 as an amendment to the Older Americans Act of 1965. Under the 1975 law, discrimination on the basis of age is prohibited for all ages. In addition, the Department of Health, Education, and Welfare (HEW), which was to monitor ADA compliance, required affirmative action on the basis of age. The nature of the affirmative action is the requirement to ensure that older minorities learn about and are encouraged to take advantage of federally funded programs for older persons. When HEW was abolished in 1978, this responsibility was transferred to the Department of Health and Human Services.

The ADA provides several exemptions from coverage. The law exempts any program in which age is considered reasonably necessary for "normal operation" of a federally funded program or activity, an exception that is clearly vague. Yet another exception is allowed when factors other than age serve inadvertently but reasonably to screen out persons in certain age ranges. Laws specifying age entitlements or age-specific statutory objectives are also exempt, including the obvious discrimination in favor of older persons under both the Social Security Act and the Older Americans Act of 1965.

In 1975, Congress also amended two earlier laws to add a ban on age discrimination. To the State and Local Fiscal Act of 1972, which provided revenue-sharing funds to the states, Congress outlawed discrimination on the basis of age with no upper or lower age limits; this law was repealed after Ronald Reagan became president in 1981. In addition, the Equal Credit Opportunity Act was amended to ban discrimination by lending institutions on the basis of age, though the act covers only those aged sixteen and over. Interestingly, a later study of the impact of the Equal Credit Opportunity Act demonstrates that most age discrimination by lending institutions is against persons in their twenties, not the elderly.

DISABILITIES

As individuals age, disabilities often handicap their ability to function as they did in their youth, and they frequently encounter barriers to participation in the mainstream of life. Accordingly, laws have been passed to outlaw discrimination based on disability. Of the approximately 43 million disabled persons in the United States, most are elderly.

Congress adopted the Rehabilitation Act of 1973 in recognition of the fact that disabled persons of all ages were often excluded from participation in programs operating with federal funds because they could not see, hear, or obtain wheelchair access to the places where such programs operated. The law provided that there should be no discrimination of this sort and that recipients of federal funds should take affirmative action to make these programs more accessible to all, which meant the removal of architectural barriers so that physically handicapped persons could gain access to buildings, the provision of translation services for the deaf, accommodation to the mobility needs of blind persons, arrangements for disabled persons to ride on public forms of transportation, and designated parking stalls for those with such mobility problems as knee arthritis and wheelchair confinement.

In 1990, Congress adopted the Americans with Disabilities Act (ADA). Under this comprehensive statute, Congress filled in gaps in earlier legislation. The term "disability" is defined in the law to mean a substantial limitation of one or more major life activities, but the statute also covers not only persons believed to have a disability but also those closely associated with disabled persons, such as partners of persons with acquired immunodeficiency syndrome (AIDS). The law prohibits both employment discrimination for otherwise qualified workers based on disability and disability discrimination in federally funded programs. A major provision in the law is the requirement for "reasonable accommodation," which means that public agencies and private firms must do whatever they can reasonably afford so that disabled persons will have equal opportunity to enjoy the benefits of public programs and private-sector facilities.

AGE DISCRIMINATION LACKING LEGAL PROTECTION

The elderly often face social discrimination. For example, in the choosing of marriage partners, older persons are often considered less desirable. No legal recourse is possible, however, for such very personal choices.

Although the Civil Rights Act of 1964 prohibits racial discrimination in public accommodations (such as buses, shopping malls, and theaters) and in public facilities (such as government offices and public parks), there is no federal protection against either form of discrimination on the basis of age, though some states have banned these forms of discrimination. In addition, age is sometimes a factor in jury selection, but there is no statutory protection for this form of discrimination.

In short, legal protection against age discrimination is incomplete but has increased considerably since the middle of the twentieth century.

—*Michael Haas*

See also Advocacy; Age Discrimination Act of 1975; Age Discrimination in Employment Act of 1967; Ageism; American Association of Retired Persons (AARP); Disabilities; Early retirement; Employment; Forced retirement; Job loss; Older Americans Act of 1965; Older Workers Benefit Protection Act; Pensions; Politics; Retirement; Social Security; Stereotypes; Townsend movement.

FOR FURTHER INFORMATION:

Butler, Robert N. *Why Survive? Being Old in America.* New York: Harper & Row, 1975. The classic statement about "ageism" by the person who coined the term.

Eglit, Howard. "Of Age and the Constitution." *Chicago-Kent Law Review* 57 (Fall, 1981): 859-914. The most comprehensive survey of age factors in the Constitution and in constitutional law.

Hushbeck, Judith C. *Old and Obsolete: Age Discrimination and the American Worker, 1860-1920.* New York: Garland Press, 1989. Discusses the historical development of corporate practices that marginalized older workers with the advent of the Industrial Revolution.

Issacharoff, Samuel, and Erica Worth Harris. "Is Age Discrimination Really Age Discrimination? The ADEA's Unnatural Solution." *New York University Law Review* 72 (October, 1997): 780-840. The authors argue that the American Associa-

tion of Retired Persons perverted the Age Discrimination in Employment Act by securing changes in the law that enable rich executives to obtain lucrative awards by suing employers.

Neugarten, Bernice L. "Age Distinctions and Their Social Functions." *Chicago-Kent Law Review* 57 (Fall, 1981): 809-825. A review of some of the reasons for age discrimination in modern society.

U.S. Department of Labor. *The Older American Worker: Age Discrimination in Employment. Report to Congress Under Section 715 of the Civil Rights Act of 1964.* Washington, D.C.: Government Printing Office, 1965. This report, submitted by the secretary of labor to Congress in 1965, galvanized support for passage of the Age Discrimination in Employment Act two years later.

U.S. Equal Employment Opportunity Commission. *Age Discrimination.* Washington, D.C.: Government Printing Office, 1998. A comprehensive review of provisions of the Age Discrimination in Employment Act, as amended.

Whitton, Linda S. "Ageism: Paternalism and Prejudice." *DePaul Law Review* 46 (Winter, 1997): 453-482. The author reviews the social and psychological bases for age discrimination.

AGE DISCRIMINATION ACT OF 1975

DATE: Signed into law on November 28, 1975

RELEVANT ISSUES: Law, work

SIGNIFICANCE: The Age Discrimination Act of 1975, its title notwithstanding, was limited in both scope and application. Nevertheless, as a safeguard against bias-based abuse, the act served as a statutory foundation stone for the antidiscrimination policies that followed in the wake of the Civil Rights movement

In its basic premises, the Age Discrimination Act of 1975 originated in the Civil Rights Act of 1964. Title VI, Section 715 of this law mandated that the U.S. secretary of labor formulate a special report on the extent of age discrimination practices in employment. In 1965, the secretary's office completed the report, which documented widespread discrimination against senior citizens.

The Age Discrimination in Employment Act of 1967 (ADEA) went so far as to prohibit discrimination in employment directed against workers aged from forty to seventy.

Though the format of the Age Discrimination Act (ADA) of 1975 follows that of Title III to the Educational Amendments of 1972 and Section 504 of the Rehabilitation Act of 1973, with their respective prohibitions against discrimination based upon gender and disability, it is most closely modeled on the 1964 Civil Rights Act. The ADA itself is not a blanket prohibition against age-based discrimination but much more narrowly affects "programs or activities receiving Federal financial assistance"; it states that no one can be "excluded from participation, denied the benefits of, or be subjected to discrimination under" such programs. The act's provisions are further limited by significant exceptions outlined in two subsections (6103-b and 6103-c). The exemptive provisions apply to cases in which age is a factor necessary to "the normal operation or the achievement of any statutory objective"; in which "differentiation" occurs based on "reasonable factors other than age"; and in which programs provide benefits based upon age (such as Social Security and Medicare) or establish "criteria for participation in age-related terms." The ADEA is set apart as being outside the provisions of the ADA; with the exception of programs "receiving financial assistance under the Job Training Partnership Act," the ADA is denied the authority to extend the enforcement of its provisions to the private sector of the economy.

The lead time given for compliance was gradual; no provision of the act was to take effect until July 1, 1979. The Commission on Civil Rights was empowered to make a study determining the possible existence of instances of unreasonable age discrimination within the affected programs and agencies and to identify the alleged violators. The resulting report was to be submitted to the president and Congress no later than November 28, 1977.

The U.S. secretary of health and human services was then required, beginning in 1980, to make an annual report to Congress by March 31 describing the degree of compliance with the provisions of the act by the relevant agencies, departments, and programs. Enforcement methods include termination of federal assistance to violators and "any other means authorized by law."

—Raymond Pierre Hylton

See also Advocacy; Age discrimination; Age Discrimination in Employment Act of 1967; Ageism; Employment; Politics.

AGE DISCRIMINATION IN EMPLOYMENT ACT OF 1967

DATE: Signed into law on December 15, 1967
RELEVANT ISSUES: Economics, law, work
SIGNIFICANCE: The Age Discrimination in Employment Act (ADEA) promotes employment of older persons based on their ability rather than age, prohibits arbitrary age discrimination in employment, and helps employers and employees to resolve problems arising from the effects of age on employment

The enactment of the ADEA by Congress was deemed necessary to protect the civil rights of workers between the ages of forty and sixty-five, many of whom who found themselves disadvantaged in retaining employment or in regaining employment following displacement from a job. The law prohibits age discrimination, or ageism, in hiring, discharge, pay, promotion, and other terms and conditions of employment. Through the ADEA, Congress intended to bar employers from setting arbitrary age limits that disregarded workers' potential for job performance. Congress recognized that the incidence of unemployment—especially long-term unemployment with resultant deterioration of skill, morale, and employer acceptability—was high among older workers and that the existence of arbitrary age discrimination in industries burdened commerce and impeded the flow of goods.

The U.S. secretary of labor administers and enforces the ADEA through the Equal Employment Opportunity Commission. The act applies to employers with more than twenty employees, to employment agencies, and to unions. The ADEA's protections apply to both employees and applicants for a job. Most states have enacted laws parallel to the federal law.

The ADEA provides for exceptions. Any action that may otherwise be unlawful under the ADEA is legal if age is a bona fide occupational qualification that is reasonably necessary for the normal operation of the particular business. In some jobs, an employee must meet certain physical qualifications that an older person cannot satisfy; for example, public safety concerns may validly affect age-related employment decisions regarding the piloting of aircraft, fire fighting, or law enforcement, whereas valid commercial considerations may affect hiring decisions regarding the modeling of clothes for teenagers. The law stipulates that an employer is not required to hire anyone who is unqualified to do a job, regardless of age, and that it is legal to discharge an older employee for good cause.

Employees or applicants may agree to waive their rights under the ADEA. For a waiver to be considered voluntary and valid, minimum standards must be met. The waiver must be in writing and be understandable, it must specifically refer to ADEA rights, it may not waive rights or claims that may arise in the future, it must be in exchange for valuable consideration, it must advise the individual in writing to consult an attorney before signing the waiver, and it must provide the individual at least twenty-one days to consider the agreement and at least seven days to revoke it after signing it.

In 1978, an amendment of the ADEA extended protection to employees up to seventy years of age. On October 7, 1998, President Bill Clinton signed the Higher Education Amendments of 1998, which allowed colleges and universities to offer age-based early retirement programs to tenured faculty without violating the ADEA. Thus, tenured faculty may be offered "supplemental benefits upon voluntary retirement that are reduced or eliminated on the basis of age," as long as the benefits are in addition to any retirement or severance benefits generally offered to tenured faculty.

—Manjit S. Kang

See also Advocacy; Age discrimination; Age Discrimination Act of 1975; Ageism; Early retirement; Employment; Forced retirement; Politics; Retirement.

AGE SPOTS

RELEVANT ISSUES: Biology, health and medicine

SIGNIFICANCE: Age spots, also known as liver spots or solar lentigo, are benign lesions found on sun-exposed skin. Age spots are seen in more than 90 percent of Caucasians sixty-five years of age and older; they typically represent no immediate danger

By the time they reach their seventh decade, most people have age spots on areas of the skin exposed to sunlight, such as the face. (James L. Shaffer)

Age spots are flat tan or brown spots with well-defined borders between 2 millimeters and 30 millimeters in size. Occasionally, they can be slightly scaly or have a rough surface. Age spots are caused by a proliferation of normal melanocytes (the cells that produce melanin) in the epidermis as the result of chronic sun exposure. These lesions are commonly found on the face, especially the forehead and temples, the backs of the forearms and hands, and the shoulders and back. They are less commonly found on the trunk and legs. Age spots have no malignant potential.

No treatment is needed for age spots. Sunscreens and sun protection are usually advised because they help to decrease the rate of appearance and darkening of these lesions. Some older adults may seek treatment for cosmetic reasons. When treatment is sought, liquid nitrogen cryotherapy is usually used to lighten or remove the spots. This therapy is usually effective because melanocytes are more sensitive to cold than epidermal cells are. Trichloracetic acid may also be used to lighten or remove age spots. Bleaching agents such as tretinoin (Retin A) or hydroquinone may lighten age spots slowly, usually over three to four months. The color will return, however, if the use of the bleaching cream is discontinued.   —*Courtney H. Lyder*

See also Aging process; Antiaging treatments; Cosmetic surgery; Skin cancer; Skin changes and disorders; Wrinkles.

AGEISM

RELEVANT ISSUES: Culture, media, psychology, sociology

SIGNIFICANCE: Ageism consists of any stereotypic perception, prejudicial attitude, discriminatory action, role assignment, or institutional structure against an individual or group purely on the basis of age

American society has been described as maintaining a stereotypic and often negative perception of older adults. This perception of aging and aged individuals is readily apparent in such areas as language, media, and humor. For example, such commonly used phrases as "over the hill" and "don't be an old fuddy-duddy" denote old age as a period of impotency and incompetency. The term used to describe bias against older adults is "ageism." While ageism usually represents a negative bias, positive stereotypes also reflect a form of ageism. Thus, the notion that all older adults are wise represents an ageist belief.

Ageism, however, is different from other isms, such as sexism and racism, for two primary reasons. First, age classification is not static. An individual's age classification changes during the progression through the life cycle. Thus, age classification is characterized by continual change, while the other classification systems traditionally used by society such as race and gender remain constant. Second, except for those who die at an early age, no one is exempt from at some point achieving the status of "old" and thus from experiencing ageism. The latter is an important distinction, as ageism can thus affect the individual on two levels. First, the individual may be ageist with respect to others; that is, the individual may stereotype other people on the basis of age. Second, the individual may be ageist with respect to self. Thus, ageist attitudes may affect self-concept.

THE CAUSES OF AGEISM

Social gerontologists have examined the negative stereotypes and myths that persist in American society concerning older adults. Based on their studies, they have developed several hypotheses concerning the causes and bases for ageism.

It has been postulated that the fear of death in Western society contributes to ageism. Western civilization conceptualizes death as outside the human life cycle. As such, death is experienced and viewed as an affront to the self. It is not seen as natural and an inevitable part of the life course. This can be contrasted with Eastern philosophy, in which life and death are all part of a continuous cycle.

Unfortunately, old age and death are viewed as synonymous in American society. Thus, as death is feared, old age is feared. Ageist attitudes and stereotypes can insulate the young and middle aged from the ambivalence that they may feel toward the elderly and death. The young and middle aged may perceive aging purely as a time of dependency, unproductiveness, and illness. This misperception represents the most commonly argued basis for ageism.

The second factor hypothesized to contribute to ageism is the emphasis on the youth culture in American society. For example, the media, ranging from television to novels, place an emphasis on youth, physical beauty, and sexuality. Older adults are primarily ignored or portrayed negatively. The emphasis on youth affects not only how older individuals are perceived but also how older individuals perceive themselves. Persons who are dependent on physical appearance and youth for their identity are likely to experience loss of self-esteem with age.

The emphasis in American culture on productivity represents the third factor contributing to ageism. It should be noted that productivity is narrowly defined in terms of economic potential. Both ends of the life cycle are viewed as unproductive—children and the aged. The middle aged are perceived as carrying the burdens imposed by both groups. Children, however, are viewed as having future economic potential. Economically, older adults are perceived as a financial liability. Upon retirement, the older adult is no longer viewed as economically productive in American society and thus is devalued.

Unfortunately, the manner in which aging was originally studied in the United States has also contributed to ageism. Researchers went to long-term care institutions where the aged were easy to find. Yet, only 5 percent of the older population is institutionalized. Thus, the early research on the aged and aging was based on institutionalized older individuals who were not physically well.

It has been proposed that individual ageist attitudes can be decreased through continual exposure to and work with older adults. However, there appears to be a large societal influence on ageist attitudes. Until these societal influences are addressed, ageism cannot be obliterated. For example, if the fear of death and therefore aging is not somehow addressed societally, then many younger individuals will continue their attempts to make the older population somehow different from themselves.

ATTITUDES TOWARD AGING AND THE AGED

Social gerontologists have examined the issue of ageism across the life span. While most studies have demonstrated a pattern of ageist beliefs and attitudes, others have not.

When studying children, researchers have demonstrated that the child's perception of older adults can be broken down to three dimensions: personality traits, affective relations, and physical abilities. Often, children may rate an older individual negative on one dimension while positive for another. For example, a child might rate an individual negatively for a personality trait dimension (they are messy or aggressive) and at the same time rate them positively for the affective relations dimension (they are fun). This multidimensionality of perceptions may explain the mixed research findings often cited concerning children's attitudes toward older adults.

Most research concerning ageism has examined the attitudes of students, ranging from junior high to graduate school, toward the aged. This research has demonstrated that students often believe many of the common stereotypes and misconceptions about older adults. For example, they tend to characterize later adulthood as a time of loneliness, ill health, rigidity, and decreased cognitive functioning. Most perceive old age as an unpleasant experience, and older adults are viewed as living in the past.

Other factors may influence students' perceptions of older adults. For example, adolescents from higher socioeconomic backgrounds have been found to view old age more positively than students from low socioeconomic backgrounds. This may simply reflect the economic realities related to aging in the United States. Additionally, older women are often perceived more positively than older men.

While some of the current research suggests that attitudes toward the elderly are becoming increasingly positive, these attitudes may be directed primarily toward stereotypically defined older adults. As such, these attitudes may not describe older adults as individuals but rather a positive stereotype that does not exist in reality. Therefore, even though the younger individual responds to the older adult more positively, the use of the stereotype still maintains a distance between the two.

Few studies have examined the attitudes of older adults toward aging and aged individuals. The majority of these studies have examined the perceptions of institutionalized older adults. Research has included hospital residents receiving medical, rehabilitative, or psychosocial treatment, as well as indigent institutionalized individuals. Therefore, the negative view of older adults reported in these studies may simply reflect the subjects' own negative experience of old age and/or life.

Studies examining the attitudes of well, community-dwelling older adults toward older adults have produced mixed results. The research suggests that older men maintain fairly neutral attitudes toward aging and the aged. Older women have been found to have extremely positive attitudes toward older adults and aging. This can be contrasted with the predominantly negative biases demonstrated by younger women regarding age. Thus, a gender difference may exist concerning attitudes toward aging and the aged.

Very little research addresses the causes of ageist attitudes. Research has examined the relationship of knowledge of aging with ageist attitudes and found no correlation. In other words, the level of one's ageist attitudes appears to be independent of one's knowledge about the aging process.

GENDER AND AGEISM

The sexless older woman is a common theme, particularly in humor and greeting cards. Jokes usually ascribe to the older woman the following characteristics: lonely, frustrated, and shriveled. Unfortunately, these attempts at humor merely reflect negative stereotypes and not reality; sexual interest and ability generally do not decrease with age for women.

Older women are often viewed as unhealthy. Older men are usually perceived as being healthier than older women even though, on the average, women live seven years longer than men. On measures of perceived physical health, however, no differences have been found between old men and women.

Older women are also often viewed as ineffective, dependent, and passive. This is particularly true for the older woman whose sole identification was with her husband. This image of the older woman can also be a self-fulfilling prophecy, particularly for new widows. In addition, women continue to experience sexism during old age and are placed, thus, in double jeopardy.

Older men, however, are perceived as becoming more "feminine" with age, femininity being equated with psychological dependency and timidity. Therefore, the perception of men as they age undergoes a shift. This does not reflect actual changes in men as they age but rather younger adults' perceptions of older men.

Ageism is readily apparent in language against both men and women. The derogatory terms with which older adults are described represent some of the more common stereotypes of older men and women. For example, the term "little old lady" suggests incompetency and impotency. "Old hag" or "witch" commonly refer to a woman who is physically unpleasant in appearance, with a disagreeable personality. Old men are commonly described using such terms as "old coot" and "codger." These terms suggest that old men are slightly odd or quaint. The commonly used term "dirty old man" suggests an unnatural sexual perversion in older men.

TELEVISION AND AGEISM

A large body of research exists in the area of television and aging. Studies have examined the depictions of older adults and aging on prime-time shows, in daytime serials, and in Saturday morning cartoons. Early research primarily demonstrated that older individuals were underrepresented on television and, when present, their image was primarily negative. Partly in response to the aging of the baby-boom generation, however, television images of aging began changing in the late 1980's.

Research found an increase in the number of older adults portrayed on family-oriented prime-time television, and old age was presented more positively on these shows. In 1989, the Nielsen ratings reported *Murder, She Wrote*, *The Golden Girls*, *Matlock*, *Jake and the Fatman*, and *In the Heat of the Night* among the top-rated shows in the United States. Each of these programs featured well-known and respected individuals over the age of fifty-five. This implies a trend toward an increase in the number of television programs that highlight positive older characters.

Images of aging in daytime serials (soap operas) have also been studied. On the whole, older men are characterized as good listeners and older women as nurturers. Often these characters are described as "advisers-in-residence." Thus, the role for each character is primarily that of a sage—a provider of wisdom to children and grandchildren. Thus, while the depiction of the older adult in daytime television is not primarily negative, it is stereotypic.

Yet there are several caveats. First, while older adults may be represented with greater frequency, the number of older characters still does not reflect the proportion of older adults within the United States. Additionally, when older adults are represented, they are often portrayed stereotypically or as comic relief. Finally, it is important to remember that this research focuses on a specific class of television programs. One cannot generalize these findings to all of prime-time or daytime television programming.

While prime-time television programming may have exhibited an increase in positive imagery of aging, this trend may not have spilled over to all media. For example, a 1994 article in *Time* magazine discussed the aging trend in detective programming on television. The article, entitled "Murder, They Wheezed," described the central characters as "arthritic whodunits" and "old codgers." Accompanying graphics displayed the detectives as broken down and decrepit.

Gerontologists have also examined the portrayal of older persons in cartoons. The results show that older adults are represented rarely in Saturday morning cartoons. If they are present, it is typically in one of two forms. The older person is presented either as the evil character in the cartoon (such as a witch) or as someone who is slower, frail, and in need of a superhero's help. Thus, images of older individuals, however infrequent, foster a negative attitude toward the elderly.

The impact of television viewing on ageist attitudes has also been examined. While the research in this area has yielded contradictory results, it does suggest that a relationship may exist. Frequent television viewers appear to be more likely to believe negative stereotypes about the aged, such as that older adults are more rigid and less open-minded. In addition, they have also been found to believe that the health and longevity of older adults are declining. These notions are contrary to empirical evidence within the field of gerontology. The impact of television viewing on attitudes toward aging has been found to have a particular impact on younger people.

CROSS-CULTURAL PERSPECTIVES

Ageism is not a universal, cross-cultural phenomenon. There appears to be a great variation as to the treatment that older adults receive, ranging from extreme reverence and respect to abandonment and deprivation. Some anthropological research suggests that attitudes toward the elderly are most favorable in traditional societies and that they decrease with increasing modernization. In other words, the more "civilized" a society is, the more likely it is to maintain negative attitudes about the aged. This appears to be an oversimplification, however, as other factors such as differences between Eastern and Western cultures must be taken into account.

The cross-cultural differences in attitudes toward the aged may in part be attributable to societal perspectives. Three of the factors hypothesized to contribute to the development of ageism may be of relevance. First, death is not viewed in Western society as a natural part of the life cycle. Those societies that view life and death as a continuous process exhibit fewer ageist attitudes. Second, older individuals are viewed as productive in many small-scale traditional societies. In fact, they are often the power brokers within those societies. This can be compared with Western society, where older adults are thought of as unproductive. Finally, not all societies are youth-oriented. Therefore, a higher value is placed on the later stages of adulthood.
                                        —*Linda M. Woolf*

See also Advertising; Age discrimination; Aging: Historical perspective; Beauty; Communication; Cultural views of aging; Death and dying; Death anxiety; Films; *Golden Girls, The*; Greeting cards; Humor; Literature; *Matlock*; Men and aging; *Murder, She Wrote*; Old age; Over the hill; Stereotypes; Television; Women and aging.

FOR FURTHER INFORMATION:

Bytheway, Bill. *Ageism.* Bristol, Pa.: Open University Press, 1995. Examines the cultural and historical context of ageism.

Falk, Ursula A., and Gerhard Falk. *Ageism, the Aged, and Aging in America: On Being Old in an Alienated Society.* Springfield, Ill.: Charles C Thomas, 1997. Discusses ageism as a form of bigotry and examines what it is like to be an older adult in the United States at the end of the twentieth century.

Featherstone, Mike, and Andrew Wernick, eds. *Images of Aging: Cultural Representations of Later Life.* New York: Routledge, 1995. A collection of conference papers focusing on images of aging as influenced by culture, history, media, health, and gender.

MacDonald, Barbara, and Cynthia Rich. *Look Me in the Eye: Old Women, Aging, and Ageism.* Duluth, Minn.: Spinsters Ink, 1991. A collection of essays concerning the experience of aging. Combines personal experience and feminist theory.

Palmore, Erdman. *Ageism: Negative and Positive.* New York: Springer, 1991. A comprehensive review of the different forms of ageism, including positive ageism. Offers a discussion regarding methods to reduce ageism.

Rosenthal, Evelyn, ed. *Women, Aging, and Ageism.* New York: Haworth Press, 1990. A collection of articles examining issues of concern to women at midlife and beyond, including sexuality, social isolation, and the feminization of poverty.

Shenk, Dena, and W. Andrew Achenbaum, eds. *Changing Perceptions of Aging and the Aged.* New York: Springer, 1994. Contributors discuss images and perceptions of aging from a variety of perspectives. including historical, cross-cultural, economic, and theoretical.

AGING: BIOLOGICAL, PSYCHOLOGICAL, AND SOCIOCULTURAL PERSPECTIVES

RELEVANT ISSUES: Biology, culture, death, psychology, sociology

SIGNIFICANCE: How and why people age and what can be done about it have a significant impact on personal well-being and societal functioning

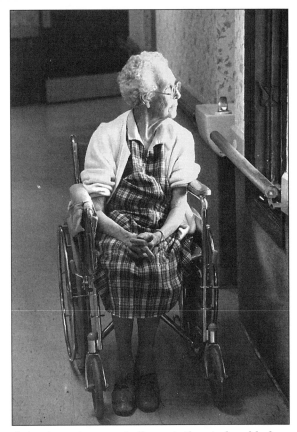

Aging presents many challenges to the mind and body as appearance, functionality, and societal roles shift. Aids such as eyeglasses and wheelchairs may be necessary, and housing options and accompanying social interactions can become limited. (James L. Shaffer)

Aging is the manifestation of biological, psychological, and social events that occur over the passage of time. Gerontologists, those people who study aging, make two important distinctions regarding the aging process. First, chronological aging, which occurs with the passage of time from birth or conception, is distinguished from functional aging, measured by how well people function over that passage of time. Second, longevity, the average number of years people can expect to live, is distinguished from life span, the theoretical upper limit on how long a person can live. These distinctions provide a necessary context for understanding the course of the biological, psychological, and sociocultural facets of aging.

HOW LONG CAN HUMANS LIVE?

Advances in medicine and health care, especially in the eradication of many childhood diseases, greatly increased the longevity of humans in the twentieth century. To illustrate, only 4 percent of Americans were age sixty-five and older at the beginning of the twentieth century. By the close of that century, that percentage more than tripled to approximately 13 percent, with life expectancy reaching to the high seventies. This optimistic picture, however, needs to be qualified in two regards. First, longevity varies greatly across culture and era. For example, Moses, living in the thirteenth century B.C., wrote in the Ninetieth Psalm of the Bible that the life expectancy of his contemporaries was between seventy and eighty years. Furthermore, extrapolations from Leonard Hayflick's work on cell division begun in the 1950's strongly suggest that there is an upper limit to how long a person can live: approximately 120 years, the same number that is told to Noah in Genesis 6:3.

Great variation is also found between the genders within most species of animals. The general rule is that females experience greater longevity than males. Among humans, female life expectancy is approximately seven years longer.

PROGRAMMED EVENTS AND RANDOM OCCURRENCES

Why are there consistent differences in the course of aging between the sexes and species? An obvious inference is that all animals are biologically determined to live a particular number of years and then die. Three main theories interpret aging as the consequence of purposeful, predetermined events.

The cellular clock theory is based on Hayflick's work with cell cultures derived from embryonic tissue. A 1990 study by Hayflick demonstrated that human cells placed in a dish and fed nutrients will grow, divide, and multiply rapidly at first. The rate of division will then slow down, however, and the cells will die somewhere between forty and sixty divisions, with male cells ceasing their doubling before female cells. Hayflick's explanation is that an intracellular clock determines an end to each cell's life.

The genetic design theory, proposed by Charles Minot in 1908, contends that the deoxyribonucleic acid (DNA) of every cell determines the course of aging in that cell. In other words, aging is designed in the "blueprint" of each organism at the time of conception. Consistency of aging in a species is therefore seen to be the consequence of similar DNA.

Extracellular mechanisms are the focus of the neuroendocrine theory. Many declines in vitality are induced by drops of particular hormones. For example, dehydroepiandrosterone (DHEA) diminishes with age, and some research indicates that supplements of DHEA in older adults restore many youthful characteristics. According to this theory, aging is predetermined by changes in endocrine gland functioning that reduce levels of various hormones.

Theories of aging based on random events can be roughly categorized into three types. The wear-and-tear approach to aging assumes that people and all biological organisms simply wear out like machines. Aging is seen to be an erosion process, and the greater the stress on the body, the greater the acceleration of aging. For example, the more skin is exposed to the sun, the more rapidly it ages.

Error theories of aging focus on something going wrong with physiological functioning. Many sorts of errors are implicated in aging. Some of these errors may be intracellular, such as flaws in the transcription process involving ribonucleic acid (RNA) that lead to the loss of DNA or flaws in enzymes that impair the production of proteins. Other errors may be extracellular, such as the immune system attacking and weakening the host body or failures to maintain proper homeostatic balances such as temperature or blood sugar level.

A third random event approach to aging emphasizes the accumulation of harmful substances which then interfere with the smooth functioning of the body. Some of the accumulated substances are produced within the body, such as waste products, genetic mutations, cross linkages (interconnections that reduce pliability in bodily tissues), and caramelization (coating of proteins by excess sugars). Some harmful substances come from outside the body. Free radicals—molecules with one or more unpaired electrons—are highly reactive and can initiate chemical changes in the wrong place and at the wrong time. Oxygen is a major source of free radicals, and breathing ensures a constant influx of these damaging substances. While free radicals are also produced in the body and play roles in digestion and immunological responses, their accumulation, if not checked by antioxidants and free radical scavengers such as melatonin, inevitably lead to physiological damage. Various pollutants and drugs can also add and subtract from the vigors of youth. For example, smokers show excessive and accelerated wrinkling of the skin as compared to nonsmokers.

No one theory of aging, whether based on random or programmed events, offers a complete explanation of the aging process. That is why many gerontologists adopt an eclectic perspective that views aging as a consequence of numerous events, designed and undesigned.

EXTERNAL AGING

Normal aging involves bone loss that is more severe in women (30 percent) than in men (17 percent). Two main consequences follow when the bones lose calcium. First, osteoporosis, in which bone loss leads to a stooping posture and a high risk of fractures, increases in incidence. Second, height decreases with aging. Lifetime average losses in height are greater for women (2.0 inches) than for men (1.25 inches), with the rate of loss increasing with age. Tooth loss is primarily a result of periodontal disease, the swelling and shrinking of infected gums, not calcium loss.

While height declines with age, the pattern is different for weight. Most studies show increases of weight until the mid-sixties and then declining weight through late adulthood. Because excess weight is a risk factor for premature death, late adulthood averages are lower, in part, because of the smaller representation of heavier individuals.

Other dimensions of human stature also change with aging. The nose and ears elongate. The chest and head increase in circumference. The trunk becomes thicker, and the legs and arms become thinner, although arm span shows only a slight decrease through the years. Muscle mass, particularly the percentage of lean muscle tissue, decreases with age and further alters physical appearance.

The aging of the skin is a consequence of both preventable and unpreventable factors. What is unpreventable is the inevitable loss of elastin and collagen proteins that help the skin retain its suppleness. What is preventable are two lifestyle choices that dramatically impact the rate and severity of wrinkling. Smoking, which accelerates the loss of collagen, leads to excessive wrinkling. In the case of heavy smokers, the wrinkling is several times more severe than in nonsmokers. Time spent in the sun also greatly influences wrinkling: The greater the exposure to the sun, the earlier and more excessive the wrinkling and the greater the risk of skin cancer.

A slowing in the growth rate of hair and fingernails (but not toenails) is observed with aging. The slowing of the growth rate in hair is more rapid in men than in women and can lead to baldness. High levels of certain androgen hormones, which men have more of, appear to play the key role in this process. Graying is caused by decreases of melanin, a pigment that gives hair its color. Body hairs also become less numerous during the aging process; an exception is that hair on the upper lip of women, particularly after the menopause, often increases.

Physical strength and capacity for exercise begin to show declines in the thirties and are related primarily to decreases in muscle tissue. In general, people who maintain good and consistent exercise patterns throughout their lives exhibit considerably smaller declines than those whose lifestyles are sedentary.

THE SENSES

Several changes occur with aging that impair the ability of the eyes to convey the physical world. Changes in the lens of the eye that affect vision are usually first noticed by people in their forties. The lens becomes thicker and harder through the years, which begins to interfere with the ability to see things close to the eyes. The result is presbyopia, or farsightedness, which is why middle-aged adults usually need reading glasses. The lens also begins to cloud with aging, a condition called cataracts, further obscuring vision in most elderly people. The opening permitting light to reach the lens is called the pupil, and its ability to dilate decreases with age. This results in less light being allowed to enter the eye and can cause night blindness. Directly in front of the pupil is a chamber containing a fluid called aqueous humor. A slowdown in the amount of aqueous humor leaving this chamber can result in a buildup of pressure called glaucoma that, if unchecked, can lead to blindness. Two other notable changes in vision are linked with aging. First, peripheral vision usually begins to decrease in the late fifties to sixties. Second, there is often a decrease in the ability to perceive blues and greens.

Hearing losses with age occur in ability to detect both pitches and loudness. By the mid-thirties, people begin a progressive loss of the ability to hear higher-pitched sounds, a condition called presbycusis. Furthermore, because the pitch range of male hearing is lower than female hearing, hearing loss enters the range of normal human conversation sooner in men than in women. There is also a diminishment in loudness perception, which is measured in decibels. Both long exposures to dangerous decibel levels (over 90 decibels) and shorter exposures to extremely high decibel levels will damage hearing cells and increase hearing deficits.

Age-related deficits in taste are the result of degenerative changes in the taste buds that reduce the perception of bitterness and saltiness more than sourness or sweetness. Thirst tends to slacken with age, increasing the risk of dehydration, especially in the elderly.

Several studies have also recorded drops in the sense of smell. This drop in the ability to detect odors includes a diminished ability to detect faint odors and a lesser ability to judge the magnitude of strong odors. The decline is steeper and more rapid for men than women.

The sense of touch is actually at least three senses, each mediated by different sense organs: skin contact and movement, temperature, and pain. Research indicates some decline in all three tactile abilities. The vestibular sense, or sense of balance, begins to decline in the fifties. Impairment of this sense combined with bone loss greatly increases the risk of broken bones as people grow older.

INTERNAL SYSTEMS

Changes in both the quality and quantity of sleep occur with age. Rapid eye movement (REM) sleep, which facilitates learning and is characterized by a high prevalence of dreaming, gradually declines from birth to death. The amount of sleep also declines from birth to late adulthood: from about sixteen hours to a little under seven hours. As people move into middle age, they typically wake up more frequently from their sleeping (maintenance insomnia) and end their sleeping periods sooner (termination insomnia).

Diseases of the cardiovascular system became the leading causes of death in most industrialized countries during the course of the twentieth century. Great variability in the rates of heart attacks, atherosclerosis (thickening and hardening of the arteries), and other cardiovascular problems between different nations demonstrate the importance of environmental factors, particularly diet, in addition to normal aging. What is normal is that both the heart and the blood vessels become less flexible. A combination of these changes and lifestyle dynamics makes several diseases more prevalent with aging. Systolic blood pressure increases and can result in hypertension (high blood pressure); diastolic blood pressure does not increase with aging. Decreased oxygen to the heart can lead to chest pains called angina or, in the case of a complete blockage, a stroke. Decreased heart output and increased blood pressure lead to increased fluid around the heart, a condition called congestive heart failure, a leading reason for hospitalization in the elderly.

Declines in the functioning of the organs of the digestive system associated with aging are generally not severe enough to cause major health problems. There are decreases in several digestive enzymes, particularly the protein enzyme hydrochloric acid, secreted by the stomach. On the other hand, bile, which is stored in the gallbladder and helps to break down fats, can increase in concentration and lead to gallstones. The liver, which produces bile and plays the major role in regulating blood contents, shows some shrinkage with age. Hardening of the liver, termed cirrhosis, is more attributable to alcohol consumption than to normal aging.

The general rule regarding the aging of the endocrine system, the cells and tissues that produce hormones, is that less hormones are produced and cells become less responsive to them. Drops in melatonin lead to sleep problems; in thyroxin, to decreases in metabolism; in insulin and glucagon, to greater difficulty regulating the blood sugar level; and in androgens and estrogens, to declining reproductive ability and deficits in muscles and bones.

Healing capacity is reduced in two ways as people age. Wound repair is slower in older people, and the strength of the repairs is diminished. Once the healing process is completed, however, the repairs are basically as good in older people as in younger individuals. Inflammatory response to irritants is reduced with increasing age, as is immune system responsiveness. Skin with greater exposure to the sun heals slower than skin that is infrequently exposed to the sun.

The body's main defense against attacking microorganisms and foreign materials is the immune system. To function effectively, the immune system must maintain a balance between the extremes of too much activity, in which immune cells attack other cells of the body as foreign, and too little activity, in which foreign invaders to the body are not repulsed. As people grow older, there is an increased tendency for the immune system to lose that necessary balance. Thus, cancers become more likely as a result of immunological underreactiveness and, conversely, overreactiveness leads to autoimmune disorders such as certain kinds of arthritis. The most significant observable change in the immune system occurs in the thymus gland, which shrinks after puberty and loses over 90 percent of its original size by the age of fifty. The effectiveness of white blood cells, such as the lymphocytes and neutrophils, also decreases with the increase in years.

One of the reasons that people typically put on excess weight during middle age is a decrease in the basal metabolic rate (BMR). Declines in the BMR mean that less food is "burned" as fuel and more food is turned into fat stores. The good news about a lowered BMR is that it is linked with greater longevity: Mammals with lower BMRs generally outlive mammals with higher BMRs, which is also one reason that females (with a lower BMR) outlive males.

Age-related changes in the nervous system have a significant impact on the physiological, psychological, and social aspects of aging. As people age, there are two primary changes observed in their nervous systems. First, the speed of messages to and from nerve cells (neurons) slows down about 10 percent. This slowing is partly responsible for increases in reaction time and a general decrease in the speed in which older people do activities. The second major change in the nervous system is a shrinkage in size. For example, measures of the size of the human brain reveal average decreases of approximately 10 percent from young adulthood to late adulthood. This decrease is partly attributable to losses of neurons and partly the consequence of shrinkage of the neurons themselves.

There are significant age-related differences in declining reproductive ability (called the climacteric) between females and males. By around the age of fifty, a decline in the number of a woman's eggs and an associated decline in estrogen levels result in irregular menstrual periods and eventually the cessation of the menstrual cycle (the menopause), ending her ability to reproduce naturally. Furthermore, by middle age a woman's remaining eggs begin to deteriorate in quality, diminishing her likelihood of becoming pregnant. Shrinkage in the size of the uterus, vagina, and breasts is also typical in postmenopausal women.

There is no naturally induced end to a male's reproductive capability. Declining hormone levels do, however, lead to a decline in the number of sperm produced as a man ages. The most problematic change associated with this gradual climacteric is the enlargement of the prostate gland and an increased risk of prostate cancer in elderly men. As men age, obtaining an erection becomes more difficult but maintaining it becomes easier.

The most significant change in the respiratory system is a drop of over 50 percent in vital capacity (the amount of air volume that can be inspired) from young to late adulthood. Calcification of air passages, increased rigidity of the rib cage, reductions of elastin and collagen in the lungs (reducing their flexibility), and decreases in muscle strength all play a role in this decline.

The ability to control body temperature is reduced as people grow older due to a reduction in sweat glands, subcutical skin (which controls the loss of body heat), and the density of the circulatory system of the skin. These changes put the elderly at greater risk in extremes of both cold and hot temperatures.

Problems with the urinary tract can be a major source of embarrassment for the elderly. Approximately half of all people over the age of sixty-five have some problems with bladder control. The functioning of the kidneys also declines about 50 percent from young to late adulthood.

PSYCHOLOGICAL AGING

Much of the work in the early twentieth century on the effects of aging on intellectual functioning was cross-sectional research comparing younger people to older adults. Deficits in the abilities of the elderly as compared to younger individuals were found and attributed to the natural course of aging. These findings were eventually criticized because generational differences, such as health care and educational background, were ignored, making it impossible to assume that only normal aging played a role in the findings. Improved research by people such as Paul Baltes has demonstrated that while there is an age-related drop in the speed of information processing, which appears to be biologically based, there is no drop in knowledge quantity, which is more experientially based. Moreover, wisdom, the ability to use knowledge, has been found in some research to increase as people grow older.

Research on memory has found that some types of memory decline with aging while others do not. Memories of personal events (episodic memories) decline with aging, but memories of how to do something (procedural memories) or of facts (semantic memories) do not. Memories of very recent events (short-term memory) decline more with aging than knowledge of more distant past experience (long-term memory).

Most basic personality traits show little change as people grow older. What does change with aging is that older adults tend to decrease participation in fast-paced activities and become more introspective. For example, life review—looking back on one's life, thinking about it, and working to find meaning in it—is more common among the elderly.

Research has not demonstrated consistently any trend toward poorer mental health associated with aging. Older adults are no more likely to suffer from major depression than younger adults, and some research indicates that older adults have greater satisfaction with their lives than younger adults. While the suicide rate does increase in later adulthood, other factors, such as poor physical health, may play a greater role in this statistic than lack of psychological well-being.

SOCIAL ACTIVITIES AND AGING

Increased mobility in society has resulted in a decreased likelihood of multigenerational families in the same home. One consequence has been an increase of the number of older people being institutionalized, such as in nursing homes. However, most people above the age of sixty-five, about 95 percent, live in their own homes.

Another trend seen in industrialized societies during the twentieth century was the increase in the number of full-time workers who retire from work. Many countries have encouraged older workers to retire in order to reduce unemployment rates for younger workers. Individuals who adjust best to retirement are those who prepare best for it (especially financially) and who find other meaningful activities in which to engage.

Adjustment to aging is greatly influenced by satisfaction with various social roles. Those in late adulthood who are married are happier and live longer than those who are unmarried. Friendships take on increased importance as people grow older, helping to buffer individuals from the inevitable stresses of losing loved ones. Approximately 75 percent of all adults above the age of sixty-five have at least one grandchild, and most grandpar-

ents find the role enjoyable. Gender roles may also change, as research finds that most men become more nurturing as the years go by.

Individuals above the age of sixty-five express more interest in spirituality than do younger adults, typically praying more, attending religious services more, and being more likely to be in positions of religious leadership. Research has found that older adults who are more religious have a greater overall sense of well-being than those who are less religious.

SOCIETAL AND CULTURAL FACTORS IN AGING

Two of the major trends in industrialized countries during the course of the twentieth century were a decrease in the number of children per woman and the increased longevity of the population. As the twentieth century came to a close, many nations grappled with the implications of these trends: a greater need for social programs to help support an aging population but a decrease in workers whose tax dollars pay for those programs. Intergenerational conflict is the consequence when societies fail to balance equitably the needs of different age segments of the population.

Different attitudes and behaviors directed toward the elderly have historically been demonstrated by Western societies, such as the United States, and Eastern societies, such as Japan. In general, greater respect has been accorded the elderly in Eastern cultures than in Western nations. Ageism, prejudice against the elderly, has been more prevalent in Western civilizations. Elderly people who are ethnic minorities within a country, such as African Americans, may face the double-edged sword of racism and ageism. The good news for elderly people is that their increasing numbers have led to stronger political influence and greater power to fight ageism.

SLOWING AGING

Three primary factors will help a person to live long and well: good genes, a good environment, and a good lifestyle. Because the first two factors are largely the result of other people's decisions, gerontologists have usually emphasized lifestyle choices for people who want to do something about how they age. Lifestyle decisions have the greatest impact on functional aging. Consistent and moderate exercise, a diet high in fruits and vegetables, lower exposure to harsh environments, maintenance of proper weight, and intellectual stimulation have all been demonstrated to improve the quality of life in the later years. Of particular interest in this regard has been work with a group of nuns in Mankato, Minnesota, who are being studied because of their mental sharpness in their elderly years and their great longevity. The nuns lead very stimulating intellectual lives, and autopsies of their brains have revealed less signs of aging than in comparable groups. The implication from this research is that intellectual activity slows the ravages of aging.

The search for the proverbial fountain of youth and immortality has been the preoccupation of scholar and nonscholar alike throughout the centuries. Many of the supposed "wonder cures" for aging have had consequences worse than the natural progression of aging itself. Research, however, has provided some hope in increasing the life span. Studies with a variety of mammalian species have found that significant drops in caloric intake translate into significant increases in both functional and chronological aging. Nevertheless, limits remain to the beneficial effects of caloric restriction.

Perhaps the best attitude toward aging is summed up in the Serenity Prayer: "God grant me the serenity to accept the things I cannot change, courage to change the things I can, and wisdom to know the difference."　　　　—*Paul J. Chara, Jr.*

See also Age discrimination; Age spots; Ageism; Antiaging treatments; Arthritis; Bone changes and disorders; Brain changes and disorders; Caloric restriction; Cancer; Cataracts; Cross-linkage theory of aging; Cultural views of aging; Demographics; Fat deposition; Free radical theory of aging; Gastrointestinal changes and disorders; Genetics; Gray hair; Hair loss and baldness; Hearing loss; Heart changes; Hypertension; Life expectancy; Longevity research; Memory changes and loss; Men and aging; Menopause; Osteoporosis; Personality changes; Prostate enlargement; Psychiatry, geriatric; Reaction time; Reading glasses; Reproductive changes, disabilities, and dysfunctions; Respiratory changes and disorders; Retirement; Sensory changes; Skin changes and disorders; Sleep changes and disturbances; Social ties; Temperature regulation and sensitivity; Vision changes and disorders; Wisdom; Women and aging; Wrinkles.

FOR FURTHER INFORMATION:
Erikson, Erik H., and Joan M. Erikson. *The Life Cycle Completed.* Extended version. New York: W. W. Norton, 1997. This final work of a noted developmental psychologist, with additional material by his wife, presents an eloquent affirmation of what elderly people can become.

Evans, William, J., Jacqueline Thompson, and Irwin H. Rosenberg. *Biomarkers: The Ten Keys to Prolonging Vitality.* New York: Simon & Schuster, 1992. Guidelines for how diet and exercise can improve the aging process are described.

Hayflick, Leonard. *How and Why We Age.* New York: Ballantine Books, 1994. A preeminent scientist offers a comprehensive examination of the aging process.

Levinson, Daniel J., et al. *The Seasons of a Man's Life.* New York: Ballantine Books, 1978. Examines the issues with which individuals grapple as they age in the book that popularized the concept of midlife crisis.

Weiss, Rick, and Karen Kasmauski. "Aging: New Answers to Old Questions." *National Geographic* 192, no. 5 (November, 1997). Presents an excellent overview on aging and the techniques used to slow it down.

AGING EXPERIENCE: DIVERSITY AND COMMONALITY ACROSS CULTURES, THE

AUTHORS: Jennie Keith et al.
DATE: Published in 1994
RELEVANT ISSUES: Culture, family, health and medicine, race and ethnicity
SIGNIFICANCE: This text offers a cross-cultural comparison of aging based on a ten-year study at seven different sites around the world

A team of seven anthropologists collaborated for more than ten years on Project AGE (Age, Generation, and Experience), a study of aging at seven research sites located in Botswana, Ireland, the United States, and Hong Kong. Their research question was, "What are the sources and consequences of the different *meanings* of age in different sociocultural settings?" In other words, they wanted to learn how beliefs about age and aging in different cultures affect older people in those societies.

The major themes developed in *The Aging Experience: Diversity and Commonality Across Cultures* were age and well-being; age and the life course; political economy and age; and age, health, and functionality. The anthropologists' conclusions were based on their observations at different sites and during individual interviews. The Age Game, a portion of the interview, involved sorting cards to learn about the names and characteristics of different age groups in each society, about how the interviewees evaluated age groups in their society, and about their perceptions of the elderly who were doing especially well or especially poorly.

The book's section on age and well-being deals with how well different societies meet the needs of the elderly and how well the elderly adapt. The researchers were particularly interested in how age and sex affect a sense of life satisfaction and whether these effects are similar in all cultures. Their work led them to believe that predictable differences exist in different life stages concerning sources of life satisfaction. They also concluded that health and material resources profoundly influence people's sense of well-being in all the cultures they studied.

The section on age and the life course deals with the results of the Age Game and interviews on the structure and meaning of different life stages. Both techniques addressed marital status, children's and grandchildren's status, composition of the household, housing arrangements, and work. The researchers found considerable differences among cultures.

Political economy deals with the influences of economic roles, resource control, and cultural and social structure on individuals in a given society. Again, the researchers found considerable differences among the study sites. In the United States and Ireland, governmental policies on aging had considerably more influence than in Hong Kong and Botswana, but in all societies, governmental policies were influenced by cultural values.

In order to understand health and functionality and how they relate to age, the researchers first had to determine what good and bad health, disease, and disability meant in each society. They found considerable variation in health care, health and disability, and the relationship between functionality and well-being in the study sites.

The researchers concluded that their cross-cultural comparison demonstrated "warnings and visions for an aging society." They also raised questions about the differences between cultural aging and physical aging and cautioned individuals to consider thoughtfully the best way to age in their own societies. —*Rebecca Lovell Scott*

See also Aging: Biological, psychological, and sociocultural perspectives; Aging: Historical perspective; Cultural views of aging; Disabilities; Politics; Successful aging.

AGING: HISTORICAL PERSPECTIVE

RELEVANT ISSUES: Culture, demographics, family, values

SIGNIFICANCE: Tracing the history of aging provides information about how aging and attitudes toward elders have been defined, understood, and changed over time; the status of elders within their communities; and the history of social provisions available to elders

The history of aging is a history of how aging and elders are perceived and what status older persons have had in various societies over time. To talk about the history of aging assumes that this stage in life has a history that is unique and develops independently of the other life stages. Thus one could look at the status and social situation of elders independently from other age cohorts to find differences over time. The number of individuals who reach old age has changed quite remarkably over time. Changes have also taken place in the way older people have been viewed politically and economically. In the 1930's, in response to changes in the perceived difficult economic and social position of elders, there was a significant growth in the number of social programs developed to meet their needs. Beliefs about the economic position of older persons seems to have changed once more, and American society is now reconsidering and possibly limiting social programs, such as Medicare and Social Security retirement benefits.

DEFINING "OLD"

For most people, "old" refers to someone over the age of sixty-five. This was the age set in Germany in 1898 for eligibility for social insurance. The same age was first used in the United States as the age of entitlement to Social Security, Supplemental Security Income (SSI), and Medicare. Sixty-five has become a commonly accepted boundary between middle age and old age. In

1935, when this age of entitlement was used in the newly enacted Social Security Act, life expectancy was about sixty-five. It is easy to see how this age could take on special meaning.

In prehistoric times, advanced age was rare, and only a few people reached fifty. It was not until the civilizations of Egypt and Mesopotamia that advanced aging existed. During ancient Greek and Roman periods, some individuals lived into their seventies and eighties, but this was a much smaller segment of the population. The critical point is at what age in these earlier societies the label "old" was used as a meaningful descriptor of a person. Sociologist David Hackett Fischer suggests that in the Greek and Roman classical period, old age was defined as over sixty; thus the definition has changed little since then.

The real change over time has been in the numbers of persons who could expect to live until their sixty-fifth year. In colonial times in America, two out of ten people survived to the age of sixty-five. By the end of the twentieth century, eight out of ten Americans could expect to live to that age, and of those reaching sixty-five, half could expect to reach eighty years of age. Thus most people will reach old age in the current definition and most likely will have a very personal stake in how aging is viewed and in the viability of social insurance provisions.

Today, the definition of who is old includes all people in later years but seems most likely to be applied to those who are debilitated. Thus the term "old" increasingly refers to frail elders, who are no longer actively involved in community affairs. In reality, fragility is more likely to be the situation for those older than seventy-five or even eighty-five years of age. As one looks to the political leadership of the United States, one finds many individuals in advanced years—for example, the justices of the Supreme Court. It would seem that old age is currently defined in terms of years, as more than sixty-five, but that the meaningfulness of this definition is limited. People who continue in positions of power are not defined primarily as old. Thus the definition seems to be influenced both by real age and by status and health.

To some extent, American society is continuing a historical pattern by adding another life stage according to level of debility through the use of such terms as the "young-old" (referring to those sixty-five to eighty-five who are active and healthy), the "old-old" (those over eighty-five), and "frail elders" (those in poor health).

LIFE EXPECTANCY

Life expectancy is the average number of years that any individual can expect to live. It is a measure that reflects the number of people who die prematurely rather than a true picture of how old the oldest individuals are at any given time. In the early years of colonial America, life expectancy at birth was thirty-five years, yet some still lived into their seventies and eighties. By 1900, this figure had jumped to forty-seven years, and by 1950 it was sixty-eight years. In 1996, life expectancy for Americans was 76.1 and was expected to increase to 77.6 by 2005 and to 82.6 in 2050. Life expectancy varies from one social group to another, with women living longer than men and Asian Americans and whites living longer than African Americans and American Indians. It is only since the 1970's that one sees increases in life expectancy that reflect the extension of life rather than the prevention of premature death.

Since life expectancy has been increasing, one should not be surprised to see that the number of older people as a percentage of the total population is growing as well. According to data from the U.S. Census Bureau, the number of persons in the United States under sixty-five tripled during the twentieth century. By contrast, the number of people over sixty-five grew to eleven times what it was in 1900. In colonial times, about 2 percent of the population was over sixty-five. In 1900, that figure was 4 percent, and in 1994, it was more than

Institutionalization of Persons 65+ in the United States

| Institutions | *Average Daily Census* | | | |
	1950	1969	1973	1980
State and county mental hospitals	141,346	111,420	70,615	36,997
Private mental hospitals	N/A	2,460	1,530	8,352
Nursing homes	N/A	96,415	193,900	383,376

An old man begs for change in the streets of New York City, c. 1900. Before the advent of Social Security, many elderly Americans, particularly the disabled, had little recourse. (Library of Congress)

life referred to by some as "overaged," the "sleeping period," or the "already dead." Some tribes killed the debilitated aged outright (sometimes with the consent and cooperation of the elder), some abandoned or neglected them, and some encouraged suicide.

The Old Testament of the Bible is full of positive references to old age: "A hoary head is a crown of glory" (Proverbs 16:31). Old age is perceived as a gift from God to the righteous. These biblical references to the old influenced Western thought about aging across time. One can see these same sentiments appearing in the attitudes of colonial America. From early Greek and Roman writings onward, however, one sees ambivalence in how elders are depicted. This level of ambivalence is illustrated by W. Andrew Achenbaum in the essay "Societal Perceptions of Aging and the Aged," in *Handbook of Aging and the Social Sciences* (1995). Achenbaum quotes Cicero:

> the crowning glory of old age is influence . . . when the preceding part of life has been nobly spent, old age gathers the fruits of influence at last. Diminishing physical strength pales in importance when compared to the opportunities advancing years provide for the mature ripening of mind and soul.

Aristotle, on the other hand, is quoted as saying that the elderly "are apt to be suspicious from distrust, and they are distrustful from their experience. . . . They should be barred from political office, since they grow increasingly inflexible and small-minded with years." These opposing viewpoints are echoed in the literature of other historical periods. While there is considerable respect

12 percent. The Census Bureau projects that by 2050, approximately 20 percent of the population will be over sixty-five.

HISTORICAL TRENDS IN ATTITUDES TOWARD AGING

In an examination of primitive societies, Fischer notes that one must first understand that in these societies, people of advanced age were very rare. Those who were perceived to be old were in their forties or fifties; few, if any, survived beyond fifty. Older persons were treated with respect and had a special place in formal ceremonial occasions. This position of respect was withdrawn, however, for those elders who were no longer able to contribute to the common welfare or to look after themselves. They were seen as a threat to the group, which often existed on the margin of sustainability. Fischer describes this final period, beyond that of respected elder, as another stage in given to elders, the literature often reflects both positive and negative views.

What has not seemed to have changed over time is the diversity among older people. It has been said that as people age, their personal characteristics become more distinct and set, so that older persons become ever more like themselves, ever more unique. It is no wonder that literature, over time, also reflects quite divergent views on aging and older persons. Perhaps what is being said is that any cohort of the population cannot be so unidimensionally defined.

It is commonly accepted that traditional cultures, which depended on older persons as the holders of traditional wisdom or understanding of the world, held aging persons in greater regard. It was elders who kept the past alive as a model for how people should conduct their lives. One must add that this was the case for the more successful and respected men of the group. It did not include those in decline and ill health, nor did it usually include women or the poor.

Fischer notes that in the colonial period of America, for the Puritans great age was seen as a special gift from God. One aspect of this attitude was the rarity of advanced age. From what is known of the behaviors of colonial Americans, one sees much evidence that they lived these beliefs. In church, the best pews were assigned to elders. (To be sure, other criteria such as wealth, power, race, and sex were also taken into account.) Community and church leadership was held by men of maturity.

Retirement was not usual; when it took place, it was for cause, not age. Colonial America was largely agrarian, and like other traditional societies, it was age-integrated. Age-integrated societies had a social arrangement in which older persons were not categorized separately or set apart. They continued to work and remained as heads of family. Physical and mental decline could ultimately make this position less possible. This is the point at which attitudes toward elders may have changed, more in response to debility than to years of age. Land ownership was at the heart of success in agrarian societies, and title stayed with the elder male in a family. This arrangement made sons dependent on their fathers, often until middle age. Respect for the old was part and parcel of the holding of land and other resources and strongest for the elite, powerful, and prosperous man.

The elderly poor, on the other hand, were treated badly. As Fischer states:

> poor, widowed, and base born women were treated with a contempt which was deepened all the more by their womanhood. Some were actually driven away by their neighbors who feared an increase in their poor rates. . . . To be old and poor and outcast in early America was certainly not to be venerated but rather to be despised. . . . Old age seems actually to have intensified the contempt visited upon a poor man.

Unattached, poor old persons were grouped with other dependents such as the mentally or physically ill. Such experiences were the case only for a small minority. Most elders unable to provide self-care were provided for by family members. One must be careful, however, about romanticizing social relationships during this period; many were troubled. In addition, those individuals who did live to advanced years often did so with considerable illness and misery. Serene old age was all but unknown. Some would say that there has never been a true "golden age" for older persons. During the early years in America, age and problems associated with it were simply seen as individual concerns. The significant social issue was premature death and the resultant problems of widows and orphans needing assistance.

This traditional family system has often been seen as breaking down with the coming of the Industrial Revolution. Commonly held beliefs are that work was transformed by technology, urbanization created by the centralization of jobs in large factories led to the breakup of extended families, and the growth of mass education provided the vehicle through which knowledge could be transferred to the young. Many believe that the social changes that accompanied the Industrial Revolution were the mechanisms that changed elders' position of respect in society.

Some suggest, however, that the change in the position of elders in society predates the Industrial Revolution. Fischer argued that the new ideas about equality and equal rights that lay behind the revolution were also behind the change from traditional social structures. Others point out that in the late eighteenth and early nineteenth centuries, many changes were taking place. New philosophies gained currency, agrarian life gave way to industrialization, and industrialization supported the growth of cities. The development of new knowledge, public education, and technologies made possible an improvement in living conditions and thus allowed more people to live longer. The view of aging and elders gradually changed. The discovery of age-linked disease helped to redefine old age as a state of illness.

Fernando M. Torres-Gil, in his book *The New Aging: Politics and Change in America* (1992), divides the history of aging in the United States into three periods: "pre-1930 (Young Aging), 1930-1990 (Modern Aging), and post-1990 (New Aging)." He argues that prior to 1930, the status of older people continued to reflect centuries-old patterns of how elders were viewed through family traditions, roles, and economic power. He saw the big change as occurring during the 1930's. It was at this time, based on new knowledge emerging in the previous decades, that elders were redefined in the public mind as poor, ill, and needy. In response to this new understanding, between 1930 and 1990, one sees increasing development of government-sponsored programs and services with requirements based on age.

SOCIAL PROVISION AS DETERMINED BY AGE

In the nineteenth century, the problem of poor elders unable to meet self-care needs was resolved by almshouses or poor farms. Because the needs of most elders at this time were met by family, one tends to forget that this was not the situation for all older individuals. Fischer states that in 1910, the first serious attempt was made to determine the number of poor elderly in Massachusetts. It was discovered that one of four elderly were receiving relief; 23 percent were public paupers or inmates of asylums and almshouses. In Massachusetts, 92 percent of those in almshouses were over sixty-five; the comparable figures were 60 percent for Ohio and 87 percent for Wisconsin. Poverty was at the heart of the problem presented by age. According to Fischer, the poverty rate for the old was 23 percent in 1910, 40 percent in 1930, and 50 percent in 1935. By 1940, two-thirds of people over sixty-five were receiving some sort of charity. This was not the idyllic scenario of elders cared for by family. At that time, family resources were often scarce, and employment was hard to find for all ages. Community resources were also strained to the breaking point.

The use of almshouses to provide care for dependent unattached elders was resolved in various ways. Many were moved to newly developed state hospitals. These elders are now most likely to be found in nursing homes. A chart taken from the report submitted by the President's Commission on Mental Health illustrates these changes.

The new information detailing the difficult circumstances of the elderly presented a new image of them as poor, frail, and without other resources. This perception formed the backdrop for the development of the age-specific social programs begun in the 1930's. The Social Security Act of 1935 firmly set the principle of retirement for older persons. Prior to such legislation, older persons worked until health problems or lack of employment made work impossible. Without employment, older persons had to rely on family assistance or community support. The tragedy of the Great Depression, which began in 1929, made that support difficult if not impossible.

The provisions of the original Social Security Act continued to expand until the 1980's. This expansion included more complete coverage for a wider number of workers and improvements in the provisions for poor elders, in survivors benefits, and in medical care. The year 1965 also brought the Older Americans Act, which provided a wide array of age-specific programs that brought increased stability to the lives of the majority of elders but still left some in poverty. The development of age-specific programs seemed to set people over sixty-five apart from other adults. It was a firm distinction of "otherness" for older persons. It is also clear that the social programs designed to meet the needs of a smaller group of older persons in 1935 need to grow dramatically to be able to provide for so many more people than once expected.

CONCLUSION

To some extent, whatever was true historically about aging is true today in different balance. American society still honors older persons of accomplishment, as reflected in its chosen leadership. Families still provide the bulk of elder care needs, whether out of duty or affection. What has changed is that more people live to advanced age than ever before. The social provisions that the U.S. government began in the 1930's need to be adjusted to this new reality. What one learns from examining historical attitudes toward aging is that the adjustment of age-specific social provisions must be visited as a new problem with new solutions.   —*Joan Hashimi*

See also African Americans; Age discrimination; Age Discrimination Act of 1975; Age Discrimination in Employment Act of 1967; Ageism; Aging: Biological, psychological, and sociocultural perspectives; American Indians; Asian Americans; Baby boomers; Caregiving; Cultural views of aging; Demographics; Employment; Family relationships; Forced retirement; Graying of America; *Growing Old in America*; Latinos; Life expectancy; Medicare; Men and aging; Multigenerational households; Older Americans Act of 1965; Pensions; Politics; Retirement; Social Security; Stereotypes; Townsend movement; Wisdom; Women and aging.

FOR FURTHER INFORMATION:

Achenbaum, W. Andrew. "Societal Perceptions of Aging and the Aged." In *Handbook of Aging and the Social Sciences*, edited by Robert H. Binstick and Linda K. George. San Diego: Academic Press, 1995. This chapter provides an overview of the humanistic view of aging from ancient times to the end of the twentieth century. Describes changes in the American view of aging and points to the colonial period through the first half of the nineteenth century as the time of an age-integrated society. Argues that since the development of age-based services and programs, the United States has become an age-segregated society.

Achenbaum, W. Andrew, Steven Weiland, and Carol Haber. *Key Words in Sociocultural Gerontology*. New York: Springer, 1996. This interesting text lists and fully defines a number of terms key to an understanding of gerontology. Some terms highlight shifting beliefs about aging that began in the 1930's. Includes references to activity theory, age discrimination (which is dated to the era immediately following the American Revolution), and modernization theory.

Bengtson, Vern L., and W. Andrew Achenbaum. *The Changing Contract Across Generations*. New York: Aldine de Gruyter, 1993. The authors define the changes that took place in family structure in the twentieth century. They point to changes in the number of generations in exis-

tence at a given point of time. The generational structure went from a pyramid to a bean pole (from, for example, one grandparent, four or five adult children, and twenty grandchildren to a great-grandmother, her daughter and son-in-law, their two children and spouses, and four great-grandchildren). An opposite generational pattern becoming more prevalent is age-gapped intergenerational structure, which results if parenting is delayed until the mid- to late thirties. When these changes are combined with higher divorce rates, one can see that family patterns and roles must change in response to these personal choices. The authors' theme is that these changes bring about changes in the social contract for expectations and obligations between the generations. This becomes a social issue when one takes up concerns of equity and fairness between age cohorts at any given time and the expectations of any cohort for resources.

Fischer, David Hackett. *Growing Old in America*. Expanded ed. New York: Oxford University Press, 1978. An older but quite readable text that describes aging in the United States. Through evidence gained from primary resources, Fischer brings out both the respect and honor for the old and the suffering among elders held in less regard. Includes much detailed information on styles of dress and hair, job continuation, social leadership roles, and many other variables to illustrate the position and status of elders over time. Fischer also delves into some controversial issues among historians that focus on the validity of the modernization model.

Hooyman, Nancy R., and H. Asuman Kiyak. *Social Gerontology: A Multidisciplinary Perspective*. 5th ed. Boston: Allyn & Bacon, 1999. This broad text in social gerontology contains an interesting chapter on the history of aging that adds a cross-cultural view. Enters the debate on the meaningfulness of the modernization theory by stating that there is not a simple "before and after" relationship of the status of older persons pre- and postindustrialization. By using cross-cultural information, the authors are able to show how modernization can have a different impact in different cultures.

Ozawa, Martha N. "The Economic Well-Being of Elderly People and Children in a Changing Society." *Social Work: Journal of the National Associa-*

tion of Social Workers 44, no. 1 (1999). The author begins with the premise that the twentieth century was a "triumph" for older Americans. Ozawa cites the Social Security Act of 1935, the Supplemental Security Income (SSI) program of 1972, the 1965 Social Security amendments establishing Medicare and Medicaid, and the Employee Retirement Income Security Act of 1974 (ERISA) as providing basic income for older persons. All this legislation was enacted at a time when there was a better numerical balance between old and young, retirees and workers. This balance is changing from 3.2 workers per retiree in 1996 to a projected 1.9 in 2050. Ozawa further shows the falling economic well-being of children, with the number of children living below poverty being greater than the number of elder persons in that state. The author argues that the United States must devote more resources to providing for the needs of children.

Skocpol, Theda. *Protecting Soldiers and Mothers: The Political Origins of Social Policy in the United States.* Cambridge, Mass.: The Belknap Press of Harvard University Press, 1992. A new interpretation of social provision for older persons in the period from 1890 to 1910. During that time, the federal government devoted over a quarter of its expenditures to pensions for Northern veterans of the Civil War. By 1910, about 28 percent of all American men aged sixty-five or older received federal benefits. Over three hundred thousand widows, orphans, and other dependents were also receiving payments from the Treasury. In addition, many more were residents of special homes maintained for veterans. As the numbers of Civil War veterans shrank early in the twentieth century, programs for women and children developed in many states. This book details that provision and its political context.

Torres-Gil, Fernando M. *The New Aging: Politics and Change in America.* New York: Auburn House, 1992. This work looks at the social provisions for elders of the twentieth century and the changes that took place in the older adult population. Also examines the changes that can be expected and how these changes influence what society will be able to provide in the coming years.

U.S. Census Bureau. "Sixty-Five Plus in the United States." http://www.census.gov/socdemo/www agebrief.html. This statistical brief provides basic census data from the twentieth century about those over sixty-five years of age.

AGING PROCESS

RELEVANT ISSUES: Biology, health and medicine, psychology

SIGNIFICANCE: The process of aging affects all the body's systems and results in physiological and psychological changes of varying dimension from person to person and even within the same individual

As people age beyond a certain point, they decline physically. From the fourth decade of life onward, a gradual decline in vigor and resistance eventually gives way to various types of illnesses. In the opinion of many authorities, people do not "die of old age"; rather, old age worsens specific conditions responsible for death. This process of decline can be described on the basis of predictable occurrences. Change is gradual. In aging, gradual changes in body structure or function occur before specific health problems are identified.

Individual differences also occur. When two people of the same age are compared for the type and extent of age-related change, major differences can be noted. Even within the same person, different systems decline at differing rates and varying extents. The greatest changes are noted in areas of complex function. The most profound effects of physiological aging are usually noted in physiological processes involving two or more major body systems. Becoming older is associated with a growing difficulty in maintaining homeostasis (the dynamic balance among body systems). In the face of stressors, an older adult's system takes longer to respond, does not respond with the same intensity, and may take longer to return to a normal state than a younger person's. Like growth and development, aging is predictable yet unique for each person. Since the process of aging is extended over the course of time, much living must occur before one is "old."

HEALTH CONCERNS OF ELDERLY ADULTS

In elderly persons, it is frequently difficult to distinguish between changes caused by aging and those caused by disease. For virtually every body system, biomedical indexes for the old and young can overlap. In the respiratory system, for example, the oxygen-uptake capacity of a man seventy years old may be no different from that of a man fifty-five years old who has a history of smoking. Is the level in the elderly man to be considered an indicator of a disease, or should it be considered a reflection of normal old age? In dealing with the elderly, physicians frequently must make this kind of distinction. In elderly persons, as in midlife persons, structural and physiological changes are routinely seen. In some cases, these are closely related to disease processes; in most cases, however, they reflect the gradual decline that is thought to be a result of the normal aging process.

The most frequently seen changes include decreases in bone mass, changes in bone structure, decreases in muscle bulk and strength, decreases in oxygen uptake-capacity, loss of nonreproducing cells in the nervous system, decreases in hearing and vision abilities, decreases in all other sensory modalities (including the sense of body positioning), slowed reaction times, and gait and posture changes resulting from a weakening of the muscles of the trunk and legs. The most common physical change seen in the elderly is the increased sensitivity of the body's homeostatic mechanism. Because of this sensitivity, a minor infection or superficial injury can be traumatic enough to decrease the body's ability to maintain its internal balance. An illness that would be easily controlled in a younger person can prove fatal to a seemingly healthy seventy-five-year-old. Health can thus be an uncertain commodity for persons beyond the age of sixty-five.

PHYSICAL CHANGES IN STRUCTURE AND FUNCTION

Living is a process of continual change. Infants become toddlers, pubescent children blossom into young men and women, and dependent adolescents develop into responsible adult citizens. The continuation of change into later life is natural and expected. The type, rate, and degree of physical, emotional, psychological, and social changes experienced during life are highly individualized. The types and degrees of these changes are influenced by genetic factors, environment, diet, health, stress, and numerous other elements.

The result is not only individual variations among aged persons but also differences in the pattern of aging of various body systems within the same individual. Although some similar elements in the pattern of aging can be identified between individuals, the unique pattern of aging in each person must be recognized.

Organ and system changes can be traced to changes at the basic cellular level. The number of cells is gradually reduced, leaving fewer functional cells in the body. Lean body mass is reduced, whereas fat tissue increases until the sixth decade of life. Bone mass is decreased. Extracellular fluid remains fairly constant, although intracellular fluid is decreased, resulting in less total body fluid. This makes the risk of dehydration significant in the elderly.

Some of the more noticeable effects of the aging process begin to appear after the fourth decade of life. It is then that most men experience hair loss, and both sexes develop gray hair and wrinkles. As body fat atrophies, the body's contours gain a bony appearance, along with a deepening of the hollows of the intercostal and supraclavicular spaces, orbits, and axillae. Elongated ears, a double chin, and baggy eyelids are among the more obvious manifestations of the loss of tissue elasticity throughout the body. Skinfold thickness is significantly reduced in the forearm and on the back of the hands. The loss of subcutaneous fat content, which is responsible for the decrease in skinfold thickness, also is responsible for a decline in the body's natural insulation, making older adults more sensitive to cold temperatures. Stature deceases, resulting in a loss of approximately 2 inches in height by seventy years of age. Body shrinkage is caused by a loss of cartilage and thinning of the vertebrae, causing the long bones of the body, which do not shrink, to appear disproportionately long. Normal oral temperatures are lower in later life than in younger years. These changes are gradual and subtle. Further differences in structure and function can arise from changes to specific body systems.

THE CARDIOVASCULAR SYSTEM

Heart size does not change significantly with age; enlarged hearts are associated with cardiac disease, and marked inactivity can cause cardiac atrophy. Heart valves become thick and rigid as a re-

The aging process is often most noticeable in the facial features: wrinkles and creases, sagging skin, thinning and gray hair, and a longer nose and chin. (Jim Whitmer)

sult of sclerosis and fibrosis, compounding the dysfunction associated with any cardiac disease that may be present. The aorta becomes dilated and elongated. The vessels lose their elasticity and accumulate calcium deposits, resulting in a narrowing of their lumen size. This reduced elasticity of the vessels, coupled with thinner skin and less subcutaneous fat, allows the vessels in the head, neck, and extremities to become more prominent.

Physiological changes in the cardiovascular system appear in a variety of ways throughout the adult years; the heart muscle loses its efficiency and contractile strength, resulting in a reduction in cardiac output of 1 percent per year. Usually, adults adjust to changes quite well; they learn that it is easier and more comfortable for them to take an elevator rather than stairs, to drive rather than to walk long distances, and to pace their activities, for example. When unusual demands are placed on the heart, however, the changes are realized.

The same holds true for the elderly, who are not severely affected by their lesser cardiac efficiency under nonstressful conditions. When older persons are faced with added demands on their hearts, however, the differences are apparent.

Although an elderly person's pulse rate may not reach the levels experienced by a younger person, a rapid heart rate (tachycardia) in an elderly person will last for a longer time. Stroke volume may increase to compensate for this situation, resulting in elevated blood pressure, although the blood pressure can remain stable as tachycardia progresses to heart failure in the elderly. Resistance to peripheral blood flow increases by 1 percent each year. Decreased elasticity of the arteries is responsible for vascular changes to the heart, kidneys, and pituitary gland. The increased rigidity of vessel walls and their narrower lumen necessitate that more force be used to pump blood through the vessels; in other words, systolic and diastolic pressures rise. The level at which the normal elevation becomes hypertension (high blood pressure) that requires treatment is a source of controversy in geriatric medical circles. Some physicians adhere to conservative practices and treat all individuals with elevated blood pressures; others do not treat higher levels if no symptoms or damages are apparent.

THE RESPIRATORY SYSTEM

As a person ages, various structural changes in the chest reduce respiratory activity. The calcification of costal cartilage makes the rib cage more rigid; the anterior-posterior chest diameter increases, and thoracic inspiratory and expiratory muscles are weaker. Alveoli are reduced in number and stretched as a result of a loss of elasticity. The lungs become more rigid and have less recoil. These changes cause less lung expansion, insufficient inflation, and decreased ability to expel foreign or accumulated matter. The lungs exhale less effectively, thereby increasing the residual volume. As the residual volume increases, the vital capacity is reduced; maximum breathing capacity also decreases. With less effective gas exchange and lack of inflation, the elderly are at high risk for developing respiratory infections.

THE GASTROINTESTINAL SYSTEM

Although not as life-threatening as cardiovascular or respiratory problems, gastrointestinal symptoms are of more bother and concern to older persons. This system is altered by the aging process at all points. Tooth loss is a consequence not of growing old but of poor dental care, diet, and environmental influences. Periodontal disease is the major reason for tooth loss after thirty years of age. Many elderly must rely on dentures, which may not be worn regularly because of discomfort or poor fit. If natural teeth are present, they often are in poor condition, having flatter surfaces, stains, and varying degrees of erosion and abrasion of crowns and root structures. Dentin production is decreased, the root pulp experiences shrinkage and fibrosis, the gingiva retracts, and bone density in the alveolar ridge is lost. The tooth brittleness of some older people creates the possibility of aspiration of tooth fragments.

Taste sensations become less acute with age because the taste buds atrophy. Chronic irritation (as from pipe smoking) can reduce taste efficiency to a greater degree than that caused by aging alone. The sweet sensations on the tip of the tongue tend to suffer a greater loss than the sensations for sour, salty, and bitter flavors. Excessive seasoning of foods may be used to compensate for taste alterations and can lead to health problems for the elderly. Approximately one-third of the amount of saliva is produced in old age as in younger years, interfering with the breakdown of starches. Esophageal motility is decreased, and the esophagus tends to become slightly dilated. Esophageal emptying is slower, which can cause discomfort because food remains in the esophagus for a longer time. Relaxation of the lower esophageal sphincter may occur; combined with the elderly's weaker gag reflex and delayed esophageal emptying, such relaxation can sometimes cause breathing problems.

The stomachs of older people have reduced motility along with decreases in hunger contractions and emptying time. The gastric mucosa atrophies, and lesser amounts of hydrochloric acid, pepsin, lipase, and pancreatic enzymes are produced, creating many of the indigestion problems experienced by older adults. Fat absorption is slower, and dextrose and xylose are more difficult to absorb. Absorption of vitamin B, calcium, and iron is faulty. Some atrophy occurs throughout the small and large intestines, and fewer cells are present on the absorbing surface of intestinal walls. Constipation is promoted by decreased colonic peristalsis. Neural impulses that sense the signal to empty are slower and duller, which can cause the need to evacuate to be postponed, resulting in constipation or impaction. The internal anal sphincter also loses its tone with age.

With advancing age, moreover, the liver becomes smaller and consequently has less storage capacity. Less efficient cholesterol stabilization and absorption cause an increased incidence of gallstones. The pancreatic ducts become dilated and distended, and often the entire gland prolapses.

THE GENITOURINARY SYSTEM

Renal (kidney) mass becomes smaller with age. Renal tissue growth declines, and atherosclerosis may promote atrophy of the kidneys. These changes can have a profound effect on renal function. Approximately a 50 percent decrease in renal blood flow and glomerular filtration rate occurs between the ages of twenty and ninety. Tubular function decreases, causing less effective concentration of urine. This decrease in function also causes decreased reabsorption of glucose from the filtrate, which can cause proteinuria and glycosuria. Urinary frequency, urgency, and nocturia accompany bladder changes with age. Bladder muscles weaken, and bladder capacity decreases. Emptying of the bladder is more difficult; retention of large volumes of urine may result. The emptying reflex is delayed. Although urinary incontinence is not a normal outcome of aging, some stress incontinence may occur because of a weakening of the pelvic diaphragm, particularly in women who have given birth to more than one child.

Prostate enlargement occurs in most elderly men; the rate and type vary between individuals. Three-fourths of men aged sixty-five and older have some degree of enlargement, which causes problems with urinary frequency. Although most prostate enlargement is benign, it does pose a greater risk of malignancy and requires regular evaluation. Older men do not ordinarily lose the physical capacity to achieve erections or ejaculations.

The female genitalia, however, demonstrate many changes with age, including atrophy of the vulva from hormonal changes, accompanied by the loss of subcutaneous fat and hair and a flattening of the labia. The vagina of the older woman appears pink and dry, with a smooth, shiny canal because of the loss of elastic tissue and rugae. The vaginal epithelium becomes thin. The vaginal environment is more alkaline in older women and is accompanied by a change in the type of flora and a reduction in secretions. The cervix atrophies and becomes smaller; the endocervical epithelium also atrophies. The uterus shrinks, and its lining (the endometrium) atrophies; however, the endometrium continues to respond to hormonal stimulation, which can be responsible for incidents of postmenopausal bleeding in older women on estrogen therapy. The Fallopian tubes atrophy and shorten with age, and the ovaries atrophy and become thicker and smaller. Despite these changes, the older woman does not lose the ability to engage in and enjoy intercourse or other forms of sexual pleasure.

THE MUSCULOSKELETAL SYSTEM

The spinal curvature, enlarged joints, flabby muscles, and decreased height of many elderly persons announce the variety of musculoskeletal changes occurring with age. Along with other body tissue, muscle fibers atrophy and decrease in number, with fibrous tissue gradually replacing muscle tissue. Overall muscle mass, muscle strength, and muscle movements are decreased; the arm and leg muscles, which become particularly flabby and weak, display these changes well. The importance of exercise to minimize the loss of muscle tone and strength increases with age. Muscle tremors may be present and are believed to be associated with degeneration. The tendons shrink and harden, causing a decrease in tendon jerks. Reflexes are lessened in the arms and are nearly totally lost in the abdomen but are maintained in the knee. For various reasons, moreover, muscle cramping frequently occurs.

Bone mineral and mass are reduced with age, contributing to the brittleness of the bones of older people, especially older women. These changes make fractures a serious risk to the elderly. Although long bones do not significantly shorten with age, thinning disks and shortening vertebrae reduce the length of the spinal column, causing a reduction in height with age. Height may be further shortened because of varying degrees of kyphosis, a backward tilting of the head, and some flexion at the hips and knees. A deterioration of the cartilage surface of joints and the formation of points and spurs may limit joint activity and motion.

THE NERVOUS SYSTEM

It is difficult to identify the exact effects of aging on the nervous system because of the dependence of the system's function on other body systems. For example, cardiovascular problems can reduce cerebral circulation and be responsible for cerebral dysfunction. Declining nervous system function may be unnoticed because changes are often nonspecific and slowly progressing. Reductions in nerve cells and cerebral blood flow and metabolism are known to occur, and nerve conduction velocity is lower.

These changes are manifested by slower reflexes and delayed responses to multiple stimuli. Kinesthetic sense lessens. Because the brain affects the sleep-wake cycle, changes in the sleep pattern occur. Frequent awakening during sleep is not unusual, although only a minimal amount of sleep is actually lost.

THE SENSORY ORGANS

Each of the five senses becomes less efficient with advanced age, interfering in varying degrees with safety, normal activities of daily living, and general well-being. Perhaps the greatest of such interferences results from changes in vision. Presbyopia (farsightedness), the inability to focus properly at a distance, is characteristic of older eyes and begins in the fourth decade of life. This vision problem causes most middle-aged and older adults to need corrective lenses.

Presbycusis is progressive hearing loss that occurs as a result of aging, and it is the most serious problem affecting the inner ear. High-frequency sounds are the first to be lost; middle and lower frequencies may also be lost as the condition progresses. Taste in the elderly becomes less acute because the number of functioning taste buds is reduced; the taste buds become inefficient in relaying flavors, although various flavors can be differentiated. The sense of smell is reduced because of a decrease in the number of sensory cells in the nasal lining and fewer cells in the olfactory bulb of the brain. Tactile sensation also diminishes, as is evidenced by the elderly's reduced ability to sense pressure and pain and to differentiate temperatures. These sensory changes can cause misperceptions of the environment and, as a result, profound safety risks.

THE ENDOCRINE AND IMMUNE SYSTEMS

With age, the thyroid gland undergoes fibrosis, cellular infiltration, and increased nodularity. The resulting decreased thyroid activity causes a lower basal metabolic rate, reduced radioactive iodine uptake, and less thyrotropin secretion and release. The thyroid gland progressively atrophies, and the loss of adrenal function can further decrease thyroid activity. Overall, however, thyroid function in elderly people generally remains adequate.

The pituitary gland decreases in volume by approximately 20 percent in older persons. Gonadal secretion declines with age, including gradual decreases in testosterone, estrogen, and progesterone. With the exception of alterations associated with changes in plasma calcium level or dysfunction of other glands, the parathyroid glands maintain their function throughout life. There is a delayed and insufficient release of insulin by the beta cells of the pancreas in the elderly. The older person's ability to metabolize glucose is reduced; therefore, it is not unusual to detect higher blood glucose levels in nondiabetic older persons.

The depressed immune responses of older adults cause infections to be a significant risk for many elderly people. Changes in T cells contribute to the reactivation of tuberculosis infections found in many older individuals. Responses to influenza, parainfluenza, pneumococcus, and tetanus vaccines are also less effective, although vaccination for such illnesses is recommended for the elderly.

THE SKIN AND INTEGUMENTARY SYSTEM

Diet, general health, activity, exposure, and hereditary factors influence the normal course of aging of the skin. Skin changes are often the most bothersome because they are obvious and clearly reflect advancing years. Flattening and reduced thickness and vascularity of the dermis and a degeneration of elastin fibers occurs. As the skin becomes less elastic, drier, and more fragile and as subcutaneous fat is lost, lines, wrinkles, and sagging become evident. Skin becomes irritated and breaks down more easily. Melanocytes cluster, causing skin pigmentation commonly referred to as age spots; these are more prevalent in areas of the body exposed to the sun. Scalp, pubic, and axilla hair thins and grays; hair in the nose and ears becomes thicker. The growth of facial hair may occur in older women. Fingernails grow more slowly and become hard and brittle. Perspiration is slightly reduced because the number and function of the sweat glands are lessened.

PSYCHOLOGICAL AND PERSONALITY CHANGES

Psychological changes during the aging process cannot be isolated from concurrent physical and social changes. Sensory organ impairment can impede interaction with the environment and other people, thus influencing psychological status. Feelings of uselessness and social isolation may obstruct optimum psychological function. Psychological changes can be influenced by general health status, genetic factors, educational achievement, and activity.

Drastic changes in basic personality normally do not occur as one ages. The kind and gentle old person was most likely that way when young; likewise, the cantankerous old person probably was not mild and meek in earlier years. Excluding pathological processes, an older person's personality will be consistent with that of earlier years, though it may be more openly and honestly expressed. The alleged rigidity of older persons is more the result of physical and mental limitations than of personality changes. For example, an older woman's insistence that her furniture not be rearranged may be interpreted as rigidity, but it may be a sound safety practice for someone coping with poor memory and visual deficits. Changes in personality traits may occur in response to events that alter self-attitude, such as retirement, death of a spouse, loss of independence, income reduction, and disability. No personality type describes all older adults. Morale, attitude and self-esteem tend to be stable throughout the life span.

MEMORY, INTELLIGENCE, LEARNING, AND ATTENTION SPAN

Aging can slow the retrieval of information from long-term memory, particularly if the information is not used or needed on a daily basis. According to one study, healthy older women have been found to have a greater ability to recall nouns presented in a list than do their male counterparts. Some age-related forgetfulness can be improved by the use of mnemonic devices and other memory aids (for example, associating a name with an image, making notes and lists, and placing objects in consistent locations).

In general, it is wise to interpret experimental findings related to intelligence and the elderly with caution, as results may be biased by the measurement tools or methods of evaluation used. For example, sick older people cannot be compared accurately to healthy persons, people with different educational backgrounds cannot be compared accurately, and individuals who are familiar with and capable of taking intelligence tests cannot be well compared to those who have sensory deficits or to those who have never taken such tests. It has been shown that basic intelligence is maintained with age; one does not become less bright or smarter with age. Verbal comprehension and arithmetic abilities do not change, although the elderly are able to use past learning and experiences for problem-solving.

Although learning ability is not seriously altered with age, other factors can interfere with an older person's learning, including motivation, attention span, delayed transmission of information to the brain, perceptual deficits, and illness. Older persons may display less readiness to learn and may depend on previous experience for solutions to problems rather than experimenting with new problem-solving techniques. The early phases of the learning process tend to be more difficult for older persons than for younger individuals; however, after a longer early phase, they are then able to keep equal pace. Learning occurs best when the information is related to previously learned information. Although little difference is apparent between the old and young in verbal or abstract ability, older persons do show some difficulty with perceptual motor tasks. Because it is generally a greater problem to learn new habits when old habits exist and must be unlearned, relearned, or modified, elderly persons may have difficulty in these areas.

Older adults generally demonstrate a decrease in vigilance performance, or the ability to retain attention longer than forty-five minutes. They are more easily distracted by irrelevant information and stimuli and are less able to perform tasks that are complicated or require simultaneous performance.

ACCEPTING THE DECLINE OF AGING

The general decline associated with the second half of the life cycle is particularly serious between the seventh and eighth decades. Emotionally, socially, and intellectually, elderly persons must accept at least some decline. Because each segment of the life cycle should be approached with the fullest level of involvement possible, experts say, the elderly also should strive to maintain the highest level of physical function possible. For areas of decline in which some measure of reversal is possible, the elderly are well advised to seek rehabilitation. Whether through individually designed programs or through the aid of skilled professionals, many elderly people can improve the level of diminished functions. Moreover, through devices such as hearing aids, assistive ambulatory devices, and household implements, many impairments of aging may be restored and improved.

Since they have already experienced so much, many elderly people have no fear of death, even though they may fear the process of dying. Like all other developmental tasks, aging is a personal experience. If the elderly approach the end of life with the same sense of purpose they used for earlier tasks, they will feel that the sense of integrity need not be destroyed by the process of aging.

—*Jane Cross Norman*

See also Age spots; Aging: Biological, psychological, and sociocultural perspectives; Antiaging treatments; Arthritis; Bone changes and disorders; Brain changes and disorders; Breast changes and disorders; Bunions; Corns and calluses; Cross-linkage theory of aging; Fallen arches; Fat deposition; Foot disorders; Free radical theory of aging; Gastrointestinal changes and disorders; Genetics; Gray hair; Hair loss and baldness; Hearing loss; Heart changes and disorders; Longevity research; Menopause; Nearsightedness; Osteoporosis; Premature aging; Reaction time; Reading glasses; Reproductive changes, disabilities, and dysfunctions; Respiratory changes and disorders; Sensory changes; Skin changes and disorders; Temperature regulation and sensitivity; Vision changes and disorders; Wrinkles.

FOR FURTHER INFORMATION:

Burrell, Lenette O., ed. *Adult Nursing in Hospital and Community Settings.* Norwalk, Conn.: Appleton and Lange, 1992. An inclusive source for nursing management of adult patients, including the elderly. Contains comprehensive, indepth information from prevention to acute care.

Carnevali, Doris L., and Maxine Patrick. *Nursing Management for the Elderly.* 3d ed. Philadelphia: J. B. Lippincott, 1993. Provides the underlying knowledge that enables nurses to make accurate diagnoses and sound treatment decisions for elderly patients.

Cookfair, Joan M. *Nursing Care in the Community.* 2d ed. St. Louis: Mosby, 1996. A comprehensive introductory text that provides undergraduate nursing students with a basic foundation for the practice of community health nursing. The special needs of the elderly are outlined.

Lueckenotte, Annette G. *Gerontologic Nursing.* St. Louis: Mosby, 1996. Contains comprehensive theoretical and practical information about basic and complex concepts and issues relevant to the care of older people in a variety of settings.

Matteson, Mary A., and Eleanor S. McConnell. *Gerontological Nursing: Concepts and Practice.* Philadelphia: W. B. Saunders, 1988. Provides a knowledge base in biological, psychological, and sociological changes in aging. Covers the expansion of health care services for the elderly, the economics of the high cost of care, and Medicare regulations.

Monahan, Frances D., and Marianne Neighbors. *Medical-Surgical Nursing: Foundations for Clinical Practice.* 2d ed. Philadelphia: W. B Saunders, 1998. Addresses complex concepts and trends in health care delivery, with specific coverage of body systems and relevant care needs.

AIDS. *See* ACQUIRED IMMUNODEFICIENCY SYNDROME (AIDS).

ALCOHOLISM

RELEVANT ISSUES: Family, health and medicine, psychology, race and ethnicity

SIGNIFICANCE: Serious problems from inappropriate use of alcohol can have potentially life-threatening effects at any age, but particularly in elders, as the physical and social changes commonly associated with age can limit a person's ability to recover from the deleterious effects of alcohol

"Alcoholism" is a vague clinical term that is sometimes used to describe the condition in which an individual is afflicted with severe physical, social, and psychological problems related to alcohol use. It is not a medical diagnostic term. Rather, it is a colloquial term used to describe the state of an individual experiencing a general set of problems associated with the more formal diagnostic conditions known as alcohol abuse and alcohol dependence. Alcohol abuse is a specific diagnosis given for alcohol problems in which physical dependence on alcohol is not indicated. In cases of alcohol abuse, repeated and significant psychological, legal, and social problems tend to occur over the course of a year. The diagnosis of alcohol abuse is distinct from that of alcohol dependence and is described in the fourth edition of the *Diagnostic and Statistical Manual of Mental Disorders: DSM-IV* (1994) by the American Psychiatric Association. Alcohol dependence refers to both physical and psychological reliance on alcohol, despite the presence of repeated significant problems associated with its use for a period of a year or more.

PREVALENCE AND SPECIAL PROBLEMS

Alcohol problems can be diagnosed in individuals of any age; alcoholism among the elderly is thus to be expected at about the same rate as it would be in other adult age groups. In the elderly, however, alcoholism can be related to more significant problems because of the physical, mental, psychological, social, and financial vulnerabilities that can accompany later life. Changes in resilience accompanying later life can magnify the impact of problems related to alcohol by making recovery from such problems more difficult. This is especially true for elderly women, as physiological differences between men and women appear to cause alcohol problems to escalate in severity more quickly in older adult women than in older adult men.

Problematic alcohol use in elders is especially complicated by the greater physiological effects of alcohol that result from changes in how alcohol is processed by the body. As the body ages, the liver and other organs are less able to process alcohol out of the body, thereby altering tolerance to alcohol. As a result, alcohol stays in the body longer and has a more pronounced effect. This slowing of the body's ability to process substances also affects the processing of other drugs, which may also stay in the body longer. This can create drug interaction problems in the elderly, as they are especially likely to take prescription and nonprescription drugs on a regular basis.

Alcohol can intensify the effects of certain drugs, and vice versa; such interactions are particularly hazardous in the elderly. Combined with sedatives, alcohol can cause severe respiratory problems and also worsen problems related to balance. For elders already having respiratory or balance problems, such intensified effects can be very dangerous, leading to increased risk for falls, other accidents, or even death. Similarly, alcohol taken in combination with diuretics can be particularly dangerous, as the combination may encourage dehydration and can affect kidney functioning and blood pressure in a dangerous manner.

TREATMENT AND INTERVENTION

Alcohol problems in the elderly can come in two important types. For some, problems with alcohol may merely represent a continuation of lifelong habits. In these cases, the problems are chronic and will most likely require intensive intervention and management. Chronic problems of this type may lead to premature aging, serious cardiovascular health problems, cancers, and death, as well as severe difficulties with memory and other mental problems such as organic brain syndromes, aphasias, and dementias.

For other elderly people, though, problems related to alcohol may be a new development. In some cases, such problems may be situational, resulting from a recent stressor such as a death or loss of a loved one. Alcohol may be being used as a means of managing grief or depression. In these cases, interventions from someone such as a psychologist or geriatric psychiatrist may be warranted. Such assistance can help to address the root problem and also decrease the chance that a secondary problem with alcohol might develop as a result of repeated use.

Similarly, short-term alcohol problems may result from a lack of knowledge about drug interactions with alcohol. In these cases, the dissemination of information from a pharmacist about the dangers of mixing drugs and alcohol can prevent the elder from using alcohol in dangerous ways. Similarly, education from a family physician about how alcohol interacts with certain health conditions, such as heart problems, blood pressure problems, diabetes, depression, anxiety, insomnia, and stomach problems can also be useful in decreasing misuse of alcohol.

Alcohol problems may be more difficult to diagnose in the elderly than in younger adults. Older adults often do not show obvious signs of intoxication and withdrawal; moreover, when such symptoms appear, they may be attributed to other problems related to aging. Additionally, confusion of alcohol problems with other age-related conditions such as tremors, forgetfulness, and disorientation may obscure an accurate diagnosis. Alcohol problems in the elderly may also be masked by other physical or psychological conditions. Such conditions may bring an elder in for treatment, but the alcohol problem may go undetected. Screening for alcohol problems and questioning by medical professionals about alcohol use are thus important, as missing such problems may predispose an elder to relapse and worsened problems in the future.

Signs of problem drinking among the elderly may include any of the following: unusual increases in falls or accidents, slurring of speech, anxiety, insomnia or other sleep disorders, irritability, social withdrawal, efforts to hide or lie about the use of alcohol or other drugs, increased consumption of alcohol following significant losses, drinking alone more often, gulping of drinks or drinking fast, loss of interest in food, or any social, medical, or financial problems that appear to be caused or exacerbated by drinking. Evidence of any of these conditions may suggest a need for further medical evaluation. —*Nancy A. Piotrowski*

See also Balance disorders; Depression; Gastrointestinal changes and disorders; Grief; Loneliness; Medications; Overmedication; Psychiatry, geriatric; Social ties; Women and aging.

FOR FURTHER INFORMATION:

The Diagnostic and Statistical Manual of Mental Disorders: DSM-IV. 4th ed. Washington, D.C.: American Psychiatric Association, 1994.

Fanning, Patrick, and John T. O'Neill. *The Addiction Workbook: A Step-by-Step Guide to Quitting Alcohol and Drugs.* Oakland, Calif.: New Harbinger Press, 1996.

Miller, William R., and Ricardo F. Munoz. *How to Control Your Drinking: A Practical Guide to Respon-*

sible Drinking. Rev. ed. Albuquerque: University of New Mexico Press, 1990.

Roukema, Richard W. *What Every Patient, Family, Friend, and Caregiver Needs to Know About Psychiatry.* Washington, D.C.: American Psychiatric Press, 1998.

ALL ABOUT EVE

DIRECTOR: Joseph L. Mankiewicz
CAST: Bette Davis, Anne Baxter, George Sanders, Celeste Holm, Gary Merrill, Hugh Marlowe, Thelma Ritter
DATE: Released in 1950
RELEVANT ISSUES: Marriage and dating, media, psychology, values, work
SIGNIFICANCE: This Academy Award-winning film analyzes the psychological and marital problems of mature women in the theater

Eve Harrington (played by Anne Baxter) is an aspiring actress whose manipulative behavior threatens aging theater star Margo Channing (Bette Davis) and her friend Karen Richards (Celeste Holm). While Eve's appearance as a supposedly starstruck fan in Margo's dressing room triggers the film's action, the focus is upon the older women's reactions as Eve attempts to supplant Margo on stage and to lure away Margo's devoted male friend, Bill Sampson (Gary Merrill), and Karen's playwright husband, Lloyd Richards (Hugh Marlowe).

Margo Channing, insecure in a profession in which youth and beauty are valued, is driven to near breakdown. She almost drives away Bill; her insecurity causes her to turn on him despite his protestations, since she cannot understand that he prefers her to the younger Eve. Karen watches helplessly as her husband is tempted by Eve, who is ruthlessly willing to destroy the older women for the sake of her own career. A third older woman, Birdie (Thelma Ritter), adds another perspective on aging. Her career past, she toils endlessly as Margo's all-purpose maid. She apparently has no alternatives; she illumines the dangers that threaten Karen and Margo.

(Left to right) Anne Baxter, Bette Davis, Marilyn Monroe (in a small role), and George Sanders act a scene from the film All About Eve. *(Archive Photos)*

Birdie and caustic theatrical critic Addison de Witt (George Sanders) see through Eve Harrington from the beginning. De Witt outmanipulates Eve to provide a happy ending for Karen, while Margo gathers strength and provides her own happy ending. Eve gains success but is faced with a future in which younger women will supplant her in turn.

Based on the short story "The Wisdom of Eve," by Mary Orr, the film was adapted by Joseph L. Mankiewicz. It received fourteen Academy Award nominations and won Best Picture for 1950. Mankiewicz won Oscars for screenplay and direction, and Sanders was named Best Supporting Actor. Davis, Baxter, Holm, and Ritter received nominations.

—Betty Richardson

See also Age discrimination; Ageism; Beauty; Films; Marriage; Sexuality; Stereotypes; Women and aging.

ALZHEIMER'S ASSOCIATION

DATE: Founded in 1980

RELEVANT ISSUES: Family, health and medicine, psychology, sociology

SIGNIFICANCE: This national organization provides aid, service, advocacy, and information on Alzheimer's disease and related issues

The Alzheimer's Association (AA) is a national voluntary health organization committed to the elimination of Alzheimer's disease. The AA, also known as the Alzheimer's Disease and Related Disorders Association, was founded in 1980 with seven original chapters. By the end of 1980, twenty chapters had been established. By the late 1990's, the organization had grown into a nationwide network of more than two hundred chapters with more than thirty-five thousand volunteers. The AA works to achieve its mission through increased education and public awareness, advocacy for government-funded research and supportive public policy, funding for relevant research projects, and access to services, information, and care.

The AA publishes a quarterly newsletter, *Advances,* for families affected by Alzheimer's disease, and a newsletter, *Research and Practice,* that provides health care professionals with information on the latest advances in the science and treatment of Alzheimer's disease. The AA also publishes books and pamphlets and produces films and videos on Alzheimer's disease. The Benjamin B. Green-Field Library and Resource Center, a national resource facility, is located at the central office of the AA. This library has a large collection of materials on Alzheimer's disease and related disorders.

The AA also sponsors an annual advocacy conference and lobbies for legislation that impacts persons with Alzheimer's disease. The AA conducts numerous conferences and training sessions on Alzheimer's disease and the treatment of Alzheimer's disease. Additionally, the AA conducts a variety of public information campaigns.

The organization has increased funding for government-sponsored research on Alzheimer's disease through its "National Program to Conquer Alzheimer's Disease" campaign and through lobbying efforts that resulted in the establishment of five Alzheimer's Disease Research Centers. The AA also supports research through its Ronald and Nancy Reagan Research Institute, the largest private funding source for Alzheimer's research.

The AA also conducts several programs designed to provide support to persons with Alzheimer's disease and their caregivers. In 1993, the AA launched the Safe Return Program to help persons with Alzheimer's disease who become lost as a consequence of disease-related wandering behavior; the program sponsors a telephone information line and a toll-free number for Safe Return telephone registration. Safe Return emergency incident lines are available and manned by social workers who provide counseling and assistance in emergency situations. Through the Connections Demonstration Program, the AA provides grant funding to promote assistance and care planning to families of persons with Alzheimer's disease. Using data collected from surveys, the AA advocates for supportive programs for caregivers.

—Colleen Galambos

See also Alzheimer's disease; Brain changes and disorders; Dementia; Forgetfulness; Memory changes and loss; Mental impairment; Psychiatry, geriatric.

ALZHEIMER'S DISEASE

RELEVANT ISSUES: Family, health and medicine, psychology

SIGNIFICANCE: Alzheimer s disease, a progressive degenerative disorder of the brain that leads to full debility, afflicts millions of Americans and is one of the most costly diseases in American society

Dementia, a disorder that mainly affects people aged sixty-five and older, may be thought of as a gradual decline of mental function. The most common form of dementia is the Alzheimer's type. Alzheimer's dementia is more fully characterized as a pathological condition in which there is progressive loss of cognitive, visual-spatial, and language skills.

Alzheimer's disease is an acquired condition, the exact causes of which are unknown. Approximately 6 to 8 percent of all people older than sixty-five have Alzheimer's dementia; roughly 1.7 percent of people from sixty-five to seventy years of age have Alzheimer's disease. The prevalence of this disorder doubles every five years after age sixty; thus, about 30 percent of people older than eighty-five have Alzheimer's disease. While Alzheimer's dementia typically begins late in life, a small percentage of sufferers experience its onset in their thirties or forties.

Although some mild decline in memory, primarily demonstrated as slowness of recall, may be considered a normal part of aging, this must be distinguished from the debilitating condition of Alzheimer's disease. Because of the progressive decline that it causes in its victims' ability to function in all aspects of daily life, Alzheimer's dementia eventually results in the need for care and supervision twenty-four hours a day.

It was estimated that four million Americans had Alzheimer's disease in the late 1990's. It was predicted that fourteen million Americans would have Alzheimer's disease by 2050. While the average life expectancy is eight to ten years after diagnosis, some patients may live twenty years or more. In 1999, the average lifetime cost per patient was about $174,000, and this cost was expected to rise. Contrary to public perception, 75 percent of people with Alzheimer's disease receive care at home, often by family members. Nevertheless, nearly half of all nursing home residents have Alzheimer's disease.

The very elderly (those aged eighty and older), as the most rapidly growing segment of the American population, are changing the way in which society copes with this disease. To adjust to the increasing needs and demands for care, assisted-

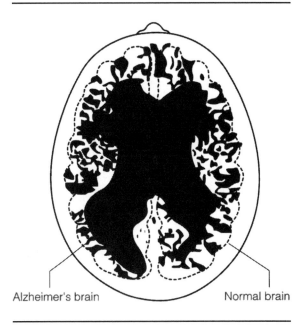

Alzheimer's brain   Normal brain

Alzheimer's disease causes the volume of the brain to shrink substantially. (Hans & Cassidy, Inc.)

living centers and nursing homes dedicated to the exclusive care of people with Alzheimer's disease are on the rise. Since most of this long-term care is not covered by Medicare or private insurance policies, families are expected to cover the expenses. The cost to families can be devastating, both financially and emotionally.

SIGNS AND SYMPTOMS

Since the rate of cognitive decline in Alzheimer's disease can be slowed with medications, early recognition of the signs and symptoms is imperative. With proper medical guidance and quality care at home or in staffed facilities, one can minimize the dehumanization and suffering that Alzheimer's disease inflicts upon its victims.

Three specific areas of decline found with Alzheimer's disease are in the learning of new information; in complex task completion, organization, and daily planning; and in communication and interactions.

The earliest symptoms of Alzheimer's dementia are noted with difficulty remembering where common items have been placed or recalling basic details of recent conversations. Common examples are forgetfulness concerning appointments with physicians, family gatherings, or meetings that were previously well known and anticipated. For example, a woman who normally goes weekly for salon appointments on a certain day and at a set time might begin to arrive on the wrong day or not at all. Additional early warnings may include inability to recall important recent family events, such as weddings or the birth of new family members.

Unfortunately, it is at this stage that family and friends are prone to dismiss these difficulties as normal aging, part of "getting older." The reluctance to recognize dementia early may arise, in part, from the tendency to dismiss abnormal behaviors as normal, particularly in loved ones. For example, most people can recall a time when, perhaps during a particularly stressful or sad time, they too had been forgetful. Nevertheless, there is a great difference between the minor and time-limited forgetfulness that nearly all people have experienced and the ever-worsening, irreversible forgetfulness of Alzheimer's disease.

Other areas of daily life become increasingly problematic as the dementia progresses. Tasks that require several steps—such as cooking a meal, doing laundry, or balancing a checkbook—may be poorly performed with erosion of the cognitive skills necessary to organize these tasks mentally and physically. Reasoning may decline so that unsound or ill-advised contracts may be signed, perhaps exploiting the victim's financial security. There is an inability to devise coping strategies or to develop solutions when problems arise. As such, relatively minor problems such as a burned-out light bulb, a leaky faucet, or a flooded basement can be viewed as insurmountable. Moreover, the skills of knowing one's space and orientation within that space, or visual-spatial awareness, also wane. As a result, navigating through a once-familiar neighborhood or within one's own home becomes increasingly difficult. Even on simple trips, demented individuals are at great risk of getting lost or endangering themselves and possibly others. While this situation is of concern when these individuals are wandering on foot, it is even more problematic when those with dementia are still driving.

Personal grooming and hygiene may also decline with Alzheimer's disease. This may start with subtle cues, such as fingernails not being polished or trimmed. The individual may forget how to shave or shampoo or be unable to remember the last time that bathing occurred. Articles of clothing may be worn in uncharacteristically bizarre or clashing combinations, such as a winter coat with summer sandals, that heretofore would have never been combined by that person. A decline in personal appearance and habits strongly suggests a problem with cognitive skills.

Increasingly, words and sentences become difficult to organize for the person with Alzheimer's disease. Often, the first sign of language decline is the inability to remember words for simple items, such as the palm of the hand or the band of a wristwatch. This inability to find the word to identify an object is called anomia, literally meaning "without name." When speaking, the patient may experience a sense of frustration while halting to recall a word or even the topic of conversation. Substituted phrases or stammering until someone rescues the patient by speaking for him or her become awkward but adaptive ways to communicate with others.

Associated with declining language skills may be an increasing tendency to withdraw from conversations and be uncommonly passive. Alternatively, previously well-mannered people may become socially inappropriate—for example, speaking only in a loud voice. As the ability to modulate behavior deteriorates, social graces are lost. Some people may develop an irritable demeanor; others may become combative or blatantly aggressive with words and actions. These behaviors almost always lead to medical attention if none was previously sought.

Alzheimer's dementia ultimately robs individuals of their personality. At first, this may appear subtly as a loss of interest in once-pleasurable things. Often, there is progression to a more socially withdrawn state, with less expression of mood and feelings evident. Eventually, people who were once full of life, each with unique facial expressions and senses of humor, somehow end up looking very similar—with expressionless, blank faces and eyes that seem to stare deeply into nothing. This flattening of expression and loss of personality usually occurs late in Alzheimer's disease.

DIAGNOSIS

Dementia of the Alzheimer's type currently cannot be diagnosed by laboratory tests or imaging techniques such as computed tomography (CT) or magnetic resonance imaging (MRI). As a medical diagnosis, Alzheimer's dementia is a diagnosis of exclusion. As such, the possibility must be evaluated that the presenting symptoms of confusion, memory loss, and poor ability to take care of oneself derive from other causes. First, other forms of dementia, some of which may be reversible, are explored. In addition, medical conditions such as delirium or depression are carefully considered, as both are generally reversible and, with medical treatment and management, of limited duration. The physician will need to know what medical problems, if any, the patient may have, as well as what prescription and over-the-counter medications are being taken. If a fall has occurred that may coincide with the onset of symptoms, it will be important to assess and evaluate the patient for possible head trauma or injury, including intracranial bleeding. Any history of excessive alcohol consumption or illicit drug use is important; such information can clarify certain health issues, such as vitamin deficiencies, that may be contributing to the clinical picture.

Once such factors are identified and resolved or found to be noncontributory, the physician can explore the possibility of Alzheimer's disease more completely. This diagnosis is made primarily from the doctor's suspicion and from clinical findings. Thus, the physician will consider the patient's symptoms as described by family and friends. The physician will observe, engage, and monitor the patient's ability to perform simple tasks, such as social greetings and recalling names of people in their family, important dates, or current events. The evaluation may include the Mini-Mental Status Exam, the Blessed Information-Memory-Concentration Test, a clock drawing test, a functional activities questionnaire, or other diagnostic aids. While helpful tools, these diagnostic assessments alone cannot diagnose Alzheimer's dementia definitively.

The physician will also ask questions regarding certain risk factors for Alzheimer's disease. Known risk factors include a family history of Alzheimer's dementia, increasing age (especially after age eighty), and head trauma in the past that caused a loss of consciousness. An additional risk factor for Alzheimer's disease is found in people who have been diagnosed with Down syndrome (trisomy 21), as almost all people with trisomy 21 who survive to age forty-five will develop early onset of Alzheimer's dementia. Lastly, although it remains unclear as to the role of estrogen as it may relate to Alzheimer's disease, the physician will probably want to know whether female patients are using or have used estrogen replacement therapy after the menopause.

Late in the disease, other signs and symptoms may appear as a consequence of neuron (brain cell) loss and the biochemical dysfunction of surviving neurons. One of these is hallucinations, such as hearing voices or seeing images of people or things that are not present yet believing fully that they are real. This condition is known as psychosis. Another familiar psychotic feature is paranoid delusions. This often presents itself in moderate dementia, typically revolving around unfounded beliefs that family members are stealing items. Sometimes the items "stolen" have no value, such as a hat or glove; more important, such paranoia is a demonstration of the confusion that results from the chaos of not having memory.

A careful history of the patient's decline and the severity of symptoms will help to establish the relative rate of cognitive loss. From these data, a prognosis for the patient in terms of both quality and, to a lesser extent, quantity of life may be made.

TREATMENT AND MANAGEMENT

There is no known cure for or prevention of Alzheimer's dementia. As a consequence, treatment focuses on managing symptoms, slowing the rate of cognitive decline, and improving quality of life.

The most commonly prescribed medications used to abate the progression of Alzheimer's dementia come from a category of pharmaceutical agents known as cholinesterase inhibitors, including tacrine and donazepril. Although the exact role of cholinergic neurons within the central nervous system is not well understood, it has been demonstrated that in Alzheimer's disease, there is both a loss in the number of cholinergic neurons and dysfunction in the cholinergic neurons that remain viable. Thus, Alzheimer's dementia is characterized by a net deficit of cholinergic neurotransmitters.

The enzyme cholinesterase biochemically degrades cholinergic neurotransmitters within the central nervous system. In health, this poses no problem, but in Alzheimer's disease, this process exaggerates symptoms. Even a little reduction of already depleted amounts of cholinergic neurotransmitters worsens the condition. Therefore, an inhibitor that halts the enzyme activity helps to increase the amount of cholinergic neurotransmitter, which, in turn, improves cognition. The optimal benefit from cholinesterase inhibitors is obtained when the medication is started as early in the dementia process as possible. With medications, some people will have improvement of cognition that is evident in their mood, speech, and self-care or in their ability to perform daily tasks. Even in moderate to severe forms of Alzheimer's disease, where cognitive decline is marked, these medications have been helpful in reducing symptoms of agitation, aggression, or restlessness.

About 25 to 30 percent of all people diagnosed with Alzheimer's disease will experience depression. Since loss of brain cells occurs with Alzheimer's disease, it is no surprise that some cells which produce neurochemicals to regulate mood are also lost. Thus, depression should be looked for in all stages of Alzheimer's disease, as it can be identified and treated with antidepressant medications. In the past, tricyclic antidepressants were used for this illness in the elderly, but because tricyclics have multiple side effects, other medications are increasingly receiving favor. Side effects and drug interactions can be particularly problematic in the elder patient who is frequently taking several medications for other medical conditions.

Additional therapies target particular symptoms. For example, paranoia can be managed and often resolved with antipsychotic medications. With the elderly, special efforts are made by physicians to use the lowest dose possible, as well as to select medications that have minimal side effects. Two other common concerns are lack of impulse control or lability of mood and disruption of sleep patterns. Often, the former can managed with mood stabilizers, such as valproic acid, as well as environmental controls, so that the patient is not overly stimulated by activities or sounds that occur in everyday life. The latter can be managed with "sleep hygiene." This therapy helps to reset the biological clock by establishing fixed hours to go to and awaken from sleep and not allowing napping. Additional aids may include medications, but caution should be exercised because some commonly used agents, such as benzodiazepines, may have paradoxical effects in the elderly. Another caution is to avoid the use of the anticholinergic medications often used to induce sleep, such as diphenhydramine, as this can worsen dementia symptoms.

How Families Cope

Although Alzheimer's disease afflicts individuals, entire families are affected by the cruel and prolonged course of this disease. Enormous emotional costs are paid by family members who care for and attend to a loved one who increasingly grows to depend on others for safekeeping. More often than not, it is adult women, many of whom are working mothers of young children or teenagers, who find themselves in the role of providing care for family members with Alzheimer's disease. In fact, studies indicate that greater than 90 percent of those providing care for patients with Alzheimer's disease in their or a family member's home are women. This role is far more demanding than simply providing meals or getting someone to a doctor's appointment. For example, traveling or even being alone is no longer a safe option for the person with Alzheimer's disease; constant supervision to prevent wandering from the home and getting lost is needed. Cooking or ironing is no longer safe for someone with Alzheimer's disease because of the potential for self-injury or household fires, yet these activities are often attempted when a brief lapse of supervision occurs. Unlike children, who lack good judgment but are small and manageable, adults with Alzheimer's disease may be physically strong and sizable. This fact makes keeping them in safe spaces a real challenge. Families need to "Alzheimer-proof" the home to reduce the risk of injury or tragedy, such as accidental death, for the patient with Alzheimer's disease and other family members. It is helpful to contact local police and fire departments and to advise them that someone with Alzheimer's disease lives at that residence. This allows ease of filing a missing person's report with police or getting a rapid response to home fires, as both events are not uncommon when someone with Alzheimer's disease lives in a family home.

At variable rates, but in a predictable manner, dependence needs grow to include making phone calls to family or friends, finding belongings, grooming and dressing, or using simple appliances such as electric shavers, lamps, or toasters.

As the progressive loss of cognition continues, simple housekeeping tasks such as clearing a table or depositing trash into proper receptacles cannot be performed. Assistance with toileting or changing adult diapers also becomes necessary. In the late stage of Alzheimer's disease, assistance with eating, sitting upright, and walking is required as the disease leads a fully debilitating course.

As may be anticipated, caregivers are at risk for emotional burnout and physical fatigue. To alleviate this problem, many areas offer adult day care programs. In these programs, people with Alzheimer's disease are assisted by trained staff in physical, social, and creative activities that help to optimize the overall well-being of participants. In better programs, such activities are tailored specifically to meet the unique needs of Alzheimer's patients. These programs also promote improved mood through socialization and offer a sense of independence from family members. Such programs are beneficial not only to participants but also to their caregivers. Clearly, adult day care offers a reprieve to the caregiver who, for a specified number of hours a day, will be relieved from the burden of having to monitor and care for an ill loved one constantly.

Although 75 percent of people with Alzheimer's disease are cared for by family members, 50 percent or more of all nursing home residents have Alzheimer's disease. This shift occurs as debility consumes the very life of the Alzheimer's patient, to the point that safety can no longer be maintained without professional supervision, proper medical care, and careful medication management. When this point is reached, family members become resigned to placing loved ones in facilities where assisted-living and medical services can be provided. With guidance from support groups, doctors, and other professionals, good to excellent facilities can be found that meet the emotional, physical, and medical needs of the family and yet fit within their financial constraints.

Patients with Alzheimer's disease require increasing amounts of assistance, usually from spouses, as their condition gradually worsens. (Ben Klaffke)

In 1999, the average monthly cost of caring for a family member with Alzheimer's disease in either an assisted-living facility or in a nursing home was $3,100. When the care was provided in the family home, the average monthly cost was $1,500. These numbers, when multiplied by twelve for the months per year and then by eight for the years of possible life expectancy, give a conservative estimate of $144,000 to $297,000 for lifetime care per person with Alzheimer's disease. Because most families do not have such resources available, great measures are taken to afford care for loved ones, sometimes at great economic risk to these families.

Another consideration is the matter of competency. In Alzheimer's disease, the ability to make important personal decisions such as writing wills or making financial and health care choices is lost. Therefore, early in the course at the disease, families are encouraged to have court-appointed guardianship or executorship established. This allows the appointed person, usually a spouse or child of the patient, to make financial, health care, and medical choices for the demented person. Court actions can assist many families with the economic aspect of Alzheimer's disease as they can manage the patient's financial matters.

As for the emotional toll, support from others who have endured or are enduring the same problem can be found in many communities at Alzheimer's Association chapters. Many turn to lifelong friends and their religious beliefs for further support and guidance.

The cruel reality of Alzheimer's disease is that at the end of the twentieth century, it was the fourth-leading cause of death in adult Americans. Therefore, end-of-life choices need to be addressed, including the "do not resuscitate" (DNR) status and the personal choice of life support. Some families are lucky to have had the patient with Alzheimer's disease designate, while they were fully competent, their wishes through drafting a living will or giving someone they trusted durable power of attorney. Such actions give chosen individuals the responsibility for making important decisions for patients in the event that they are unable to do so themselves. DNR status allows a person to die without resuscitation if it will simply delay death rather than maintain life in anticipation of recovery. Some members of society consider resuscitation an intrusion of modern medicine into the natural course of dying; others want everything done to sustain life, regardless of the ultimate outcome. Often these emotions are based on deeply held personal beliefs. DNR requests are generally made by the patient (while in good health) or by family members to the patient's physicians without court involvement. Rather, dialogue about prognosis, the pros and cons of DNR status, and family meetings with doctors and other professionals contribute to the family's decision.

INSIGHTS FROM PAST AND PRESENT RESEARCH

It was Alois Alzheimer who, in 1907, first described certain brain abnormalities during the autopsy of a female patient whom he had observed to be in mental decline for nearly five years. He found a uniformly atrophic (small and wasting away) brain with no other grossly visible abnormalities evident. Microscopically, he recorded what is now known to be the hallmark of descriptive pathology in the brains of Alzheimer's patients: the presence of neurofibrillary tangles. These neurofibrils, he found, were abnormal biochemically and physically. More important, the tangles appeared to have formed as the once-viable and encompassing neurons, within which these neurofibrils reside, began dying.

Through neuron death, the mass of the entire brain is reduced to between 900 and 1,100 grams; this contrasts with the average brain mass of healthy elderly, which spans 1,200 to 1,400 grams. Further evidence of brain atrophy includes widened sulci (spaces between brain folds) and thinned gyri (brain matter).

Additional microscopic findings include neuritic (senile) plaques, which have a central core rich in a substance known as beta-amyloid. The periphery of the plaque contains diverse fragments of brain cells. The presence of amyloid led to research on amyloid precursor protein (APP) in the hope of better understanding the pathology of Alzheimer's disease. The gene for APP was found to be on chromosome 21; thus a link to Down syndrome (trisomy 21) was established. Perhaps gene mutations on chromosome 21 in families with early-onset Alzheimer's disease could account for the cognitive decline.

Additional findings have suggested the role of a substance known as apolipoprotein E, which binds highly to APP. This prompted research that may provide insight into late-onset Alzheimer's disease. There appears to be an association of a certain region, or allele, on chromosome 19 that occurs at a rate that is four times greater in families prone to late-onset Alzheimer's disease than in other families. The culprit region seems to reside within the E4 allele of chromosome 19. The task before researchers is to determine if the E4 allele is causal or contributory to increasing an individual's risk for developing Alzheimer's disease late in life.

Investigation continues concerning to what extent, if any, estrogen protects an individual from Alzheimer's disease. Preliminary studies suggest that estrogen, or estrogen replacement therapy in postmenopausal women, may prevent the onset of Alzheimer's disease in women. Therefore, many physicians use estrogen in the management of Alzheimer's disease in female patients. In addition, some research teams are looking at nutritional aspects of Alzheimer's dementia. Many people believe that antioxidants, in particular vitamin E (alpha-tocopherol), may be protective. Other studies hold promise for the possibility of performing a simple blood test to assess who may be at risk for Alzheimer's disease. This information would allow planning in advance of the onset of disease so that many difficult decisions can be made while the individual is still in good health.

SUMMARY

Alzheimer's dementia is a progressive, abnormal loss of one's ability to think, learn, communicate, and care for oneself. The illness leads to full debility and a dependence on others in order to sustain life. By the end of the twentieth century, because of the prolonged course of Alzheimer's disease and the need for medical and high-level nursing care, it was the third most costly medical condition, ranked after heart disease and cancer. As people live longer and the "aging of America" continues, the number of people with Alzheimer's disease will increase. As a result, more nurses and physicians will be needed in geriatric medicine.

—Mary C. Fields

See also Alzheimer's Association; Brain changes and disorders; Caregiving; Communication; Dementia; Depression; Durable power of attorney; Forgetfulness; Living wills; Memory changes and loss; Mental impairment; Personality changes; Psychiatry, geriatric; Sleep changes and disturbances.

FOR FURTHER INFORMATION:

Larkin, Marilynn. *When Someone You Love Has Alzheimer's.* New York: Dell, 1995. An excellent resource for caregivers. Offers tips on daily management of people with Alzheimer's disease, including diet, toileting, exercise, and medical care. A comprehensive resource list is provided.

Mace, Nancy L., and Peter Rabins. *The Thirty-six-Hour Day: A Family Guide to Caring for Persons with Alzheimer's Disease, Related Dementing Illnesses, and Memory Loss Later in Life.* 3d ed. Baltimore: The Johns Hopkins University Press, 1999. An excellent resource for caregivers who find comfort in fighting this disease with knowledge. The book also offers tips on coping with typical problems encountered in caring for someone with Alzheimer's disease.

Markin, R. E. *Coping with Alzheimer's: The Complete Care Manual for Patients and Their Families.* Secaucus, N.J.: Carol, 1998. A quick read that is helpful in the organization process for caring for someone with Alzheimer's disease. Some of the medication information is outdated, but otherwise this is a good, practical guide.

Nolan, K. A., and R. C. Mohs. "Screening for Dementia in Family Practice." In *Alzheimer's Disease: A Guide to Practical Management, Part II,* edited by Ralph W. Richter and John P. Blass. St. Louis: Mosby-Year Book, 1994. The source from which the clock drawing test was obtained. Although this book is written for physicians, some of the information can be comprehended easily by laypeople who may have a diagnostic interest in Alzheimer's disease.

Oliver, Rose, and Frances Bock. *Coping with Alzheimer's: A Caregiver's Emotional Survival Guide.* New York: Dodd, Mead, 1987. Designed to help caregivers take care of themselves and avoid burnout, this is a must-read before beginning to care for a family member with Alzheimer's disease. It anticipates the common mixture of emotions that accompany this role, helping caregivers avoid the pitfalls that can undermine their efforts.

Powell, Lenore S., and Katie Courtice. *Alzheimer's Disease: A Guide for Families.* Rev. ed. Reading, Mass.: Addison-Wesley, 1993. This excellent book is divided into three sections: "The Burden of Love," "Understanding and Dealing with the Patient's Problem," and "Taking Care of

Yourself." Nontechnical chapters about the nature of this disease are helpful. Examples of a living will and a resident's bill of rights (for nursing homes or assisted-living facilities) are given.

Statistics Fact Sheet. Chicago: Alzheimer's Disease and Related Disorders Association, 1998. Some of the statistics reported in this entry were obtained from the Alzheimer's Association. This support group is an excellent resource for facts, information, and updated treatment options for families who struggle with Alzheimer's disease. An abundance of information can be obtained by visiting their Web site at http://www.alz.org, by calling (312) 335-8700, or by writing to 919 North Michigan Avenue, Suite 100, Chicago, IL 60611-1676.

AMERICAN ASSOCIATION OF RETIRED PERSONS (AARP)

RELEVANT ISSUES: Economics, health and medicine, recreation, work

SIGNIFICANCE: The American Association of Retired Persons is the major advocacy group for the elderly in the United States

Founded in 1958 by Ethel Percy Andrus, a retired Los Angeles high school principal, the American Association of Retired Persons (AARP) was created to "promote independence, dignity, and purpose" among the elderly. With rapidly growing membership that reached thirty-three million in 1998, AARP has come to represent the American elderly, seeking to improve every aspect of their lives. It publishes the *AARP Newsletter* and the nation's largest circulation magazine, *Modern Maturity,* mailed to twenty-two million households, which contains articles on such topics as careers, science and health, investments, and personal relationships.

AARP is a tax-exempt, nonprofit organization that provides its members with an unusual blending of social welfare and commercialism. Yet despite its tax-exempt status, AARP is a moneymaking organization, with an income that exceeds $300 million per year. Its membership dues, income from products and services, fees from established firms that pay AARP for joint ventures, and yearly federal grants to run government-funded programs for seniors fill AARP's coffers handsomely.

In 1988, Horace Deets, a former Jesuit priest, became AARP's executive director. AARP is run by the executive director and a staff of lobbyists who attempt to influence government decision makers. They report to a board of directors and national officers, who control a network of more than two thousand volunteers from across the country. Other key decision makers are AARP's chief legal advisers.

LOBBYING AND LEGISLATION

AARP's moneymaking has drawn fire from critics, and the organization is also perceived by many as lobbying for legislation that goes against the wishes of its members. Some critics insist that AARP pursues an aggressively liberal political agenda at the expense of the elderly. AARP polls its members periodically to determine broad policy positions, but the actual task of determining political priorities falls to a committee of AARP volunteers who meet with the professional staff. Moreover, while the unpaid AARP lobbyists in each state determine their own priorities, they must abide by the guidelines laid down by headquarters. To the dismay of some members, AARP's interests range far and wide; for example, the organization pushes aggressively for tax increases and for the spending of money on acquired immunodeficiency syndrome (AIDS) research rather than on Alzheimer's disease and cancer research.

The philosophical and political diversity of AARP gives it less clout than other, more cohesive groups. Only 14 percent of the group's members join AARP's lobbying activities, while the large majority seek only discounts, bargains, and price reductions, all of which are made available to members for a membership fee of only eight dollars a year.

One of AARP's largest concerns is the financial stability of Medicare. The Balanced Budget Act of 1997 was estimated to have extended the solvency of the Medicare Trust Fund until 2008. Shortly thereafter, members of the baby-boom generation will become eligible for Medicare, and the additional number of Medicare beneficiaries is expected to place great strain on the fund's stability. Less-populous succeeding generations may also prove unwilling to pay for the baby boomers' Medicare and Social Security. AARP thus defends both programs, while admitting that both will need to change in order to survive; at the same time, it maintains that all members should share the sacrifice to see the plans through.

Social Security also faces adjustments in order to ensure its ongoing stability. The AARP has maintained that any Social Security solvency reform package should maintain the earned-right nature of the program's benefits, should provide benefits to workers and their families, and should ensure Social Security as a base of retirement income for as many workers as possible.

AARP has also developed a set of principles by which it evaluates tax-reform proposals. The organization maintains that any tax reform must ensure the generation of enough income to meet the government's obligations to programs vital to older Americans, specifically Medicare and Social Security.

BENEFITS AND SERVICES

From its inception, AARP saw its priority as providing health care for the elderly. In 1958, the sum of fifty thousand dollars was put up by Leonard Davis, an insurance broker from Poughkeepsie, New York, who convinced Continental Casualty of Chicago to take a risk covering Andrus's group. As AARP became popular and its membership soared, Davis in 1963 founded his own insurance company, Colonial Penn, which replaced Continental as AARP's insurer. By the mid-1970's, as other companies began to offer health insurance for the elderly with similar or greater benefits, AARP turned to other underwriters for its health insurance.

AARP's health insurance plans are a mixed bag. Its Medicare supplemental policy, or Medigap, provides coverage for some health costs that Medicare does not cover. Standard plans featuring different degrees of coverage are relatively inexpensive. Married couples receive a discount, and all sub-

Volunteers from AARP sort through mail collected as part of the organization's Project Senior Sting to fight fraud against the elderly. (AP Photo/ Patricia McDonnell)

scribers pay the same premium, regardless of age. Also, Medigap coverage is automatic for those who choose any of the basic plans; others include prescription drug coverage. AARP's hospital-surgical policy, Hospital Advantage, covers part of the cost of hospital stays and surgical treatments. However, the Hospital Indemnity Plan, which pays a flat amount for each day of hospitalization, is of little real benefit to most policyholders.

AARP's long-term care, which covers Alzheimer's disease and all types of nursing homes, at-home care, and adult day care centers, costs more and covers less than plans available from other insurers. In addition, AARP provides for its members other health services: discounts on prescription drugs; information concerning resources available to individuals with chronic disorders; help for alcohol abuse; news about the latest medical breakthroughs and about alternative medicine, caregiving, and managed care; and help with nursing home contracts and the rights of nursing home residents.

AARP sells a variety of life insurance policies. Although most life insurers charge women less than men of the same age because women on average live longer, AARP charges high rates for women. Similarly, its rates for healthy men, usually discounted in other policies, are high.

AARP offers members inexpensive homeowner's and mobile home owner's insurance with comprehensive coverage that insures mobile homes of any age or value. The group's automobile insurance, though guaranteeing rates for a full year, is more costly.

Also offered is an investment program from which members can choose from eight mutual funds, each designed to provide competitive returns. AARP also offers guidance and educational materials for members who lack investment experience. Designed with AARP's less-affluent investors in mind, the funds offer a low minimum investment as well as training on other matters. VISA cards designed for AARP members boast low interest rates, no annual fee, free additional cards, and convenience checks. Also available is a pharmacy service that includes prescriptions, over-the-counter medications, and health and beauty aids for shopping-at-home convenience.

AARP's travel bargains, a prime reason for its large membership, are offered to members over fifty and their spouses. Travel programs tout discounts in car rental, lodging, and tours. AARP reviews route itineraries, monitors the programs, and follows up on criticisms. Prospective travelers fill out questionnaires about hearing, vision, allergy, mobility, and other problems and receive key considerations, such as extended trips by bus or foot, often denied to the general public. Though costly, AARP tours are designed for the elderly.

AARP provides help for independent living for the elderly, advice about home-modification devices, information about coping with grief and loss, tips on driving safety, and aid for grandparents who raise their grandchildren. —*Mary Hurd*

See also Advocacy; Consumer issues; Discounts; Early retirement; Income sources; Leisure activities; Life insurance; Long-term care for the elderly; Medical insurance; Medicare; Politics; Retirement; Retirement planning; Social Security; Vacations and travel.

FOR FURTHER INFORMATION:
Birnbaum, Jeffrey H. "Washington's Second Most Powerful Man." *Fortune* 135 (May 12, 1997).
Klein, Joe. "AARP? Arrgh." *Newsweek* 125 (May 15, 1995).
McArdle, Thomas. "Golden Oldies." *National Review* 47 (September 11, 1995).
Novack, Janet. "Strength from Its Gray Roots." *Forbes* 148 (November 25, 1991).
O'Connell, Vanessa, and Ellen Stark. "Taking a Hard Look at AARP's Deals." *Money* 24 (July, 1995).

AMERICAN INDIANS

RELEVANT ISSUES: Culture, demographics, economics, health and medicine

SIGNIFICANCE: Race, age, ethnicity, and tribal membership define a high-risk population of American Indian elders; the heterogeneity of more than six hundred distinct and evolving cultures complicates the picture and challenges assumptions

Even a superficial understanding of American Indian elders requires some background on Native Americans. As the first peoples to inhabit North America and to organize civilizations there, Indians have variably resisted colonization since European invaders "discovered" the Americas in 1492. The complete occupation of the eastern half of the continent can be symbolized by a yearlong event the Cherokee called *Nunahi-Duna-Dlo-Hilu-I,* commonly translated as the Trail of Tears. In the spring of 1838, the military and the executive branch of the federal government conspired to ignore the U.S. Supreme Court by unlawfully arresting and interning Southeastern Indians in concentration camps throughout the summer and then forcibly expelling them from the Union. Under armed guard and without preparation, the Cherokee were forced on an arduous thousand-mile march through winter snows to territories unknown. Thousands died on the trail in a prelude to apartheid encountered on reservations west of the Mississippi. Subsequently, the reservation system too was slowly undermined in an uncoordinated century-long effort to engineer the partial assimilation and near cultural genocide of American Indians. Nevertheless, according to Robert L. Schneider and Nancy P. Kropf, Indian peoples maintained their wide-ranging diversity of language, religion, lifestyle, culture, and tribal politics.

Federal policy toward indigenous North Americans has resulted in the numerical and geographical marginalization of Indians on their own continent. Once the entire population of what is now the United States, American Indians are frequently grouped under "other" or "too small to be statistically significant" by contemporary demographic reports. Some individuals have attempted to assuage the effects of the most savage federal policies, but most attempts have been paternalistic lone efforts lacking a critical mass of the electorate to reverse fully the genocidal tide.

The most notable exception was the Indian Self-Determination Act of 1975. Through this single law, tribal governments have increasingly seized control of, and provided direction to, federal programs that permeate reservation life. In related developments, the Smithsonian Institution's National Museum of the American Indian (NMAI) is making authentic strides toward the empowerment of Indian communities. They can tell their own stories, start dialogues with one another, and construct their own representations for mainstream America. With NMAI's help, the Internet is linking reservations and bringing Native Americans together in virtual reality. As a consequence, solidarity among indigenous peoples of the Americas is beginning to have real meaning for the first time in history.

DEMOGRAPHICS

American Indians, including Aleuts and Inuits (Eskimos), are members of 558 distinct sovereign nations that peacefully coexist, by treaty, within the borders of the continental United States. R. John's

Some elder American Indians try to preserve and pass on tribal customs. This Ottawa woman displays her crafts. (Ben Klaffke)

demographic review in *Full Color Aging* (1999) asserted that there were 165,842 Indian elders in 1990, defining elders as those with a chronological age of sixty years or more. At the time, this figure represented 8.5 percent of the total American Indian population of 1,959,234 individuals, an estimated 52 percent increase among Indian elders from 1980 to 1990. According to a 1998 report by Robert N. Butler, Myrna I. Lewis, and Trey Sunderland, a majority of Indian elders live in five Southwestern states—Oklahoma, California, Arizona, New Mexico, and Texas—while a substantial portion of the remainder reside on widely scattered reservations, trust lands, tribal jurisdictions, and reservation proximal environs near the Canadian border.

Indian Health Service (IHS) verification of entitlement offers the most reliable count of federally recognized American Indians. In 1997, IHS reported 1.8 million system users, while researchers estimated 2.2 million people self-identifying as American Indians. Some allege that recent American Indian census counts are 33 percent inflated by a second population that began embracing their distant Indian ancestry after 1970. Much like Irish Americans and Italian Americans, they fall into a category of so-called hyphenated Americans sharing wide-ranging degrees of unverified descent. This second Indian population lacks a legal claim to treaty protections and entitlements. Demographics are further complicated by variations in tribal membership rules and the fact that any given tribe's sovereignty remains vulnerable to the vicissitudes of federal recognition. Though many of the tribes that were previously legislated out of existence have been restored, more than one hundred groups still pursue federal recognition. These anomalies give rise to a third population of individuals who self-identify as "full-blooded Indian" by descent from grandparents with tribal affiliations but who are unable to meet the tests of any single tribe's membership rules.

Putting aside the debate surrounding a Census overcount of the gross Indian population, there are strong arguments that the Census specifically undercounts American Indian elders. This paradox is understandable in the light of the fact that younger U.S. citizens are more likely than elders to be influenced by multiculturalism, accepting themselves as hyphenated Americans and self-identifying as "Indian Americans." Simultaneously, elders, who are more rural and more culturally isolated than the Indian population generally, are more susceptible to underrepresentation in the Census count, even as other subpopulations are being inflated.

MEDICAL, PSYCHOLOGICAL, AND SOCIAL CHARACTERISTICS

Schneider and Kropf report that in 1997, 61 percent of Indian elders (those sixty-five and older) fell below the poverty line, as compared to only 13 percent of whites. These authors note that starting at age forty-five, consistent with socioeconomic status, American Indians suffer a higher incidence of chronic health problems and functional impairments than the general elderly population and that American Indians who are forty-five and older show startling similarities across several dimensions to the non-Native American population over age sixty-five.

Regarding mental health, a 1998 study by K. J. Curyto and colleagues reported that living in an urban area is a significant predictor of depression among Great Lakes Indians, along with fewer years of formal education. These findings are consistent with earlier data, from D. Lester in 1995, that suicide rates for American Indians correlate with a cluster of variables that measure wealth and urbanization, in stark contrast with data on white Americans. J. Kramer and J. C. Barker's 1996 study revealed that 16 percent of all Indian elders in Los Angeles County were homeless, a much higher percentage than those of other urban minority elder populations. Therefore, over a wide range of indicators, Indian elders appear to be a highly vulnerable population.

As such, membership anomalies, which on the surface may appear to be merely annoying, can have an adverse impact on both medical and psychological health. For example, if family caregivers expect to be refused IHS services on a trip to town, how easily will an offer of transportation be made to, and accepted by, rural Indian elders who feel ambivalent about going to IHS for medical treatment in the first place? Taken together, it appears that Indian elders are undercounted, increasingly underrepresented as a proportion of the total Indian population, and then at personal risk for underutilization of needed services due to political and social forces.

The situation takes on added poignancy since rural Indians are more likely, relative to urban Indians, to be over age sixty and lacking formal education, according to John. Data from the 1990 census revealed that 26.3 percent of Indian elders lacked access to a car. On a positive note, John noted that long-term residential stability is a pronounced characteristic of older American Indians living on reservations. Therefore, it is not surprising that 1990 Census data also revealed that 71.9 percent of households headed by an Indian elder over age sixty were also owner-occupied.

According to the U.S. Department of Commerce, however, 10.6 percent of all Indian elders (over age sixty) who lived in owner-occupied units lacked complete plumbing, while 9.4 percent lacked complete kitchens. Monthly housing costs were reported to exceed 50 percent of household income for 9.2 percent of Indian elders living in owner-occupied units. Renters fared still worse, with 22.2 percent of Indian elders paying rent in excess of 50 percent of household income. In the context of rural isolation and the occasion of dire need, it is striking that 31.3 percent of rural households headed by Indian elders also lacked phone service. To provide a broader context, John pointed out that among all housing units in the United States lacking telephone service, 77 percent were headed by rural Indian elders and 40.4 percent were headed by rural Indian elders living alone.

If reservation Indians are "old" by forty-five years of age, then it may be argued that Indian elders are additionally undercounted because gerontologists identify elders based on chronological age, following a European knowledge tradition that is inappropriate in this cultural context. Numerous authors report that traditional Indian communities define age not by years but by function and role in society. If this redefinition is proper, and it probably is, then the needs of Indian elders are most assuredly underestimated in policy analysis and Indian elders are underserved by the institutional safety nets that provide services to low-income elders in America.

—*Sherry Cummings and Clifford Cockerham*

See also Alcoholism; Cultural views of aging; Depression; Diabetes; Family relationships; Grandparenthood; Health care; Heart disease; Homelessness; Housing; Hypertension; Multigenerational households; Obesity; Poverty; Religion; Suicide; Wisdom.

FOR FURTHER INFORMATION:
Butler, Robert N., Myrna I. Lewis, and Trey Sunderland. *Aging and Mental Health: Positive Psychosocial and Biomedical Approaches.* Boston: Allyn & Bacon, 1998.
Curyto, K. J., et al. "Prevalence and Prediction of Depression in American Indian Elderly." *Clinical Gerontologist* 18 (1998): 19-37.
John, R. "Aging Among American Indians: Income Security, Health, and Social Support Networks." In *Full Color Aging*, edited by T. P. Miles. Washington, D.C: Gerontological Society of America, 1999.
Kramer, J., and J. C. Barker. "Homelessness Among Older American Indians." *Human Organization* 55 (1996): 396-408.
Lester, D. "Social Correlates of American Indian Suicide and Homicide Rates." *American Indian and Alaska Native Mental Health Research* 6 (1995): 46-55.
Schneider, Robert L., and Nancy P. Kropf. *Gerontological Social Work: Knowledge, Service Settings, and Special Populations.* Chicago: Nelson-Hall, 1997.

AMERICAN SOCIETY ON AGING

DATE: Founded in 1954
RELEVANT ISSUES: Media, psychology, sociology, work
SIGNIFICANCE: With more than eight thousand members, the American Society on Aging is one of the largest organizations that provides education and training to professionals in aging and aging-related fields

The American Society on Aging (ASA) was founded in 1954 as the Western Gerontological Society (WGS). The WGS, a regional association of researchers, writers, scholars, and teachers of gerontology, represented fifteen Western states. The organization continued to grow in terms of both membership and sponsored events. Its activities were managed by volunteers until 1975, when paid professionals were hired to manage the workload. By 1985, three thousand people belonged to the WGS, and as membership expanded into other geographical regions, the organization was renamed the American Society on Aging.

The ASA's mission is "to promote the well being of aging people and their families by enhancing the abilities and commitment of those who work with them." This mission is achieved through the provision of education, training, and resource materials. The ASA provides opportunities for professionals to develop a sense of community and cooperation through its sponsorship of conferences and meetings, which focus on various aspects of aging in society. It promotes innovative approaches to providing services to older persons. The ASA also influences policy through the identification of issues in the field of aging.

The organization is multidisciplinary. Its membership is made up of a wide variety of professionals in various service areas: representatives of public and private agencies, researchers, educators, advocates, health and allied health care workers, mental health providers, students, retirees, and policymakers and planners.

The ASA has a National Learning Center that provides educational resources. These resources include speaker directories, trainers, consultants, distance technologies, and products for learning and teaching about aging issues.

—*Colleen Galambos*

See also Advocacy; Aging: Biological, psychological, and sociocultural perspectives; Geriatrics and gerontology; Politics.

AMERICANS WITH DISABILITIES ACT

DATE: Signed into law on July 26, 1990
RELEVANT ISSUES: Economics, law, work
SIGNIFICANCE: The Americans with Disabilities Act guarantees equal opportunity for disabled individuals in public accommodations, employment, transportation, state and local government services, and telecommunications; many elderly people with disabilities are protected by its provisions

The Americans with Disabilities Act (ADA) prohibits discrimination on the basis of disability in employment, programs, and services provided by state and local governments, private companies, and commercial facilities and mandates establishment of telecommunications devices for deaf persons. The employment provision covers all companies that employ fifteen or more people. American Indian tribes, tax-exempt private-membership clubs (not including labor unions), and the federal government are not covered by the ADA. However, the federal government is covered by the Rehabilitation Act of 1973, which prevents the federal government, federal contractors, and educational programs receiving federal funds from discriminating against disabled persons. Religious organizations are governed by the ADA but may give employment preference to people of their own religion or religious organization.

QUALIFIED INDIVIDUALS UNDER THE ADA

Only individuals who are qualified under the ADA may claim discrimination under the act. The act establishes three categories of criteria for such qualification. To qualify as a disabled individual, a person must have a physical or mental impairment that substantially limits one or more major life activities, have a record of such an impairment, or be regarded as having such an impairment. Persons discriminated against because they have a known association or relationship with a disabled individual are also protected by the act.

The first category includes disabilities such as impairments in seeing, hearing, speaking, walking, breathing, performing manual tasks, learning, caring for oneself, and working. It does not include minor, nonchronic conditions of short duration such as sprains, influenza, and broken limbs. However, an individual with a broken limb that does not heal within a few months or that fails to heal properly may be considered disabled; determining whether a condition is a disability under the ADA is done on a case-by-case basis.

The second category covers people who have recovered from cancer, heart disease, mental illness, or other debilitating illness. It also includes individuals who were misdiagnosed with such illnesses if the misdiagnosis leads to discrimination. The third category protects individuals who are regarded as having a substantially limiting impairment, even though they may not. This would include individuals with controlled high blood pressure, individuals rumored to be infected with the human immunodeficiency virus (HIV), and individuals with observable deformities such as severe facial disfigurement.

Characteristics that are not considered disabilities under the ADA include current illegal drug use (although rehabilitated drug abusers may be covered), homosexuality, bisexuality, various sexual disorders (including pedophilia, exhibitionism, and voyeurism), certain behavior disorders (such as compulsive gambling, kleptomania, and pyromania), and such personality traits as poor judgment, a quick temper, or irresponsible behavior. Environmental, cultural, and economic disadvantages, such as lack of education or a prison record, are not covered by the ADA.

TITLE I: EMPLOYMENT

The ADA prohibits discrimination against qualified individuals in all employment practices, including job application procedures, hiring, firing, advancement, compensation, and training. A qualified individual is a person who meets legitimate skill, experience, education, or other requirements of an employment position and who can perform the essential functions of the position with or without reasonable accommodation. A written job description can provide evidence of the essential functions of a position but is not necessarily definitive. Whether an activity is an essential function must be determined on a case-by-case basis. Reasonable accommodations are those that would not impose an undue hardship on the operation of the employer's business; an undue hardship is an action that requires difficulty or expense when considered in the light of the size, resources, nature, and structure of the employer's operation. Reasonable accommodations may include remodeling existing facilities to make them readily accessible and usable by an individual with a disability, restructuring a job or work schedule, providing qualified readers or interpreters, or modifying examination or training to allow a disabled individual to demonstrate the knowledge or skills actually required for the position.

An employer may not ask or require a job applicant to have a medical examination before making a job offer but may condition a job offer on the satisfactory result of a postoffer medical examination or medical inquiry if such an examination or inquiry is required of all entering employees in the same job category. Information from all medical examinations and inquiries must be kept apart from general personnel files as a separate, confidential medical record. Drug testing is not a medical examination under the ADA. An employer cannot make any preemployment inquiry about the nature or severity of a disability but can ask about an applicant's ability to perform specific job functions and may ask for a reasonable demonstration of the required ability.

Employers may refuse to hire or may terminate the employment of disabled individuals if such individuals would pose a direct threat to the health and safety of themselves or others. This type of discrimination is allowed only if there is significant risk of substantial harm. The direct threat must be based on valid medical analyses or other objective evidence, not on speculation by the employer. The employer must attempt to eliminate the threat or reduce it to acceptable levels with reasonable accommodations. If elimination or reduction is not possible, the employer may refuse to hire or may terminate the employment of a disabled person. For example, an employer at a day care center might refuse to hire an individual with an active tuberculosis infection if no reasonable accommodation could be made to reduce the risk of infection to others.

TITLE II: PUBLIC SERVICES

Under the ADA's provisions, state and local government facilities, the National Railroad Passenger Corporation, and public transportation systems cannot deny services to people with disabilities. This prohibition extends to publicly owned buildings and vehicles and also affirmatively requires state and local governments to provide access to programs offered to the public. The ADA also covers effective communication with people with disabilities that may restrict or prevent their access to such programs. The act does not require that state and local governments provide all documents in Braille if workers are present to read documents to persons with vision or reading disabilities, nor does it require that sign-language interpreters be available if communication can be accomplished via note-writing.

However, the act does require reasonable modifications of policies and practices that may be discriminatory. For example, if a town council were to meet on the second floor of a building with no elevator, it would discriminate against disabled persons with mobility problems who could not walk to the second floor. Such an act would violate the ADA's provisions. However, if the town council were to meet without a sign-language interpreter, it would not discriminate against a deaf person who chooses to attend the meeting alone.

TITLE III: PUBLIC ACCOMMODATIONS

The ADA requires that construction of and modifications to structures that house entities providing goods or services to the public must be accessible to the disabled. Organizations that provide goods or services to the public, regardless of their size or number of employees, are considered to be public accommodations; these include stores, banks, libraries, hotels, restaurants, nursing homes, and privately owned transportation systems such as taxis and cruise ships. Residential facilities, independent-living centers, and retirement communities are covered by Title III if they provide a significant enough level of social services such as medical care, assistance with daily-living activities, provision of meals, transportation, counseling, and organized recreational activities.

The ADA also contains requirements for improving access to existing facilities. The act requires public accommodations to remove architectural barriers in existing facilities when such alteration is readily achievable without much difficulty or expense. Examples of readily achievable alterations include the ramping of one or a few steps, the installation of a bathroom grab bar, the lowering of towel dispensers, the rearranging of furniture, the installation of offset hinges to widen a doorway, and the painting of new lines to create an accessible parking space.

TITLES IV AND V: TELECOMMUNICATIONS AND MISCELLANEOUS PROVISIONS

The ADA mandates establishment of TDD/telephone relay systems and prohibits telecommunications companies from substituting a seven-number emergency line for the 911 emergency line for hearing-impaired individuals. The ADA prohibits coercing, threatening, or retaliating against disabled persons when those persons assert their rights under the act. Further, it prohibits threats or retaliation against individuals who attempt to aid disabled persons in asserting their rights under the ADA.

Complaints concerning violations of the ADA may be filed with the Equal Employment Opportunity Commission or with designated state human rights agencies. Available remedies include hiring, reinstatement, promotion, back pay, restored benefits, reasonable accommodation, attorneys' fees, expert witness fees, and court costs as well as real and punitive damages. —*Lisa M. Sardinia*

See also Advocacy; Disabilities; Employment; Hearing loss; Mental impairment; Mobility problems; Politics; Transportation issues; Vision changes and disorders; Wheelchair use.

FOR FURTHER INFORMATION:

Anderson, Robert C. *A Look Back: The Birth of the Americans with Disabilities Act.* Binghamton, N.Y.: Haworth Press, 1997.

Gostin, Lawrence O., and Henry A. Beyer, eds. *Implementing the Americans with Disabilities Act: Rights and Responsibilities of All Americans.* Baltimore: P. H. Brookes, 1993.

Johnson, William G. *The Americans with Disabilities Act: Social Contract or Special Privilege?* Thousand Oaks, Calif.: Sage Publications, 1996.

Shapiro, Joseph P. *No Pity: People with Disabilities Forging a New Civil Rights Movement.* New York: Times Books, 1993.

U.S. Equal Employment Opportunity Commission Staff. *Americans with Disabilities Act with Resource Directory.* Indianapolis: JIST Works, 1992.

ANTIAGING TREATMENTS

RELEVANT ISSUES: Biology, death, health and medicine, psychology

SIGNIFICANCE: Through a greater understanding of the mechanisms of aging, it is hoped that the healthy, active years of life for all people can be extended

Aging is a distinct process as yet to be fully understood by the scientific community. Several effects come into play that result in such characteristics of aging as a decrease in physiological functions of the body, diminished capacity for cellular protein production, a decline in immune function, an increase in fat mass, a loss of muscle mass and strength, and a decrease in bone mineral density. The risk that an illness or an injury will prove fatal increases with age. Most elderly individuals die as a result of arteriosclerosis, cardiovascular disease, cancer, or dementia.

Research continues to investigate the progressive, nonpathological biological and physiological changes that occur with advancing age and the abnormal changes that are risk factors for or accompany age-related disease states. While it is highly doubtful that scientists can ever stop aging completely or drastically extend the maximum life span of humans, there is a good chance that they will develop interventions to reduce or delay age-related degenerative processes in humans, hence improving the quality of late life.

GENETICS OF AGING

The life span of each species is determined by genetic makeup and altered by environmental exposure and behaviors. Within the human population, individuals vary greatly in their rate of aging and vulnerability to age-related diseases. Many genes may act together in determining the longevity and the manner in which individuals age. Several "longevity genes" have been isolated in mammals and lower organisms. Scientists are now pushing to find the biological limit and redefine it despite humans' inherent genetic makeup. For example, longevity genes discovered in fruit flies have increased their life expectancy by 30 percent. Similar genes that affect human longevity are being sought by both public-sector and private-sector research institutions.

Success in this area will lead to new means to improve the ability of humans to age in a healthy manner, with minimized frailty and disability. This involves a shift to the belief that the aging process, along with its fundamental cellular changes that occur in age-related diseases, is modifiable. Three main approaches to aging research emerged in the 1990's. The first focuses on the genetic analysis of senescence using hybridization techniques to examine how aging is affected by gene expression. The second approach focuses on dissecting the steps in growth factor signal transduction, and the third on how chromosomal structure such as telomere shortening affects the aging process. In most of these studies, however, the relationship between the basic aging mechanism and age-related diseases were not defined. The unraveling of this relationship should prove vital for antiaging treatments through gene therapy or related genetic approaches.

OVERVIEW OF TREATMENTS

Age-related diseases account for 90 percent of all diseases. It is virtually impossible to provide an exhaustive list. The best definition would be diseases that one typically does not develop before middle age. They include (but are not limited to) Alzheimer's disease, Parkinson's disease, diabetes, cancer, heart disease, osteoporosis, arthritis, stroke, and various disabilities related to the malfunction of the brain or immune system.

The recent belief is that aging is a series of degenerative processes that can be slowed and in some cases reversed (at least temporarily) through existing medical interventions. Future antiaging measures, however, will go far beyond the traditional preventive therapies. They may apply cutting-edge biotechnology such as improved magnetic resonance imaging (MRI) and sonogram imaging for the very early detection of age-related diseases. They may use advanced methods of genetic engineering therapeutics, hormonal growth factors, dietary supplements and products, or cloned stem cells for the repair and rejuvenation of the elderly immune and nervous systems. These medical methods will undoubtedly transform society in profound ways, eliminating the need for retirement at age sixty-five, pushing back the period of degenerative age-related disease to the very last few years or perhaps months of life, and vastly improving both the quality and the quantity of the human life span.

MEDICINE

Even though humans have been searching for the fountain of youth for centuries, the practice of antiaging medicine has been around for only a few decades. This medical field, which is based on the realization that aging is a treatable condition, seeks to slow, suspend, and in some cases even reverse the biological deterioration and diseases of the body. Insulin produced via genetic engineering was the first example of this approach. It was first used to treat diabetes in 1982. By 1997, genetically engineered insulin was being used by approximately 16 million diabetics, of which more than half were fifty-five or older. A daily prescribed dose of insulin keeps a patient's blood sugar and pressure at normal levels, hence eliminating or reducing the incidence of heart failure and other complications associated with diabetes.

Another age-related condition is Alzheimer's disease, the most common form of dementia that affects as many as four million older people. This progressive brain disorder is marked by gradual, abnormal changes in the brain that eventually leave patients oblivious to the outside world and unable to perform even the most basic tasks. As a result, Alzheimer's disease has a profound effect on the millions of family members and others who provide the care for people with this disease. Epidemiologists have found three potential interventions that may reduce the incidence of Alzheimer's disease: antioxidants, nonsteroidal anti-inflammatory drugs (NSAIDs), and estrogen replacement therapy. Studies of these three protective factors were reported in 1997. The use of NSAIDs such as ibuprofen was associated with a 50 percent reduced risk of Alzheimer's disease. Estrogen replacement therapy in postmenopausal women also led to a 50 percent reduction in the risk of developing this disease, compared to women who did not receive hormonal therapy. Use of the antioxidants selegiline or vitamin E, or a combination of the two, was evaluated to assess the effect on the progression of Alzheimer's disease in moderately impaired patients. Selegiline and vitamin E were found to slow development of functional signs and symptoms of the disease by about seven months, although they did not affect cognitive measurements. These antioxidants also decreased the rate of loss of the ability to perform daily activities such as bathing, dressing, and handling money by about 25 percent. Findings from such research are helping to launch new clinical trials for Alzheimer's disease.

Furthermore, human growth hormone was approved by the Food and Drug Administration (FDA). It was projected that millions of baby boomers would take the hormone to help forestall the diseases or conditions associated with aging, such as heart failure, muscle and bone loss, wrinkling, obesity, and failing memory. New drug therapies will undoubtedly improve the quality of later life, and prevention will save the cost of medications to treat diseases.

NUTRITION AND DIETARY SUPPLEMENTS

In the United States, many leading causes of death among aged people—heart disease, cancer, stroke, and diabetes—are rooted in the sedentary American lifestyle and poor dietary practices and are mostly preventable. Prevention through good nutrition, dietary supplements, and exercise is un-

doubtedly an important facet of antiaging treatments. This integrative approach tries to ensure that endurance, strength, and balance are kept at the highest possible levels and that the risk of disease and disability are kept to the minimum.

Healthy eating not only increases longevity but also significantly enhances quality of life. Numerous studies have demonstrated that the consumption of fruits and vegetables in variety and quantity has significant life-improving and life-extending effects. These positive effects are likely a result of hundreds of compounds acting in concert. Another simple eating habit that leads to an increased vitality is the consumption of fish. The omega-3 fatty acids in fish have been found to help prevent or reduce the risk of cancer, heart disease, and stroke.

Dietary supplements that increase the intake of calcium and vitamin D are found to help fight osteoporosis. Each year in the United States, the loss of bone mass caused by osteoporosis contributes to 1.5 million fractures, resulting in pain and dysfunction in later life. In a three-year trial that ended in 1998, daily dietary supplementation with 500 milligrams of calcium and 700 International Units of vitamin D prevented bone loss and was associated with a 50 percent reduction in the rate of symptomatic nonvertebral fractures. The benefits of these low-cost, low-risk, and easily available supplements are clear. They help older people maintain bone density and prevent hip fracture, a leading cause of nursing home entry for the elderly.

Simple daily routines established long before old age may improve the quality of later life, such as eating enough fruits and vegetables, drinking an appropriate quality and quantity of water, and taking an active interest in health.

EXERCISE AND PHYSICAL THERAPY

A regular exercise program should be an integral part of maintaining quality of life throughout the aging process. Mild exercise helps improve function and reduce pain in patients with osteoarthritis, a common condition and a major cause of pain and activity limitation in senior citizens. Although no cure has been found for this degenerative joint disease, aerobic training (walking) and resistance training (weight lifting) were found to be a safe and effective treatment option to help older people with osteoarthritis maintain function and quality of life without inflicting injuries. Moderate exercise can reduce the death rate from 30 to 50 percent, when compared to control groups that do not exercise. The amount and type of such exercise amounts to little more than a brisk daily walk.

A variety of physical therapies have been designed as antiaging treatments. Antihypertensive therapy is designed to reduce the risk of heart failure and major cardiovascular disease. Isolated systolic hypertension, the major risk factor for heart disease and stroke, affects more than 3 million older people. A low dose of diuretic-based medication has been found to lower the risk of heart failure by 50 percent for seniors with no previous heart failure and by 80 percent for persons who have already had a heart attack. The increased use of such inexpensive medication to reduce heart failure caused by isolated systolic hypertension could contribute greatly to quality of life and reduce the associated hospital and medical costs.

Another important area of aging prevention treatment is occupational therapy. This therapy designs specific instructions for people aged sixty or older that alter their approach to everyday activities such as shopping, exercising, and socializing in order to maximize function, productivity, and vitality. People who receive occupational therapy experience more gains (such as better physical and mental health, increased vitality, higher-quality social interactions, and greater life satisfaction) and fewer declines in important health-related areas (such as fewer role limitations and less bodily pain). Occupational therapy appears to be a useful tool to preserve function in older people.

GENE THERAPY

Gene therapy is a state-of-the-art technology that allows the addition of a functional gene or group of genes to a cell by gene insertion to correct a hereditary disease, cancer, or other age-related diseases. Patients are diagnosed through genetic testing, which allows for the early detection and treatment of cancer, Alzheimer's disease, and heart disease. It is believed that genetic testing will lead to real cures through detection and treatment years before diseases become clinically significant, giving physicians the ability to interrupt the disease process early on rather than waiting for symptoms to appear.

In 1998, scientists successfully used gene therapy in mice to show that it may be possible to prevent age-related muscle atrophy and preserve muscle size and strength in old age. The treatment increased muscle strength by 15 percent in young adult mice and, even more strikingly, by 27 percent in older mice. For older mice, muscle strength was restored to levels equivalent to those normally observed in young adulthood. To produce these results, the investigators engineered a virus to deliver into mouse muscle a normally occurring gene called insulin-like growth factor I (IGF-I), which plays a critical role in muscle repair and is believed to become less effective with age. While technical and ethical issues must be overcome if the procedure is to be tested in humans, this therapeutic approach holds promise for reducing age-related muscle loss, for strengthening muscles, and for treating muscle diseases.

Another example of gene therapy is the insertion of genes that prevent cellular aging. Findings in early 1998 about the process and control of cellular aging and death provided valuable insights into telomeres, the segments of deoxyribonucleic acid (DNA) on the ends of chromosomes that shorten with each cell division until at some point, cell division ceases. The enzyme telomerase adds DNA segments to the ends of chromosomes, compensating for telomere loss. Human cells do not naturally produce telomerase. Researchers showed that by inserting the gene for telomerase into normal, telomerase-lacking cells in mice, shortened telomeres grow longer and cells replicate far beyond the limits observed for normal cells while retaining the function of young cells. This discovery may aid in the development of a gene therapy for effective antiaging treatments in humans.

—Ming Y. Zheng

See also Aging: Biological, psychological, and sociocultural perspectives; Aging process; Alzheimer's disease; Antioxidants; Arteriosclerosis; Bone changes and disorders; Brain changes and disorders; Cancer; Cross-linkage theory of aging; Estrogen replacement therapy; Exercise; Free radical theory of aging; Genetics; Longevity research; Memory changes and loss; Nutrition; Osteoporosis; Sarcopenia; Vitamins and minerals.

FOR FURTHER INFORMATION:

Finch, Caleb, E., and Rudolph E. Tanzi. "Genetics of Aging." *Science* 278 (October, 1997). A discussion about the genetic basis of aging as well as the influence of lifestyle and other environmental factors.

Isaacson, Walter, et al. "The Future of Medicine." *Time* 153, no. 1 (January, 1999). A collection of eighteen articles that provide a wonderful outlook on the trends, directions, and concerns for medicine in the twenty-first century.

Klatz, Ronald. *Hormones of Youth.* Chicago: American Academy of Anti-Aging Medicine, 1999. A general and useful guide for the use of antiaging hormone replacement therapy.

Klatz, Ronald, and Robert Goldman. *Brain Fitness.* Chicago: Doubleday, 1998. A list and description of new drugs and therapies that can stop or reverse the memory loss and cognitive decline associated with aging.

Lange, Titia de. "Telomeres and Senescence: Ending the Debate." *Science* 279 (January, 1998). A good summary of the debate about the role of telomere shortening in the senescence of cells and possibly entire organisms and the implications of contemporary research in this area for longevity studies and antiaging treatments.

ANTIOXIDANTS

RELEVANT ISSUES: Biology, health and medicine
SIGNIFICANCE: Antioxidants are substances that neutralize the harmful effects of free radicals in the body; their role in preventing aging has received considerable interest in recent years

Free radicals are highly reactive chemicals that form in normal metabolism or are produced by radiation and environmental stress. These volatile chemicals react with cell components, causing mutations in deoxyribonucleic acid (DNA) and destroying cell proteins and lipids. The aging process and various degenerative diseases of aging are believed to be caused in part by the lifetime accumulation of cell damage caused by free radicals.

Antioxidant defenses occur naturally in the body to inactivate free radicals and repair damaged tissues. The body's natural supply of antioxidants is limited, however, and a small amount of destruction occurs to cells daily. Dietary antioxidants—in the form of fruits and vegetables or vitamin supplements—are believed to improve health and to prevent aging by boosting the body's natural supply of antioxidants.

Extensive research, including many large-scale studies, has demonstrated the beneficial role of dietary antioxidants in preventing such age-related disorders as cardiovascular disease, cancer, immune dysfunction, brain and neurological disorders, and cataracts. Fruits and vegetables, long recognized for their protective and healthful effects, are particularly rich sources of antioxidants, which may be the basis for their antiaging and anticarcinogenic properties.

Vitamin E, vitamin C, and beta carotene are the main dietary antioxidants. Vitamin E (tocopherol) is a fat-soluble antioxidant found in oils, nuts, seeds, and whole grains. This antioxidant appears to protect arteries against damage. Two recent studies have shown that taking vitamin E supplements appears to reduce the risk of heart disease dramatically. In addition, studies in mice suggest that vitamin E supplements slow the decline of brain and immune system function caused by aging. Vitamin C (ascorbate) works in the water-soluble part of tissues. Citrus fruits, strawberries, sweet peppers, and broccoli are good sources of vitamin C. This antioxidant boosts the immune system, strengthens blood vessel walls, and increases levels of a natural antioxidant, glutathione. Vitamin C also helps restore levels of active vitamin E in the body. Beta carotene, a precursor of vitamin A, is found in carrot juice, sweet potatoes, and apricots. Many studies have demonstrated the anticancer and antiaging effects of beta carotene.

Other antioxidants include coenzyme Q10, gingko, lipoic acid, grapeseed, and various substances found in green and black teas. The micronutrients zinc and selenium also have antioxidant properties; they aid the immune system and boost the levels of natural antioxidant enzymes in the body. Antioxidants appear to work together, as a combination of antioxidants is more potent than each substance alone.

Evidence for the beneficial role of antioxidants in human health is growing. Clinical studies have not definitively confirmed, however, whether consuming large amounts of antioxidants offers increased protection against aging. It is not clear what the optimal levels of antioxidants are to prevent the damaging effects of aging. Adequate levels of vitamins may vary greatly for each person, depending on levels of environmental stress, smoking, how well supplements are absorbed, and other factors. In addition, it is unclear whether vitamin supplements are superior to fruits and vegetables, since other factors in these foods (fiber, micronutrients) may be responsible for their healthful effects. —*Linda Hart*

See also Aging: Biological, psychological, and sociocultural perspectives; Aging process; Antiaging treatments; Cross-linkage theory of aging; Free radical theory of aging; Malnutrition; Nutrition; Vitamins and minerals.

ARTERIOSCLEROSIS

RELEVANT ISSUES: Health and medicine

SIGNIFICANCE: Arteriosclerosis, a general term for thickening and hardening of the arterial walls, is a progressive condition, the consequences of which account for the majority of morbidity and mortality in the United States

The most common type of arteriosclerosis is atherosclerosis, which is often the cause of heart attacks and strokes. Collectively, arteriosclerosis and other types of heart disease, such as congestive heart failure, are the leading cause of death in the United States for those over the age of sixty-five as well as for all age groups combined.

DEVELOPMENT OF ARTERIOSCLEROSIS

The changes that lead to atherosclerosis involve the arterial wall, which is the inside lining of the arteries. There are three parts to the arterial wall: the intima, the media, and the adventitia. The intima is a single layer of endothelial cells that line the artery. It rests on connective tissue of the media, which is the thickest layer of the wall. The intima and media are both involved in atherosclerotic changes. The third and outer segment of the arterial wall is the adventitia. It contains collagen, blood vessels, nerves, and lymphatic tissue.

Most scientific evidence supports the concept that injury to the epithelial cells of the intima begins the atherosclerotic process. An important function of the epithelial cells is to provide a barrier to keep blood and its components within the artery. Injury to these cells leads to increased permeability, which can allow components to pass

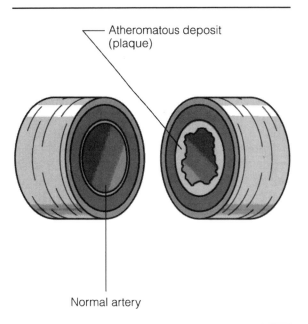

Arteriosclerosis leads to the buildup of fatty plaques on arterial walls, which inhibits blood flow and may lead to obstructions resulting in strokes and heart attacks. (Hans & Cassidy, Inc.)

through the intima and into the media that would normally be kept out. One of these components is low-density lipoproteins (LDLs).

LDLs are composed of protein, triglyceride, and cholesterol. The quantity of LDLs secreted from the liver is determined by several factors, including genetics and dietary fat. Fat is absorbed in the gastrointestinal tract and secreted into the blood and lymphatics as chylomicrons. The chylomicrons are partially degraded, leaving a chylomicron remnant. This remnant is taken up by the liver and secreted back into the blood as very low-density lipoproteins (VLDLs). The VLDLs are degraded to LDLs. Therefore, the more chylomicrons that are secreted in response to a high-fat diet, the higher the production of LDL.

After the LDLs have been transported into the intima of the arterial wall, they may become oxidized. The consequences of oxidation include recruitment of white blood cells. The white blood cells then initiate synthesis of adhesion molecules on the surface of the endothelial cells. The adhesion molecules attract proteins and fats in the blood to also adhere to the inside of the arterial wall. This produces a narrowing and inflexibility in the artery.

The earliest visible lesions in the arterial wall are fatty streaks, which do not protrude or disturb blood flow. Fatty streaks have been found to begin in early adulthood or even childhood. They do not contain the adhesion molecules or white blood cells.

Fibrous plaques appear to develop from fatty streaks after the LDLs have permeated the intima. They may protrude into the artery, making the diameter of the vessel narrower. They can also make the arterial wall thicker and less flexible, and thus more easily injured. Plaque may partially or totally block the blood's flow. Bleeding into the plaques can also occur, or a blood clot can form on the plaque's surface. In any of these situations, a heart attack or stroke may result. A heart attack occurs when the blood is blocked at the heart, while a stroke occurs when blood is blocked going to the brain. Left undisturbed, fatty streaks develop very slowly, becoming widespread only in old age. However, fatty streaks may be triggered into plaque development during middle age.

RISK FACTORS FOR ATHEROSCLEROSIS

Several factors have been associated with the progression or development of plaques in the artery and subsequent heart disease. Elevated levels of blood cholesterol or LDLs, high blood pressure, cigarette smoking, diabetes mellitus, obesity, and genetic disposition toward heart disease are all risk factors for the development of atherosclerosis. The Framingham Heart Study, begun in 1948, was the first to identify cardiovascular risk factors. The Framingham reports also include advancing age as a risk factor.

The National Institutes of Health (NIH) divides cardiovascular risk factors into those that one can do something about and those factors that cannot be changed. The latter category includes age: being forty-five years old or older for men and fifty-five years old or older for women. (Estrogen plays a protective role for women until they are past the menopause.) Another risk factor that cannot be changed is having a family history of early heart disease: a father or brother who developed heart disease before the age of fifty-five, or a mother or sister who developed heart disease before the age of sixty-five.

Risk factors that can be changed include high blood cholesterol, high LDL levels, low high-density lipoprotein (HDL) levels, high blood pressure (hypertension), diabetes, being physically inactive and overweight, and smoking. All these factors have been shown to be associated statistically with atherosclerosis. However, there is also a physiological basis for their being associated statistically. High blood cholesterol and LDL levels are thought to increase the probability that LDL will adhere to or permeate the epithelial cells of the intima. The HDL transports excess cholesterol in the blood back to the liver. Therefore, a higher level of this lipoprotein is a "risk reducer." Although people cannot be cured of high blood pressure or diabetes, having their blood pressure or blood sugar under control is less of a risk than uncontrolled high blood pressure or elevated blood sugar. Physical inactivity is believed to decrease the levels of HDL in the blood, to decrease uptake of LDL, and to contribute to obesity. Cigarette smoke is thought to directly injure the epithelial cells of the intima in the arterial wall, thus making them more susceptible to LDL adherence to the intima and invasion of the media of the arterial wall.

Because fatty streaks are believed to continue to develop throughout life, health policy has aimed at reducing those behaviors that may contribute to the acceleration of the fatty streaks into dangerous plaque formation. National health campaigns and health policies have suggested the elimination of smoking and the control of high blood pressure as ways to decrease the morbidity and mortality associated with atherosclerosis. Professional organizations have also promoted increasing physical activity, screening and treating those with diabetes, and achieving an optimal weight.

The reduction of dietary fat is also a national health guideline. Dietary fat is more of a risk factor in the development of atherosclerosis than is dietary cholesterol. Dietary cholesterol is also transported in the intestinal chylomicrons, but there is much less of it. Usual intakes of cholesterol fall well within the recommended 300 milligrams per day. In contrast, even a low-fat diet of 30 grams of calories from fat will result in an intake of 66,000 milligrams of fat when consuming a 2,000 calorie diet. It is clear that dietary fat has more of an impact than dietary cholesterol.

Other foods and nutrients continue to be investigated for their role in the prevention and treatment of atherosclerosis. Omega-3 fatty acids may have a role in the prevention or treatment of atherosclerosis, although their contribution remains to be clarified. In general, guidelines suggest that consuming fish once per week as a source of omega-3 fatty acids may be of benefit. Increasing the fiber in the diet can also help in lowering blood cholesterol and LDLs. Soluble fiber reduces blood cholesterol by decreasing absorption of cholesterol or fatty acids. Soluble fiber can be found in some fruits and grains, most notably oats. A variety of other dietary manipulations continue to be investigated. These include soy protein, garlic, isoflavones, and several vitamins.

Medications can also be used to lower elevated blood cholesterol or LDLs. Generally, dietary modification is recommended before medications are used because diet changes have no appreciable side effects. Medications for treating elevated blood lipids include a classification of drugs known as the statins, which work to decrease liver synthesis of cholesterol. Bile acid sequestrants reduce the reabsorption of bile acids and cholesterol. Nicotinic acid is a vasodilator that has been used to decrease blood lipids.

Prevention of atherosclerosis begins during young adulthood and continues into old age. Maintaining the integrity of the arteries is a process that must continue over the life span. When arteries are damaged, treatment and repair is much easier if they have been kept in good shape all along. —*Karen Chapman-Novakofski*

See also Antioxidants; Heart attacks; Heart changes and disorders; Heart disease; Hypertension; Malnutrition; Nutrition; Obesity; Strokes.

FOR FURTHER INFORMATION:

American Heart Association. *American Heart Association Guide to Heart Attack: Treatment, Recovery, and Prevention.* New York: Times Books, 1996.

_____. *Your Heart: An Owner's Manual.* Englewood Cliffs, N.J.: Prentice Hall, 1995.

Caplan, Louis, J. Donald Easton, and Mark L. Dyken. *The American Heart Association Family Guide to Stroke: Treatment, Recovery, and Prevention.* New York: Times Books, 1993.

Kris-Etherton, Penny, and Julie Burns, eds. *Cardiovascular Nutrition: Strategies and Tools for Disease Management and Prevention.* Chicago: American Dietetic Association, 1998.

Kris-Etherton, Penny, Patricia Volz-Clarke, Kristine Clark, and Anne Dattilo, eds. *Cardiovascular Disease: Nutrition for Prevention and Treatment.* Chicago: American Dietetic Association, 1990.

ARTHRITIS

RELEVANT ISSUES: Health and medicine

SIGNIFICANCE: In its many varied forms, arthritis causes joint difficulties ranging from discomfort and limitation of motion to loss of motion and extreme pain. Medical treatment is mainly palliative, although recent advances promise to arrest development of the disease or even cure it

Arthritis (from the Greek *arthron,* or "joint," and *itis,* a suffix referring to inflammation) is not one but a number of diseases with the common factor that they affect joints in some way. The term itself is misleading, because joint inflammation is absent in most forms of arthritis. Swelling around the affected joint is not uncommon, and pain is frequent, particularly with extreme muscular effort or range of motion. These symptoms, however, are characteristic of only certain kinds of arthritis. Other kinds can produce growth of nonjoint type tissue in joints, causing pain and sometimes immo-

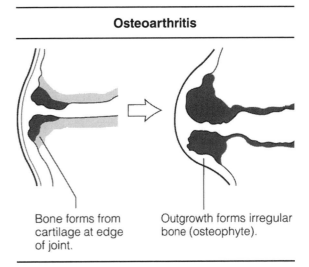

Osteoarthritis

Bone forms from cartilage at edge of joint.

Outgrowth forms irregular bone (osteophyte).

Osteoarthritis results when irregular bone growth occurs at the edge of a joint, causing impaired movement of the joint and pressure on nerves in the area. (Hans & Cassidy, Inc.)

Rheumatoid Arthritis

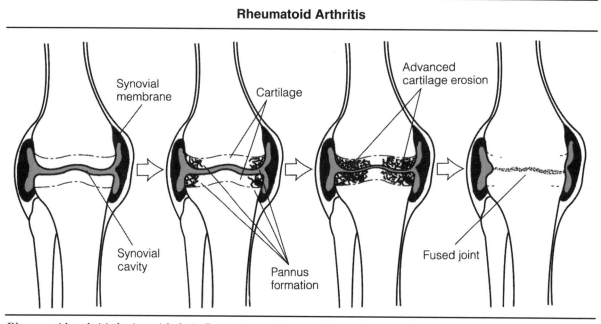

Rheumatoid arthritis begins with the inflammation of the synovial membrane and progresses to pannus formation and erosion of cartilage; eventually, the joint cavity is destroyed and the bones become fused. (Hans & Cassidy, Inc.)

bilization of joints; can produce secondary effects such as fatigue or fever; or can operate through interference with the immune system.

OSTEOARTHRITIS

Osteoarthritis is the most common form of arthritis. In 1999, it affected an estimated sixteen million Americans, about three-quarters of them women. Osteoarthritis usually occurs in older persons ("older" is a flexible term, as osteoarthritis can appear in one's forties or may appear two decades or more after that) and is often thought of as the result of wear and tear on the material of joints. In most of the joints in the body, the bone ends that come together are padded with cartilage on each side. Cartilage, or gristle, is a protein somewhat similar to that which forms the matrix of bones; this matrix is filled with calcium salts for load-bearing strength. Cartilage has no calcium salts and is porous, spongy, and elastic. With age, joint cartilage can lose its elasticity or develop rough surfaces. This makes for slowed or restricted motion, sometimes with accompanying pain. In addition, the tendons and ligaments that hold the joint together may loosen, allowing slippage in the joint and further wear on the cartilage pads.

With the restricted motion of the worn cartilage padding, the surrounding muscles get less exercise, and a slow decay in strength results. This brings on the problems often ascribed merely to age, such as a slowed gait, limited motion in limbs or neck, and loss of hand strength so that opening jars and bottles becomes difficult. Osteoarthritis can occur in any joint in the body—knees, hips, shoulders, fingers, or toes—but usually is confined to a relatively small number: one hip, or a thumb or a few fingers, for example. Debilitation is rarely complete but can be a thoroughgoing nuisance.

RHEUMATOID ARTHRITIS

Rheumatoid arthritis is the second most common type of arthritis. In 1999, there were an estimated two million sufferers in the United States, two-thirds to three-quarters of them women. This is the affliction that many people think of as "arthritis," typified by swollen joints, crooked fingers, and slow and painful movement. Unlike osteoarthritis, rheumatoid arthritis can affect many (or all) joints at once, usually symmetrically—that is, if the left knee and hip are affected, the right ones are almost certain to be affected also. Rheumatoid arthritis is a disease of the synovial membrane, which is the membrane that surrounds the joint (somewhat in the fashion of the rubber boot that seals the joint of the gear lever in a stick-shift car). The synovial membrane holds in the fluid that lubricates the joint, nourishes the joint cartilage, and keeps the joint flexible. The origin of the disease is unknown (a virus has been suggested), but the results are clear: the synovial membrane is invaded by inflammatory cells that cause it to thicken and release enzymes that initially irritate the joint cartilage but that can eventually cause it to dissolve. It is often replaced by scar tissue, which can restrict the joint's normal motion and sometimes freeze it altogether. Pain is chronic to acute. Rheumatoid arthritis usually begins in the patient's forties; it can be a one-time (though damaging) bout of a few weeks or months, or a series of recurrences, or an ongoing condition. The synovitis can be treated, and even in chronic cases the disease tends to lessen its effects over time—but the initial damage remains regardless.

JUVENILE RHEUMATOID ARTHRITIS AND GOUT

Despite its name, this form of arthritis is not related to the adult form of rheumatoid arthritis. Three kinds are known: a form that affects only one or a few joints and that usually goes away without recurrence; a form that shows itself as very high fever with little joint involvement (though this can occur in later life); and the form known as rheumatic fever, which is not an arthritis but a streptococcal infection that sometimes invades the joints. All these forms do not usually persist into adulthood.

Gout is a crystalline form of arthritis, in which crystals of uric acid actually deposit in the joint and cause excruciating pain, though usually for only a few days. Sufferers are mainly male. The joints most often affected are those of the foot, usually the big toe, and sometimes the third (metatarsal) joint of the little toe. It was at one time thought that this was a disease of excess—of rich food, much drink, and little exercise. Current thinking suggests that these excesses may be involved but also implicates genetic factors. As animals at the top of the food chain, most humans ingest too many amino acids, from plant and animal sources, that they cannot use in building proteins. The excess nitrogen from these amino acids must be excreted. This is done by passing water-soluble

urea in the urine. Some uric acid passes also, but uric acid is only slightly water-soluble; thus, it persists in relatively high concentration in the blood. Some persons are genetically predisposed to precipitate this uric acid, and for some this occurs in the joints, leading to gout. A pseudogout, in which the precipitated crystals are calcium phosphate, is also known. This usually occurs after age seventy, in both men and women; though it may recur, it tends to disappear spontaneously.

ANKYLOSING SPONDYLITIS

Ankylosing spondylitis (AS) is an arthritis mainly of the spine, though it sometimes affects other joints in the central part of the body. The name means an inflammation of the vertebrae (spondylitis) that results in ankylosis (stiffening of a joint, with the bones fusing together in late stages). AS is a genetically connected disease, and the gene site is known and can be detected by standard DNA analysis. AS shows up in early adulthood, predominantly in men. Most cases begin with fusion of the sacroiliac joint, immobilizing the lower back. Many never go beyond this stage, and the majority of persons with AS lead perfectly active lives. A few percent of cases progress to general spinal fusion, but even in these cases, mobility is not seriously impeded. Perhaps one case in a hundred freezes the entire spine, the neck, and even the cartilages of the ribs and breastbone, which restricts breathing but is rarely life-threatening. Most AS victims, in fact, have full lives and die of natural causes, despite the agonizing appearance of spinal rigidity and deformity in extreme cases.

It should be noted that kyphosis, the "dowager's hump" seen in elderly women and in some men, is not a result of this or any other arthritis; rather, it comes from osteoporosis, or loss of bone density, which leads to compression and partial collapse of vertebrae.

SYSTEMIC LUPUS ERYTHEMATOSUS AND OTHER FORMS OF ARTHRITIS

Systemic lupus erythematosus is an autoimmune disease—that is, one in which the system's tissues are attacked by its own antibodies. Arthritis results when the synovium or the joint cartilage is attacked. The symptoms resemble those of rheumatoid arthritis but are much milder and usually do not result in the bone damage of rheumatoid arthritis. On the other hand, the arthritis and its pain persist for the duration of the disease, which can be five to ten years or longer. The overwhelming majority of lupus victims are women.

More than a hundred other kinds of arthritis are known, but they affect relatively fewer people. They include psoriatic arthritis; Reiter's syndrome; fibromyalgia; arthritis associated with gonorrhea, tuberculosis, or Lyme disease; and polymyositis. Descriptions, treatment, and prognosis of these and other forms of arthritis can be found in the books cited at the end of this entry.

MEDICAL TREATMENT FOR ARTHRITIS

Until the mid-1990's, most of the medications used for arthritis were painkillers. The most notable exceptions were the corticosteroids, which gave dramatic results in relieving inflammation and swelling, though not without undesirable side effects.

The most common pain relievers are the nonsteroidal anti-inflammatory drugs (NSAIDs). They have have no chemical similarity to one another except that they are not steroids. NSAIDS include some of the oldest and cheapest drugs in the pharmacopeia, as well as some newer and correspondingly more expensive drugs. The oldest NSAID is aspirin (acetylsalicylic acid). Other over-the-counter analgesics include acetaminophen, ibuprofen, and naproxen. Although these drugs are available in such brand-name pain relievers as Tylenol and Advil, most of these NSAIDs are available as generic or in-house drugs. They are generally effective pain relievers, but they can cause side effects; for example, all except acetaminophen can cause ulcers and gastric bleeding, sometimes unexpectedly after many months' use. Acetaminophen in protracted high dosage has been shown to cause liver and kidney damage. In addition, NSAIDs can further damage joint cartilage, an effect that has also been demonstrated with the prescription NSAID indocin (indomethacin).

All the standard NSAIDs are cox (short for "cyclooxygenase") inhibitors that that interfere with the production of prostaglandins, which control cell chemistry. Only recently was it found that what had been thought to be a single cox that controlled both inflammation and pain as well as ulceration of the stomach and duodenum was in fact two separate compounds: Cox-1, which protected the stomach lining from acid degradation, and Cox-2, which produced joint inflammation. Thus, a compound that inhibited only Cox-2 could relieve arthritis symptoms without irritating the stomach. In 1999, two Cox-2 inhibitors were submitted for Food and Drug Administration (FDA) approval: celecoxib (Celebrex) and rofecoxib (Vioxx).

Two other osteoarthritis drugs are available that work on a totally different principle. These are hyaluronan (Hyalgan) and hylan G-F20 (Synvisc). Both are substitutes for hyaluronic acid, which appears to lubricate and increase the viscosity of joint fluid. As such, they must be injected directly into the joint in question, in a weekly series that typically costs from five hundred to seven hundred dollars. Large joints such as the knee fare best in this treatment; small joints are nearly impossible to inject with the large needle required for the viscous fluid. Relief is reported to last for six months to a year.

The NSAIDs are used extensively in osteoarthritis treatment, although they may be recommended in any case where pain must be controlled. Drugs to treat rheumatoid arthritis have been less effective than the NSAIDs, often merely reducing inflammation and performing a holding action on development of the disease. Historically, the first of these was a corticosteroid. With its use, inflammation and pain were virtually eliminated, and the disease appeared to be arrested. Side effects soon occurred, however, and in ensuing decades have been well documented: possible ulcers, mental changes, fat accumulation in the body, muscular weakness and wasting, loss of bone calcium, and other symptoms. Steroids are now used sparingly and as a kind of last resort.

A variety of treatments has sprung up to lessen swelling and ease other symptoms of rheumatoid arthritis: methotrexate, injectable gold salts, penicillamine, azsulfidine, and hydroxychloroquine, among others. Some of these have serious side effects, and in any case they do not reverse the effects of the disease; moreover, it is generally unclear whether they actually arrest the arthritic damage or merely slow it down. Three newer drugs may actually halt the disease. The first of these, leflunomide (Arava), is an immune suppressor that targets the cells of the joint. General immunosuppressors like methotrexate have been used, but leflunomide is the first that is tailored to the inflammatory cells that attack the synovium. Standard treatment costs about three thousand dollars per year, however, and requires careful monitoring by a physician and laboratory tests to observe effects on the body.

The other two drugs are the anti-TNF (tumor necrosis factor) compounds infliximab (Remicade) and etanercept (Enbrel). TNF is a cytokine that seems to cause inflammation and bone damage, so a drug that suppresses it suppresses its effects. Both drugs are administered by injection—intravenous in the case of infliximab—and both are expensive, about ten thousand dollars per year for etanercept.

One other new treatment for rheumatoid arthritis has been devised, involving blood-serum filtration with a protein called Prosorba, which seems to clear out inflammatory substances. This is a procedure prescribed for those who are getting no help from regular medication; it is very expensive (about twenty thousand dollars per year). None of these drugs or procedures had received FDA approval by mid-1999.

Drugs and treatments for other types of arthritis are usually some combination of those given for osteoarthritis and rheumatoid arthritis. No herbal, naturopathic, homeopathic, or other "alternative" treatment has been shown by laboratory testing to give reproducible results other than occasional pain relief. 　　　　—*Robert M. Hawthorne, Jr.*

See also Aging: Biological, psychological, and sociocultural perspectives; Aging process; Bone changes and disorders; Canes and walkers; Disabilities; Medications; Mobility problems.

FOR FURTHER INFORMATION:

Ahmed, Paul I., ed. *Coping with Arthritis.* Springfield, Ill.: Charles C Thomas, 1988. Views of nineteen contributors on coping with various types of arthritis. Highly varied and informative.

Calin, Andrei, and John Cormack. *Arthritis and Rheumatism: Your Questions Answered.* London: Churchill Livingstone International, 1996. Entire book in the form of questions and answers, frequently rather chatty. Thorough, well informed; excellent index.

Dunkin, Mary Ann. "The New Drugs: What to Expect." *Arthritis Today* 12, no. 6 (November/December, 1998): 31-35. Fuller discussion of new drugs mentioned above. *Arthritis Today,* published by the Arthritis Foundation (www.arthritis.org), contains well-balanced popular articles on all aspects of the disease.

Fries, James F. *Arthritis: A Comprehensive Guide to Understanding Your Arthritis.* 3d ed. Reading, Mass.: Addison-Wesley, 1990. Thorough discussion of types of arthritis, treatments, and prognoses, followed by an extensive guide to personal management methods and suggestions for problem-solving.

Lorig, Kate, and James F. Fries. *The Arthritis Helpbook.* 3d ed. Reading, Mass.: Addison-Wesley, 1990. Gives a brief introduction to the disease along with much valuable advice on exercise, pain management by self-suggestion, sleep, depression, nutrition, medication, working with one's physician, and other topics. Less technical than the preceding text.

Sands, Judith K., and Judith H. Matthews. *A Guide to Arthritis Home Health Care.* New York: John Wiley & Sons, 1988. Down-to-earth advice on changes in arthritis patients and how to manage them. Includes chapter bibliographies and patient-education materials. Good index.

_____. "Medications: Arthritis Drugs Hit Their Mark." *Harvard Health Letter* 24, no. 4 (February, 1999): 4-5. Evaluates new arthritis drugs.

ASIAN AMERICANS

RELEVANT ISSUES: Culture, family, race and ethnicity, values

SIGNIFICANCE: Older Asian Americans, coming from different cultural backgrounds with different values and attitudes toward the elderly, face social and psychological problems in coming to terms with aging

Asian Americans face many of the same problems with the aging process as do other Americans, such as financial and employment issues, retirement, and health problems. In addition, they face special psychological and social problems that arise out of their own racial and ethnic cultural backgrounds.

All people whose racial and ethnic origins lie in Asia but who are now permanently settled in and usually citizens of the United States are classified as Asian Americans. This definition encompasses people whose origins lie in the Middle East (countries from Turkey to Iran), the Far East (Pakistan, Afghanistan, India, and Bangladesh), and the Orient (from Burma to China and Japan, including countries in between). With such a vast array of differing cultures and religions, it is difficult to make generalizations on the problems faced by Asian Americans—except on the issue of aging. In their attitudes toward the elderly, all these Asian cultures show a remarkable similarity in the care that is given and the respect that is accorded to aging parents.

CULTURAL ATTITUDES TOWARD AGING

In all Asian cultures, the prevailing model has been the joint family system, in which aging parents live in the same household with at least one of their children. While this is usually a son and his family, it can also be a favorite daughter and her family. If the family has unmarried sons or daughters, they are a part of the joint family, unless they choose to live independently. This joint family system became a part of these cultures for socioeconomic reasons. If the parents had accumulated wealth but the children were struggling financially, it became more economical for the children to live with and care for their aging parents. If, on the other hand, the parents were destitute but one child was doing well, it became easier for social reasons, in countries that had no system of organized nursing homes, for the parents to be cared for at home. In addition, because of the respect shown to aging parents, there was a social stigma in the community against caring for aging parents anywhere except in the home.

Such an arrangement, however, could not have survived over the centuries in any of these cultures for merely economic reasons. There was a positive advantage to having aging parents living in the home. They continued to manage the household (including the cooking and the servants, if any) and looked after the grandchildren, thereby permitting the younger generation more time to pursue careers and other interests. The wisdom and advice of elderly parents was sought (although not always taken), and, as respected elders, the aging parents were always secure in the

Two older men admire plants at a bonsai club. Many Asian American elders living in the West find ways to stay connected to their cultural heritage. (Ben Klaffke)

knowledge that even if extreme health problems arose—such as senility or a broken hip causing them to become bedridden—they would not be abandoned.

OLDER GENERATIONS IN THE UNITED STATES

Asian Americans often find that the cultural values and attitudes toward aging that they brought from their homelands no longer apply in the United States. The overriding cultural value that dominates the thinking of all Americans, not simply the younger generation, is freedom. This concept brings to the forefront all the disadvantages ingrained in the joint family system. The younger generation was not totally free to run their lives because of the presence of aging parents in the household. This loss of freedom could take many forms, ranging from being overruled in the decision-making process in the running of the household to chafing under restrictions placed on their lives by the mere presence of parental authority in the home. A resentful daughter-in-law or son-in-law only aggravated the feelings of lost freedom, sometimes leading to a breakup of the joint family system, with the aging parents either surrendering authority or moving to the home of another, more accommodating child.

It is not only the younger generation of Asian Americans that feels this loss of freedom under the joint family system. There is an inherent loss of freedom for the parents themselves. If in good health and financially stable, those in the older generation feel some reticence toward being cared for, in old age, by an adult child. Having seen the advantages that freedom brings in the United States, even in old age, the thought of losing it creates the dichotomy of being caught between two cultures. This problem is particularly aggravated if the son or daughter has married outside the culture or faith, to someone who might not appreciate the cultural sensitivities of deep and abiding respect for the wisdom of an aging parent. For example, to address a parent by his or her first name would be considered disrespectful in most Asian cultures. There is also some sense of foreboding associated with living with a son or daughter who is married outside the culture or faith. This feeling arises from the fact that the majority of such marriages do not survive, with divorce rates similar to the general divorce rate in the United States. When divorce does occur, the aging parents may feel that they were, in some part, responsible for the breakup of the child's marriage. The accompanying guilt is a heavy burden to bear.

THE GENERATIONAL RESPONSE

Many of the same problems that face all Americans also face Asian Americans in particular, although some distinction has to be drawn between the generation of Asian Americans who were born and brought up abroad and then emigrated to the United States and the generation of Asian Americans who were born and brought up in the United States and who are facing retirement. In the first group, the response to other issues is also deeply influenced by culture. First-generation Asian Americans, having lived in their home countries for a considerable period of time and experienced the aging process in the generation that preceded them, are faced with reacting to various issues of their own aging in a different culture.

For later-generation Asian Americans, the response is modified by culture, but not to the extent that it is radically different from the response of most other Americans. The assimilation is slow, and possibly never complete, but with third-generation and fourth-generation Asian Americans, the differences in the response to aging tend to disappear.

RETIREMENT

Most Asian Americans come from poor, developing countries (a notable exception being Japan). In such countries, there is generally no Social Security or similar government-sponsored retirement net that provides for people in old age. As a result, most older Asian Americans have a deep-rooted sense of obligation to save over the years, far in excess of the average American. This bodes well for aging Asian Americans, except that these retirement funds are still far below the costs of nursing home care for even one incapacitated parent, let alone both parents.

With the extended joint family system now a footnote in history and nursing home care often beyond their reach, many aging Asian Americans have few alternatives left but to survive on their own at reasonable levels of proper living until they become incapacitated, at which point they swallow their pride and move in with the most accommodating of their children. A child who has married within the culture is the most likely candidate for the role of caregiver, but human relations play a large part in determining this decision. Sometimes a "mixed" marriage child is better suited, by virtue of compatibility, to performing the gracious role of caregiver.

HEALTH ISSUES

The medical problems that accompany old age are both physical and mental. Strokes, heart attacks, arthritis, and pulmonary diseases are examples of the medical problems faced by aging Asian Americans, and their response to these illnesses is becoming no different from that of other Americans. In most Asian countries, little emphasis is placed on fat-free diets or on the importance of regular cardiovascular exercise, especially for women. In traditional societies, women cannot jog or go to health clubs, even if men do. In the United States, however, older Asian Americans are becoming increasingly aware of the health risks that they run because of traditional fat-rich diets or lack of exercise. Later-generation Asian Americans, both men and women, are not inhibited in joining health clubs or exercising in other ways, on a regular basis, and by doing so they have become aware of the importance of preventive measures in maintaining good health in the aging years.

It is, however, in the area of mental illness, such as senility, Alzheimer's disease, and dementia, that there is a marked difference in the cultural attitudes of most Asian Americans of older generations. In most Asian countries, these mental illnesses have been considered shameful, partly because they are frustratingly incurable and partly because the parent suffering from such mental illness, if exposed to the outside world, may perform shameful acts that bring disgrace to the family name. Mental illness has often been hidden, with the aging family member closeted within the family environment. While this response had negative effects, both socially and psychologically, not only on the patient but on the rest of the family as well, it had one very great advantage: It forced the family to take care of the mentally ill parent or family member. Within the United States, however, this stigma against mental illness no longer

exists, and so the compelling social need to care for a mentally ill parent at home has disappeared. In those households that can afford it, placing the aging parent in a nursing home that has better facilities to care for such a physically or mentally ill parent has become acceptable among Asian Americans.

POLITICAL POWER

In all Asian countries, without exception, aging parents have been looked at with deep respect for their wisdom and experience gained over the years. This respect did not translate into political power, however, because the aging parents were past the career stage. Therefore, political decision making was left to the younger generation, which was thought to be better equipped to handle such issues. Nevertheless, movements in many countries, particularly Japan, have now raised the idea of "old people power." This concept has become a meaningful one to politicians, particularly since the percentage of the aging population in their retirement years has increased tremendously as a result of increased longevity. This change in attitude, coupled with the tradition of activism in the United States, has led many Asian Americans to become more politically involved.

RELIGION

Older-generation Asian Americans come from strong religious backgrounds, whether Jewish, Christian, Muslim, Hindu, or Buddhist. While individuals may be agnostics, or even atheists, in their early years, most people turn toward religion in their later years. Jews, Christians, and Muslims yearn for union with God and a place in heaven. Hindus and Buddhists wish to stop the cycle of rebirth and achieve nirvana. Whatever the end goal, it is the ever-looming thought of death that seems to make religion a prime focus of attention in the aging years.

Increasing periods of time are spent by older Asian Americans in religious ritual and prayer. Such activities seem to bring a sense of peace that was not sought in earlier years but has now become a necessary part of their lives. While mental illness and disease cannot be overcome by these practices, religion does seem to provide solace and to help overcome the frustration that can accompany the aging process. In some Asian Americans, this turning toward religion in the later years is augmented by increased financial donations to charitable causes and sometimes by volunteer service to the community as well, with a spirit of caring for the less fortunate in society.

—*Bezaleel S. Benjamin*

See also Aging: Historical perspective; Caregiving; Cultural views of aging; Family relationships; Multigenerational households; National Asian Pacific Center on Aging; Religion; Wisdom.

FOR FURTHER INFORMATION:

Dandekar, B. B. *Bene Israel Tales.* Lawrence, Kans.: A. B. Literary House, 1991. A collection of short stories about the Bene Israel of India. The story "Photograph of a Son" deals particularly with the loneliness of old age and the intense desire to belong to a family.

Kageyama, Yuri. "Japan Relearns Joys of Aging." *Chicago Tribune,* February 11, 1999. This newspaper article deals with *rojinryoku,* or "old people power" in Japan, where by government estimates one in four people will be over sixty-five by the year 2015.

Kitano, Harry H. L., and Roger Daniels. *Asian Americans: Emerging Minorities.* 2d ed. Englewood Cliffs, N.J.: Prentice Hall, 1995. Various immigrant Asian American communities are profiled, including Chinese, Japanese, Filipinos, Indians, Koreans, and Pacific Islanders. The book discusses a host of issues, such as family life and acculturation or integration into the United States. Provides statistics.

Lee, Joann Faung Jean. *Asian American Experiences in the United States.* Jefferson, N.C.: McFarland, 1991. Offers oral histories of first- to fourth-generation Americans from China, the Philippines, Japan, India, the Pacific Islands, Vietnam, and Cambodia.

Min, Pyong Gap, ed. *Asian Americans: Contemporary Trends and Issues.* Thousand Oaks, Calif.: Sage Publications, 1995. This series of essays by the editor and five other contributors on various Asian American communities covers a variety of issues.

AUTOBIOGRAPHY OF MISS JANE PITTMAN, THE

AUTHOR: Ernest J. Gaines

DATE: Published in 1971

RELEVANT ISSUES: Race and ethnicity, religion, values

SIGNIFICANCE: This inspiring novel tells how an unprepossessing, elderly African American woman served as a quiet heroine in the struggle for civil rights

The Autobiography of Miss Jane Pittman begins in the 1960's when a young historian interviews the aged Miss Jane Pittman as part of his project to gather an oral history of the black community in Louisiana. It is her longevity that makes her a historical resource, and she proves a valuable repository for the history of her people. She recollects her life as a young slave girl, the Civil War, and its aftermath, when she is forced to become a poor sharecropper. In these early years, her adopted son Ned and her husband, Joe Pittman, are the ones who are active in the struggle for genuine African American empowerment. When Joe dies and Ned is murdered by local whites, Jane gains strength and fortitude from her religion, which allows her to endure these losses.

It is only when Jane becomes an old woman that she truly comes into her own. Despite her troubles, she survives to a great old age with dignity and grace and comes to represent courage, perseverance, and strength of character to the people around her. She particularly inspires a young black man named Jimmy, who, like Dr. Martin Luther King, Jr., emerges in the 1950's as a leader in the cause of civil rights. When Jimmy is murdered, Jane herself finally becomes an active part of the Civil Rights movement. At over one hundred years of age, she gallantly joins a rally in honor of the fallen Jimmy, openly challenging the racism she fought quietly for many generations.

This novel was made into a film for television in 1974.

—*Margaret Boe Birns*

See also African Americans; Centenarians; Films; Literature; Politics; Women and aging.

BABY BOOMERS

RELEVANT ISSUES: Demographics, economics, family, sociology

SIGNIFICANCE: Profound economic and demographic changes in American society resulted from the significant increase in the annual birth rate between 1946 and 1964

During the economic depression of the 1930's and World War II, the annual birth rate in the United States was relatively low. Between 1930 and 1945, there were fewer than 3,000,000 live births each year. With the end of World War II and the relative economic prosperity of the postwar years, men and women were more motivated to have children, and the birth rate increased significantly between 1946 and 1964. The average annual U.S. birth rate during this period was approximately 4,000,000; it approached 4,500,000 annually by the late 1950's before declining to around 3,500,000 by the late 1960's.

ECONOMIC AND DEMOGRAPHIC CHANGES

The significant increase in the birth rate had a very real effect on American society. During the Great Depression and World War II, relatively few new schools had been built and few teachers hired. Thus a crisis in education began in 1952, when the first of the baby boomers entered elementary schools.

Municipal governments across the United States almost doubled the number of teachers in elementary, middle, and high school between 1945 and 1960, and thousands of new schools were built for the education of millions of baby boomers. As the number of children in public schools increased dramatically, parents of baby boomers insisted on better-educated teachers. Until World War II, almost half of elementary teachers had not earned a B.A. degree, but parents and government officials required higher standards. By the 1950's, most school boards required both a B.A. degree and teacher certification for elementary-school teachers, and high-school teachers were expected to be working on master's degrees as well. The relative shortage of qualified teachers forced school boards to pay higher salaries to hire and retain their teachers. Local and state governments had no real choice but to increase funding for public schools.

Many states turned to the federal government for financial assistance, but the federal government declined to offer massive assistance for several reasons. First, members of the executive and legislative branches believed that public education should remain a responsibility of local and state governments, which could then retain control over their own curricula. Second, the federal government did not want to support segregated schools in many states, and it certainly did not want to begin subsidizing parochial schools, as such support would violate the constitutional separation between church and state. The federal government did support certain aspects of public education with the passage of the National Defense Act of 1958 and the Elementary and Secondary Education Act of 1965, but federal assistance constituted a relatively small portion of the annual budgets for school boards. Federal assistance was largely targeted for handicapped and economically disadvantaged children.

Other significant demographic changes also took place during the two decades after World War II. Many parents of baby boomers decided that the quality of life for their families would improve if they moved from crowded cities to new and spacious suburbs. New towns with planned subdivisions were created throughout the United States. Just as the United States had been transformed from an agricultural to an urban society in the decades after the Civil War, it was gradually transformed from an urban to a suburban society in the decades after World War II.

These social changes had unintended adverse effects. Businesses began to leave major cities for the suburbs, and economic conditions in cities deteriorated as there were fewer and fewer well-paying jobs in cities. Those who were financially unable to move to the suburbs saw a marked decrease in their standard of living. Baby boomers who were raised in cities developed significantly different outlooks from those baby boomers who lived in suburbs. This contributed to alienation among urban baby boomers, who felt that they had little in common with relatively affluent suburban baby boomers. Suburban baby boomers came to realize that their lives were not necessarily any better than those of their urban contemporaries because suburban life had not helped them to understand the complex fabric of American diversity.

Urban and suburban baby boomers got to know each other in college. Until World War II, relatively few Americans had been able to attend college. After the war, however, attitudes changed and people concluded that higher education was absolutely essential for individual success and American economic growth. The G.I. Bill enabled millions of veterans to earn college degrees, and state governments began to build more colleges and to increase enrollments at existing colleges and universities. Starting in the mid-1960's, baby boomers began to graduate from high school. Unlike earlier generations, a significantly higher percentage of baby boomers attended college, and this trend changed the United States in subtle but real ways.

In college, baby boomers were exposed to a wide variety of opinions, and many began to question the religious, political, and ethical values of their parents. As the baby boomers started to attend college, the Vietnam War began to escalate and the number of American fatalities in this controversial war increased significantly. Many baby boomers started to question both the reasons for American involvement in this war and their parents' belief that the government always based its decisions on what was best for its citizens. Overt racism against African Americans and the violence manifested by rioting in many cities and by assassinations of such respected leaders as President John F. Kennedy, Dr. Martin Luther King, Jr., and Senator Robert F. Kennedy persuaded many baby boomers that the social problems in the United States were much more profound than their parents seemed to realize. The political maneuverings of Presidents Lyndon B. Johnson and Richard Nixon only increased the baby boomers' feelings of alienation from politics and their parents' generation.

Changing U.S. Birthrates, 1910-1996

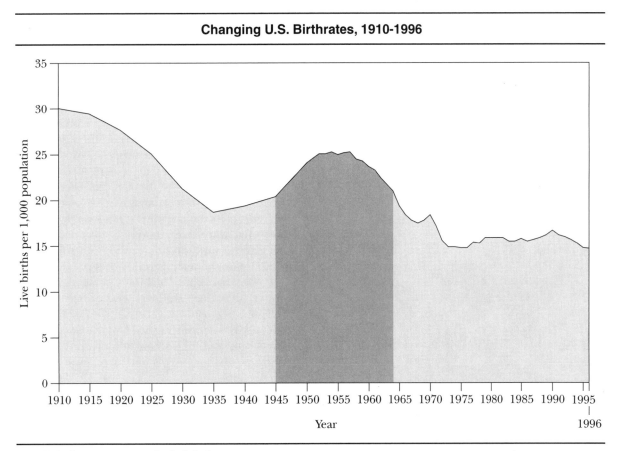

Note: Baby-boom years are shaded dark gray.
Source: The Time Almanac 1998. New York: Information Please, 1997.

ECONOMIC REALITIES FOR ADULT BABY BOOMERS

Baby boomers had been led to believe that they would enjoy economic success and a comfortable lifestyle if they simply studied diligently and obtained university degrees. They mistakenly thought that the extended period of economic growth that had started after World War II would be permanent. They were psychologically unprepared for the serious economic downturn that began in 1973 with the oil crisis and continued well into the 1980's. Extremely high inflation reduced their spending power, and job insecurity became a way of life for millions of American baby boomers. Their parents had taught them that they should have faith in government programs such as Social Security and Medicare. Furthermore, baby boomers believed that they could supplement Social Security with company pensions. Economic changes in the 1980's caused much anxiety among baby boomers who experienced corporate downsizing, and many came to realize that they would probably not work long enough with any single company to receive a meaningful pension during retirement.

Baby boomers adapted to changing economic conditions in a variety of ways. In order to make up for the company pensions that they might never receive, they began to invest heavily in individual retirement accounts (IRAs) and other tax-deferred investments so they would have money to live on during retirement. To deal with job insecurity, baby boomers recognized the importance of continuing education and the need for job flexibility. They realized that they might work not only in several different jobs but in several different fields and regions of the country as well. Their parents had believed in company loyalty to workers, but baby boomers had no such illusions. The loyalty of baby boomers was to themselves and their families—a realistic reaction, not a cynical one.

As for Social Security, baby boomers had very low expectations. When the Social Security program was created in 1935, it was established on a "pay as you go" basis. The payments received each month in taxes from employees and employers were used to pay benefits to retirees. Taxpayers did not have IRAs, but rather they were promised a certain level of payments based on the number of years of paying Social Security taxes and the amount of these taxes. This system worked very well during the early years of Social Security because there were more than ten active workers for each retiree. By the late 1990's, however, it was estimated that when baby boomers began to retire during the second decade of the twenty-first century, there might be only three workers for each retiree. Demographic realities persuaded baby boomers that they would receive either nothing for Social Security or very reduced benefits in comparison to those received by earlier generations. A 1985 poll of working adults indicated that two-thirds of them expected to receive nothing from Social Security.

It is not known how the federal government will deal with the impending financial crisis for Social Security. Some sociologists predict "age wars" if the federal government proposes decreasing benefits for current retirees so that future retirees can receive comparable benefits. Some economists and

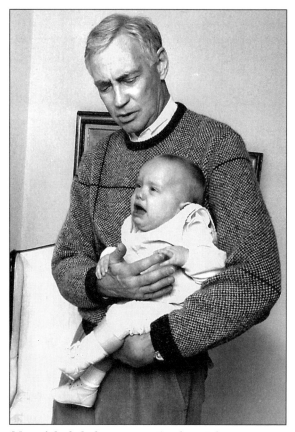

Men of the baby-boom generation have taken a more active role in the raising of children and grandchildren. (Jim Whitmer)

politicians propose that some Social Security taxes be invested in the stock market in IRAs so that each taxpayer can enjoy higher Social Security benefits if the stock market does well. Such a system of combining guaranteed government-sponsored retirement benefits with variable IRAs was implemented in Great Britain in the 1980's. By the end of the twentieth century, however, it was not clear whether such a modified Social Security system could be approved by an American Congress and signed into law by an American president.

OTHER CONCERNS OF BABY BOOMERS

As they aged, baby boomers came to believe that their lives were much more complicated than their parents' lives had been. The divorce rate continued to increase, resulting in more single parents and in numerous blended families in which children have different biological parents. Such trends created both emotional stress and financial strain on families. Baby boomers with children worried about raising them and saving enough money for their higher education. Paying for higher education became a serious issue for baby boomers because college tuition in the 1980's and 1990's increased at a rate higher than the national inflation rate.

Another serious problem for baby boomers became the care of their aged and ill parents. In the late 1990's, approximately four million elderly Americans suffered from Alzheimer's disease, and many others had suffered strokes or had other debilitating illnesses that made it impossible for them to care for their own needs and continue living by themselves. In ever-increasing numbers, baby boomers had to become caregivers for their own parents. Such responsibilities are emotionally demanding for caregivers. Many baby boomers realized that they would have to take care of their own children but found themselves unprepared for the full commitment required of caregivers for elderly parents as well. When adult children become caregivers, the traditional parent-child role is reversed.

If the aged parent is seriously ill or mentally incompetent, the adult child may have to make all financial and medical decisions for the parent. As the parent's medical condition deteriorates, the caregiver's responsibilities increase. The parent may no longer to able to live with his or her adult child. Placing a parent in a nursing home is never an easy decision, but often adult children run out of choices. Medical care at home or in a nursing home may become increasingly more expensive, and the caregiver may have to make life-or-death decisions for the parent. Even if the parent has signed an affidavit requesting not to be resuscitated and for no extraordinary measures to be taken to extend life, doctors and nurses will still turn to the caregiver and ask him or her to make a decision concerning medical care. Such decisions are often difficult because there are no good choices. Approving the insertion of feeding tubes, for example, extends life, but if no hope exists that the patient's condition will improve, it extends suffering as well. Refusing medical treatment, however, brings about a parent's death. Caring for an ill parent may last years, which takes a terrible toll on the patient, the caregiver, and the caregiver's spouse and children. Many baby boomers find themselve unable to meet all the demands from parents, spouses, children, and jobs. Frequently, the caregiver and other family members seek psychological counseling in order to cope both before and after the parent's death.

Some sociologists have been rather harsh in their comments on baby boomers, whom they accuse of being self-centered. Although there may be some truth in this value judgment, it overlooks the fact that baby boomers have had to deal with profound differences between the reality of their complex lives and the excessively optimistic promises made to them in the 1950's and 1960's. Most baby boomers did their best to cope with significant changes in American society that began with the end of World War II.   —*Edmund J. Campion*

See also Aging: Historical perspective; Caregiving; Children of Aging Parents; Death of parents; Demographics; Divorce; Early retirement; Employment; Filial responsibility; 401K plans; Graying of America; Income sources; Individual retirement accounts (IRAs); Marriage; Medicare; Middle age; Midlife crisis; Parenthood; Pensions; Politics; Remarriage; Retirement; Sandwich generation; Single parenthood; Social Security; Stepfamilies.

FOR FURTHER INFORMATION:

Gerber, Jerry, and Janet Wolff et al. *The Future of Baby Boomers and Other Aging Americans.* New York: Macmillan, 1989. Discusses the effect of social policies on the working and retirement years of baby boomers.

Greeler, Martin M., and David M. Nee. *From Baby Boom to Baby Bust: How Business Can Meet the Demographic Challenge.* Reading, Mass.: Addison-Wesley, 1989. Analyzes the need for human resource managers to be more sensitive to the needs of baby boomers so that companies and individuals can profit from business changes and mergers.

Jones, Landon Y. *Great Expectations: America and the Baby Boom Generation.* New York: Coward, McCann & Geoghegan, 1980. Contains much useful statistical information on the economic and social lives of baby boomers.

Russell, Cheryl. *The Master Trend: How the Baby Boom Generation Is Remaking America.* New York: Plenum Press, 1993. Contains a rather harsh judgment of baby boomers as self-centered free agents who never fully accepted their social responsibilities.

Russell, Louise B. *The Baby Boom Generation and the Economy.* Washington, D.C.: Brookings Institution, 1982. Contains a well-researched analysis of the influence of baby boomers on schools and the labor market in the United States.

BACK DISORDERS

RELEVANT ISSUES: Biology, health and medicine

SIGNIFICANCE: Although well documented in medical literature, back disorders are the most expensive ailment in thirty- to sixty-year-olds and remain controversial in diagnosis and treatment.

Back disorders are among the most prevalent, debilitating, and costly medical conditions in Western society. About 80 percent of adults experience back pain sometime in life, with most serious cases beginning around age forty. Back problems are the second leading reason for missed work, causing full-time employees to lose five working days annually, and only 50 percent of persons missing work longer than six months return to their previous capacity. Direct and indirect medical and economic consequences of spinal problems are estimated between 16 and 40 billion dollars annually in the United States. Degenerative disorders of the aging spine manifest themselves as bone abnormalities, degenerative disk and joint disease, increased laxity in supporting ligaments, and muscle and tendon weaknesses and imbalances.

VERTEBRAE

A normal spine contains thirty-three bones called vertebrae—seven cervical, twelve thoracic, five lumbar, five sacral, and four coccygeal—which enable mobility and protect the spinal cord. The spine also contains the origins of thirty-one pairs of spinal nerves. The cervical and lumbar regions normally exhibit a lordotic curve (anterior concavity), whereas the thoracic, sacral, and coccygeal regions have a kyphotic curve (posterior convexity). From the second cervical to the first sacral vertebra, adjacent vertebrae are connected by disks anteriorly and facet joints posteriorly.

Vertebrae, which are approximately six times stiffer and three times thicker than disks, are filled with blood and are much spongier than the skeletons hanging in anatomy classrooms. Healthy vertebrae deform about half as much as disks during compression, with vertical height often reduced by nearly 1 inch throughout the day. The body's center of gravity gradually shifts downward beginning in middle age as a result of the constant force of gravity and blood circulation adjustments.

Increased compression on the spine occurring simultaneously with osteoporosis (bone weakening) strongly contributes to vertebral fractures. Bone weakening depends on the amount of bone mass gained from adolescence to age thirty-five and the rate of bone loss that follows. Cortical bone decreases by about 3 percent and trabecular bone by 7 percent per decade, with postmenopausal women losing bone three times faster than the rest of the population. As the skeleton adapts to stresses put upon it, 90 percent of women over age seventy-five develop conditions such as kyphosis (humpback or dowager's hump), scoliosis (lateral curvature), flat back, or sway back. Scoliosis can be congenital (present at birth) or can develop later in life, possibly as a result of rickets or tuberculosis. The cartilaginous endplates of vertebrae progressively lose minerals over time until only minimal layers of bone separate disks from vascular channels after age sixty.

Other disorders can affect the disks. Adjacent vertebrae form the intervertebral foramen, through which sensory and motor neurons and blood vessels pass. These neurons can become irri-

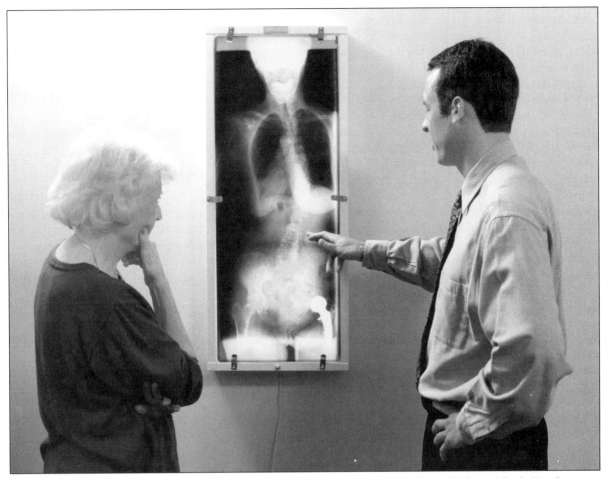

Changes in the bones with age, especially in postmenopausal women, put older people at risk for such back disorders as osteoporosis, scoliosis, and slipped disks. (PhotoDisc)

tated or compressed, causing numbness, tingling, pain, and weakness in the extremities. Spondylosis is a unilateral fracture of the pars interarticularis, an isthmus at the lamina-pedicle junction. Excessive loading in extension—the spine's position when facet joint surfaces are maximally congruent and ligaments are maximally taut—is often the cause. Dancers may experience spondylolisthesis, a bilateral fracture of the pars interarticularis that causes forward slippage of the lumbar vertebrae. Thoracic outlet syndrome may develop from compression of the brachial plexus (the network of nerves in the armpits) and the blood vessels below the collarbone near the cervical vertebrae. Bony abnormalities of the thoracic vertebrae include a sharp posterior angulation and kyphosis associated with postmenopausal osteoporosis. Scheuermann's

disease, or osteochondrosis of adolescence, leads to thoracolumbar kyphosis and anterior wedging of the vertebrae. Deviations from the range called the neutral spine progressively require greater more reliance on support structures to maintain balance.

INTERVERTEBRAL DISKS

The spine exhibits three ranges of motion: flexion-extension, sidebending, and rotation. The degree and type of motion, and resting position, at various spinal levels is determined by the ratio of intervertebral disk to vertebral height and the orientation of the facet joints. Young adult disks contribute 20 to 33 percent of total vertebral height and function like a universal joint in providing the fulcrum for movement. The disks of newborns possess a direct blood supply that enhances protein synthesis, but this circulation is terminated when compressive weightbearing begins. Adult disks resemble a wedge-shaped, jelly-filled donut and rely on diffusion for nourishment.

As early as age thirty, type I collagen fibers of the outer disk annulus (ring) begin losing their ability to stabilize against tensile forces; the rate of degradation may be genetically influenced. Aging also degrades type II collagen fibers within the inner nucleus pulposus of the disk, decreasing resistance against compression. The nucleus normally takes up about 25 percent of a disk, is largest in the cervical and lumbar areas, and contains about 80 percent fluid. Biochemical imbalances and a reduction in the amount of substances called glycosaminoglycans, possibly greater than 50 percent by age thirty, reduce fluid attraction and retention in the nucleus, curtailing its ability to absorb and distribute shock. The result is disk bulges that often have a half-life of several days. Pressure on mature disks is estimated to increase 200 percent when one changes from a supine position to standing and by 400 percent during slumped sitting. The spine attempts to attenuate forces from a bulging disk by increasing vertebral surface area, often leading to spur formations that can interfere with nerve roots.

A herniated disk is a protrusion in which the disk remains contained because of an intact outer annulus or posterior longitudinal ligament. A prolapsed or extruded disk involves a rupture in the fibers of an annulus or ligament, allowing bulging of the nucleus into the neural canal. A noncontained disk involves the extrusion of a disk through the posterior longitudinal ligament. Compressed material from disks generally protrudes posteriorlaterally, as this direction is furthest from the spine's axis of motion and is provided less resistance by the posterior longitudinal ligament. Invasions of the nucleus into adjacent vertebrae with advanced osteoporosis are called Schmorl's nodes or the vacuum phenomenon. Disk collapse in the lumbar spine increases lordosis, causing Baastrup's "kissing spine" syndrome.

Intervertebral disks were considered to be without nerves until research indicated that superficial layers of the annulus are very pain-sensitive. Degenerative disease increases pain sensation in the disk, particularly while sitting, as an ingrowth of nervous tissue occurs during healing of a torn annulus. Rotation produces shear stress to the disk, whereas bending movements produce tensile and compressive stress. Compressive testing of cadaver spines has shown that the disks of individuals younger than forty can withstand more than twice the compressive force of the disks of individuals older than sixty, which often degenerate into disorganized fiber.

FACET JOINTS

Facet (or zygapophyseal) joints are oriented differently throughout the spine and contain lubricating synovial fluid within a capsule to enhance movement. When degenerative disk disease reduces the toleration of compressive force in the anterior spine, the facets become increasingly loaded and degenerative joint disease begins. The facets can experience cartilage wear, osteophyte development, and swelling, causing discomfort and pain that is often relieved by sitting or bending forward. Articular cartilage is not sensitive to pain, so that degeneration often progresses to the point of subchondral bone deformation before medical care is sought.

Osteoarthritis, which is present in 85 percent of persons over age sixty, involves collagen degradation, spur formation, sclerotic (dense) bone, joint space narrowing, and cartilage thinning at joint margins which reduces joint nourishment. Rheumatoid arthritis involves inflammation of joint linings, which reduces lubrication and increases swelling, tenderness, and stiffness. Meniscoids (pieces of cartilage, adipose tissue, or connective tissue often still attached to the joint capsule) may migrate into the facet during forward flexion and become pinched during extension. Acute conditions include lumbago, a low back locking restriction, and torticollis, a tilting of the neck that motivates patients to find the position of optimal comfort. Osteophyte formation around the spinal canal can impinge on either the spinal cord or the spinal nerve roots. Spinal stenosis (narrowing) is now considered inevitable during aging, although it often does not cause pain or disability.

SOFT TISSUES

Technological advances in the twentieth century have enabled a sedentary lifestyle. Unfortunately, the result has been a reduction in healthy physical stress, causing earlier deterioration of the soft tissues supporting the spine. Muscles, tendons, ligaments, and fascia, which act as spinal guides, become weak or change in length with prolonged inactivity while maintaining poor posture and are further aggravated by sudden overloads of strenuous work or recreational activities. The cervical spine is particularly vulnerable to whiplash-type injuries, with rear-end vehicle collisions often damaging the thirty-two complexly related anterior neck muscles. Temporomandibular joint (jaw) problems and headaches often follow.

Soft tissue injuries are prevalent during combination lifting and twisting movements that require muscles to control the rate of tilting before returning the back to the upright position. Small tranversospinalis muscles such as the multifidi are at a tremendous mechanical disadvantage during tilting, particularly in the lumbar region. The distance from the upper body to the point on the low back where pivoting occurs is considerably longer than the distance from the lateral attachment of the muscles to their medial attachment on the spine near the pivot point. As with all lever systems, shorter lever arms require more force to be exerted at the pivot point to resist the longer lever arm, with forces greatly magnified by rapid changes in torque. Small posterior spinal muscles weaken with disuse atrophy, inappropriately spasm when attempting to protect the spine (a phenomenon called muscle guarding), or create imbalances and instabilities when paired muscles on one side becomes stronger. Myofascial "trigger points" develop from repeated trauma, both large and small, resulting in twisting and knotting that causes restrictions in blood circulation and nourishment during critical phases of healing. Spinal ligaments, which have many nerves, increase the stress on facet joints with increases in laxity, forcing the surrounding muscles to compensate. Degradation of the elastic ligamentum flavin reduces its ability to check facet joint movement and to prevent intra-articular cartilage from shearing joint surfaces with age, particularly in sedentary persons.

SPINAL PAIN

Mechanical spinal pain can be divided into spondylogenic and radicular pain. Spondylogenic pain involves deep, dull, aching discomfort referred to a poorly localized area, with no neurologic signs. Insidious in onset and relieved by rest, spondylogenic referred pain from the lumbar spine, for example, can be incorrectly perceived by the brain to be originating within the buttock and sacroiliac region of the pelvis, or even as far down as the legs and calves. Spondylogenic pain is often caused by irritation within deep skeletal structures, such as protrusions placing mechanical pressure on the annulus, anterior dura mater, or posterior longitudinal ligament.

Radicular pain, which is common in the cervical and lumbar regions of the back, involves pressure on the spinal nerves or their roots, often near the intervertebral foramen, resulting in sharp pain localized to related areas. Radicular pain caused by protruding disks occurs most often before age fifty, whereas radicular pain from arthritis is more common in older individuals. Sources of pain outside the nerves include tethering of a nerve with scar tissue; pain can also be caused by scarring and inflammation within the nerve itself. Spinal pain is extremely complex and often requires extensive diagnostic testing.

MEDICAL MANAGEMENT

Research has consistently shown that a majority of patients with acute back pain experience spontaneous relief within approximately four weeks. Longer-lasting symptoms require complete medical examination for serious "red flag" conditions such as fractures, tumors, bacterial infections, upper motor neuron lesions, fibromyalgia, cauda equina syndrome, or visceral or systemic problems such as vascular claudication that can mimic back disorders. Pain that increases while lying down at night and is associated with recurrent fever; chills; bladder, bowel, and erectile dysfunction; or other neurologic symptoms (particularly if progressive) may indicate an underlying pathology.

Examination of disks by magnetic resonance imaging (MRI) and vertebrae by X rays is common. Myelograms, diskograms, computed tomography (CT or CAT) scans, bone scans, electromyograms, nerve and joint blockage, and blood and urine testing are also utilized. The spines of people over age sixty generally appear unhealthy on X rays, but many visible abnormalities do not cause chronic pain or disability.

Oral analgesic and muscle relaxant medications, injections, immobilization via bracing, and surgical techniques such as laminectomy, fusion, ablative neurosurgery, and Harrington rod insertion are also options. Surgery is generally reserved for cases in which a specific cause is clearly identified and nonoperative therapies have failed. Estrogen replacement therapy and supplemental calcium help maintain skeletal strength. Nonsteroidal anti-inflammatory drugs (NSAIDs) are often given to relieve discomfort. Long-term usage of some medications blocks protein synthesis during healing, however, which has led to experimentation with supplements such as shark cartilage.

PHYSICAL THERAPY

Back disorders, the most frequent source of musculoskeletal pain and disability in Americans, account for 25 percent of outpatient visits to physical therapists, who have become the primary care providers for musculoskeletal problems. Comfort and healing can be enhanced through thermal energy using hot packs or acoustic energy using ultrasound, but physical therapists primarily use mechanical energy to modify and improve postural alignment and retrain movement patterns. Posture issues often include reductions in forward head and shoulder posture and maintenance of proper cervical and lumbar posture during activities of daily living, recreation, work, and sleep. Immediate treatment, appropriate rest, and an injury-specific clinic and home rehabilitation regimen, which focuses on appropriate collagen realignment during progressive stages of healing, often restores back health effectively. Patient education regarding coughing, smoking, and alcohol use, along with the management of psychological stressors, can alleviate some symptoms.

Spinal muscles and joints, but not ligaments, generally respond well to medical exercise therapy, with mobility in specific spinal regions often improved by segmental strengthening and varying grades of joint movement. Neuromuscular reeducation assists in coordinating agonist muscles, which initiate and continue movement, and antagonist muscles, which control and modify movement. Transcutaneous electrical stimulation utilizes the "gate theory of pain," which argues that direct stimulation of mechanoreceptors blocks the transmission of nociceptive (pain) signals traveling up the spine in a similar manner to "scratching an itch." Pain is an important protective mecha-

nism that keeps damaged regions undisturbed so that healing can proceed. Therefore, treating the cause of pain, not just pain itself, is critical.

Electromyography enables biofeedback regarding the amount of muscular tension and also assesses inappropriate compensatory movement patterns. Movement, rather than rest, enhances healing once the patient is past the acute stage of injury. The benefits of regular aerobic exercise include weight loss, the internal analgesic effects of endorphin release, and enhanced local circulation bringing oxygen, nutrition, antibodies, and white blood cells to the injury site and removing inflammatory and metabolic end products.

Some back disorders are managed with orthotic devices to compensate for leg length discrepancies, sacral base and pelvic misalignments, and structural imbalances in the hip, knee, ankle, and foot during standing and walking. Modifying home and workplace ergonomics, particularly at computer workstations, is also effective. Imbalances between low back and anterior abdominal muscles and tightness in ligaments, muscles, and fascia commonly cause discomfort. A tight piriformis muscle or sacroiliac subluxation may lead to sciatic pain down the leg. Therapies such as oscillatory direct or indirect joint articulation techniques, muscle energy, proprioceptive neuromuscular facilitation, inversion and traction for spinal decompression, strain-counterstrain, acupressure, myofascial release massage, craniosacral rhythm therapy, cryokinetics, and specialized taping have proven effective. Also helpful are techniques taught at back schools such as work hardening and McKensie extension exercises. Sensation, motor coordination, deep tendon reflexes, range of motion, strength, joint play, and pain are continually monitored, with improvement in severe disorders often taking months. Lengthening tight and strengthening weak soft tissues, in combination with retraining the nervous system and managing pain, are the primary goals of manual physical therapy.

—Daniel G. Graetzer

See also Aging: Biological, psychological, and sociocultural perspectives; Aging process; Arthritis; Bone changes and disorders; Canes and walkers; Exercise and fitness; Fractures and broken bones; Health care; Injuries among the elderly; Kyphosis; Mobility problems; Osteoporosis; Vitamins and minerals.

FOR FURTHER INFORMATION:

Esses, Stephen Ivor. *Textbook of Spinal Disorders.* Philadelphia: J. B. Lippincott, 1995. This medical text on developmental and progressive spinal disorders highlights biomechanics, physiology, joint structure, and anatomy.

Frymoyer, John W. *The Adult Spine: Principles and Practice.* Philadelphia: Lippincott-Raven, 1997. This clinical text provides in-depth examinations of spinal physiopathology, wounds, diseases, and surgery.

Herkowitz, Harry N., Richard H. Rothman, and Frederick A. Simeone. *The Spine.* 4th ed. Philadelphia: W. B. Saunders, 1999. Offers an overview of the spine and related disorders.

Hertling, Darlene, and Randolph M. Kessler. *Management of Common Musculoskeletal Disorders: Physical Therapy Principles and Methods.* Philadelphia: J. B. Lippincott, 1996. An often-referenced physical therapist text on the evaluation and treatment of cervical, thoracic, and lumbar spine disorders.

Magee, David J. *Orthopedic Physical Assessment.* Philadelphia: W. B. Saunders, 1997. A clinical text on systematic approaches to the assessment and treatment of neuromuscular disorders.

BALANCE DISORDERS

RELEVANT ISSUES: Biology, health and medicine

SIGNIFICANCE: Balance disorders are among the most common health concerns in an aging population. Frequently, balance disorders result in falls and other accidents. Problems with balance may be described by sufferers as dizziness or vertigo and usually are associated with the inner ear

Being able to stand upright and walk with a steady gait is the result of a complex of body systems. For example, sight and hearing provide information about an individual's location and movement, and proprioceptors in muscles and joints help evaluate the individual's position in the environment. Age affects many of these systems, and age-related changes often impair the sense of balance.

Balance disorders include light-headedness, unsteadiness, or imbalance in walking. Such disorders also include vertigo, the feeling that a person's surroundings are moving or spinning around or that the person is spinning. Vertigo is sometimes accompanied by nausea. Because the ears often are involved, dizziness or vertigo may also be accompanied by tinnitus, a hissing, buzzing, or ringing sound in one or both ears.

Balance disorders often involve the labyrinth, a membrane-lined inner-ear chamber filled with fluid. The labyrinth consists of three canals, each at right angles to the other two. Any head movement—shaking, nodding, or tilting—is sensed by the canals, and the information is transmitted to the brain. Sometimes the labyrinth becomes inflamed, often from a viral infection, thus interfering with the signals relating to movement. Interference also occurs in motion sickness, in which the eyes see one kind of movement while the body, via the labyrinth, senses another kind of movement. The result is a confusion of signals and, often, the familiar sensations of dizziness, nausea, and vomiting.

Other causes of balance problems include neural dysfunctions and restrictions on the supply of blood to the brain. Light-headedness, for example, may be the result of changes in the flow of blood to the brain; if the flow is diminished, the result often is a "graying out," or darkening of vision. In extreme cases, the sufferer faints.

A balance disorder such as unsteadiness in walking may be the result of a dysfunction in the cerebellum, the back part of the brain. If the condition persists or worsens, it may be a symptom of a serious neurological disorder. Also, as part of the aging process, fine hairs in the inner ear may be reduced in number or size and thus function imperfectly. This frequently results in balance dysfunctions. Ear pain, nasal congestion, or discharge from the ears may result from middle-ear disorders and accompanying balance problems. Other causes include some medications, poor sleep habits, and vision problems.

Balance disorders may be symptomatic of serious physical problems and are best dealt with by a physician. If a balance problem is occasional and of short duration, relief may be gained simply by lying down for a brief while in a darkened room.

—*Albert C. Jensen*

See also Brain changes and disorders; Canes and walkers; Illnesses among the elderly; Injuries among the elderly; Vision changes and disorders; Wheelchair use.

BALDNESS. *See* **HAIR LOSS AND BALDNESS.**

BEAUTY

RELEVANT ISSUES: Culture, sociology

SIGNIFICANCE: While standards of appearance have varied by time and place, the United States and other Western societies generally value youthful looks, especially for women

Though both women and men age, and their appearance alters significantly as they grow old, people often do not perceive women's and men's aging in the same way. According to Susan Sontag in her classic 1972 article "The Double Standard of Aging," many consider the physical signs of women's aging to be less acceptable than the physical signs of men's aging. Sontag argues that there are two standards of beauty for men, those of the boy and mature man, but only one for women, that of the young girl. Yet not all societies and eras have emphasized the importance of women remaining young-looking. Cross-cultural research shows that some societies place a higher value on women's craft abilities and technical knowledge than on their appearance. In these societies, women's status improves with age, and middle-aged and old women do not strive to maintain the appearance of youth. In societies where women are more valued for their appearance than for other traits, women's status does not improve with age, or improves little.

In her 1994 article "Growing Old Gracefully: Age Concealment and Gender," Mary B. Harris reports on her research on the double standard of aging. It indicates that men and women of varying ages see women's physical aging as less attractive than men's. Women, however, consider the changes in men's body shape to be as unattractive as changes in women's body shape, though they are more accepting of men's facial wrinkles than men are of theirs. Women also give more positive evaluations to women's white and gray hair. They are nevertheless more likely than men to say that they do or would in the future hide signs that they are aging. In general, males have been found to have a stronger youth bias than females, with some evidence that this is especially true when the person being considered is female. Older subjects also see aging as somewhat more attractive than do younger ones. People who try to hide signs of ag-

ing by coloring their hair, getting a face lift, using wrinkle creams, or lying about their age are viewed more negatively than people who do none of these things. This is especially true if the person altering his or her appearance or lying about his or her age is male.

Thus, the tendency for people to evaluate negatively those who try to hide physical aging suggests that women and men face different dilemmas of aging and beauty. Altering one's appearance to look younger is viewed negatively, but women also are more severely evaluated on their aging appearance, especially by males. Signs of aging in men are also evaluated negatively, though less so, but their efforts to hide these markers of age meet with more criticism than do women's efforts.

CLOTHING

In some places and historical periods, men have been encouraged to display their good looks through clothing. From the eleventh to the nineteenth century in Europe, for example, male bodies were displayed through fashions that emphasized, to varying degrees, their feet, legs, and genitals. Though these fashions involved class competition, the intent of sexual allure was also present.

In the West, there is also a tradition of questioning the importance of beauty. In societies which value age more than youth, clothing may symbolize these relative values. Clothing during the United States colonial period of the 1600's and 1700's, for example, flattered age. Clothes were cut to make men's waists and hips seem broader and to make their spines appear bent. Women wore long dresses that were flattering to all ages. White, powdered wigs were fashionable for both genders.

Today in the United States and other Western countries, clothing symbolizes the value placed on young women's beauty. Much of younger women's clothing emphasizes their beauty by displaying or hugging the body. In general, older women's clothing does not expose as much flesh, which would also expose signs of aging. Some older women are dissatisfied with the clothes available to them; they prefer the revealing clothing that symbolizes female youth and sexual attractiveness. Men's clothing, however, except that worn by some subcultures of adolescent boys, remains constant through the life span, indicating greater status continuity.

WORK

The tendency for men to evaluate women's aging more harshly than other women can be examined in the light of the fact that men hold more positions of power. In general, corporations remain male-dominated, with men in most of the top positions. Those who do the hiring and promoting are more likely to be male than female. While the exact role of attractiveness in employment depends on the nature of the job, men's stronger youth bias with regard to females puts older women at a job disadvantage. Their youth bias also puts older men at a disadvantage, but to a lesser degree.

Physical attractiveness in women is especially valued when jobs are considered to require feminine characteristics. Women applying for, or already in, these jobs may consider physical attractiveness to be part of the job and may not consider appearance requirements to be a type of discrimination. Middle-aged and old women are found mostly in service or administrative support positions. Service jobs require cooking, cleaning, and/or caregiving. Administrative support jobs are nonmanagerial corporate positions, usually requiring some sort of secretarial work. Both of these types of positions are thought to require feminine characteristics, and appearance may be considered in hiring, retention, and promotion decisions. Professional women are also subject to the double standard of aging. Colleagues and superiors may consider the woman who does not cover up physical signs of aging to be "unprofessional." Women in all these types of positions face competition from younger, more recently trained women who also better fit societal standards of beauty. Realizing the bias toward youth and youthful attrac-

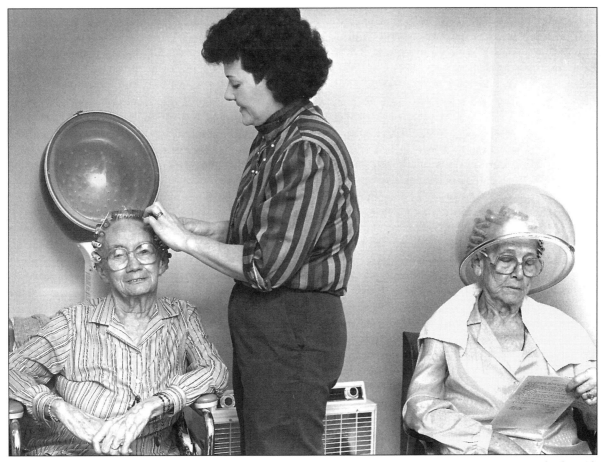

Despite the emphasis on youthful looks in American culture, most elderly women keep up a beauty routine and take pride in their appearance. (James L. Shaffer)

tiveness in the workplace, many women choose to dye their hair or otherwise alter physical characteristics that mark them as middle-aged or old.

THE MEDIA

Magazines present women and men with pictures of "ideal beautiful women," as do television advertisements, television shows, and films. The body types depicted have changed considerably over the years, indicating that the concept of beauty varies in different eras. The ideal body is thinner than in the past, and therefore less attainable by middle-aged and old women. Female models are almost invariably young. Older female models are found mostly in magazines specifically produced for the "mature." When older women, such as female celebrities, are pictured in women's magazines, they are made up, photographed, airbrushed, and transformed by computer imaging to appear younger than they are. In contrast, men of varying ages are depicted in magazines, often with no attempt to make them appear youthful. Though the majority of male models are young, more middle-aged male models are seen.

Female actors are usually young or young-appearing and are filmed in such a way that signs of their physical aging are minimized or erased. When older women appear in television and film roles, they are rarely presented as beautiful or sexual beings, though middle-aged and old men are presented as attractive and sexual and are often paired with younger women. Female television news anchors may be young or middle-aged, but the latter present a youthful appearance. Few theatrical roles go to women over forty, and the middle-aged and old women who receive them generally appear younger than their true ages. A greater diversity of age is seen in males on television and in film and theater roles.

Also of import are the antiaging products advertised in the media. Almost everyone in the United States is exposed to many such advertisements each day. The majority of antiaging products are for women, though there are more antiaging products for men than in the past. Men as well as women color their hair, use skin exfoliators, and seek cosmetic surgery. The advertisements aimed at men are different, however, from those aimed at women. They associate the products with sports and business and often suggest that the product will help an older man maintain his "edge" at work when competing with younger men. Advertisements aimed at women generally do not use these associations but rather use women's fear of aging.

According to Susan Hillier and Georgia M. Barrow in their book *Aging, the Individual, and Society* (7th ed., 1999), the Food and Drug Administration (FDA) believes that the claims for some of these products are false. They either do not work or are limited in their effectiveness. For example, the FDA has approved Retin A (tretinoin) to treat wrinkles, but Retin A does not have permanent results. No skin care product exists that can alter skin structure. Rogaine (minoxidil), also FDA-approved, is used by men for baldness, but it does not always work and generally does not result in a full head of hair. Hair dyes are temporary, and even face lifts must be repeated every three to five years for a youthful face to be maintained. A majority of these products are aimed at the female market, and aging women spend much more money than men of the same age on products that promise a more youthful appearance.

CLASS, RACE, AND SEXUAL ORIENTATION

Given class differences in diet, access to exercise programs, and the ability to afford the more expensive beauty aids, poor people tend to show the signs of aging more quickly than affluent ones. The importance of beauty to women of all classes, however, is shown in the availability of beauty shops in most communities. They are used by women from all socioeconomic strata except the most destitute. Wealthier women have available a broader array of means to maintain a young appearance than do less affluent women, including repeated cosmetic surgery on the face and body.

Not all these efforts are healthful, however, and some can be dangerous. Surgery always carries some risk, both from the procedure itself and from anesthesia. Occasional deaths from cosmetic surgery have been reported. Liposuction removes fat cells, a source of estrogen production. Estrogen declines after the menopause, and modest weight gain by some women of that age may be healthy. The women undergoing these procedures may, however, receive a psychological boost or may benefit in the workplace or in relationships.

Just as it is easier for the affluent older woman to mold herself to the youthful cultural ideal, so too it is easier for the affluent man to be perceived as desirable. Men are increasingly using methods such as cosmetic surgery to transform an aging appearance. Older men may be described as "distinguished," however, on the basis of an unaltered aging appearance. This term has a class basis. Only men of at least adequate financial means are labeled "distinguished"; poor men are not.

Though research is lacking, it is possible that many men view changes in their appearance as they age with regret. For men who wish to hide some of the more obvious signs of aging, simple means of appearance alteration such as hair dye are available. As already noted, however, men who use these products meet with more social disapproval than women who use them.

Little research exists as well on racial differences in aging and beauty. The most examined are differences between African American and white women. The skin of African American women has a greater amount of melanin, which limits damage from the sun. Their skin remains youthful longer than does the skin of white women. African American girls generally report that women get more beautiful with age, and they may cite their mothers as examples. Most white girls think that their mothers may have been beautiful once but no longer are. The hair of white women also turns gray about ten years earlier, on average, than that of African American women. Though African American women show signs of aging more slowly, Midge Wilson and Kathy Russell argue in their book *Divided Sisters* (1996) that African American women and white women share a common challenge in the double standard of aging.

Care must also be taken in discussing older gays and lesbians, since research for this population is largely anecdotal and little is known about these two groups from a social science perspective. The limited evidence available suggests that lesbians do not escape Western culture's emphasis on youthfulness, with many older lesbians reporting that they are invisible or unattractive to younger lesbians. Some middle-aged and old lesbians, however, believe that youthful age bias is less pronounced in the lesbian community than among heterosexuals. Both views make sense in the light of research showing that women have a bias toward youthful appearance but that women's "youth preference" is less pronounced than that of men. Standards of beauty are more diverse in the lesbian community, since lesbians value both feminine and masculine appearance in women.

Many gay men value a strongly masculine appearance and may be more concerned about aging than are heterosexual men. *Beauty Before Age*, for example, is a film that explores the fears of many homosexual men about looking older. Some research suggests that older gay men prefer men somewhat younger, but not necessarily young, as partners.

CONCLUSION

Though beauty standards for women in Western societies are more exacting than those for men and demand a more youthful appearance, this does not mean that all women accept or try to follow these standards. Some women, for varying reasons, do nothing to try to maintain youthful looks. Others use only the means that are the easiest and/or the least expensive. Still others use multiple methods, including surgery, to look as young as possible. The extent to which women accept or resist societal pressures toward maintaining a youthful appearance needs to be explored further by scholars.

It is clear, however, that utilization of the simpler and more affordable means of appearance alteration, such as hair dye, are common among women and are becoming more frequently adopted by men. Procedures such as cosmetic surgery are also being pursued by more people, with the numbers of women using them still far surpassing the number of men who do so. Male usage, however, is no longer uncommon. It remains to be seen whether the numbers of middle-aged and old people who pursue youthful appearance will continue to increase; the Western tradition of questioning the importance of beauty might reassert itself in new forms as the population ages.

—*Roxanne Friedenfels*

See also Advertising; African Americans; Age spots; Ageism; Antiaging treatments; Cosmetic surgery; Cultural views of aging; Exercise and fitness; Face lifts; Fat deposition; Films; Gay men and lesbians; Gray hair; *In Full Flower: Aging Women, Power, and Sexuality*; Men and aging; Midlife crisis; Premature aging; Poverty; Sexuality; Television; Women and aging; Wrinkles.

FOR FURTHER INFORMATION:

Banner, Lois. *In Full Flower: Aging Women, Power, and Sexuality.* New York: Alfred A. Knopf, 1992. Mostly a discussion of older women's sexuality, but with some material on beauty interspersed in various places in the text.

Friday, Nancy. *The Power of Beauty.* New York: HarperCollins, 1996. Argues that the pursuit of beauty benefits women and contains a chapter on the double standard of aging.

Gerike, Ann E. "On Gray Hair and Oppressed Brains." In *Aging for the Twenty-First Century: Readings in Social Gerontology,* edited by Jill Quadagno and Debra Street. New York: St. Martin's Press, 1996. Possibly the only article on women and gray hair from a feminist perspective.

Harris, Mary B. "Growing Old Gracefully: Age Concealment and Gender." *Journal of Gerontology* 49, no. 4 (July, 1994). A study testing the concept of the double standard of aging on 269 adults, both male and female, aged eighteen to eighty, with some mix of race among the respondents.

Hillier, Susan, and Georgia M. Barrow. *Aging, the Individual, and Society.* 7th ed. Belmont, Calif.: Wadsworth, 1999. A readable general text on aging, with material on appearance found in several sections of the book.

Rodeheaver, Dean. "Labor Market Progeria: On the Life Expectancy of Presentability Among Working Women." In *Gender and Aging,* edited by Lou Glasse and Jon Hendricks. Amityville, N.Y.: Baywood, 1992. Examines the influence of aging women's appearance on their employment opportunities.

Sontag, Susan. "The Double Standard of Aging." In *The Other Within Us,* edited by Marilyn Pearsall. Boulder, Colo.: Westview Press, 1997. The classic article that originated the influential concept of the double standard of aging. Originally published in *Saturday Review* 55 (September 23, 1972).

Stanford, Barbara. "Winter Beauty." In *Gift of a Lifetime: A Woman's Guide to Triumphant Aging.* Cambria, Calif.: Lodge Hill Press, 1997. Argues that a woman who accepts her age is beautiful.

Wilson, Midge, and Kathy Russell. "Surface Divisions: Issues of Beauty and Style." In *Divided Sisters: Bridging the Gap Between Black Women and White Women.* New York: Anchor Books, 1996. Discusses the attitudes of black and white women about appearance, with a short discussion about aging. Mostly on beauty and young women.

Wolf, Naomi. *The Beauty Myth: How Images of Beauty Are Used Against Women.* New York: William Morrow, 1991. Focuses on the damage that "the beauty myth" does to women; contains some material relevant to aging.

BEQUESTS. *See* **WILLS AND BEQUESTS.**

BIOLOGICAL CLOCK

RELEVANT ISSUES: Biology, culture, family, psychology, values

SIGNIFICANCE: The psychological need of some women to have children increases with age and can affect decisions concerning careers, the timing of childbearing, and their identity as women, as well as society's perceptions of them

The concept of the biological clock is a phenomenon created both by hormonal changes and by psychological and societal perceptions that increase the need for some women to conceive and bear children. As the complex series of hormonal changes necessary to bring about menstruation (and hence the ability to have children) is interrupted and becomes irregular, the time between menstrual periods increases and the amount of blood loss gradually diminishes until menstruation ceases altogether (the menopause). If a woman wants to experience childbirth, the inevitability of this process, which is brought on by a decline in estrogen production by the ovaries generally between the ages of forty-five and fifty-five, further exacerbates her urgency to bear children.

Many women decide to delay having children in order to pursue a career. Some of them, after reaching a level of success and stability in their careers, feel the need to embrace more traditional female roles, such as motherhood. Women may also delay having a family because of a lack of financial resources, job stability, personal commitment, or a suitable partner. In addition to wanting to have children, women often face societal pressures to do so. When a woman does not conform to societal expectations, many people conclude that something must be wrong with her. This situation is further compounded by the fact that at midlife, major preoccupations concern the potential loss of certain identity-conferring roles or ways of being—in this case, motherhood and the roles associated with it. —*Kristine Kleptach Jamieson*

See also Change: Women, Aging, and the Menopause, The; Childlessness; Infertility; Menopause; Middle age; Midlife crisis; Parenthood; Reproductive changes, disabilities, and dysfunctions; Women and aging.

BLACKS. *See* AFRICAN AMERICANS.

BLESS ME, ULTIMA
AUTHOR: Rudolfo A. Anaya
DATE: Published in 1972
RELEVANT ISSUES: Race and ethnicity, psychology, values
SIGNIFICANCE: In this novel, a young boy develops a bond with an old *curandera* (healer).

In the novel *Bless Me, Ultima*, readers are invited to view life in a small, unpretentious town in rural New Mexico, but the real excitement of the story is described through the eyes of the young Antonio. In his relationship with a old woman, a *curandera* named Ultima or La Grande who knows no sin, he wrestles with his identity, his parents' desires for him, and his own growth.

While his association with La Grande provides little direct guidance, she becomes his strength. In her clear, wise eyes, Antonio learns about the duality of being a good Christian and the need to believe in something tangible in the here and now. All his questions about good and bad, the Church versus belief in witches, and whether he will be a priest (as his mother wishes) or a vaquero (as his father wishes) are left unanswered except for the teachings of La Grande. Life in a rural town is difficult for the young boy who knows no English when he goes to school and learns to eat his lunch of beans and tortillas away from the laughs that ridicule him. His relationship with La Grande, however, is very powerful. From her he learns to live in an English-speaking world that for a Spanish-speaking person presents another constant duality.

From La Grande, Antonio learns about the history of his family and the land. He learns about the god that lives in the water whom he can count on for protection. He learns that La Grande's owl

knows what goes on; it warns them of approaching harm. In all these experiences, he begins to grow in ways that neither of his parents considered. His bond with this old woman ultimately gives him the strength to believe in himself.

A *curandera* is a healer who learns from another healer. It is thought that to be a *curandera*, one must be born with special gifts. La Grande is such a person. Much of her work with Antonio is teaching him about the herbs that she uses. He learns to be considerate of the earth and of nature. In this relationship, she is his guide both mentally and spiritually. They depend on each other, as when she heals Antonio's uncle who has been "witched." Antonio accompanies her because, with her, he is fearless. This is the gift that she leaves him.

Through Anaya's novel, the reader is transported to a world of the rural Spanish-speaking indigenous people in the United States. The role of elders in this culture is better understood through the eyes of a child. —*Sara Alemán*

See also Cultural views of aging; Latinos; Literature; Mentoring; Multigenerational households; Wisdom.

BLINDNESS. *See* VISION CHANGES AND DISORDERS.

BONE CHANGES AND DISORDERS
RELEVANT ISSUES: Biology, health and medicine
SIGNIFICANCE: Beginning around thirty-five, a progressive decline in bone strength, coupled with the disintegration of bone trabeculae in elderly women, results in increasing fracture risks and deformities with increasing age

Like most physiological processes, bone development follows a building pattern up through puberty and the early reproductive years and then begins a gradual deterioration with increasing age, a breakdown that accelerates past age sixty. The approximately 206 bones in the skeletal system provide several critical functions for the body, including body support, protection of internal organs (such as the skull protecting the brain, the rib cage protecting the heart and lungs), bodily movements, fat storage in yellow bone marrow, and production of all blood cell types from red bone marrow. Bone also stores several key minerals in the tough spaces between bone cells.

BONE STRUCTURE AND DEVELOPMENT

Osteology is the study of bone structure and function. In a newborn child, nearly 90 percent of the skeleton is cartilage. Before and continuing after birth, much of the cartilaginous skeletal elements begin ossification, the deposition of bone cells. In long bones such as the humerus, radius, and ulna of the arm and the femur, tibia, and fibula of the leg, this endochondral ossification starts with primary ossification centers in the middle shaft called the diaphysis, followed by secondary ossification centers at the ends called the epiphyses. These ossification centers involve the activity of osteoblasts, or bone-building cells, which deposit collagen protein plus minerals such as calcium and phosphate into the intercellular space, or matrix, surrounding the osteocytes, the principal bone cells. Furthermore, embryonic mesenchymal cells differentiate into osteocytes.

By birth, the primary and secondary ossification centers are well formed and growing toward each other, a process that replaces the cartilage that initially formed the morphological pattern for the bone. At birth, a flexible cartilage-dominated skeleton enables many bones such as those of the skull to compress through the birth canal without damaging the baby's internal organs.

Throughout infancy, bone ossification accelerates with a high-calcium diet, principally from breast milk. The primary and secondary ossification centers grow together, separated by thin epiphyseal disk regions of fibrocartilage. These thin cartilaginous regions allow for the longitudinal growth of bones under the influence of growth hormone as the skeleton grows larger throughout adolescence. Additionally, many bones such as those forming the skull cranium grow together and are separated by very fine strips of fibrocartilage to create bone sutures allowing for increased longitudinal bone growth as the child's body matures. Cartilage is maintained at the ends of bones articulating with other bones at joints, although this articular cartilage decays with increasing age.

The two major types of bone are cortical bone and cancellous bone. Cortical bone, which constitutes about 80 percent of body bone mass, is compact and dense. It is located primarily in the diaphyses of long bones and in vertebral ends. Cancellous or spongy bone makes up the remainder of the skeletal mass and is located primarily at the epiphyses of long bones and in the vertebrae. Cancellous bone, which has higher metabolic activity, consists of a loose web of trabeculae that makes the bone resistant to mechanical stress.

A diet high in calcium from such food sources as dairy products, green vegetables, and legumes (peanuts, for example) promotes bone growth in healthy individuals. Bone mass generally increases up to age thirty-five and often increases even into the middle forties. The bone osteocytes arrange themselves into concentric circular/cylindrical units of several thousand cells each called a Haversian system. Tens of thousands of Haversian systems run longitudinally through a bone. Each Haversian system contains a central Haversian canal through which nerve and capillary blood supplies extend. Materials diffuse to and from the surrounding osteocytes via minute channels called canaliculi. The osteocytes and bone-building osteoblasts establish the toughness of bone in each Haversian system by secreting the protein collagen and minerals such as calcium, phosphate, and strontium into the intercellular matrix between the osteocytes of the Haversian system.

BODY CHEMICAL HOMEOSTASIS AND BONE REMODELING

Throughout life, bone structure is recycled and remodeled at the level of the Haversian system. This remodeling is performed because of the body's need to maintain steady levels, or homeostasis, for various blood substances such as calcium. When blood calcium levels rise, the thyroid gland releases the protein hormone calcitonin, which stimulates bone osteoblast cells to build bone by depositing collagen and calcium phosphate into the intercellular matrix between the osteocytes of the bone Haversian systems. The calcium phosphate crystallizes in the matrix to form the tough hydroxyapatite that dominates mature bone.

When blood calcium levels are low, the parathyroid gland releases parathyroid hormone, a protein hormone that activates bone osteoclast cells to break down bone by dismantling the hydroxyapatite matrix between the osteocytes. This back-and-forth process of bone building and bone breakdown occurs daily throughout all the bones for an individual's entire life span and depends on the amount of calcium in the bloodstream from moment to moment. Dynamic bone remodeling is essential to the body's calcium homeostasis and to its proper distribution to the roughly one thousand trillion cells making up a person's body.

Thus, blood calcium homeostasis and the accompanying bone composition depend on the body's intake of calcium. A diet high in calcium should promote bone building because resulting high blood calcium levels will activate increased thyroid production of calcitonin, thereby stimulating the osteoblast cells to build bone. In contrast, a diet low in calcium should elicit the opposite response, with the parathyroid gland releasing parathyroid hormone to stimulate the bone-destroying osteoclasts.

Beginning in the middle thirties to middle forties, or at the menopause in women, bone density begins to decrease with age as a result of changes in calcium metabolism. The loss of bone density accelerates faster in women than in men and specifically involves the collagenous-hydroxyapatite intercellular matrix. Factors that can contribute to this calcium loss include higher parathyroid hormone levels and/or lower calcitonin levels because of physiological changes in the parathyroid and thyroid glands, respectively. Additionally, decreased body calcium intake and decreased intestinal absorption of calcium can contribute to the serious loss of bone density in older people.

The maintenance of bone density also depends on the hormone cholecalciferol, or vitamin D, and the steroid hormone estrogen, the latter hormone being especially important in women. Vitamin D is critical because it is needed by cells of the duodenum, the absorptive region of the small intestine, to transport calcium into the bloodstream. If intestinal cells are deficient in vitamin D, very little calcium will be absorbed by the body, and bone building plus bone replacement will stop. Vitamin D can be obtained from dairy products, eggs, codliver oil, and reasonable exposure of the skin to sunlight.

Additional important vitamins for bone building include vitamin A, called retinol, and vitamin C, called ascorbic acid. Vitamin A stimulates the osteoblasts to build bone. Vitamin C increases the release of collagen into the intercellular matrix, thereby increasing the density and hardness of bone. Vitamin A can be obtained by eating beta carotene, a photosynthetic pigment found in red, yellow, and green vegetables. Vitamin C can be obtained by eating citrus fruits.

Estrogen, produced by the ovaries, maintains bone structure and density in women by inhibiting the osteoclastic breakdown of the bone matrix. In contrast, the glucocorticoid steroid hormones produced by the adrenal cortex activate bone breakdown by blocking the intestinal absorption of calcium into the blood; the resulting decreased blood calcium levels trigger parathyroid activation of osteoclasts to break down bone. The protein hormones growth hormone and insulin, produced by the pituitary gland and the pancreatic islets of Langerhans, respectively, both promote bone growth by activating the insulin-like growth factor I in target bone tissue. Therefore, a variety of hormones and vitamins are critical for balancing body calcium levels and thereby affecting bone remodeling.

The science of bone histomorphometry has enabled precise measurements of bone changes with age, even at the microscopic level. With age, there is no substantial loss of cortical bone in the long bone diaphyses of the arms and legs for women and men. Much of the bone loss with age seems to be in the cancellous bone, which has a loose, spongy trabecular arrangement and which is located primarily in the ends of long bones, the vertebrae, and the pelvic bones. These three bone regions represent the major sites of physical disability in the aging skeletal system, especially for women.

BONE DISORDERS

Osteopathy is the study of bone disease. Several bone disorders and diseases are intricately associated with aging or with disruptions of calcium metabolism that are indirectly linked with aging. Overwhelmingly, the major bone disorder plaguing the elderly is osteoporosis. Osteoporosis involves the breakdown of mostly cancellous trabecular bone at the ends of long bones, in the pelvic girdle, and in the vertebrae. This disease can involve the cortical bone in the diaphyses of the arms and legs, but it usually occurs in cancellous bone. Women are five times as likely to suffer from osteoporosis than are men.

Contributing factors to osteoporosis include overall body and bone calcium deficiencies, excess phosphate, vitamin D deficiency, decreased estrogen production after the menopause in women, metabolic disorders affecting bone or the hormones that control bone remodeling, or a combination of these factors. The effects on bone include a higher turnover rate (particularly for cancellous bone), increased osteoclast and decreased osteoblast activities, and the resulting loss of trabecular bone from such critical body support bones as the vertebrae, the pelvic girdle or hips, and the long bones of the arms and legs.

Victims of osteoporosis develop progressively more brittle bones, weakness, and fractures. In many individuals, the decay of vertebral bones can lead rapidly to a hunchback appearance, or kyphosis, as the bones lose the strength to support the upper body. Fractures of the hip and forearm bones are common. One-half of women age sixty-five and older have some degree of osteoporosis. One-third of women age sixty-five to seventy-four have significant loss of upper body strength as a result of osteoporosis. Fractures and physical deformities incapacitate many victims, who subsequently require daily care.

Osteoporosis can be detected early via X rays or photon absorptiometry and by quantitative computed tomography. Often, the disease is identified too late following serious bone deformities or fractures. Treatment for osteoporosis includes increased calcium intake and vitamin A, C, and D dietary supplements, bearing in mind that aging decreases the intestinal absorption of calcium. Daily exercise is very important for slowing the progression of osteoporosis. Medications such as alendronate sodium mimic natural phosphate and bind to bone matrix hydroxyapatite, thereby strengthening bone and slowing the progression of osteoporosis.

The best approach to stopping osteoporosis is prevention. Because women have less bone mass and a looser cancellous trabecular bone structure than men, and because women generally do not consume enough of their recommended daily calcium requirements, doctors recommend calcium dietary supplements as early as age twenty-five. Daily exercise throughout life is important. Also, estrogen replacement therapy, even with the slight increase in associated cancer risks, is recommended for women after the menopause and after hysterectomies in order to counteract bone loss.

Closely related to osteoporosis is osteoarthritis, the degeneration of fibrocartilage at bone joints, particularly the knee and intervertebral joints, accompanied by outgrowths of bone. Osteoarthritis leads to painful movement and physical deformity. Bracing or surgery can be effective for treating knee osteoarthritis. Little can be done, however, for vertebral osteoarthritis. Like other arthritic joint diseases, osteoarthritis involves the progressive loss of cartilage with increasing age.

Osteomalacia can cause serious spinal and long bone deformities in the elderly. It is usually caused by the failure of the intestines to absorb adequate amounts of calcium to maintain blood calcium homeostasis. This disorder is treated with increased dietary supplements of vitamin D and calcium. Similarly, osteopenia can weaken the cancellous bone matrix at the ends of long bones and vertebrae. It is usually caused by elevated levels of corticosteroids in the bloodstream.

Paget's disease, also known as osteitis deformans, involves bone deformities in the vertebrae, skull, pelvic girdle, and long leg bones as a result of the destruction of bone followed by irregular bone replacement. It happens more often to very elderly individuals, is more prevalent in men, and is poorly understood.

Glandular disturbances that weaken bone include hyperthyroidism and hyperparathyroidism. Both conditions, involving enlargement and increased activity of the respective glands, stimulate increased bone breakdown and the corresponding loss of bone density. Hyperparathyroidism can contribute to osteopenia as well. In contrast, hypothyroidism (underactive thyroid) reduces bone turnover and causes a small increase in both cancellous and cortical bone masses.

A healthy skeleton can add many active, productive years to a person's life. Bone is dynamic, living tissue. Therefore, proper bone maintenance with aging includes daily exercise; a diet rich in dairy products, fruits, and green vegetables; vitamin and calcium dietary supplements as needed; and postmenopausal estrogen treatment for women.

—David W. Hollar, Jr.

See also Aging process; Arthritis; Back disorders; Bunions; Canes and walkers; Disabilities; Exercise and fitness; Fallen arches; Foot disorders; Fractures and broken bones; Hammertoes; Hip replacement; Injuries among the elderly; Kyphosis;

Malnutrition; Nutrition; Osteoporosis; Safety issues; Vitamins and minerals; Wheelchair use; Women and aging.

FOR FURTHER INFORMATION:
Audesirk, Teresa, and Gerald Audesirk. *Biology: Life on Earth.* 5th ed. Upper Saddle River, N.J.: Prentice Hall, 1999. This general biology textbook contains several chapters devoted to human and vertebrate animal skeletal systems, development, and nutrition, plus health essays devoted to topics such as osteoporosis.

Eriksen, Erik F., Douglas W. Axelrod, and Flemming Melsen. *Bone Histomorphometry.* New York: Raven Press, 1994. This short book is a concise presentation of bone anatomy, bone remodeling, bone measurement, and metabolic disorders of bone. Considerable information is presented in color photographs, data tables, and illustrative figures.

Gaudin, Anthony J., and Kenneth C. Jones. *Human Anatomy and Physiology.* San Diego: Harcourt Brace Jovanovich, 1989. This textbook for premedical students provides clear chapters on the development and anatomy of the human skeletal system with illustrations and health essays.

Guralnik, Jack M., Linda P. Fried, Eleanor M. Simonsick, Judith D. Kasper, and Mary E. Lafferty, eds. *The Women's Health and Aging Study: Health and Social Characteristics of Older Women with Disability.* Bethesda, Md.: National Institute on Aging, 1995. This comprehensive survey of aging in women compiles data collected from physician assessments of over two thousand elderly women, disease conditions, strength tests, laboratory tests, and follow-up surveys of patients. Data are reported in useful tables accompanying clear chapter summaries.

Sandford, Mary K., ed. *Investigations of Ancient Human Tissue: Chemical Analyses in Anthropology.* Langhorne, Pa.: Gordon and Breach Science Publishers, 1993. A collection of nine research papers, this work emphasizes the difficulties involved in assessing ancient peoples based on chemical analysis of bone. Offers clear, detailed summaries of bone composition and the metabolic control of bone remodeling.

Saunders, Shelley R., and M. Anne Katzenberg, eds. *Skeletal Biology of Past Peoples: Research Methods.* New York: Wiley-Liss, 1992. This work is a collection of twelve technical papers dealing with chemical and physical measurements of preserved bone tissue, including determinations of age at death, evidence of disease present in bones, bone changes with aging, and paleolithic diet.

Wallace, Robert A., Gerald P. Saunders, and Robert J. Ferl. *Biology: The Science of Life,* 4th ed. New York: HarperCollins College Publishers, 1996. This general biology textbook includes chapters summarizing the vertebrate skeletal system, animal development, and digestion.

BOOSTERS. *See* **IMMUNIZATIONS AND BOOSTERS.**

BRAIN CHANGES AND DISORDERS

RELEVANT ISSUES: Biology, health and medicine, psychology

SIGNIFICANCE: During normal aging, the brain undergoes a number of changes; distinguishing these changes from those that are pathological is important to the understanding of normal aging and to the treatment of neurological disorders

Like all tissue, the brain experiences a number of changes during the normal aging process. These changes are expressed anatomically, physiologically, functionally, and chemically. An important goal in the study of brain changes with age is the careful distinction between changes that occur during the normal aging process and those that are the result of disease states (such as Parkinson's, Huntington's, and Alzheimer's diseases).

CHANGES IN THE HEALTHY BRAIN WITH AGE

Studies have shown that the human brain is "plastic," or malleable, throughout the life span. As a result, the kind of life that a person leads—the level of activity, type of diet, exposure to environmental toxins, education level, environmental stimulation, and mental exercise—can produce either positive or negative changes in brain structure and function. This finding makes a description of normal aging changes in the nervous system problematic.

Typically, there is a decrease in brain size with age. In addition, there is a widening of the sulci (grooves on the surface of the brain) and an enlargement of the ventricles, the fluid-filled cavities in the brain. The extent to which these changes reflect a loss of brain cells (neurons), however, is questionable.

In some brain structures and systems, cell loss with age is fairly well established. Such is the case with the hypothalamus, the cortex, and the limbic system, a group of structures (hippocampus, amygdala, parts of the thalamus) involved in a variety of functions such as learning, memory, and emotion. In other structures, cell loss is minimal. Even within a given structure, such as the hippocampus, the extent of loss still varies as a function of the specific brain site. In addition, cell loss is a phenomenon that is a part of normal brain development across the life span. Indeed, the greatest amount of cell loss in the nervous system occurs during prenatal development. As a result, the importance of cell loss in the healthy brain with age is unclear.

The function of the brain can change as a result of modifications in its connectivity, the pattern of connections between brain cells that enables communication within the nervous system. Synapses are functional connections between neurons. It has been estimated that the number of synapses decreases with age, with some areas of the brain showing decreases of up to 25 percent. Once again, however, these decreases vary from one brain region to the next, with decreases in synaptic connections being minimal in many brain structures. In fact, some research has shown that the number of synaptic connections can increase during old age. In other words, the brain of an older person is modifiable, in a positive direction, like that of a younger individual. The direction of the modification, increases or decreases in the number of synaptic connections, is influenced to a great extent by physical activity, lung function, and environmental stimulation (that is, education and mental exercise). Other factors found to influence the extent to which positive brain changes can occur with age are lack of chronic disease, high standard of living, willingness to change, and satisfaction with life accomplishments.

While there is some decrease in brain size and possibly cell loss with age, there are few changes in brain metabolism. The brain uses approximately 20 percent of the body's oxygen (even though it represents only around 2 percent of total body weight) and derives most of its energy metabolism from glucose. Oxygen consumption in a normal brain remains relatively unchanged from early adulthood through old age. There is, however, some decrease in glucose metabolism with age, and this decline is thought to be a mechanism involved in age-related effects on memory.

Neurotransmitters, chemical messengers that are involved in communication between brain cells, can also show changes with age. These changes, typically decreases in the amount of transmitter substance or in the number of receptors (sites on cell membranes with which transmitters associate), vary from one brain site to another and also depend on the type of neurotransmitter involved. Two neurotransmitters studied extensively are acetylcholine and dopamine, both of which show declines in the hippocampus, cerebral cortex, and basal ganglia (a group of structures called the caudate nucleus, the globus pallidus, and the putamen). Reductions in transmitter activity also occur in parts of the brain stem (for norepinephrine and serotonin) and the thalamus (for gamma aminobutyric acid, or GABA).

Brain Changes Associated with Disease

While the normal age-related changes that occur in the brain are undetermined, definite changes are seen in disease states that are more likely to occur as a person ages. Various neurodegenerative disorders can develop, including Parkinson's, Huntington's, and Alzheimer's diseases. While these disorders are not limited to the elderly, the incidence of them clearly increases with age.

There is some overlap of affected brain structures in these disorders, which suggests the possibility that common mechanisms induce the symptoms. For example, both Parkinson's and Huntington's diseases are accompanied by damage to the basal ganglia, a brain region involved in movement. One possible mechanism by which these neural structures might be damaged is through activation of excitatory amino acid receptors. (Excitatory amino acids are a type of neurotransmitter.) This activation is hypothesized to result in increased calcium influx into the neurons, which results in a number of cellular changes leading to cell death. Oxidative stress, the deleterious effects of oxygen by-products such as free radicals, is another putative mechanism producing the neural damage associated with these neurodegenerative disorders.

PARKINSON'S DISEASE

In the late 1990's, this disease affected 1.5 million people worldwide, typically around middle age. It is named after James Parkinson, who first described the disorder in 1817. The symptoms of Parkinson's disease include tremor (especially at rest), muscular rigidity, slowness in initiating movements, instability, and postural abnormalities.

The primary brain dysfunction associated with the disorder is a decrease in the neurotransmitter dopamine, particularly in the basal ganglia. The cause of this deficiency in dopamine activity is the death of cells in the brain pathway connecting the substantia nigra (a midbrain structure) and the caudate nucleus and putamen in the basal ganglia. Dopamine levels can be reduced to 10 percent of normal values in this pathway. Other brain areas can also exhibit reductions in dopamine activity to varying degrees. The hippocampus, hypothalamus, and nucleus accumbens are only three structures where dopamine activity has been found to be deficient in Parkinson's disease. These findings suggest that while the primary deficiency is in the substantia nigra-basal ganglia pathway, a general involvement of the dopaminergic system is a part of the disorder. In addition, more subtle deficiencies occur in the neurotransmitters norepinephrine and serotonin.

Lewy bodies, inclusions in the cells of neurons, are found in various brain areas such as the substantia nigra, cortex, and basal forebrain. While sometimes seen in normal brains of older people, Lewy bodies are present in approximately 90 percent of subjects diagnosed with Parkinson's disease.

A typical treatment for Parkinson's disease is the administration of L-dopa, a dopamine precursor which is changed into and replenishes dopamine in the brain. Other treatments include surgeries, for example pallidotomy and thalamotomy (selective destruction of cells in the basal ganglia and thalamus, respectively), high-frequency stimulation of brain areas in and around the thalamus, and brain transplants of fetal tissue.

While the exact cause of the neuropathological changes that produce Parkinson's disease remains elusive, one theory postulates a breakdown in intracellular calcium maintenance as a probable mechanism. According to this theory, prevention of these deleterious brain changes could be accomplished through the use of calcium-channel blockers, which would reduce the influx of calcium through the cell membrane and help to maintain intraneuronal calcium homeostasis. Alternatively, blockade of the receptor site for the excitatory amino acid neurotransmitter glutamate has also been shown, in animal models, to reduce the cell death that results from excessive calcium entry into neurons.

HUNTINGTON'S DISEASE

Another neurodegenerative brain disorder whose incidence increases with age is Huntington's disease; in the late 1990's, it affected approximately 25,000 people in the United States alone and threatened another 150,000. First described by George Huntington in 1872, this disorder is characterized by involuntary, jerky movements; abnormal voluntary movements which can affect control of vocalization, chewing, and swallowing; declines in the cognitive abilities of attention and memory; and emotional dysfunction such as depression, apathy, and irritability. The disease is progressive, fatal, and incurable. There is loss of neurons in the basal ganglia, cortex, and hippocampus, as wells as deficiencies in the neurotransmitters GABA, dopamine, and acetylcholine.

The cause of Huntington's disease is a mutation on chromosome 4, specifically an abnormal repeating sequence of three nucleotides near the beginning of a gene on that chromosome. In people without the disorder, this sequence repeats approximately thirty-four times; in those individuals with Huntington's disease, the sequence repeats between forty-two and one hundred times. The gene product of this abnormality is called huntingtin and is thought to be related, in some manner, to the death of cells in the brain structures mentioned.

As is the case with Parkinson's disease, a putative mechanism for the cell death seen in Huntington's disease is thought to be overactivity of the glutamate neurotransmitter system. Another proposed mechanism is a breakdown in the function of mitochondria, structures responsible for energy production within cells.

ALZHEIMER'S DISEASE

Affecting approximately 20 million people worldwide in the late 1990's, Alzheimer's disease is a progressive, fatal disease that typically develops during the seventh or eighth decade of a person's life. The modern description of this disease comes from a case study published by Alois Alzheimer in 1906. Early signs include memory decline, but eventually a variety of cognitive, personality, and motor abilities are lost. Clear neuropathological signs of Alzheimer's disease include senile plaques, neurofibrillary tangles, and neuron loss.

Senile plaques are areas of cell loss and scar tissue that have a central core of amyloid protein. Amyloid protein is a product of amyloid precursor protein (APP) whose gene is located on chromosome 21. A mutation of the gene coding for this protein results in the excessive production and accumulation of amyloid protein. These plaques are a marker for Alzheimer's disease in the human nervous system and are found principally in the limbic and association cortices. Neurofibrillary tangles, another hallmark of Alzheimer's disease, consist of twisted protein filaments within a brain cell. These tangles are prevalent in various brain regions, including the hippocampus, basal forebrain, locus ceruleus, and raphe nucleus. Both senile plaques and neurofibrillary tangles disrupt the normal operation of the brain and are thought to result in the early memory loss and eventual cognitive impairment seen in the disorder. A third clear indicator of Alzheimer's disease is cell loss, particularly in limbic areas and the cerebral cortex.

In addition to these hallmarks of Alzheimer's disease are decreases in various neurotransmitters, including acetylcholine, norepinephrine, serotonin, and glutamate. Genetic research indicates that Alzheimer's disease is associated with mutations on chromosomes 1, 14, and 19, in addition to the already mentioned abnormality on chromosome 21. The specific mutation seems to determine, to some extent, the age of onset of the disease. For example, early onset (forties and fifties) is associated with mutations on chromosomes 1, 14, and 21, while later onset (sixties and older) is associated with mutations on chromosome 19. All these genetic alterations seem to influence the accumulation of amyloid, the key substance in the formation of senile plaques. The exact mechanism whereby amyloid accumulation and deposition results in brain loss and plaque formation is unknown. Research, however, is investigating the possible link between amyloid accumulation and both calcium flow into cells and the release of damaging free radicals.

—*Kevin S. Seybold*

See also Aging process; Alzheimer's Association; Alzheimer's disease; Dementia; Forgetfulness; Free radical theory of aging; Memory changes and loss; Mental impairment; Parkinson's disease; Psychiatry, geriatric.

FOR FURTHER INFORMATION:

Arking, Robert. *Biology of Aging: Observations and Principles.* 2d ed. Sunderland, Mass.: Sinauer Associates, 1998. A good overview of aging from a biological point of view. Includes material on changes in the nervous system.

Beldotti, Stephanie. "The Human Brain." *Popular Science* 252, no. 1 (January, 1998). Discusses the effects of age on the operation of the human brain.

Finch, Caleb E., and George S. Roth. "The Biochemistry of Aging." In *Basic Neurochemistry,* edited by George J. Siegel et al. 6th ed. Philadelphia: Lippincott-Raven, 1999. Discusses the cellular and chemical changes that take place in the brain with age.

Kotulak, Ronald. "Keeping the Brain Sharp as We Age." *Saturday Evening Post* 268, no. 6 (November/December, 1996). Reviews evidence that the brain does not lose large numbers of cells with age, that the brains of younger and older people are remarkably similar, and that the brain is plastic throughout adulthood.

Morrison, John H., and Patrick R. Hof. "Life and Death of Neurons in the Aging Brain." *Science* 278, no. 5337 (October 17, 1997). Discusses qualitative and quantitative brain changes seen in normal aging and in Alzheimer's disease.

Scheibel, Arnold B. "Structural and Functional Changes in the Aging Brain." In *Handbook of the Psychology of Aging,* edited by James E. Birren and K. Warner Schaie. 4th ed. San Diego: Academic Press, 1996. A chapter describing the gross, microscopic, regional, and vascular changes that occur in the healthy brain during aging.

BREAST CANCER

RELEVANT ISSUES: Biology, death, demographics, health and medicine

SIGNIFICANCE: Breast cancer usually occurs in older women, in part because of age-related decline in the body's various defense mechanisms against such disease

Breast cancer is one of the most common forms of cancer among American and European women. Usually, this disease is detected in women who are well into or have passed middle age. In fact, occurrence of breast cancer among women older than sixty-five years is ten times as high as the incidence among women younger than forty-five years. The proportion of elderly women who survive breast cancer is also decreased relative to younger victims of this cancer type.

A number of other kinds of cancer also increase sharply later in life. This pattern of cancer development can be explained in part by deterioration in function of some of the body's organs during advanced age. Several changes in these systems have been identified as contributing specifically to breast cancer.

How Breast Cancer Forms

Breast cancer is a complex disease that results from a sequence of defects in the mammary gland. A key feature of breast cancer is the malfunctioning (mutation) of at least two of the genes that specifically regulate the growth of these cells. Not only is growth increased as a result but unfortunately these cells also become immortal; they do not die when no longer needed, as do most normal cells.

In breast cancer, the first of these mutations may be inherited from one of the parents. In this situation, called familial breast cancer, the second mutation may occur at any age, often leading to breast cancer in young women. Familial breast cancer is rare, making up only about 5 percent of all cases. In the more common forms of breast cancer, called spontaneous breast cancer, at least two genetic changes must occur in a single cell during the actual life span of the individual woman (or man, sometimes). This altered cell then becomes cancerous; that is, it begins to grow when it should not. It usually takes much longer for these two genetic accidents to occur in the same cell, and as a result spontaneous breast cancer typically does not emerge until a woman has reached the age of the menopause or later.

The features of spontaneous breast cancer differ among individual cases because different kinds of genetic defects can lead to the disease and it can occur in different functional structures in the breast. The most common forms of breast cancer occur in the epithelial cells of the mammary gland, which are the cells that produce milk and that line the ducts that convey milk to the nipple. The least dangerous kinds of cancer, called benign cancer, may simply plug some of the milk-producing structures and the ducts with excess cells. Progressively more aggressive cancer cells may literally digest surrounding structures and spread further. In the most advanced cases, the cancer cells may enter the circulatory system and form additional tumors elsewhere in the body, a process called metastasis. Breast cancer can also develop within the supportive (connective) tissue, the fatty tissue, or the lymphoid tissues of the gland, although these sites are less common.

Aging and Additional Breast Cancer Risks

The longer a person lives, the more time has passed during which genetic damage can occur by accident in the body. Because genetic damage is a key event in breast cancer development, it is clear that the risk of breast cancer must increase with age.

Even so, cancer may not develop and grow unless the conditions within a woman's body encourage the mutant cells to begin growing. Of particular importance are the female hormones, estrogen and progesterone. The levels of these hormones change during puberty, the menstrual cycle, pregnancy, and, most important, the menopause. Various lifestyle factors are also thought to influence how breast cancer develops, including diet, exercise, drug use, and exposure to other harmful chemicals. Notably, these factors may all change as a woman ages.

Many other factors also contribute to development of the disease. For example, the younger human body has superb defense systems that work to eliminate genetically damaged cells and to prevent cells from growing inappropriately. One of these is the immune system. When functioning properly, this system is very efficient at producing antibodies that can eliminate malfunctioning cells. Unfortu-

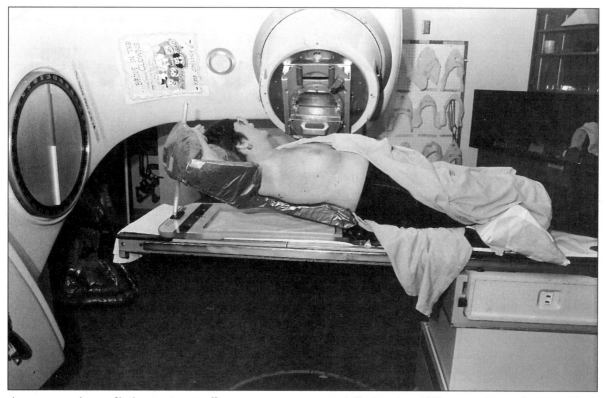

A woman receives radiation treatment; all women over twenty, especially those in middle age and beyond, are at risk for developing breast cancer. (Ben Klaffke)

nately, the immune system typically weakens during advanced age. Damaged cells are increasingly likely to escape detection, survive, and grow to produce breast tumors.

Other life-sustaining systems in the body also tend to weaken and become damaged with age. The result can be development of disease states other than breast cancer. These other diseases can, in turn, impair the body's ability to fend off breast cancer. This situation is termed "comorbidity." For example, high blood pressure, high blood cholesterol, and other related difficulties can impair the function of the circulatory system to deliver antibody-producing cells, and subtle changes in blood chemistry may actually enhance the growth of breast tumors.

As methods are developed to prevent these other diseases, deaths from such relatively common events as strokes and heart attacks have decreased among the elderly. Yet, those who elude these other diseases are still at risk for breast cancer as they age. Indeed, as the average life span in-

creases, for whatever reason, the chances of contracting breast cancer also increase. Thus, with the aging of the U.S. population, the incidence of breast cancer will continue to rise until the disease can be successfully prevented or eradicated among elderly victims.

BREAST CANCER CHARACTERISTICS IN ELDERLY WOMEN

All breast cancers have the same basic feature, that of abnormal growth, regardless of the age of the women in which the cancer occurs. Several of the more subtle characteristics of the disease, however, tend to differ somewhat in older and younger women. For example, cancers in older women are often more responsive to female sex hormones. Often, the tumors in women of advanced age are of a type that is less life-threatening.

Several other characteristics of the growth process can be more favorable in older women. Although these characteristics differ among individuals, it is clear that breast cancer in older women is often treatable using the therapeutic tools available, if care is taken to tailor therapy to the characteristics of each patient.

TREATMENT

Several different kinds of therapy are commonly used in the treatment of breast cancer. All of them can be used successfully with older patients. Some are preferable, however, because they are less risky for individuals of advanced age, producing fewer complications that may themselves threaten the well-being or life of the patient.

The most straightforward way of dealing with breast tumors is surgery. There are well-known risks associated with any surgery, and older people are at increased risk because of age-related debilities. Given this limitation, conservative surgery is an acceptable way of controlling breast cancer in the elderly. Among women whose disease is still localized—that is, has not yet spread to other parts of the body—surgery is about as effective among older as among younger women.

Radiotherapy is treatment with radioactive substances or X rays, which are designed to kill any cancer cells in the irradiated area. Again, there are risks, because the radiation may also affect nearby normal tissues and can itself cause cells to grow abnormally. Available information suggests that women over sixty respond well to radiotherapy as postoperative treatment to prevent local regrowth of any remaining cancer cells. Indeed, some studies suggest that this procedure may be slightly more effective in elderly patients than in younger women.

Hormone therapy was among the first treatments for breast cancer. As long ago as 1896, G. T. Beatson realized that in women with advanced breast cancer who had just lost their ovaries, the malignancy tended to regress. This observation has since led to several strategies for manipulating hormones in order to modify the growth of tumor cells.

Breast tissue contains certain proteins called receptors that make the tissue responsive to the various hormones that affect its normal function. These hormones include estrogen, which controls the normal growth and development of breast tissues, and progesterone, which helps prepare the breast for milk production after pregnancy. These hormones cycle regularly in premenopausal women. Some breast tumors retain these receptor molecules, while others do not. Those that still have the receptors often are capable of responding to these hormones; as a result, the tumor grows more. Likewise, as in Beatson's study, tumors may stop growing if the hormones are removed. It is clear that knowledge of the presence or absence of receptors for these and some other hormones is important information for selecting a therapy. In some studies, up to 80 percent of the breast tumors of women over the age of fifty have been found to carry estrogen receptors. This is actually higher than the percentage in cancers of younger women. This high percentage makes the modification of estrogen levels a particularly attractive type of therapy for many older women. About half the cancers of older women also carry progesterone receptors, making this an attractive target for therapy as well.

Hormone therapies that target the estrogen receptor are the best developed of hormone treatments. The primary source of estrogen is the ovaries, so their removal is an effective way to reduce estrogen levels in the body. Unfortunately, this can produce some significant side effects, because estrogen has beneficial effects as well in older women. Of particular importance is that estrogen helps prevent weakening of the bones, called osteoporosis. An alternative way to deal with the estrogen problem is to use an "antiestrogen." This is a molecule that counteracts the effects of estrogen, often by competing for the estrogen receptors on cancer cells. A number of antiestrogens have been developed for therapy; the best of these inhibit cancer growth while also providing some of the benefits of estrogen, such as preventing osteoporosis. One well-known drug of this type is tamoxifen. Unfortunately, tamoxifen and similar drugs may have damaging effects on other estrogen-responsive organs. For example, tamoxifen has been associated with an increased risk of endometrial (uterine) cancer. Promising new antiestrogens are continually being developed.

In general, hormone therapy is less traumatic for the elderly than are more invasive treatments like surgery and radiation. Another advantage is that it can be used to treat advanced stages of breast cancer, in which cancer cells have already spread to distant parts of the body. The costs and risks of other treatments need to be weighed carefully, but the advantages of hormone therapy may be of particular importance in older women.

Chemotherapy is the use of certain drugs to kill cancer cells. They are not selective for this cell type, however, and can cause other kinds of damage to the body as well. These side effects can be more severe in older women because they are not as capable of responding to the stress. Physicians are advised to adjust the doses of such drugs to allow for these age-associated declines in the ability of the body to cope with them. For example, the kidneys of a person of advanced age are not as efficient at removing the waste products resulting from such drug-caused damage. Survival rates of women who undergo chemotherapy are nearly as good as those of women treated with hormone therapy, but because of these age-related side effects, hormone therapy is generally preferable for older women.

Other promising strategies have been and are being developed that take advantage of the specific defects of breast cancer cells to target the damaged cells for treatment. For example, cancer drugs can be attached to hormones or antibodies that recognize the hormone receptors on breast cancer cells. The drug is delivered at high dosage to the target cells, and other cells nearby are more likely to escape harm. Similar targeting methods can be used to insert specific genes into breast cancer cells that can then function normally to replace the damaged genes whose defects contribute to features of the disease. It is expected that many such novel strategies will become available for use in the future.

CONCLUSIONS

Many variables must be considered in designing breast cancer therapy for older women. Unfortunately, the disease is often well advanced before a physician is consulted, making treatment more challenging. Breast cancer in older women is often hormone responsive, however, and typically their cancers are slower-growing than those in younger patients. These features make treatment more likely to succeed. On the other hand, the decline in normal body function must be taken into account because the treatments themselves can be very stressful. Breast cancers in many older women will respond to traditional therapies, but the best therapy needs to be designed individually. This therapy plan should recognize other illnesses af-

flicting the patient, her ability to tolerate certain therapies, and the effect of the aging process on functioning of the patient's other bodily systems. Because older patients can expect fewer years of life remaining in any case, the quality of life of those women can be greatly improved during their remaining years even when the long-term outlook may be less hopeful.   —*Howard L. Hosick*

See also Breast changes and disorders; Cancer; Death and dying; Estrogen replacement therapy; Free radical theory of aging; Health care; Hospice; Terminal illness; Women and aging.

FOR FURTHER INFORMATION:
DiGiovanna, Augustine G. "Reproductive System." In *Human Aging: Biological Perspectives.* New York: McGraw-Hill, 1994. This book is a broad overview of all aspects of getting old. Offers very straightforward comments on how breast cancer develops.

Holliday, Robin. "Human Disease and Aging." In *Understanding Aging.* New York: Cambridge University Press, 1995. Holliday is a prominent British biologist who has the ability to make unfamiliar concepts clear. This entire book is recommended reading for anyone with a particular interest in aging.

National Cancer Institute. *Understanding Breast Cancer Treatments: A Guide for Patients.* Bethesda, Md.: National Institutes of Health, 1998. One of a series of excellent pamphlets that explain with understandable diagrams and sketches what is happening with various breast cancer therapies. A glossary of terms is included, and other resources are listed.

Ross, Ian K. "The Body Changes I: Cancer and Cardiovascular Disease." In *Aging of Cells, Humans, and Societies.* Dubuque, Iowa: Wm. C. Brown, 1995. This book describes the cell-level defects that lead to cancer more so than the other titles listed here. The book as a whole is also a much broader consideration of the aging process.

Tannock, Ian F., and Richard P. Hill. "Pharmacologic Applications of Hormones in Breast Cancer: Treatment of Breast Cancer." In *The Basic Science of Oncology.* 3d ed. New York: McGraw-Hill, 1998. This is essentially a textbook on cancer. The chapter on hormone therapy for breast cancer should be accessible to those with a particular interest in this subject.

BREAST CHANGES AND DISORDERS

RELEVANT ISSUES: Biology, health and medicine, psychology

SIGNIFICANCE: Normal breast changes occur throughout life, while benign disorders, which require attention and sometimes necessitate treatment, are rarely precancerous conditions

The basic structures of the female breast are all present at birth. Their development is stimulated by hormone production at puberty and by twenty years of age are complete. Thereafter, depending on her stage of life and state of health, a woman's breasts will vary in size, shape, coloring, and skin texture. Breast screening, by self-examination, by a doctor, or by mammography, is strongly recommended, as it can detect abnormal changes in the breast.

PHYSICAL STRUCTURE OF THE NORMAL BREAST

The breast consists of three types of tissue: breast, fat, and fibrous. Breast tissue extends from the breastbone to the back of the armpit, from the collarbone to the lower few ribs, and from the skin to the chest muscle. Sandwiched between layers of fat, breast tissue lies mostly in the upper breast and toward the armpit, while fat tissue lies mainly in the middle and lower part of the breast. As a woman ages, the amount of breast tissue decreases and the amount of fat tissue increases. Bands of flexible, fibrous tissue, called Cooper's ligaments, pass between the lobes from the chest muscles to the skin, providing support to the breast. With age, the ligaments stretch, causing the breast to droop. The breast also has arteries, veins, and nerves.

Nipples, which are highly responsive to touch, may protrude slightly, lie flat against the skin, or be inverted. Hair follicles are found around the nipple. The areola, a pigmented area surrounding the nipple, varies in size and shape. Its color reflects a woman's complexion and changes during sexual arousal and orgasm.

Within each breast are lobules and ducts that during lactation produce and transport milk to an ampulla (reservoir) under the areola, where it remains until it is released. The parts of the breast involved in producing, transporting, or storing milk are called the parenchyma, while all other parts, including the fat cells and fibrous tissue, are called the stroma.

NORMAL CHANGES AND BENIGN BREAST DISORDERS

Throughout her life, a woman will have to contend with and adjust to various breast changes. Prior to and during menstruation, these changes may include swelling, tenderness, and lumpiness. Some women experience a more severe breast pain known as mastalgia. Cyclical mastalgia, the most common type, appears to be related to hormonal fluctuations. Beginning two weeks before menstruation and at times continuing after it has begun, the pain can radiate down the arm. Noncyclical breast pain, also known as target zone breast pain, since it frequently occurs in one specific site, can result from trauma such as a blow or a surgical biopsy. At times, what appears to be chronic breast pain may be referred pain originating elsewhere in the body.

Physiological changes in the breasts occur during sexual activity. During the excitement phase, the breasts plump, the areola swells, and the nipples harden and become more erect. Immediately before orgasm, at the plateau phase, the nipples and areola enlarge further, peaking at orgasm, after which they gradually subside.

Throughout pregnancy and during lactation, the milk-producing glands swell. During breastfeeding, sebaceous glands lubricate the nipple and areola. Breast size increases during feeding and lactation. Following pregnancy, the areola usually darkens.

Included within the category of benign breast disorders are general breast lumpiness, individual lumps, nipple discharge, infections, and inflammation. In *Dr. Susan Love's Breast Book* (1990), Susan M. Love, an authority on breast disease and innovative treatments, criticizes the use of the term "fibrocystic disease" because it covers several entirely unrelated symptoms, ranging from swelling, pain, tenderness, and lumps to the density differences of breast tissue observed in mammograms and the normal microscopic findings by a pathologist. Only one pathological finding, atypical hyperplasia, suggests an increased risk for breast cancer.

LUMPS IN THE BREASTS

Lumpiness in the breast tends to disappear after the menopause unless the woman is receiving hormone replacement therapy. Cysts and fibroadenomas, however, are formed during premenopausal years but may become apparent only later in life.

Cysts, which are spherical sacs filled with fluid, most commonly appear in the years immediately prior to the menopause. A woman may find one or several lumps in one or both breasts with no other symptoms present or her breasts may feel full and painful. If the lumps can be felt, they are usually tender and firm, and can be slightly moved. Cysts can be seen with mammography, when they appear as a dense area. They can also be detected using an ultrasound. Because a cyst is not a solid mass, the sound waves will travel through it. A cyst

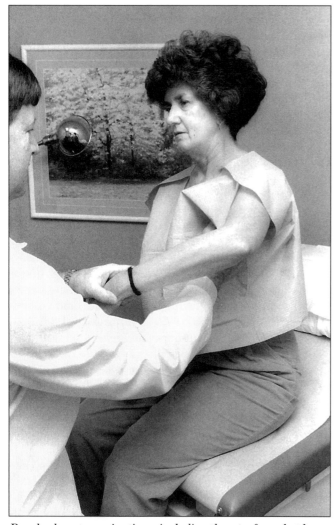

Regular breast examinations, including those performed at home, are crucial screening tools for breast cancer and other breast disorders that increase in frequency in middle age. (Ben Klaffke)

can be differentiated from a solid mass by using fine-needle aspiration to withdraw fluid, thereby avoiding a biopsy. When a cyst is detected, it can be drained. If a solid component is found within the cyst, then a biopsy is indicated.

A fibroadenoma is a smooth, round, and hard lump that easily moves around in the breast tissue. The size can range from 5 millimeters to 5 centimeters. When viewed on mammograms and ultrasounds, fibroadenomas are usually clear. To further examine the lump, cell tissue can be removed by fine-needle aspiration. Fibroadenomas are usually removed in women who are middle-aged or older. Like cysts, they will not appear after the menopause unless the woman is receiving hormone replacement therapy.

Sclerosing adenosis involves excessive growth of lobular tissue in the breast. On a mammogram, it shows up as microcalcifications. Since the changes are microscopic, a biopsy is required to rule out cancer.

Atypical hyperplasia describes an increased number of cells lining the ducts or the lobules. The cells are slightly abnormal in appearance. This condition indicates an increased risk for breast cancer, with the degree of risk depending on the severity of the cell growth.

INFECTIONS AND NIPPLE DISCHARGE

The two major categories of breast infections are intrinsic (those occurring in the breast itself) and extrinsic (those showing first in the breast but also involving the whole body, such as tuberculosis and syphilis). Within the former category, lactational mastitis occurs in nursing mothers when a duct becomes infected as a result of a milk blockage. Occasionally, in about 10 percent of cases, an abscess develops that requires draining. Nonlactational mastitis describes a similar, usually more generalized infection in a nonlactating woman that produces swelling and heat and is accompanied by a high fever. It is treated with antibiotics. The second most common infection is a chronic subareolar abscess, an abscess in the area of the areola.

Most women secrete a small amount of discharge from their nipples when their breasts are squeezed. This discharge occurs mainly at puberty and at the menopause and does not indicate a medical condition. A nipple discharge becomes pertinent only when it is spontaneous, persistent, issuing from only one breast, and either clear and sticky or bloody. Then the possible causes include an intraductal papilloma (a small wartlike growth on the duct lining), intraductal papillomatosis (many small growths), and an intraductal carcinoma in situ, which is a precancer that blocks the duct. Very rarely, in about 4 percent of cases, a spontaneous unilateral bloody discharge can indicate cancer. Other nipple problems include allergic skin reactions and eczema.

THE CONTROVERSY REGARDING SILICONE BREAST IMPLANTS

Developed in 1962 and used mainly for cosmetic augmentation and reconstruction after breast surgery, silicone breast implants have been associated with some risks. Among them are a hardening in surrounding tissue caused by calcium deposits, which can cause pain; occasional leaks and ruptures so that the silicone gel is released into surrounding tissue; problems with the lymph nodes in the implant area; and a temporary or permanent loss of sensation in the nipple and breast tissue. For several years, the Food and Drug Administration disallowed use of most silicone implants. Although a number of legal cases charged that the implants were the cause of systemic connective tissue disease, no clear evidence supported the contention. Furthermore, in December 1998, an independent scientific panel, appointed by a federal court, concluded there was little or no justification for believing that breast implants caused diseases of any kind.   —*Susan E. Hamilton*

See also Aging process; Breast cancer; Cosmetic surgery; Cysts; Women and aging.

FOR FURTHER INFORMATION:

Apgar, Barbara. "Changes in Breast Biopsy Results at Age Fifty Years." *American Family Physician* 54, no. 6 (November 1, 1996): 2071.
Cooper, Cyrus, and Elaine Dennison. "Do Silicone Breast Implants Cause Connective Tissue Disease?" *The British Medical Journal* 316, no. 7129 (February 7, 1998): 403.
Fiorica, James V., et al. "Benign Breast Disorders: First Rule Out Cancer." *Patient Care* 31, no. 7 (April 15, 1997): 140.
Gabriel, S. E., et al. "Risk of Connective-Tissue Diseases and Other Disorders After Breast Implantation." *New England Journal of Medicine* 330, no. 24 (June 16, 1994): 1697-1702.
Love, Susan M., with Karen Lindsey. *Dr. Susan Love's Breast Book.* 2d ed. New York: Addison-Wesley, 1995.
National Cancer Institute. *Understanding Breast Changes: A Health Guide for All Women.* Bethesda, Md.: National Institutes of Health, 1997.
Segal, Marian. *A Status Report on Breast Implant Safety.* Rev. ed. Rockville, Md.: Department of Health and Human Services, Public Health Service, Food and Drug Administration, 1997.

BRIDGES. *See* CROWNS AND BRIDGES.

BUNIONS

RELEVANT ISSUES: Health and medicine
SIGNIFICANCE: Bunions are joint disorders of the feet that can develop during the aging process, producing deformity, pain, and discomfort

A bunion, or hallux valgus, is a swelling on the foot, usually at the joint of the big toe, that is caused by a misaligned bone in the joint. Bunions often develop with aging as a result of widening of the feet, arthritic conditions, or the wearing of improperly fitted shoes. Typically, the misaligned bone protrudes outward at the joint of the big toe, giving the bunion its bulging appearance. The bursa, a fluid-filled sac in the joint, becomes inflamed and swells, often twisting the big toe toward the second toe. Since the big toe supports most of the body's weight every time an individual pushes off the ground, a bunion can cause severe pain and discomfort. In addition, because bunions can change the shape of the feet, it becomes much harder for an aging sufferer to find shoes that fit properly.

While bunions themselves cannot be inherited, an individual can inherit the tendency to develop bunions by being born with extra bone near a toe joint. The risk of developing bunions can be reduced by exercising daily to keep the muscles of the feet and legs in good condition and by wearing wide-toed shoes that fit well. Women tend to de-

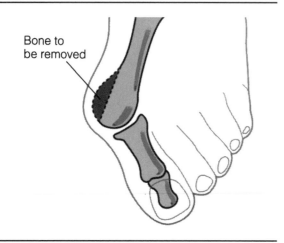

Bone to
be removed

A bunion, a bony overgrowth of the big toe, can be re-moved surgically by cutting off the excess bone segment, thus reshaping the foot. (Hans & Cassidy, Inc.)

velop bunions more than men do, possibly be-cause many women wear shoes that are too small or narrow. Symptoms of bunions include pain, redness, stiffness, swelling, thickness of the skin over the bunion, fluid accumulation under the thickened skin, and the eventual development of osteoarthritis that impairs the joint's flexibility.

If a bunion is not severe, greater comfort can come from simply wearing a different style of shoe, including those that have been stretched in the big toe area, that are made of soft leather, or that have cushioned insoles. Sandals with cross straps and athletic shoes are best for providing maximum comfort for people with bunions. Other ways to re-lieve the pain include using shoe inserts called bunion pads, using a moist heating pad on the bunion at night, applying an ice pack to reduce swelling, and taking an over-the-counter anti-inflammatory medication such as aspirin or ibuprofen (Advil or Motrin). Aging persons with medical conditions should read product labels carefully and consult their doctor or a pharmacist before taking pain-relieving medications. If home care measures do not provide relief, a podiatrist (foot doctor) may prescribe a special shoe insert known as an orthotic device.

For severe bunions, outpatient surgery may be required. The most common surgery reduces the angle between the big and second toes. Bones in the big toe are realigned, and the bunion is shaved away. Ligaments and tendons on the outside of the toe may be tightened to hold the joint properly, while any tight tendons on the inside of the toe are released. Bunion surgery can reduce pain and im-prove the appearance of the feet. Recovery in-volves the use of crutches to keep weight off the foot, and the majority of healing typically occurs within a few weeks. After surgery, pain will gradu-ally subside and deformity of the foot will improve. However, tight shoes must still be avoided.

—Alvin K. Benson

See also Bone changes and disorders; Fallen arches; Foot disorders; Hammertoes; Mobility problems.

CALLUSES. *See* **CORNS AND CALLUSES.**

CALORIC RESTRICTION

RELEVANT ISSUES: Biology, health and medicine
SIGNIFICANCE: Roy Walford, a physician and member of the Biosphere 2 team, conducted studies indicating that the human life span can be increased by implementing a regimen of caloric restriction

Humans have been interested in ways to extend their life span since time immemorial. The science of gerontology, the study of aging, seeks to understand the biological causes of aging, to extend the maximum human life span, and to improve the quality of the later years of life. This science was on the fringes of mainstream scientific thought until the 1970's and 1980's, when the studies and theories of Roy Walford suggested that this dream could become a possibility. As a professor of pathology at the University of California, Los Angeles (UCLA) School of Medicine, Walford focused his research on the biology of aging.

According to the results of Walford's many studies on animals (and one unplanned human study), life span can be increased through dietary restriction, the limitation of total caloric intake without loss of critical nutrients. This might best be described as "undernutrition without malnutrition"—a limiting of the total intake of calories without causing a lack of critical nutrients such as vitamins, essential amino acids, fatty acids, and minerals. Dietary restriction has been found to retard aging and extend life span in nearly all species that have been tested, from unicellular organisms to mammals such as rodents.

ANIMAL STUDIES OF DIETARY RESTRICTION

Clive McCay of Cornell University performed the first reliable studies of dietary restriction on rats in the mid-1930's. He found that in some cases, both the maximum life span and the 50 percent survival rate (the age at which half of the studied population is still living) of rats were doubled when their food intake was restricted, as compared to those rats who ate as much as they wanted. In the 1960's and 1970's, Morris Ross of the Institute for Cancer Research conducted experiments that yielded a 60 percent increase in the life span of rats on a calorically restricted dietary regimen.

Beginning in the 1970's, Walford and his colleagues performed experiments on how nutrient-rich caloric limitation affects the physiology of the body of the restricted animal. They found that dietary restriction causes lowered blood pressure, lowered blood cholesterol levels, lowered fasting blood sugars, borderline low leukocyte (white blood cell) counts, prevention or delay of cancer and other age-related diseases, increases in vitality, and minimal bone loss. However, these animals were smaller in size as compared to regularly fed animals. In addition, calorie-restricted animals are more functionally fit than those of the same age who eat as much as they like. In fact, in one test of "athletic ability," thirty-two-month-old calorie-restricted mice tested as well as twelve-month-old fully fed mice and far better than fully fed thirty-two-month-old mice.

The increase in life span is proportional with an increase in restriction. In one study, the maximum life span of a certain strain of mice was close to thirty-eight months for fully fed mice. When mice of this same strain ate 10 percent fewer calories than the fully fed mice, the maximum life span was increased to forty-three months. A 50 percent calorie reduction resulted in a life span expansion to more than fifty-four months. Most of these animal experiments were conducted on mice that began the restricted diet at weaning, resulting in rodents about two-thirds the size of fully fed rodents. However, further research indicated that dietary restriction begun in adult life can still prolong life span and retard aging.

MECHANISMS OF THE RESTRICTED DIET

The largest question facing researchers studying dietary restriction pertains to how a low-calorie, nutrient-dense diet can increase life span. One complication is that many different theories exist regarding how the aging process works. Dietary restriction positively influences every age-related function and resistance to major diseases.

Dietary restriction seems to fit every major theory of aging. It counteracts the immune system's tendency to lose the ability to attack foreign objects and to begin to attack itself, as the immunological theory of aging suggests. It increases the body's ability to repair injury to its deoxyribonucleic acid (DNA), which is thought to be lost according to the DNA repair theory of aging. It also increases the body's production of antioxidants, which keep free radicals from attacking the body, as suggested by the free radical theory of aging. The search for these mechanisms is the next big phase in dietary restriction research.

BIOSPHERE 2

Walford served as the team physician during the first two-year closing of Biosphere 2, a 3.15-acre, closed ecological space in the desert near Tucson, Arizona. Biosphere 2 contained rain forest, ocean, savannah, and desert biomes; an agricultural space; and living quarters for its residents. It was "closed" to the exchange of any physical material, but sunlight and electric power were allowed to enter and heat could leave. From 1991 to 1993, eight scientists lived and worked in this structure, along with over 3,800 carefully selected species of plants and animals. These "Biospherians" had to grow all of their own food within the complex after the closing, and all organic material, water, and air had to be recycled. As a result of problems with the crops, the projected daily diet of 2,500 kilocalories per person was reduced to an average of 1,780 kilocalories per day during the first six months. The nutritional quality of the food grown inside the compound, however, was excellent; it was mainly vegetarian and consisted of varieties of fruits, cereal grains, legumes, vegetables and greens, white and sweet potatoes, and small amounts of goat milk and yogurt, goat meat, pork, chicken, fish, and eggs. Walford had an opportunity to record the results of this low-calorie, nutrient-dense diet on the eight subjects.

As Walford had predicted, the physiological changes in the Biospherians corresponded closely to those seen in his experiments with rodents. During the first eight months, the Biospherians underwent gradual but substantial weight loss, an average of 10 percent for women and 18 percent for men. Though their weight loss was dramatic, the Biospherians did not feel any undue hunger, even though there was substantial physical exercise involved in running Biosphere 2. Body fat content stabilized at 6 to 10 percent for the men and 10 to 15 percent for the women, despite a gradual increase in calorie consumption after the first few months. After six months, the Biospherians experienced reductions in blood pressure, blood cholesterol, blood sugar, and white cells in their blood;

in addition, they were more resistant to disease and showed increased vitality. Even the acne of two of the Biospherians cleared up. Though it is difficult to draw convincing conclusions from a two-year experiment, Walford believed that there was no reason to doubt that the other effects of the low-calorie, nutrient-dense diet—retardation of aging and health enhancement—would also occur if one stayed on this diet for a longer period of time.

In 1994, Walford published *The Anti-Aging Plan*, his first book since the human dietary restriction experiment in Biosphere 2. In this book, Walford and his daughter Lisa provided an easy-to-understand explanation of the strategy of dietary restriction and a plan for the implementation of this diet by the average person. This plan is based on the diet and caloric intake of the Biospherians, although it has a little more variety and may be tastier because of the availability of seasonings not found in Biosphere 2. The diet provides 100 percent or more of the recommended daily allowance of all essential and important nutritional items with a low-calorie intake. The second half of *The Anti-Aging Plan* contains over one hundred recipes and techniques that can be used by anyone interested in losing weight, increasing resistance to disease, and adding additional quality years to one's life.   —*Karl Giberson and Sara Turmenne*

See also Aging process; Antiaging treatments; Antioxidants; Free radical theory of aging; Life expectancy; Longevity research; Malnutrition; Nutrition; Vitamins and minerals; Weight loss and gain.

FOR FURTHER INFORMATION:

Walford, Roy L., et. al. "The Calorically Restricted Low-Fat Nutrient-Dense Diet in Biosphere 2 Significantly Lowers Blood Glucose, Total Leukocyte Count, Cholesterol, and Blood Pressure in Humans." *Proceedings of the National Academy of Sciences, USA* 89 (December, 1992).

_____. *Maximum Life Span.* New York: W. W. Norton, 1983.

_____. *The 120-Year Diet.* New York: Simon & Schuster, 1986.

Walford, Roy L., and Lisa Walford. *The Anti-Aging Plan.* New York: Four Walls, Eight Windows, 1994. Web site: http://www.walford.com

Weindruch, Richard, and Roy Walford. *The Retardation of Aging and Disease by Dietary Restriction.* Springfield, Ill.: Charles C Thomas, 1988.

CANCER

RELEVANT ISSUES: Biology, death, health and medicine

SIGNIFICANCE: The incidence of cancer increases with age; about one-half of the people afflicted with cancer each year are over age sixty-five

Cancer is an abnormal growth of cells. It begins when a single cell is transformed to a state where it reproduces itself without the constraints that are normally placed on cells. Each new cell produced also divides uncontrollably. The dividing cells produce a mass of tissue that may spread to other organs. Illness and death from cancer are caused by infection, hemorrhage, and impairment of vital body functions, such as digestion or breathing.

CAUSES OF CANCER

Cancer may result from environmental factors, such as chemicals, radiation, and viral infections, or internal factors, such as inherited or accidental gene mutations. Cancer is caused by permanent genetic changes in cells that allow them to divide without control. Other factors, such as hormones, drugs, and such irritants as particles in cigarette smoke may stimulate cell division without actually changing the cells permanently.

Cancer is believed to develop in three stages: initiation, in which a mutation occurs in a gene that controls some aspect of cell division; promotion, in which the cell with the mutation is induced to divide by irritants, local cell growth promoting factors, and hormones; and progression, in which more mutations and other growth-related changes occur in the cell line that eventually allow it to grow uncontrollably. It is believed that most cancers have about four to seven mutations in growth-controlling genes. During progression, the body's immune system tries to kill as many cancer cells as possible, but the surviving malignant cells often develop resistance and become more aggressive and lethal to the host. This is similar to the resistance bacteria develop to antibiotics.

Chemicals, especially such organic chemicals as benzo(*a*)pyrene in cigarette smoke, are to known to cause mutations in genes involved in controlling cell division (for example, p53). Radiation from such sources as radon in the environment and nuclear accidents can also cause mutations that can lead to cancer. Certain viruses cause cancer by al-tering processes in cells that control cell division or by stimulating activity in cellular genes involved in controlling cell division. Cancer or the predisposition to cancer can be inherited. For example, the predisposition to one form of breast cancer is caused by an inherited gene called BRCA1.

Aging contributes to the incidence of cancer in several ways. The immune system and other regulatory systems begin to decline with age and thereby reduce the body's ability to protect itself against cancer and other diseases. It often takes many years for cancer to develop and become a threat to the body. In addition, older people have been exposed over a longer period to factors that can cause cancer. Thus, older people are quite vulnerable to cancer and need to be more vigilant in detecting possible cancers and seeking immediate diagnosis and treatment.

A DISEASE OF THE GENES

All cell activity is controlled by genes—including the misbehavior of cancer cells. Errors (mutations) in the genes cause alterations in the proteins they encode. If these proteins are involved in cell division, breakdowns may result that cause the cell to divide uncontrollably. Scientists have discovered two categories of genes that are involved in most cancers: proto-oncogenes and tumor suppressor genes.

Proto-oncogenes are genes that code for proteins involved in promoting cell division. When a mutation occurs in only one of the two copies of the gene coding for these traits (either the one from the father or the one from the mother), increased cell growth may occur. When mutated, these dominant transforming genes are called oncogenes. They code primarily for factors both external and internal to the cell that signal the cell to divide. For example, the *sis* proto-oncogene codes for a growth factor that combines with a receptor on the cell surface, which initiates a cascade of other signals inside the cell to commence cell division. Mutation or overexpression of *sis* may lead to increased cell division.

Other proto-oncogenes code for growth factor receptors and signal molecules inside the cell and nucleus. As mentioned, proto-oncogenes are usually activated by mutation, but they may also transform cells if they are overexpressed because of amplification (extra copies of the gene) or deregulated by other factors, such as chromosomal translocation (when part of one chromosome attaches to another). An example of an oncogene involved in human cancer is *ras*, found in 50 percent of human colon cancers and in many other malignancies. The *ras* proto-oncogene codes for an internal cell protein involved in controlling growth-promoting signals going to the cell nucleus. A mutation in this gene causes a one-hundred-fold increase in the growth-promoting signal. An analogy for such an oncogene would be a defective switch for a car horn that becomes stuck in the "on" position, causing the horn to sound continuously without control.

A second category of cancer genes are the tumor suppressor genes, which code for proteins that block or slow cell division. Because both genes of the pair code for suppressor proteins, they both must be mutated or deleted for unregulated cell division to occur. People who have inherited one faulty tumor suppressor gene are more likely to develop cancer because only one gene of the pair needs to mutate sometime during their life. This is true of familial adenomatous polyposis, a form of colorectal cancer that involves the tumor suppressor gene adenomatous polyposis coli (APC). This gene codes for a protein that facilitates colon-cell maturation and thus when mutated allows immature cells to accumulate and begin to form a tumor. Another important tumor suppressor gene is p53, which has been found to be altered in more than 50 percent of human cancers. Tumor suppressor genes are analogous to the brakes on a car in that they slow or stop cell division.

In addition to these two categories of genes, other inherited traits may also influence the occurrence and progression of cancer in the body. People with inherited forms of immunodeficiency (weakened immune system) are not able to mobilize white blood cells known as T-killer cells that seek out and kill cancer cells. Inherited diseases, such as xerderma pigmentosum, result in the inability of cells to repair errors in deoxyribonucleic acid (DNA) at the time it is duplicated, which eventually leads to errors in genes that control cell division and thus greatly increases the risk of cancer. Other inherited traits, such as race and sex, also influence the risk for certain cancers. For instance, people with fair skin are more vulnerable to skin cancer.

CANCER RISK

The population of the United States suffers from about 1.2 million new cases and 550,000 deaths from cancer each year, second only to heart disease. Cancer accounts for about one in five deaths, while heart disease kills two in five. While most cases occur in midlife or later, cancer is still a scourge to the young, causing more deaths than any other disease in children aged one to fourteen. These statistics do not include most skin cancers and early noninvasive cancers, which easily add up to more than 1 million cases per year. The most common cancers are lung, prostate, and colorectal in men, and lung, breast, and colorectal in women. More men (272,000) die each year from cancer than do women (242,000). Lung cancer has increased dramatically since the invention of the cigarette and now is the most common type of serious cancer, estimated to have killed about 150,000 people per year in the late 1990's—more than breast, prostate, and colorectal cancers combined. Breast and prostate cancers are on the increase, possibly because of better diagnostic techniques and longer life expectancy. Stomach and cervical cancers have declined dramatically since the 1930's, probably because of improved food quality and the invention of the Pap smear.

The risk for cancer increases with age. Men and women aged sixty to eighty have a one in three and a one in four chance of developing invasive cancer, respectively; the risk is reduced to one in thirteen and one in eleven for those aged forty to fifty-nine and one in fifty-eight and one in fifty-two for those aged thirty-nine and under. The risk of developing cancers that are promoted by hormones, especially breast and prostate, increases with age because the hormones act on the target organs over a longer time. Ironically, men who lead healthy lifestyles and live longer assume higher risk of developing prostate cancer simply by virtue of their longer exposure to testosterone. Women who have their first menstrual cycle at an early age or have a late menopause have increased risk of breast cancer because of longer exposure to estrogen. Cancers of the skin, colon, lungs, and other organs occur more frequently in elderly people because they have been exposed for a longer period to carcinogens and have provided enough time for the precancerous cells to develop into full-blown cancer.

DIAGNOSIS AND TREATMENT

Early detection and diagnosis of cancer is highly correlated to survival. Survival increases 25 to 50 percent if the tumor is detected before it metastasizes to other organs. Sadly, more than two-thirds of cancers are not diagnosed until they reach this stage. Early detection could be increased by following the recommendations of the American Cancer Society. Screening for breast cancer should begin at age forty, and women aged fifty and older should have a mammogram yearly. Colon cancer screening should also begin at age forty and include a digital rectal examination and stool blood test. After age fifty, a sigmoidoscopy should be performed every three to five years. Prostate cancer can also be detected with the digital rectal examination, and men over fifty should have an annual prostate-specific antigen (PSA) blood test.

A yearly physical is a good idea for everyone because it includes routine checks for cancer. Self-examinations and awareness of cancer signs and symptoms are of utmost importance to ensure early detection. Once cancer is suspected, the physician can order an array of tests to determine the location, size, and type of malignancy. Knowing the stage (degree of spread) that the cancer is in and its grade (abundance of abnormal cell types) will help the oncologist determine the type of treatment to be used.

Treatment of cancer is constantly changing and improving. If the tumor is confined, it can usually be removed successfully by surgical techniques that lead to a cure. Surgery may also be used to prevent or lower the risk of cancer, to aid in diagnosis, to relieve symptoms, to support other therapies, and to reconstruct damaged organs. Radiation therapy can be used to cure the cancer or to relieve symptoms. It is used when the cancer is inaccessible or not easily or fully removed by surgery. It can be used in combination with surgery or chemotherapy. Radiation from a beam, such as high-energy X rays, is aimed at the tumor. Radiation from radioactive isotopes implanted near the tumor or injected into the bloodstream may also be used. All types of radiotherapy cause tumor cells to die by damaging their DNA and other cellular molecules by ionization. Since normal tissues in the path of the radiation can also be damaged, there may be some side effects, depending on the organs involved. For instance, radiation treatment of the upper abdomen may cause nausea and vomiting.

Chemotherapy involves treating cancer with chemical drug agents that specifically interfere with cell growth and division. Chemotherapy is often used to treat cancer that has spread beyond its site of origin and would not easily be treated by surgery or radiotherapy. It can achieve complete remission, partial remission, or stabilization. Drugs are given in precise doses and schedules orally, by injection, or by various intravenous delivery systems. Treatment may last several weeks or months. One of the major side effects of chemotherapy is reduced blood cell production, which increases the danger of infection and bleeding. Other side effects include temporary hair loss, mouth sores, nausea, vomiting, and diarrhea.

Biological therapy involves the use of products made from living body cells. This type of therapy is still experimental, and only a small percentage of cancer patients receive it. One strategy is to boost the body's own immune system with bacterial or chemical boosters or with tumor-associated vaccines. Another is to use antibodies against the tumor produced in the laboratory (monoclonal antibodies such as herceptin for breast cancer). A third method is to remove some immune cells from the patient and condition them in the laboratory so that they will have a stronger anticancer effect when they are returned to the body. Biological agents are also being developed to discourage the tumor from making new blood capillaries to supply itself with blood (an example is angiostatin), others to encourage cancer cells to die on schedule (proapototic substances), and others to prevent cancer cells from dividing perpetually (telomerase inhibitors). Bone marrow transplants are used to restore the bone marrow of cancer patients who have undergone aggressive therapy or need to replace cancerous marrow.

CANCER PREVENTION

Two general strategies can help prevent cancer: avoiding carcinogens as much as possible and protecting the body against the effects of carcinogens through dietary and other means. Carcinogen avoidance should begin with not smoking or using any kind of tobacco product since it is well documented that these products may cause cancer. Excess alcohol also increases the risk of liver, oral, and breast cancer. Certain occupations that allow higher-than-normal exposure to chemicals and radiation increase cancer risk and therefore should be considered cautiously. Living in urban areas and near industries that utilize chemicals and radiation may increase exposure to carcinogens. Sunbelt inhabitants are exposed to more intense ultraviolet rays and therefore have a higher risk of skin cancer. Foods cooked at high temperature, charred foods, and pickled, smoked, and nitrite-cured foods may contain excess amounts of chemical carcinogens. Excess fat may, through its metabolism, increase cancer-causing chemicals in the body. Living in buildings with high amounts of radon and at high altitudes, where there is less atmospheric protection against cosmic radiation, may also increase the risk of cancer.

The skin can be protected against cancer by wearing protective clothing and using sunscreens. Protective equipment, proper ventilation, and other safety measures are important to guard against occupational carcinogens. Cancer researchers believe that eating a diet high in fiber is protective against cancer because fiber in the digestive system absorbs carcinogens and promotes motility of wastes through the bowel. Fruits and vegetables contain vitamins such as A, E, and C, as well as other substances that protect against the effects of mutation-causing free radicals formed during metabolism. Some drugs, such as tamoxifen, are protective against cancer. This drug competes with cell-growth-promoting estrogen for receptors in breast cells, thus helping to prevent cancer. A healthy lifestyle is very important in the prevention of cancer. For most people, the risk of cancer could be cut in half by not smoking and eating primarily a vegetarian diet.   —*Rodney C. Mowbray*

See also Breast cancer; Death and dying; Free radical theory of aging; Genetics; Health care; Hospice; Illnesses among the elderly; Prostate cancer; Skin cancer; Smoking; Weight loss and gain.

FOR FURTHER INFORMATION:

Dollinger, Malin, Ernest H. Rosenbaum, and Greg Cable, eds. *Everyone's Guide to Cancer Therapy.* 3d ed. Kansas City: Somerville House Books Limited, Andrews McMeel Publishing, 1997. A thorough discussion or cancer diagnosis and treatment written in layman's terms by medical specialists.

Landro, Laura. *Survivor: Taking Control of Your Fight Against Cancer.* New York: Simon & Schuster, 1998. Excellent personal account of one woman's fight against chronic myelogenous leukemia.

McGinn, Kerry A., and Pamela J. Haylock. *Women's Cancers: How to Prevent Them, How to Treat Them, How to Beat Them.* Alameda, Calif.: Hunter House, 1998. Comprehensive treatment of women's cancer presented by two experienced oncology registered nurses.

McKinnell, Robert G., Ralph E. Parchment, Alan O. Perantoni, and G. Barry Pierce. *The Biological Basis of Cancer.* Cambridge, England: Cambridge University Press, 1998. This text is designed for an undergraduate course in cancer. Excellent presentation of the basic biology of cancer.

Murphy, Gerald P., Lois B. Morris, and Dianne Lange. *Informed Decisions: The Complete Book of Cancer Diagnosis, Treatment, and Recovery.* New York: Viking Press, 1997. An American Cancer Society-sponsored publication written specifically to help cancer patients make decisions concerning their medical care.

Steen, R. Grant. *A Conspiracy of Cells: The Basic Science of Cancer.* New York: Plenum Press, 1993. A book written for cancer patients describing the basis of cancer and providing thorough coverage of the most common human cancers.

Weinberg, Robert A. *One Renegade Cell: How Cancer Begins.* New York: Basic Books, 1998. A leading cancer researcher explains how scientists greatly increased the understanding of the underlying causes of cancer during the 1980's and the 1990's; interesting and informative.

CANES AND WALKERS

RELEVANT ISSUES: Health and medicine

SIGNIFICANCE: Numerous styles of canes and walkers are prescribed by health care providers or are available for purchase; the choice and fit of these devices are important to ensure safety and maximal benefit

Many types of canes and walkers are available for purchase in drugstores and variety stores. Many older individuals using these assistive devices purchased them in such stores or borrowed one from a friend or family member. Often, these devices are prescribed by a physician or therapist for either temporary or long-term use. Regardless of how the device was obtained, proper choice and fit are important for many reasons. A poor choice or fit can result in decreased stability, increased energy expenditure needed to walk, and unsafe walking.

A cane or walker properly fit for an individual results in the handgrip of the device being level with the user's wrist crease when the user is standing with arms at the sides. The fit can also be checked by ensuring that the elbow is bent approximately twenty to thirty degrees when the user stands and holds the device. (For individuals with decreased leg strength, walkers may be fit a bit lower to allow greater use of the arms.) A combination of these methods should be used to check for proper fit, since individuals sometimes have proportionally long or short arms. In addition, the device should be measured with the user in the footwear normally worn, since shoe height will affect the fit.

The choice of device should be made considering the user's needs and abilities. Canes are more functional on stairs and in confined areas, and they are easier to transport than are walkers. Canes do not provide as much support, however, and are not recommended for use with any weight-bearing restrictions, such as after total knee or hip replacement surgery. Walkers offer maximal support and stability, but mobility is somewhat restricted because of their size. Walkers are often prescribed for mobility with weight-bearing restrictions, with the goal of advancing to a cane or another assistive device as healing progresses.

Several styles of canes and walkers are available, and the choice should depend on the user's needs and abilities. Standard *J* canes are inexpensive; most are wooden and can be cut to the proper height. They are not the most stable choice, however, since the user's hand is not directly over the foot of the cane. Offset canes have a bend in the shaft that places the user's hand over the cane's foot, thereby increasing stability. Often, these canes are also adjustable in length and, therefore, can be used with varying footwear or by different individuals. Quad canes have four feet and offer the most

Some elderly people find that the added stability provided by walkers allows them to remain more active. (James L. Shaffer)

stability. They are more difficult to use, however, and can be very unstable if all four feet do not come in contact with the ground with each step.

Standard walkers are the most inexpensive type, but they are relatively awkward and difficult to transport since they do not fold. This problem is solved with folding walkers, but these devices can collapse if they are not set up properly. Wheeled varieties are available for individuals without the arm strength to pick up and advance a walker with each step. They also allow increased speed and provide good stability if used with brakes that activate when the user pushes down with each step.

—*Mary Ann Holbein-Jenny*

See also Balance disorders; Bone changes and disorders; Foot disorders; Hip replacement; Injuries among the elderly; Mobility problems; Osteoporosis; Safety issues; Transportation issues; Wheelchair use.

CARDIOVASCULAR DISEASE. *See* **HEART DISEASE.**

CAREGIVING

RELEVANT ISSUES: Family, health and medicine, sociology

SIGNIFICANCE: As the population of the United States ages, caregiving for older family members becomes an increasingly common experience for spouses, adult children, and other family members

Two population factors have resulted in a greatly increased need for elder care in the United States. First, the population has aged. Life expectancy has increased dramatically, and the birth rate has decreased. As a result, the proportion of people aged sixty-five and older in the population is expected to be over 22 percent by 2050, up from about 4 percent in 1900 and about 13 percent in 1990. Second, the fastest-growing age group in the United States is people age eighty-five and over. These elders, the old-old, are most likely to have multiple chronic health problems and to need help with daily living.

Contrary to popular belief, the majority of older people are not warehoused in nursing homes. On a given day, only 5 percent of people over sixty-five are in such institutions. Families provide the vast majority of care for older members. Estimates vary, but approximately 70 to 80 percent of care for impaired older people is given by family members.

Relatives give more care than in past centuries. There is a misconception that, in days gone by, older people enjoyed special protection within the family no matter what their health status. Social historians have shown that this is not true. Much more family care is given now than in the past, probably because, between the eighteenth century and the early twentieth century, families could not easily afford to support dependent people. In the agricultural societies of those times, all household members were expected to work. When people became ill or old, they were often forced to leave.

DEFINING CAREGIVING

Researchers often evaluate the extent of care given by asking questions about activities of daily living. This way of defining caregiving has become so common that there are standard lists of activities. They include most of the tasks an adult must accomplish to be independent, such as preparing foods, doing laundry, getting around by car or public transportation, and doing light cleaning. If an older person needs help with even one of these tasks, their helper is defined as a caregiver. In addition, there are personal tasks required of independent adults, such as bathing, dressing, and taking medication. If help is needed for one such task, again the helper is typically defined as a caregiver. Help with either of these groups of tasks is what commonly defines caregiving. However, both researchers and family caregivers know that much more is involved.

Caregiving often includes social or emotional support, financial aid, and spiritual support. Caregivers commonly accompany the care recipients through many kinds of losses and provide advice, comfort, and security. For example, loss of the ability to drive a car is a shock and a disabling event in most areas of the United States, where driving is recognized as a sign of adulthood. In this case, a caregiver is often called upon to take over transportation and chores in addition to comforting the spouse or parent who may be upset and depressed about the loss of his or her independence.

The list of chores a family caregiver might be required to accomplish is very long because caregiving situations change and needs change. In addition to the actual caregiving, there may be communication tasks such as talking with doctors, home care services, family members, and friends. Often, a number of phone calls are required to establish and maintain a service, such as home health aid help with bathing the older person. Family members who live at a distance may want to hear detailed accounts of the elder's condition. Friends, coworkers, neighbors, and church members typically contact the primary caregiver for information about the elder.

There is a great variety in caregiver-care recipient living situations. However, caregiving is not defined by the caregiver and care recipient living together because coresidence does not necessarily mean there is caregiving. Naturally, most spouse caregivers live with the care recipient. Although sometimes the adult children who give care live with parents or take parents into their homes, much caregiving is done for parents who live alone or together with spouses. Even when a person is living in an assisted-living apartment or a nursing home, family members often still contribute a lot of time and work to caregiving. This is the reason that caregiving is almost always defined by the tasks done for the older individual rather than the family's living arrangement.

DEFINING THE CAREGIVER

There is a hierarchy of caregiving, an order in which family and friends accept the role of caregiver. If an ill elderly person's spouse is available, he or she is most likely to fill the caring role. An adult child is likely to help, or, if a spouse is unavailable, a daughter or son usually becomes caregiver. Siblings follow daughters and sons as likely caregivers. However, the overwhelming majority of family members giving care are spouses and adult children. Older sibling relationships are more often based on companionship than helping with care. Grandchildren, nieces and nephews, and friends and neighbors also provide help, but not usually primary care. These groups are more often involved with giving extra help to caregivers of old-old rather than young-old (those aged sixty-five to seventy-nine) people. The young-old tend to be more active and have fewer needs. Finally, for the most impaired elders, paid services may be included in their care. Workers who are paid for caring services are known as formal care providers. Home health aids, bath nurses, and social workers who develop caregiving plans are examples of formal providers. Again, the majority of caregivers are spouses and adult children.

Most elder care is given by women. They may be spouses, daughters, or daughters-in-law. This is not to say that husbands and sons do not give care. Many husbands are busy primary caregivers. Because older women have a longer life expectancy than men and also tend to marry men who are a few years older, however, many are widowed and have no spouse to fulfill the caregiver role. Only one of three older women is living with a spouse. Thus, the majority of spouse caregivers are wives. Sons typically care for older parents if no daughter is available. Also, sons often help the primary caregiver with specific tasks, such as balancing a checkbook, mowing the lawn, or maintaining the car.

The fact that so many female family members, especially daughters, are caregivers has led to the term "women in the middle," which refers to "sandwich generation" women caught between the demands of children, jobs, and aging parents. There is no question that the great proportion of middle-aged women in the workforce has diminished the number of women available to be caregivers, but research shows that many caregiving women work and often arrange their jobs around that role.

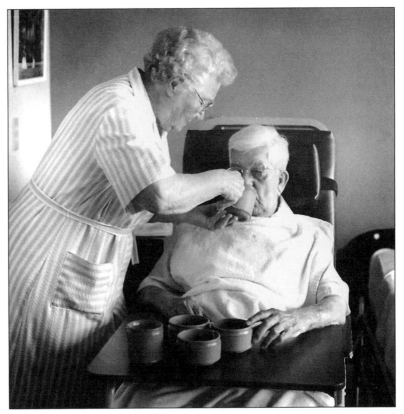

Most elder care takes place within families and is provided by spouses and children, usually wives and daughters. (James L. Shaffer)

Women in their fifties are more likely to have old-old parents with many needs. The children of women in their fifties are commonly young adults who have left or are preparing to leave the parental home. Therefore, women with the oldest parents usually have older children who often share the demands of giving care. In general, women in their thirties and forties who have younger children are likely to have young-old parents who need less help. Also, some researchers have noted that many midlife women say that providing care for parents is fulfilling and that they enjoy having several important roles in their lives, such as careers and parent care. Caregiving often fills the nurturing role given up when children are grown.

A number of factors have a potential for affecting caregiving daughters and daughters-in-law and changing the situations described here. First, couples are having children later in life. Thus, they may still be raising children when their parents have great need of help. Second, compared with earlier times, many more adult children return home to live after college or divorce. This is likely to put some additional pressure on midlife caregiving daughters. Third, health researchers have been discovering a new phenomenon: increasing rates of chronic illness among the young-old. This suggests more need for care of people who are only in their sixties or seventies.

CARE RECIPIENT IMPAIRMENT AND CAREGIVER BURDEN

Older family members with care needs may be physically or cognitively (mentally) impaired, or both. Research shows cognitive impairment is often more difficult for caregivers. Care recipients with cognitive impairment are likely to be institutionalized earlier than care recipients with only physical limitations. With physical health problems, the spouse or adult child still has the companionship of the loved one. Particularly for spouses, cognitive impairment means stressful full-time caring and isolation from friends and family.

Alzheimer's disease is an example of serious cognitive impairment that affects many older people, especially in the old-old group. Alzheimer's victims provide a constant challenge. The disease disrupts normal waking and sleeping patterns, and the caregiver may not be able to rest at night. Also, caregivers of some Alzheimer's patients must cope with caring for someone who seems to be a stranger and to be unappreciative of the care. Thus, it is not surprising that studies find family members find dealing with physical ailments easier than dealing with mental ones, even when they have a great amount of work to do.

When family members give care, there is less pressure on society and government to provide services for the elderly. Thus, much caregiving research has focused on the stresses and strains of caregiving. First, there are some problems that relate more to spouse caregivers and some that relate more to adult children. Spouses have a lot of stress relating to their own health and worries that if they become ill, the couple will need care or will go to a nursing home. Second, when spouses give care, often other family members and friends assume everything is fine and the caregiver-care recipient couple is socially isolated. Especially if they are mostly housebound, friends and family may stop including them in plans and reduce personal contact.

For adult child caregivers, stress or burden relates to time limitations, which result in conflicts with work schedules, marriages, family time, and social events. Adult children often report giving up leisure activities, social events, and time spent on themselves. The burden of caregiving is generally demonstrated in diminished participation in social events, physical health symptoms, and depression.

The burden is increased by such things as grief and role reversal. Both spouses and adult children grieve for the losses that they see their loved ones experience. Again, they grieve for lost companionship when there is cognitive impairment. Husbands may find themselves in unfamiliar territory as homemakers and nurturers, roles formerly filled by their wives. Likewise, wife caregivers may take over such tasks as home repairs. Adult children may be making decisions for and advising their parents. Reversing these roles is often difficult and disturbing to caregivers and adds to the burden of caring.

Several decades of great numbers of caregiving studies have highlighted the problems and needs of caregivers in general and of caregivers in specific situations. This has resulted in many community services. Examples include meals-on-wheels programs, which deliver low-cost or free meals to homebound elders, and adult day care centers that help working caregivers have safe, interesting environments for elders who cannot stay home alone. Another example is respite services begun by many churches and community organizations. Volunteers are trained to be friendly visitors for shut-in older people. The caregivers are then freed to have some time for themselves.

There are also caregiver support groups, some of which are specifically for Alzheimer's caregivers. Programs for supporting caregivers in their roles have been developed in rural and small-town areas, which commonly have a disproportionate number of elderly people. All such programs—such as the Area Agencies on Aging, which exist all over the United States—supplement government programs.

Finally, despite the hard work and stress involved, family members who are caregivers often report that the process enhances the quality of family relationships. Spousal relationships are often enriched by the time spent together. For example, spouse caregivers say, as couples, that they learned patience or reviewed their relationship together. Male spouse caregivers who are retired and have given up their productive work roles in the world may appreciate the sense of authority caregiving gives as they oversee household maintenance and their wives' care. Many adult children say they have renewed bonds with parents that had been either neglected or strained. Some talk about learning family history and hearing new stories from their parents' lives. Understanding the full circle of life, the meaning of families and traditions, and the ties across generations are other benefits that caregivers describe. They often say that this enriches their lives and gives them insights into parenting their own children.

Perhaps the most general positive outcome that caregivers report is the feeling of accomplishment that comes from having been helpful to their loved one. The knowledge that they have been available and that they have given a gift that was very meaningful and unique is often what they have left to keep when caregiving is over.

—*Virginia L. Smerglia*

See also Abandonment; Absenteeism; Aging: Biological, psychological, and sociocultural perspectives; Aging: Historical perspective; Alzheimer's disease; Baby boomers; Brain changes and disorders; Children of Aging Parents; Communication; Cultural views of aging; Death and dying; Death of parents; Disabilities; Elder abuse; Family relationships; Filial responsibility; Health care; Home services; Hospice; Illnesses among the elderly; Independent living; Long-term care for the elderly; Meals-on-wheels programs; Multigenerational households; Neglect; Nursing and convalescent homes; Old age; Sibling relationships; Terminal illness; Widows and widowers; Women and aging.

FOR FURTHER INFORMATION:

Butler, Robert N., and Kenzo Kiikuni, eds. *Who Is Responsible for My Old Age?* New York: Springer, 1992. An in-depth discussion of individual, family, and government responsibility for the needs of older persons by a group of experts and people in public life.

Fradkin, Louise G., and Angela Heath. *Caregiving of Older Adults.* Santa Barbara: ABC-Clio, 1992. Contains information about who provides care, as well as the stresses involved; includes a complete listing of resources for solving caregivers' problems.

Jackson, Billie. *The Caregiver's Rollercoaster.* Chicago: Loyola University Press, 1993. An experienced family caregiver uses easy-to-understand language and humor to discuss all aspects of the caregiving role.

Kaye, Lenard W., and Jeffrey S. Appelgate. *Men as Caregivers to the Elderly.* Lexington, Mass.: Lexington Books, 1990. A complete reference explaining the caregiving role as it is fulfilled by male family members.

Romaine-Davis, Ada, Jennifer Boondas, and Ayeliffe Lenihan, eds. *Encyclopedia of Home Care for the Elderly.* Westport, Conn.: Greenwood Press, 1995. This handbook for caregivers and potential caregivers includes a comprehensive list of topics related to caring for elders.

Springer, Dianne, and Timothy H. Brubaker. *Family Caregivers and Dependent Elderly.* Beverly Hills, Calif.: Sage Publications, 1991. Gerontologists discuss caregiver stresses, problems, and specific types of support caregivers need.

Thompson, Neil. *Age and Dignity: Working with Older People.* Brookfield, Vt.: Arena, Ashgate, 1995. A reader for professionals or family helpers that focuses on age-related problems and policies.

CATARACTS

RELEVANT ISSUES: Health and medicine

SIGNIFICANCE: Cataracts are a common defect of vision among the elderly in which the lens of the eye develops dark spots that interfere with the transmission of light

The human eye is the most important sense organ for people to gather information about their environment. An amazingly high 40 percent of all nerve fibers going to the brain come from the retina of the eye. Any defect or deterioration from normal vision is a serious limitation. In modern society, people with poor eyesight are greatly handicapped. Everyday activities such as reading a newspaper, driving a car, watching television, participating in sports, operating machinery, or using a computer all depend on good vision.

The formation of cataracts in the lens of the eye is a normal part of the aging process, like wrinkled skin or gray hair. The initial symptom is a gradual deterioration of vision, usually in one eye at a time. There is no known treatment other than to remove the lens surgically. After surgery, neither the lens nor the cataracts can grow back. Cataract removal is the most frequently performed surgery in the United States and gives rise to the single largest expenditure of Medicare funds.

WHAT CAUSES CATARACTS?

The front of the eyeball has a tough, transparent outer skin called the cornea. It has no blood vessels, but its many nerve cells make it sensitive to touch or irritation. Immediately behind the cornea is a layer of clear, aqueous fluid that carries oxygen and nutrients for cell metabolism. Next comes the colored portion, the iris, with a variable-size opening, or pupil, at its center that regulates the amount of light entering the eye. The pupil has no color but appears black, like the entrance to a cave. Behind the pupil is the lens of the eye, enclosed by an elastic capsule. The lens is not a simple homogeneous fluid but has an internal structure that continues to grow throughout the life of an individual. New cells originate at the front surface of the lens, just inside the capsule membrane. These cells divide and grow into fibers that migrate toward the middle of the lens. The structure of the eye lens has been compared to the layers of an onion, with the oldest cells at the center. The older protein molecules in the middle are more rigid than those in the outer part of the lens. By the age of forty, in most people the firm center has enlarged until the lens has lost much of its elasticity. The eye eventually loses its power of accommodation, and glasses are needed for near and distant vision.

The mechanism by which cataracts form in the lens is not yet clearly understood. Like the loss of accommodation, it is a normal part of the aging process. One proposed biochemical explanation is the Maillard reaction, in which protein molecules and glucose combine when heated to form a brown product. The Maillard reaction is responsible for the browning of bread or cookies during baking. The same process is thought to occur even at body temperature, but very slowly over a period of years. Some scientists have theorized that wrinkled skin, hardening of the arteries, and other normal features of aging may be caused by this reaction. The biochemistry of aging is an active area of research, in which the deterioration of the eye is only one example. Some studies have suggested that diet, exercise, and a healthy lifestyle can delay (but not prevent) the onset of cataracts.

The most common cataracts are those attributed to aging, called senile cataracts. (This has nothing to do with the use of the term "senility" to describe declining mental ability.) Secondary cataracts can develop in special circumstances such as exposure to X rays or other ionizing radiation. Certain medications such as cortisone, which is used for arthritis treatment, increase the risk of cataracts. A diet deficient in protein, a frequent occurrence in developing countries, has been associated with cataract formation. A blow to the eye from a sports injury or other accident can lead to a cataract. Diabetics are more likely to develop cataracts than the general public. Some studies have suggested that electric shock, ultraviolet rays, and environmental pollutants may be other causes. Some babies are born with cataracts. These congenital cataracts are frequently associated with the mother having had German measles (rubella) during the first three months of the pregnancy. Some ophthalmologists believe that early onset of cataracts runs in families, suggesting a genetic influence, but the evidence is not conclusive. What causes cataracts is much less understood than how to treat them surgically.

DIAGNOSIS AND TREATMENT

The most common symptom of cataracts is a loss of clear vision that cannot be corrected with eyeglasses. Cataracts are not an infection, a growth, a disease, or a film over the surface of the lens. They do not cause pain, redness, teardrops, or other discomforts of the eye. When cataracts begin to form in the lens, no medication can remove them, and they will not improve on their own. The patient's vision will continue to deteriorate as the cataracts mature, although the process may be quite slow.

Consider a typical middle-aged man who believes that his vision is getting worse. When he goes to an optometrist, he is informed that his eye examination reveals the onset of senile cataracts. He is referred to an ophthalmologist, who finds no need for surgery at this time but recommends more frequent, semiannual checkups. The patient is told that reading or other eye-straining activities will not accelerate cataract growth but that brighter lighting will help him to see more clearly. Eventually, the patient's vision may deteriorate until his ability to read or to drive a car is seriously impaired, and surgery is indicated.

The basic steps in cataract surgery are to cut a small slit in the cornea, remove the lens, insert a plastic lens, and close the incision in the cornea with a fine needle and thread. The surgeon performs the operation while looking through a microscope whose focus controls are operated using foot pedals so that both hands are free.

Two types of cataract extraction are performed. The intracapsular method removes the lens along with its capsule. The advantage of this method is that no part of the lens is left behind to cause possible infection later. The disadvantage is that the incision at the edge of the cornea must be fairly large, requiring five to ten stitches. The lens is rather slippery, so the extraction is usually done with a cold temperature cryoprobe, rather than with forceps. The lens freezes against the probe

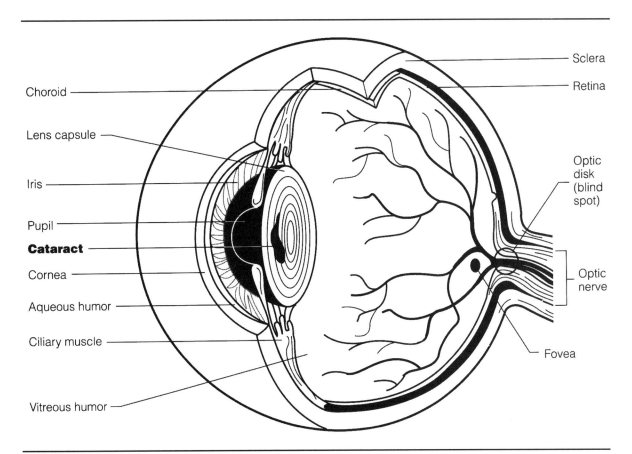

Cataracts are dark regions in the lens of the eye that lead gradually to obscured vision and even blindness. (Hans & Cassidy, Inc.)

and can be pulled out in one piece. A second method of cataract surgery is called extracapsular extraction. An ultrasonic probe is used to break the lens into small fragments, which are then suctioned out. The main advantage is that the incision can be quite small because the lens is brought out in fragments. This method requires specialized training because surgeons must learn to operate the microscope, the ultrasonic generator, and the suction apparatus all with their feet.

After the eye lens has been extracted, an artificial lens is inserted. The implant is made of clear plastic and is about the size of an aspirin tablet. Two spring loops embedded in the plastic are used to center the implant and to keep it in place permanently.

While recuperating from surgery, the patient is instructed to avoid strenuous exercise and to protect the eye from any hard contact. Normally there is little pain, although some eye irritation should be expected during the healing process. The plastic implant lens has a fixed focal length with no power of accommodation. It works like a box camera that gives a sharp image only at one set distance, while near and far objects are blurry. After the eye has fully healed, the patient can be fitted with prescription glasses.

All operations have some risk, however, and a small percentage of cataract surgeries lead to complications such as a detached retina, glaucoma caused by scar tissue, and hemorrhaging from the retina. Fortunately, such problems are rare. In the United States, more than one million cataract surgeries are performed annually, with a success rate greater than 95 percent. —*Hans G. Graetzer*

See also Aging: Biological, psychological, and sociocultural perspectives; Aging process; Nearsightedness; Reading glasses; Sensory changes; Vision changes and disorders.

FOR FURTHER INFORMATION:

Anshel, Jeffrey. *Healthy Eyes, Better Vision.* Los Angeles: Body Press, 1990.
Eden, John. *The Physician's Guide to Cataracts, Glaucoma, and Other Eye Problems.* Yonkers, N.Y.: Consumer Reports Books, 1992.
Houseman, William. "The Day the Light Returned." *New Choices for Retirement Living* 32 (April, 1992).
Kelman, Charles D. *Cataracts: What You Must Know About Them.* New York: Crown, 1982.
Rubman, Robert H., and Howard Rothman. *Future Vision: Space-Age Techniques to Save Your Sight.* New York: Dodd, Mead, 1987.
Shulman, Julius. *Cataracts: The Complete Guide—from Diagnosis to Recovery—for Patients and Families.* New York: Simon & Schuster, 1984.
Van Heyningen, Ruth. "What Happens to the Human Lens in Cataracts." *Scientific American* 233 (December, 1975).

CENTENARIANS

RELEVANT ISSUES: Biology, demographics, health and medicine, sociology

SIGNIFICANCE: Studies of people one hundred years and older suggest that lifestyle, individual health choices, and heredity all play a role in determining longevity

Reliable information on the ages of centenarians is most readily available in countries with a national birth registration system. Even where these systems exist, however, researchers can encounter a variety of data problems. In the absence of these records, investigators must use such sources as family bibles, marriage certificates, school and war records, and census records. Despite these difficulties, demographers have established that in a number of countries, including the United States, mortality rates of those aged one hundred and older have been falling since about 1950. Consequently, centenarian status is less rare than in the past. Reasons for this change continue to be debated, but they may include income and health care advantages enjoyed by centenarians as compared to younger age groups.

Census information taken in a particular year cannot be considered adequate verification of age because people do not necessarily tell the truth. Inflation of ages, typically starting around seventy, is not uncommon. People may round their ages up, causing "heaping" at numbers such as 90, 100, and 105. Reasons can vary from laziness to vanity. Moreover, extremely old people are rewarded with at least modest recognition and approval in most areas of the world; in some countries claiming a high proportion of centenarians, they are feted and considered a source of national pride. Men are especially likely to say that they are older than they are. It is more difficult to check men's ages against those of their children; women who have children may choose not to claim extra years, even in societies where age is revered, because they know their claims may seem unlikely upon examination of their children's birth dates. It may be plausible, for example, that a man fathered children between the ages of 60 and 100; it is much less likely that a woman who claims to be 115 and has a 50-year-old child gave birth at age 65.

For these reasons, centenarian age claims require verification. Where such verification exists, the female-to-male ratio of centenarians is typically about two to one. If a region or nation claims to have a predominance of male centenarians, the assertion is to be doubted. In the following three studies, researchers made significant attempts to verify the accuracy of centenarians' age claims.

ABKHAZIAN STUDY

One body of research on centenarians, emanating from the 1960's and 1970's, comes from the Abkhazian Institute of Gerontology. Abkhazia was a region of the Republic of Georgia in the Soviet Union before its breakup. Possible Abkhazian centenarians were identified through the census, and institute team members attempted to verify ages during visits to the centenarians' homes. Centenarians were interviewed and given physical examinations.

Abkhazians valued old age and treated elders with reverence. Consequently, people looked forward to becoming old. Family members sought the counsel of elders, and elders participated in village and regional political life. Women gained new freedoms after the menopause.

The arduous life in the Caucasian mountains appeared to benefit their cardiovascular systems. As centenarians, the majority continued to work, though for fewer hours per day. They never labored to exhaustion, and they exhibited a dislike of hurry. They believed that eating quickly was impolite, as was eating too much. About 70 percent of their diets consisted of vegetables and dairy products. Fruits, grain, and nuts made up most of the remainder. They ate meat only occasionally, and they exhibited a strong preference for fresh foods. The combination of heavy physical exertion and healthful diet led to low body weight. Though tobacco was a local crop, few of the centenarians had ever smoked. Some long-lived Abkhazians drank small amounts of alcohol daily and on festive occasions.

Most of the Abkhazian centenarians had been married, and many had taken second or third spouses. As centenarians, they lived with their families. Half of the centenarians were able to take care of their daily needs; the other half required assistance.

The region was beset by civil war in the 1990's. It is possible that records have been destroyed, which would make further study of centenarians difficult. The war may have increased the mortality of centenarians. The disruption of stable community

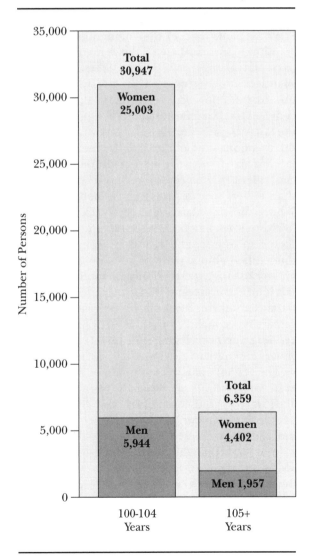

Centenarians in the United States, 1990

Source: U.S. Bureau of the Census.

life does not benefit long-lived people, who depend on community support.

GEORGIA CENTENARIAN STUDY

A U.S. study in the state of Georgia began in 1988. It compared forty-eight centenarians with fifty-seven octogenarians and sixty people in their sixties. Of the 165 participants, 63 were men and 102 women, and 119 were white and 46 black. These are overall totals; some of the conclusions are based on smaller numbers. The state of Georgia did not begin to collect birth records until the 1920's, so ages were confirmed through relatives and one other source such as a family Bible. In some cases, secondary government sources such as Social Security records were used.

Participants lived in the community and were cognitively intact. Many of the centenarians said they had always been healthy. They consumed slightly more vegetables than the two younger groups, but none were vegetarians. About 52 percent had used vitamin and mineral supplements in the last year, with more women and whites likely to do so. Among the centenarians' less healthful habits were high intakes of total and saturated fat. African American men consumed more fat and sugar than either African American women or whites. Whites ate breakfast regularly; blacks were less likely to do so. Few of these centenarians had ever dieted to lose weight. Blacks consumed less sodium than whites, perhaps because they are at greater risk for hypertension and may have limited salt intake as a precaution. On average, the centenarians drank one alcoholic beverage a week. The researchers concluded that the African American centenarians had a higher nutritional risk than the white centenarians and were in poorer health.

The centenarians were found to be more dominant and less conformist than the younger groups. They were also quite suspicious, which in studies of people in "younger" old age predicts increased mortality. They scored lower on intelligence and memory tests than the comparison groups in their sixties and eighties. The centenarians with higher fluid intelligence were better able to manage everyday needs. Intelligence predicted memory and mental health, with those having higher intelligence scores having lower levels of depression.

The centenarians were more likely than those in the younger groups to use religion as a coping device. It was unclear whether this pattern had developed as they aged or if they had been religious throughout their lives.

BEARD STUDY

Belle Boone Beard began a study of centenarians in the United States around 1940 and collected information until the late 1970's. She found centenarians in every state and in Puerto Rico and the U.S. Virgin Islands. Age verification was made through a wide variety of sources, including birth, death, and marriage certificates; Social Security records; and slave deeds.

Lifelong health was one attribute of most of the centenarians in this study. Some had major illnesses, but they were in the minority. Most had never been to a doctor, and some attributed their longevity partly to this fact. Some were in wheelchairs at the time of the study, but most remained active. Generally, they were slim or average in weight. Only a few had smoked tobacco. Slightly more than half used alcohol, having typically one drink a day.

A majority had a grade-school education or less. Most considered themselves to be middle class. A few were destitute, and ten were millionaires. (Information on actual incomes was not published.) Most had strong work ethics, and many had engaged in hard physical labor for much of their lives. A majority remained active but had altered their work patterns to suit their current capacities. Many considered hard work to be one reason for their longevity.

More than 90 percent said that religion was very important to them. Almost one-half attended church services at least once a month; most had not become religious in their old age but had been religious throughout their lives.

Friendship was important to the majority of these centenarians, and many were involved in community organizations. Most valued romance and marriage. Many had large families and enjoyed family gatherings.

FACTORS PREDICTING CENTENARIANISM

Though the subject remains under debate, these studies point to some likely causes of extreme longevity. The majority of centenarians have been and remain physically active. Their diets vary significantly, but centenarians generally eat more fruits and vegetables than those less long-lived. Most maintain body weight at slender-to-average levels; obesity is rare among those living to be one hundred. Living in a locale that reveres the elderly appears to encourage longevity, but strong social bonds with family and friends may offset the less positive attitudes toward aging found in societies such as the United States. The religiosity of most people living to one hundred or beyond is also marked. Finally, the influence of genetics cannot be dismissed. Women clearly have an advantage. Having long-lived parents adds an average of three extra years to the life span, and many, though not all, centenarians say that they have been healthy all of their lives.

—Roxanne Friedenfels

With the rise in life expectancies for both men and women, the United States has seen an increase in the number of people reaching one hundred. (James L. Shaffer)

See also Aging process; Antiaging treatments; Cross-linkage theory of aging; Cultural views of aging; Demographics; Free radical theory of aging; Life expectancy; Longevity research; Nutrition; Old age; Social ties.

FOR FURTHER INFORMATION:

Adler, Lynn Peters. *Centenarians: The Bonus Years.* Santa Fe, N.Mex.: Health Press, 1995. Centenarians from throughout the United States recall stories from their lives.

Beard, Belle Boone. *Centenarians: The New Generation.* New York: Greenwood Press, 1991. The outcome of almost forty years of research, this book discusses numerous case studies of centenarians.

Buono, Marirosa Dello, et al. "Quality of Life and Longevity: A Study of Centenarians." *Age and Ageing* 27, no. 2 (March, 1998). A study assessing the quality of life of thirty-eight Italian centenarians in comparison with two groups of younger "old age" adults.

Georgakas, Dan. *The Methuselah Factors: Learning from the World's Longest Living People.* Chicago: Academy Chicago, 1995. A readable discussion of longevity studies. Examines changes that individuals can make to increase their life span.

Poon, Leonard W., ed. *The Georgia Centenarian Study.* Amityville, N.Y.: Baywood, 1992. Summarizes mostly quantitative findings of a study of 165 community-dwelling centenarians in the U.S. state of Georgia.

CENTER FOR THE STUDY OF AGING AND HUMAN DEVELOPMENT

DATE: Founded in 1955

RELEVANT ISSUES: Biology, health and medicine, sociology

SIGNIFICANCE: This center conducts research into aging, educates professionals on the aging process, and provides services to older adults

This research center, known in full as the Duke University Center for the Study of Aging and Human Development, is located at Duke University in Durham, North Carolina. Founded in 1955, the center was designated one of five regional resource centers on aging by the United States Public Health Service in 1957.

In 1956, the center began the Duke Longitudinal Studies, a twenty-year project to study the physical, mental, social, and economic status of about eight hundred older adults. This project, which documented the ability of most older adults to age well, won the 1983 Sandoz International Prize for multidisciplinary research in aging. In 1975, the Older Americans Resources and Services Program developed the first comprehensive technique for assessing functional impairment in the elderly. The center continues to conduct research on the biological, medical, and social aspects of aging. In addition to research, it provides education on the aging process to physicians and other health professionals, social workers, psychologists, and undergraduate students.

In 1967, the center opened the Geriatric Evaluation and Treatment Center to provide medical care to older adults throughout the southeastern United States. Other services provided to the community include the Duke Family Support Program, which assists those who care for older adults with chronic illnesses, including Alzheimer's disease. In 1988, the Center for the Study of Aging and Human Development established the Duke Long-Term Care Resources Program, which assists the state of North Carolina in developing and implementing public policies involving the long-term care of older adults. This program also maintains an archive of information on long-term care issues and manages the Aging at Home Program, a community-based long-term care initiative.   —*Rose Secrest*

See also Advocacy; Aging: Biological, psychological, and sociocultural perspectives; Geriatrics and gerontology; Home services; Long-term care for the elderly.

CHANGE: WOMEN, AGING, AND THE MENOPAUSE, THE

AUTHOR: Germaine Greer
DATE: Published in 1991
RELEVANT ISSUES: Biology, culture, health and medicine, values
SIGNIFICANCE: Greer's account of the menopause addresses a much-misunderstood and mistreated aspect of a significant phase in the lives of women

Germaine Greer, a native of Australia, made her literary debut with the publication of *The Female Eunuch* (1971) four years after she received a Ph.D. from Oxford University. That book and subsequent books by Greer examined the social, psychological, and political restraints placed on women. *The Change: Women, Aging, and the Menopause* explores the physical and psychic stresses that women face when they undergo the adjustments associated with the combination of aging and the cessation of ovulation.

Greer's approach to the topic was prompted both by her long commitment to understanding cultural restraints on women and by her personal experience with the impact of the menopause. The book contains seventeen chapters and more than four hundred pages of text and notes. Her research includes literary as well as medical sources, and she uses both an anthropological and a historical approach to the subject. Her goal is to educate an audience of women who are either unaware or afraid of the changes associated with the menopause. She notes that in some primitive societies, older women past the stage of childbearing were held in high regard but that in modern societies, where the emphasis for women has been to be young, physically attractive, and capable of reproduction, "the change" has signaled a time when a woman is no longer a cultural or social asset.

In the past, women going through the menopause, Greer notes, were sometimes told that the resulting physical changes were only in their imagination, should be hidden from others, or could be made to go away if they followed the advice given by the medical profession. This advice, according to Greer, usually was not of much assistance. In the past (sometimes the not-too-distant past), women were told that such activities as bloodletting; bombardment with X rays; electrogynecology; treatment with special herbs; abstinence from coffee, tea, and chocolate; hypnosis; or the use of special oils would cure them of the physical changes experienced during the menopause. In the chapter titled "Medical Ignorance," Greer suggests that hormone replacement therapy (HRT) is an attempt by the male medical and pharmaceutical institutions to convince women that they can remain forever feminine and attractive. She admits that HRT has some advantages but believes that the premise on which it is based should make women as suspicious of its value as previous therapies.

Greer argues that the menopause and its debilities can be an asset if women will accept that they no longer need to be bound by the false definitions that they have allowed to be given of themselves. Aging, and the changes associated with it, Greer asserts, can be liberating rather than debilitating. —*Robert L. Patterson*

See also Aging process; Beauty; Estrogen replacement therapy; Menopause; Reproductive changes, disabilities, and dysfunctions; Women and aging.

CHILDLESSNESS

RELEVANT ISSUES: Death, demographics, family

SIGNIFICANCE: Older adults who are childless may face a number of difficulties that those with children do not, include loneliness, dependence on nonfamily members for care and financial support, and narrower social networks in old age

Gerontologists have long been interested in the role that family plays in the aging process. Family members have been shown to be instrumental in providing a wide variety of services and support for older family members. While spouses are the most likely people to provide social support for older adults, adult children have been viewed as being particularly important, as they are the second most likely to provide assistance, both financial and otherwise, to aging parents. They are seen as a "natural" support system. The adage that "your children will take care of you in your old age" is true to some degree. Approximately 20 percent of older people, however, do not have adult children.

TYPES OF CHILDLESSNESS

Social demographers and family sociologists have discussed a number of ways through which older adults would become childless. First, there are those couples who made conscious decisions

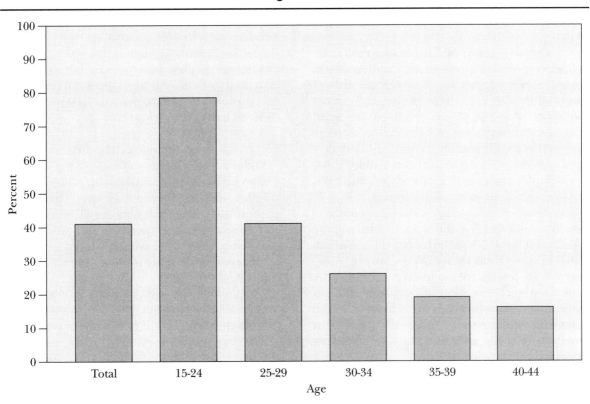

Childlessness Among American Women in 1992

Source: U.S. Bureau of the Census.

not to have children, the so-called voluntarily childless couples. The decision not to bear children is made for a number of reasons, including career considerations, a desire to focus on the marital partner, personal issues (such as the freedom to pursue hobbies and other interests), and questions about one's suitability for parenthood. Antinatalist forces or institutions in society that discourage people from having children also play a role. About 5 percent of all married couples consciously choose to be child-free. The number is three times higher among college graduates.

A second reason for childlessness is the postponement of childbearing until it becomes too late for the woman to conceive. The extent to which this occurs is unknown. The third type of childlessness results from infertility, a condition that affects some 15 to 20 percent of couples. New reproductive technologies have increased the probabilities that a woman will conceive, but a substantial fraction are not successful. Of couples experiencing infertility, a small percentage adopt, but most remain childless into their older years. Finally, there are those older adults whose children die before the parents reach their older years.

CONSEQUENCES OF CHILDLESSNESS

The conventional wisdom on childlessness in the older years suggests that those who are without adult children are much more likely to suffer from a number of social, physical, and psychological maladies. Although there is some truth to the contention that childlessness in old age has some negative consequences, it is also a fact that older childless couples and individuals cope with this situation in unique and creative ways.

It is also true that having children does not necessarily ensure that one will not suffer from these problems. The quality of the parent-child relationship is of critical importance in terms of the consequences of having adult children in the older years. That is, if the relationship was contentious in the younger years, then it is likely to be so in the older years and thus not provide the buffer against some of the social and psychological challenges presented by the aging process.

PHYSICAL AND SOCIAL HEALTH

There is some evidence that the overall physical health of older adults without children is worse than those with them. There is also some indication that older childless women, especially those from racial and ethnic minorities, suffer poorer health, but then older women as a group have more health problems than do men. Part of the reason for this is that women tend to live longer than men do and thus to be single. In some cases, this longer life means that they outlive their children.

Child-free elderly have fewer social contacts than do those with children. This is especially true for those with health problems. However, when marital status is taken into account, a somewhat different pattern emerges. Unmarried childless older adults have more interactions with friends and neighbors than do married childless adults. It may be that the married child-free couples focus more on each other, thus limiting other social interaction. In contrast, the unmarried realize that they may need a support network at some point in their lives and so work actively to develop and sustain such a network. Childless elderly women are more likely than men to develop "kin-like" relationships, especially with other older women, but they are also at greater risk of institutionalization. Another aspect of social relationships is marital satisfaction. Middle-aged and older childless couples report higher levels of marital satisfaction than do those with children. Nearly all couples report greater levels of marital satisfaction after the children have left home.

PSYCHOLOGICAL HEALTH

Older adults without children do not exhibit a greater incidence of mental health problems. Specifically, childless elders do not have higher levels of depression or other functional disorders. Some evidence suggests that those who are childless and widowed have overall lower feelings of well-being, but that may result more from poor health and isolation.

The great advantage of having children seems to lie in whether the older adults are emotionally close to their children. Those without them compensate by developing other social networks to sustain them in the older years. However, few social programs exist that address the needs of those who have not developed those networks or who have lost them to death. Older women are particularly vulnerable in this regard. —*David Redburn*

See also Biological clock; Caregiving; Cohabitation; Death of a child; Family relationships; Friendship; Infertility; Marriage; Singlehood; Social ties.

FOR FURTHER INFORMATION:

Cantor, M. H., and V. Little. "Aging and Social Care." In *Handbook of Aging*, edited by Robert H. Binstock and Ethel Shanas. 2d ed. New York: Van Nostrand Reinhold, 1985.

Chappell, N. "Living Arrangements and Sources of Caring." *Journals of Gerontology* 46, no. 1 (1991).

Choi-Nmakea, G. "Patterns and Determinants of Social Service Utilization: Comparison of the Childless Elderly and Elderly Parents Living with or Apart from Their Children." *The Gerontologist* 34 (1994).

Himes, C. L. "Future Caregivers: Projected Family Structures of Older People." *Journals of Gerontology* 47, no. 1 (1992).

Hobbs, F. B., and B. C. Damon. *Sixty-five Plus in the United States*. Washington, D.C.: U.S. Bureau of the Census, 1996.

CHILDREN OF AGING PARENTS

DATE: Founded in 1977

RELEVANT ISSUES: Family, health and medicine, law, recreation

SIGNIFICANCE: Children of Aging Parents is a national organization that provides assistance and numerous resource services to caregivers of elderly persons

Begun in Levittown, Pennsylvania, Children of Aging Parents (CAPS) is a charitable organization that assists the caregivers of the elderly with information, referrals, and support. The organization also works to heighten public awareness that the health of family caregivers is essential to ensure quality care of the growing U.S. elderly population. The idea for CAPS evolved from the informal sharing of problems by several neighbors who were caring for their elderly parents and who discovered they had similar needs, concerns, and limitations. CAPS was incorporated as a nonprofit organization in 1980. CAPS offers advice and answers to questions and issues about the health and care of the elderly and also provides numerous resource assistance services. Specific information provided by CAPS includes phone numbers and names of nursing homes, retirement communities, and independent-living facilities; home care agencies; elder-law attorneys; elder day care centers; medical insurance providers; respite care; assisted-living residences; and state and area agencies on aging.

Children of Aging Parents also writes, collects, and disseminates fact sheets on various topics related to the health and well-being of elderly persons and their caregivers. It publishes a bimonthly newsletter for caregivers of the elderly and arranges conferences and workshops on issues affecting caregivers and professionals who work with the elderly. CAPS further provides information on new products and seeks to improve the public understanding of caregiving and aging issues through broadcast and print media. For nominal fees, representatives from the CAPS speakers bureau present lectures and workshops on aging and elder care issues to civic clubs, church groups, and companies. Moreover, CAPS refers caregivers of the elderly to appropriate support groups in various cities throughout the United States and encourages the formation of new CAPS-affiliated groups.   —*Shirley Rhodes Nealy*

See also Advocacy; Caregiving; Death of parents; Family relationships; Home services; Hospice; Housing; Independent living; Medical insurance; Nursing and convalescent homes; Retirement communities; Senior citizen centers.

CHOLESTEROL

RELEVANT ISSUES: Health and medicine

SIGNIFICANCE: Cholesterol is a fatlike substance found in certain foods and in the human body; blood levels increase with age and are associated with heart disease

The body needs cholesterol for a variety of purposes. It is a component of cell membranes, for example, and is needed for the production of bile and certain hormones (estrogen, testosterone, and adrenal hormones). It is a component of brain and nerve cells.

Cholesterol circulates in the blood attached to proteins called lipoproteins. Major lipoproteins include chylomicrons, which carry digested and absorbed dietary fats in the blood; very low-density lipoproteins (VLDLs); low-density lipoproteins

(LDLs), which are also called "bad" cholesterol; and high-density lipoproteins (HDLs), also called "good" cholesterol because HDLs seem to have protective functions.

The liver manufactures about half of the cholesterol needed by the body; the rest comes from foods. Dietary sources of cholesterol include animal fats and oils such as egg yolk, whole milk, butter, cream, cheeses, ice cream, sour cream, lard, and meats, especially fatty meats. Dietary cholesterol raises LDLs and total cholesterol in the blood, but to a lesser extent than foods high in saturated fatty acids. Saturated fats are found in many of the same foods as cholesterol as well as in some vegetable oils, including coconut, palm, and palm kernel oils.

Despite the body's need for cholesterol, excessive amounts over long periods of time can accumulate in blood vessels, increasing the risk of atherosclerosis, coronary artery disease, or carotid artery disease. These increase the risk of heart attack or stroke. The American Heart Association recommends a blood cholesterol level of 200 milligrams per deciliter or less to lower the risk of heart disease. Elevated levels of LDLs increase the risk the most and should be below 130 milligrams per deciliter in the general population.

Blood cholesterol levels increase with age, especially LDL levels. Cholesterol levels are generally higher in men than in women until women reach the menopause, when their levels begin to increase. For both men and women, heart disease is the number one cause of death in the United States.

Both people with elevated blood cholesterol levels and the general population are advised to reduce their consumption of cholesterol (300 milligrams daily or less), of total fat (30 percent of dietary calories or less), of saturated fat (8 to 10 percent of total calories), and trans fats (or transfatty acids) in hydrogenated foods such as margarines and shortenings. One should choose lean cuts of meats with the fat trimmed, limit meat portions to 6 ounces daily, choose low-fat dairy products, use small amounts of monounsaturated vegetable oils such as olive and canola oils, and eat increased amounts of fruits, vegetables, and whole grains.

Reading the nutrition labels on foods to learn the grams of total fat, saturated fat, and cholesterol the foods contain is helpful in selecting appropriate foods. Increasing exercise, losing weight if overweight, and stopping smoking are also recommended for those with high levels of blood cholesterol. In addition, some people with high levels of blood cholesterol may need to take lipid-lowering drugs.
—*Betsy B. Holli*

See also Arteriosclerosis; Heart attacks; Heart disease; Malnutrition; Nutrition; Obesity; Strokes.

CIRCADIAN RHYTHMS

RELEVANT ISSUES: Biology, death, health and medicine

SIGNIFICANCE: Circadian rhythms are cycles by which living things facilitate their adaptation to periodic environmental changes; disruptions in these cycles with age may contribute to an increase in various disorders

From the rotation of giant galaxies to the orbiting of electrons in atoms, cycles are the basic rhythms of the universe. On Earth, many organisms, from algae to humans, have life processes that exhibit cycles. Because of Earth's daily rotation, a particular rhythm called circadian (corresponding to the twenty-four-hour solar day) regulates such animal activities as sleep and waking. Strikingly stable, these physicochemical timing systems are intrinsic and unaffected by such extrinsic factors as temperature changes and chemical agents. These accurate biological clocks are "entrained" or locked into circadian cycles, which develop even when animals are raised from birth in nonperiodic conditions and which persist even when animals are isolated from regular light changes.

Although circadian rhythms are intrinsic, they are also programmed to keep in step with such environmental changes as light periodicity. The best known example of desynchronization of circadian rhythms is the phenomenon of jet lag, a feeling of fatigue, discomfort, and reduced efficiency caused by the failure of the body's various biological clocks to synchronize with a new local time. This malaise that jet-lagged travelers experience has similarities to some of the symptoms of malfunctioning biological clocks among the aged. Scientists have indeed discovered age-related changes in circadian rhythms, but little consensus exists about their nature. Evidence for deterioration in circadian rhythms derives principally from studies of sleep-wake rhythms in elderly humans. Older people commonly show an increased fragmentation of nocturnal sleep and increased napping during the day. Although no probative data exist that these disrupted sleep-wake patterns are caused by the arrhythmicity of biological clocks, several researchers attribute these variations to abnormalities in the circadian timing system. Indeed, some scientists speculate that aging and death are associated with the programmed decay of the body's many biological clocks.

These age-dependent changes in the circadian system have several consequences for the aged. For example, malfunctions in the circadian timing system may be causally related to the increase of depression among the elderly. Such abnormalities in primary depressives as early morning waking, disrupted nocturnal sleep, and changes in various hormonal rhythms can be debilitating, though these dissociations of physiological rhythms might emanate from many sources—illnesses, viruses, and emotional stresses, as well as from a desynchronization of circadian rhythms.

During the twentieth century, scientists made dramatic progress in understanding circadian rhythms, leading to the development of a new field, chronobiology. This improved understanding includes evidence that the circadian system changes with age and raises the question of whether biological clocks can be maintained in all of their youthful accuracy as a person ages. Data on exercise, diet, hormonal balance, and even social and emotional conditions suggest that the efficiency of circadian rhythms can be preserved, even in old age. On the other hand, those neurons within the hypothalamus of the brain that are important in the generation of circadian rhythmicity appear to be selectively lost in older people. The aging of a sixty-trillion-celled human is a very complex process, and for those scientists interested in slowing the aging process, the task is daunting. How does anyone confer immortality on cells that have inside them so many ways to live and die?

—*Robert J. Paradowski*

See also Aging process; Depression; Psychiatry, geriatric; Sleep changes and disturbances.

Cocoon

DIRECTOR: Ron Howard

CAST: Don Ameche, Hume Cronyn, Jack Gilford, Maureen Stapleton, Jessica Tandy, Gwen Verdon, Steve Guttenberg, Wilford Brimley, Brian Dennehy, Tahnee Welch, Tyrone Power, Jr.

DATE: Released in 1985

RELEVANT ISSUES: Media, values

SIGNIFICANCE: In this science-fiction/fantasy film, older adults find themselves rejuvenated by contact with alien cocoons maintained in an indoor pool

Cocoon addresses the question "What if a group of senior citizens were to discover the fountain of youth?" Aliens arrive on Earth to retrieve hibernating friends from cocoons left behind millennia ago. Once retrieved from the ocean depths, these

Hume Cronyn in a scene from the film Cocoon. (Archive Photos)

pods are placed in a specially prepared indoor pool in a mansion. Senior citizens residing at a retirement community adjacent to the mansion sneak in to take a swim and discover the rejuvenating powers of the water. After swimming in the pool, they can engage in activities long ago forgotten and find renewed life energy and spirit. Unfortunately, their revitalization costs the cocoons their needed life energy, and some of the aliens die. The remaining cocoons are returned to the ocean, and the aliens prepare to leave. In an act of generosity, however, the aliens offer to take the seniors with them to their planet, where they will stay forever rejuvenated. As one of the seniors explains to his grandson, "When we get where we're going, we'll never be sick, we won't get any older, and we won't ever die."

While the film portrays older adults engaged in life and active living, it implies that this situation results solely from the magical powers transfused through contact with the pool and cocoons. A contrast is made between those who reap the benefit of the pool and those who do not. Those who have been rejuvenated experience renewed energy, romantic interest, and an active nightlife, including break dancing; those who have not are portrayed as tired, depressed, and moving toward death. Thus, the film unintentionally supports the premise that old age is characterized by disability and dying.

Cocoon won Academy Awards for Best Supporting Actor for Don Ameche and Best Visual Effects.

—Linda M. Woolf

See also Antiaging treatments; Films; Old age; Stereotypes.

COHABITATION

RELEVANT ISSUES: Economics, family, marriage and dating, values

SIGNIFICANCE: Cohabitation between aging singles has become an increasingly viable living arrangement as economic and social pressures make marriage a more difficult lifestyle choice

Many older family members who are single as the result of the death of a spouse or divorce or because they never married are reevaluating the option of cohabitation with another single senior, often of the opposite sex. In fact, unmarried couples older than age forty-five were the fastest-growing type of household in the United States in 1995. In 1999, an estimated 370,000 men and women over age sixty-five were living together—nearly double 1980 levels.

While younger singles who live together often do so as a way to "test the waters" before marriage, many older adults look at cohabitation as a permanent arrangement that may increase or maintain economic status and avoid family conflicts. Although a relaxation of social mores against living together without marriage may contribute to the increase in cohabitation among seniors, the vast majority of those opting for this arrangement cite economic issues and pressure from family members to remain single as primary reasons to cohabit.

FINANCIAL ISSUES

The financial advantages associated with living together are frequently the most common reason for seniors to choose cohabitation over marriage. In the United States, seniors who marry can often anticipate a significant drop in combined incomes. Tax rates may increase both because of so-called marriage penalties and because the combined income puts the couple in a higher tax bracket. Social Security benefits may go down or be discontinued or taxed. Retirement benefits from a deceased or divorced spouse, as well as alimony payments, may also be decreased or cut altogether.

Under the U.S. Tax Code, married couples receiving Social Security benefits are taxed at a higher rate than two single recipients. At the 1997 tax rate, married couples who jointly earned more than $32,000 were forced to pay taxes on their Social Security benefits. For example, a couple who each receive $8,400 in annual Social Security benefits and a $16,000 pension each take in $24,400 per year. If they marry and file jointly, their combined income of $48,800 would force them to pay tax on a portion of their Social Security income. If they remained single but lived together, their incomes would be assessed separately and would be below the $25,000 individual threshold for taxation of Social Security benefits, saving them $2,435 in taxes.

Social Security benefits may also be affected by marriage. This is especially true of Supplemental Security Income (SSI) benefits, which are administered by the Social Security Administration and designed to help low-income seniors with few assets and those with disabilities. These benefits are based on income and may be cut or eliminated based on the inclusion of a new spouse's income.

Many companies extend retirement benefits to the spouse of a deceased employee only as long as the spouse remains single. Although an unmarried partner is usually not eligible for any survivor benefits—a potential downside to living together—retirees often have the option of taking a lump-sum distribution and buying an annuity that provides survivor benefits for the partner.

Home ownership is another issue that can affect the decision of older singles considering marriage. Homeowners over fifty-five can take a one-time capital gains tax exclusion on the profits from a house sale of up to $125,000. If, however, one partner has already taken this exclusion, marriage will make the other partner ineligible, unless the partner who has not used the exclusion becomes widowed or divorced. Although laws and rules regarding joint purchase of a home by two unmarried individuals have changed significantly, the process remains more complex than that applied to married couples.

State rules vary, but married couples may be forced to use up many of their jointly owned assets before Medicare will pick up the tab for long-term nursing home care. If a couple lives together, the assets of the healthy partner cannot be touched, unless they include joint assets or assets transferred by the sick partner during a three-year period prior to Medicare application or following entrance into a nursing home.

SOCIAL FACTORS

Seniors who live together often do so for different reasons. Men may be looking for the care and companionship involved in a long-term relationship, while women may be interested in the economic stability that such an arrangement can provide. As people live longer and enjoy better health later in life, the sexual aspects of such a relationship are also frequently a factor. Many seniors are reluctant to give up a sex life simply because they have become widowed or divorced.

In addition to financial concerns, some singles opt to live together as a result of family pressure against remarriage after the death of a spouse. Many children, in particular, find it difficult to ac-

cept that an aging parent may still be sexually active and attracted to someone other than the deceased parent. Remarriage may also be considered an insult to the deceased parent. In these circumstances, children may find cohabitation a more palatable arrangement by ignoring the potential sexual aspects of cohabitation and viewing the relationship between a parent and partner as purely platonic.

Children who understand that such a cohabitation relationship may be sexual in nature may object to a parent living with another single senior. While these same children may hold relaxed sexual attitudes toward relationships between younger people, the attitude pervades that it is unseemly for older adults to engage in sexual activity.

Cohabitation among seniors still remains relatively rare, accounting for only about 3 percent of all seniors in 1995. In fact, cohabitation was illegal in at least eight states as of 1997. Still, the number of those who choose to cohabit appears to be rising. This increase is apparently attributable to both the acknowledgment by peers of the economic disadvantages of marriage and a relaxation of social taboos associated with cohabitation. The aging of the baby-boom population, which frequently embraced the relaxed sexual attitudes of the 1960's and beyond, may also be a factor contributing to the acceptance of cohabitation among older adults.

CONSIDERATIONS

Although studies indicate that couples who live together have a higher rate of domestic abuse, conflict, and other relationship problems, research also suggests that seniors may be less prone to these problems. In any case, studies indicate that cohabiting couples of all ages have a significantly lower long-term success rate than those who choose to marry.

Older men and women who cohabit are still subject to statutes in many states regarding common-law marriage. In states that allow common-law marriage, couples who present themselves as husband and wife are generally considered to be legally married and bound by tax, Social Security, and other rules that apply to married couples. In addition, cohabiting couples may face discrimination when seeking rental housing or joint credit or when making major purchases.

An unmarried couple living together at any age should consider preparing a cohabitation contract, since the law provides few protections for unmarried mates. Such contracts should identify what property belongs to whom and should also specify the division of jointly owned property or other assets if one person dies or the relationship is dissolved. Purchase of a jointly owned home is usually handled as a separate legal agreement.

In most states, the law offers few provisions to allow unmarried partners to make health care decisions for their mates. A durable power of attorney can remedy this situation, however, allowing partners to designate each other to make health care decisions should one of them become incapacitated.

Likewise, seniors living together are especially in need of an updated will to ensure the security of the surviving partner. Seniors couples who face objections to their relationship from children for inheritance reasons may want to consider creating a trust that allows the surviving partner to use part of the assets of the deceased partner, with the remainder passing on to the deceased partner's children when the surviving partner dies.

Cohabitants can expect many of the same challenges faced by couples who choose to marry. Older people have a lifetime of habits and lifestyle choices that may seem attractive when dating but can become annoying when living together. Such problems may be exacerbated by the specter of a deceased or former spouse who may have been more competent in some areas than the new partner. While married couples may be inclined to put more energy into working through such problems, older adults living together, like cohabiting couples of all ages, may be more likely to walk away from the challenges of a cohabitation relationship.

—Cheryl Pawlowski

See also Ageism; Caregiving; Children of Aging Parents; Demographics; Divorce; Dual-income couples; Durable power of attorney; Estates and inheritance; Family relationships; Home ownership; Housing; Income sources; Long-term care for the elderly; Marriage; Medicare; Men and aging; Old age; Pensions; Relocation; Remarriage; Sexuality; Singlehood; Social Security; Social ties; Stepfamilies; Trusts; Widows and widowers; Wills and bequests; Women and aging.

FOR FURTHER INFORMATION:
Battle, Carl W. *Senior Counsel: Legal and Financial Strategies for Age Fifty and Beyond.* New York: Allworth Press, 1993.
Blieszner, Rosemary, and Victoria Hilkevitch Bedford, eds. *Handbook of Aging and the Family.* Westport, Conn.: Greenwood Press, 1995.
Ihara, Toni, and Ralph Warner. *The Living Together Kit.* 8th ed. Berkeley, Calif.: Nolo Press, 1997.
Kirwan, Roberta. "Why Seniors Don't Marry." *Money,* July, 1995.
Maddox, George L., ed. *The Encyclopedia of Aging.* 2d ed. New York: Springer, 1995.
Silverstone, Barbara, and Helen Kandel Hyman. *Growing Older Together.* New York: Pantheon Books, 1992.
Solomon, David H., Elyse Salend, Anna Nolen Rahman, Marie Bolduc Liston, and David B. Reuben. *A Consumer's Guide to Aging.* Baltimore: The Johns Hopkins University Press, 1992.

COMMUNICATION

RELEVANT ISSUES: Culture, media, psychology
SIGNIFICANCE: The human need to communicate and maintain relations does not decrease with age, but it is altered because of social stereotypes and the communicative changes such labels and prejudices produce

Aging influences communication, and communication influences aging. These processes are intimately connected to each other. A person's ability to adapt to the aging process depends, in large part, on the person's interaction with others, and aging itself influences various aspects of communication. These changes in communication can be positive and negative. Changes in communication influence both how older people view themselves and how others view them. Reactions to change can influence a person's self-esteem or sense of self-worth in empowering, affirming ways, or such reactions can cause a person to feel diminished, unseen, and worthless. As many researchers and writers have noted, communication processes define, form, maintain, and dissolve all social relationships.

CHANGE AND IDENTITY

A theme evident in many articles and books about communication and aging is that of the heterogeneity, or mixed make-up, of the group of people who are variously referred to as "elderly," "aged," "older," or "over sixty-five." This diversity applies to their communication skills as well. While there are hundreds of articles that focus on what happens to communication when a disorder (of speech, language, or hearing) is present in older individuals, there are as many works devoted to challenging the ideas of normal aging.

At the bottom of such challenges are recognitions that throughout life, individuals communicate to themselves about themselves and that this internal message—called body image—is affected by physiological, psychological, sociological, and cultural pressures. Age, illness, or disability can alter or threaten this image of the self. When body image adjustment is considered too great, a person may retreat rather than adjust. When overwhelming change occurs, some people choose to disengage or separate themselves from others. Some people choose isolation or death, whereas many others are able to adapt to their new images and then assist others in adapting to them. Change is a constant in life, and one of the greatest communicative challenges is human interaction and support as people of all ages survive change, restructure their body images, and collaboratively work to look to the future with hope rather than despair.

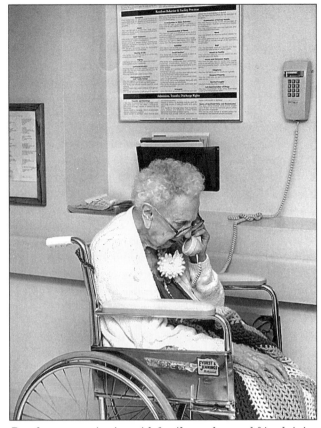

Regular communication with family members and friends is important for elders, especially those who have relocated to care facilities. (James L. Shaffer)

STEREOTYPES AND COMMUNICATION

Stereotypes occur when perceptions of age and aging solidify as images, labels, or categories. Sometimes such images are useful to understanding experience, but there is always the danger of inflexibility, which restricts abilities to see beyond the labels, or images. Many researchers have examined both positive and negative stereotypes that shape perceptions of older adults. Most people's images of aging come from their experiences of aging and the old. These images are often shaped by mediated images—images of the elderly in print, photography, music, television, and film—and by interpersonal interactions and relationships with older adults. Stereotypes can influence expectations and perception, creating a distorted image of an individual or group of individuals. In short, the processes of labeling, or developing descriptive metaphors for people, shape what is then believed about those people. The forming of myths and prejudices about growing old can cause substantial harm, as some people begin to behave in the ways they hear and see themselves described, or behave toward others on the basis of myths and prejudice.

The attitudes and emotions one has toward aging and the elderly affect communication. Researchers have shown that American teenagers develop negative stereotypes of elders as withdrawn, reclusive, and passive. The questions raised by this involve the origins of these images. Why does aging mean this to so many young people? What is it about cultural practices that creates and perpetuates these stereotypes about aging and elders? Meanings of aging differ for different age groups; thus, thirty-year-olds and seventy-year-olds differ in their views of aging. Elders are less likely than younger people to believe that age-related stereo-types are typical of aging, because their own experiences of aging have led them think about aging in more complicated ways. Also, the historical era in which one is reared influences how one thinks about aging, as does one's unique cultural background.

SOCIAL GROUPS AND COMMUNICATION

People get a tremendous sense of personal worth from the groups to which they belong, in which they participate, and with which they identify—family groups, religious groups, community service organizations, recreational teams, or groups of any other sort. Growing older involves a number of changes in lifestyle and life opportunities. The particular age identity that one wishes to claim for oneself changes with the situation. Young people often seek the credibility that comes with age and accomplishments and will often try to pass themselves off as older than they actually are. People categorize themselves and others in terms of age, health, marital status, the ages of a family's children, and the employment status of a family's adults.

As people come to identify with groups purely on the basis of age, much intergenerational communication is lost; in Western cultures, moreover, a greater value is placed on youth. For persons with access to money and privilege in these cultures, the absorbing of an older identity has often involved the creation of a more youthful identity.

In addition to keeping mindful of fashion and appearance, an older person may avoid particular markers of being old, such as using a cane or asking for a senior discount. Yet as more people enter age-identity groups, emerging communication strategies include re-creating age groups in more positive terms, redefining images and taking pride in the uniquenesses of being old. In other words, the connection between identity and aging involves two issues: the degree to which people are able to establish and maintain lifelong identities into old age and the degree to which people can take on new age-related identities.

COMMUNICATION NEEDS TAKE MANY FORMS

To make meaning of the experiences of aging involves the composition and recomposition of the life stories of individuals, families, and commu-nities. As people move toward the end of their lives, the achievement of personal story, of telling that story and having it heard, seen, witnessed, and appreciated by others, is tremendously important. It is often easy, however, for people to become desensitized to the communication needs both of others and of themselves. There is always a need for careful monitoring of communication behaviors. The physiological health factors that play a role in the communication of and with many older adults can effect changes in the voice, in hearing, in language function, and in intellectual abilities. Changes of these sorts are factors in how people are judged, and they necessitate different communication environments and interaction patterns from family and other care providers.

The dynamics of interaction in health care contexts are too frequently marked by insensitivity, the kinds and degrees of which are varied as caregivers respond to a sense of burden. For example, gerontologist Mary Lee Hummert and others have examined how stereotypes contribute to a type of communication known as "patronizing speech." To be on the receiving end of patronizing speech is rarely pleasant. This type of speech is motivated by a desire to adapt one's talk to one's perception of another's abilities to comprehend. It is an adaptive, accommodating strategy in interaction that involves shorter sentences, slow, careful articulation, and a very simple and concrete vocabulary. Alone, these are common features of "elderspeak," a type of language used by caregivers and some elderly as they make adjustments to the perceived needs of their conversational partners. It becomes patronizing when a demeaning emotional tone is present or felt or when the quality of talk is superficial. Extreme patronizing speech takes the form of secondary baby talk. Hummert's studies show that patronizing speech is often addressed to adults in extended care facilities, retirement homes, and assisted-living arrangements.

IMPROVING COMMUNICATION

The work of improving communication involves paying attention to how images of self and other affect, create, and perpetuate stereotypes. Much of that monitoring involves investigating the following types of questions: How do stereotypes about aging and the aged influence the ways in which elders are treated by other age groups? How do such stereotypes influence how elders behave toward younger individuals, particularly people to whom they are not related by blood or family? What stereotypes are similar or different across cultures?

One particular feature of communication research that distinguishes it from other work in the social sciences is its focus on the development, expression, and adaptation of messages. Such an emphasis requires attention to the social-psychological origins of language and ideas, the technical and artistic aspects of the expression of messages, and the social understandings necessary for effective adaptation of those messages. The human need to communicate and maintain relationships does not decrease with age, but it is altered because of social stereotyping. —*C. Turner Steckline*

See also Advertising; Advocacy; Ageism; Cultural views of aging; Depression; Family relationships; Friendship; Films; Hearing aids; Hearing loss; Humor; Internet; Leisure activities; Literature; Loneliness; Mentoring; Old age; Personality changes; Sensory changes; Social ties; Stereotypes; Television.

FOR FURTHER INFORMATION:

Al-Deen, Hana S. Noor, ed. *Cross-Cultural Communication and Aging in the United States.* Mahweh, N.J.: Lawrence Erlbaum Associates, 1997.

Davis, A. Jann. *Listening and Responding.* St. Louis: C. V. Mosby, 1984.

Hummert, Mary Lee, John M. Wiemann, and Jon F. Nussbaum, eds. *Interpersonal Communication in Older Adulthood.* Thousand Oaks, Calif.: Sage Publications, 1994.

Huntley, Ruth A., and Karen S. Helfer, eds. *Communication in Later Life.* Newton, Mass.: Butterworth-Heinemann, 1995.

Mace, Nancy L., and Peter V. Rabins. *The Thirty-Six-Hour Day.* Rev. ed. New York: Warner Books, 1992.

Minister, Kristina. "Rehearsing for the Ultimate Audience." In *Performance, Culture, and Identity,* edited by Elisabeth Fine and Jean H. Speer. Westport, Conn.: Praeger, 1992.

Myerhoff, Barbara. "Life History Among the Elderly: Performance, Visibility, and Remembering." In *Remembered Lives: The Work of Ritual, Storytelling, and Growing Older,* edited by Barbara Myerhoff and M. Kaminsky. Ann Arbor: University of Michigan Press, 1992.

Rust, Laurel. "Another Part of the Country." In *Women and Aging,* edited by Jo Alexander et al. Corvallis, Oreg.: Calyx Books, 1986.

COMPULSORY RETIREMENT. *See* FORCED RETIREMENT.

CONSUMER ISSUES

RELEVANT ISSUES: Economics, health and medicine, law

SIGNIFICANCE: As the number of senior citizens in the United States continues to grow, aging-related consumer issues, previously ignored by merchants and manufacturers, have become increasingly important

Many of the consumer issues that are of importance to senior citizens are also important to all segments of society. All consumer issues relate to the desire of consumers to obtain value for their money. All consumers want safe, dependable, and effective goods and services at a reasonable price. Every consumer wants to be assured that in the event of problems with goods and services, safeguards are in place to handle these problems.

In many ways, however, a senior citizen represents a special consumer; some consumer issues related to being a senior citizen are of less importance to other consumers. These issues include the availability of products that satisfy the special needs of senior consumers, prices for products that are needed specifically by seniors, and concerns about people who might take advantage of the most elderly American citizens.

NEED FOR SPECIAL PRODUCTS

As people become older, their bodies, living conditions, and goals change. These changes create the need for special products. In some cases, manufacturers and providers of goods and services have been slow to recognize these needs. In other cases, the needs have been apparent, but businesses have not seen providing goods and services for the elderly as an economically profitable enterprise and, therefore, have been reluctant to market specialty products usable only by senior citizens. However, as the large and affluent baby-boom generation, those born between 1946 and 1964, reaches senior citizen status, manufacturers, merchants, and service providers will likely see an economic benefit in providing goods and services designed specifically for the elderly.

One general issue associated with providing products for senior consumers is related to changes in the human body. While the body changes in a variety of ways as people get older, manufacturers often do not produce goods or provide services that accommodate these changes. One area affected by changes in the body's shape and size is fashion. People who reach senior status often find that the only fashions available are ill-fitting or unbecoming clothes that have been designed for younger consumers. Clothing manufacturers have concentrated their efforts on designing clothing for the youth market and have largely ignored the needs of the elderly. However, members of the baby-boom generation have tended to be concerned about personal appearance and are likely to demand attractive clothing as they age. This demand, along with the affluence of the baby boomers, is likely to prompt manufacturers to put more effort

and resources into designing fashionable clothing for the aging population.

Manufacturers have also failed to consider the comfort of senior citizens in their product designs. The aging process may cause changes in the body's center of gravity, shape, weight, or overall size. Clothing, furniture, and even homes that seem comfortable to a thirty-year-old may cause pain and discomfort among the elderly. Among the industries that began to address this problem in the 1990's were automobile manufacturers. Engineers began designing cars with wider and more comfortable driver's seats and with easily reachable accessories, such as radios and air-conditioning controls. Many cars have been made easier to get out of with the addition of swivel seats and chassis designs that better accommodate the elderly body.

Safety is another area of concern for elderly people. Since the aging body is less agile than a young body, senior citizens have an interest in promoting the production of furniture, household

An older woman shops at a department store that offers a 10 percent discount for seniors on Wednesdays. Such opportunities and curtailed finances are significant factors in consumer habits. (AP Photo/Douglas Healey)

appliances, recreational equipment, and tools that are as stable as possible. Because safety is not just a senior issue and because all consumers may benefit from having products that are more stable and generally safer, the manufacture of such items has proven to be economically beneficial to the companies that produce them. Since the market is large for such products, manufacturers are able to provide them at competitive prices.

As people age, their living conditions often change, creating the need for products that support and reflect new lifestyles. Many senior citizens go from living in family groups to living alone or with just one other person. The growing elderly population may lead to an increased demand for ground-level, one-bedroom housing units; easily prepared food packaged for one person; and compact appliances, such as smaller washing machines and freezers. In addition, manufacturers may recognize the economic potential of marketing appliances and furniture designed for use by people in wheelchairs.

Aging people also experience changes in their life goals. Such changes often demand the creation of new goods and services, some of which may be of a financial nature. People who retire at age sixty or sixty-five often have many years of life ahead of them. Many of them need financial services to help them invest their pensions and develop long-term financial plans. Many people who see many years of retirement ahead of them set goals for self-improvement, such as completing college degrees, engaging in fitness programs, learning new skills, volunteering, or exploring their inner selves. Finding ways to provide low-cost, effective ways for seniors to improve their lives during retirement is a consumer issue of growing importance.

SENIORS AS VICTIMS

The elderly are among society's most vulnerable citizens, often because they are in poor health; thus, they may not be able to leave their homes or engage in an active social life. These seniors may become easy prey for people who wish to take advantage of them by selling goods and services that are defective, insufficient, or nonexistent. Such schemes often involve the sale of services that the elderly person desperately needs but because of poor health or disability, cannot perform, such as

home repair. Each year, elderly people are cheated out of millions of dollars that they paid for repair services that were not done or were done improperly. Other scam artists identify senior citizens who may be lonely enough to talk with a stranger for a long period of time, call them, engage them in conversation, and trick them into buying unneeded goods and services. Others trick the seniors into giving them their credit card numbers, which the scam artists then use to make purchases of their own.

It is likely that deception of the elderly will receive more attention as greater numbers of Americans become senior citizens. Consumer advocate groups have already identified several tactics that the elderly can use to make sure that they are not victims of consumer fraud. One important measure includes asking friends, relatives, or paid advisers for advice before making a major purchase or paying for a service, such as home repair. Consumers who are the victims of deceptive service providers are advised to report their problems to the consumer protection division of their state's attorney general's office.　　　*—Annita Marie Ward*

See also Advertising; Ageism; Antiaging treatments; Baby boomers; Beauty; Canes and walkers; Dentures; Discounts; Driving; Fraud against the elderly; Home services; Loneliness; Retirement; Safety issues; Scams and con artists; Wheelchair use.

FOR FURTHER INFORMATION:
Cheney, Walter J., William Diehm, and Frank E. Seeley. *The Second Fifty Years: A Reference Guide for Senior Citizens.* Weed, Calif.: Writers Consortium, 1992.

Dychtwald, Kenneth. *Age Wave: How the Most Important Trend of Our Time Will Change Our Future.* New York: Bantam Doubleday Dell, 1990.

Walker, Malcolm, and Bob Fiegel. *Senior Citizens' Survival Guide.* New York: CCC, 1999.

COPING SKILLS. *See* STRESS AND COPING SKILLS.

CORNS AND CALLUSES
RELEVANT ISSUES: Health and medicine
SIGNIFICANCE: Corns and calluses become increasingly common as one ages; they can cause foot discomfort and thereby impair mobility

Both corns (clavi) and calluses (tylomas or tyloses) are areas of thickened skin that occur as a result of constant pressure or friction over a bony prominence. Chronic pressure or friction causes hypertrophy of the dermal skin layer and a proliferation of keratin as a protective response. Both corns and calluses usually occur on the feet. Corns develop from pressure on normally thin skin. Calluses develop over areas where the skin is normally thicker. They commonly develop on the plantar (sole) surface of the foot and on the palmar (palm) surface of the hand. Corns are frequently painful, whereas calluses usually are not painful. Corns are small, flat, or slightly elevated lesions with a smooth, hard surface. Calluses cover a larger area than corns and are less well demarcated.

There are two classifications of corns: hard and soft. Hard corns have a conical structure composed of keratin, with the point of the cone directed inward, causing pain when pressed into the soft, underlying tissue. Hard corns have a circumscribed border that demarcates the lesions from the surrounding soft tissue. Hard corns usually develop on the top or sides of the toes, where shoes press on the interphalangeal joints of the toes, or the plantar surface of the foot, where pressure is exerted against bony prominences.

Soft corns develop in areas where a bony prominence causes constant pressure against soft tissue, resulting in a blanched thickening of the skin. Because soft corns commonly develop on interdigital surfaces, such as between the fourth and fifth toe, they are characteristically moist and macerated and can become inflamed.

Calluses develop as a protection against continual pressure. They do not have the central core of keratin and as a result are not sensitive to pressure. Normal skin markings are present over callused areas. Calluses usually develop on weight-bearing areas of the foot under the metatarsal heads and the heel. Calluses on the palm are frequently the result of manual occupations.

Treatment of corns and calluses depends on symptoms. Since corns and calluses are caused by chronic pressure, preventive measures include removing the source of friction or pressure. Well-fitting shoes that do not crowd the toes relieve pressure on interdigital areas. Soft, sufficiently wide or open-toed shoes are good choices. Soft insoles and properly fitting stockings also reduce pressure. Wrapping lambs wool or other padding over pressure points can increase air circulation and reduce pressure and discomfort. Corns and calluses can be treated with over-the-counter keratolytic agents. Salicylic acid plasters are used to soften the tissue, which can then be removed with a pumice stone. When corns, or occasionally calluses, become inflamed or painful, they can be removed by paring or trimming. This should be done by a health care provider, especially in patients with compromised circulation to the feet. In rare circumstances, surgery may be required if a corn or callus becomes infected or if the chronic pressure on particular areas is caused by a structural abnormality of the foot, such as a hammertoe. *—Roberta Tierney*

See also Bunions; Foot disorders; Hammertoes; Mobility problems; Skin changes and disorders.

COSMETIC SURGERY

RELEVANT ISSUES: Health and medicine, psychology, sociology

SIGNIFICANCE: Cosmetic surgery helps to minimize the visible effects of aging, giving the person a more youthful, rested appearance

Plastic surgery is a type of surgery that focuses on remodeling a part of the body. It comes from the Greek word *plastikos*, which means to mold or form. Many people think it is a new type of surgery, but it is actually one of the oldest forms. Documentation has shown that members of the potter (tilemaker) caste in India reconstructed noses as early as 1000 B.C. Gaspare Tagliacozzi, of Bologna, wrote the first textbook on plastic surgery, *On the Surgical Restoration of Defects by Grafting*, in 1597. Great strides in plastic surgery occurred during World War I and World War II as plastic surgery centers were established for the large number of soldiers whose wounds required reconstructive surgeries.

Plastic surgery can be divided into two basic types: reconstructive and cosmetic. Reconstructive surgery is done to restore function to a damaged body part, as with congenital abnormalities or traumatic lesions. Cosmetic surgery is done to remove blemishes or change contours. In some instances, such as traumatic injuries or cancer surgeries, plastic surgery may be used both to restore function and to remove blemishes or change contours. This entry focuses on cosmetic surgery that is done to counteract some of the effects of the aging process.

THE AGING PROCESS

Changes in skin appearance readily reflect the aging process. Wrinkles, sagging skin, gray hair, and baldness can begin as early as the third decade of life. Several factors contribute to these normal changes.

The skin has three layers. The outer layer is the epidermis, which tends to thin with age. This layer also decreases in moisture content, which leads to dry skin. The thinner, dryer skin is more prone to develop wrinkles. The second layer is the dermis. Collagen, a gel-like protein, constitutes 80 percent of this layer and accounts for the elasticity of the skin. Beginning in the third decade, collagen decreases at a rate of 1 percent each year. Since the dermis layer is thinner in women than in men, women begin to show signs of aging skin earlier. The dermis blood supply also decreases with age. This results in destruction to the hair glands and sweat glands. These natural changes contribute to hair loss and the development of wrinkles. The third layer is the subcutis layer, which is composed mainly of fat tissue. With age, this layer thins in the face, hands, and lower legs. It tends to increase in other areas. Decreased fat tissue in the face can cause the skin to sag or look hollow.

Hair color and distribution are other main identifiers of aging. By the age of fifty, 50 percent of people have some degree of gray hair. This condition is caused by a decline in the production of melanin and the gradual replacement of pigmented hair with nonpigmented hair. Hair distribution is affected all over the body. Hair on the head tends to decrease, while hair of the upper lip and lower face (in women) and the ears, nose, and eyebrows (in men) increases with age. Big business is involved in the development of creams and drugs to either remove or increase hair growth or to slow the change in distribution of hair.

Several changes affect physiological processes. Temperature regulation and the sensations of pain and touch may be altered. Social function can also be altered by the changes of aging. Skin and hair communicate many things about a person: age, race, gender, work status, and other personal characteristics. They also play a role in how people define themselves. Many people strive always to look their best and do not want to look older than they are. Additionally, many people believe that they need to look young to remain competitive in the business and social worlds. Thus, there are many reasons to have cosmetic surgery.

TYPES OF COSMETIC SURGERIES

Cosmetic surgery may be requested to counteract the normal changes of the skin that appear with aging. The area around the eye is the first to show signs of aging. The procedure that removes excess skin and fatty tissue from eyelids and eye area is called blepharoplasty. Areas involved can include one or both eyes and either upper or lower lids, or both. Incisions are made in the eyelid fold and extend out toward the smile lines.

A later sign of aging is the gradual stretching downward of the cheeks and deep wrinkling of the forehead. Face lifts (rhytidectomy) and brow lifts are procedures to address these issues. Rhytidectomy tightens the skin of the face and neck. The face and neck are often done together because aging changes occur in both at the same time. A brow lift relieves sagging eyebrows and a wrinkling forehead. Tightness occurs after these procedures because skin and sometimes underlying tissue and muscles are moved. Extra skin is cut off. Incisions are made in existing creases and in the hairline around ears.

While there are many reasons for hair loss—severe infection, thyroid disease, some medications, chemotherapy—the main reason is heredity. Hair loss can begin in the twenties or thirties. It occurs both in men and women, but women seldom go bald. There are many treatments: systemic steroids or hormones, ointments, and antibiotics. Hair transplantation is another method. The older type of hair transplantation takes grafts from the back and side of the scalp and places them in the bald areas. Several sessions are usually required. A disadvantage of this method is that it often gives the appearance of "doll's hair." A newer method is microtransplantation, or minigrafts, which takes a few hairs with each graft. The result is a more natural look.

The surgeries outlined here are only a few of the numerous procedures that are offered. Surgical protocol varies with each procedure. Many of the cosmetic surgeries can be done in an outpatient setting, while others can be done only in a hospital. The surgical time can last from thirty minutes to four or five hours. All procedures will produce some degree of swelling and bruising—which can last for several weeks.

OPINIONS ABOUT COSMETIC SURGERY

There are two basic camps regarding cosmetic surgery: those who think that it is a waste of money and those who believe that it is the best thing offered. Those in the first group believe no cream, drug, or surgery can stop or reverse the aging process. They are quick to point out that cosmetic surgery is temporary and that the aging process continues, which means that wrinkles and sags will reappear. The money wasted on attempts to defy reality could be better used to meet more basic needs. Many also argue that American society tends to take the "quick fix" approach and jump at medication or surgeries to solve their problems. This group of people is more likely to avoid the sun, maintain proper nutrition, and not smoke as more natural methods to slow the signs of aging.

Members of the other group acknowledge that cosmetic surgery does not stop the aging process but seem pleased at the temporary reversal of the process. These people believe there is a positive impact on their daily life. Studies have demonstrated that there is an increase in self-esteem, more self-confidence, more satisfaction with appearance, and less depression after a person undergoes cosmetic surgery.

ISSUES TO CONSIDER

Before cosmetic surgery is performed, several issues need to be addressed. The first is the general health of the person considering surgery. With age and the natural decline of some body functions, there can be a greater likelihood of adverse reactions to anesthesia and a delay in healing.

The desired results of the surgery need to be reviewed. Cosmetic surgery will not yield a "model-like" appearance. People with unrealistic expectations will not be satisfied with the results. It is important to remember that the results of surgery are not seen immediately. There can be extreme bruising and swelling for several weeks after most surgeries. It may take up to a year for healing to be complete.

While cosmetic surgery is not the fountain of youth, it can be an effective method to aid people in looking their best. *—Jennifer J. Hostutler*

See also Age spots; Antiaging treatments; Beauty; Communication; Cultural views of aging; Face lifts; Fat deposition; Gray hair; Hair loss and baldness; Men and aging; Middle age; Midlife crisis; Obesity; Old age; Premature aging; Sexuality; Skin changes and disorders; Varicose veins; Weight loss and gain; Women and aging; Wrinkles.

FOR FURTHER INFORMATION:

Henry, Kimberly A., and Penny S. Heckaman. *The Plastic Surgery Sourcebook*. Los Angeles: Lowell House, 1997.

Marfuggi, Richard A. *Plastic Surgery: What You Need to Know Before, During, and After*. New York: Berkeley, 1998.

Perry, Arthur W., and Robin K. Levinson. *A Complete Question and Answer Guide*. New York: Avon Books, 1997.

Sarnoff, Deborah S., and Joan Swirsky. *Beauty and the Beam: Your Complete Guide to Cosmetic Laser Surgery*. New York: St. Martins Griffin, 1998.

Wyer, E. Bingo. *The Unofficial Guide to Cosmetic Surgery*. New York: Simon & Schuster/Macmillan, 1999.

CREATIVITY

RELEVANT ISSUES: Psychology
SIGNIFICANCE: Psychological factors that accompany aging also support creative potential; however, actual creativity depends on the value that individuals place on the specific components of creativity during each life stage

Creativity may be defined as a new (original) product that works (accomplishes some goal). This general definition is intentionally flexible. The twin elements of novelty and effectiveness apply equally to everyday tasks (such as baking), creative expression, and technological advances in the public arena. The definition does not, however, imply a social value judgment of the "worthiness" of a created product, only that it is somehow innovative and effective.

Psychologist Theresa Amabile used this general understanding of creativity to articulate a more useful componential definition that clarifies why creative potential increases with aging. Her approach identified domain-relevant skills, creativity-relevant skills, and intrinsic motivation as three necessary and sufficient components for creativity. As predicted by this definition, creative potential varies with stage of life and the particular demands of a discipline. For example, creative musicians must know the fundamentals of a particular instrument (domain skills), but this is insufficient for creativity. In addition, musicians must be able to use that knowledge to reinterpret existing music or create new music in original ways (creativity skills) and enjoy the process so thoroughly that they will persevere in their music even if their efforts are unrecognized and unrewarded (intrinsic motivation). The strength of each of these components varies with stage of life and the demands of particular creative endeavors.

PSYCHOLOGICAL FACTORS SUPPORTING CREATIVITY

Three psychological factors support a positive correlation between creative potential and growing older: breadth and depth of personal experience, spontaneous life review, and a tendency toward disinhibition. These three factors conspire to create a reservoir of creative potential. However, creative potential is not the same as creative productivity, and creative potential is often not realized by aging individuals or supported by family or institutions. The resulting challenge becomes a personal and social choice regarding whether to support the creative potential that accompanies aging.

The first psychological factor supporting simultaneous increases in creative potential and aging is the breadth and depth of life experience. Studies of academically talented youths suggest that most components of creativity are present but relatively immature. One study met with seventh- through tenth-grade students who had scored above the ninety-eighth percentile on the SAT. Students displayed intrinsic motivation by their eagerness to learn and discover. Within the fields identified by the SAT, their domain-relevant skills were sharper than most but still unrefined. Similarly, their creativity skills (including risk taking) were high.

Many seniors use the newfound free time that comes with retirement to express their creativity. (Donna Shaffer)

However, each component was relatively undeveloped. These academically high-achieving students clearly had creative potential. As such, they were likely to play a role in the type of generational disagreements that lead to scientific revolutions and eventual paradigm shifts, as discussed by Thomas Kuhn in his book *The Structure of Scientific Revolutions* (1962). However, they were simply too young and inexperienced, for the most part, to make significantly creative contributions.

The second factor supporting creative potential and aging is spontaneous life review. A distinct developmental shift occurs for many individuals as they approach forty years of age. They begin to count their own lives in terms of "years left" rather than "years lived." The consequent search for personal meaning supports the intrinsic motivation necessary for personal creativity. However, creativity in midlife tends to be undermined by cynicism, or a loss of intrinsic motivation. A study of government employees in mid-career reported a strong urge to "play it safe," not to jeopardize future promotions, and to protect the status quo that held their growing retirement funds. Nevertheless, spontaneous life review contributes to distinguishing between what activities are perceived as meaningful and those likely to be frivolous and unproductive.

The third factor supporting the positive correlation between creative potential and age is increasing disinhibition. Disinhibition refers to lack of self-control. It suggests an absence of the internal mechanisms that restrain harmful impulses. Especially during youth, many negative consequences are associated with disinhibition, most notably self-destructive social deviance. However, the tempered disinhibition that seems to accompany aging holds more promise for producing positive, creative consequences. Some of the rudeness that appears to accompany some aging is an expression of individuals finally allowing themselves to tell other people what they really think.

One study of government bureaucrats revealed an increased willingness to experiment and start new projects among those who were within one to five years of retirement. Of the people studied, one had increased the use of bicycle safety helmets through innovative advertising campaigns, another had initiated long-needed training and education programs for bureaucrats, and a third had created a new mentoring system in New York State's complicated budget processes to support the next generation of lawmakers. These people were disinhibited by the recognition that they had achieved their highest career ranking, that they had earned their last promotion, and that the time for meaningful action had arrived. The personal networks of influence were not yet retired, and their bureaucratic (domain-relevant) skills were wonderfully refined.

CREATIVITY AMONG NURSING HOME RESIDENTS

The three creativity-supporting factors are strongly represented among people living in nursing homes. For these very old and frequently disabled individuals, life experience is rich and grow-

Physical changes in reaction time and dexterity that accompany aging can be offset by a lifetime of practice to master such skills as playing a musical instrument. (James L. Shaffer)

ing richer as they continue to experience institutional life. Spontaneous life review appears to function as both a pleasurable activity and a way to strengthen coping mechanisms in a highly disorienting, often discouraging, environment. Disinhibition is encouraged by stark, daily reminders of dying and death.

The joining of these three factors produces widespread creative potential. A variety of demonstrations have acknowledged the penetrating wisdom and imagery available to those living in nursing homes. Kenneth Koch's work in supporting poetry through workshops in nursing homes, described in his book *I Never Told Anybody* (1977), helped inspire Thomas Heinzen's *Many Things to Tell You* (1996), a collection of "accidental poetry" gleaned through a variety of psychological interventions. The chief detriment to realizing this particularly unusual form of creativity appears to be limitations of domain-relevant skills: Arthritis, stroke, dementia, and other common deficits make word production and writing difficult. Each of these may be overcome by careful listening and recording by others.

Consequently, aging represents a period of creative potential, supported by life experience, deep reflection, and disinhibition. The most dramatic and counterintuitive population discussed in this essay are the very old and disabled who live in nursing homes. Amabile's useful componential definition of creativity articulates the kinds of supports needed for creativity, even at this distressing stage of life. The chief means of communication among very old people is words, since motor, visual, and other abilities have tended to decline. Some language facility generally remains, and creativity skills seem to naturally spring from a now disinhibited life review.

Koch and Heinzen discovered that it is relatively easy to prompt meaningful utterances among people living in nursing homes. When the very act of speaking significantly reduces limited reservoirs of strength, carefully selected words become the only tools of influence and coherence. Intrinsic motivation similarly evolves out of these combined stressors that conspire to "squeeze" individual personality. Words are used economically and meaningfully. The natural consequence is creative poetry, even if the creators themselves are unlikely to identify their own words in that manner.

Each stage of life represents a different mix of the components of creativity. Similarly, each life stage suffers from inherent weaknesses and can benefit from a variety of supports. Open-minded mentors can assist enthusiastic youth. Visionary leaders can help the middle aged avoid inappropriate compromises. Careful listeners can capture the accidental creativity of very old age. The perceived social value of what is created at each stage of life, within each discipline and specialty, constantly varies. A useful componential definition of creativity leads to a simple conclusion: Whatever the age, creative productivity is almost always a possibility.

—*Thomas E. Heinzen*

See also Adult education; Aging: Biological, psychological, and sociocultural perspectives; Communication; Cultural views of aging; Leisure activities; Literature; Maturity; Nursing and convalescent homes; Personality changes; Social ties; Successful aging; Wisdom.

FOR FURTHER INFORMATION:

Amabile, Theresa. *The Social Psychology of Creativity.* New York: Springer-Verlag, 1983. Defines and describes a componential definition of creativity.

Heinzen, Thomas. *Many Things to Tell You.* New York: Seaburn Publishing, 1996. Demonstrates and discusses how to elicit natural poetry from people living in nursing homes.

Koch, Kenneth. *I Never Told Anybody.* New York: Random House, 1977. Describes poetry workshops and the resulting poetry of nursing home residents.

Kuhn, Thomas. *The Structure of Scientific Revolutions.* Chicago: University of Chicago Press, 1962. Describes the process by which scientific perspectives are gradually undermined and then replaced.

CROSS-LINKAGE THEORY OF AGING

RELEVANT ISSUES: Biology

SIGNIFICANCE: According to this theory, large, complex molecules that have important functions in the body can become modified during aging so that they stick together and fail to function properly

The human body is a very complex machine. In order for it to work properly, thousands of chemical reactions must occur at just the right time and place. In addition, the materials that support and give shape to the body must also function correctly for good health to be maintained. Small changes can occur in the molecules of the body so that these reactions and structures become impaired. Such subtle alterations may accumulate slowly throughout life, and as they accumulate they become the reason for many of the symptoms that accompany advancing age.

The cross-linkage theory is one of about a dozen major theories that attempt to explain the accumulation of such defects with age. This particular theory describes a change that occurs most commonly in large molecules such as proteins. As individuals age, proteins tend to become stuck to one another chemically, which is called cross-linking. When they are fastened together in this way, their shape may be slightly changed and they do not work as efficiently. This is particularly damaging for enzymes, which are the proteins that catalyze (accelerate) the many chemical reactions in the body.

Another kind of protein, collagen, serves as scaffolding to support parts of the body. When collagen in the skin becomes highly cross-linked during aging, the skin becomes stiffer and less able to stretch. Such cross-linking of structural proteins might also contribute to the stiffening of the walls of blood vessels, a disease known as arteriosclerosis. Cross-linking of proteins surrounding air sacs in the lungs can contribute to a decline in efficiency of respiration later in life.

Cross-linking can also occur in genes, which are the blueprints for making proteins. The proteins produced from such a cross-linked blueprint can be malformed or may never be produced at all. It is possible for proteins to cross-link to genes, impairing the function of both. Also, some kinds of fats may cross-link, contributing to clogging of the arteries.

Cross-linking is believed to occur during aging because certain small molecules that are the by-products of energy production in the body tend to accumulate during aging. These molecules are very active chemically and can cause the reactions that lead to cross-linking, as well as other kinds of chemical damage. Clearly, any improvement in the body's ability to deal with these dangerous waste products makes it less likely that proteins and other important molecules will be impaired by them. A proper diet can help minimize the harm caused by these substances. Vitamins C and E are called antioxidants; they appear able to help keep proteins working properly by counteracting the effects of the waste products. Exercise can also help the body rid itself of these damaging chemicals. As with other symptoms of aging, a healthy lifestyle can minimize the potential damage of cross-linking. —*Howard L. Hosick*

See also Aging process; Antiaging treatments; Antioxidants; Arteriosclerosis; Exercise and fitness; Free radical theory of aging; Genetics; Heart disease; Nutrition; Respiratory changes and disorders; Skin changes and disorders; Vitamins and minerals; Wrinkles.

CROWNS AND BRIDGES

RELEVANT ISSUES: Health and medicine

SIGNIFICANCE: Crowns and bridges are used to restore proper functioning and aesthetics of the teeth

With the aging process, the teeth undergo wear, increased sensitivity, decay, and in some cases, disease that may result in the loss of some or all of the teeth. This is particularly true in the elderly. Dentists can restore natural teeth that are damaged, decayed, or lost by using crowns and bridges. A crown may be constructed to restore an individual damaged tooth back to its original form and function, while a bridge may be utilized to replace one or more missing teeth. Each of these restorations is cemented onto the teeth and is referred to as fixed dentistry, in contrast to a restoration of missing teeth with a removable appliance or partial denture.

A crown, or cap, fits over a tooth. It strengthens and protects the covered tooth structure and can improve the overall appearance of the teeth. Crowns and bridges can be made from different materials, which include natural-looking porcelain, porcelain fused to a metal crown, or an all-metal crown. The patient and the dentist decide which type is the most appropriate, depending on the strength requirements and aesthetic concerns of the tooth or teeth involved. Cost will be a primary concern for many elderly.

A crown is produced using an indirect procedure. The tooth to be capped is modified by drilling and then prepared using special instruments. A copy of the prepared tooth is made by taking an impression, which is sent to a laboratory where the crown is constructed. Once the impression stage is completed, the dentist places a temporary plastic or acrylic crown on the prepared tooth to protect it and the gum tissues until the permanent crown is ready to be cemented onto the tooth.

When one or more teeth are lost, five or more other teeth may be affected. Remaining teeth may shift or tilt into the open space, changing the bite, which may result in sore jaws, gum disease, or decay. When teeth are missing and there are teeth on either side of the open space, a bridge is the best way to replace the missing teeth. Replacement teeth can be attached to two crowns constructed for the two teeth on either side of the open space.

A fixed bridge is used to replace one or several teeth. To prepare the bridge, diagnostic models are used to study the optimum way to perform the procedure. After these studies are completed, the tooth on each end of the open space is carefully reshaped, impressions are taken, and crowns are made for the end teeth so that they can serve as anchors for the bridge. While the permanent bridge is being prepared, which usually takes about two to three weeks, a temporary acrylic bridge is cemented into place. Since the bridge and attaching crowns are made as one solid piece, it is necessary to use a special type of dental floss that goes under the bridge in order to keep this area of gum tissue healthy.

—*Alvin K. Benson*

See also Aging process; Bone changes and disorders; Dental disorders; Dentures; Health care.

CULTURAL VIEWS OF AGING

RELEVANT ISSUES: Culture, psychology, sociology
SIGNIFICANCE: Aging is a dynamic multidimensional process, the meaning of which has been woven with the fabric of individual experiences, shaped by social, economic, and cultural forces, constructed and reconstructed continuously along historical time

Life and death are omnipresent in people's terrestrial experiences. Death is the endpoint of a process called "aging," during which the organism's functioning is irreversibly deteriorating. Over thousands of years, human beings have been trying to understand this mysterious process. His-

torically and almost universally, positive and negative meanings have been constructed associated with aging and old age.

HISTORICAL VIEWS OF AGING

In this section, views of old age from antiquity to the Renaissance are discussed first, based on Georges Minois's *History of Old Age* (1987), followed by views of aging in early America, based on Thomas Cole's *The Journey of Life* (1992). Literature of old age in those time periods excluded women; therefore, the historical descriptions of aging were of old men and the language used was masculine.

From the very beginning, human understanding of old age immediately registered ambiguity in meaning and ambivalence in emotion. Old age was awed and honored but at the same time feared and despised. The pendulum is usually swung to the nasty extreme when supplies become scarce, competition fierce, and society industrialized. In prehistoric years, when means of production were primitive and living conditions were harsh, old people, seen as a useless burden, were often eliminated. Senile, old African chiefs had to commit suicide. Unhealthy old people were suffocated in the Turco-Mongols. Healthy old men were sacrificed and devoured in the Padaei.

Unfortunately, such barbaric treatment of the old continued. In late nineteenth century capitalist America, George Miller Beard's curve of productivity (a sharp intellectual and moral decline after the peak age of forty) "justified" retirement as social euthanasia. Nineteenth century physician William Osler appreciated Anthony Trollope's plot of chloroform and cremation for those who had "outlived" their usefulness at age sixty-seven in his satire *The Fixed Period* (1882) and advocated "men stopping working after sixty." As recently as 1984, Governor Richard D. Lamm of Colorado asserted that elderly, if very ill, had a duty to die.

The rebellion from the young kings in the Hebraic monarchic world demonstrated the first sign of the decline of the "beards." Longevity became "a long individual tragedy, a sequence of misfortunes." Ancient Greek mythological literature, poems, and plays were merciless toward old men. Even death was preferred over the divine curse of old age. Aristotle argued that a weakened, aging body could never host a sound mind, so the old man was a

Within the African American community, aging often has a positive image, with old people accorded a special "survivor" status. (Jim Whitmer)

Yet, there have also been positive views of aging throughout history. The scarcity of old people in prehistorical eras put a halo over longevity. Old age was awed as a miracle and a divine reward. Oral traditions valued old men as "a fund of knowledge" and "living archives." Old men in the Hebraic world before the Hebrew exile were respected as natural leaders and "the bearers of the divine spirit." In ancient Greece, Plato acknowledged mental refinement and rational advantages in old age, a compensation for the physical decline. All senators in the Roman republic were men of years.

In Dark Ages, "venerable" old men were attributed such qualities as "purity of heart," "wisdom," "prudence," "experience," and "sweet fruits." Catholic religions viewed old age as a testimony of piety and self-discipline, which could lead to salvation. They employed only the old as the moral authority to play the exemplary and educational roles. Age was honored for entry into holy orders. Monasteries were created, and expanded in the Middle Ages, for old men to retire from the secular world into eternity. For merchants, old age meant substantial wealth accumulation. After the plague epidemics during the fourteenth and fifteenth centuries, old men's contributions in the transmission of knowledge in extended families and communities were recognized. An interesting paradox existed in the sixteenth century: The cultural opinion demeaned the old, whereas the government empowered them with more responsibility than ever before.

In the seventeenth century, English colonists brought Protestant ideas about aging to the New World. The Puritans saw aging as a sacred pilgrimage to God and the final judgment of lifetime conduct. Aging was not a bad experience when the young remained dependent in the patriarchal structure (the young served and the old ruled) until young people migrated to the city and earned independence. American revolutionaries challenged authoritarian figures, and equality of gen-

hopelessly hesitant coward. The Roman elders were deprived of authority during civil wars and the Empire. Christian morality in the Dark Ages equated miserable old age to sin, a curse and punishment from God. Old men in the Middle Ages were illustrated in terms of "coughs," "loss of reason," and "filth." The worship of youthful creativity and beauty in the Renaissance implied a profound despair associated with loss of all vitality in old age. Eternity was an illusion because all achievements and beauty would vanish with aging and death. Old age was hated, demeaned, blackened, and damned. Even William Shakespeare mocked the "childish" and "oblivious" last stage of life.

erations was advocated. By the end of the eighteenth century, old age was devalued. The paradox of old age, however, still existed in the nineteenth century. In the spiritual world, old age was looked up to. Old age was believed to be the best time for retrospective life reviews and inner reorganizations. Aging was the transition from darkness to light. Sentimentalism toward old age was also reflected in the understanding of its existential significance: As a public good, living to old age was useful in itself. The metaphor of old age as winter was changed into the autumn season, the time of ripeness. In the secular world, however, old age was looked down upon.

Toward the end of the nineteenth century, American culture became increasingly democratic, competitive, and urban. The "civilized morality" code of "personal responsibility and internalized self-restraint" facilitated hostility against aging because an individual's ambition and independence diminished with aging. Felix Adler, leader of the New York Ethical Culture Society, tried to help the public with his conceptual distinction between "being" and "doing"—the spiritual life was engendered in a person through "doing" in earlier years but was manifested in "being" in old age to be honored and appreciated. Still, the American public was afraid of aging. This great fear was behind their zest for youth-prolonging and rejuvenation techniques (still very much so today). By the early twentieth century, scientists were working to demystify the aging phenomenon. Modern gerontology (coined in 1904 by Elie Metchnikoff) and geriatrics (coined in 1909 by I. L. Nascher) emerged. The great psychologist G. Stanley Hall published his book *Senescence, the Last Half of Life* in 1922. The cultural shift from viewing aging primarily as a mystery or an existential problem to a scientific and technical problem had taken place.

VIEWS OF AGING IN WOMEN

In early times, the menopause could signify a promoted status. Aging to women could mean a relief from domestic chores and sexual taboos as well as more power and public exposure. For example, in the Lemba tribe, the postmenopausal woman was allowed to play a role alongside the men in important affairs. More often, though, the old woman was a synonym of evil. As in modern times, according to Minois, aging was difficult for poor women, especially childless widows.

In late nineteenth and early twentieth century America, old women escaped the attacks at old men, probably owing this "mercy" to their domestic "usefulness," according to Cole. In modernized America, gender discrimination, divorce, single-mother responsibilities, and Social Security benefits based on job incomes have made old age a difficult time for women. Old women are likely to be victims of a double jeopardy: being old and belonging to the "minority" group of women. Old women from ethnic minorities suffer even more.

In a woman's life, the menopause carries biological and physiological as well as psychological and social meanings. To some women, the menopause means discomfort from negative physiological symptoms (such as hot flashes), anxieties about reduced sexual appeal or desire, despair from loss of reproductive ability, worries about osteoporosis (bone loss), and depression and fear of aging in general. Yet, according to K. Warner Schaie and Sherry L. Willis in *Adult Development and Aging* (4th ed., 1996), recent research suggests that many educated women understand the menopause as a normal event in development and view it positively as a relief from menstruation and worries about contraception, as well as freedom for new experiences.

Men and women construct meanings of aging and old age differently because of the differences in their biological makeup, socializing practices, social roles and expectations, and the social treatment they receive. To women, aging could mean the end of reproduction with the menopause; empty nest syndrome, especially for homemakers; new roles as primary caregivers of aging parents, typically for daughters in their fifties; widowhood, as women have a longer life expectancy than men; living alone, as old women are less likely than old men to remarry because of discrepancies in age and number; or limited financial resources, a consequence of historical gender discrimination. In a culture that presents the young woman as the symbol of beauty, love, and worldly pleasure, the older woman is destined to suffer when youth is lost in aging. On the other hand, aging could mean an exciting time for women, with new directions available and freedom for personal growth.

VIEWS OF AGING IN ETHNIC MINORITY GROUPS

The meaning of aging is also influenced by an individual's ethnicity. As noted in *Aging and Ethnicity* (1987), edited by Kyriakos S. Markides and Charles H. Mindel, in discussing the aging experiences of ethnic minority groups in America, many researchers remind people of "double jeopardy": Elderly minority members suffer from the additive effects of being old and ethnically different. The vast diversity within each ethnic group, however, should be kept in mind.

African Americans have a long tradition of viewing old age as survival and a sign of dignity, something to be proud of. The elderly are valued as educators of cultural heritage and family history. African American elders generally view old age as a reward, are glad to be alive, and enjoy families and friends. Yet, to those who are homeless and mentally ill, inner-city residents in particular, aging means a bleak experience.

Although the overall condition for African Americans has improved, the history of racial discrimination bears its long-term consequences into old age. For example, a 1997 study by Jim Mitchell and colleagues published in the journal *Research on Aging* showed that Caucasian elders were about twice as likely as African American elders to visit health care specialists, even though there was little difference among older adults in primary care physician visits by race.

The meaning of aging as measured in life satisfaction among Mexican American elders reflected their general contentment in a study published in *Hispanic Elderly: A Cultural Signature* (1988), edited by Marta Sotomayor and Herman Curiel. Some of these Latino elders might have thought that their life was improving, or they might have been insulated from a broader society holding negative views toward the old. Life satisfaction for old men was lower than for old women, suggesting that role continuity might exist for the elderly woman but not for the elderly man.

Examination of the meaning of growing old to Puerto Ricans in *Hispanic Elderly*, in terms of their relationship to their children and grandchildren, revealed a living arrangement pattern typical of the dominant American culture: Most of the elderly were living either alone or with their spouse. Grandchildren meant love and happiness to these elders, but the day-to-day relationship between the two generations appeared not to be very close. These findings have challenged the belief that older Hispanic Americans benefit from extended families.

According to Susan Hillier and Georgia M. Barrow in *Aging, the Individual, and Society* (7th ed., 1999), aging could mean a tough time for Hispanic elders because they have suffered major linguistic and cultural barriers to assimilation and have occupied a low socioeconomic status.

Aging in Asian cultures is believed to mean enjoying filial care from next generations. Research in the United States has found a prevalence of intergenerational residence among Asian Americans. In a 1997 study, however, Masako Ishii-Kuntz observed differentiated filial support, depending on factors such as proximity in residence, financial resources, number of years the children have lived in the United States, and parental need for assistance.

Different degrees of cultural assimilation across generations, language barriers, insulation from the larger society, and lack of culture-compatible social services may cause difficulties for elderly Asian Americans.

Various American Indian tribes have different views of aging. A traditional Ojibway story depicts human life as a journey to conquer four hills. Many will die and will never reach the last hill. Old age means great success and deserves respect, as noted in *The Oxford Book of Aging* (1994), edited by Thomas R. Cole and Mary G. Winkler.

Susan Mercer's 1996 ethnographic research indicated that growing old in Navajo culture meant being addressed as "Grandparent," being less visible, having specific foods, and having more flexibility. Any "Grandparent" near the last stage of an illness was transferred to the Indian Health Service. Many American Indians were still unwilling to touch a dead body because of taboos.

Hillier and Barrow argue that lower education level, meager income, poor nutrition, and lack of health care have placed older American Indians in an enormously needy group, possibly the most deprived of all ethnic groups in the United States.

CONTEMPORARY THEORETICAL PERSPECTIVES OF AGING

Driven by cosmic curiosity and pressure from a graying globe, natural and social scientists—especially those working in the fields of or related to gerontology, what Hillier and Barrow call "the scientific study of the aging process from maturity into old age and the elderly as a special population"—have been busy searching for the meaning of aging.

Aging in biomedical models. Unless otherwise noted, the definitions cited in this section, as well as information about the full names and works of original authors, can be found in David Hall's *The Biomedical Basis of Gerontology* (1984).

Biological gerontology and biomedical models of aging basically deal with physical aging involving senescence. Senescence is defined as "a deteriorative process . . . associated with a decrease in viability and an increase in vulnerability" and shows itself as an increased probability of death with increasing chronological age" (Comfort, 1979). Hall summarized the meaning of aging in many definitions, as follows: Becoming more noticeable in the postreproductive period, aging lowers the functional capacity of cells, organs, and entire organisms; results in the degradation of structural elements within the body; lowers the effectiveness of the response of the organism to internal and external factors; and increases the likelihood of the ultimate dysfunction—death. Aging also means a decline in the production of free energy (Calloway, 1964).

In the endogenous view, aging is an involuntary process that operates cumulatively with the passage of time to result in the adverse modification of cells, such as Leonard Hayflick's theory of cellular aging caused by damage to deoxyribonucleic acid (DNA) or errors in protein synthesis. In the exogenous view, aging is a consequence of impairments attributable to infections, accidents, or poisons in the external environment, such as skin aging due to sun exposure (Cowdry, 1942—see *Adult Development and Aging*). Aging involves both endogenous and exogenous processes as genetic and environmental factors interact.

Aging can be seen as a developmental continuum that is genetically controlled and preprogrammed over evolution in all living things, as if there were an "internal clock of age," as also discussed by John J. Medina in *The Clock of Ages* (1996).

Hall integrates many other biomedical theories of aging (cross-linkage theory, free radical theory,

immunological theories) into this conclusion: Aging is "the superimposition of accumulating errors on a programme. The programme is predictable, whereas the errors, being stochastic, cannot be."

James E. Birren's definition of aging as "the transformation of the human organism after the age of physical maturity—that is, optimum age of reproduction—so that the probability of survival constantly decreases and there are regular transformations in appearance, behavior, experience, and social roles," in *Emergent Theories of Aging* (1988), edited by Birren and Vern L. Bengtson, obviously includes other domains in addition to biology.

Aging in psychological theories. Psychological theories of aging focus on psychological aging or changes in sensation and perception, behavior, intelligence and cognition, emotions, motivation, identity, personality, personal relations, and social roles.

Developmental psychologists view aging as a later stage or life experience built upon the outcome of earlier stages or life experiences. Aging means developing a new identity and solving new developmental tasks. For example, in 1972 Robert Havighurst listed six developmental (adjusting) tasks of late life, as discussed in *Adult Development and Aging*. Crisis models explain life crises as normative events in development, such as the menopause for women or the loss of a spouse. The best representative crisis theory is Erik H. Erikson's psychosocial theory. The last of his eight developmental stages involves the crisis of integrity versus despair and the task of balancing the two. Integrity matures from wisdom, the crystallized meaningfulness from life experiences. Integrity is a sense of coherence and wholeness as a person. Integrity also means demonstrating to young people what to anticipate in ripe old age and "reritualizing" them. The counterpart to wisdom is despair in an increasing state of feeling finished, confused, and helpless. According to Erikson in *The Life Cycle Completed* (1982), up to a point, despair is "a natural and necessary reaction to human weakness." In discussing wisdom, Birren asserted that wisdom can enable older people to use self-generating strategies proactively (as opposed to merely reactively) in order to create a favorable environment to override their biological and social limitations. That some retirees migrate to warmer regions is an example of such "niche-finding" strategies.

The meaning of aging is dependent on what research design was used. Cross-sectional studies usually give an impression of steady decrements after the prime time. Longitudinal studies, however, often demonstrate remarkable psychological stability over time in the same individual. For example, as noted in an essay by Nathan W. Shock, the Baltimore Longitudinal Study on Aging showed that psychological changes in vigilance, reaction time, logical problem solving, paired-associate and serial learning of verbal material, and memory for visual designs were not major before age seventy in normal aging adults.

In cognitive aging, it is generally agreed that fluid intelligence (genetically and biologically determined "native" mental ability) tends to decline with age but that crystallized intelligence (general world knowledge acquired through education and life experiences) may be maintained or even improved in later life, as discussed by Johannes J. F. Schroots in his 1996 article "Theoretical Developments in the Psychology of Aging." Furthermore, the elderly are well equipped to develop compensatory skills to perform complex tasks. In information-processing models, empirical studies with healthy aging adults do not support the myth that aging means a universal cognitive decline.

In discussing personality shift in *The Human Elder in Nature, Culture, and Society* (1997), David Gutmann proposed a universal developmental process in the human species driving aging women to be more "masculine" (for example, more decisive) and aging men more "feminine" (for example, more nurturing and pacific), both becoming androgynous.

In 1996, Schroots reviewed psychologists' efforts to distinguish normal aging (typical changes as one ages) from pathological aging (atypical, abnormal changes). Primary aging refers to disease-free changes intrinsic to the aging process that are ultimately irreversible, such as the menopause; secondary aging refers to changes caused by illnesses that are correlated with age, such as Alzheimer's disease; and tertiary aging refers to rapid losses and a marked decline shortly before death. Successful aging shows few signs of change.

The continued-potential view of aging, what Gutmann calls the "strong face of aging," suggests that positive psychological aging is possible.

Aging in sociological theories. Social gerontology and sociological theories of aging focus on social aging, the meaning of the mutual influences from aging individuals on society and vice versa.

Patricia Passuth and Bengtson gave an excellent review of the major theories in social gerontology in *Emergent Theories of Aging*; the full names of authors and the sources of references cited in this section can be found in that work.

Within structural functionalism, four sociological theories of aging have been developed. The disengagement theory (Cumming and Henry, 1961) contends that aging involves "a decreased level in the number and frequency of social interactions as well as decreased emotional involvement in old age." The mutual withdrawal of the aging person and society from each other is functional to both parties: Society will have room for the young and the individual will have time to prepare for the final complete withdrawal (death). The modernization theory (Cowgill and Holmes, 1972) argues that "the status of the aged is inversely related to the level of societal industrialization." Aging being devalued in highly industrialized America is seen in people's intense fear of aging and craving to prolong youthfulness. The age stratification model is based on "cohort flow" (Riley, 1971). A birth cohort is a group of people born at the same time in history who age together. Each cohort is unique because it has its own characteristics (size, gender, social class distribution) and each experiences particular historical events. For example, aging has a different meaning for the cohort that underwent the two world wars and the Great Depression than for baby boomers. The life course perspective is a framework including "social clock," as proposed by Bernice Neugarten in 1965, and the timing of role transitions across the life span. Transitional models understand aging as a progress in the life course, predictable from the expected timing of events based largely on societal and cultural age norms.

Symbolic interactionism has generated three theories of aging. The activity theory (Havighurst and Goldhamer, 1949) includes central conceptions of "adjustment," "activity," and "individual life satisfaction," which are also discussed in the

1996 article "Tracing the Course of Theoretical Development in the Sociology of Aging" by Robert Lynott et al. To make aging meaningful and satisfying, an elderly person must substitute new roles for those lost in old age (through retirement or widowhood) to maintain a positive sense of self and must engage in new activities to remain active. The social competence and breakdown theory (Kuypers and Bengtson, 1973) suggests that a negative spiral of feedback can occur as a result of the vulnerability of the aging person, resulting in a "social breakdown syndrome that might destroy the individual's self-concept. Successful aging depends on a supportive environment as well as self-reinforcement. The subculture theory (Rose, 1964) holds that the aged are developing their own subculture in American society. Their decreased interaction with other age groups and increased interaction among themselves inspire them to create their own norms and values.

The social exchange theory predicts that aging means reduced power for the aged in social exchanges because they possess fewer resources to offer (Dowd, 1975).

Karl Marx's conflict theory argues that those who control the means of production control the distribution of power, profits, and resources. The political economy of age (for example, Estes, 1979) looks at the political and economic conditions that give rise to problems of growing old. The old are usually perceived as deprived and impoverished in a capitalist society.

Social phenomenological theories of aging concern the interpretation of the subjective reality. With an interdisciplinary approach incorporating phenomenological and humanistic psychology and symbolic interactionism in sociology, personal narrative models conceptualize that meanings are both subjective and intersubjective, in that they derive from interactions and one's interpretations of these interactions (Reker and Wong, 1988). Older people's narratives or personal stories are the products of the past and future interacting with the present, reflecting the continuity and the function of historical time.

Chronological age. Using chronological age to divide up a life course (so that "old age" is defined) is a convenient and ancient practice. In the United States at the end of the twentieth century, the legal definition of old age (for receiving Social Security benefits) was sixty-five, with a transition to age sixty-seven anticipated in the next twenty years or so. People over sixty-five can be divided into "the young-old" (sixty-five to seventy-five or eighty), "the old" or "the old-old" (seventy-five or eighty to ninety), and the "very old" or "the oldest-old" (eighty-five or ninety and older).

Aging as dependency. According to Margret M. Baltes in *The Many Faces of Dependency in Old Age* (1996), dependency is defined as "a product of decline and deterioration, as a loss in both physical and mental functioning . . . an inevitable consequence of growing old." An aging person has to balance between security and autonomy. There are many types of dependency: financial dependency, physical dependency, behavioral dependency, emotional dependency, and structured dependency.   *—Ling-Yi Zhou*

See also African Americans; Ageism; Aging: Biological, psychological, and sociocultural perspectives; Aging: Historical perspective; *Aging Experience: Diversity and Commonality Across Cultures, The*; American Indians; Asian Americans; Baby boomers; Death and dying; Death anxiety; Erikson, Erik H.; Filial responsibility; Funerals; *Growing Old in America*; Latinos; Maturity; Men and aging; Middle age; Midlife crisis; Neugarten, Bernice; Old age; Over the hill; Religion; Stereotypes; Successful aging; *Why Survive? Being Old in America*; Wisdom; Women and aging.

FOR FURTHER INFORMATION:

Baltes, Margret M. *The Many Faces of Dependency in Old Age.* New York: Cambridge University Press, 1996. Vignettes and the author's research on dependency in old age.

Birren, James E., and Vern L. Bengtson, eds. *Emergent Theories of Aging.* New York: Springer, 1988. Selected articles review theories of aging in biological, psychological, and social/sociological disciplines.

Cole, Thomas R. *The Journey of Life: A Cultural History of Aging in America.* New York: Cambridge University Press, 1992. Reviews the images of the human life course and the meaning of later life in Northern middle-class culture, first in Europe and then in America between the Reformation and World War I.

Cole, Thomas R., and Mary G. Winkler, eds. *The Oxford Book of Aging.* New York: Oxford Univer-

sity Press, 1994. Citations from great writers, po-
ets, and philosophers as well as folklore stories
in many cultures about the meaning of aging
organized into nine theme chapters.

Erikson, Erik H. *The Life Cycle Completed.* New York:
W. W. Norton, 1982. This monograph discusses
major stages in psychosocial development.

Hall, David A. *The Biomedical Basis of Gerontology.*
Littleton, Mass.: John Wright, 1984. Discusses
various definitions and theories of aging based
on biomedical models.

Hillier, Susan, and Georgia M. Barrow. *Aging, the
Individual, and Society.* 7th ed. Belmont, Calif.:
Wadsworth, 1999. A college textbook focused
on the sociological aspects of aging.

Ishii-Kuntz, Masako. "Intergenerational Relation-
ships Among Chinese, Japanese, and Korean
Americans." *The Family Coordinator* 46, no.1
(January, 1997).

Lynott, Robert, et al. "Tracing the Course of Theoretical Development in the Sociology of
Aging."*The Gerontologist* 36, no. 6 (December,
1996).

Markides, Kyriakos S., and Charles H. Mindel, eds.
Aging and Ethnicity. Newbury Park, Calif.: Sage
Publications, 1987. Examines the status and experience of growing old in the United States as
related to ethnicity.

Medina, John J. *The Clock of Ages: Why We Age—How
We Age—Winding Back the Clock.* New York: Cambridge University Press, 1996. Discusses the biological basis for aging.

Mercer, Susan O. "Navajo Elderly People in a Reservation Nursing Home: Admission Predictors
and Culture Care Practices." *Social Work* 41, no.
2 (March, 1996).

Minois, Georges. *History of Old Age: From Antiquity
to the Renaissance.* Translated by Sarah Hanbury
Tenison. Chicago: University of Chicago Press,
1987. Discusses the cultural views of old age reflected in literature, religion, and the arts.

Mitchell, Jim, et al. "Health and Community-Based
Service Use: Differences Between Elderly African Americans and Whites." *Research on Aging*
19, no. 2 (June, 1997).

Schaie, K. Warner, and Sherry L. Willis. *Adult Development and Aging.* 4th ed. New York:
HarperCollins, 1996. A college textbook focused on adult development and aging in the
perspective of developmental psychology.

Schroots, Johannes J. F. "Theoretical Developments in the Psychology of Aging." *The Gerontologist* 36, no. 6 (December, 1996).

Settersten, Richard A., Jr. Reviews of *Adulthood and
Aging: Research on Continuities and Discontinuities,*
edited by Vern L. Bengtson; *The Human Elder in
Nature, Culture, and Society,* by David Gutmann;
and *The Meanings of Age: Selected Papers of Bernice
L. Neugarten. The Gerontologist* 37, no. 5 (October, 1997). Settersten reviews three books on
the meaning of aging.

Shock, Nathan W. "Longitudinal Studies of Aging
in Humans." In *Handbook of the Biology of Aging,*
edited by Caleb E. Finch, Edward L. Schneider,
et al. 2d ed. New York: Van Nostrand Reinhold,
1985. Reports the major results of the Baltimore
Longitudinal Study of Aging as well as other
similar studies.

Sotomayor, Marta, and Herman Curiel, eds. *Hispanic Elderly: A Cultural Signature.* Edinburg,
Tex.: National Hispanic Council on Aging,
1988. Essays discuss and report research results
about the well-being of Hispanic elderly in psychological and sociological perspectives.

CYSTS

RELEVANT ISSUES: Health and medicine

SIGNIFICANCE: Cysts are benign (noncancerous)
tumors that usually do not cause health problems unless they put pressure on another organ
of the body

Sebaceous cysts are noncancerous tumors or
growths that consist of a cyst wall filled with either
solid or liquid material. Other names for sebaceous
cysts include epidermal, keratin, or epidermoid
cysts. They usually occur with increased frequency
following puberty. Sebaceous cysts usually occur
within the layers of the skin or directly beneath it.
These cysts are usually firm and freely movable
with clear borders, as opposed to cancerous tumors
that tend to have a "stuck down" feeling and are
generally rock hard with irregular edges. It is important, however, to have cysts evaluated by a health
care provider to be sure that they are not cancerous growths. Sebaceous cysts are usually filled with
a solid or liquid material that is white and bad
smelling. Sometimes this material will drain from
an opening known as a "punctum." Cysts occur
most often on the face, scalp, neck, back, and scro-

tum, and they range in diameter from 0.5 centimeter to 5 centimeters. Sebaceous cysts do not usually cause symptoms unless they become infected, rupture, or are traumatized. Their cause is not entirely understood, but they are thought to arise spontaneously when a hair follicle becomes blocked.

Sebaceous cysts may be left in place if they are not causing any difficulties or if they do not create a cosmetic problem. They may be removed if they are in areas that expose them to rubbing or trauma or if they are unsightly. The entire cyst, including the wall, must be removed so they do not recur. If a cyst becomes infected, the usual treatment is to cut it open and drain it. The health care provider may also prescribe antibiotics for the infection. Once the infection has resolved, the cyst wall can be "shelled out" by a surgeon, thereby preventing recurrence.

Cysts may also occur in areas of the body other than skin, including the brain, breast, and bone. Cysts in other locations also have a cyst wall and may be filled with clear, watery fluid; dark, syrupy material; or other substances. They may cause symptoms because of pressure on the surrounding body organs or because they are preventing the normal flow of blood or lymph throughout the body. Bone cysts may lead to fractures as the cyst invades the bone and replaces normal bone tissue. Treatment is directed at the specific type of cyst, its location, and the symptoms it is causing.

—*Rebecca Lovell Scott*

See also Bone changes and disorders; Brain changes and disorders; Breast changes and disorders; Cosmetic surgery; Skin changes and disorders.

DEAFNESS. *See* **HEARING LOSS.**

DEATH AND DYING

RELEVANT ISSUES: Death, family, psychology, sociology

SIGNIFICANCE: Consideration of personal death and the experience of the deaths of others shape the lives of middle-aged and older adults and the society in which they live

The relationship of death and dying to aging is complex and continually changing. Three primary areas of interest to researchers are the increase in life expectancy and the effects of that change, the personal experience of multiple deaths, and increasing choices in the dying process.

LIFE EXPECTANCY

Richard Kalish notes that, while the old always have died, the dying have not always been old. In the early twentieth century, death was common at all ages; the life expectancy for individuals born in 1900 was only forty-seven. One hundred years later, however, with the eradication of many catastrophic diseases, the advancement of medical treatment for life-threatening conditions, and the decrease in maternal deaths caused by childbirth, age has become more predictive of time of death. Individuals now expect to die in old age, and for most, that expectation is fulfilled. More and more, death has become the province of the old.

A child born in the United States in 1999 was expected to live approximately seventy-six years and was most likely to die of heart disease, cancer, or cerebrovascular disease (stroke). Exact life expectancy figures are related to general characteristics such as gender, ethnicity, and income in addition to individual factors such as genetic inheritance and personal lifestyle (for example, nutrition, exercise, habits, and exposure to stress). Common causes of death are related to these variables as well. In most cases, appropriate medical care will make death a slow process, very unlike the quick deaths of earlier times.

As people live longer, the experience and expectations of adulthood change accordingly. For most, there will be a healthier, more active middle and early old age; however, advances in medicine also have condemned many to live longer in a debilitated state prior to death. This last change fuels debates about quality of life, particularly in the later years.

The expectation of death in old age also has affected personal grieving and larger societal issues. For example, as death becomes associated with old age, deaths in middle adulthood or earlier become more unexpected and more difficult for survivors to accept. In addition, as death becomes linked to old age, there is a transfer of the fears of death and dying to the process of aging, and the fear that they are close to death can affect the treatment of the elderly themselves. Increases in life expectancy also are shaping public policy debates. For example, decisions about eligibility for Social Security benefits first were made in the 1930's, when life expectancy was much lower than at the end of the century. One side of the policy debate questions whether eligibility should be postponed as life expectancy increases. At the same time, research on life extension is increasing, sparking debates about who will be permitted to postpone death and at what cost. While life expectancy has increased for all gender, ethnic, and income groups, it has not done so equally. Many fear that successful life extension technologies will exacerbate existing inequalities.

In summary, increases in life expectancy have changed the experience of living, aging, and dying as well as the social policy governing them. As medical technology becomes more advanced and life expectancy continues to change, both individuals and society will undergo further adaptation.

DEATH ANXIETY

Early research on death anxiety assumed that, because they were closer to dying, the old would be the most anxious about death. However, few studies have found a relationship between age and death anxiety. When a correlation has been found, the middle aged have been the most anxious about death, not the old. Further studies have noted that while the old report thinking, dreaming, and talking about death more than other age groups, these activities are not due to fear or anxiety. Kalish has theorized that at least three factors contribute to diminished death anxiety in the old. First, in old age many individuals have lived longer than they expected, consequently they do not feel cheated by death. Second, older adults have had more experience with death and therefore have become more socialized to and comfortable with death. Third, old age is devalued in American society and the elderly, as members of that society, share the perception that the deaths of the old (now, their deaths) are less significant than those of younger persons.

Erik H. Erikson's theory of psychosocial development provides another reason that older adults may be less anxious about death than other age groups. Erikson writes that the primary developmental task of old age is to engage in life review through reminiscing and making sense of one's life. According to Erikson, a successful life review will lead to a sense of ego integrity, that one's life has been meaningful and well spent. When a person is satisfied with his or her life there are fewer regrets, fewer tasks left undone, and death is less frightening.

DEATH OF PARENTS

One of the unavoidable consequences of living to old age is the experience of multiple deaths. Most individuals expect that the deaths will follow a natural order, with the oldest dying first and the youngest surviving until much later. Generally, the death of parents is experienced in middle age and often the death of a parent is the first significant death in an individual's life. By the age of fifty-four, one-half of all adults have lost both parents, although with increased life expectancy parental death is becoming more common when children are in old age. Regardless of the timing, the death of a parent is an important loss for most adult children.

Psychologist Therese Rando notes that the death of a parent initiates several losses for most adult children, including the losses of unconditional love, shared memories of the past and childhood, present and future relationship, possible resolution of unfinished business, and a generational barrier between the adult child and death. In adulthood, parents serve as a buffer against death; regardless of their age, as long as parents are alive there is the expectation that personal death is not imminent. Death of the last parent, especially in middle or old age, signals that the adult child is in the next generation to die, making death unavoidable.

When adult children become part of the oldest generation, they often report feeling more autonomous, mature, and more responsible for themselves and others. However, these positive feelings typically are the result of contemplation of one's own death and the intense questioning and reevaluation of personal priorities caused by the pain of parental death. Erikson's seventh stage of psychosocial development, generativity versus stagnation, occurs when middle-aged adults focus on the legacy that they will leave after death. The death of parents, with the consequent consideration of one's own mortality, adds to the focus on generativity in middle age.

Although the death of parents is difficult for most adult children, the impact of parental death depends on several factors, including the closeness of the relationship and the prior health of the parent. In dysfunctional families or in cases where

Leading Causes of Death in the United States in 1900 and 1995

1900	*1995*
1. Pneumonia and influenza	1. Heart diseases
2. Tuberculosis	2. Cancer and other malignant tumors
3. Diarrhea, enteritis, and ulceration of the intestine	3. Strokes
4. Heart diseases	4. Chronic obstructive pulmonary diseases
5. Senility (ill-defined or unknown)	5. Accidents
6. Strokes	6. Pneumonia and influenza
7. Nephritis	7. Diabetes mellitus
8. Accidents	8. HIV-AIDS
9. Cancer and other malignant tumors	9. Suicide
10. Diphtheria	10. Chronic liver disease and cirrhosis

Source: The Time Almanac 1998. New York: Information Please, 1997.

there was unfinished business, parental death precludes the possibility of reconciliation and consequently may be especially difficult for the adult child. Parental health prior to death affects children's grief in several ways; for example, deaths can be easier to accept when the parent has been severely incapacitated or in great pain. In these cases, grieving starts earlier, at the loss of functioning, so that physical death is the last of many losses experienced in the parent's decline. After a parent dies, adult children who have been their caregivers report feelings of relief and gratefulness for the extra time they now have for themselves, in addition to the more typical grief reactions to parental death.

In summary, the death of a parent usually is tragic but, to some extent, expected. Most adult children anticipate outliving their parents. Death of the last parent separates adult children from their childhood and makes personal death seem more imminent, often causing an upheaval in their lives. However, the end result of parent death can be greater feelings of personal maturity and responsibility for others.

DEATH OF A SPOUSE

Death in one's own generation becomes more common in middle age and a frequent occurrence in old age. The majority of older women experience death of a spouse; for those over seventy-five, 64.9 percent of women and 21.6 percent of men are widowed. Death of a spouse is a disorganizing experience involving major role losses. One is no longer part of a couple, with the shared experiences and shared responsibilities that have come to characterize married life. The widowed individual must adapt to singlehood, which may mean a change in finances, meal preparation, hobbies, activities, and perceived safety as well as a different status in their social network. Recently widowed individuals not only must cope with bereavement but also face an increase in daily hassles, leading to extreme stress. It is not surprising that the newly widowed display higher levels of depression than married adults of the same age and show an increase in mortality rates for the year after spousal death.

Adaptation to the loss of a spouse varies by age, gender, and the status of the relationship. In general, studies have found that adaptation is better

for the old than the young, probably because the death of a spouse is expected in old age. However, being widowed greatly increases the chances of nursing home placement in older adults. Studies examining gender issues have found mixed results, but all note that men are more likely to remarry and their remarriages occur more quickly than those of women. In cases where traditional gender roles were followed, it has been found that men have poorer adjustment to loss of spouse than women. Researchers hypothesize that in traditional families, widowed men have to learn more new roles, are less likely to seek help, and are less likely to discuss their feelings than women are, making their adjustment to the loss of a spouse more difficult. Consequently, it is not surprising that older widowers are more likely to die within the first year after the death of their spouses than are widows. The status of the relationship also affects adjustment to the death of a spouse; those who experienced happy, close marital relationships appear to adjust better to the loss of a spouse than those who had conflicted marriages.

Although most of the research studies examine legally married couples, many authors have written about the death of a partner in homosexual relationships. Most of the general principles on death of a spouse apply to homosexual couples, but gay men and lesbians face additional issues stemming from their marginal status in society. Many hospitals restrict access to the dying, except in cases of legally recognized relationships such as close relatives and spouses. At death, decisions on body disposition and funeral services are expected to come from those relatives. Consequently, unless prior arrangements were made to include them, partners in homosexual relationships (like partners in other unmarried couples) may have restricted access to the dying environment of and bereavement rituals for their partner. In addition, homosexual partners are less likely to be supported in their grief by the surrounding community. Lack of support may lead to disenfranchised grief, a grief that is intense and difficult to resolve.

DEATH OF FRIENDS

For most individuals, middle age is the first time that a noticeable number of people from their own generation start to die; the total death rate rises from approximately 180 deaths per 100,000 in young adulthood to 790 deaths per 100,000 in middle age. About 65 percent of the deaths in middle age are the result of conditions that may have been developing for years, cardiovascular disease and cancer. The death of others in their age group reminds the middle aged of their own mortality and susceptibility to disease. By old age, friend death is a common occurrence and the number of people alive who knew the older adult in their youth dwindles.

Friends serve important functions at all ages, but research on friends in old age suggests that having a strong social network improves physical health. In addition, the maintenance of close relationships with friends has been found to be more important to a sense of well-being than having close relationships with family members. Friends in old age provide a special type of companionship, and consequently, older adults report greater loneliness after the death of a close friend. Grief at the death of a close friend is similar to the grief for a close family member and both diminish the social networks so vital to older adults. Unfortunately, the older one becomes, the more friends one loses to death, and those losses come more rapidly with age. Because of the number of deaths experienced, theorists have suggested that many older adults feel bereavement overload.

Most older adult pet owners keep animals for companionship, making pets a special type of friend. For older adults, pets relieve loneliness, increase social interaction, give a sense of purpose and responsibility, provide a sense of continuity and structure, increase self-esteem, and give unconditional love that is independent of the changing appearance and ability level of the pet owner. Research has demonstrated that older pet owners are healthier, requiring fewer medications than the elderly without pets, and that stroking a pet reduces blood pressure. Pet ownership can lower stress levels, and the responsibility of owning a pet can help maintain cognitive functioning. Because of the importance of pets in so many areas of life, the death of a pet can have devastating effects on the elderly, removing some of the purpose, structure, and love from their lives. For many older adults the death of a pet causes reconsideration of their own mortality and can signal the end of an era, where their impending deaths make it unwise to acquire another pet who will outlive them.

Thus, pet death in old age not only creates loss in the present, but can highlight the unavailability of certain positive interactions in the future. Not surprisingly, most elderly pet owners report keeping articles associated with their deceased pet (for example, bowls, leashes) as mementos of their special relationship.

DEATH OF A CHILD

To many, the death of one's child is the most tragic death, regardless of the child's age. A metaphor commonly used to describe the feeling of losing a child is amputation; a part of oneself is gone. Death of a child violates the natural order, the expectation that children will outlive their parents. The death of a child also violates a primary assumption of the parental role, that parents can and will protect their children from harm. Regardless of the child's age at death, parents usually feel guilty for not having been able to protect them. In addition, some loss of the past and a reorganization of the future accompany the death of a child. However, for some parents there is a complete loss of role, as in the loss of being a mother when an only child dies.

The death of a child elicits many of the same reactions from parents regardless of whether the death is through miscarriage or stillbirth or occurs in infancy, childhood, or adulthood. At all ages, the death of a child puts a strain on marital relationships because spouses often grieve differently. Among middle-aged parents, the death of a child also may trigger a crisis in Erikson's seventh stage of generativity versus stagnation, in which the middle aged focus on the legacy they will leave after death. Because children play a strong part in that legacy, child death can be particularly difficult in middle age.

Approximately 10 percent of parents over the age of sixty have experienced the death of at least one child, and that percentage grows dramatically with increasing age. While the elderly experience the death of a child in ways similar to parents of other ages, in old age the death of a child also signals the loss of a potential caregiver. Parents whose children have died are at an increased risk of institutionalization in their later years.

In old age, several factors may diminish the support available for parents grieving the death of a child, including the age of their child, the shrinking social networks of older adults, and the possible health problems of the elderly parents. Because their child is an adult (often in middle or old age), they typically have a family of procreation and those family members will be the first to be given the resources available for grieving. The child's family also will have easy access to rituals that aid in the acceptance of death such as planning the funeral and sorting through belongings. The relationship of the elderly parent to the child's family will dictate to what extent they are excluded from support provided to the grieving family and rituals associated with the death. In addition, the social networks of the elderly often are strained by the number of deaths and other losses occurring within them, making their resources inadequate to support parents at the death of a child. Finally, the health status of the parent affects the number of options available for gaining support in their grieving, such as participating in support groups and attending rituals for the dead. Health status also affects the likelihood of having diversions from their grief and the number of opportunities for reinvesting energy in new relationships. Among the frail elderly, parental health also affects the amount of information they are provided about their children; studies have found that caregivers of the frail elderly frequently fail to disclose information about their children's serious illnesses and sometimes they are not told of a child's death.

In summary, the death of a child is a devastating and life-changing experience for all parents. To parents, the death of a child represents the loss of a future, and as children get older their deaths also represent losses of the past and the specific roles that they played. As parents and their children age, grieving for a child's death becomes more complex due to changes in the family, social, and health systems.

MULTIPLE LOSSES

A consequence of living to old age is the experience of multiple deaths, generally starting in middle age and accelerating in older adulthood. Psychologist Robert Kastenbaum has noted that the elderly are likely to experience losses in greater number, variety, and rapidity than any other age group. One effect of experiencing multiple deaths can be bereavement overload, where the older adult does not have time to mourn and accept one death before another occurs. Often at the same time they are experiencing multiple deaths, other personal losses are occurring such as the end of work life, changes in physical ability, and the shrinking of social networks, all of which contribute to feelings of overload. Multiple losses of various types can contribute to depression in the elderly, causing symptoms of fatigue and withdrawal that are too often misdiagnosed as being part of the natural aging process.

While few would volunteer for the experience, positive outcomes also are associated with living through multiple losses. It has been hypothesized that one of the reasons older adults are less anxious about death than other age groups is their vast experience with the deaths of others.

"And death shall have no dominion" is a line repeated throughout the famous poem by Dylan Thomas. Studies indicate that this sentiment accurately describes the experience of most people, who continue to have bonds with the dead long after physical separation from them. These bonds may be especially important to the elderly, who typically have encountered multiple losses and outlived many of their relatives and friends. Psychologist Lillian Troll, in her work with the old-old (those over age eighty-five) described the survivorship of the dead, where older adults periodically consult their deceased loved ones about decisions and give them updates on recent events. These consultations provide continuity and comfort for older adults, continuing the relationships that they have treasured throughout their lives.

DYING OPTIONS

One of the ongoing revolutions in health care concerns the provision of choices in the dying process and the related public dialog about quality-of-life issues. Spurred both by advancements in medical technology and the original hospice movement in England and Europe, the questions of how to die and under what circumstances have been changing the experience of dying in America. Many choices about the dying experience are permitted under present law and experiments in other types of choice are being conducted on a statewide or agency-level basis. State laws govern the use of living wills (in which an individual can state in advance the medical procedures they would like performed or would want to avoid should they become incapacitated) and durable power of attorney for health care (in which an individual designates a representative who will make their health care decisions should they become incapacitated). These documents, in which the individual stipulates conditions of medical treatment or individuals who will make their medical decisions, are known as advance directives. In 1991, the U.S. Congress enacted the Patient Self-Determination Act, giving all patients in hospitals receiving government funds the right to execute an advance directive.

At the same time that the right for advance directives was being written into law, the hospice movement was growing in the United States. Advocates for advance directives

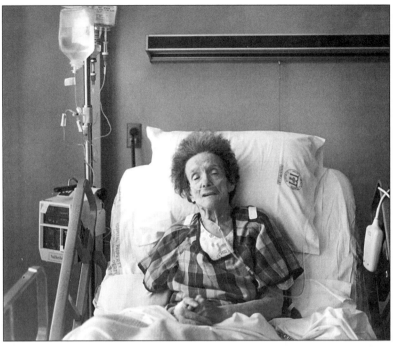

The terminally ill have many choices to make concerning hospitalization, painkillers, and life support or other life-extending measures. Many now opt for hospice care at home. (James L. Shaffer)

and hospice questioned prevailing medical procedures that attempted to prolong life regardless of the quality of that life or the cost to the individual. For the first time, dying in a sterile environment while attached to machines was publicly questioned. Hospice advocates argued for a different view of dying, where the philosophy was not to prolong the lives of the dying, but to give life quality and dying dignity. In hospice, these goals are achieved by allowing people to die at home or in other comfortable surroundings, in as little pain as possible, with loved ones nearby. For those with no hope of medical cure, the choice of dying under hospice care has become increasingly popular, and most major medical plans cover the costs.

Another choice in the dying process is the use of euthanasia. Although passive euthanasia, in which the individual is allowed to die of medical conditions, is legal and part of the advance directive process, active euthanasia, in which death is hastened by a third party, generally is not. Debates continue to rage over cases in which active euthanasia might be acceptable, but the possibility of abuse and the moral implications of its practice

make it unlikely that active euthanasia will become a widely accepted procedure in the near future. Studies of advance directives have found no age differences in their acceptance and use, but older adults are less likely than other age groups to accept measures that actively hasten death.

Physician-assisted suicide is one last, controversial choice in the dying process that currently is under debate. At the end of the twentieth century, it was legal only in one state, through the Oregon Death with Dignity Act. Under that legislation, individuals who have a terminal illness with less than six months to live can request medication from their physician that will hasten their deaths. Strict guidelines require a waiting period, assessment by multiple physicians, and that the dying be of sound mind for the medications to be prescribed. Data from the first years of the legal use of physician-assisted suicide in Oregon are available to the public and reveal no age trends in utilizing this choice. One of the most interesting aspects of the data is that a number of individuals requested and received lethal doses of medication from their physicians but never used them and died natural deaths.

Far less systematic were the over one hundred cases of suicide assisted by Dr. Jack Kevorkian. Kevorkian began his practice of assisting in suicide before passage of the Oregon Death with Dignity Act, and the publicity of his cases helped focus the national debate on physician-assisted suicide. Working outside of the law, Kevorkian's decisions to accept suicide cases appeared haphazard, and his cases differed from those allowed under the Oregon Death with Dignity Act in several important ways, including verification that the patient had a terminal illness; consultation with other physicians; requirement of a written request for aid signed in front of witnesses; an imposed waiting period between the request and provision of the means for committing suicide; and an ongoing relationship between the physician and the patient. In addition, while Oregon physicians were given license to dispense medications for subsequent suicide, Kevorkian's patients were attached to a suicide machine, an apparatus that dispensed various lethal drugs when a button was pushed by the patient. An examination of Kevorkian's cases reveals that the majority of his patients were middle-aged and older women despite the fact that, when no physician is involved, the suicide rate is highest for elderly men.

In summary, changes in medical technology and the hospice movement have generated questions about the conditions under which individuals would rather die than live. While the debates about advance directives and hospice care appear to be resolved in favor of more choice for the dying individual, the debates about active measures to end life are far from over.

OPTIONS AFTER DEATH

Other choices in the death process involve events that take place after death, such as the dissemination of assets and the plans for ritual. The few studies that have examined age differences in writing wills have found that significantly more older adults have wills than middle-aged and younger adults, probably because they have accumulated more assets and feel closer to death. Although close to one-half of Americans die without indicating preferences for services and internment, older adults are more likely to leave such arrangements than are young or middle-aged adults. Surveys indicate that older adults are more likely to have ongoing relationships with funeral directors and to find funerals more comforting than other age groups.

Finally, preferences for body disposition have been changing, with cremation increasingly chosen. No age differences have been found in choosing cremation over burial.

CONCLUSIONS

Most issues of death and dying are consistent across adult age groups, however changing expectations about the timing of death are modifying the experience of death and grief. One important effect of age is the sheer magnitude and diversity of deaths experienced, which highlights the preciousness of life but also can result in bereavement overload. Finally, as more options become available in the dying process, older adults embrace the majority of choices but are cautious about giving up control where it may be abused too easily.

—Pamela Roberts

See also Acquired immunodeficiency syndrome (AIDS); Breast cancer; Cancer; Cultural views of aging; Death anxiety; Death of parents; Death of a child; Depression; Durable power of attorney; Erikson, Erik H.; Estates and inheritance; Euthanasia; Friendship; Funerals; Gay men and lesbians; Grief; Heart attacks; Hospice; Life expectancy; Living wills; Loneliness; Middle age; Pets; Prostate cancer; Remarriage; Singlehood; Social ties; Stress and coping skills; Strokes; Suicide; Terminal illness; Widows and widowers; Wills and bequests.

FOR FURTHER INFORMATION:

Akner, Lois F., and Catherine Whitney. *How to Survive the Loss of a Parent: A Guide for Adults.* New York: Quill/Morrow, 1994. A support group led by the first author is followed through several meetings, with the stories of participants used as illustrations of typical grief reactions to the death of a parent.

Albom, Mitch. *Tuesdays with Morrie: An Old Man, a Young Man, and the Last Great Lesson.* New York: Doubleday, 1997. An extraordinary dying man reaches out to his pupil to give lessons on life and the dying process.

Byock, Ira. *Dying Well: Peace and Possibilities at the End of Life.* New York: Berkley Publishing Group, 1997. Rich stories of the individuals and families that Dr. Byock has known through hospice illustrate varying facets of dying with dignity and meaning.

Colgrove, Melba, Harold H. Bloomfield, and Peter McWilliams. *How to Survive the Loss of a Love.* Los Angeles: Prelude Press, 1993. One of the best selling books on grief, this revised and expanded edition provides short, easy-to-read chapters on feelings typical in the grieving process and prescribes simple actions that aid in healing.

Delany, Sarah L., and Amy Hill Hearth. *On My Own at 107: Reflections on Life Without Bessie.* New York: HarperSanFrancisco, 1997. Sarah Delany lived with her sister for over one hundred years. Excerpts of her diary, written after her sister's death, illustrate both the enormity of losses that accompany the death of a loved one and the hope that previous experiences with death can provide during the grieving process.

Ericsson, Stephanie. *Companion Through the Darkness: Inner Dialogues on Grief.* New York: HarperPerennial Library, 1993. Diary entries and short essays present Ericsson's experiences after her husband died. The on-line resource WidowNet notes that if they could recommend one volume to the widowed, this would be the book.

Finkbeiner, Ann K. *After the Death of a Child: Living with Loss Through the Years.* New York: Free Press, 1996. Finkbeiner uses the stories of her own child's death and the losses of other bereaved parents to illustrate the continuing effects of a child's death and the ongoing love that parents feel for their deceased children, even decades after their deaths.

Lewis, C. S. *A Grief Observed.* San Francisco: HarperSanFrancisco, 1994. Written originally in the 1960's, this ever-popular book portrays the disillusionment and destabilization encountered by Lewis, an Oxford professor famous for his unshakable convictions and theology, when his wife died.

Rosof, Barbara D. *The Worst Loss: How Families Heal from the Death of a Child.* New York: Henry Holt, 1995. Rosof, a psychotherapist, uses case histories to illustrate the effects of the death of a child on parents and siblings and their relationships.

Webb, Marilyn, Timothy Quill, and Joanne Lynn. *The Good Death: The New American Search to Re-shape the End of Life.* New York: Bantam Books, 1997. This book uses individual stories and interviews with the dying, their family members, health care workers, lawyers, and religious leaders to illustrate the practical, moral, and legal complexity of end-of-life decision making.

DEATH ANXIETY

RELEVANT ISSUES: Death, psychology, religion

SIGNIFICANCE: Death anxiety—a term which typically refers to a cluster of death attitudes characterized by fear, threat, unease, discomfort, and other negative emotional reactions, as well as anxiety that has no clear object—can have an impact on the lives of all individuals, regardless of age

Death anxiety can affect anyone but is particularly relevant in the work of grief counseling, organ donation, hospice adjustment, and midlife transition. Death anxiety may be manifested in avoidance behaviors. A person may avoid visiting a dying friend in the hospital or use euphemisms (such as "passed away") in discussing death. Western society encourages avoidance, for example by providing institutions for the dying and making certain that death-related aspects of funeral homes are not conspicuously displayed. Death anxiety may also be manifested in overt behaviors. Individuals with lower levels of anxiety are more likely to make prudent arrangements for the disposal of their bodies after death (such as through funeral plans) than individuals with higher levels of anxiety. Thus, death anxiety has practical, behavioral consequences.

RISK FACTORS FOR DEATH ANXIETY

Death anxiety is not necessarily associated with age. Indeed, it diminishes with age, so that the elderly as an age group have less death anxiety than younger individuals. Death anxiety is associated low life satisfaction. It is also associated with the personality factor of external locus of control, which is the feeling that external forces such as chance or luck control one's life rather than internal forces such as determination or ability. Death anxiety is also associated with physical illness. Therefore, death anxiety is associated with some aspects of personality and with illness, but not with age.

Though the elderly as a group have low death anxiety, some elderly individuals, such as those with low ego integrity who are institutionalized rather than living independently, have high death anxiety. The specific death-related concerns of the elderly include fear of pain and suffering, fear of abandonment, concerns about sensory loss, concerns about personal safety, and fear of what lies beyond death. Coping strategies used by the elderly to combat these fears include reminiscences, social support, and prayer.

Although elderly individuals are more accepting and less fearful of their own deaths than younger people, elderly individuals think about death more than younger people do. The increased thoughts of death may be the result of increased exposure to death in the people they know or an awareness that their life expectancy is short. Whatever the reason, the attitude is typically one of acceptance rather than fear.

MEASURING DEATH ANXIETY

Herman Feifel made pioneering contributions to death anxiety research with his 1955 article "Attitudes of Mentally Ill Patients Toward Death" in the *Journal of Nervous and Mental Disease*; in the forty-five years that followed, more than one thousand articles were published on the topic of death anxiety. Information about death anxiety can be found in professional journals in many areas, including psychology, medicine, nursing, and geriatrics. Two national, peer-reviewed journals that frequently publish information about death anxiety are *Omega: Journal of Death and Dying* and *Death Studies*.

According to R. A. Neimeyer in 1998, an estimated 95 percent of research literature on death anxiety used conscious reports in the form of written scales or questionnaires. One early and often-used measure is the Death Anxiety Scale, which consists of fifteen true-or-false statements such as "I am very much afraid to die." Because of methodological shortcomings, it was modified in 1994 into the Revised Death Anxiety Scale, which has twenty-five five-point items on a Likert scale. A second measure of death anxiety is the Threat Index. Originally a theoretically derived, structured interview, a revised version of the Threat Index asks respondents to rate "self" and "death" on seven-point Likert scales such as "predictable versus random" or "secure versus insecure." These early instruments are still widely used in research on death anxiety.

Three more recent research instruments represent advances in the understanding of death anxiety. The Multidimensional Fear of Death Scale has forty-two Likert items such as "I am afraid of dying very slowly" in eight factors: fear of the dying process, fear of the dead, fear of being destroyed, fear for significant others, fear of the unknown, fear of conscious death, fear for the body after death, and fear of premature death. The Fear of Personal Death Scale has thirty-one seven-point Likert items such as "Death frightens me because of the necessity to cease all plans and goals" in six factors: loss of self-fulfillment, self-annihilation, loss of social identity, consequences to family and friends, transcendental consequences, and punishment in the hereafter. Originally constructed in Hebrew to investigate death fears in an Israeli context, it was subsequently carefully translated into English for use in cross-cultural research. The Death Attitude Profile-Revised has thirty-two seven-point Likert items such as "Death is a natural aspect of life" in three subscales: neutral acceptance, approach acceptance, and escape acceptance. These newer research questionnaires add to current understanding of the different aspects of death anxiety.

In addition to paper-and-pencil questionnaires, another way to measure death anxiety is open-ended, free-form narratives that are later analyzed. For the Revised Twenty Statement Test, respondents give twenty brief, narrative responses to the prompt "What does your own death mean to you?" The investigator codes each response using ten mutually exclusive content categories (such as positive, negative, or religious). For the Death Construct Coding Manual, respondents write narratives that are first segmented into units or phrases for coding, then analyzed using a nonexclusive twenty-five-category system. Finally, a projective measure of death anxiety is to ask the person to describe death as if it had a human form (such as a macabre figure, a gentle comforter, or a faceless automaton). These alternative research instruments contribute qualitatively to the present understanding of death anxiety.

Rather than being a unitary concept, death anxiety has several facets. Aspects of death anxiety include death fear, desire to avoid death and reminders of death, denial of the reality of death and the possibility of one's own death, reluctance to interact with dying persons, preoccupation with thoughts of dying, negative reaction to pain, and concerns about the afterlife.

As critical as emotional reactions to death are, it is equally critical to acknowledge that humans have a long history of coping with death. One instrument to measure such coping is Bugen's Coping with Death Scale, which consists of thirty seven-point Likert items such as "I am aware of the full range of services offered by funeral homes." A second measure of coping is the Death Self-Efficacy Scale, which consists of forty-four specific tasks relevant to hospice work and personal mortality (such as "write a living will") that respondents rate from 1 to 100 according to how certain they are that they could perform them. These instruments have in common the fact that they are straightforward, experimenter-framed inquiries into respondents' attitudes. Also, the items are all brief, declarative statements with similar wording. These questionnaires contribute to an understanding of how people cope with death anxiety.

CONCLUSION

Fear of death is a human preoccupation that has at least two positive outcomes. First, fear of death causes people to expend much effort in avoiding it. Second, there is much speculation that death anxiety is the inspiration for many great individual achievements. For example, an artist may hope that his works will impact people long after he dies or a politician may hope that her accomplishments will be recorded in history books.

—*Lillian M. Range*

See also Death and dying; Death of a child; Death of parents; Depression; Durable power of attorney; Estates and inheritance; Euthanasia; Funerals; Geriatrics and gerontology; Grief; Hospice; Life insurance; Living wills; Psychiatry, geriatric; Religion; Stress and coping skills; Suicide; Terminal illness; Trusts; Wills and bequests.

FOR FURTHER INFORMATION:

Durlak, J. A., W. Horn, and R. A. Kass. "A Self-Administering Assessment of Personal Meanings of Death: Report on the Revised Twenty Statements Test." *Omega: Journal of Death and Dying* 21, no. 30 (1990).

Florian, V., and S. Kravetz. "Fear of Personal Death: Attribution, Structure, and Relation to Religious Belief." *Journal of Personality and Social Psychology* 44, no. 3 (March, 1983): 600-607.

Hoelter, J. "Multidimensional Treatment of Fear of Death." *Journal of Consulting and Clinical Psychology* 47, no. 5 (October, 1979): 996-999.

Krieger, S. R., F. R. Epting, and L. M. Leitner. "Personal Constructs, Threat, and Attitudes Toward Death." *Omega: Journal of Death and Dying* 5 (1974): 299-310.

Neimeyer, R. A. "Death Anxiety Research: The State of the Art." *Omega: Journal of Death and Dying* 36, no. 2 (March, 1998): 97-121.

Neimeyer, R. A., D. J. Fontana, and K. Gold. "A Manual for Content Analysis of Death Constructs." In *Personal Meanings of Death*, edited by F. R. Epting and Neimeyer. Washington, D.C.: Hemisphere, 1984.

Robbins, R. A. "Bugen's Coping with Death Scale: Reliability and Further Validation." *Omega: Journal of Death and Dying* 22, no. 4 (November, 1991): 298-299.

Templar, D. I. "The Construction and Validation of a Death Anxiety Scale." *Journal of General Psychology* 82 (April, 1970): 165-177.

Thorson, J. A., and F. C. Powell. "A Revised Death Anxiety Scale." In *Death Anxiety Handbook: Research, Instrumentation, and Application*, edited by R. A. Neimeyer. Philadelphia: Taylor & Francis, 1994.

Wong, P. T., G. T. Reker, and G. Gesser. "Death Attitude Profile-Revised." In *Death Anxiety Handbook: Research, Instrumentation, and Application*, edited by R. A. Neimeyer. Philadelphia: Taylor & Francis, 1994.

DEATH OF A CHILD

RELEVANT ISSUES: Death, family, psychology
SIGNIFICANCE: The death of a child has been described as life's greatest tragedy; it has particularly deleterious psychological, social, and physical effects on the well-being of older parents

When a child dies, the special and complex bond between the parent and the child seeks resolution; the many factors that accounted for the unique relationship between parent and child are those same factors that intensify the parental grief experience. For example, a child is seen as the best and the worst of the parent, as a source of hope, as a validation of self-worth and adult status, and as a symbol of immortality. The loss of a child creates an existential and narcissistic wound, often referred to in terms of an amputation, signifying the permanence of the loss and the enduring changes that are required to cope with it.

A child's death is often interpreted by bereaved parents as violating a basic sense of justice and the natural order of the universe: The old die before the young. While a parent may have anticipated (at least on an abstract level) his or her own death, the expectation has been that the child would be the survivor. This violated worldview makes life chaotic and unpredictable. Further, the untimeliness and dissynchrony of the death is often equated with wrongdoing, failure, or incompetence as the parents search for meaning. These factors necessarily complicate the grief experiences of bereaved parents. Parental bereavement (that is, the parental responses to the death of a child) has been identified as unparalleled in grief reactions with a duration that falls outside the parameters of what is considered to be typical. Psychoanalysts view parenthood as a process ending with the death of the parent, not with the death of the child. Accepted models of grief and bereavement do not go far enough in their attempts to account for the complex reactions evidenced by parents following the death of a child.

The study of parental bereavement largely has been restricted to the effects of infant death on relatively young parents. Analyses of stillbirths, miscarriages, death in the neonatal period, and sudden infant death syndrome (SIDS) have characterized the area with a distinct medical perspective. Although the term "child" has connotations of youthfulness, it is a family label unencumbered by age boundaries; correspondingly, the death of a child is not an event restricted to any particular age group. Mortality curves evidence a decrease following infancy to their lowest point at about age ten, with consistent increases throughout the remainder of the life course. In an odd pairing of forces, life expectancies are increasing, as are age-specific rates of fatalities from accidents and particular diseases, as well as suicides and homicides. Together, these elevate the potential for parental bereavement at all stages of the family life course.

A FAMILY PERSPECTIVE

Children create for parents a sense of community and help define a family in its traditional sense—that is, children create parents out of partners. The life of the parent may revolve around the child both emotionally and physically. These issues are made even more salient with the death of an only child. Innocuous questions such as "Do you have any children?" become heavy with emotions as bereaved parents struggle between denying the existence of their child—their family—and opening the wound of the loss to public scrutiny.

Accompanying the change in identity occasioned by the transition to parenthood is a change in the social organization of these parents. Recreation patterns are changed, as are social contacts, since socializing often involves contacts initiated through their children. With the death of a child, parents lose contact with their social sphere. Friends and acquaintances may avoid the bereaved parents out of the fear of saying something that might cause the parents pain or discomfort and out of the fear that they too may be vulnerable to such a tragedy.

Family developmental theorists operate from the premise that families experience distinct stages of development and that parents and children engage in different developmental tasks at different periods of the family life course. This conceptualization of family development allows for predictions to be made about families and about the particular vulnerability of families dependent on their current stage. By extension, the death of a child may be perceived differently and associated with different issues and patterns of response as a function of the family stage or position in the developmental sequence at the time of death. This is not to say that one death is easier or more difficult than another; rather, different deaths may be associated with different issues and kinds of pain.

DEATH OF AN INFANT

Author Therese Rando has written extensively in the area of parental bereavement. She notes that an infant signifies new life and is the antithesis of death. A child's death is thus an incongruous and incomprehensible loss. Infants hold for parents the potential to achieve all that the parents could not or did not; the death of an infant robs parents of this potential and leaves them with a sense of unfinished business. Even many years following the death, parents report tracking the development of the child should he or she have survived—thinking, for example, "My child would have graduated from high school this year." This suggests that the attachment to the child, which has its origin prior to the birth, does not end with the death of the child but probably changes in form over time.

Accidents and congenital birth defects are some of the leading causes of the death of infants and young children. Such deaths are often associated with parents feeling that they had somehow failed to protect or even to produce a healthy child. Guilt and self-recrimination are frequent accompanying emotions. Parents whose children died from SIDS experience significant hopelessness in that there is no ready, explainable cause of the death; they may be plagued by thoughts of "if only." Such intense feelings, coupled with distinct gender-based patterns of grieving, may lead to misunderstandings between bereaved parents and a perceived absence of support from one's marital partner. Young parents may attempt to conceive other children, a coping strategy that is often not entirely successful. Some authors have suggested that young mothers in particular are at an elevated risk for a prolonged grief.

Support is not readily forthcoming from social networks. Author Dennis Klass reports that bereaved parents find themselves in a network of social relations that fail to understand the enormity of their loss. For example, neonatal deaths are sometimes interpreted as a nonevent by those adhering to the naïve and erroneous belief that there is no loss to grieve as no relationship had yet been established. Within such an environment, bereaved parents are expected to resume their lives as though nothing had happened.

DEATH OF A YOUNG CHILD OR ADOLESCENT

In contrast to those parents bereft of an infant, the mothers and fathers of deceased young children or adolescents are perceived by society to have suffered an enormous loss. This perception provides a great deal of initial support from friends and relatives, but the expectation is that parents will recover, and their grief will subside. When such expectations are not met, as is most of-

ten the case with bereaved parents, support diminishes. Parents in this age group, particularly the well educated, frequently make use of bereaved parent support groups, such as Compassionate Friends.

The guilt and recrimination experienced by the bereaved parents of infants are similarly experienced by bereaved parents of young children and adolescents, often exacerbated by the cause of death. For example, suicide is among the top ten leading causes of death and often ranks in the top five causes of deaths of adolescents and young adults. Stigmatization often accompanies such a death, contributing to a sense of shame, social disdain, and blame by parents themselves and others in their social environment. Parents often describe the death in terms of rejection, abandonment, and punishment.

The death of a child is the loss of the future, and the bereaved parents of young children and adolescents describe such a loss with a sense of futility for the efforts they have put into the rearing of the child—on the verge of making societal contributions and making use of his or her education and training—only to feel deprived of this potential. Parents ask how children who avoided harm as an infant could die before their "natural" life expectancies had been reached. Moreover, relationships between adolescent children and their parents are frequently characterized by conflict and strained communication, primarily around issues of independence and autonomy. The loss of a child prior to the resolution of such conflicts may complicate responses to the death.

DEATH OF AN ADULT CHILD

It has been reported that the most distressing and long-lasting grief responses are found in the experiences of those parents who have lost adult children. The characterization of parents bereft of infants, young children, and adolescents largely apply to those mothers and fathers bereaved of an adult. Age exacerbates, rather than attenuates, the grief responses. For example, later life has been described as a time of many personal, health, and social changes, most often framed as losses, which have been interpreted as harbingers of mortality. In this context, the death of a child is an especially dissynchronous event: Older parents perceive that their own deaths are more immediate than the death of their offspring. Their resulting survival guilt is pronounced. Furthermore, the death of a child may have an even greater impact for the surviving parents in later life given the longevity of their relationships with their children, the effectively richer memories, and the greater intertwining of lives. Older parents may feel as though they have lost not only their child but also their confidant and friend, as well as their extended kinship connection.

Bereaved older (postclimacteric) mothers are unable to bear other children, and they report this experience as something that sets them apart from all other grieving parents, including their husbands. Across the family life course, mothers tend to report higher levels of grief than do fathers. The difference between mothers and fathers is greatest over the death of an infant and least over the death of an adult child; the age of the deceased child does not make a difference in the experience of mothers, whereas fathers show greater grief intensity with increasing age of the child at death. Mothers bereft of a daughter and fathers bereft of a son have been found to exhibit the highest levels of distress.

The grief of frail, elderly parents in particular may be exacerbated by their anxieties about future sources of help and support. Their deceased child may have been a caregiver or potential caregiver to her or his elderly parents, and the death may now mean that the elderly person will require services from formal and community agencies or may not be able to sustain independent living. The institutionalized elderly have fewer living children than the community-dwelling elderly, and a significant number of hospital and long-term care admissions were initiated by the death or severe illness of an adult child. Several studies report poorer perceived health and intensified health problems among bereaved older parents. There is even some suggestive evidence that the death of an adult child is associated with increased mortality rates for the older surviving parents.

The death of an individual in his or her midlife may leave bereft parents as well as bereft children. These grandchildren may serve as ongoing reminders, both comforting and stressful, for the older parents of their deceased child. The absence of grandchildren may lead older bereaved parents to see their hobbies, crafts, and skills as futile in the absence of beneficiaries. Similar to the relationship with the grandchildren, the relationship between the surviving spouse and the bereaved parents may be mutually supportive, or it may be strained by the surviving spouse's attempt to form new relationships, something bereaved parents may perceive as inappropriate or disrespectful of their child's memory.

This middle generation and their children (the family of procreation of the deceased individual) are typically seen as experiencing more intense grief than are the families of origin (the older parents) over the loss of the midlife adult. Older parents typically do not share a residence with the adult child who died and often had minimal involvement in the medical and health care issues of their deceased child; such decision making was often left to the surviving spouse and the children. Consequently, older parents often have less information about the death and the circumstances that led to it, factors that may complicate the grieving process. Furthermore, condolences are primarily oriented toward the surviving spouse and young children, whose loss seems more direct. This relative absence of social recognition of their loss may make older parents feel especially isolated.

—*Brian de Vries*

See also Death and dying; Death anxiety; Death of parents; Family relationships; Funerals; Grief; Parenthood; Single parenthood; Suicide; Terminal illness.

FOR FURTHER INFORMATION:

De Vries, Brian, Rose Dalla Lana, and Vilma T. Falck. "Parental Bereavement over the Life Course: A Theoretical Intersection and Empirical Review." *Omega: Journal of Death and Dying* 29, no. 1 (1994). A journal article review of research and theory on the death of a child for parents at three different stages of the family life course.

Klass, Dennis. *Parental Grief: Solace and Resolution.* New York: Springer, 1988. Klass addresses the course and substance of grief of bereaved parents.

Klass, Dennis, and Samuel J. Marwit. "Toward a Model of Parental Grief." *Omega: Journal of Death and Dying* 29, no. 1 (1994). This journal article proposes a theory to address the special issues of parental loss of a child.

Margolis, Otto S., Austin H. Kutscher, Eric R. Marcus, Howard C. Raether, Vanderlyn R. Pine, Irene B. Seeland, and Daniel J. Cherico, eds. *Grief and the Loss of an Adult Child.* New York: Praeger, 1988. Contains chapters on the particular issues surrounding later life parental bereavement, including interdisciplinary approaches to bereavement and the roles of funerals.

Rando, Therese A., ed. *Parental Loss of a Child.* Champaign, Ill.: Research Press, 1986. Contains chapters on a variety of perspectives on and issues in the death of a child, including socially unacknowledged parental losses, accounts on the subjective experiences, and sources of professional help and support organizations.

Schiff, Harriet Sarnoff. *The Bereaved Parent.* New York: Crown, 1977. An account of the death of a child, including resources to assist bereaved parents.

DEATH OF A SPOUSE. *See* WIDOWS AND WIDOWERS.

DEATH OF PARENTS

RELEVANT ISSUES: Death, family, health and medicine, psychology

SIGNIFICANCE: Dealing with the death of parents may be the single most difficult task faced by the aging adult; as such, it may have persistent, long-term effects

Dealing with the death of a parent is difficult at any age. Research by Christopher Tennant found that there is no evidence indicating that the death of a parent in childhood places one at significant risk for depression later in life, except in cases in which there was significant child-parental discord. Phyllis Silverman conducted research dealing with college students whose parent had died while the child was in grade school, adolescence, or young adulthood. Her research indicated that the time of the parent's death did not have an effect on the individual's reactions to the death, their bereavement, or the long-term impact of the death. In all cases, regardless of the child's age at the death of the parent, the impact on the individual was extensive and long-term.

According to Lauren Saler and Neil Skolnick, those children who had greater opportunity to en-gage in activities that foster mourning (attending the funeral, talking about the parent, keeping mementos, visiting the grave) were less likely to demonstrate subsequent depression. Research by Andrew Scharlach investigating the impact of parental death in middle age found that the extent of the grief reaction was influenced mainly by the degree of expectedness of the death and the level of independence of the adult child. No matter how independent the adult, one's parents had always been there to depend on throughout one's formative years. To be faced first with role reversal (as parents become increasingly dependent) and then their loss seems incomprehensible to some.

PARENTAL DEATH AS LOSS OF BUFFER

While one's parents are alive, there exists a cushion between that person and the grave. People rarely think of their own potential illnesses or demise while their parents still exist. With the loss of parents comes the loss of the psychological buffer between the individual and death. It is partially for this reason that anyone who has been orphaned at any age becomes very much aware of his or her own mortality. People become aware that if death can happen to their parents, then it can happen to them. If parents happen to die at an early age (whether accidentally or of natural causes), one becomes very much aware that deaths do occur early in life and that the same thing could happen again.

According to Veronika Denes-Raj and Howard Erlichman, adults who had at least one parent die prematurely (prior to age fifty-five) estimate that their life expectancy will be shorter than is true for other people of their age. Furthermore, they indicate that this expectation of a shorter life is based on personal feelings rather than on objective data. Many of the subjects went on to indicate that they expected their cause of death to be the same as their parent's, and this group exhibited significantly poorer general health practices, as if they were resigned to the inevitable.

The death of one's parent generally does occur during the course of one's lifetime. Researcher Debra Umberson considers loss of a parent to be the most common type of bereavement. Umberson's data indicate that 5 percent of the population in the United States loses a parent each year, most typically in middle age. The single most common decade for a person to lose a parent is in the fifties. By the time they reach age sixty-two, 75 percent of adults have lost both of their parents. It should be realized that dealing with the death of a parent is now very different than it was a hundred years ago, in part because of increased life expectancy. Parent and child now very often share many years of an adult relationship, something that was relatively uncommon in the past when adults died at much earlier ages. While people are aware throughout this relationship that their parents will die someday, they still have difficulty dealing with the reality of the loss when the time comes.

The death of one's parents is difficult at any age but takes on added meaning in middle age, as the torch is permanently passed from one generation to the next. (Jim Whitmer)

REACTIONS TO PARENTAL DEATH

Death of a parent is typically met with a combination of pain, fear, and sadness. All these feelings are present in the individual who is grieving and are necessary to deal with the loss of the emotional ties to the individual who has died. How grief is experienced by the individual who has lost the parent is affected by a number of factors. As indicated by Tennant, the nature and extent of the individual's relationship with the parent will strongly influence both the immediate and the long-term reactions to the death. Additionally, the age of the parent at the time of the death, and whether it was an appropriate time for death, will affect the grieving process. The death of a parent that occurs suddenly may well be grieved more intensely than one that follows a long illness. Further factors that affect the reactions to parental death include the individual's age, sex, previous experience with death, religious beliefs, and presence of social support systems.

Responses are different for the death of the first parent and for the final parent. There are, however, some elements of the grieving process that are common reactions to most deaths, including the death of a parent. The initial response is typically one of shock or denial, which eventually gives way to a feeling of numbness. At this point, one may feel like a spectator in life, viewing without emotion events which seem that they cannot really be taking place. As the reality of the death dawns on the individual, numbness may give way to anger. This anger may be directed at the medical profession for not saving the parent, at God for taking the parent, or at the parent for daring to abandon the child. This same anger turned inward is often experienced as guilt. The adult child whose parent has died will often feel that he or she should have been able to do something to prevent the death from occurring. One might have insisted that a parent see a doctor sooner or might have been present to prevent an accident from happening. If any disagreements or arguments had occurred shortly before the death, the individual may feel guilty about those as well. People often find themselves becoming preoccupied with thoughts of the dead parent both in their waking hours and during sleep.

There may also be physical sequelae that accompany the grieving process over time. The preoccupation with thoughts of the deceased parent may result in sleeplessness, as well as irritability or restlessness. Related anxiety may be accompanied by shortness of breath or weight loss.

There are many secondary losses as well related to the death of a parent. With their demise, one may well have lost a valued friend, advisor, and role model. For most people, the parent is one person apt to be proud of accomplishments. Judith Viorst indicates that many individuals have a desire to be the adored and approved-of child, with parents as the number-one fans. For those individuals who have positive relationships with their parents, the death means the loss of the person who showed them absolute love and devotion. For those people who did not have positive relationships with their parents, the loss may be just as hard to bear because one loses the opportunity to please the parent and establish that desired relationship.

IMPACT ON FAMILY

With the death of the parent, one may also lose the glue that binds the family of origin together. The site for family reunions may cease to exist, and contact with adult siblings may diminish as parents die. Parental death also means loss of grandparents for one's children and the related loss of affection, love, approval, and role model. Research by Herta Guttman indicates that in some cases the death of a parent may serve to precipitate conflict in a previously peaceful long-term marriage. A bereaved spouse may attack or withdraw from the partner, or may become irrationally angry. In such a case, marital therapy often focuses on the facilitation of mourning for the dead parent.

The effect of parental loss on the family often begins long prior to the actual death of the individual. Adult children often find themselves serving as caregivers during illnesses that precede the death. The existence of the role of caregiver for a dependent parent generally creates stress for both individuals and their families. Caregivers are typically faced with other work and family responsibilities, with little time for themselves. If they still have dependent children at home, they now become members of the "sandwich generation" (sandwiched between dependent children and dependent older adults) and clearly the subjects of major stress. Attempts may be made to share responsibility for caregiving among siblings, often leading to disagreements or shirked responsibilities by some. If the illness is prolonged, or caregiving requirements become too extensive, or if great distances are involved, decisions may have to be made about nursing homes or hospice care.

Following some extended illnesses, the death of a parent may be viewed as a relief and as a release. The parent's death may restore to family members the parent whom they previously knew. In these cases, the parent is no longer defined by the illness and can be remembered as the person he or she once was. Adult children in this situation also report that they can stop being terrified at the ringing of the phone because they have already received the dreaded news. In other instances, death is viewed as liberating, since the parent can no longer define who the child should be, so that the adult child can come to be his or her own person. In many situations, the death of a parent is viewed with regret since more should have been done by the individual to please the parent. In most instances, the death of the parent is met with pain at the loss, leaving the individual missing, needing, and wanting the deceased parent, and missing their own role as "somebody's child."

COPING WITH PARENTAL DEATH

Psychologists often stress the importance of working through one's grief with no shortcuts. If a remaining parent exists, he or she is usually counseled not to make major decisions hastily and should be helped to work through grief. Legal and technical issues must be taken care of, and again this should not be done in haste. Advance planning with the parents before death helps alleviate the need for many decisions at this time. If wake and funeral plans were discussed ahead of time (hopefully along with the issuance of advance directives) and wills or living trusts were put in place, this will lessen the present ordeal.

Psychologists also maintain that one must feel free to vent feelings, taking time to cry and expressing anger. Family and friends serve as important support systems on which to lean. The bereaved should feel free to talk openly and let others know of their needs. Doctors and clergymen may serve as a source of support, and, if necessary, support groups can be contacted. When possible, the bereaved's schedule should be lightened, allowing quiet time to put things into perspective. Becoming comfortable with the memory of the deceased parent allows children to share memories with other family members and friends. Years after the death of the parent, children will still sense their presence and feel their loss. By dealing effectively with this loss and the resulting grief, one can gain strength and insight to better help deal with the future.

—*Robin Kamienny Montvilo*

See also Caregiving; Children of Aging Parents; Death and dying; Death of a child; Death anxiety; Durable power of attorney; Estates and inheritance; Euthanasia; Family relationships; Filial responsibility; Funerals; Grief; Hospice; Illnesses among the elderly; Living wills; Terminal illness; Widows and widowers; Wills and bequests.

FOR FURTHER INFORMATION:
Akner, Lois F., and Catherine Whitney. *How to Survive the Loss of a Parent: A Guide for Adults*. Austin, Tex.: Quill, 1994. This popular guide was written for the individual who needs help dealing with parental death. Based on interviews with adults who have suffered parental loss, the book suggests tools for coping.

Kamerman, Jack. *Death in the Midst of Life: Social and Cultural Influences on Death, Grief, and Mourning*. Englewood Cliffs, N.J.: Simon & Schuster, 1988. This text provides an overview of death in America. It covers topics ranging from planning for death to dealing with grief at any age in life.

LeShan, Eda. *Learning to Say Goodbye: When a Parent Dies*. Englewood Cliffs, N.J.: Simon & Schuster, 1976. This book is intended to help children deal with parental death. It focuses on questions, fears, and fantasies that children experience at the death of a parent and can serve as a resource for the surviving parent to promote discussion with their children.

Lustbader, Wendy, and Nancy Hooyman. *Taking Care of Aging Family Members: A Practical Guide*. New York: Free Press, 1994. This book serves as a guide for family members taking care of older adults. It includes necessary information concerning advanced planning, making caregiving and coping with death much easier.

Moss, Miriam, and Sidney Moss. "The Death of a Parent." In *Midlife Loss: Coping Strategies*, edited by Richard Kalish. Newbury Park, Calif.: Sage Publications, 1989. This chapter focuses on the experience of parental death in the lives of middle-aged individuals. Deals with the effects of parental death on identity, daily activities, and social relationships.

Viorst, Judith. "No One Loved You More." *Redbook*, November, 1993. This simple, straightforward article accurately describes the common feelings experienced by adults who have lost a parent. Viorst stresses the fact that this loss is often felt for the remainder of one's life.

Worden, James. *Children and Grief When a Parent Dies*. New York: Guilford Press, 1996. This book presents current and historical research on grief and mourning in children. It delves into the mourning process in children, as well as delineating factors that put bereaved children at risk.

DEMENTIA

RELEVANT ISSUES: Health and medicine, psychology

SIGNIFICANCE: It is estimated that the prevalence of dementia ranges from two to four million cases in the United States

Dementia is a chronic global impairment of intellectual abilities characterized by the presence of multiple cognitive deficits. The incidence of dementia increases with age and the prevalence among the population over eighty-five years of age can approach 50 percent. The caregivers of persons with dementia often experience burdens in the form of declines in their own physical and mental health.

ALZHEIMER'S DISEASE

Alzheimer's disease, a specific type of dementia, is the most common cause of dementia in the elderly. The neuropathology of the disease was first documented by Alois Alzheimer in 1907. Alzheimer's disease is a progressive neurodegenerative disease (that is, a disorder of the brain and nervous system) of unknown etiology. It is characterized by diffuse atrophy (shrinkage of the brain and brain cell loss) throughout the cerebral cortex, with distinctive brain tissue changes of neuritic plaques (abnormal neurons) and neurofibrillary tangles (abnormal filamentous structures within the cytoplasm of abnormal neurons).

Advancing age is the only established risk factor for Alzheimer's disease to date. The diagnosis of probable Alzheimer's disease or senile dementia of the Alzheimer's type (SDAT) is a diagnosis of exclusion. The differential diagnoses include infectious and metabolic disorders, toxicity, neoplasms, head trauma, nutritional deficiencies, Wernicke-Korsakoff syndrome, Pick's disease and other neurodegenerative disorders, psychiatric disorders, extrapyramidal syndromes, depression, vascular dementias, post-traumatic dementias, postanoxic dementias, and hydrocephalus. Autopsy is currently the only way to make a definitive diagnosis of Alzheimer's disease.

The six specific diagnostic criteria for the diagnosis of Alzheimer's disease, according to the fourth edition of the *Diagnostic and Statistical Manual of Mental Disorders: DSM-IV* (1994), are as follows. First, the development of multiple cognitive deficits manifests as both impaired short-term and long-term memory and at least one of the following: aphasia (language disturbance), apraxia (impaired ability to carry out motor activities despite intact motor function), agnosia (failure to recognize or identify objects despite intact sensory function), and disturbance in executive functioning (that is, planning, organizing, sequencing, abstracting). Second, these cognitive deficits each cause significant impairment in social or occupational functioning and represent a significant decline from a previous level of functioning. Third, the course is characterized by a gradual onset and progressive cognitive decline. Fourth, the cognitive deficits are not the result of any of the following: other central nervous system conditions that cause progressive deficits in memory and cognition, systemic conditions known to cause dementia, or substance-induced conditions. Fifth, the deficits do not occur exclusively during delirium (an acute or subacute global cognitive impairment that occurs as a consequence of an underlying medical problem). Sixth, the disturbance is not better accounted for by another psychiatric disorder.

A patient suffering from dementia takes part in an art class. (Ben Klaffke)

ETIOLOGY AND ASSESSMENT

One goal of the diagnostic process is to elicit treatable causes of dementia, which include pseudodementia caused by depression, vitamin B_{12} deficiency, hypothyroidism (underactive thyroid), hyperthyroidism (overactive thyroid), normal pressure hydrocephalus (NPH), neurosyphilis, alcohol-associated dementia, toxins (such as heavy metals), and environmental exposures (such as insecticides and industrial solvents). In addition, medications can produce a subacute delirium that is manifested as a dementia.

Consequently, the assessment evaluation consists of a detailed history gathered from the patient and caregivers that includes a medication review and exposure history. There should be general physical, neurological, and psychiatric examinations, as well as formal tests of cognitive function. Laboratory tests should include a complete blood count (CBC), sedimentation rate (the rate at which red blood cells sink), electrolyte levels, blood chemistries, liver and thyroid function tests, syphilis serology, urinalysis, and B_{12} levels. If indicated, human immunodeficiency virus (HIV), folate, heavy metal, and toxicology screening should be performed. Other testing may include lumbar puncture (spinal tap), computed tomography (CT or CAT) scanning, magnetic resonance imaging (MRI), and electroencephalography (EEG). According to a 1991 article by J. L. Cummings, early on the following should be assessed: caregiver stress, the home environment, the financial situation, services needed and barriers to those services, legal issues such as guardianship and durable power of attorney, and end-of-life issues such as an advanced directives, including living wills, "do not resuscitate" (DNR) orders, and durable power of attorney for health care.

Care of Clients with Dementia

Several planning issues are associated with care management for clients with dementia. The goal of care with Alzheimer's disease is to preserve recipients' autonomy as much as possible without compromising their own or their caregivers' health and safety. The most difficult change will be not allowing patients to drive once it becomes apparent that this has become a dangerous activity. The most emotional issue for many clients and their families is nursing home placement. Many families rely on professionals for guidance as to when it is appropriate to place individuals, and they may need encouragement or even "permission" not to feel guilty when their loved one is no longer able to be maintained at home.

Managing affective problems (such as anger, depression, fear, or any other negative emotion) and behavioral problems is challenging at best. Characteristic problems include depression, anxiety, wandering, psychotic symptoms, aggressive behavior, and "sundowning" (confusion, agitation, or sleep disturbances that occur in the evening or at night). Management requires evaluation of the role of each of the possible causes and treatment if possible. It must be determined which, if any, of the symptoms are substantial enough to warrant intervention. Interventions may include

health promotion and disease prevention strategies.

Implementation of interventions for the client with dementia begins with the education of caregivers about the disease process, prognosis, treatment, management, and realistic expectations, as well as about what behavior patterns can be expected and what environmental modifications might be beneficial. According to Cummings, precipitating or aggravating factors, superimposed medical problems, and household psychological stress should be sought out and relieved if possible.

Managing Difficult Behaviors

For the client or patient with dementia, wandering can be a problem. It can result in an individual getting lost for long periods of time and possibly end in death from medical illness requiring routine medications, inclement weather, wild animals, dehydration, or starvation. Wandering may be attributed to confusion from being relocated, pain, the need for more frequent toileting, boredom, anxiety, psychosis; the cause may be idiopathic (unknown). Therapy may include constant reorientation, regular exercise, scheduled voiding, increased time spent completing disruptive tasks (such as bathing), or pharmacological therapy. Environmental manipulations such as door locks, electronic warning systems, stop signs, or night-lights are often helpful. Environmental manipulations that may alleviate the symptoms of sundowning include providing a quiet room with reduced but not absent sensory input and day-night cues. All clients should be provided with armbands or nonremovable necklaces, pins, or identification bracelets; these items are available through the Alzheimer's Association. Only disruptive psychotic or aggressive behavior need be treated with low-dose antipsychotic drugs. According to Cummings, medications in this situation should be avoided as they can paradoxically increase agitation and confusion.

According to the *NGNA Core Curriculum for Gerontological Nursing* (1996), early in the illness, memory-enhancing techniques such as note-taking, signs, or calendars are helpful. Other interventions include reality orientation, remotivation, life review, reminiscence, pet therapy, validation therapy, personal choice enhancement, involvement in activities that focus on client strengths or past roles and abilities, memory enhancement, and other cognitive stimulation methods. Several of these interventions are health promotion and disease prevention strategies. Health care providers should stress the importance of following regular routines, simplifying the environment, removing clutter, providing better lighting, using strategically placed lights (such as leaving the bathroom light on), and avoiding stimulants in the evening that may cause sleep disturbances. Speech, physical, or occupational therapy may be beneficial in selected patients. Correction of vision and hearing problems is imperative, since sensory deficits contribute to the cognitive dysfunction. The cognitively impaired do better with ongoing sensory and social stimulation that is tailored to their abilities.

These interventions are appropriate in multiple settings, including the home, adult day care facilities, and nursing homes. Thus, using such techniques provides an opportunity for continuity of care and smoother transitions between long-term care situations.

MEDICATIONS

Although there is no curative therapy for Alzheimer's disease, certain drugs are utilized to manage its symptoms. Pharmacological treatment is aimed at either enhancing cognitive function or managing troublesome behavior. Medications used to manage behavioral problems included antidepressants, antianxiety drugs, propranolol, and carbamazepine. The symptom relief provided by these drugs is variable and must be balanced against potential side effects. Currently, tetra-hydro-aminoacridine (also known as THA, Tacrine, or Cognex) and Aricept are the only drugs approved for the treatment of Alzheimer's disease by the Food and Drug Administration (FDA). They are associated with modest improvements in cognition, primarily memory function. There is no evidence to date, however, that they alter the course of the underlying dementia. On the other hand, modest improvements in scientific terms may translate into significant changes to an individual family. For example, if the modest improvement is a slightly longer attention span that allows the Alzheimer's disease patient to have increased nutritional intake, the result may be some decrease in caregiver stress.

CAREGIVER ISSUES

Interventions for the caregiver must also be considered. Caregivers undergo a tremendous amount of stress and are vulnerable to depression, anxiety, guilt, substance abuse, medical illness, and stress-related disorders. Caregivers need as much support and education as possible. Although they do not seem to improve depression or anxiety in caregivers, assistance with problem solving, respite, and support groups do result in a better quality of life. Appropriate referrals should be made for services, including legal services. Evaluation of interventions is an often-neglected phase of working with clients. Regular follow-up with the client and caregivers to ascertain what their concerns and problems are will assist professionals in determining if the various interventions are working or if they need to be adjusted or changed. Clients should be in safe environments and have their needs met, while caregivers should be able to cope without ruining their own physical or emotional health.   —*Mary E. Allen*

See also Aging process; Alzheimer's Association; Alzheimer's disease; Brain changes and disorders; Caregiving; Forgetfulness; Memory changes and loss; Mental impairment; Psychiatry, geriatric.

FOR FURTHER INFORMATION:

Cummings, J. L. "Geriatric Syndromes: Dementia." In *Geriatrics Review Syllabus: A Core Curriculum in Geriatric Medicine*, edited by J. C. Beck. New York: American Geriatrics Society, 1991.

Diagnostic and Statistical Manual of Mental Disorders: DSM-IV. 4th ed. Washington, D.C.: American Psychiatric Association, 1994.

Luggen, A. S., ed. *NGNA Core Curriculum for Gerontological Nursing.* St. Louis: C. V. Mosby, 1996.

DEMOGRAPHICS

RELEVANT ISSUES: Death, demographics, economics, sociology

SIGNIFICANCE: In most industrialized societies, including the United States, the proportion of older people to younger people has been increasing, and this population aging affects virtually every aspect of social life

Demography is the study of the social characteristics of human populations. It deals with how many people there are in a population and with how many people there are with various characteristics in that population. Demographic information includes the relative numbers of men and women, sizes of ethnic and racial groups, levels of education, areas of employment, percentages of people unemployed, and ages of people in the population.

Birth, death, and migration are the three basic demographic forces that determine the makeup of populations. Age is closely linked to all three of these forces. The age of a population may change because more people are born in some decades than in others. Populations with many women past childbearing age have fewer births, and therefore smaller rates of growth, than populations with many women in their late teens and early twenties. Declining death rates generally mean more older people. Societies with large numbers of older people also tend to have large numbers of deaths and high medical expenses, as these societies have many individuals who are at the ends of their natural lives. Older people tend to move less than younger people, so that migrants tend to come from relatively young societies and to go to relatively old societies.

Percentages and Projected Percentages of the U.S. Population Aged 65+ and Median Age of the U.S. Population, 1900-2050

Year	%65+	Median Age
1900	4.1	22.9
1910	4.3	24.1
1920	4.7	25.3
1930	5.5	26.5
1940	6.9	29.0
1950	8.1	30.2
1960	9.2	29.4
1970	9.8	27.9
1980	11.3	30.0
1990	12.7	33.6
2000	13.1	36.4
2010	14.1	38.9
2020	18.2	40.2
2030	22.9	41.8
2040	23.9	42.6
2050	24.9	45.0

Sources: U.S. Bureau of the Census, *1990 Census of Population* (1990) and *Historical Statistics of the United States* (1993), Washington, D.C.: U.S. Government Printing Office.

POPULATION AGING

Population aging occurs whenever the proportion of older people in a society increases relative to the proportion of younger people. Over the course of the twentieth century, the populations of almost all industrialized countries aged. One indicator of this change is a country's median age—the age that divides the country into two, with half of the people older than that age and half of the people younger. In 1900, the median age in the United States was 22.9. By 1996, according to U.S. Census records, the median age had risen to 34.6 years and was expected to reach 36.4 by 2000. In 2010, according to projections, the median age would be 38.9. It was projected to continue to rise, reaching 40.2 in 2020 and in 41.8 in 2030.

When the median age increases, there are more people in older age categories. In 1900, only 4.1 percent of the people in the United States were sixty-five years of age or older. Fifty years later, 8.1 percent of the U.S. population was sixty-five or older. By 1990, this figure had risen to 12.7 percent, roughly the same percentage of the population as the nation's largest minority group, African Americans. According to U.S. Census projections, the proportion of older people will continue to grow through the first half of the twenty-first century, reaching 22.9 percent of all those in the country in 2030 and 23.9 percent in 2040. By 2050, according to these estimates, one out of every four Americans will be over the traditional retirement age. This trend is often referred to as the graying of America, but a similar "graying" can be found in most other economically developed nations. For example, in 1990, 18 percent of the Swedish population was over sixty-five, as was almost 16 percent of the population of Great Britain and 15 percent of the population of Germany.

THE DEMOGRAPHIC TRANSITION

Most demographers argue that the population patterns of societies are linked to the levels of technological development in those societies. Demographic transition theory divides human societies into three stages of technological and economic development. The first stage is found in preindustrial agricultural societies. This stage is characterized by high birthrates, because children provide agricultural labor and because effective birth control is not available. However, there are also high death rates in the first stage, because pre-industrial people have a low material standard of living and primitive medical technology. Low life expectancies, with great increases in the probability of death accompanying each year of age, make young people the overwhelming majority in pre-industrial societies.

The second stage, with early industrialization, brings about a surge in population, or a demographic transition. Industrialization greatly expands the available food supply and, in modern times, provides improved access to medical care. This brings about a fall in death rates, while birthrates remain high. European societies entered this second stage during the late 1700's, during the Industrial Revolution. Many developing nations in Latin America and Asia entered this stage during the twentieth century. These industrializing societies also tend to have young populations, since each younger generation is larger than the preceding generation.

In the third stage, advanced industrialization, population growth begins to slow; some highly industrialized societies may even reach zero population growth. Technologically sophisticated, widely available medical care greatly extends life expectancy. The United States, for example, has seen a tremendous increase in life expectancy over the course of the twentieth century. In 1900, only about 63 percent of white females, 32 percent of nonwhite females, 55 percent of white males, and 28 percent of nonwhite males would live to age sixty. By 1990, 93 percent of white females, 91 percent of nonwhite females, 88 percent of white males, and 83 percent of nonwhite males could expect to reach age sixty. Over time, then, a continuing pattern of fewer births combined with longer lifetimes has produced the "graying" of the industrialized societies of North America, Western Europe, and Japan.

Population aging and the slowdown in population growth in the third stage occur for a number of additional reasons. As standards of living improve, individuals develop greater expectations. The perception of television sets, washing machines, spacious houses, and other consumer goods as necessities leads many people to limit family size in order to be able to purchase these goods. Children no longer contribute to family income, as they do in agricultural societies. Instead, in advanced industrial societies, children need long years of education and training before they are able to become economically active. In general, children whose parents can give them many years of education will have more prestigious and better-paying jobs than children who are able to finish only minimal levels of education. Parents in advanced industrial societies therefore often have fewer children in order to invest more in the children they do have.

The changing status of women in advanced industrial societies also tends to promote the slowing of population growth and to promote population aging. As higher education becomes more common for women, women tend to delay childbirth and to have fewer children. The entry of women into the labor force means that women have smaller families in order to pursue careers and that women are less available as full-time caretakers for large numbers of children.

THE BABY BOOM

Even though developed societies have a general tendency toward growing proportions of older adults as a result of declining birthrates and long life expectancies, these societies still show some fluctuations in population age. Historical events continue to influence how many children people have, and relatively high birthrates at any given point in history mean a dip in the age of the population. For example, in the United States the median age increased steadily over the first half of the twentieth century, from 22.9 in 1900 to 30.2 in 1950. Over the following two decades, though, the U.S. population grew younger, with a median age of 29.4 in 1960 and a median age of 27.9 in 1970.

American society became more youthful during these decades because men and women began settling into family life in record numbers from the end of World War II until 1965. The three- and four-child family became a widespread ideal, so that about 75 million babies were born in the United States during the two decades of the "baby boom." By the second half of the 1990's, four out of every ten Americans were members of the baby-boom generation. The United States was not unique in this respect, since many nations experienced a similar spurt in population size following World War II. The reasons for this phenomenon are not entirely clear, but it appears that a desire for settled family life often becomes common among people after the disturbing events of a war.

During the 1960's and 1970's, as members of the baby-boom generation reached their teens and early twenties, they created a worldwide youth culture. During the early twenty-first century, the baby boomers will make an enormous contribution to the graying of the industrialized world, since they will become the largest generation of senior citizens in history. Not only will this generation of older people be numerous, it will also be huge compared to other age groups as well. The baby boom produced a "baby bust," since Americans born during the boom tended to have fewer children than their parents did. In the late 1990's, however, U.S. public schools began to experience a rapid rise in enrollments termed the "baby boom echo" as the children of baby boomers, who often delayed childbearing, converged with the children of later generations.

DEMOGRAPHIC CHARACTERISTICS OF OLDER PEOPLE

One of the most notable demographic characteristics of older people is the imbalance between the numbers of men and the numbers of women. Women tend to live longer than men do, so there are more older women than older men. In the United States, there were an estimated 20,022,000 women and 13,850,000 men aged sixty-five or older in 1996, or 1.4 women for every man. Among the oldest people, the imbalance was even greater. There were 2,697,000 women and 1,049,000 men eighty-five or older, or 2.6 women for every man. As a population grows older, then, women make up a growing proportion of its people.

The economic circumstances of older people in the United States and in a number of other developed countries improved markedly during the last third of the twentieth century. In the 1960's, about 30 percent of people in the United States aged sixty-five and above lived in poverty, making older people among the most likely to be poor. By 1995, however, only 10.5 percent of Americans aged sixty-five and older were poor, compared to 13.8 percent of all Americans. Despite the fact that older people were less likely to be poor than others, in part as a result of Social Security, private retirement plans, and high rates of home ownership, they also tended to have less income than others.

The median income in the United States in 1992 was only $14,548 for men aged sixty-five and older and $8,189 for women in this age group, compared to $22,013 and $11,803 for men and women aged less than sixty-five.

In the United States, whites tend to have lower birthrates than members of racial and ethnic minority groups. Since 1965, moreover, the majority of immigrants to the United States have come from Latin America and Asia. As a result, by the end of the twentieth century, America's older population contained more white non-Hispanics than the younger population did. White non-Hispanics made up 71.5 percent of those aged eighteen to twenty-nine but 86.6 percent of those aged sixty-five and older in 1991. By contrast, 13.4 percent of those between the ages of eighteen and twenty-nine were African American, and 11.6 percent were Latino. African Americans and Latinos made up only 8.0 percent and 3.7 percent, respectively, of those who were sixty-five and older. Numbers of older minority group members were, however, expected to grow rapidly during the twenty-first century.

CONSEQUENCES OF AN AGING POPULATION

Some criminologists have maintained that crime rates can be expected to go down as a population ages, since most property and violent crimes are committed by people aged under sixty-five. Some have even attributed the decrease in the U.S. crime rate in the late 1990's partly to the aging of the population. Social commentator Theodore Roszak has argued that aging baby boomers will become a great political and social asset by combining the wisdom of old age with the idealism of their generation's youth.

Despite the possible positive consequences of population aging, many policymakers and social scientists are concerned about the problems that may result from having increasing percentages of older people. The sophisticated technology that has increased life expectancy has also driven up health care costs. As people get older, moreover, they rely increasingly on health care, which causes costs to go up even more. Further, as older, retired people grow as a proportion of the population, they must be supported by fewer young people. In 1960, there were five workers for every retiree; by 2025, it was estimated that there would be only 2.2 workers for every retiree. These trends have led to debates about reforming the Social Security system and to suggestions that the retirement age should be raised from sixty-five to seventy or even higher.

One interesting consequence of population aging is that old age itself is gradually being seen less as a stage of life and more as a series of stages. It has become common for gerontologists, specialists in old age, to divide the last part of life into three stages: the young-old, aged sixty-five to seventy-four; the middle-old, aged seventy-five to eighty-four; and the old-old, aged eighty-five and above. As the demographic makeup of the United States and other developed nations changes, it will become increasingly common to find families made up of different generations of the old.

—*Carl L. Bankston III*

See also African Americans; American Indians; Asian Americans; Baby boomers; Childlessness; Gay men and lesbians; Graying of America; Health care; Homelessness; Latinos; Life expectancy; Marriage; Men and aging; Middle age; Old age; Politics; Social Security; Voting patterns; Women and aging.

FOR FURTHER INFORMATION:

Callahan, Daniel. *Setting Limits: Medical Goals in an Aging Society.* New York: Simon & Schuster, 1987. Argues that the graying of American society makes it necessary for citizens to recognize that medical resources are limited and that, therefore, there must be limits to medical spending on the elderly.

Dunn, William N. *The Baby Bust: A Generation Comes of Age.* Ithaca, N.Y.: American Demographics Books, 1993. Examines the consequences of a low birthrate among baby boomers.

Owram, Douglas. *Born at the Right Time: A History of the Baby Boom Generation.* Toronto: University of Toronto Press, 1996. Follows major changes in American society from the birth of the baby boom generation through the 1990's.

Roberts, Sam. *Who We Are: A Portrait of America Based on the Latest U.S. Census.* New York: Times Books, 1993. Provides a readable description of major demographic characteristics of the United States. Based on the 1990 U.S. Census.

Roszak, Theodore. *America the Wise: The Longevity Revolution and the True Wealth of Nations.* Boston: Houghton Mifflin, 1998. Looks at a wide variety of topics related to the aging of American society and argues that a large population of older people will be an economic, social, and political asset.

Russell, Cheryl. *The Master Trend: How the Baby Boom Generation Is Remaking America.* New York: Plenum Press, 1993. Discusses consequences of the large cohort of children born in the years following World War II.

Wolfe, John R. *The Coming Health Crisis: Who Will Pay for Care for the Aged in the Twenty-First Century?* Chicago: University of Chicago Press, 1993. Examines and attempts to offer solutions for the health care crisis the author believes will result from the aging of America's baby boomers.

DENTAL DISORDERS

RELEVANT ISSUES: Health and medicine

SIGNIFICANCE: Proper dental care prevents diseases of the mouth, teeth, and gums that affect the health and general well-being of the older adult and is important for the overall health of an aging population

As the geriatric population increases in the United States, the provision of dental services for the elderly will have to expand to provide adequate regular dental follow-ups. This population will also need to be educated about how to care for their teeth, gums, and dentures in order to maintain good dental health and retain their natural teeth as long as possible.

NORMAL AGE-RELATED CHANGES

Approximately 90 percent of the elderly have some form of mouth disorder. Normal age-related changes of the mouth have a minimal effect on overall functioning. Muscle weakening and decreased bone density in the jaw, decreased elasticity in the gums and cheeks, reduced secretion of saliva, and increased alkalinity in saliva make chewing foods more difficult. Thinning and staining of tooth enamel leads to chipping of teeth. The soft dentin in the teeth slowly and gradually dissolves as a result of exposure to the acid in saliva. Receding gums encourage the trapping of food in crevices between teeth and gums and in tooth borders. This accumulation of food and debris can promote gum irritation and tooth decay if proper dental hygiene, such as brushing and flossing, is not followed.

DISORDERS OF THE TEETH

Being toothless (edentulous) is not a normal part of aging. The major causes of tooth loss in adults are tooth decay and periodontal disease. Lack of water fluoridation, limited access to dental care, and inadequate dental hygiene are also causes of tooth loss in adults. Today, there are fewer cases of adults who are edentulous because of increased availability of preventive dental care and early diagnosis and intervention to prevent disease that causes tooth loss. Treatment for tooth loss includes bridges that replace one or more teeth and anchor onto teeth on either side of the bridge, partial dentures to replace missing teeth, full dentures to cover the entire gum of missing teeth, and dental implants to replace individual teeth by anchoring a post in the jaw and placing an artificial tooth over it.

Cavities (caries) are the major cause of all tooth loss in the United States. Because of their receding gums, most caries in older adults form at the gum line and the roots of teeth. Caries are areas in a tooth in which enamel has thinned (demineralized), causing weak areas in tooth enamel that eventually decay. This decay is a result of the acid in saliva, which increases during eating. Fluoride helps to slow enamel demineralization. Fluoride is present in many water supplies, toothpaste, and mouth rinses. Brushing the teeth at least twice daily and flossing between teeth help to prevent enamel demineralization.

An abscessed tooth is an inflammation and infection in the pulp of a tooth. It most frequently results from a cavity that exposes the tooth pulp to bacteria. The major symptom is a constant, severe pain in the affected tooth. The pain increases when the tooth is exposed to heat and cold. Treatment includes drainage of the abscess by a dentist. If the pulp of the tooth is severely infected, a root canal may be the only means to save the tooth. A root canal is a procedure in which the diseased pulp is removed and the remaining space is filled with a compound that will maintain the integrity of the tooth.

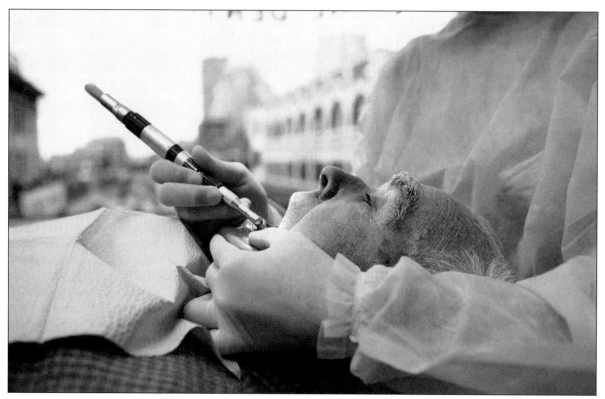

Regular checkups and cleanings are crucial in the later years to avoid tooth loss and other serious dental problems. (PhotoDisc)

A fractured tooth is one that has cracked from trauma, poor health, or demineralized enamel. If the fracture is severe, a crown may be placed over the tooth to protect, strengthen, and prevent tooth loss.

Malocclusion occurs when the teeth do not align in the mouth properly. This condition causes uneven wear on the teeth. Over time, it can create dental problems that require dental procedures to correct the damage that is caused. Common malocclusions are an overbite, in which the upper teeth greatly overhang the lower teeth, and an underbite, in which the lower teeth jut out beyond the upper teeth.

When the gums recede or teeth are chipped or fractured, the dentin of the teeth allows the nerves to be exposed to irritants that cause pain or discomfort. The result is sensitive teeth. Frequently, these irritants are heat, cold, and sweet or sour foods and drinks. Using toothpaste for sensitive teeth and a soft toothbrush may help to relieve discomfort.

Age-related color changes that occur in the teeth are normal. Years of exposure to coffee, tea, colas, fruit juices, and smoking gradually and steadily stain the teeth, causing color changes from whiter to more yellow. Professional bleaching by a dentist can help to restore some of the whiteness of teeth.

DISORDERS OF THE GUMS

Periodontal disease, also called gum disease or pyorrhea, is a major cause of tooth loss in older adults. It results from an inflammatory process caused by the accumulation of plaque and tartar that destroys the bones supporting the teeth. Plaque is composed of sticky components of bacteria and saliva that adhere to the gum line and the crevices of the teeth. It forms constantly and must be brushed away to prevent tartar. Tartar is the hardened mineral deposits that are formed from plaque that is not removed. The accumulation of plaque and tartar may be the result of food impurities, malnutrition, vitamin deficiencies, endocrine disorders, certain medications, breathing through the mouth, poor dental hygiene, poor-fitting dentures, and inadequate access to dental care. The incidence of periodontal disease increases with age because of a reduction in saliva. Saliva aids in rinsing food particles from the teeth and gums and prevents plaque from forming.

There are early and late stages in periodontal disease. Gingivitis is the earliest and least-invasive stage; it involves only the gums surrounding the teeth. The major cause of gingivitis is poor dental hygiene. Gingivitis produces bleeding, tender gums. Periodontitis is a more severe stage of periodontal disease in which the gums recede and separate from the teeth and the bone depletes. If this condition is left untreated, the gums recede and bone depletes even further. Food becomes trapped in the pockets that form between the gums and teeth; the resulting infection causes the teeth to loosen and fall out.

Tobacco use also leads to periodontal disease, ulcerative gingivitis, tooth staining, delayed healing, and precancerous mouth tissue. Regular brushing of the teeth, gums, and tongue helps to fight periodontal disease.

Receding gums shrink away from the gum line and expose the root of the tooth, which is normally covered. Improper tooth brushing techniques, firm-bristle toothbrushes, and periodontal disease cause the gums to shrink away from the gum line. Once the gums shrink, they do not grow back, even when there is an improvement in tooth brushing techniques and soft-bristle toothbrushes are used. Exposing the root of the tooth increases the chances for periodontal disease.

Overgrowth of gum tissue (gingival hyperplasia) can result from irritation caused by plaque from poor dental hygiene or from physical or chemical irritant to the gums. Medications such as phenytoin and cyclosporine commonly cause gingival hyperplasia.

OTHER MOUTH DISORDERS

Many older adults have the misconception that wearing dentures indicates that they no longer need to make regular visits to the dentist. This misconception causes many to experience dental problems that could be prevented. If identified in early stages of development, many dental problems are treatable or preventable. Denture wearers have 50 percent of the chewing and biting ability of those who have their natural teeth. Dentures that do not fit well can cause pain or discomfort that causes even more difficulty in chewing foods. Poor-fitting dentures may also cause speech problems because of the inability to enunciate words clearly. Poor-fitting dentures are an indication that a dentist visit is needed. Over time, the bone in the mouth that supports the dentures shrinks. Adjustments must be made to ensure that the denture fits properly and comfortably and to prevent additional dental problems.

Individuals in their seventies have the highest incidence of mouth cancer. Malignant oral lesions are most associated with iron deficiencies and tobacco and alcohol use. Approximately 90 percent of the oral lesions that are identified are squamous cell cancers. A white coating in the mouth or on the tongue or lips and painless lumps or sores in the mouth that last more than a month should be examined.

Oral candidiasis is a fungal infection that appears as a white or cream-colored coating on the tongue, throat, and inner cheeks of the mouth. It is identified as either acute or chronic in nature. Acute oral candidiasis (thrush) is associated with antibiotic and immunosuppressive therapies. Chronic oral candidiasis is associated with iron and folate deficiencies and the wearing of acrylic dentures. The space between the roof of the mouth and the upper denture is an ideal place for candidiasis to grow. Chronic candidiasis is sometimes accompanied by painful cracks at the corners of the mouth (cheilitis). Obtaining proper-fitting dentures, cleansing and soaking the dentures regularly to remove debris, and taking antifungal medication will cure this condition.

A burning tongue (glossopyrosis) or painful tongue (glossodynia) usually cannot be explained. It may be accompanied by increased redness and inflammation of the tongue, increased size of the tongue, and pronounced taste buds (papillae). These symptoms may be the result of malnutrition, vitamin deficiencies, infection, medications, mental or physical diseases, or changes associated with the menopause, as well as other dental conditions. Medical assistance should be accessed to diagnose the problem. The goal is the relief of symptoms and the treatment of underlying causes.

Bad breath (halitosis) is the result of poor dental hygiene, cavities, periodontal disease, or simply the type of foods that are eaten. Proper brushing and flossing and the avoidance of large quantities of foods that cause bad breath may alleviate halitosis. Bad breath may also be a symptom of other medical conditions, such as sinus infection, gastrointestinal disease, or diabetes.

Dry mouth (xerostomia) results from decreased excretion of saliva from the salivary glands. This condition may occur with normal aging, but it is more frequently caused by medications, such as those for cardiac problems, high blood pressure, allergies, gastric problems, depression, and Parkinson's disease. Xerostomia can be helped with warm water rinses and with oral lubricating preparations or hard candies.

Temporomandibular (TMJ) disorders occur in cycles and increase in times of stress and during strenuous activities. TMJ disorders cause chronic facial pain and include conditions that involve the jaw muscles, temporomandibular joints, and the nerves of the jaw. These conditions are most frequently a result of grinding and clenching of the teeth (bruxism), osteoarthritis, osteoporosis, congenital misalignment of the jaw, or partial or complete tooth loss. TMJ disorders are treated with stress reduction, relaxation techniques, and resting of the TMJ joint.   —*Sharon W. Stark*

See also Aging process; Bone changes and disorders; Cancer; Crowns and bridges; Dentures; Health care; Malnutrition; Medications; Nutrition; Smoking; Vitamins and minerals.

FOR FURTHER INFORMATION:
Academy of General Dentistry. *AGD Impact* 13 (August/September, 1998).
Crest Dental Resource Net. www.dentalcare.com/soap/patient.htm.
Epidemiology and Oral Disease Prevention Program. National Institute of Dental Research. *Oral Health of the United States Adults: The National Survey of Oral Health in U.S. Employed Adults and Seniors, 1985-1986—National Findings.* NIH Publication no. 87-2868. Bethesda, Md.: U.S. Department of Health and Human Services, Public Service, National Institutes of Health, 1987.
Little, J., and D. Falace. *Dental Management of the Medically Compromised Patient.* 4th ed. St. Louis: Mosby Year Book, 1993.

DENTURES
RELEVANT ISSUES: Health and medicine
SIGNIFICANCE: Dentures replace missing teeth and restore both facial appearance and the ability to speak clearly and to chew food by maintaining the shape of the jaw

With the aging process, disease of the teeth and surrounding tissues often increases, leading to the eventual loss of some or all of the teeth. When teeth are missing, the remaining teeth can change position, drifting into the surrounding space. Teeth that are out of position can damage tissues in the mouth. It is also more difficult to clean thoroughly between crooked teeth, resulting in an increased risk of tooth decay, gum disease, and additional loss of teeth. The solution is to replace the missing teeth with a denture. In 1999, more than thirty-two million Americans were wearing some type of denture, and the majority were over fifty-five years of age.

When a large number of teeth are missing, and a sufficient number of adjacent teeth are not present to support a bridge, or fixed partial denture, a removable partial denture is the solution. It consists of replacement teeth attached to pink or gum-colored plastic bases, which are connected by a metal framework. This prosthetic device is usually secured by clasping it to several of the remaining teeth. The clasps are typically made out of gold or a cobalt-steel alloy. Although more costly, precision attachments are nearly invisible and generally more aesthetically pleasing than metal clasps. Crowns on the adjacent natural teeth may improve the fit of a removable partial denture, and they are usually required with precision attachments.

When all the teeth need replacement, a full denture is constructed. It is usually made of acrylic, occasionally reinforced with metal. Full dentures replace all the teeth in either jaw and are generally held in place by suction created between saliva and the soft tissues of the mouth. A temporary soft liner can be placed in a new or old denture to help improve the health of the gum tissues by absorbing some of the pressures of mastication and providing maximum retention by fitting around undercuts in the bone and gums.

A common misconception is that when all the teeth are extracted and replaced by full dentures, all teeth problems cease. In fact, properly fitted full dentures at best are only about 25 to 35 percent as efficient as natural teeth. Many elderly have little trouble adjusting, but some find it difficult to adapt to and learn to use dentures properly. Furthermore, the tissues of the mouth undergo constant changes, which may result in loose or bad-fitting dentures, which may cause damage to the mouth tissues. Consequently, a person who wears dentures should continue to see a dentist for regular annual checkups.

Full and partial dentures are removable and must be taken out frequently and cleansed. In addition, the supporting soft tissues of the mouth need thorough cleansing with a soft mouth brush two to three times daily. It typically takes a few weeks to get used to inserting, wearing, eating with, removing, and maintaining dentures. Careful attention to all the instructions given by the dentist is vital.   —*Alvin K. Benson*

See also Aging process; Bone changes and disorders; Crowns and bridges; Dental disorders; Health care.

DEPRESSION

RELEVANT ISSUES: Health and medicine, psychology

SIGNIFICANCE: Depression is the most common psychological illness among the elderly

Community surveys have reported depressive symptoms in 30 percent to as many as 65 percent of people over the age of sixty. Depressions severe enough to warrant psychiatric intervention are generally estimated to affect 10 to 15 percent of the geriatric population, and depressive disorders are estimated to account for nearly one-half of the admissions of older adults to acute-care psychiatric hospitals in the United States.

DEMOGRAPHIC ASPECTS

Strong associations have been found between geriatric depression and a number of demographic variables. Many of these variables involve decreases or losses in social, physical, and financial resources. Geriatric depression has been found to increase as financial status, the quality of interpersonal relationships, and general health decreases. Additional factors frequently associated with geriatric depression include marital discord, marital separation or divorce, living alone, lack of children (childlessness), lack of a confiding relationship, decreases in social support, deaths of relatives and friends, physical disabilities affecting employment, high levels of stress, physical pain, chronic medical conditions, and lower levels of attained education.

Considered together, these factors suggest that quality-of-life issues are crucial in understanding

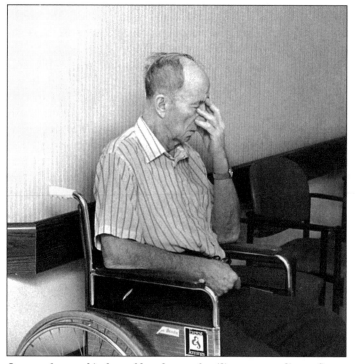

Losses of many kinds—of loved ones, familiar surroundings, financial resources, and physical or mental abilities—can result in depression in some older people. Elderly men in particular have an increased risk for suicide. (James L. Shaffer)

the onset, severity, and chronicity of geriatric depression. These factors do not cause geriatric depression per se but, in general, make the older individual much more vulnerable to its occurrence. On an individual basis, the effects of any one of these factors may be significantly mitigated by the attitude and psychological resources of a given individual. Specifically, greater overall coping with social, medical, and environmental stressors seems to be related to a given individual's overall mental health before the onset of the stressors. Those older individuals who manifest more extensive psychological strengths and a greater repertoire of social and interpersonal skills tend to succumb to stressors much less frequently than individuals with histories of poor coping or impaired social functioning.

PSYCHOLOGICAL ASPECTS

Susceptibility to geriatric depression has been linked to a number of psychological variables. Extensive research has focused on the areas of self-esteem, engagement in general life activities, and learned helplessness. Lowered self-esteem has been consistently associated with geriatric depression. Many elderly feel stigmatized or marginalized, especially after leaving positions of importance or prominence. The elderly in Western societies lack the high levels of respect and reverence shown toward the elderly of Eastern societies and many tribal cultures. Poor adjustment to retirement can often result in newly acquired feelings of inferiority or uselessness. Low self-esteem in elderly individuals has also been associated with overall poor coping following the death of a spouse. In addition to its association with geriatric depression, low self-esteem has been linked with greater levels of reported pain, lower levels of self-reported health, higher levels of physical disability, and increased anxiety.

Investigation into the relationship between geriatric depression and "engagement" has produced fairly consistent results. Engagement theory conceptualizes geriatric depression as resulting from an overall "disengagement" from general life activities, especially social activities, recreational activities, volunteer work, and meaningful interactions within the larger community. According to this theory, many older individuals "withdraw inside themselves," increasingly narrowing their personal worlds and levels of activity, eventually reaching a psychological state of stagnation and boredom resulting in depression. Depressed geriatric individuals do report a greater use of avoidance coping behaviors than their nondepressed peers. However, older individuals who engage in volunteer work have been found to manifest higher levels of life satisfaction, stronger desires to live, and overall fewer symptoms of anxiety and bodily complaints. In addition, nursing home residents who volunteer in a range of activities within their facilities have been found to manifest significant reductions in perceived hopelessness and depression. Overall, general activity and age-appropriate work appear to result in greater social contacts, reduced boredom, and increased sense of usefulness and satisfaction.

A theoretical framework that has been quite influential in explaining the cognitive, motivational, and psychological deficits associated with depression is the learned helplessness model proposed by Martin Seligman. According to this model, depression is often the result of a perceived condition of "independence" between one's actions and the results of one's actions. A "helpless" individual is one who increasingly sees aspects of life as uncontrollable. It is this very feature of uncontrollability that, over time, leads to the perception of personal helplessness; the perception of helplessness, in turn, leads to depression. A factor that has been thought to encourage perceptions of noncontrol and helplessness in the aged is the widespread stereotyping of this population as infirm and fragile. It has been found that nurses who view their aged patients as dependent reinforce helplessness and "sick role" behaviors. It has also been found that residents from private retirement homes who were given control of both the frequency and duration of the visits they received were consistently superior on measures of physical and psychological well-being to residents who had not been given this control.

MEDICAL ISSUES

Given the psychological, cultural, and medical issues frequently faced by the elderly, the phenomenon of depression is highly complicated and frequently not detected. Adding to this complication is the phenomenon of pseudodementia, in which an elderly individual is incorrectly evaluated as manifesting severe cognitive impairments while the true diagnosis of depression is missed.

The relatively extensive number of medical issues faced by the elderly often focuses the attention of medical professionals and the elderly themselves on bodily and pain-oriented complaints. What is often missed is a coexisting depression that preceded the onset of medical issues or occurred during the onset of medical issues but is unrelated to medical issues; a coexisting depression that is the elderly individual's reaction to medical issues; or both. Nondetection of geriatric depression may also result from the hesitation of many elderly individuals to discuss psychological or emotional issues. The stigma sometimes associated with psychological issues is often a forceful factor in the elderly individual's tendency to minimize them in favor of a wholly medical or pain-oriented presentation of symptoms. A medical or mental health professional who accepts this presentation without inquiring about issues related to emotional well-being may fail to uncover a coexisting depression underlying medical issues or even a depression unaccompanied by true medical difficulties.

Another phenomenon involving the nondetection of geriatric depression is pseudodementia, in which the elderly individual is diagnosed as manifesting significant deficits in memory and intellectual processing typical of true dementia victims. This misdiagnosis can result from the unrecognized fact that depressions of all kinds, affecting individuals of all age groups, typically involve temporary deficits in memory processing, concentration, and general intellectual functioning; the fact that temporary deficits in memory and cognitive functioning are often brought on by prescriptions of drug dosages beyond the delicate physiological needs of the elderly; or the inaccurate assumption that severe memory and intellectual deficits are a normal part of aging.

Medical issues can often mask the presence of a concurrent depression. It is therefore important for medical and mental health professionals to inquire about mood states, life satisfaction issues, self-esteem issues, and issues related to hopefulness and hopelessness as experienced before and during the onset of medical and pain complaints. Instruments such as the Beck Depression Inventory and the geriatric depression scale can be helpful in evaluating both the degree of depression and the content areas associated with a depression. Accurate diagnosis of depression can result in medical and psychotherapeutic treatment that can significantly speed the course of recovery.

—*John Monopoli*

See also Childlessness; Death of parents; Death and dying; Death of a child; Dementia; Disabilities; Divorce; Friendship; Grief; Loneliness; Marriage; Medications; Memory changes and loss; Pets; Psychiatry, geriatric; Social ties; Stress and coping skills; Volunteering; Widows and widowers.

FOR FURTHER INFORMATION:
Billig, Nathan. *To Be Old and Sad: Understanding Depression in the Elderly.* Lexington, Mass.: Lexington Books, 1987.

Brink, Terry L. *Clinical Gerontology: A Guide to Assessment and Intervention.* New York: Haworth Press, 1986.

Gallagher, Dolores, and Larry W. Thompson. *Depression in the Elderly: A Behavioral Treatment Manual.* Los Angeles: University of Southern California, Ethel Percy Andrus Gerontology Center, 1981.

Knight, Bob G. *Psychotherapy with Older Adults.* Thousand Oaks, Calif.: Sage Publications, 1996.

Sloane, R. Bruce, and Gene D. Cohen. *Handbook of Mental Health and Aging.* San Diego: Academic Press, 1992.

DIABETES

RELEVANT ISSUES: Biology, health and medicine

SIGNIFICANCE: Diabetes mellitus is a metabolic disorder characterized by high blood glucose concentration and excessive urination and thirst; it is a significant risk factor for complications, disability, and mortality among the aging

Diabetes is one of the top health issues in the United States. It can strike anyone, regardless of age and sex, but it develops most often in adults who are overweight, older, less active, and genetically predisposed to the disease. The prevalence of this disease is also known to increase with advancing age. According to the Centers for Disease Control and Prevention (CDC), a major agency of the United States Public Health Service, more than 15 percent of elderly adults have diabetes. Diabetes also develops regardless of ethnicity. In the United States, however, African Americans, Latinos, and especially American Indians are at greater risk than are Caucasians; American Indians are known to have the highest rates of diabetes in the world.

It is estimated that diabetes afflicts more than sixty million people worldwide, more than fifteen million of them Americans. Of those fifteen million, ten million are diagnosed and about five million are undiagnosed. Diabetes is one of the leading causes of death in the United States. The National Center for Health Statistics at the CDC reported that diabetes was the seventh leading cause of American deaths listed on death certificates in 1996, although the disease is underreported. Diabetes is also the leading cause of disability, kidney failure, blindness, and lower extremity amputations in the aging in the United States. According to the CDC, diabetes accounts for 45 to 70 percent of all nontraumatic lower extremity amputations. Approximately half of these amputations occur in people over sixty-five years of age.

ABSORPTION OF GLUCOSE

The primary source of energy for the human body is glucose, a simple sugar obtained from the digestion of food rich in simple carbohydrates such as sugar, jams, jellies, and soft drinks or complex carbohydrates such as cereal, bread, rice, and pasta. When a nondiabetic eats a carbohydrate-rich meal, glucose is absorbed from the digestive tract into the blood, and the blood glucose concentration rises automatically. In response to the elevated glucose concentration in the blood, beta cells in the pancreas, which are found in clusters called the islets of Langerhans, become stimulated to increase the secretion of the hormone insulin. The role of insulin is to decrease the glucose concentration, bringing it back to a normal range of less than 110 milligrams of glucose per deciliter (0.1 liter) of blood. Insulin accomplishes its function by stimulating target cells such as fat, muscle, and liver cells to take up glucose from the blood and convert it immediately to energy needed for daily life. Unconverted glucose becomes stored for future use as fat in fat cells or as glycogen, a large molecule consisting of glucose molecules, in the liver and muscles.

In diabetics, after a meal rich in carbohydrates, glucose is absorbed into the blood but is not taken up by the cells in the body and is therefore not converted to energy. Consequently, the glucose accumulates in the blood, causing hyperglycemia (abnormally high levels of glucose in the blood). The accumulated glucose is removed by the kidneys, two bean-shaped organs that filter wastes and remove excess water and salts from the blood, and is excreted in urine. Glucose draws water along with it, causing the volume of urine to increase and subsequently requiring frequent urination. The presence of glucose in urine is called glucosuria; it is a clinical indication of diabetes.

When the body is unable to utilize glucose as an energy source, it turns to fat and protein as alternative sources. The liver breaks down fat incompletely to ketone bodies, a group of compounds which include acetone, acetoacetic acid, and beta-hydroxybutyric acid. The ketone bodies are then used as an alternative energy source. Excess ketone bodies are released from the liver into the body, causing ketosis, a condition in which the blood and body fluids become too acidic. If severe, ketosis can lead to diabetic coma—a state of unconsciousness—and death. The presence of ketone bodies in urine is another clinical indication of diabetes. A quick test for diabetic coma is the fruity odor of acetone on the breath of a diabetic.

A fasting blood glucose value of 126 milligrams per deciliter or greater has been determined to be diagnostic of diabetes. (Previously, a value of 140 milligrams per deciliter or greater was considered diagnostic of diabetes.) Certain individuals have fasting blood glucose levels of 110 to 125 milligrams per deciliter, which lies between normal and diabetic. These individuals do not have diabetes, but they are thought to have impaired glucose tolerance and are therefore at risk for developing diabetes.

Types of Diabetes

There are two major clinical types of diabetes mellitus. Type I, referred to as insulin-dependent (formerly juvenile-onset) diabetes mellitus, occurs abruptly in about 10 percent of all diabetics before the age of thirty years in genetically susceptible children and teenagers, even when there is no known family history. It is not uncommon to find individuals over fifty years of age living with type I diabetes. This type of diabetes is called an autoimmune disease because the beta cells in the pancreas are destroyed by the person's own immune system, the body's defense against disease; consequently, little or no insulin is produced by the beta cells. Some researchers believe that a viral infection triggers the destruction of the beta cells.

Type II, referred to as noninsulin-dependent (formerly maturity-onset or adult-onset) diabetes mellitus, occurs in 90 percent of all diabetics. It is a common occurrence in the aging. This disease starts in middle to late life, usually after forty, and is most common in people over fifty-five years of

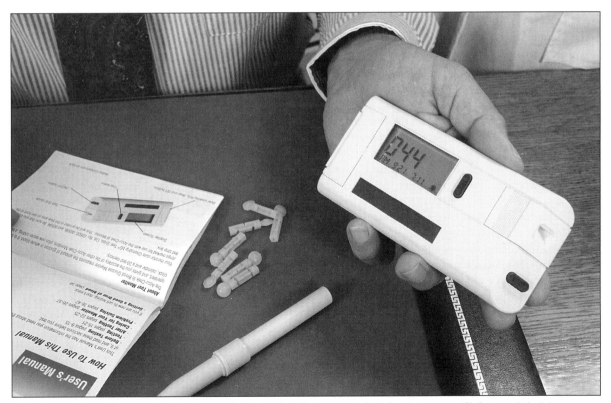

A device can be used to monitor blood sugar levels in the effort to control moderate to severe diabetes, minimizing or even eliminating its effects on the body. (Digital Stock)

age. Older, overweight adults are at high risk for type II diabetes and related complications. Approximately 80 percent of adults with type II diabetes are obese. Because the onset of symptoms is gradual, developing over a period of months or even years, many in the aging population are unaware of their condition. When adults with undiagnosed diabetes experience fatigue and other symptoms of the disease, they often attribute them to aging and therefore do not seek medical care. The chance of an adult developing diabetes increases if one or both parents had the disease. In such an individual, excessive intake of carbohydrates can trigger the onset of the disease. An older woman is also at high risk of developing type II diabetes if she developed gestational diabetes during pregnancy. Type II diabetes in older people is not the result of insulin deficiency. In fact, the pancreas secretes sufficient amounts of the hormone; the problem is that the target cells in the aging body become resistant or less sensitive to the insulin signal that allows them to take up glucose from the blood.

Symptoms and Complications

Symptoms associated with diabetes include frequent and excessive production of sugary urine, insatiable thirst, increased appetite, extreme fatigue caused by the loss of the body's primary source of energy, and sudden unexplained weight loss resulting from the breakdown of fats and proteins for energy. Other symptoms are blurred vision, slow wound healing, numbness or tingling in the feet from the disruption of nerves, and genital itching in women. The occurrence of heart attacks, strokes, and hypertension (high blood pressure) is higher in elderly diabetics than in non-diabetics in the general population.

Other long-term complications include nerve damage; atherosclerosis (hardening of the arteries), especially in the elderly; kidney failure, which can be treated through a kidney transplant or by an artificial kidney machine in a process called dialysis; gangrene of the feet and eventual amputation; blindness; eye damage; cataracts (clouding of eye lens); and glaucoma (pressure in the eye).

Treatment

In order to stay alive, patients with type I diabetes—including children, young adults, and the aging—are treated with insulin, hence the term "insulin-dependent" diabetes. It was not until 1921, when Frederick Banting and Charles Best isolated insulin from the pancreas of a dog, that type I diabetics had a chance for survival. Insulin cannot be taken orally because it is digested in the intestine; therefore, two or more insulin injections per day are needed for treatment. Prior to 1982, insulin was extracted from the pancreases of pigs and cows because of its structural similarity to human insulin. Unfortunately, insulin from these sources provoked allergic reactions in some patients. Today, insulin is manufactured, either by altering pig insulin chemically to form human insulin or by genetically engineering human insulin. Pharmaceutical company Eli Lilly has marketed genetically engineered human insulin under the trade names Humulin and Humalog.

A proper and strict diet is essential in controlling diabetes. Three healthy low-calorie meals per day based on a physician's personal plan are recommended. Some healthy food choices are bread, cereal, pasta, rice, meat, poultry, fish, dry beans, eggs, nuts, vegetables, fiber, dairy products, nuts, and fruits. Restricting the intake of simple carbohydrates, saturated fats, cholesterol, sodium, and alcohol is crucial. Changes in lifestyle are also beneficial. For example, abstaining from smoking reduces the risk of stroke and heart attack. An exercise regimen reduces weight, improves blood pressure, builds muscle strength, improves sense of well-being, and reduces depression.

Often, proper diet, weight loss, and exercise are enough to control type II diabetes. If not, then treatment advances to oral medications. Physicians may prescribe any of a class of oral hypoglycemic drugs called sulfonylureas, such as tolbutamide, tolazamide, acetohexamide, glyburide, and glipizide or the newer oral drug glucophage (brand name Metformin). The sulfonylurea drugs stimulate the secretion of insulin, but they are known to increase the risk of complications such as heart disease, blindness, and weight gain. Glucophage does not cause some of the serious side effects of the sulfonylurea drugs. It is known to reduce the risk of heart attacks and perhaps facilitate weight loss. Although type II diabetics generally do not require insulin injections, they may be recommended by a physician if diet, exercise, and oral drugs are unable to control glucose levels. About one-third of older patients with diabetes take insulin injections.

The most common adverse effect associated with insulin therapy is a drastic drop in blood glucose concentration, a condition known as hypoglycemia. Hypoglycemia is a risk factor in individuals who receive an overdose of insulin injection or in individuals who are starving. The result may be insulin shock, in which the patient suddenly becomes hungry, weak, and drowsy; is trembling, dizzy, and sweaty; and has a rapid heartbeat. In severe cases, patients become disoriented, suffer seizures, go into a state of unconsciousness, or even die because the brain is deprived of glucose for energy. It is absolutely vital to the well-being of the human body that a constant or normal blood sugar level be maintained, even during fasting periods, because brain cells rely completely on a continuous supply of blood glucose. Insulin and another hormone, glucagon, which is secreted by alpha cells in the pancreas, work oppositely to keep blood glucose level within normal ranges. When the glucose level rises, insulin lowers it; when the level falls, glucagon raises it.

When a person suddenly begins to experience the symptoms of hypoglycemia, a quick self-treatment is a sugar-containing snack or drink. If the person is unconscious, however, immediate medical attention is required. A medical alert identification bracelet or tag usually notifies health care providers about a patient's condition.

There is no doubt that insulin injections prolong the lives of diabetics, but they cannot fully replace the precise insulin secretion from a normal, functional human pancreas. Consequently, pancreatic islet transplants have been considered the best hope as a cure for diabetes. Improved transplantation techniques may prevent recipients from rejecting their new islets and allow them to live healthy lives.

SELF-MONITORING OF BLOOD GLUCOSE

Physicians recommend self-glucose monitoring before symptoms appear in order to guard against both hypoglycemia and hyperglycemia. Many diabetics detect glucose with the aid of a blood test usually performed in the morning before breakfast, after a meal, or several times a day, based on the physician's recommendation.

The test involves pricking a finger with a lancet in order to draw blood. A drop of blood is placed on a strip impregnated with glucose reagent, and a color develops. The more glucose there is in the blood, the darker is the color of the strip. A meter translates and then measures the color change in the strip to give a blood glucose reading. Many patients keep a written log of their blood sugar results. Ongoing research into a continuous blood glucose monitor inserted under the skin, however, may eliminate the need for finger-pricking.

BURDEN OF DIABETES

Diabetes imposes a heavy personal and financial burden on patients. Besides long-term complications, many diabetics experience stress and anxiety. Many also experience clinical depression and therefore need professional counseling. The disease also imposes an astronomical cost to society. According to the American Diabetes Association, in 1997 the United States spent ninety-eight billion dollars on diabetes. Direct medical costs were in the amount of forty-four billion dollars, and indirect costs in time off work, disability, and death accounted for the rest.

Through public awareness, education, public programs, innovative projects, campaigns, prevention and control strategies, early diagnosis, and treatment, the CDC has been making efforts to reduce the burden of diabetes on patients, their families, and society. For diabetics, a modification in lifestyle, self-care, a positive outlook on life, proper treatment, exercise, and dietary control are essential to the management of diabetes and its associated long-term complications.

—Oluwatoyin O. Akinwunmi

See also Cataracts; Exercise and fitness; Gastrointestinal changes and disorders; Glaucoma; Health care; Heart attacks; Hypertension; Illnesses among the elderly; Medications; Nutrition; Obesity; Strokes; Vision changes and disorders; Weight loss and gain.

FOR FURTHER INFORMATION:

Atkinson, Mark A., and Noel K. Maclaren. "What Causes Diabetes?" *Scientific American* 263 (July, 1990). The authors discuss how the immune system attacks the body's insulin-producing cells.

Bellenir, Karen, and Peter D. Dresser, eds. *Diabetes Sourcebook.* Detroit: Omnigraphics, 1994. A health reference book for the general public that describes diabetes—its symptoms, complications, treatments, and statistics on prevalence, morbidity, and mortality. Includes source listings for further help and information.

Ezzell, C. "New Clues to Diabetes' Cause and Treatment." *Science News* 140 (December 21 and 28, 1991). A short article that discusses the cause and treatment of diabetes.

Lienhard, Gustav E., Jan W. Slot, David E. James, and Mike M. Mueckler. "How Cells Absorb Glucose." *Scientific American* 266 (January, 1992). The authors discuss how glucose enters the cell through transporter proteins.

Orci, Lelio, Jean-Dominique Vassali, and Alain Perrelet. "The Insulin Factory." *Scientific American* 259 (September, 1988). The authors describe how insulin is made in the pancreas.

Saudek, Christopher D., Richard R. Rubin, and Cynthia S. Shump. *The Johns Hopkins Guide to Diabetes for Today and Tomorrow.* Baltimore: The Johns Hopkins University Press, 1997. Written by a team of specialists at The Johns Hopkins University for people with diabetes, their families, and the general public.

DIET. *See* **NUTRITION.**

DISABILITIES

RELEVANT ISSUES: Demographics, family, health and medicine, psychology

SIGNIFICANCE: Most of the attention given to age and disability has focused on children and youth. Only recently have professionals begun to address the challenges encountered by adults, altering the overall perspective of aging and disability and broadening the views of many professionals and consumers

Aging is defined here as the systematic reduction in the quality in functioning of human body systems. Disability is a general term used for a functional limitation that interferes with a person's ability, for example, to walk, hear, learn, or have strength or endurance. It may refer to a physical, mental, or sensory condition.

In 1999, an estimated forty-three million Americans were significantly limited in their capacity to participate fully in work, education, family, or community life because they had a physical, cognitive, or emotional condition that required societal accommodations. Public Law 101-336, the Americans with Disabilities Act (ADA) of 1990, declares that individuals with disabilities have fundamental rights of equal access to public accommodations, employment, transportation, and telecommunications. The recognition of these rights, and of society's obligation to facilitate their attainment, provides the opportunity for major improvements in the daily lives of individuals with disabilities.

Common disabilities identified with age are mobility limitations, sensory limitations, and intellectual limitations. These conditions may result in difficulty or inability to perform activities of daily living such as eating, bathing, dressing, or toileting without assistance or devices. They may also limit the ability to perform activities related to basic home care, shopping, meal preparation, telephone communication, and money management.

For most people, adulthood is a time when one leaves home, gets a job, and becomes more self-reliant, no longer dependent on parents or caregivers. For adults with disabilities, however, living conditions and lifestyles vary greatly. Many people with disabilities lead a somewhat typical existence, living and working in their community, perhaps marrying, and for the most part supporting themselves financially. These adults still need support, however, as do people who are not disabled. That support may be time-limited (such as vocational rehabilitation services) or informal (such as attention from family members and friends). Those with more severe disabilities need opportunities for paid employment, housing in the community, and access to recreation and leisure experiences.

Adults with mild disabilities have a better prognosis than those with more severe disabilities. For adults with more severe disabilities, ongoing government-funded and natural supports are critical in order to ensure access and participation in employment, supported residential living, and recreation in the local community. Parents and family members of people with severe disabilities often face the stark reality that their caregiving role may not diminish during the adult years and could well extend through a lifetime.

Quality of life during the adult years is most often characterized by employment, useful work, and valued activity; access to further education when desired and appropriate; personal autonomy and independence; social interaction and community participation; and participation within the life of the family. As one reaches the adult years, decisions have to be made relative to each of these areas.

Aging and acquiring a disability are the normal sequelae of human development. Acquiring a dis-

ability prior to age sixty-five is common among those individuals who did not already have a disability that manifested itself during the prenatal period. Common causes of such disabilities are dis-

Residential Alternatives for Persons with Disabilities

Residential Model	Characteristics
Public Residential Facilities	Institutionalized facilities with trained staff and full-time supervision for residents. Residents are segregated from the community.
Sheltered Villages	Institutionalized facilities with trained staff and full-time supervision for residents. Privately supported, the facilities are often located in rural areas with the residents segregated from the community.
Public Community Facilities; also called Intermediate Care Facilities	Institutionalized facilities with trained staff and full-time supervision for residents. Residents are segregated from the community for some activities but integrated for others.
Public Group Homes	Government-operated homes shared by groups of persons and supervised by a staff which may be part-time. Residents may be segregated from the community for some activities but integrated for others.
Private Group Homes	Privately operated homes with the same characteristics as public group homes.
Cooperatively Owned Group Homes	Homes owned jointly by residents and for which full-time or part-time staff may be employed. Residents may be segregated from the community for some activities but integrated for others.
Foster Care	A situation in which persons with disabilities live in a home and under the supervision of a caregiver, who may be paid a stipend for these services. The degree to which residents are integrated into the community varies according to the attitudes of the caregivers.
Publicly Managed Supervised Apartments	Government-operated apartments leased to individuals. Persons are supervised or assisted by an apartment manager who may be part-time. Residents may be segregated from the community for some activities but integrated for others.
Privately Managed Supervised Apartments	Privately managed apartments with the same characteristics as publicly managed supervised apartments.
Cooperatively Owned Supervised Apartments	Cooperatively owned apartments or condominiums leased to individuals with the same characteristics as publicly or privately managed supervised apartments.
Independent Living	A wide range of residential options that may include renting or purchasing a residence in ways similar to those by which residences are selected and maintained by persons without disabilities. Persons with disabilities have unrestricted access to community activities and can request assistance from agency personnel as appropriate.

eases and accidents. During the aging process, many conditions are ontogenetic (age-related). Research into gerontology and disabilities is in its early stages of knowledge acquisition.

MIDDLE AGE

The period of aging from forty to sixty-five, the transitional years to late adulthood, is typically fraught with the acquisition of ontogenetic disabilities. The developmental stages for the middle-age period are described in three categories: physical development, cognitive development, and social-emotional development.

Physical development manifests itself as some deterioration of physical health, stamina, and prowess; declines in seeing and hearing; shortening in height; less frequent sexual behavior but generally a moderate-to-strong interest; and the menopause in women. Cognitive development manifests itself as high degrees of wisdom and practical problem-solving skills; a decline in the ability to solve novel problems; and some decline in memory, with deficits greater in long-term than in short-term memory. Social-emotional development manifests itself as continuing development of a sense of identity; double responsibilities of caring for children and elderly parents, which may cause stress; launching of adult children into the world, which may result in empty nest syndrome; a peak in career success and earning power for some but burnout for others; the search for meaning in life; and a midlife crisis for some individuals.

LATE ADULTHOOD

This period of aging from age sixty-five to death is usually the time when medically related conditions occur that result in disabilities.

Physical development manifests itself as general health and activity for most but some decline in health and physical abilities; an increase in chronic disorders; and a slowing of reaction time which affects many aspects of functioning. Cognitive development manifests itself as mental alertness and an increase in wisdom for most people but declines in the speed of processing declines and in memory; and compensation for some deterioration in intelligence and memory for most. Social-emotional development manifests itself as retirement from the workforce, which may create more leisure time but reduce economic circumstances; a focus on life satisfaction and aging; coping with losses in many areas (loss of one's own faculties, loss of loved ones) and one's own approaching death.

The stereotypes of aging are the desolate empty nest, the volcanic midlife crisis, the dependency of aging parents, and the trauma of the menopause. A 1999 study conducted by the MacArthur Foundation of a nationally representative sample of 7,852 Americans aged twenty-five to seventy-four, however, revealed a different picture. Overall, middle-aged people were less nervous and worried than those under age forty; they felt a growing sense of control at work and greater financial security. They found life to be overfull but rewarding. Although often bombarded by challenges, they showed excellent coping skills.

Respondents aged thirty-five to sixty-five enjoyed remarkably good health, but in some cases poor physical fitness and self-destructive habits signaled potential trouble. Seven of ten people in midlife said that they were overweight, and more than half over age forty-five said that they were less fit than five years ago. Although 73 percent strongly agreed they could do things to lower their risk of a heart attack, only 23 percent strongly agreed they worked hard to stay healthy. The majority of smokers did not believe that they had a higher-than-average risk of developing cancer or heart disease.

Such denial about diseases caused by poor health habits is likely to result in more heart and lung diseases in the future. Many more individuals will have serious medical and disability-causing conditions in the year 2030, when sixty-nine million Americans are expected to be sixty-five or older, nearly double the thirty-five million in 1999; nine million will be eighty-five or older, compared with four million.

SERVICE DELIVERY

During middle age and late adulthood, three levels of service delivery are considered: no special services, time-limited services, and ongoing services. No special services refers to an individual who does not need any specialized services for an age-related or disability-related condition. Time-limited services refers to an individual who needs services such as medical aid, home care, or therapy for a limited amount of time. Ongoing services refers to an individual who needs some type of

The special needs of individuals with nonfatal birth defects, such as flipper-like limbs caused by thalidomide use in pregnant women, may need to be addressed throughout the life span. (James L. Shaffer)

health-related or personal service through the remainder of life.

Those persons who are aging and have a disability should have an array of services available to them in addition to Social Security. Services should be individualized and provided in settings that match the person's needs. The intensity of services may range from intermittent to pervasive. Examples of these support levels are intermittent, limited, extensive, and pervasive.

Intermittent support occurs on an as-needed basis. It is episodic in nature, with the individual not always needing support or requiring short-term support during life span transitions such as job loss or acute medical crisis. Intermittent support may be of high or low intensity when it is provided.

Limited support is of an intensity characterized by consistency over time. It is time-limited but not of an intermittent nature and requires fewer staff members and less cost than more intense levels of support. Examples are time-limited employment

training or transitional supports during the school-to-adulthood period.

Extensive support is characterized by regular involvement (such as daily) in at least some environments (such as work or home). It is not time-limited (such as long-term support and long-term home living support).

Pervasive support is characterized by constancy and high intensity. It is provided across environments and is of a potential life-sustaining nature. Pervasive support typically involves more staff members and intrusiveness than do extensive or time-limited support.

PROGRAMS FOR ADULTS WITH DISABILITIES

In the United States, two types of adult service programs for those with disabilities are supported by the government: entitlement and eligibility. Under an entitlement program, everyone who meets the eligibility criteria must receive the service. Income support such as Supplemental Security Income and medical assistance programs such as Medicaid and Medicare are government-supported programs for adults with disabilities. Entitlement programs require that services be provided to eligible individuals with disabilities without respect to the availability of funds.

Under an eligibility program, in contrast, the person with a disability may meet the eligibility criteria but not receive the service because not enough funds are available to serve everyone. When funds are insufficient, some people with disabilities are placed on waiting lists for months or even years. Residential services, housing, and many employment programs such as supported employment are examples of eligibility programs.

ISSUES FOR AGING ADULTS WITH DISABILITIES

Life expectancy for all adults, including those with disabilities, continues to improve. According to projections, between the years 2020 and 2030 about 20 percent of U.S. citizens will be over the age of sixty-five. The fastest-growing age group in the United States is people between the ages of seventy-five and eighty-five. As life expectancy increases for people with disabilities, concerns have arisen among family members, service providers, and the individuals themselves related to life satisfaction, health care, and living arrangements as they age.

In the area of health care, more researchers are attempting to expand knowledge about the functional competence and health status of older people with disabilities. As suggested in the article "Health and Medical Issues" by B. A. Hawkins in *Older Adults with Developmental Disabilities* (1993), "maintaining health and functional status is clearly central to enhancing inclusion, independence, and productivity of adults with disabilities as they grow older."

Similar research is being conducted in the area of community living. Research findings on community living options for older people with disabilities parallel those concerning adults with disabilities in general: a trend toward using smaller community living options. A 1993 survey by M. C. Martinson and J. A. Stone found that, although large congregate care facilities (such as nursing homes) remain as a major service provider for older people with disabilities, there is a clear trend toward smaller establishments. These authors note that older adults with developmental disabilities

should have the opportunity to participate in the communities in which they live, instead of being neglected and made "invisible."

Although a precise and universally agreed-upon definition of independent living is elusive, community integration is a philosophic assumption that people with disabilities should be integrated into the mainstream of community life. If community integration of people with disabilities occurs, then patterns of life should approximate unrestricted conditions of living to the greatest extent possible. A variation of this theme has emerged in the concept of quality of life. Although a subjective term, it carries connotations of happiness, personal well-being, contentment, success, and individualism; it is rooted in the rights of persons with disabilities to be independent, employed, and participants in their communities.

Section 701 of the 1993 Amendments to the Rehabilitation Act of 1973 underscored the need for

> a philosophy of independent living, including a philosophy of consumer control, peer support, self-help, self-determination, equal access, and individual and system advocacy, in order to maximize the leadership empowerment, independence, and productivity of individuals with disabilities, and the integration and full inclusion of individuals with disabilities in the mainstream of American society. . . .

From the late 1960's to the late 1990's, the proportion of persons with disabilities in public residential facilities progressively decreased. This attrition was in response to challenges about whether public institutions could develop the highest possible quality of life for residents. At the same time that this change in attitudes toward public residential facilities occurred, state governments increased funding for alternative, community-based facilities such as group homes, supervised apartments, foster care, and independent living. Only a small percentage of individuals who are aged and disabled own or lease their own homes. Community-based living arrangements are preferred overwhelmingly by persons with disabilities. The accompanying table contains a list and definitions of popular residential models for people with disabilities. It is organized from the most restrictive residential model (public residential facilities) to the least restrictive model (independent living).

DISABILITY AND EMPLOYMENT

In 1996, M. P. La Plante and D. Carlson reported that nineteen million Americans with a disability or health problem, aged eighteen to sixty-nine, were unable to work or limited in the amount or type of work they could do. Back disorders, heart disease, and arthritis were frequently reported causes of work disability. Mental illness, however, was one of the most-disabling conditions; data showed that among adults with serious mental illness, an estimated 3.3 million persons, 29 percent were reported to be unable to work or limited in their ability to work because of their disorder.

While the presence of any disability reduces the likelihood of employment, the effect is closely tied to the severity of the disability. In 1993, J. M. McNeil reported estimates that among persons twenty-one to sixty-four years old, the employment rate was 81 percent for persons with no disability, 67 percent for persons with a disability that was not severe, and 23 percent for persons with a severe disability. Disabled persons who work full time typically earn less than nondisabled workers, with the earnings gap widening with age and severity.

Supported employment models are currently available for individuals with disabilities who have reached adulthood. Supported employment is defined as paid employment for persons with disabilities for whom competitive employment at or above the minimum wage is unlikely and who need ongoing support to perform their work because of their disabilities. Support is provided through activities such as training, supervision, and transportation. Supported employment is conducted in a variety of settings, particularly in work sites in which persons without disabilities are employed. The most common models available to adults with disabilities are those described by P. Wehman, P. Sale, and W. Parent in *Supported Employment: Strategies for Integration of Workers with Disabilities* (1992): enclave, mobile work crew, benchwork or small business, and entrepreneur.

The enclave model places a group of individuals with disabilities in competitive industry while providing full supervision and support in the setting. Enclaves are usually comprised of three to eight individuals. The enclave is often presented as a vocational option for individuals with more severe disabilities and behavior problems because the work is often repetitious and relatively stable over time. Individuals with severe disabilities are placed in companies in industry, often called host companies. In exemplar programs, workers receive pay that is commensurate with nondisabled workers producing the same amount and are given comparable fringe benefits. Supervision can be provided by either the host company or job coaches from a nonprofit organization.

A mobile work crew provides group vocational opportunities for a small group of individuals with disabilities (typically three to eight people). Supervised by one or two individuals, the mobile work crew travels from site to site in the community to provide services. The mobile work crew model is often recommended for individuals with severe disabilities and behavioral problems. Advantages of this particular model include flexibility in meeting the varied needs of different communities, opportunities for community integration, and high public visibility.

Benchwork, also referred to as a small business model, can offer manufacturing services or subcontract work. Small businesses typically operate a small, single-purpose, nonprofit business in which individuals with disabilities can receive training and supervision for contract work. The benchwork model has been suggested for individuals with the most severe disabilities, who may need constant supervision.

The entrepreneur model is one in which an individual with a disability establishes his or her own business. This business can be in a community store, mall, or building. In a number of cases, the business is run out of the person's own home.

In addition, many individuals with disabilities operate street vending stands or work concession stands in governmental buildings. Others may be employed by a corporation but perform the essential job functions at home because of the hardship imposed on them with coming to an office.

CONCLUSION

Although people are living longer, they are not necessarily living better. Many elderly and disabled persons are not receiving the kind of care that they need; others have unmet needs for a variety of noninstitutional services, including home care, employment, and supportive living arrangements. Key issues that need to be addressed are community care, self-care, family care, and funding for services needed by the elderly.

—*Bruno J. D'Alonzo*

See also Americans with Disabilities Act; Arthritis; Back disorders; Canes and walkers; Cataracts; Dementia; Employment; Hearing loss; Hearing aids; Heart disease; Independent living; Mental impairment; Mobility problems; Psychiatry, geriatric; Reading glasses; Sensory changes; Vision changes and disorders; Wheelchair use.

FOR FURTHER INFORMATION:

Brim, O. J. *Midlife Research*. Vero Beach, Fla.: John D. and Catherine T. MacArthur Foundation, 1999. This resource is a primary and definitive work containing a description of a national study on aging and disabilities that includes research data and analysis.

Butler, R. N., M. Lewis, and T. Sunderland. *Aging and Mental Health*. New York: Charles E. Merrill, 1991. This textbook contains extensive information about aging and disabilities related to mental health.

Diagnostic and Statistical Manual of Mental Disorders: DSM-IV. 4th ed. Washington, D.C.: American Psychiatric Association, 1994. This manual is the primary resource for individuals who practice psychiatric and psychological interventions. It is used for diagnostic and classification purposes and contains descriptions of mental conditions.

Hardman, M. L., C. J. Drew, and M. W. Eagan, eds. *Human Exceptionally: Society, School, and Family*. 6th ed. Boston: Allyn & Bacon, 1999. This textbook contains comprehensive information regarding laws, litigation, issues, and in-depth description of the various disability types.

Hawkins, B. A. "Health and Medical Issues." In *Older Adults with Developmental Disabilities*, edited by E. Sutton et al. Baltimore: Brookes, 1993. This chapter contains information that provides the reader with a general overview of health and medical issues relevant to the aged with disabilities.

Health Care Financing Administration. *Medicare and You*. Baltimore: U.S. Department of Health and Human Services, 1999. This manual provides the reader with a comprehensive overview of Social Security, Medicare, and Medicaid.

La Plante, M. P., and D. Carlson. *Disability in the United States: Prevalence and Causes*. Washington, D.C.: National Institute on Disability and Rehabilitation Research, 1996. This report contains a description of data on disability prevalence and etiology in the United States.

Luckasson, R. *Mental Retardation: Definition, Classification, and Systems of Supports*. Washington, D.C.: American Association on Mental Retardation, 1992. This manual is used by professionals to determine if an individual should be classified as mentally retarded. It gives a description of the various causes of mental retardation and the levels of support needed by such individuals.

McNeil, J. M. *Americans with Disabilities: 1991-92*. Washington, D.C.: U.S. Bureau of the Census Reports, U.S. Government Printing Office, 1993. This report is a composite of data collected on Americans with Disabilities from the U.S. Bureau of Census Reports of 1991 and 1992.

Martinson, M. C., and J. A. Stone. "Small-Scale Community Living Options Serving Three or Fewer Older Adults with Disabilities." In *Older Adults with Disabilities*, edited by E. Sutton et al. Baltimore: Brookes, 1993. This chapter contains a description of community living facilities for aged adults with disabilities.

Savage, R. C., and G. F. Wolcott, eds. *Educational Dimensions of Acquired Brain Injury*. Austin, Tex.: Pro-ed, 1994. This textbook contains information about the various types of acquired brain injury and the types of therapy, rehabilitation, and educational protocols needed for recovery.

Wehman, P., P. Sale, and W. Parent. *Supported Employment: Strategies for Integration of Workers with Disabilities*. Boston: Andover Medical Publishers, 1992. This textbook provides comprehensive information regarding supported employment research and descriptions of the various models of supported employment.

DISCOUNTS

RELEVANT ISSUES: Economics, recreation

SIGNIFICANCE: Senior citizen discounts are of value not only to the elderly but also to merchants, who use them to capture a share of the billions of dollars that older people spend each year

Discounts to seniors began in the 1970's when it became apparent that middle-aged people whose children had left home, as well as retired people, had a great deal of disposable income to spend on goods, services, travel, and leisure activities. As the percentage of people over fifty increased within the total population, so did the number, variety, and appeal of senior citizen discounts.

AVAILABLE DISCOUNTS

Discounts can be found on virtually any product or service used by consumers. In most parts of the United States, groceries, haircuts, pedicures, restaurant meals, airline tickets, theaters, car insurance, vacation packages, prescription medicines, eyeglasses, crematory urns, and a host of other goods and services carry senior citizen discounts. Knowledgeable consumers will locate the discounts that are best for them.

Discounts vary in value, depending on the merchant and the nature of the goods and services that are offered. These discounts usually range from 5 to 25 percent (and in rare cases as high as 50 percent) and generally cannot be combined with other discounts, although this is not always the case. Sometimes the discounts do not specify a percentage of discount but will rather be in the form of an added good or service. For example, some airlines give a senior citizen a free ticket for young grandchildren when the grandparent pays full price. Some merchants give a discount for a spouse when a senior citizen pays full price for a meal, ticket, or service. Hotels and motels may give a senior a free day of lodging after the senior has paid for a specified number of days.

Many businesses offer discounts to people who are as young as fifty years old. Generally, the more monetary value a discount has, the more restrictive is the age requirement. Some businesses require seniors to join a club in order to obtain the discount. In order to join, seniors complete an application to obtain a membership card. The senior then must show the card in order to take advantage of the discount. Sometimes the information on the application will be used by the business to market goods and services. Information may even be sold to other businesses that want to target products to specific groups of senior citizens.

While many businesses do not require seniors to obtain a card in order to get a discount, some of them require people to establish proof of age by showing a birth certificate, a government-issued identification card, or a driver's license when they attempt to take advantage of the senior discount. This is particularly true in cases where there is no membership card and the monetary value of the discount is relatively large. Where the monetary value is small, many merchants and service providers accept people's assertions that they are eligible for the discount. Consumers almost always have to ask for the discount, however, since a businessperson who presumes a customer to be of senior status may inadvertently insult the customer.

Membership in certain organizations or professional groups may offer senior citizens discounts that are not available to people who do not belong to the organization. For example, anyone fifty or older is eligible for membership in the American Association of Retired Persons (AARP). This membership gives seniors a variety of discounts, such as reduced rates on Internet connections and service. These special rates are generally available only to people who have AARP membership.

SENIOR DISCOUNT DAYS

Many merchants have one day each week, often a midweek day when business might be slow otherwise, designated as "senior citizen day." On this day, seniors can receive a special discount on goods and services. Designating one day each week as a senior citizen day not only is a boon for seniors but also makes it possible for merchants to handle efficiently the special needs that seniors might have when shopping, such as special assistance in carrying packages to their vehicles. Senior citizen days create a target audience for stores and malls that can, on these days, set up special displays of products that may have particular appeal to the elderly.

On senior discount days, community service organizations may work with merchants to provide special programs geared toward seniors. Thus, the Red Cross may send a bloodmobile to a mall or supermarket once each month on senior citizen day, giving seniors an opportunity to provide blood donations. Health clinics may periodically have special events on a merchant's senior discount day. At these events, health news of interest to older people may be disseminated, and routine medical procedures, such as blood pressure readings, may be administered free or for very small fees. Some merchants or groups of merchants may have events that are somewhat social in nature, such as shows or refreshment tables.

VALUE TO SENIORS

While many people do not like to think of themselves as growing old, most who are eligible for senior citizen discounts are quite willing to take advantage of them. Some people are willing to do so because they believe that after spending decades raising children, nurturing marriages, starting businesses, developing careers, paying utility bills, and retiring mortgages, they have invested enormous time, energy, and money into developing the economy and preserving society. These people regard a senior citizen discount as something that is owed to them.

Others see the discounts from a different perspective. They view them as proof that merchants, businesses, and society as a whole appreciate the efforts that these citizens have made to further the interests of their communities and their nation. Thus, for this group, senior citizen discounts contribute not only to economic well-being but also to feelings of self-esteem and social worth.

Discounts help a large group of senior citizens maintain a standard of living comparable to the one that they had before retirement. Many older Americans have income only from Social Security benefits. Others have both Social Security and pension benefits. Nearly all retirement benefits represent fixed incomes and are generally less than what workers received when employed. Thus, retirees must find ways to live on fixed incomes and within budgets that might be smaller than when the retirees were younger. The discounts offered to senior citizens on discount days and at other times help the seniors maintain these smaller budgets. Therefore, senior discounts contribute to the economic security of older Americans.

Senior citizen discounts also help citizens maintain social and family contacts. Senior citizen days at malls and grocery stores give older people a chance to shop together and to meet on a regular basis. Such social contact helps them maintain a social network. Discounts on meals, theater tickets, vacation packages, and airline tickets help make it possible for seniors on a tight budget to enjoy social events and holiday trips with family and friends.

Some major airlines give seniors drastic discounts on a grandchild's ticket when seniors pays full price. Such a discount makes it possible for grandparents to provide grandchildren with special trips and to spend time with them at a price that will fit the seniors' budget. This sort of discount can help seniors maintain family ties and makes their family appreciate the grandparents' kindness and generosity.

Some bus companies have special promotions that allow the senior who pays full price for a tour or a trip to take a companion at a reduced price or, in some cases, even free. Such an arrangement helps seniors build special relationships with companions or nurture marriages as partners share new travel experiences with each other.

Senior discounts can also make it possible for people to keep up with developments in fields in which they were employed or still may be employed. Many professional organizations offer discount memberships to people who are classified as seniors. These organizations may also offer discounts on attendance at professional meetings and on professional journals. Such discounts may be among the most important to senior citizens who have had long careers in professional fields. These seniors may see the discounts as evidence that their professions still value them as active members; this perception may be a real boost to the morale of the senior citizen. Also, the discounts may make it possible for seniors to participate in conferences where they can serve in a mentoring position to junior members of the profession. The possibility of mentoring others makes many seniors feel satisfied with life, since they will consider themselves to be productive and to be contributing to the furtherance of their profession. Discounts on professional conference attendance may make it possible for seniors, who could not otherwise attend professional conferences, to do so. Interacting with other professionals at these conferences stimulates seniors, keeps them mentally alert, and helps them continue to develop knowledge, skills, and professional relationships.

VALUE TO BUSINESSES

Offering senior discounts has both economic and social values for businesses. In the year 2000, more than 35 million Americans were over sixty-five years of age. This group controlled billions of dollars, much of it disposable income. Thus, mail-order businesses, airlines, travel agents, supermarkets, hair salons, theaters, tour groups, and a multitude of other producers and providers of goods and services, hoping to snag a share of this money, used marketing strategies, such as senior citizen discounts, to attract customers. A visit to any grocery store on senior citizen day illustrates to even the most casual observer the effectiveness of such a marketing strategy.

Another economic aspect of the senior citizen discount strategy involves a senior's extended family. The majority of senior citizens have family members who value and respect them. Family members who see that their father, mother, grandfather, or other relatives shop at a certain business because of a special discount is offered may also shop there. They may appreciate the consideration that has been given to older people in their family, or they may trust the older person's judgment and choose to shop at businesses recommended by the older person.

While the senior discount strategy has economic value to the merchants, businesses, and service providers who employ it, the strategy also has social value. Offering a discount to older people sends the message that these consumers are valued by the business offering the discount. Seniors often interpret this to mean that their contributions to society and their sacrifices have been recognized and are valued. When people feel that their contributions are valued, society is enhanced. Thus, in offering the discounts, merchants make the society a more harmonious place for everyone.

THE FUTURE OF THE SENIOR CITIZEN DISCOUNT

In 1996, the first of the post-World War II baby-boom generation reached fifty years of age. For the first time, members of this well-educated, affluent generation became eligible for many senior citizen discounts. Baby boomers, many with large disposable incomes, have had access to spending money since early childhood, when they received their first allowances. Thus, members of this generation developed savvy consumer knowledge. Merchants who want to get part of the billions of dollars that baby boomers have to spend each year must develop innovative marketing strategies that will be accepted by this group. One such strategy will be new variants of the senior citizen discount.

As merchants seek to develop new variations on the senior citizen discount, they will have to keep in mind the nature of people who will become se-

nior citizens in the first decades of the twenty-first century. As a group, people who were born during the fifteen-year period following World War II have always valued good health, physical attractiveness, youthfulness, freedom, and sex appeal. It will be quite a challenge for businesses to persuade members of this generation to accept the idea of being a senior citizen. Merchants and service providers will have to emphasize discounts on goods and services that appeal to the values associated with the baby boomers. Perhaps senior citizen days at malls will occasionally feature senior athletic events. The affluence and number of baby-boomer retirees will make it likely that senior citizen discount days will no longer be offered primarily by pedestrian businesses, such as grocery stores, but will become part of the marketing strategy of upscale department stores, spas, and computer companies. —*Annita Marie Ward*

See also Advertising; American Association of Retired Persons (AARP); Baby boomers; Consumer issues; Grandparenthood; Income sources; Social ties; Vacations and travel.

FOR FURTHER INFORMATION:

Cheney, Walter J., William J. Diehm, and Frank E. Seeley. *The Second Fifty Years: A Reference Manual for Senior Citizens.* Weed, Calif.: Writers Consortium, 1992. This manual serves as a catalog for all sorts of issues and problems that senior citizens have, including those related to being a senior consumer.

Dychtwald, Kenneth, and Joe Flower. *The Challenges and Opportunities of an Aging America.* New York: Bantam Books, 1990. Aging is seen as the most important trend in the latter part of the twentieth and the first part of the twenty-first centuries. Changes that this trend will bring about are delineated.

Heilman, Joan Rattner. *Unbelievably Good Deals and Great Adventures That You Absolutely Can't Get Unless You're over Fifty.* 10th ed. Lincolnwood, Ill.: NTC/Contemporary, 1999. Discounts on adventure travel, lifetime admission tickets to national parks, hotels, and restaurants, with up to 50 percent off, are identified. The last chapter presents an overview of tax and insurance breaks available to senior citizens.

Spade-Kershaw, Sylvia. *Discounts and Good Deals for Seniors in Texas: The Best Bargains and Deals from*

Abilene to Zavalla for Ages Fifty and Up. Houston: Gulf, 1997. A presentation of senior citizen discounts found while the author traveled throughout Texas.

Walker, Malcolm, and Bob Fiegel. *Senior Citizens Survival Guide.* New York: CCC, 1999. Every aspect of being a senior citizen is explored.

DISCRIMINATION. *See* AGE DISCRIMINATION.

DIVORCE

RELEVANT ISSUES: Family, marriage and dating, psychology, sociology

SIGNIFICANCE: More midlife and older people than ever before must cope with the challenges and possibilities that divorce presents as the rate of divorce among older persons continues to rise

Divorce and remarriage are major components of the social and psychological landscape in North America; at the end of the twentieth century, 46 percent of all marriages were, in fact, remarriages. Divorce and remarriage have been scientifically studied since the 1950's. By 1999, more than one hundred scientific papers had examined forty-five thousand older marriages. Yet, divorce from midlife to old age remains understudied relative to other psychosocial groups of interest, with little attention paid to its scope and impact and the adjustments that older couples face.

The rate of divorce among first-time marriages that have lasted into middle adulthood and beyond is increasing, and seniors are divorcing in greater numbers. In the late 1990's, twenty-five thousand marriages of thirty to forty years of duration were legally dissolved each year. While this number represented less than 2 percent of the divorces taking place in a given year, most people, even geriatric professionals, were surprised that fifty thousand seniors aged sixty and older divorced each year.

REASONS FOR DIVORCE

Every individual, every couple, and every marriage is unique, and so are the reasons that a particular divorce occurs. There are common experiences why people dissolve their marriages, but these tend to differ between those married for lon-ger periods versus those married for shorter periods. For example, younger divorced often cite their former spouses' failure to be responsible in the relationship or failure to commit actively to make the partnership their primary relationship as the most important reason for divorce. They often say that the person they dated, even lived with, turned out not to be the person they married.

Older divorced know their former partners better. They lived long enough together that surprises and revelations were rare. Rather, many older couples cite that they had grown far enough apart to have too little in common or that decision making was nearly always a matter of conflict; they became incompatible. Pleasant times were few; fights were frequent.

With jobs and careers established, home base secured, and children grown, the older divorced gradually had less and less in common until they reached a point where there was no point in staying together. They often report that the years preceding the dissolution were marked either by great conflict and discord or by great emotional detachment and indifference. Their lives were increasingly parallel with fewer intersections, fewer coupled activities, less affirming and nurturing time given and less received.

Younger couples often divorce in response to single precipitating events such as infidelity, failure to establish the marriage as the primary relationship (for example, the problems with in-laws or oversocialization with one spouse's friends), or the discovery that one partner has an addictive disease and will not pursue treatment. Younger couples have invested less of themselves than older couples. They tend to believe that they will have more of themselves left to live with someone else when they do divorce.

Older couples are less likely to end their marriage because of a single episode of insult or injury to the relationship. This does not suggest that the discovery of extramarital affairs, covert monetary mismanagement, or other marital hurdles are not as stressful for midlife and older couples. It does reflect, however, that with a greater shared history, severing a marriage has greater life consequences as aging offers fewer options.

Another factor for older married couples, as distinct from younger ones, is the onset and sometimes onslaught of age-specific stressors. As midlife approaches the end of life, many people become ill or disabled, and nearly all eventually suffer significant psychological or functional loss. These stressors can bring instability and eventual dissolution to what were previously stable, if not emotionally close, relationships.

Another distinction between the older and younger divorced is the assumption made about marital permanence. Younger people married in an era of divorce, when it was commonly believed that one in two marriages would "succeed" and that one in two would "fail." The cultural credo, "For better or worse, for richer or poorer, in sickness and in health, until death do us part," is not taken literally among the younger married. This was not necessarily so in the previous generation. For many midlife and older divorced, marriage and family had been roles aspired to and maintained so that life itself would have meaning. The marital vow was permanent, commitment to it lifelong. Divorce meant that the vow was broken, the commitment severed. For individuals with these values, the psychological impact is often not "My marriage failed" or "We could not make it work no matter how hard we tried," but "I failed; I am no good" or "If I were better or stronger, I would have saved my marriage."

MEN AND WOMEN

While few studies examine gender differences in divorced and divorcing couples, those that do tend to find differences between men and women. In couples married thirty or more years, husbands initiate divorce more often and wives more often strongly contest it. Frequently cited psychological and social circumstances are related either to the husband's impending or recent retirement and the accompanying sense of lost identity or to the husband's liaisons with significantly younger women, usually interpreted as attempts to recapture youthful vigor and prowess and often accompanied by extended self-grooming and significant purchases like a sportier car. Among older divorced men, there is also a subset whose fathers' died at preretirement or near retirement ages. This group seems to pursue activities and pleasures more reminiscent of older adolescence than later adulthood. It is as if they are trying to get in all the living they can before their genetically inherited longevity ends.

There is a subset of women whose marriages dissolve later in life who often blame themselves. They explain that they no longer look appealing and have lost their physical allure; they were failing in their roles as homemaker and spouse; their declining health had made them burdens to their former husbands; or they had become stagnant in their own personal development and were no longer stimulating companions to their husbands.

That older women often blame themselves while older men tend not to blame themselves is of social and psychological significance. As a group, older divorced women have greater degrees of personal docility and passivity. They may have incorporated their roles as wife, homemaker, and mother as their total personal identity. When the crisis of divorce strikes, the roles and routines by which they have defined themselves for decades crumble and their sense of themselves collapses. Their personal identity was never sufficiently encouraged and thus never sufficiently developed. Women who have worked hard for many years, supporting and organizing the lives of many others, who have been caring and competent, can feel incomplete, lost, empty, and despairing. Among the women who blame themselves for the loss of their marriage is the existential question, "If I am not his wife, then who am I?"

It must be stressed, however, that these findings represent trends in the research; they are not findings that apply necessarily to any one individual man or woman. There are always exceptions. There are men, for example, whose individuality is underdeveloped and whose sense of autonomy is precarious. Men too ask the question, "If I am not her husband, then who am I?" There are also women whose divorce has freed them from chronic aggravation and stress and who now feel a stronger sense of identity than ever before.

THE IMPACT OF DIVORCE

There are no winners in divorce. Everyone experiences loss and profound disruption in their personal world. Men and women do survive it, and many eventually go on to lead healthier, more fulfilling, and less stressful lives. The process of psychosocial, familial, and financial healing, however, is gradual and painful. One does not come out ahead in divorce; one gets through it, survives it, recovers from it.

Divorce represents the dissolution of life's centering and organizing mechanism: marriage and (in most cases) family. Not surprisingly, the longer the marriage, the greater the postdivorce despair and the longer the recovery. Divorce in midlife and beyond is as painful as at any other point in the developmental life cycle, but it is painful for much longer. On average, clinical depression from any cause will lift within six to eighteen months. Among all ages who divorce, depression and/or its major features are commonly evident even five years later. For those divorcing after thirty or forty years, depression and unresolved hostility can be present ten years later, and often to the same degree as the period of separation and breakup just before the divorce itself.

SUCCESSFUL AND HEALTHY COPING

Postdivorce adjustment, however, need not be experienced as the psychological equivalent of a ten-year criminal sentence. Many factors play a role in how well and how fully each divorced person recovers and moves on. Like the death of a loved one, divorce requires acceptance of the fact, accommodation to the resulting changes, and a period of concomitant grief. The goal can never be to revive the marital relationship, no more than the goal of dealing with death can be to revive the deceased loved one. Even those couples who divorce and later remarry the same partner had to go through sincere mourning and accommodation for their remarriage to be successful.

Other variables affect how well and how quickly one can recover from a divorce in midlife to later life. What was the degree of anticipation? (For how long was the divorce expected?) What was the amount of predivorce separation? (Had the couple been physically separated? Had they continued to attend social gatherings together?) What will be the immediate impact on one's lifestyle? (Who is moving out? How far does he or she need to go? What happens financially?) What will be the impact on family relationships? (Is one person moving in with an adult child who already has stresses from his or her own marriage and children? Do the adult children blame one parent more than the other? Are visits to and by grandchildren curtailed?) What is the existing social network? (Are there friends to talk to, to do things with, to help blunt the sense of isolation?) What attribution of blame does one make? (Whose fault was it? If one partner had stopped drinking, gambling, or working too hard, had not gotten sick, or had been more understanding, helpful, or sensitive, would the couple still be together?) Does one have a surrogate primary friend? (Is there someone to date and socialize with who could be a potential other partner?)

Many of these variables are outside one's direct control—but not all of them. Denial about how one actually feels, fostering of unresolved anger, refusal to move on, determination to get even, absence of hope, and the presence of inappropriate guilt adversely affect postdivorce adjustment.

Many divorced people do not allow themselves to express what they actually feel, believing their emotions to be wrong, unjustified, or inappropriate. They may think that they should not have lingering affection, positive regard, or love for their former spouse. They may think that their underlying sadness and grief means they are weak or lack personal strength, that their feelings signify yet another victory for their former spouse, who has cost them so much of their lives already. Sometimes, divorced people believe they should not have the mix of emotions that they have. The black-on-white legal divorce decree, they think, is supposed to mean psychological clarity of thought and consistency of emotion.

After decades of marital ups and downs, divorce can leave people feeling that their former spouse is to blame for all the aggravation of the past, the pain of the present, and the paucity of future options. They might think, "I am old and unattractive. How can I meet people? How can I have a relationship with someone else when I am so set in my ways?" Some may believe that their former spouse should suffer too. In the interests of retribution and recompense, they hold onto their unresolved anger until it ages to bitterness. As bad as the postdivorce period is, this decision, made more with passion than with logic, will make it worse.

Profound losses such as divorce that occur later in life challenge people's underlying hopefulness. In earlier years, divorce is often considered a setback, not a conclusion. There is time to move on, to find another relationship, and to achieve goals. Seniors implicitly know that there is less time for them to get to where they wish to be. It is harder to be hopeful.

Concurrent with how hopeful people are is their intrinsic faith in themselves and their understanding of what caused their divorce. Do they believe that they are naturally no good, insincere, selfish, or duplicitous, that they could never sustain honest human relationships? Do they believe that there must be something essentially wrong with them, so how could anyone find them interesting, like them, or want to grow old with them?

Relationships fail when the unique mix of fuel and air that keeps them powered runs too rich, runs too lean, or runs out altogether. A couple's relationship is as unique as each partner is individually. When the relationship dissolves, both are responsible, both are to blame, and both will need to change themselves if their next relationships are to run better. Divorced people who primarily point the finger at only one person—whether it is at themselves or their former spouses—miss the painful lessons that divorce offers.

Healthy friends, genuine family ties, prayer, social involvement, support groups, and psychological counseling can all help reduce the anxiety, demobilization, and despair suffered by people who divorce at midlife and beyond. Feeling frightened, scared, self-doubting, and vulnerable is often more intense, more difficult, and more challenging to the elderly. This psychological state comes at a stage in life when personal resources, flexibility, and options may be decreasing. These individuals need support; no one should have to work through this period alone.   —*Paul Moglia*

See also Cohabitation; Depression; Empty nest syndrome; Family relationships; Loneliness; Marriage; Middle age; Midlife crisis; Parenthood; Remarriage; Retirement; Sexuality; Single parenthood; Singlehood; Social ties; Stepfamilies.

FOR FURTHER INFORMATION:

Berry, Dawn Bradley. *The Divorce Sourcebook*. 2d ed. Los Angeles: Lowell, 1998. A helpful guide through preparing emotionally and legally for divorce and its myriad implications, including economic and emotional recovery.

Fisher, Bruce. *Rebuilding: When Your Relationship Ends*. 2d ed. San Luis Obispo, Calif.: Impact, 1992. In its ninth printing, this book reviews many conceptual and emotional aspects to the process of divorce and its aftermath. Includes sections on being single and for children.

Kirshenbaum, Mira. *Too Good to Leave, Too Bad to Stay*. New York: Penguin, 1996. A balanced work to help sort the confusing, often chaotic, and always painful process of deciding about the future of one's primary relationship.

Osing, Richard A. *Love at Midlife: Building and Rebuilding Relationships*. San Francisco: Rudi, 1998. Well-reasoned and practical discussions on characteristics of loving relationships and strategies for forming new ones.

"DR. HEIDEGGER'S EXPERIMENT"

AUTHOR: Nathaniel Hawthorne
DATE: Published in 1837
RELEVANT ISSUES: Values
SIGNIFICANCE: This early short story about the consequences of drinking from a fountain of youth shows the benefits of aging gracefully

Dr. Heidegger, nearing eighty himself, owns a flask of water taken from the fountain of youth in Florida that Ponce de León once sought. After placing a dried rose in the water to prove its effectiveness—the rose reverts to a beautiful, blushing bud—he asks four of his acquaintances to drink from it. The friends eagerly begin to sip the champagne-like fluid. The first glass brings color back to their cheeks. The second glass makes them middle aged.

The four friends all react differently to the miracle. The woman, Widow Wycherly, runs to the nearest mirror to admire her recovered beauty. The merchant, Mr. Medbourne, begins devising outrageous business schemes. The politician, Mr. Gascoigne, gives ringing speeches and mutters diabolical political intrigues. The soldier, Colonel Killigrew, sings drinking songs and flirts with the widow.

A third glass returns them to their twenties. The four friends choose this time to mock their former elderly condition by laughing at what they are wearing. They act out their former infirmities and mimic Dr. Heidegger's stiff bearing and hobby of scholarly activity. The three men, as they had done in their youth, then begin to fight over who gets the privilege of dancing with Widow Wycherly. During their struggles, they break the bottle of elixir and quickly return to their elderly state. Dr. Heidegger thanks them for convincing him not to drink the water, implying that the wisdom and accomplishments that come with old age make it worthwhile. The four friends leave to search for the fountain of youth so that they may remain forever foolishly young. —*Rose Secrest*

See also Antiaging treatments; Literature; Old age; Wisdom.

DOWAGER'S HUMP. *See* **KYPHOSIS.**

DRIVING

RELEVANT ISSUES: Demographics, health and medicine, recreation, sociology

SIGNIFICANCE: One of the common consequences of growing older is a reduction in the skills necessary to operate a motor vehicle safely. As people age, their individual capabilities are so diverse, however, that few generalizations about the elderly can be made concerning driving

The link to the many and varied activities of Americans is travel. Access to family, friends, jobs, shopping, entertainment, personal care, education, and religious services depends on the ability to get from one location to another. Access to transportation can mean high levels of choice, opportunity, and enrichment. Lack of access to transportation can lead to isolation and impoverished lives for the elderly.

Americans have come to depend on automobiles as a means of achieving the mobility necessary to maximize access to personal and social opportunities. People with automobiles have the

Class members perform neck exercises as part of a course for older drivers that teaches tips to help compensate for the losses in vision, hearing, and reaction time that come with age. (AP Photo/Dave Martin)

luxury of making choices about where they want to live, work, shop, and interact with other people. People who do not drive are left to find alternatives to bridge the distances and reach the destinations that drivers take for granted as within easy reach. Despite the large numbers of persons who do not rely on automobiles, modes of transportation by means other than driving have not been readily available in most American cities. Furthermore, many of the same disabilities that lead to a decrease in a person's ability to continue driving are the same difficulties that make using mass transportation inaccessible. Many cities offer little in public or private transportation services, providing few alternatives to driving as a means to accessing services.

THE SENIOR BOOM

By the end of the twentieth century, as the baby boomers began to advance to the age of "senior boomers," increasing numbers of elderly were driving on America's roads. Few people plan for a time when they will not be driving, but many people will eventually outlive their ability to operate an automobile safely. Advanced age, coupled with increased frailty and chronic health problems, raises the question of the elderly person's ability to continue driving. Societal concern with the ability of the elderly to drive is not only for the interest and protection of the elderly themselves but for the safety of other motorists. These concerns need to be measured appropriately against the preservation of the elderly person's dignity and ability to remain independent.

In the latter half of the twentieth century, America aged rapidly. According to the *Social Work Almanac* (1995), less than 7 percent of the American population was over the age of sixty-five in 1940. By 1980, that number grew to 11 percent; by 1990, 13 percent of the population was over age sixty-five. By 2025, it was projected that more than 18 percent of the American population would be over the age of sixty-five. In 1990, the population of persons aged sixty-five years and over in the United States was 32 million; it was projected that 61.5 million Americans would be over the age of sixty-five by 2025.

According to Jon Burkhardt, Arlene Berger, Michael Creedon, and Adam McGavock, in *Mobility and Independence: Changes and Challenges for Older Drivers* (1998) from the Administration on Aging, elderly drivers are a major concern because by 2020 the number of older drivers on America's roads was expected to more than double. In addition, older women were expected to drive in greater numbers. The number of older drivers could be greater than 2.5 times 1996 levels within thirty years. By 2030, the number of drivers over the age of eighty-five could be four to five times greater than in 1998. As the aging of American society creates more older drivers, there will also be a larger number of elderly who are unable to operate an automobile safely, as a result of an increase in the number of persons with disabilities and a reduction in driving skills. When elderly persons with diminished capacities continue to drive, an increased safety risk is created for all members of society.

ELDER TRAFFIC ACCIDENTS

According to 1998 estimates by the Administration on Aging, the number of elderly traffic fatalities will more than triple by 2030. If this expected increase actually occurs, this would mean the number of elderly in traffic fatalities in 2030 could be up to 35 percent greater than the total number of alcohol-related traffic fatalities that occurred in 1995.

Jennifer Cox, Margery Fox, and Linda Irwin provide evidence in their article "Driving and the Elderly: A Review of the Literature" (1990) that the skills needed to maintain safe driving practices deteriorates between the ages of fifty-five and seventy-five. Data collected from fourteen state traffic authorities in 1986 indicated that the highest rate of accidents per number of drivers was among persons under the age of twenty-five. After that, accidents lessen until around the age of sixty, when an increase in the number of traffic accidents is again noted. The accident rates double for drivers over the age of seventy for every 100,000 miles driven.

According to Fox in her article "Elderly Drivers' Perceptions of Their Driving Abilities Compared to Their Functional Visual Perception Skills and Their Actual Driving Performance" (1990), elderly persons demonstrate a more cautious approach to driving in order to compensate for deteriorating sensory skills. The elderly tend to drive shorter distances and to stop more frequently.

They are less likely to drive in the evening hours, and they try to avoid peak traffic hours, major freeways, highways and expressways, and bad weather. Studies on the number of accidents in the United States caused by elderly drivers indicate that persons aged sixty to sixty-nine have fewer motor vehicle accidents than the national average and that persons over seventy have a number of accidents equal to the national average.

On the other hand, according to the U.S. Department of Transportation's *Fatality Analysis Reporting System* (1997), there is cause for concern when the elderly do drive. Many of the accidents that involve elderly drivers can be attributed to deficits in vision, memory, and motor skills. Elderly drivers do not cope as well as younger drivers with complex traffic situations, and multiple-vehicle crashes at intersections increase markedly with the age of the driver. Elderly drivers are more likely to receive traffic citations for failing to yield, improper turning, and running stop signs or traffic lights. The U.S. Department of Transportation reports that per licensed driver, persons seventy-five and older have higher fatality rates in motor vehicle accidents than drivers in any other age group and that people over seventy-five have more automobile accidents per 100,000 people than any other group except for persons age twenty-five and younger.

ELDER DRIVERS AND HEALTH

For many elderly persons, the ability to drive assists in maintaining an active and independent lifestyle. Unfortunately, a person's ability to drive is vulnerable to the aging process. Hearing, vision, reaction time, memory, and mobility—all necessary components to safe driving—tend to diminish as people age. In their book *Taking Care of Aging Family Members* (1994), Nancy Hooyman and Wendy Lustbader discuss some of the more common health problems that affect older drivers: vision problems; memory loss; slower reaction time; heart problems; deficits from strokes; fainting, dizziness, drowsiness, or seizures; high blood pressure; back problems; arthritis; and diabetes.

The elderly are more prone to loss of vision, depth perception, peripheral vision, and the ability to read road signs from a distance, particularly at night. Some elderly may forget their intended destination. They may forget the directions, where

they parked the car, or the meaning of road signs. Elderly have slower reflex times and may suffer from muscular weaknesses or have tremors in the hands or feet. Physicians may advise against driving for elderly patients with heart problems because of the danger in episodes of incapacitation. Seniors who have suffered a stroke may experience loss of vision, one-sided weakness, or paralysis that can interfere with the handling of a steering wheel or foot pedals. Some suffer from communication problems that can impair driving abilities. Seniors with neurological, respiratory, or inner-ear problems or insomnia, as well as those taking certain medications, may be unable to operate a motor vehicle safely. Some physicians may advise their geriatric patients with hypertension (high blood pressure) against driving. Back problems such as disk deterioration and spinal fractures may be aggravated by driving. Problems with dexterity, shoulder pain, and reduced range of motion in the arms and neck may restrict driving by some seniors with arthritis. Some seniors with diabetes may experience numbness or weakness in the hands and feet or episodes of low blood sugar during which mental acuity may be compromised.

In *Mobility and Independence*, the Administration on Aging presented the mobility consequences model, which traces the typical sequence of events associated with age-related driving. First are physical and mental changes, which include changes in hearing and vision and health problems that lead to reductions in the skills necessary for safe driving. Second is age-related functional decline, which includes a reduction in driving-related skills such as driving shorter distances, not driving at night, and driving less often. These functional declines also can lead to an increased risk of accidents. Third are reductions in mobility, which include fewer trips by all modes of transportation, higher transportation costs, and reduced mileage traveled. Fourth are quality-of-life changes, which include reductions in all activities such as less social interaction, reduced use of community services, and fewer outings in the community.

Seniors may develop a rigid driving posture in an attempt to compensate for many of the health problems associated with aging. They may sit forward in the seat, grasp the steering wheel too tightly, and focus directly ahead in an attempt to concentrate on the road. Maintaining a rigid posture can contribute to a reduction in the ability to attend to peripheral activities, such as a pedestrian entering the crosswalk or another car changing lanes or merging into traffic.

THE LOSS OF A DRIVER'S LICENSE

Despite the many problems faced by elderly drivers, many seniors continue to cling to their automobiles and driver's licenses as representations of their independence. Older drivers facing the prospect of reducing or terminating their driving may find the consequences quite undesirable. According to *Mobility and Independence*, these consequences include loss of personal independence, social isolation, and a reduction or lack of access to essential services. The majority of older American drivers have grown up in a society that depends on automobiles as the sole mode of transportation. Driving occupies a central role in many Americans' lives, including the elderly. Therefore, it is not surprising that no longer being able to drive is a major loss for a great number of older people. Many gerontologists consider the loss of a driver's license to be a major crisis in an elder's life.

The Administration on Aging provides the following suggestions for family members who wish to consider transportation alternatives for elders who are still driving. Before they propose that the elder relinquish automobile privileges, a geriatric physician should be consulted to make recommendations about the elder's medical fitness to drive. Family and friends should offer their services to the elder for transportation needs. The local Area Agency on Aging (AAA) is available to discuss community transportation designed for the elderly and disabled. Taxis and public transportation are also viable alternatives for some elders.

Concerned family members and friends might need to appeal to incapacitated elders' sense of social responsibility and the guilt that would result if others were killed or crippled in a crash caused by them. Elders may be asked to consider the legal charges that could result if they were found at fault in a car accident. The high costs of car maintenance and automobile insurance may also be discussed. When addressing the termination of driving privileges with the elderly, it is best to be not only honest but also understanding of the difficulty the senior driver faces with the loss of the

American dream of freedom and independence represented by the automobile.

—*Cathleen Jo Faruque*

See also Arthritis; Back problems; Balance disorders; Diabetes; Disabilities; Hearing loss; Heart attacks; Home services; Hypertension; Independent living; Injuries among the elderly; Memory changes and loss; Mobility problems; Reaction time; Safety issues; Sensory changes; Strokes; Transportation issues; Vision changes and disorders.

FOR FURTHER INFORMATION:

Burkhardt, Jon E., Arlene Berger, Michael Creedon, and Adam McGavock. *Mobility and Independence: Changes and Challenges for Older Drivers*. Bethesda, Md.: Ecosometrics, 1998. The authors discuss the consequences of the elderly with mobility- and age-related changes in their driving patterns. They address possible interventions and methods to assist the elderly in the termination of driving as well as implications for social policy.

Cox, Jennifer L., Margery D. Fox, and Linda Irwin Cox. "Driving and the Elderly: A Review of the Literature." In *Assessing the Driving Ability of the Elderly*, edited by Ellen D. Taira. New York: Haworth Press, 1989. The authors provide an overview of literature related to the characteristics of the elderly driver. The focus is on evaluation measures in assessing the abilities of elderly drivers.

Fatality Analysis Reporting System. Washington, D.C.: U.S. Department of Transportation, National Highway Traffic Safety Administration, 1997. The Department of Transportation provides statistical data on the automobile accident rates of elderly persons in 1997. This information is also available from the Highway Loss Data Institute on the Internet as *1997 Fatality Facts: Elderly* at http://www.hwysafety.org/facts/elder.

Fox, Margery D. "Elderly Drivers' Perceptions of Their Driving Abilities Compared to Their Functional Visual Perception Skills and Their Actual Driving Performance." In *Assessing the Driving Ability of the Elderly*, edited by Ellen D. Taira. New York: Haworth Press, 1989. Fox's research examined the elderly drivers' perceptions of their own driving abilities, compared to clinically tested functional skills in the area of visual perception and their actual driving performance. Results indicated that elderly drivers tend to overrate their own driving abilities and that actual driving performance is affected by visual perception skills.

Ginsberg, Leon, ed. *Social Work Almanac.* 2d ed. Washington, D.C.: National Association of Social Workers Press, 1995. This almanac provides demographic data on older adults in the United States beginning in 1900 and with projections up to the year 2030. Attention to older adults is referenced throughout because so many issues in social welfare are associated with aging.

Hooyman, Nancy R., and Wendy Lustbader. *Taking Care of Aging Family Members: A Practical Guide.* Rev. ed. New York: Free Press, 1994. Hooyman and Lustbader discuss the health problems commonly experienced by older drivers and how they can affect driving ability. They discuss the use of transportation resources to help seniors maintain their independence without having to rely on automobiles.

DRIVING MISS DAISY

DIRECTOR: Bruce Beresford

CAST: Jessica Tandy, Morgan Freeman, Esther Rolle, Dan Aykroyd, Patti Lupone

DATE: Play produced in 1987, published in 1988; film released in 1989

RELEVANT ISSUES: Culture, family, psychology, race and ethnicity, religion, values

SIGNIFICANCE: This film, adapted by Alfred Uhry from his play, is a poignant story about aging that explores loss of independence, evolving friendship, race relations, and family ties

The story spans from shortly after the end of World War II until the 1980's. Daisy Werthan (played by Jessica Tandy), a well-to-do older Jewish widow, lives alone in a large home in Atlanta with the daily help of Idella (Esther Rolle), her housekeeper. After Daisy has a minor automobile accident, her son Boolie (Dan Aykroyd) insists that she no longer drive and hires a middle-aged African American man named Hoke (Morgan Freeman) to act as her chauffeur. Daisy, a southern lady, resents having to accept help, and at first she ignores the newly hired chauffeur. Finally, she relents to being driven by him. The two will develop an understanding and friendship over the next several decades.

Daisy is argumentative and disagrees with anything suggested to her. Hoke uses tact, persistence, and persuasion to sway her toward accepting a driver and planting a garden. Early in the relationship, Daisy realizes that Hoke can neither read nor write. In a no-nonsense manner, Daisy, a former teacher, proceeds to teach him to do both. There is humor in their relationship. Once before starting a long journey, Daisy asks Hoke if he has checked the car's air conditioning. He answers that he does not know why he should because she does not allow him to use it. Daisy is quick to let Hoke know she came from humble beginnings. As a child, she could not have a pet because there was not enough spare food to feed it. Even with her current comfortable situation, she does not want to appear to be spending money foolishly.

Boolie manages the family business, Werthan Industries. He often plays the role of a peacemaker for his mother and her relationships. On issues of importance, he remains firm, as when Daisy can no longer drive and must enter a nursing home in her very advanced years. Boolie also serves as a buffer between his wife and mother. Daisy and her daughter-in-law, Florine (Patti Lupone), never see eye to eye. Florine does not measure up to Daisy's standards, as she decorates the home for Christmas, socializes with Episcopalians, and serves as a Republican committee person.

Racial and religious issues of the times are woven into the story. A state police officer refers to the elderly Hoke as "boy." Daisy's temple is bombed by anti-Semites. Daisy attends a dinner where Martin Luther King, Jr., is the speaker. Her son avoids the dinner because he feels it may affect his business adversely.

As longtime friends aging together, Daisy and Hoke often reminisce. At the end of the film, Hoke, now an old man who can no longer drive himself, comes to visit Daisy in the nursing home. She asks him how he is. He says that he does the best he can. Both of them have realized that they must accept what neither can change.

Uhry's play *Driving Miss Daisy* won the 1988 Pulitzer Prize in Drama. The film won Academy Awards in 1989 for Best Picture, Best Actress for Tandy, and Best Adapted Screenplay for Uhry.

—*Phyllis J. Reeder*

See also African Americans; Caregiving; Cultural views of aging; Driving; Family relationships;

Friendship; Home services; Independent living; Jewish services for the elderly; Transportation issues; Widows and widowers.

DRUGS. *See* MEDICATIONS.

DUAL-INCOME COUPLES

RELEVANT ISSUES: Family, marriage and dating, sociology, work

SIGNIFICANCE: As the number of older dual-income couples has grown, it has become increasingly important to understand the particular issues faced by families in which both spouses are part of the workforce

Economic and societal changes in the United States since the 1960's have led to a significant increase in the number of dual-income families. According to the Bureau of Labor Statistics, in 1960 only 23 percent of all married women in the United States were in the labor force, compared to 60 percent in 1992. In American society, the family in which both spouses are employed outside the home has changed from being the exception to being the norm.

Dual-income couples generally fall into two categories: Those couples in which both spouses work at careers are considered to be "dual-career" couples, while those couples in which both spouses work at jobs are usually termed "dual-earner" couples. A career is an occupation that tends to require high levels of training and education. Subsequently, compared to people in jobs, people in careers are inclined to be more committed to their occupations and are more likely to stay in one particular field of work longer.

Interest in and research on dual-career and dual-earner families has surged since the 1960's. Early studies saw employment of the wife as secondary to the husband's employment. The working wife was expected to adjust her work schedule to meet the nurturing needs of her family and attend to household tasks. The husband's career or job was more important for the total benefit of the family. Historically, it has been the role of the husband to provide economic support for his family and the role of the wife to provide for the emotional care of the family.

Many members of the baby-boom generation, those born between 1946 and 1964, reached their middle years during the 1980's and 1990's. By the year 2010, many will have entered their elder years. As a group, elderly baby boomers will be better educated and healthier than previous generations. Those older workers with more education are more likely to be in a career to which they are committed. Health is also directly related to length of employment. As medical knowledge increases, so does the health of the nation's older people. This may well mean that older dual-career couples will be able to stay in the workforce longer. Declining birth rates also indicate that older employees will make up a larger percentage of the workforce. During the 1990's, employees aged fifty and over composed almost one-quarter of the workforce in the United States.

WORK-FAMILY CONFLICT

Research has indicated a conflict between work and family roles for both men and women. As Arlie Hochschild's *The Second Shift* (1989) described, the conflict has been more difficult for women balancing work demands and demands of the family. As children grow up and move out of the home, an employed woman may feel relief from the demands of children and begin to focus more on her work or spend more time with her spouse. However, just as the demands from children decline, a middle-aged woman may face demands from her own or her husband's parents. Women historically have been caregivers of children as well as caregivers of the elderly.

During the 1990's, approximately 12 percent of the population was over the age of sixty-five. The fastest-growing segment of this elderly population consisted of men and women over age eighty-five, one-half of whom required assistance with personal care or activities of daily living. As the older population, especially the very old, increases, they will require more assistance. Family size has also declined, resulting in fewer adult children on which elderly parents may rely. This could mean heavy reliance on only one family member. Balancing work and family demands can be especially challenging for women who are caring for an elderly parent or parent-in-law. Some may still have children in the home. This group of women caring for both children and parents has been referred to as "the sandwich generation." It may be necessary for the employed woman with ailing parents to reduce hours at work, take a leave of absence, or leave the workplace altogether. Any of these choices may have negative repercussions for the career development of an employed woman.

RETIREMENT

Most research on retirement has focused on the effects of the husband's retirement. It had long been assumed that husbands retire and wives continue being homemakers. Little research has been accomplished in the area of dual-income couples and retirement. Health status, retirement income, job satisfaction, family responsibilities, and the retirement of one's spouse are all factors to be considered in discussing the effects of retirement.

Improvements in the economic status of the elderly have received much attention. Income and financial resources are a major indicator of happiness in retirement. Increased labor force participation of wives among dual-income couples results in more retirement income and resources than relative to single-income families.

The lower economic status of some dual-income couples may result in continuous employment throughout their lives, not because they choose to keep working into old age but because employment is a financial necessity. Compared to majority group members, elderly minority group members in dual-earner families are more likely to be employed in service and domestic labor occupations. These types of occupations typically offer little in terms of retirement benefits, and workers must continue to work for pay literally until they die. Retirement may not be an option for some.

Many men, though not all, enjoy retirement. Because men have traditionally been the breadwinners in the family, much of their identity is based on that role. Male retirees may experience severe stress as they lose their sense of identity as the source of financial support for the family. Involvement in masculine household tasks helps lessen the sense of role loss and is positively related to feelings of well-being for retired men.

While retirement has traditionally been seen as a major life transition for men, the transition for women has not been well explored. A study by Maximiliane E. Szinovácz in 1982 indicates that employed women actually do have difficulty with retirement and often take longer to adjust to retirement than their husbands. Gerontologists used data from the 1987-1988 National Survey of Families and Households to assess the impact of employment and retirement patterns among older dual-income couples. Analyses revealed lower marital quality among dual-income couples when husbands retire first and their wives are still employed. On the other hand, compared to husbands in dual-income couples in which both spouses are currently employed, employed husbands with retired wives report somewhat higher marital quality. The division of labor based on gender generally does not change regardless of who retires first. Few dual retired couples report any changes in the division of household labor.

LIFE SATISFACTION

Analyses of data from general social surveys (1993) showed that levels of life satisfaction are similar among women and men regardless of employment status. However, the contributors of life satisfaction are different, depending on whether one is part of a dual-income couple and whether one's job is a career. For all married couples surveyed, marital happiness is the largest contributor of life satisfaction. Job satisfaction plays a bigger role in life satisfaction for employed men and women in careers than it does for those in jobs. Job satisfaction is especially important to women in dual-career families. Job satisfaction does not appear to be an important contributor of life satisfaction for women with jobs. The main reason these women are employed may be out of financial need.

Women from dual-career families tend to draw more equally from the two aspects of their lives—marriage and career—for their life satisfaction than do women with jobs or homemaking women. The old adage of "not putting all your eggs in one basket" is exemplified here. The dual-career lifestyle has been reputed as being stressful. Perhaps men and women in dual-career families are finding that balance is an important part of life satisfaction in this living situation.   —*Naomi J. Larsen*

See also Caregiving; Employment; Income sources; Marriage; Men and aging; Retirement; Sandwich generation; Women and aging.

FOR FURTHER INFORMATION:

Barnett, Rosalind G., and Caryl Rivers. *She Works/ He Works: How Two-Income Families Are Happier,*

Healthier, and Better-Off. San Francisco: Harper, 1996.

Hochschild, Arlie. *The Second Shift: Working Parents and the Revolution at Home.* New York: Viking Press, 1989.

Reeves, Joy, and Ray Danville. "Aging Couples in Dual-Career/Earner Families: Patterns of Role-Sharing." *Journal of Women and Aging* 4, no. 1 (1992).

Sheehy, Gail. *New Passages: Mapping Your Life Across Time.* New York: Random House, 1996.

Szinovácz, Maximiliane E. "Couples' Employment/Retirement Patterns and Perceptions of Marital Quality." *Research on Aging* 18, no. 2 (June, 1996).

_____, ed. *Women's Retirement.* Beverly Hills, Calif.: Sage Publications, 1982.

DURABLE POWER OF ATTORNEY

RELEVANT ISSUES: Death, family, law

SIGNIFICANCE: A durable power of attorney allows an individual to designate another person to act legally on his or her behalf

A power of attorney allows a competent adult individual (the principal) to appoint another competent adult individual or institution (the agent or attorney-in-fact) to perform any legal function or task which the principal has a legal right to do for himself or herself. A general power of attorney allows the principal to appoint an agent to conduct business affairs. A power of attorney for health care allows the appointment of an agent to act in making most health care decisions in the case of incapacity. Such a health care power of attorney can contain specific instructions about treatments and end-of-life issues. In some states, two separate documents are required for financial affairs and health care; in other states, the two powers of attorney can be combined.

A durable power of attorney is one that continues to be in force and effective even if the principal becomes legally incapacitated. A durable power of attorney can become effective as of the signing of the document or at some later time or event designated in the document, such as when the principal becomes incompetent. However, some states do not allow such "springing" powers of attorney and require that all powers of attorney become effective upon signing by the principal. If a springing power of attorney is allowed, the procedure for determining competency can be specified in the document.

The powers granted in a durable power of attorney can be broad or narrow and may include granting the agent the right to, on behalf of the principal, engage in real estate transactions, pay bills, endorse checks, make and perform contracts, deposit and withdraw bank funds, prepare and sign tax returns, and conduct stock, bond, and securities transactions. A power of attorney cannot grant the right of the agent to vote, sign witness statements, or create or revoke a will on behalf of the principal, or to perform under a contract executed by the principal for personal services. A power of attorney also cannot be used to give anyone authority to care for minor children in the case of incapacity; however, the agent can be authorized to use the principal's property to pay for the needs of minor children while the principal is incapacitated.

A durable power of attorney can be revoked by the principal, if competent, by destroying the document, providing the agent with a written revocation, or recording a written revocation in the appropriate government office, or through other state-specified notification procedures. A durable power of attorney terminates at the death of the principal, at the passage of a date of expiration or occurrence of an event specified in the document, or in the event of the appointment by a court of a guardian for the principal. However, court appointment of a guardian does not terminate a power of attorney for health care. If a spouse is named agent, the power of attorney terminates upon divorce from the principal.

—Lisa M. Sardinia

See also Adult Protective Services; Death and dying; Euthanasia; Health care; Living wills; Long-term care for the elderly; Mental impairment; Terminal illness.

DYING. *See* DEATH AND DYING.

EARLY RETIREMENT

RELEVANT ISSUES: Economics, psychology, recreation, work

SIGNIFICANCE: With the downsizing of many corporations and an expanding economy, it is increasingly common for people to retire before the once-conventional retirement age of sixty-five

Retirement is a relatively recent concept. Government pensions were first granted in Germany in 1880, where Chancellor Otto von Bismarck instituted them for largely political reasons. These pensions were available at age sixty-five. Because few people lived to be that old, the cost of funding this scheme was negligible.

The political advantages of instituting such plans were apparent to leaders in other countries who realized that supporting legislation to provide pensions could strengthen their positions. By 1920, plans similar to Bismarck's were in effect in Great Britain, Switzerland, the Netherlands, Belgium, France, and the Scandinavian countries.

The United States was slow to move in this direction, fearing governmental intrusion upon the lives of its citizens. The Great Depression of the 1930's, however, made Americans amenable to accepting the safety net that a governmental pension system could provide.

CHANGES IN AMERICAN SOCIETY

The U.S. economy was agricultural until the last quarter of the nineteenth century. Farmers living on their own property in extended families worked for as long as they were physically able. When their health failed, family members cared for them. Their life expectancy after they quit working was short.

As the United States became more industrialized, skilled and unskilled workers joined the labor force, but they were generally expected to provide for their own long-term futures. Most of them, like the farmers of previous generations, worked for as long as they could, after which they usually were dependent on their children or other family members for their care and support. Until the 1930's, retired people were essentially sick people with short life expectancies. Only the rich could retire before there was a physical necessity for them to do so. It was unthinkable that common workers could accumulate sufficient financial reserves to permit comfortable early retirements. Most of them worked for wages barely sufficient to cover their day-to-day expenses.

In a sense, the question of early retirement in the period from 1900 to 1930 was moot; the average life expectancy in the United States for males who were born in 1900 was forty-eight years. Females could expect to live just short of fifty-one years. By 1984, the life expectancy for males had risen to seventy-two years, whereas for females it had risen to nearly seventy-nine years. These increases in life expectancy drastically changed the concept of retirement.

NORMAL RETIREMENT AGE

In order to define early retirement, it is necessary to determine what is considered the normal retirement age. The age at which full Social Security benefits are available to retirees is sixty-five, with reduced benefits available to everyone in the system between ages sixty-two and sixty-four years and eleven months. Increased benefits are offered to those who begin drawing their benefits later than age sixty-five. Benefits are also available to those who have suffered disabilities at any age as long as they have sufficient quarters, usually forty, to qualify for full coverage.

Assuming that sixty-five is a normal retirement age, anyone who leaves the workforce short of this age has taken an early retirement. By the end of the nineteenth century, 25 percent of men had retired by age sixty-four. It must be remembered, however, that more men had died short of age sixty-four than had survived.

By 1950, 47 percent of men over sixty-four were still in the workforce. By the late 1990's, a mere 20 percent of men over sixty-four worked full time. (Historical statistics regarding retirement are usually given for men rather than for both sexes because few women worked outside the home until the 1940's.)

THE ECONOMICS OF RETIREMENT

Today's early retiree usually receives a regular income, adjusted periodically for inflation, through Social Security. This payment was never intended to do more than supplement one's retirement income. In many cases, retired employees receive payments from their employers' pension plans or draw income through various savings plans their employers have instituted, often 401K plans, to which both employees and employers contribute.

The government also encourages personal savings through individual retirement accounts (IRAs), to which people can contribute up to a given maximum amount each year, usually two thousand dollars. The money in such accounts can be invested in stocks, bonds, mutual funds, and a broad range of other vehicles. Left intact until the account holder is at least fifty-nine and a half years old, these accounts grow on a tax-deferred basis, allowing them to compound and increase substantially if the money in them is invested wisely.

In recent years, the number of people investing in the stock market either directly or through mutual funds has grown exponentially. Such increases in individual investing have provided the means for many people to build up considerable wealth through their investments, which can supplement their retirement incomes.

CORPORATE DOWNSIZING

When corporate downsizing occurs, some employees are encouraged to retire before they can qualify for Social Security benefits at age sixty-two and for Medicare at age sixty-five. In such cases, employers usually offer potential retirees attractive separation packages. These packages usually include temporary extra income to tide early retirees over until their Social Security benefits are available and sufficient health and accident insurance to cover their medical expenses until they qualify for Medicare.

Such packages may also include attractive lump-sum separation settlements based on the number of years one has been with the company. In some instances, those who are forced into early retirement through downsizing are employed as consultants or other part-time employees by the organization from which they have retired. Some organizations also help retirees to be retrained in other fields and assist them in finding work if they wish to continue working.

EARLY RETIREMENT IN EDUCATIONAL INSTITUTIONS

Public school districts and academic institutions also have encouraged early retirement, mak-

ing it attractive in a number of ways. In some public school, state college, and university retirement systems, anyone who has taught for a set number of years, usually thirty, is eligible for full retirement benefits regardless of age.

Some such systems also enhance retirement benefits by allowing early retirees to add a specified number of years to their service, usually three to five years, and to add a like number of years to their ages, so that someone retiring with thirty years service at age fifty-eight might, for retirement purposes, receive retirement credit for as much as thirty-five years of service and be paid at the rate that someone sixty-three would be paid.

Other academic venues permit one to retire with full pension benefits but to teach regularly for half of each year up to a specified age, often seventy. Sometimes, doing this immediately increases an employee's income by as much as 25 percent. Such people are also free to teach elsewhere or to hold other employment without affecting the benefits they receive from their home institutions.

WHAT HAPPENS TO EARLY RETIREES?

The transition from full-time work to retirement is sometimes difficult for those accustomed to the structure and routine a full-time job imposes. About 75 percent of retirees go from full employment to total retirement. People who have no hobbies and few outside interests are often discouraged from retiring early and, if they do, may languish for lack of social interaction or intellectual challenge. Early retirement sounds the death knell for some people.

On the other hand, many people revel in the freedom retirement offers them. Some move to other parts of the country, develop new interests, or begin to travel extensively when they are no longer tied to a job and to one specific place. Half the population of the United States over age sixty-five is concentrated in nine states: California, Florida, New York, Pennsylvania, Texas, Illinois, Ohio, Michigan, and New Jersey. For those who relocate upon retirement, California and Florida are by far the places to which they most often move.

In 1950, only 20 percent of retirees were dependent upon their children for support. That figure decreased steadily through the rest of the century. Today's retirees seldom live with their children. Rather, they often seek out retirement communities where living expenses are low and recreational opportunities extensive.

Such states as Florida, Texas, Nevada, Wyoming, Washington, New Hampshire, and Alaska have no state income tax, making them attractive to many retirees considering relocation. Some states also exempt most retirement income from state income taxes, and many grant people over a certain age substantial relief on their property taxes.

THE FUTURE OF EARLY RETIREMENT

In assessing the future of early retirement, it is necessary to take into account two seemingly contradictory elements. On the one hand, corporations and institutions of higher learning are well served by being able to prune their workforces. On the other hand, the Social Security system is facing a critical problem in that when the baby boomers born between 1945 and 1955 reach retirement age beginning in 2010, the number of retirees will grow enormously. Ensuing generations will thus be faced with ever-increasing Social Security contributions that will in no way equal the amount being expended in benefits. The baby-boom generation that will begin drawing full Social Security benefits will likely be the first to have a life expectancy of more than eighty years, and many will exceed the one hundred mark. Indeed, one of the fastest-growing segments of American society is the one-hundred-plus age group. Nevertheless, few people save enough to provide for themselves past one hundred. According to a Merrill Lynch report, most baby boomers save only 39 percent of what they should to preserve their accustomed lifestyles through the decades of retirement many of them will face.

As industry becomes increasingly automated, it requires fewer and fewer people to perform the same tasks. In addition, people are living longer. In public schools and in academic institutions, entry-level teachers and instructors command much smaller salaries than those who have reached the top of the salary range. In some instances, nearly two new people can be hired for every senior person who is lured into taking an early retirement.

Experts thus predict that the Social Security system will have to change drastically to meet the mounting economic pressures brought about both by increases in the number of people drawing Social Security benefits and by increased life expectancy. To meet the needs of this burgeoning population, the age at which full Social Security benefits can be drawn will probably be increased in gradual increments to seventy.

With life expectancy approaching eighty for men and exceeding eighty for women, such an increase in retirement age is, although unpopular, not unreasonable. Such an increase would not necessarily bring about a decline in the number of people taking early retirement because, in many cases, their employers will offer them early retirement packages to see them through financially until they can draw full benefits from Social Security.

THE SURVIVAL OF SOCIAL SECURITY

Many observers have predicted that the Social Security system will collapse before those born after 1965 are eligible to collect benefits from it. In the worst-case scenario, these people would find that they had paid oppressive contributions into the Social Security system only to have the system go bankrupt before they became eligible to collect their benefits. The likelihood of such a grim scenario is much reduced, however, by political realities; the political futures of numerous public officials are bound up with the fate of the system, making it unlikely that they would permit the system to founder.

It is predicted that shortly after 2010, there will be more retirees than workers who are still contributing to the system. If changes are not made to the system, Social Security reserves will run out by 2029. By then, the combined contributions of employees and their employers would have risen from the 1990's level of 13 percent to 17 percent. Some relief could be gained by taxing all Social Security benefits. Such benefits were once tax-free, although 85 percent of benefits for people in higher-income brackets are now taxed as regular income.

Besides proposing an increase in the age at which full benefits will be available to retirees, national leaders have considered other options. President Bill Clinton suggested that Social Security funds should be invested in ways that would generate more income than they currently do, although increased income means increased risk.

Clinton also suggested that private, personal investing should be encouraged through the liberalization of regulations on IRAs. One major change has been the establishment of the Roth IRA. With a traditional IRA, the amount contributed can be deducted from taxable income in the year the contribution is made, but the proceeds are fully taxable as income upon withdrawal. With Roth IRAs, participants cannot deduct the original contributions from their incomes. When the proceeds are distributed, however, they are fully exempt from income tax and capital gains tax.

—*R. Baird Shuman*

See also Baby boomers; Employment; Forced retirement; 401K plans; Income sources; Individual retirement accounts (IRAs); Job loss; Leisure activities; Retirement; Retirement planning; Social Security; Vacations and travel; Volunteering.

FOR FURTHER INFORMATION:

Achenbaum, Andrew W. *Social Security: Visions and Revisions.* Cambridge, England: Cambridge University Press, 1986. This is one of the most complete earlier books on the subject of Social Security and its future. It poses thorny questions about what will happen when the baby boomers retire.

Anderson, Patricia M., Alan L. Gustman, and Thomas L. Steinmeier. *The Trend to Earlier Retirement Among Males.* Working Paper no. 6028. Cambridge, Mass.: National Bureau of Economic Research, 1997. Using current statistics, the authors plot the trend toward early retirement and the impetus employers give to promote it.

Costa, Dora L. *The Evolution of Retirement: An American Economic History, 1880-1990.* Chicago: University of Chicago Press, 1998. Costa's book is filled with valuable statistics about retirement. She is thorough in her approach and is particularly strong in her predictions regarding the fate of the Social Security system.

Kasky, Jillian. "Retiring Well." *Time* 153, no. 6 (February 15, 1999). Kasky provides a prescient overview of early retirement, citing specific instances of people who have retired early or are planning to do so.

Williamson, Robert C., Alice Duffy Rineart, and Thomas O. Blank. *Early Retirement: Promises and Pitfalls.* New York: Plenum Press, 1992. This study, based on responses to questionnaires sent to 115 retired men, is largely anecdotal. Its case studies are informative and suggestive.

EATING HABITS. *See* **NUTRITION; OBESITY.**

ELDER ABUSE

RELEVANT ISSUES: Family, health and medicine, law, psychology, sociology, violence

SIGNIFICANCE: Abuse of older family members has increasingly become the concern of social scientific research, legislation, and social service and law-enforcement agencies as it has developed into a major social problem in America

Social gerontologists and other professionals who study and work with older persons report that the prevalence of elder abuse is much greater than was previously realized and that it takes multiple forms. Neglect and verbal, psychological, physical, economic, and sexual abuse do not typically occur at the hands of strangers or in unfamiliar surroundings. More often, the perpetrators of elder abuse are the primary caretakers or neighbors of the victims, and the setting is the victims' own homes, neighborhoods, or institutions charged with their care. Researchers, social workers, medical professionals, and law-enforcement officials have agreed that documented cases of elder abuse represent a small proportion of all such incidents, which are increasing in frequency.

ABUSE BY FAMILY CARETAKERS

The phrase "graying of America" alludes to the fact that the fastest-growing American age group is the sixty-five-and-over population and that the category of Americans older than eighty-five has the fastest growth rate of all. As Americans become ever older, the probability of their experiencing a degree of physiological or cognitive dysfunction that makes them dependent on others for their care increases. Members of any age group who depend on others for survival are the most likely targets of domestic abuse. The infirm elderly are the most often abused; they typically become more submissive to protect themselves from abandonment by their family caretakers.

Although the prevalence of elder abuse, as with other forms of domestic violence, is impossible to assess accurately, of greatest concern are cases involving perpetrators closely related to the victims. Not only is the specter of abuse by a family member, as opposed to a stranger, especially disturbing, but a majority of incidents occur in domestic settings. The number of documented cases of domestic elder abuse, a mere fraction of real existing instances of the problem, is increasing geometrically. Between 1986 and 1994, officially reported cases steadily increased from 117,000 to 241,000. Most cases go unreported, and 70 percent or more of documented cases are reported by someone other than the victim. Estimates of the actual number of such cases range between one and two million annually.

Data from the 1990's show that substantiated cases of reported domestic elder abuse took every form imaginable. Neglect accounted for 58.5 percent of these cases, physical abuse 15.7 percent, financial exploitation 12.3 percent, psychological and emotional abuse 8.1 percent, and sexual abuse 0.5 percent. These same data indicate that close relatives of the victims are responsible for two-thirds of the cases. Perpetrators were victims' adult children in about 38 percent of the reports, spouses in about 14 percent, and other family members in about 15 percent.

Sociologists assert that, given the strong cultural normative prescriptions for intergenerational support and affection, domestic elder abuse constitutes a violation of a social taboo—the most serious category of social infractions. This form of deviant behavior is difficult to analyze because of the complexity of its causes. Researchers who attempt to understand such dysfunctional behavior in family settings contend that like all forms of domestic violence, the causes involve a combination of psychological, social, economic, and health-related characteristics of the perpetrators and the victims.

In some cases, the stress associated with caring for an infirm elderly family member may lead to abuse, especially if the caregiver perceives the demands on time, energy, and financial resources as excessive or if the caregiver is not well prepared for the task. Some studies have found that the incidence of abuse increases when the continued physical or mental decline of the older person heightens the caretaker's responsibilities. Some domestic elder abuse is related to the perpetra-

tor's personal problems, such as chronic financial difficulties, pathological emotional or mental conditions, or addiction to alcohol or other drugs. In these cases, the abuser is often dependent on the victim for financial support and housing, and the frustration of failing to function as an independent adult manifests itself in abusive episodes. Furthermore, some researchers report that abusers who have experienced or witnessed domestic violence in their households as children may have learned to abuse in response to conflicts or stress, resulting in an intergenerational transfer of violence. Complex combinations of these and other possible factors underlie each individual case of domestic elder abuse.

ABUSE IN INSTITUTIONAL SETTINGS

Although only about 5 percent of older Americans reside in nursing and convalescent homes, they represent half of the long-term-care patients. As the eighty-five-and-over population continues to increase, the population of institutionalized older Americans is projected to grow from 1.5 million in 1990 to 2.6 million by the year 2020. The risk of abuse is especially high for this group of elderly Americans. Physicians have often recommended institutionalization as a way to prevent or stop abuse, but a potential for serious abuse in these settings has been demonstrated.

Assessing the prevalence of elder abuse in health care settings is difficult. Studies in which nursing home staff were assured of confidentiality and anonymity, however, have shown that a problem does exist. In one such study involving almost six hundred nursing home workers, 45 percent said that they had yelled, cursed, or threatened residents; 10 percent admitted physically abusing patients by hitting, pinching, or violently grabbing them; another 3 percent stated that they had hit patients with objects or thrown objects at them; and 4 percent had denied patients food or privileges. Such research efforts have probably underestimated levels of abuse by paid caregivers, and none are likely to produce reliable results regarding sexual abuse and theft.

ADULT PROTECTIVE SERVICES

A number of public agencies include elder abuse among their concerns: police and sheriffs' departments, district attorneys' offices, acute-care licensing and certification agencies, and State Long-Term Care Ombudsman's offices, which were created by the federal Older Americans Act of 1965 and organized under State Agencies on Aging to investigate elder abuse in nursing homes. However, the agencies most responsible for investigating, intervening in, and resolving cases of domestic elder abuse in most states are Adult Protective Services (APS), which are usually part of the county departments of social services. Although APS offices deal with abuse of anyone older than eighteen, 70 percent of their cases involve elder abuse.

APS responses to elder abuse have varied according to the severity and nature of the abuse. The problem is often addressed by APS caseworkers with a plan to provide assistance to family caregivers by linking them to public service, volunteer, and church-related agencies that assist in caregiving functions and even counsel abusive family caretakers. Caseworkers monitor caregiving plans to determine their effectiveness and the need for adjustments. In the most severe cases, the APS offices take more drastic measures, such as institutionalizing elderly persons or calling in law enforcement agencies. In cases requiring institutionalization, the State Long-Term Care Ombudsman program is often called upon to monitor the safety of abuse victims.

APS faces great challenges in its attempts to prevent future abuse and improve the quality of life of abuse victims. Investigators' interactions with family members are usually tense at best, because elder abuse, like spousal and child abuse, is often a well-kept family secret. Furthermore, caseworkers are prohibited from revealing the identities of the persons who report abuse, which often frustrates the families, and the interventions sometimes confuse the victims because they seldom report the abuse themselves.

Not all APS elder abuse cases are successfully resolved. Agency intervention in cases involving chronic domestic violence, regardless of the victims' ages, is especially difficult. Moreover, elder abuse intervention is often thwarted because older persons, unlike children, are beyond the age of majority and can thus refuse assistance if they fear institutionalization, abandonment, or retribution. APS caseworkers must be able to investigate cases, assess victims' physical and psychological health,

know about available elder services, work within the criminal justice system, deal with crisis situations, and protect themselves from violence at the hands of abusers. There are only a few thousand APS investigators in the United States, and their large caseloads are growing constantly.

CRIME

Although most forms of elder abuse, including willful neglect in many states, are illegal, crimes against elderly victims committed by noncaretakers are of growing concern to law enforcement officials and older persons. Conventional analyses of crime statistics have indicated that the elderly have been far less victimized than the general adult population. There is a growing consensus, however, that these statistics have grossly underestimated the magnitude of elderly victimization. Older Americans appear to be the targets of certain types of crime, and the incidents most often occur in the victims' homes or neighborhoods. Most victims of con artists, for example, are older persons. Con games take many forms, including phony insurance schemes, hearing aid scams, medical quackery of all types, real estate swindles, and investment fraud. Moreover, elderly persons are the main victims of purse snatchers, pickpockets, and petty thieves, whereby the victims are often assaulted. The perpetrators of these attacks are most often young males who live in their victims' neighborhoods.

Another form of crime-related elder abuse stems from older persons' fear of crime, which research has indicated is the greatest single concern among older Americans. Although crime statistics indicate that the elderly are less likely than younger adults to be victims of most violent crimes, the consequences of physical abuse can be especially devastating to the aged. Young or middle-aged persons might sustain minimal injuries during an assault that would cripple older victims. Even a purse snatching can result in an older person requiring hip replacement surgery or long-term medical care for internal injuries. In addition, larceny can significantly affect the economic independence of older persons with limited and fixed incomes. Fear of crime itself compromises the quality of life of many older Americans, causing them to live reclusively, afraid to leave their homes. Furthermore, some studies have concluded that few crimes against the elderly are reported, because the victims fear retribution by neighborhood criminals and pressure from family and friends to give up living independently because of their limited ability to protect themselves.

ELDERLY HOMELESSNESS

Some authors have contended that homelessness among the elderly in North America represents a serious and increasing form of abuse. Although the perpetrators are more difficult to identify and profile, there is no question that homeless older persons suffer most severely from every type of elder abuse. They experience constant absolute neglect and face daily threats of violent attacks and theft of their meager belongings. Studies have documented the brutality of their lives. Their first priority is the search for a place to sleep that is safe from attack, harassment, and the elements. Older homeless Americans have no dependable source of sustenance. They eat out of garbage cans or at soup kitchens, wherever they exist. They largely lack health care and suffer from high rates of debilitating and chronic ailments.

There are many causes of elderly homelessness in America, and the list has grown. Some researchers have pointed to family abandonment; the refusal of older persons to accept the loss of their independence represented by institutionalization, opting instead for life on the streets; and mental illness and alcoholism. Other authors have asserted that it is insufficient to blame the victims or the breakdown of principles of intergenerational reciprocity. They argue that society itself is responsible because of its unwillingness or inability to alleviate the problem socially. The failure of the economic system to stem the growth of impoverishment has played a part, as have government domestic policy changes that have cut back or eliminated funding for low-income housing, antipoverty programs, and the care of the mentally ill. These changes have left many confused, "deinstitutionalized" older persons with few residential options. Another factor is the lack of comprehensive government policies to eradicate homelessness. The official response in many cities has been to clear the streets of the homeless by forcing them to move on or arresting them for vagrancy and public drunkenness.

The face of elderly homelessness has changed in modern America. Older homeless people are of every gender, race, ethnicity, and socioeconomic background; many experience poverty for the first time in their older years. One author has commented that history will judge societies more by how they care for their helpless and vulnerable citizens than by any other criteria.

—Jack Carter

See also Abandonment; Adult Protective Services; Alcoholism; Caregiving; Family relationships; Fraud against the elderly; Homelessness; Loneliness; Multigenerational households; Neglect; Nursing and convalescent homes; Older Americans Act of 1965; Poverty; Psychiatry, geriatric; Scams and con artists; Violent crime against the elderly.

FOR FURTHER INFORMATION:

Baumhover, Lorin A., and S. Coleen Beall, eds. *Abuse, Neglect, and Exploitation of Older Persons: Strategies for Assessment and Intervention.* Baltimore: Health Professions Press, 1996. Collection of essays focusing on the causes and nature of elder abuse, with an emphasis on responses to the problem by health-care professionals.

Byers, Bryan, and James E. Hendricks, eds. *Adult Protective Services: Research and Practice.* Springfield, Ill.: Charles C Thomas, 1993. Papers by social scientists from several disciplines examining elder abuse, highlighting the challenges facing government agencies.

Filinson, Rachel, and Stanley R. Ingman, eds. *Elder Abuse: Practice and Policy.* New York: Human Sciences Press, 1989. Contributors discuss the problem, focusing on federal and state policy responses to it.

Lustbader, Wendy, and Nancy R. Hooyman. *Taking Care of Aging Family Members.* New York: Free Press, 1994. Discusses neglect and abuse and the caregiving stress that can lead to it.

O'Connell, James J., Jean Summerfield, and F. Russell Kellogg. "The Homeless Elderly." In *Under the Safety Net: The Health and Social Welfare of the Homeless in the United States,* edited by Philip W. Brickner et al. New York: W. W. Norton, 1990. Essay examining the demographics of elderly homelessness, the problems that plague these people, and the programs designed to help them in several large American cities.

ELDER CARE. *See* CAREGIVING.

EMPHYSEMA

RELEVANT ISSUES: Health and medicine

SIGNIFICANCE: Emphysema, a lung disease characterized by increased shortness of breath on exertion that affects two million individuals in the United States, is often a natural accompaniment of aging but can also be initiated or aggravated by cigarette smoking or a heritable specific protein deficiency

Emphysema is one of the two major clinical conditions encompassed in the terms "chronic obstructive pulmonary disease" (COPD) and "chronic airflow obstruction" (CAO). Fourteen million individuals in the United States suffer from emphysema or the other, more frequent condition, chronic bronchitis.

Chronic bronchitis results from exposure of the trachea and bronchial tree to irritants and is characterized by coughing and excessive mucus or sputum production on most days for three months over a period of two years or more. The symptoms result from inflammation occurring in the lining of the bronchi and bronchioles (the epithelium), with enlargement and increased activity of the mucous glands. Emphysema, in contrast, involves the lung tissue associated with the exchange of oxygen and carbon dioxide between the blood and the air. There is destruction of the walls of the alveoli, the small sacs where blood and air are in closest contact, so that permanent enlargement of the alveolar volume occurs. Clinically, patients with chronic bronchitis tend to an extreme characterized by marked decrease of oxygen in the blood, a bluish discoloration of the skin (cyanosis), and swelling of the legs (peripheral edema) as a result of heart failure. Such patients are sometimes referred to as "blue bloaters." In contrast, patients with emphysema tend to an extreme characterized by marked shortness of breath on exertion, a pinkish complexion, and little, if any, peripheral edema. Such patients are sometimes referred to as "pink puffers." Chronic bronchitis and emphysema may coexist in a given individual to a greater or lesser degree.

With the increases in life expectancy and actual longevity in the United States, the number of individuals significantly affected by emphysema can be expected to increase with time. Most older individuals show some evidence of emphysema at death. Even without emphysema, however, aging is associated with a decrease in lung or pulmonary functions such that physical activities become more limited. These normal declines in pulmonary function cannot yet be reversed or even arrested and are the result of tissue changes occurring over time. They can be markedly aggravated if emphysema, such as that caused by cigarette smoking, is superimposed on the normal processes. The life span of affected individuals may be shortened significantly.

RISK FACTORS, EPIDEMIOLOGY, AND NATURAL HISTORY

The incidence of emphysema increases with age and is much more common in men than in women. The dominant cause is cigarette smoking. The one other major identified cause is a deficiency of alpha-1 antitrypsin, a protein that inhibits the destruction of alveolar walls by enzymes. Other factors that may play significant but less certain roles are environmental pollution (including oxidants), hazardous occupations, socioeconomic status, diet, low birth weight, and severe childhood respiratory illnesses.

Although the diagnosis of emphysema is made in slightly less than 1 percent of the population, the incidence is much higher in cigarette smokers. Thus, in one study, 2.9 percent of nonsmoking males showed moderate changes associated with emphysema at autopsy, 25 percent of individuals smoking less than twenty cigarettes per day showed moderate changes, and 32.7 percent of those smoking twenty or more cigarettes per day showed such changes. Of the latter group, nearly 20 percent showed marked changes.

COPD was the fourth leading cause of death in the United States at the end of the twentieth century. Between 80 and 90 percent of the cases of COPD could be attributed to cigarette smoking. Cigarette smoking clearly limits longevity; cessation of smoking increases life expectancy and decreases the rate of decline of pulmonary functions. One measure of pulmonary function is the volume of air that can be expelled forcibly from the lungs in one second after a maximal inspiratory effort; this is referred to as the FEV_1. This measure normally peaks at age twenty-five and decreases to 75 percent of the value at age twenty-five when age seventy-five is reached. In those individuals whose

Emphysema

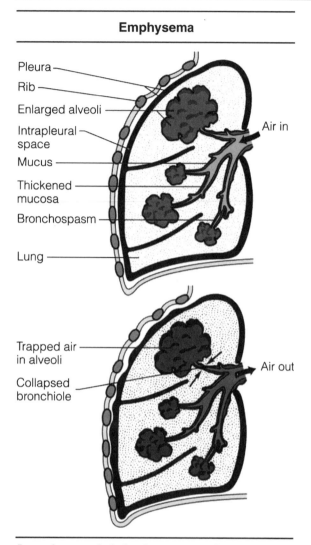

Pleura
Rib
Enlarged alveoli
Intrapleural space
Mucus
Thickened mucosa
Bronchospasm
Lung
Air in

Trapped air in alveoli
Collapsed bronchiole
Air out

In emphysema, the body releases enzymes in response to irritants such as cigarette smoke; these enzymes reduce the elasticity of the lungs, compromising the ability of the bronchioles to expand and contract normally. Air becomes trapped in the alveoli upon inhalation (top) and cannot escape upon exhalation (bottom). (Hans & Cassidy, Inc.)

pulmonary functions are affected by cigarette smoking, the FEV_1 drops to about 75 percent at age forty-five. If smoking continues, the life expectancy falls to well below seventy-five years. If smokers stop at about age fifty, however, the deterioration of the FEV_1 is slowed and their life expectancy is increased, although they may show significant disability by age seventy-five or eighty. Cessation of

smoking beyond the age of fifty, for example at sixty-five, is associated with lesser benefits because much damage has already been done and there is superposition of the damage caused by cigarette smoking on the changes occurring with age.

Of major importance to the cigarette smoker is the number of cigarettes smoked, calculated as pack years (number of packs of cigarettes smoked per day times the number of years the individual has smoked). For smokers with twenty-one to forty pack years, the FEV_1 declines to about 90 percent of the predicted value for that age. For smokers with sixty-one or more pack years, it declines to less than 80 percent of the predicted value.

Not all smokers are so affected. Indeed, 10 to 15 percent of smokers escape the effects mentioned, for reasons unknown. That some smokers are affected so much more than others might stem from intrinsic sensitivity of the airways, effects in childhood of environmental pollution or passive smoking, genetic factors, or manner of smoking (for example, whether they inhale deeply).

Functional and Tissue Changes

The patient with emphysema is generally thin, may purse the lips during expiration, is older (fifty to seventy-five years of age), and experiences increased limitation of exercise tolerance because of shortness of breath (dyspnea on exertion). This portrait is in contrast with the patient with chronic bronchitis, who has a chronic cough, excessive sputum production, and cyanosis at forty to fifty-five years of age. Chest radiographs (X rays) and computed tomography (CT) and magnetic resonance imaging (MRI) scans typically show that the patient with emphysema has a small heart, an increased lung and chest volume, lowering and flattening of the diaphragm, and areas of radiolucency (indicating decreased lung tissue density) and large bubbles or bullae (indicating the absence of any lung tissue in those areas). The patient with chronic bronchitis, in contrast, may show increased markings indicating changes in the walls of the bronchial airways and of vascular engorgement.

Pulmonary function tests (PFTs) in patients with emphysema typically show marked increases in lung volumes, particularly the total lung capacity (essentially the maximal air content) and the residual air volume (RV), the volume remaining after full expiration. The RV is an indicator of air trapped because of airway closure. The FEV_1, the rate of flow in expiration, is decreased. The elastic recoil, the driving pressure of the lungs during expiration, is decreased because of tissue changes. The action of the diaphragm is also decreased because these muscles are flattened instead of being domed and cannot move as freely as in normal individuals. In addition, because of the destruction of lung tissue there is a reduction in the pulmonary diffusing capacity, which indicates that the rate of exchanges of oxygen between the air and the blood in the pulmonary vessels is reduced. The lungs must work at a mechanical disadvantage so that with the decrease of alveolar ventilation, the work of breathing and oxygen consumption are increased. With the destruction of lung tissue, the surface of the lungs available for gas exchanges is decreased. So while the demand for oxygen is increased, the delivery is decreased, particularly during exertion.

The tissue changes in cigarette smokers differ somewhat from those observed in patients with alpha-l antitrypsin deficiency. In the former, the respiratory bronchioles are mainly affected, with relatively normal alveolar ducts and alveoli. The bronchioles widen and may fuse. In the latter, the alveolar walls are destroyed more uniformly throughout the lungs, so that mainly vascular, bronchial, and supporting structures are left. In both types of emphysema, proteases, enzymes that degrade structural proteins such as collagen and particularly elastin, overwhelm their inhibitors such as the antitrypsins. In cigarette smokers, the inflammatory response to the irritants in smoke is associated with macrophages (scavenger cells) and neutrophils, cells that respond to inflammation and produce proteases which not only attack tissues but also destroy antiproteases. Individuals with antiprotease deficiency have impaired defense mechanisms and are at greater risk of serious damage. Emphysema can be considered to occur as the result of imbalance between proteases and antiproteases. The resultant irreversible tissue changes in the peripheral parts of the lungs lead to overinflation of the alveolar air sacs and in turn may lead to compression of some of the remaining unaffected lung tissue.

PREVENTION AND TREATMENT

In cigarette smokers, the single most effective treatment is cessation of smoking. In most cases, cessation will slow the decline in respiratory functions and in exercise tolerance. The best prevention is discouraging young individuals from ever starting to smoke. Only 10 to 15 percent of cigarette smokers develop emphysema, and relatively few of them have alpha-1 antitrypsin deficiency. Nevertheless, abolition of cigarette smoking could have not only major health benefits but also major economic benefits in reducing the costs of care for an aging population already faced with declining respiratory function and exercise tolerance.

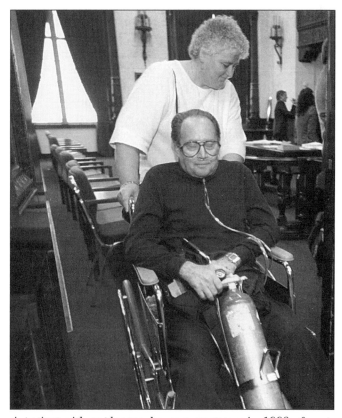

A patient with emphysema leaves a courtroom in 1998 after appearing at a hearing for a Florida smokers' class-action suit against the tobacco industry. Such lawsuits became common as older people suffered the effects of a lifetime of smoking. (AP Photo/Victor R. Caivano)

Other recognized measures for the treatment of emphysema include long-term supplemental oxygen administration as needed, bronchodilators, corticosteroids when airway inflammatory changes are present, antibiotics for infections, and diuretics and vasodilators for heart failure. Physical training programs and mechanically assisted ventilation can be extremely helpful. In patients with homozygous alpha-l antitrypsin deficiency, replacement therapy with the purified protein should be considered.

Controlled clinical trials employing the surgical reduction of lung volume began in 1997 under the joint auspices of the National Institutes of Health (NIH) and the Health Care Financing Administration. This approach is based on the fact that the overinflation of the lungs is not uniform throughout the organs. It had been suggested in the 1950's that surgical removal of the overinflated areas could improve pulmonary functions by permitting more normal positioning of the diaphragm and increasing elastic recoil. Early attempts in this direction were associated with marked subjective improvement in some patients, but the overall postoperative morbidity and mortality were very high. More recently, improved surgical techniques and intensive care procedures have resulted in better clinical results. However, the criteria for application of the procedure, the short-term benefits, and the long-term outcomes, together with cost-benefit considerations, have not yet been evaluated fully. The prospects for the controlled program, undertaken at nineteen centers in the United States, are encouraging.

Emphysema will remain a major issue in an aging population for many years. Probably the most effective means of limiting the problem will be cessation of smoking for those who do smoke and efforts to discourage younger generations from ever smoking at all. —*Francis P. Chinard*

See also Exercise and fitness; Illnesses among the elderly; Respiratory changes and disorders; Smoking.

FOR FURTHER INFORMATION:

Auerbach, O., E. C. Hammond, L. Garfinkel, and C. Benante. "Relation of Smoking and Age to Emphysema: Whole Lung Section Study." *New England Journal of Medicine* 286, no. 16 (April 20, 1972): 853-858.

Burrows, B., R. J. Knudson, M. G. Cline, and M. D. Lebowitz. "Quantitative Relationship Between Cigarette Smoking and Ventilatory Function." *American Review of Respiratory Diseases* 115, no. 2 (February, 1977): 195-205.

Cherniack, N. S. *Chronic Obstructive Pulmonary Disease*. Philadelphia: W. B. Saunders, 1991.

Fishman, A. P., ed. *Pulmonary Diseases and Disorders*. 3d ed. New York: McGraw-Hill, 1998.

Fletcher, C., and R. Peto. "The Natural History of Chronic Airflow Obstruction." *British Medical Journal* 1, no. 6077 (June 25, 1977): 1645-1648.

Knudson, R. J., R. C. Slatin, M. D. Lebowitz, and B. Burrows. "The Maximal Expiratory Flow-Volume Curve: Normal Standards, Variability, and Effects of Age." *American Review of Respiratory Diseases* 113, no. 5 (May, 1976): 587-600.

Staton, G. W., and R. H. Ingram. "Chronic Obstructive Diseases of the Lungs." In *Scientific American Medicine*, edited by D. C. Dale and D. D. Federman. New York: Scientific American, 1998.

EMPLOYMENT

RELEVANT ISSUES: Demographics, economics, race and ethnicity, work

SIGNIFICANCE: How older Americans leave the labor force is a function of the country's extensive system of public and private pensions. Facing less economic security than older white men, aging women and, to a lesser extent, minorities are less likely to withdraw from the labor force

The prime working years, thought to be between twenty-five and fifty-four, suggest that fifty-five is an appropriate starting point in the life cycle to be considered an older person. This view is supported by the notably higher levels of labor force participation rates among those aged forty-five to fifty-four, which closely match rates of younger persons.

As figure 1 shows, men and women aged forty-five to fifty-four consistently have higher labor force participation rates over time than their counterparts fifty-five to sixty-four years old, although rates vary by age and sex. The labor force participation rate of men aged forty-five to fifty-four declined only about six percentage points, from 95.8 percent in 1950 to 89.5 percent in 1997. The decline in the labor force participation rate of men

Figure 1. Civilian Labor Force Participation Rates by Sex and Age, 1950-1997

Source: Jacobs, Eva J., ed. *Handbook of U.S. Labor Statistics.* 2d ed. Lanham, Md.: Bernan Press, 1998.

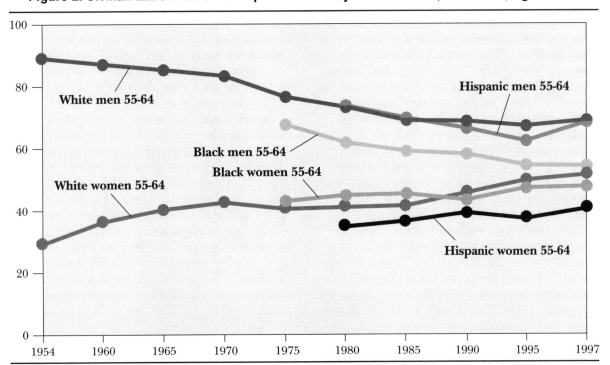

Figure 2. Civilian Labor Force Participation Rates by Sex and Race, 1954-1997, Ages 55-64

Source: Jacobs, Eva J., ed. *Handbook of U.S. Labor Statistics.* 2d ed. Lanham, Md.: Bernan Press, 1998.

Figure 3. Civilian Labor Force Participation Rates by Sex and Race, 1954-1997, Ages 65+

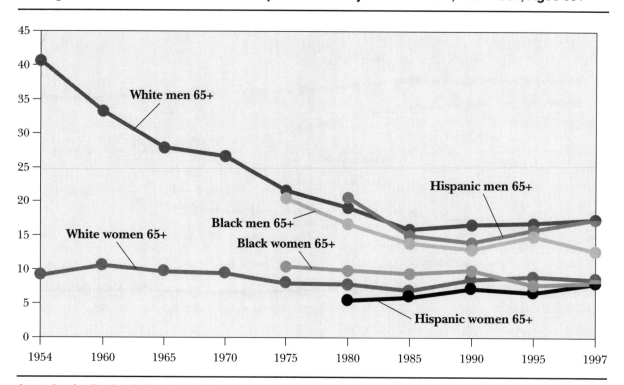

Source: Jacobs, Eva J., ed. *Handbook of U.S. Labor Statistics.* 2d ed. Lanham, Md.: Bernan Press, 1998.

aged fifty-five to sixty-four nearly doubled that of those aged forty-five to fifty-four, from 80 percent or higher in the early 1970's to a low of 66 percent in 1995, then rising slightly to 67.8 percent in 1997. The labor force participation rate of women aged forty-five to fifty-four rose steadily and dramatically by nearly forty percentage points, from 39.1 percent in 1950 to 76 percent in 1997. The increased labor force participation rates of women aged fifty-five to sixty-four was also steady, but more gradual over the entire period, from 27 percent in 1950 to 51 percent in 1997.

The labor force participation rate of those sixty-five and older is much lower than that of those aged fifty-five to sixty-four and varies over time by sex. For men aged sixty-five and older, the labor force participation rate declined from about 46 percent in the 1950's and leveled off at just below 20 percent in the mid-1980's and throughout the 1990's. The rate for women aged sixty-five and older was fairly stable between 7 percent and 11 percent, the lowest levels of any group, over the en-

tire period. Comparable data of men and women's labor force participation rates by race/ethnicity are available beginning in 1954 for whites, 1972 for African Americans, and 1980 for Latinos, who for purposes here may be of any race.

Figure 2 shows the trends in labor force participation rates by selected years and race/ethnicity for men and women aged fifty-five to sixty-four, while figure 3 does so for those aged sixty-five and older. The downward trend in labor force participation for men and the upward trend for women aged fifty-five to sixty-four occurred regardless of race/ethnicity, at remarkably similar levels among women throughout the 1980's and 1990's. Women aged sixty-five and older demonstrated very little variation in labor force participation rates over time by race/ethnicity, also at remarkably similar levels.

PART-TIME EMPLOYMENT OF OLDER PERSONS

Since the 1970's, the importance of part-time work in the United States has increased overall, especially for older workers. Although fewer than 7 percent of men aged twenty-five to twenty-nine in the nonagricultural sector currently work fewer than thirty-five hours per week, 16 percent of those aged sixty to sixty-four, 42 percent of those sixty-five to sixty-nine, and well over half of those aged seventy and older do so. For women, part-time work is more prevalent at all ages. In 1999, about 20 percent of employed women aged twenty-five to fifty-nine worked part-time. Nearly a third of women aged sixty to sixty-four, 57 percent of those aged sixty-five to sixty-nine, and two-thirds of the women aged seventy and older worked part-time. Among older workers, the proportion working part-time increased from 38 percent in 1970 to 48 percent for men aged sixty-five and older and from 50 to 60 percent for women this age.

The long-term early retirement trends may still be continuing, though not through labor force departure but rather through reduced hours of those still employed. Studies in the late 1990's indicated that between 30 and 40 percent (depending on age) of those fifty-eight to sixty-three worked in postcareer "bridge" jobs, many of which are part-time.

THE RETIREMENT AGE AND LIFE EXPECTANCY

The retirement age and life expectancy are important considerations for financial planning for individuals, as well as for organizations, both public and private. In an August, 1998, *Monthly Labor Review* article entitled "Trends in Retirement Age in Four Countries, 1965-95," Murray Gendell reports that the average five-year interval age of exit from the labor force declined for both men and women. For men, the average age of retirement declined by 1.9 years, from 64.1 years old in the 1965 to 1970 interval to 62.2 years old in the 1990 to 1995 interval. For women, the average age of retirement declined by 2.6 years, from 65.3 in 1965 to 1970 to 62.7 in 1990 to 1995.

As measured by life expectancy at the average age of labor force withdrawal, the average duration of retirement increased substantially between 1965 and 1995. For elderly men, years of life expectancy at the average age at labor force exit increased 3.9 years (by 28.9 percent), from 13.5 years in 1965 to 1970 to 17.4 years in 1990 to 1995. For elderly women, years of life expectancy at the average age at labor force exit increased 4.8 years (29.6

percent), from 16.2 years in 1965 to 1970 to 21.0 years in 1990 to 1995. The gain in retirement years is a result of the drop in the average age at retirement and the rise in longevity. Life expectancy at age sixty-five between 1965 to 1970 and 1990 to 1995 increased 2.4 years (by 18.5 percent), from 13.0 to 15.4 years, for men and 2.8 years (by 17.1 percent), from 16.4 to 19.2 years, for women. The proportion of those surviving to age sixty-five between 1965 to 1970 and 1990 to 1995 also increased, from 64 percent to 75 percent for men and 80 percent to 81 percent for women.

THE ELDERLY DEPENDENCY BURDEN

What impact have these changes in the retirement age and life expectancy had on the elderly dependency burden in the recent past, and what do they portend for the next several decades? The United States relies on a pay-as-you-go system to support retired persons and their dependents. The rise of the ratio of retirees to those working increases the likelihood of reducing the balance of income and outgo of public pension systems and increasing the dependency ratio. Declines in the average age at retirement tend to raise the system dependency ratio by increasing the number of pensioners and reducing the number of workers. The aging of the population, because of declines in fertility and mortality, also tends to raise the system dependency ratio.

In the United States, the number of persons sixty-five years of age and older per 100 persons aged fifteen to sixty-four increased from 15.4 in 1960 to 19.1 in 1990, yielding a dependency burden ratio of 1.24. Table 1 shows the projected trends of this dependency burden ratio, with a second measure comprising the number of pension beneficiaries per 100 pension contributors in the United States through 2030, when anticipated costs of Social Security payments are estimated to exceed revenues. The difference between these two measures is that the first (dependency burden-1) is an indicator of the potential elderly dependency burden in the population, whereas the second (dependency burden-2) is a measure of the actual pension system dependency ratio. As can be seen in table 1, the two measures correspond closely. Both measures grow more slowly between 1995 and 2010, with the dependency burden-1 ratio of 1.06 compared to 1.03 for dependency

Table 1: Projected Trends in Two Measures of the Elderly Dependency Burden in the United States, 1995-2030

Year	Dependency Burden-1	Dependency Burden-2
1995	19.2	23.8
2010	20.4	24.4
2030	36.8	40.0
Ratio 2010/1995	1.06	1.03
Ratio 2030/2010	1.80	1.64

Note: Dependency Burden-1 = number of persons 65+ for every 100 persons aged 15-64; Dependency Burden-2 = number of pension beneficiaries per 100 pension contributors.

Source: Adapted from Murray Gendell's "Trends in Retirement Age in Four Countries, 1965-95." *Monthly Labor Review* 121, no. 8 (August, 1998).

burden-2, than between 2010 and 2030, with the dependency burden-1 ratio of 1.80 compared to 1.64 for dependency burden-2.

The strong projected growth in both elderly dependency measures between 2010 and 2030 reflects the retirement of the baby boomers, those born between 1946 and 1964. By 2040, there will be about forty million more elderly than in the late 1990's, reflecting a 120 percent increase, compared to a projected 24 percent increase in the number of working-age adults aged twenty to sixty-four. The pace of anticipated change in the elderly dependency burden is consistent with the projection of the balance between pension revenue and expenditures. Assuming the contribution rate remains the same, pension expenditures in the United States were projected to decrease slightly from 4.4 percent of the gross domestic product in 1995 through 2010 before increasing to 7.4 percent in 2030. The balance of revenues and expenditures was expected to double from a 0.8 percentage surplus in 1995 to a 1.7 percentage surplus in 2010, then decline to a 2.2 percent deficit in 2030.

EMPLOYMENT-RELATED PROBLEMS OF OLDER WORKERS

Aging workers face special job problems, including discrimination in hiring, job obsolescence, and managerial policies. In addition, older workers, while often protected by seniority against job loss, generally find themselves as vulnerable as younger workers to plant shutdowns, corporate downsizing, and other dislocations arising from mergers and government cutbacks. These problems create immediate difficulties for workers and their families, and they often have an economic impact on their situation during the retirement years. Long-term unemployment, for example, makes saving for retirement difficult if not impossible. Moreover, periods of unemployment often result in lower pension benefits. Workers between the ages of fifty-five and sixty-four are particularly vulnerable to job dislocation, that is, job losses where it is unlikely that workers would be rehired. Once dislocated, older workers are also likely to experience longer periods of unemployment.

Older workers continue to face discrimination in hiring and other work-related practices. The 1967 Age Discrimination in Employment Act sought to protect individuals from age discrimination in hiring, discharge, compensation, and other terms of employment. The act originally covered most persons between the ages of forty and sixty-five. It was amended in 1978 to include workers up to age sixty-nine and again in 1986 to prohibit mandatory retirement at any age. Since then, most overt signs of discrimination—such as newspaper advertisements restricting jobs to younger persons and forced or mandatory retirements—have virtually disappeared. Nonetheless, it is difficult to determine the total extent to which actual discrimination has lessened, in part because little comprehensive evidence exists in regard to this matter.

Other work-related factors older persons face include lacking the necessary skills to qualify for available jobs and living in areas remote from job opportunities. Given their educational backgrounds, older persons compete less well for jobs in the growing electronics and computer industries, while skills developed in older, established industries do not transfer as readily to new, high-tech industries. Further, having established roots, many older workers with usable skills are left behind with little hope for new employment with comparable responsibility or pay as industries shift to geographic areas offering lower labor costs. Older workers also have difficulty finding new jobs because of their job-seeking behavior and lower priority given to them by various employment agencies. Evidence suggests that older job seekers display less willingness to change the types of work methods or methods of looking for work, to engage in job training, to adjust salary expectations, and to move to areas of higher employment opportunity.

Although unemployed older workers are as likely as others to seek assistance from employment services, significantly fewer older workers are tested, counseled, enrolled in training, referred to employers for job interviews, or actually placed on the job. Even when employed, older workers are less likely than others to receive job training. In 1995, for example, 50.7 percent of employees age fifty-five years and older received formal training within the previous twelve months, compared to 69.8 percent overall.

Older workers also cost more in terms of total compensation benefits than younger workers do. Group health insurance rates are likely to cost employers more to the extent they have greater numbers of older employees whose use patterns tend to be more extensive than younger employees. Employers may be reluctant to hire older workers because of higher costs associated with defined benefit pension plans. In these plans, the employer promises to pay a particular benefit, with the amount determined by an agreed-upon formula, usually based on some combination of earnings, often over the last few years of work, and years of service and age at retirement. Further, total compensation costs may be increased with newly hired older employees because such employees have shorter work histories over which employer pension contributions must be made, thereby lowering investment income arising from the pension contributions.

PROBLEMS FACED BY OLDER FEMALE AND MINORITY WORKERS

Some employment problems faced by older women differ from those of older men. Related problems stem from women's previous commitments to family roles, necessitating part-time or intermittent work over the life course. Longitudinal studies indicate that 40 percent of white women and 60 per-

cent of African American women aged forty-five to fifty-nine first returned to work before their first child reached age six. A great majority of these mothers had additional absences from the labor force. Further, after the age of twenty-five, the average woman will reenter the labor force 2.7 times during her remaining life. In addition to repeated entries to and exits from the labor market, long interruptions are also common. Women who are in their forties and fifties are likely to spend about fifteen years at home and about eleven years in the labor market upon completion of schooling. Such work patterns contribute to women's economic vulnerability during retirement and to their tendency to remain attached to the labor market on a part-time basis to make ends meet.

By old age, most people have given up strenuous manual labor, but economic circumstances and the desire to use skills acquired over many years lead some to continue such work. (James L. Shaffer)

Older women are less likely to retire from the labor force completely. Some return to work in their later years, either full-time or part-time, when children leave home or husbands die. (James L. Shaffer)

Women also face sex discrimination and occupational segregation whose adverse consequences continually erode their ability to achieve economic self-sufficiency in retirement. Earnings differentials between women and men, about $0.75 to $1.00, cannot be explained by differences in education and work experience alone. Despite recent gains in women's entry into male-dominated occupations such as medicine and law, overwhelmingly greater proportions of women hold low-paying service-sector jobs. Further, even women who hold higher-paying jobs face a glass ceiling, that is, a level of corporate responsibility with commensurate pay beyond which women seldom reach. Although women have made advances in managerial positions in recent years, younger women account for most of the increases in employment in the male-dominated professions. Working women are also less likely than men are to participate in pension plans. Married low-wage women may not want to contribute if their husbands participate in a pension plan. Because of shorter job tenure,

women are less likely to be vested than men are. Women are also about twice as likely as men are to receive a lump-sum distribution in lieu of a monthly pension benefit. When women do have pensions, they are generally less, about half, than those for men.

The prospect of less retirement income provides incentives for aging women to work beyond the normal retirement age. Although labor force participation rates of men are considerably higher than those of women at age sixty-two and older, men and women are equally likely to continue working among those drawing only Social Security benefits as retired workers. When comparing only those who work shortly before beginning to receive benefits, women are more likely than men are to continue working. The greater likelihood of retired women working reflects lower economic status.

Compared to whites, blacks are more likely to retire at earlier ages, retire because of poor health, be forced to retire, be unemployed in the twelve-month period preceding retirement, and report job dissatisfaction and job search discouragement prior to retirement. On the whole, poor health and disadvantaged labor force experiences are more influential determinants of the retirement decision and process for blacks, whereas financial readiness is more influential for whites. The current generation of older African Americans is more likely to have worked in low-status jobs characterized by sporadic work patterns over time and subjected to discrimination due to race, age, occupational segmentation, and, for women, sex. As is the case with women in general, these work patterns threaten African Americans' economic security as they reach old age. Work in old age in the same low-status jobs remains a necessity for many. Among African American women aged fifty-five and older, studies show that nearly one-quarter (22.9 percent) work twenty hours or more per week, compared to 36.1 percent of African American men aged fifty-five and older.

Older female and African American workers, and to a lesser extent Latino workers, share one problem that distinguishes them from older white workers: an increased likelihood to live in poverty. Table 2 shows the poverty rates among female and male workers aged sixty-five and older for 1996. The percentages of women living in poverty nearly doubled for male and female year-round, full-time workers aged fifty-five to sixty-four years old and tripled for non-year-round, full-time workers aged fifty-five to sixty-four. For those not working, however, the percentages in poverty were often three to four times higher than for those working, and disproportionately more so for women than for men, depending on age group. On the whole, evidence suggests that work serves less as a buffer against poverty for women and minorities than is the case for

men, particularly among women aged sixty-five and older. Although the available data are less complete for race and ethnicity, older white workers are less likely to live in poverty than are older African American and Latino workers. Table 2 also shows the poverty rates among white and minority workers aged sixty-five and older and aged fifty-five to sixty-four for 1996.

Although work serves less as a buffer against poverty for women than it does for men, this is not necessarily the case when taking race into account, although it holds for ethnicity. In 1996, of 0.2 million African American working women aged sixty-five and older, 4.9 percent were poor; of 0.2 million African American working men aged sixty-five and older, 6.2 percent were poor. The percentages of poverty among working African American men and women aged fifty-five to sixty-four were nearly equal: Of the 0.6 million African American working women in this age group, 7.0 percent were poor, while of the 0.5 million African American

Table 2: Poverty Rates Among Workers in 1996

Male and Female Workers Aged 65+

2.8 million male workers	1.7%
2.1 million female workers	2.3%
1.8 million non-year-round, full-time male workers	2.3%
1.6 million non-year-round, full-time female workers	3.0%
1.1 million year-round, full-time male workers	0.9%
0.6 million year-round, full-time female workers	0.5%

White and Minority Workers Aged 65+

4.5 million white workers	1.6%
0.3 million African American workers	5.5%
0.2 million Latino workers	8.4%
3.1 million non-year-round, full-time white workers	2.0%
0.2 million non-year-round, full-time African American workers	9.3%
0.1 million non-year-round, full-time Latino workers	2.9%

White and Minority Workers Aged 55-64

12.2 million white workers	3.1%
1.2 million African American workers	6.9%
0.9 million Latino workers	8.6%
8.0 million year-round, full-time white workers	1.1%
0.8 million year-round, full-time African American workers	2.2%
0.6 million year-round, full-time Latino workers	3.3%
4.2 million non-year-round, full-time white workers	7.0%
0.3 million non-year-round, full-time African American workers	18.4%
0.3 million non-year-round, full-time Latino workers	19.4%

working men in this group, 6.7 percent were poor. In what is perhaps implausible, the advantageous effects of employment in reducing poverty among the aged appear to be similar for white men and black women. Historically, the employment opportunities and lifetime work experiences of white men and black women are polar opposites, with most of the advantages resulting in greater economic well-being enjoyed by white men.

PENSIONS AND EMPLOYMENT

The Social Security Act of 1935 contains some provisions that encourage early retirement and others that reward continued labor force attachment. On the one hand, until 1956 workers could not receive their old-age benefits until they reached the age of sixty-five. In 1956, the law was changed to permit female workers to receive reduced benefits between the ages of sixty-two and sixty-four; and in 1961 this option was extended to men. The early retirement option proved increasingly popular. In 1970, 36 percent of male beneficiaries and 59 percent of female beneficiaries received reduced benefits, increasing to 65 percent and 73 percent respectively in 1990. Earnings tests also discourage work. An earnings test reduces benefits paid to nondisabled beneficiaries under age seventy who earn more than a certain amount. The earnings exemption for beneficiaries ages sixty-five to sixty-nine was $15,500 in 1999; benefits over this amount are reduced one dollar for every three earned above the exemption. A lower exemption applies to beneficiaries under age sixty-five ($9,600 in 1999), with benefits reduced by 50 percent of earnings over the ceiling.

On the other hand, in 1983 Congress amended the Social Security Act to provide incentives for delayed retirement and disincentives for early retirement, while gradually increasing the age for full Social Security benefits from sixty-five to sixty-seven by 2022. Delayed retirement credits encourage older workers to maintain their labor force attachment. These credits are given to workers age sixty-five or older who continue working and, as a result, do not receive their entitled benefits. An additional amount is added to benefits (of persons reaching age sixty-two in 1979 or later) for each year between ages sixty-five and seventy that they delay benefit receipt. The delayed retirement credit was expected to rise gradually, from 3 percent per year in 1989 to 8 percent in 2008. On the whole, studies suggest that historically Social Security has encouraged workers to retire earlier than they would have otherwise. Most projections done to assess the impact of congressional action to raise the future social retirement age, liberalize the retirement test, and improve benefits through the delayed retirement credit, however, indicate that these actions are not likely to raise retirement ages.

Like Social Security, employer-sponsored pension plans have an impact on retirement and employment decisions. In response to favorable tax treatment, employers encourage earlier retirement by setting the age of normal retirement specified by the company's pension plan below age sixty-five. In addition, some employers provide early retirement options, often absorbing all or most of the added costs of paying pensions out over a longer period of time and thereby allowing workers to retire early without major penalties in the form of significantly lower pension income. Other early retirement incentive programs include offering a credit to increase pension levels or a lump-sum payment, often equal to one-half to two years of salary, in addition to the regular pension. To receive these benefits, workers must terminate employment during a limited window period usually ranging from one month to one year. Studies suggest that the growing availability of private pensions at early ages contributed significantly to the higher percentages of retirees throughout the 1980's at age sixty-two compared to all retired workers, especially for married men.

The extent to which changes in the Social Security system will affect exits from the labor force remains in doubt, particularly if early-exit opportunities in private pension plans remain the same. As long as employers sanction and prefer such possibilities, and as long as they, in so doing, benefit in the form of corporate tax savings and workforce size (or labor-cost) control, there is little chance of the legislative reforms of Social Security having much impact on retirement decisions.

—*Richard K. Caputo*

See also Absenteeism; Adult education; African Americans; Age discrimination; Age Discrimination Act of 1975; Age Discrimination in Employment Act of 1967; Americans with Disabilities Act; Baby boomers; Disabilities; Dual-income couples; Early retirement; Executive Order 11141; Forced retirement; 401K plans; Income sources; Individual retirement accounts (IRAs); Job loss; *Johnson v. Mayor and City Council of Baltimore*; Latinos; *Massachusetts Board of Retirement v. Murgia*; Men and aging; Mentoring; Older Americans Act of 1965; Older Worker Benefit Protection Act; Pensions; Poverty; Retirement; Retirement planning; Social Security; *Vance v. Bradley*; Volunteering; Women and aging.

FOR FURTHER INFORMATION:

Binstock, Robert H., and Linda K. George, eds. *Handbook of Aging and the Social Sciences.* 4th ed. San Diego: Academic Press, 1996. A collection of essays addressing multidimensional aspects of aging and its impact on society, with separate chapters focusing on economic and social implications of demographic patterns, work and retirement, the political economy of aging, the economic status of the elderly, and economic security policies.

Kingston, Eric R., and James H. Schultz, eds. *Social Security in the Twenty-first Century.* New York: Oxford University Press, 1997. A collection of essays focusing on the role of Social Security in the economy and society, including chapters on the effects of Social Security on work effort and the economic security of women.

Quadagno, Jill, and Debra Street, eds. *Aging for the Twenty-first Century: Readings in Social Gerontology.* New York: St. Martin's Press, 1996. A collection of thirty-one essays about the social dimensions of aging in general, with several chapters addressing work and retirement, intergenerational equity issues, and race/ethnicity and gender issues.

Quinn, Joseph F., Richard V. Burkhauser, and Daniel A. Meyers. *Passing the Torch: The Influence of Economic Incentives on Work and Retirement.* Kalamazoo, Mich.: W. E. Upjohn Institute for Employment Research, 1990. A comprehensive review of related literature and findings of research based on national-level data demonstrating the role of pension systems across the life cycle, particularly in regard to transitions from full-time to a combination of part-time work and retirement prior to complete withdrawal from the labor market.

Schulz, James A. *The Economics of Aging.* 2d ed. Westport, Conn.: Auburn House, 1995. A comprehensive work examining changes in patterns of retirement, problems of older workers, and complexities of preparing for retirement.

Treas, Judith, and Ramon Torrecilha. "The Older Population." In *State of the Union: America in the 1990's. Volume II: Social Trends*, edited by Reynolds Farley. New York: Russell Sage Foundation, 1995. A comprehensive overview of the aging of America, with particular attention to changing circumstances affecting economic well-being, work, and retirement among aging adults and the elderly.

EMPTY NEST SYNDROME

RELEVANT ISSUES: Family, marriage and dating, psychology, sociology

SIGNIFICANCE: Once thought to be an important problem for married couples after their children left home, the concept of the empty nest syndrome has been used to describe those married couples who need support in adjusting to the absence of their mature children—a normal phase of the life cycle

The empty nest syndrome refers to the emotional problems experienced by some parents when all their children have grown up and left the home. Initially the term referred to mothers, but it was later expanded to include fathers who experienced the same symptoms. The concept of the empty nest was very popular in the 1950's and 1960's and was coined by professional therapists who feared that mothers would have a difficult time adjusting to the departure of their children. It was reasoned that when women become mothers, their role would be heavily influenced by their duties and responsibilities toward their children. These roles would dominate a significant portion of their married lives.

INCREASING LONGEVITY

By 1950, average Americans were expected to live into their sixties, which meant that a significant demographic change was taking place in the population as a result of medical advances and better health. The majority of parents had an excellent chance of raising their children and living ten to fifteen years after their last child left home. Before the 1950's one or both parents commonly died before their last child left home. For example, one demographic study found that Quaker women born before 1786 were at a median age of 50.9 years when their first spouse died and 60.2 years when their last child married. By 1960 the average American woman's first spouse died at an average age of sixty-seven, while her last child left home when she was in her mid-fifties. Thus, for the first time in U.S. history, women continued to live with their spouses long after their last child left home.

As longevity has continued to increase among Americans, it has become common for people to live into their seventies. U.S. census data have indicated that with increased longevity, marriages enjoy a new stage in the family life cycle between the departure of the last child from the home and parents' retirement from the workforce. Therapists previously warned that when parents were relieved of their significant child-rearing roles, a vacuum would form that would be difficult for parents to fill. Because husbands in this phase of the family life cycle continued to be primary breadwinners, their major role change did not occur until they retired. Wives, on the other hand, faced a major role change when they were relieved of the primary care of their children. To compound the problem, such women experienced this phase while they were undergoing the menopause.

CONCERN OVER THE EMPTY NEST

The concern over empty nest syndrome was overemphasized by therapists and the popular media, who foresaw a dismal period for women as they struggled to adjust. A small percentage of parents become severely depressed and lonely when their children leave home, and researchers have discovered that there are also parents who make this phase a stressful time for both themselves and their children. However, most parents do not experience empty nest syndrome or undergo a stressful period upon the departure of their last child. The concept of empty nest syndrome gripped public attention until the first studies began to appear in the early 1960's. Couples reported feeling relieved from the strains of child rearing and claimed to be experiencing the best time of their lives. Evidence indicated that when child-rearing roles were carried into midlife, mothers felt the impact of the empty nest less strongly.

In the 1990's, the employment, educational, and family choices open to women provided them with new opportunities for making a successful transition to a new period of the family life cycle. Wives have been able to resume the plans and projects they postponed during parenting. Most important, such women have asserted that they have pursued such activities because they want to, not because they wish to escape from loneliness. Parents have also reported that with the departure of their last child, they have had increased time for shared activities with each other. It is not uncommon to observe middle-aged couples enjoying each other's company and getting reacquainted after the pressures of parenting.

POSITIVE CHANGES

Couples have reported that marital conflicts subside to their lowest level after their last child has left the home, a situation that is most common among couples who have been married for twenty-five to thirty years and have developed teamwork, problem-solving skills, and the understanding that comes from cooperative effort over a long period of time. Evidence suggests that husbands and wives resume the provider and domestic roles that prevailed in their marriages before their children were born, with greater earning power and experience to take advantage of their time alone together.

One carefully researched study of middle-aged couples in the mid-1970's found that women's personal happiness increased after their children left home and that both men and women reported greater marital happiness during this stage. Couples reported that they were relieved to switch from the parental role of rulegivers and enforcers to the role of advisers to their grown children. In this phase of the family life cycle, couples have the resources to make improvements in their lives; many children are distressed to find that the parental home has been remodeled or refurnished and that their mothers and fathers are not available because they decided to get away for a few days. The developmental tasks that are important for couples at this stage include adjusting to the departure of their children, dealing with the realities of aging, deciding if this stage will be one of stagnation or one of recreating and improving life, and taking stock of how family relationships have changed because of the changed roles that men and women play at this stage of the life span.

POTENTIAL AREAS OF CONCERN

Some couples decide to get divorced when their last child leaves the home, but the percentage of divorces among couples in the "empty nest" age group is small. A small percentage of persons discover that as marital partners, they have grown apart and have little in common. Getting reacquainted again can be a difficult process and may not seem to be worth the effort. Parents may identify too closely with their children, but the social norm requires that parents raise their children to be independent. Parents who overidentify with their children may feel lonely and abandoned.

There is much discussion about the sexual relationships of couples at this stage of life, since men and women undergo similar midlife changes. Men report that they experience many of the same menopausal changes that women experience. At this stage, persons slow down and lose interest, but most research has reported that these changes are easily accommodated once couples understand what to expect. While a small number of midlife couples visit therapists because of sexual dysfunction, such complaints reflect a long-term pattern of dysfunction during the course of marriage. Couples in their middle years usually take these changes in stride. Women have generally reported being more responsive sexually after the menopause because the concern of pregnancy has ceased.

In general, the empty nest syndrome or the period of midlife crisis seems to have been exaggerated by the general public. The reporting of a few dramatic cases as examples of the problems of the empty nest may catch the public imagination, but the facts do not warrant the conclusion that it is a significant problem for most married couples.

—*Robert Christenson*

See also Depression; Divorce; Family relationships; Full nest; Loneliness; Marriage; Men and aging; Menopause; Middle age; Midlife crisis; Parenthood; Single parenthood; Women and aging.

FOR FURTHER INFORMATION:

Duvall, Evelyn. *Marriage and Family Development.* 5th ed. Philadelphia: J. B. Lippincott, 1977.
Glenn, N. "Psychological Well-Being in the Post-Parental Stage: Some Evidence from National Surveys." *Journal of Marriage and the Family* 37 (1975).
Sheehy, Gail. *New Passages: Mapping Your Life Across Time.* New York: Random House, 1995.
_____. *Passages: Predictable Crises of Adult Life.* New York: E. P. Dutton, 1974.

ENJOY OLD AGE: A PROGRAM OF SELF-MANAGEMENT

AUTHORS: B. F. Skinner and Margaret Vaughan
DATE: Published in 1983
RELEVANT ISSUES: Psychology, values
SIGNIFICANCE: Skinner and Vaughan urge elders to attack old age as a problem to solve, or at least one to be managed, by making adjustments to their environment and by examining what rewards are still effective in motivating them

B. F. Skinner (1904-1990) was a noted professor of psychology at Harvard University and the leader of behavior analysis, a viewpoint in psychology which argued that environmental circumstances and consequences control behavior. *Enjoy Old Age: A Program of Self-Management* is an elaboration of a paper that he prepared at the age of seventy-eight that described some of his own methods derived from behavior analysis for remaining intellectually active. It was written in collaboration with a younger colleague, Margaret Vaughan.

Many of the problems of old age stem from the loss of reinforcer effectiveness or sensory sensitivity: For example, some foods lack taste, and reading small print becomes impossible. Sometimes new reinforcers can be found or external adjustments can be made (such as the addition of a magnifying glass). The authors propose that planning behaviorally for old age is just as important as planning financially. The literal world in which elders live may need to be changed to allow for continuing to do what they like or for discovering new sources of satisfaction.

This short book contains little theory. Instead, it offers many practical tips and suggestions for dealing with problems that arise with aging. For example, as peripheral vision weakens, older people should learn to look farther in both directions before crossing a street. When forgetting to take pills becomes a problem, elders should match the requirement to another routine activity—for example, attaching the pill case to a toothbrush with a rubber band. Retirement may bring a lack of routine, and learning to structure one's day takes on a new importance. The authors advise, however, that elders should be willing to experiment with different schedules and structures. They suggest rearranging the environment so as to accommodate failings of the body and nervous system. Older people should not necessarily do old things in old ways. They should develop precise routines for such things as getting in and out of the bathtub, as a routine will lessen the chance of a fall. If done with restraint, they suggest, gambling may add excitement to life, and pornography can stimulate the sex drive. A large graph of the distance walked each day, measured by a pedometer, may be an incentive to regular exercise.

The fear of death can be best dealt with by preparing a will, making the other necessary arrangements, and then forgetting about it. Brooding about death occurs when there is too little else to do. Fears should be confronted directly with whatever action is possible. When nothing can be done, distraction may be the only answer.

Enjoying old age is doing the things one likes to do, while minimizing the imperfections brought on by aging. Doing is the best protection against depression and boredom, Skinner and Vaughan argue, and behaviorism is the science of doing.

—Terry J. Knapp

See also Aging: Biological, psychological, and sociocultural perspectives; Aging process; Death and dying; Death anxiety; Depression; Forgetfulness; Geriatrics and gerontology; Independent living; Leisure activities; Mental impairment; Psychiatry, geriatric; Safety issues; Successful aging; Vision changes and disorders.

ERIKSON, ERIK H.

BORN: June 15, 1902; Frankfurt, Germany
DIED: May 12, 1994; Harwich, Massachusetts
RELEVANT ISSUES: Culture, psychology, values, work
SIGNIFICANCE: Erikson expanded the interest of psychologists in the development of the ego and the crises that it faces periodically throughout an individual's lifetime, especially during the adult and mature years

Erik Homburger Erikson was trained as a child psychoanalyst by Anna Freud and was graduated from the Vienna Psychoanalytic Institute in 1933. He spent the remainder of his career in the United States, where he extended Freudian psychology by focusing on the ego and the varied conflicts and crises that it undergoes as the individual develops from childbirth to adolescence and throughout the decades of adulthood.

Erikson's work introduced the concepts of identity and identity crisis, ego strength, and the importance of the historical and cultural setting in understanding the individual. Thus, for Erikson, psychosocial adolescent and adult development was just as important as the early childhood psychosexual development that Sigmund Freud had described. Erikson's work is critical to the study of aging, as it advances a theory of the developmental changes that accompany the unfolding of life, including issues of psychological growth unique to old age and senescence.

EARLY LIFE AND WORK

Erikson was born of Danish parents who separated before his birth. His mother later married a German pediatrician and settled in Frankfurt, where Erikson was graduated from the Gymnasium (high school), his only formal education. He then traveled about Europe, finally settling, at the age of twenty-five, in Vienna. There he became acquainted with Sigmund Freud while serving as a tutor for a family friendly with the Freuds. His natural ability with children lead to the suggestion that he receive training in child psychoanalysis, which at the time was a field largely limited to the practice of Anna Freud, Sigmund's daughter.

Erikson held a variety of appointments during his career, changing his place of employment about every ten years. When he first arrived in the United States, he settled in Boston and became the city's first child psychoanalyst. Later he was affiliated with the Institute of Human Relations at Yale University, where he undertook field studies with several American Indian tribes. In the late 1930's, he served on the faculty of the University of California at Berkeley. He left there in 1950, after refusing to sign the required loyalty oath, and began doing clinical work with adolescents at the Austen Riggs Center in Massachusetts. In the 1960's, Erikson was Professor of Social Relations at Harvard University (one of only a few individuals without an academic degree to hold such an appointment). Following his retirement from Harvard, he was associated with Mount Zion Hospital in San Francisco, finally returning to Harvard at the Erikson Center, established in his name.

Most of Erikson's research took the form of direct observation or clinical interviews conducted in the course of therapy sessions. In the early years of his career, nearly all of his published work concerned children and youths in various cultural settings. His best-known works are *Childhood and Society* (1950), *Insight and Responsibility* (1964), *Vital Involvement in Old Age* (1986), and *Young Man Luther* (1958). This last work added greatly to the development of psychohistory, a special field that joins biography and psychoanalysis in constructing life narratives of influential individuals.

Erikson's theory of development divided the life of the individual into eight stages. Each stage represented a crisis for the ego as it confronted two dialectical alternatives or polarities, which must be delicately balanced. The crises formed the individual's personality. Ego qualities would emerge that defined the individual and that could persist throughout life. The crises could reappear as new age-related features of living were faced. The eight stages and their corresponding polarities were infancy, with trust versus mistrust; the early childhood stage, with autonomy versus doubt and shame; the play age, with initiative versus guilt; the school age, with industry versus inferiority; puberty or adolescence, with identity versus role confusion; young adulthood, with intimacy versus isolation; middle adulthood, with generativity versus stagnation; and maturity and old age, with integrity versus despair.

ERIKSON AND THE LATER DAYS OF LIFE

The latter three stages are especially relevant to issues of aging. Though they are influenced by the resolution of all the earlier stages, they present their own problems for the individual. In young adulthood, the individual resolves to merge his or her identity with that of another, so as not to remain isolated. Loving and being loved become the critical features of the developmental pattern. In middle adulthood, the individual either stagnates in self-absorption or moves toward generativity, the concern for future generations. Care now emerges as an important feature, as the individual may assume the role of parent, teacher, and care-

giver to others. The alternative is an egocentric focus on one's own activities, as though becoming a child again.

The last of Erikson's psychosocial stages deals directly with the closing decades of life and the resolution of integrity versus despair. Erikson viewed integrity as having a sense of wholeness or completeness, of being able to integrate one's failings and successes into a sense of a complete life. The alternative to integrity is despair, a regret over one's life activities and a deep fear of death. Wisdom can emerge with integrity because the individual is able to have a detached perspective of life and to live in the face of death. There is ultimately an acceptance of one's life and acceptance of the inevitable end to which it must come.

The psychosocial stages described by Erikson suggest that personality is a lifelong development process of periodic crises or challenges as succeeding decades arrive. Various life periods bring new developmental tasks, even in the final decades of life. Crises once resolved, or "balanced," can arise again, and new crises may be met with greater or lesser ego strength, depending on the resolution of prior issues.

Erikson often illustrated his concept of the human life cycle with the fictional character Isak Borg, from Ingmar Bergman's classic 1957 film *Wild Strawberries*. It is the story of a doctor in his seventies who assesses his life through reminiscences, fantasies, and recalled dreams. Erikson used the film at the close of his Harvard course and later in his writings. The film illustrated the need for "communal context" in assessing the developmental success of an individual's relationships. It showed the utility of Erikson's stages, which eventually came full circle to life's completion. Thus, for Erikson the interesting questions of psychological development did not end with the arrival of adolescence, or even adulthood.

One of Erikson's later books, *Vital Involvement in Old Age* (1986), written with Joan M. Erikson and Helen Q. Kivnick, dealt directly with old age. The book contained reflections on aging by its authors and by several dozen octogenarians who were interviewed about their life history. The participants were drawn from a study begun in the late 1920's in Berkeley, California. In the original study, the development of their children was studied, and Erikson interviewed many of the children again in the 1940's when they were teenagers. Then, the parents were studied in their later years. Erikson and his coauthors were interested in the concept of "vital involvement," defined as "a heightened awareness" that can accompany all stages of ego development, but which must in the life cycle eventually face the necessity of "disinvolvement" as brought on by aging. The interviewees provided evidence of varied solutions to these matters and of how the elderly can be "integral coworkers in community life." Erikson found that participation in relationships with extended family and grandchildren was especially valued. It brought an "enthusiasm for procreativity" but also a sense of "venerability" and the end of one's time. The life cycle in old age may come full circle as the individual once again becomes dependent on others and the issues of trust and mistrust last visited in infancy reappear.

As individuals started living longer, Erikson considered the possibility of adding a ninth stage to his cycle of life, centered on the "sense or premonition of immortality," but nothing came of the idea.

—*Terry J. Knapp*

See also Death and dying; Death anxiety; Middle age; Midlife crisis; Old age; Psychiatry, geriatric; *Wild Strawberries*; Wisdom.

FOR FURTHER INFORMATION:

Albin, M., ed. *New Directions in Psychohistory: The Adelphi Papers in Honor of Erik H. Erikson.* Lexington, Mass.: Lexington Books, 1980.

Coles, Robert. *Erik H. Erikson: The Growth of His Work.* Boston: Little, Brown, 1970.

Erikson, Erik H. *A Way of Looking at Things: Selected Papers from 1930 to 1980.* Edited by Stephen Schlein. New York: W. W. Norton, 1987.

Evans, R. I. *Dialogue with Erik Erikson.* New York: Harper & Row, 1967.

Gross, F. L. *Introducing Erik Erikson: An Invitation to His Thinking.* Lanham, Md.: University Press of America, 1987.

Roazen, P. *Erik H. Erikson: The Power and Limits of a Vision.* New York: Free Press, 1976.

Stevens, R. *Erik Erikson: An Introduction.* New York: St Martin's Press, 1983.

Wallerstein, R. S., and L. Goldberger. *Ideas and Identities: The Life and Work of Erik Erikson.* Madison, Conn.: International Universities Press, 1998.

ESTATES AND INHERITANCE

RELEVANT ISSUES: Death, family, law
SIGNIFICANCE: An estate is the aggregate of all property owned by a decedent at the time of death; an inheritance is property received from one who has died

In the United States, both the federal government and the states levy taxes on estates, but the federal tax is far greater than state inheritance tax. The Internal Revenue Code defines the taxable estate as the gross estate minus allowable deductions and exclusions. Tax considerations, therefore, are among the most important in estate planning. In order that the most substantial portion of the estate pass to the designated heirs under a will or according to the laws of intestacy if there is no will, various techniques are used to minimize taxes and maximize inheritance.

WILLS

Wills, legally enforceable documents defining in writing how a person wishes his or her property distributed after death, take effect on death and are revocable at the discretion of the testator during his or her lifetime. Wills require certain legal formalities and may vary from one state to another according to state law. Because wills are revocable, they can be amended, supplemented, condensed, or revoked in favor of a new will or living (inter vivos) trust during one's lifetime. Wills are affordable, and testators can choose what will happen to their property after death. Wills are the only document that can be used to name guardians for minor children.

There are, however, also disadvantages to wills. Wills must be probated, which is a time-consuming and often-expensive process. Probate consists of "proving" the decedent's last will (proper signature, validity, and the fact that it is the last will). If the will is determined to be in order, the estate will be distributed according to the terms of the will. If it is invalid or the decedent dies intestate, the estate will be distributed according to the state intestacy statute. Assets are not distributed until debts, fees, expenses, and federal and state taxes have been paid. Probate is avoided when the gross value of the estate is relatively small (between $5,000 and $60,000, depending on the state, in 1998).

Wills are public and can be viewed by any interested party, and their validity is dependent on state law. If the testator moves, therefore, his or her will may be inapplicable in a new state, or its intended outcome may change because of different state laws.

Trusts, especially living trusts, are the favored vehicle for older individuals with significant assets. Trusts provide privacy and flexibility. Settlors (creators of the trust) can choose their trustees and control who will manage their affairs, thereby ensuring that a court will not appoint the wrong person. If a settlor is both trustee and beneficiary of a trust and has transferred all his or her assets into the trust, there remains nothing to probate. Therefore, the trust corpus (holdings) is rapidly distributed to beneficiaries. It should be emphasized, though, that trusts are expensive to set up and manage, however beneficial they might appear.

GIFTS AND ESTATE TAXATION

Any individual is permitted to make a gift of $10,000 or its equivalent in assets to any number of individuals each year without tax. Gifts in excess of that amount incur a substantial tax. Therefore, for example, parents who wish to reduce their taxable estate and at the same time provide for their children may do so by each making a gift in the amount of $10,000 per year.

As of 1998, there was a lifetime exemption of $625,000; this was scheduled to increase to $1,000,000 in 2006. That amount may be passed tax-free. After the threshold amount is exceeded, the tax is substantial. Taxes are imposed on the true market value of the assets transferred. At the time of death, the value of all assets and property owned must be reported to the Internal Revenue Service (IRS) if the combined value exceeds a threshold amount. The value of marketable securities is determined by referring to the market prices on the date of death or at an alternate date (nine months later), whichever is lower. All real estate must be appraised, and the value of closely held business interests must be determined by experts.

In 1982, an unlimited marital deduction was instituted, meaning that almost any property transferred from one spouse to another during that person's lifetime or at death would not be subject to estate or gift tax.

JOINT OWNERSHIP AND PROBATE ESTATE

Three types of joint ownership of property exist: tenancy in common, joint tenancy, and tenancy by the entireties. Tenancy in common creates an interest whereby, upon the death of the first cotenant, one-half interest will pass by will or intestacy. Each co-owner's one-half interest is treated like individually owned property. One can sell or mortgage it, and it will pass along with individually owned property. If property is owned in joint tenancy with the right of survivorship between husband and wife, one-half of the value will be included in the estate of the first deceased regardless of who purchased the property. If the joint tenants are not spouses, a portion of the value of the property corresponding to the proportionate contribution toward the purchase of the property will be included. Record-keeping, therefore, becomes extremely important. Tenancy by the entireties is created only between husband and wife. Its operation is similar to joint tenancy with the right of survivorship in that, on the death of the first cotenant, the entire asset automatically passes to the survivor. The principal difference is that a creditor of either husband or wife cannot attach entireties property. While it is not subject to claims of creditors of either co-owner, a creditor of both husband and wife may attach the property. The nature of joint ownership of property should be clearly stated.

Only property that is owned individually can be bequeathed by will. Property that cannot be transferred by will includes life insurance, pay-on-death accounts, joint tenancy property, and retirement benefits. Property held jointly with right of survivorship will pass to the co-owner regardless of the terms of the will ("by operation of law"). Insurance proceeds will be paid to the named beneficiary in the insurance contract and will not pass under the will unless the estate is named as beneficiary. Individual retirement accounts (IRAs) and other retirement plans pass to the beneficiaries named in the document. Revocable living trust assets will not be probated. In community property states (Arizona, California, Idaho, Louisiana, Nevada, New Mexico, Texas, Washington, Wisconsin, and Puerto Rico), only 50 percent can be given because the spouse already owns the other 50 percent.

Commonly owned assets owned individually—such as real estate, stocks, bonds, cash, bank accounts, certificates of deposit, jewelry, furniture, clothing, automobiles, art work, and any debts owed by the testator or monies owed to the testator—will be included in his or her probate estate.

PROVIDING FOR SPOUSE AND CHILDREN

The testator can leave assets to the surviving spouse outright or create a marital support trust in the will naming the other spouse as beneficiary and appointing a trust advisor to help the beneficiary use the money wisely. The trustee can be given as much or little discretion as the situation warrants.

The most commonly used marital deduction trust is the qualified terminable interest property trust (Q-TIP). This trust permits the settlor to leave property in trust for the benefit of the spouse and be assured that, on the surviving spouse's death, the remaining assets will pass to beneficiaries designated by the settlor. This is especially useful if there are children from a previous marriage. If the surviving spouse is not a U.S. citizen, transfers to him or her will not qualify for the marital deduction unless they are transferred to a special trust designated for that purpose.

In 1999, in every state except Louisiana there was no legal requirement that one leave a child a testamentary bequest. If the testator intends to disinherit a child, however, this should be so stated so that a probate judge will understand that this was the testator's intent and not an oversight. This is done by leaving the child $1.00 in the will, stating the intent that the child receive no more.

Because minor children cannot own anything aside from small amounts (generally under $5,000 in most states), a property guardian can be appointed to manage the child's inheritance, leaving explicit instructions concerning the finances. This person must report annually to the probate court to prove that the money is not being squandered or misused. Often a bond must be posted, but this requirement can be waived by will. Generally, the inheritance passes outright when the child turns eighteen.

Another method by which to provide for a child is through creation of a custodian account under the Uniform Transfer to Minors Act, which permits custodial supervision of money without court review. A third method is through the creation of a trust for the child. There is no time limit on the length of time the trust remains in effect.

—*Marcia J. Weiss*

See also Death and dying; Death of parents; Income sources; Individual retirement accounts (IRAs); Trusts; Widows and widowers; Wills and bequests.

FOR FURTHER INFORMATION:

American Bar Association. *The ABA Guide to Wills and Estates.* New York: Times Books, 1995.

Bove, Alexander A., Jr. *The Complete Book of Wills and Estates.* New York: Henry Holt, 1989.

Daly, Eugene J. *Thy Will Be Done: A Guide to Wills, Taxation, and Estate Planning for Older Persons.* Buffalo, N.Y.: Prometheus Books, 1990.

Doane, Randall C., and Rebecca G. Doane. *Death and Taxes: The Complete Guide to Family Inheritance Planning.* Athens: Ohio University Press/Swallow Press, 1998.

Rottenberg, Dan. *The Inheritor's Handbook: A Definitive Guide for Beneficiaries.* Princeton, N.J.: Bloomberg Press, 1999.

Strauss, Steven D. *Ask a Lawyer: Wills and Trusts.* New York: W. W. Norton, 1998.

ESTROGEN REPLACEMENT THERAPY

RELEVANT ISSUES: Biology, health and medicine

SIGNIFICANCE: Estrogen replacement therapy is a pharmacological treatment whereby clinicians prescribe this hormone in order to replace an estrogen deficiency occurring either naturally (the menopause), medically, or surgically (total hysterectomy)

The most common use of estrogen replacement therapy is to supplement a woman's natural loss of this ovarian hormone at the menopause, when the ovaries no longer function. An adult woman's body needs estrogen for normal growth and reproduction for nearly forty years between puberty and the menopause.

Beginning at puberty, a specialized area of the brain, the hypothalamus, stimulates the pituitary gland located directly underneath to secrete a pulsatile pattern of hormones that stimulate the ovaries to produce increasing amounts of estradiol (the major estrogen) and progesterone. The monthly menstrual cycle is controlled by a well-orchestrated group of hormones from the brain and pituitary that regulate the production and secretion of estradiol and progesterone as well as egg (ovum) maturation. While the pituitary hormones are stimulating the follicles within the ovary to produce a mature ovum, estradiol and progesterone are acting on several areas of the female body. The breasts develop and prepare for potential milk production in the event of a pregnancy. The vagina thickens somewhat and produces more secretions. The inner lining of the uterus, the endometrium, is stimulated to grow by estradiol and become secretory by the combination of estradiol and progesterone. Each month, if the ovum is not fertilized, an embryo does not develop and the ovaries stop the production of estradiol and progesterone, which would be required to maintain the endometrium during pregnancy. The loss of estradiol and progesterone causes the monthly loss of the endometrium and is known as menses. This cycle is repeated nearly monthly until interrupted by pregnancy or the loss of ovarian function at the menopause.

THE BENEFITS AND RISKS OF ESTROGEN REPLACEMENT

Estradiol has many physiological roles besides its role in reproductive function and development. It aids in maintaining bone structure and thus strength by preventing the loss of calcium salts from the bone matrix. The connective tissue of the skin maintains more elasticity, and cells of the skin are exposed to more protective skin oils when estradiol is present. Estradiol provides a favorable blood lipid profile that appears to have a beneficial effect on slowing atherosclerosis and arteriosclerosis (hardening of the arteries) and thus reduces the risk of stroke and heart attack. Additionally, it may make the blood vessels themselves more resilient to the stresses of aging. This hormone may also slow the potential of developing Alzheimer's disease by a yet unknown mechanism. Similarly, estrogen may reduce the risk of developing colon cancer by nearly one-half. Estrogens, however, are not without deleterious effects, as they potentially stimulate breast and uterine cancers.

The menopause begins at approximately fifty years of age. Most women will begin having irregular monthly cycles as the ovaries lose their function, a period which can last up to five years. The loss of ovarian function at this time causes numerous signs and symptoms, which vary widely from woman to woman. A common symptom is hot flashes, in which blood vessels to the skin open rapidly, resulting in a warm, flushed feeling. Dwindling levels of estradiol also cause losses in bone mass of about 1 percent per year, which can produce osteoporosis (bone loss) and may increase the risk for fractures and of disability or even death from complications of fractures. The skin may lose some tone and advance the onset of wrinkles, and the oil-producing glands may decrease function, leaving the skin and hair less supple. For similar reasons, the vagina may become dry, making intercourse less enjoyable. Estrogen replacement therapy can reverse these signs and symptoms and may seem to be a magic solution to many women's problems. Studies beginning in the 1960's, however, began to sort out the risks and benefits of estrogen replacement therapy. Not all the results since the early studies have been so positive.

A woman's choice about estrogen replacement therapy is a complex and highly personal one. Thoughtful discussion with a health care provider is essential in making the decision to start or continue such therapy. Almost without question, estrogen replacement therapy significantly reduces osteoporosis. In fact, some postmenopausal women actually gain bone, even when beginning treatment in their seventies. Medical studies first suggested that hormone replacement therapy reduced the chance of developing cardiovascular disease or at least slowed its development. These data were well received by the medical community, as cardiovascular disease is the number one cause of death in women over sixty-five. Later studies, however, reported that women who already have cardiovascular risk factors may be at higher risk for heart attacks and strokes when they first begin therapy, which is followed by a slower, longer-term reduction in risk. Most of the early deaths in these high-risk women was the result of blood clots, which developed and may have been correlated with smoking in combination with estradiol. Overall, most women without significant cardiovascular risk factors will reduce their risk of heart disease while taking estrogen replacement therapy.

The scientific debate about whether estrogen replacement therapy increases the risk of developing breast and uterine cancer added to the complex decision of using supplementing estrogen at the time of the menopause. Most well-designed studies indicate that there may be a slight increase

Actress Valerie Harper promotes Healthy Woman, an over-the-counter soy supplement claiming to treat hot flashes and other menopausal symptoms. Some women seek natural alternatives to estrogen replacement therapy. (AP Photo/Tina Fineberg)

vorable blood lipid profile of high HDL and low LDL cholesterol helps prevent atherosclerosis and arteriosclerosis. Progesterone reduces estradiol's effect on lowering LDL-cholesterol and raising HDL-cholesterol.

The overall risk of death from heart disease, however, is still greater than the risk of dying from breast or uterine cancer. Additionally, the first studies on estrogen supplementation used higher doses than in current therapy and also showed an increase in the incidence of blood clot formation in the legs, increasing the risk of pulmonary emboli (clots in the lungs) and the potential for stroke and heart disease. More recent studies have shown that the lower doses are without such high risk. Yet, adding progesterone, which reduces the risk of breast and uterine cancer, dampens the favorable blood lipid response and has little effect on blood clot formation.

PHARMACOLOGICAL AND NONPHARMACOLOGICAL OPTIONS

Several drugs and combinations are available for patients wishing to take estrogen replacement therapy. The first choice is a hormone extracted from the urine of pregnant horses, conjugated equine estrogen. This drug essentially mimics estradiol. If the woman has not had a hysterectomy and wants to reduce the risk of endometrial cancer, progesterone is typically added, such as medroxyprogesterone. Conjugated equine estrogen and medroxyprogesterone can be given together daily, virtually eliminating menses, or can be given in a cyclical fashion over a month to mimic the premenopausal menstrual cycle, causing monthly bleeding.

Newer drugs have been introduced that can be used in estrogen replacement therapy, but with different results. For example, tamoxifen blocks most of the effects of estradiol on breast tissue, reducing the possibility of breast cancer, and may protect against osteoporosis, but it may also increase the risk of uterine cancer. Raloxifene preserves bone mass, reduces the risk of breast and uterine cancers, increases HDL cholesterol, and lowers LDL-cholesterol, but it may actually make hot flashes worse.

in breast and uterine cancer risk but that the cancers tended to be less aggressive (more easily treated) and that the addition of progesterone to the therapy may negate some of the risk.

The addition of progesterone, however, also seems to remove some of the protective effect of estrogen replacement therapy for cardiovascular disease. Postmenopausal women taking estrogen replacement therapy have elevated levels of high-density lipoprotein (HDL) cholesterol, which is protective against heart disease, and reduced levels of low-density lipoprotein (LDL) cholesterol, which increases one's risk of a heart attack. This fa-

All patients, whether they chose to use estrogen replacement therapy for medical or personal reasons, can use nonpharmacological methods to aid their health. Exercise, particularly weight-bearing exercise such as walking, can reduce the risk of osteoporosis and cardiovascular disease and may even reduce hot flashes when combined with a healthy diet. Extra calcium and a diet high in fruits and vegetables may also reduce the risk of death without the aid of estrogen replacement. Some researchers recommend the high consumption of soy products, which may act as a natural estrogen.

In the light of ongoing studies, several common results have been supported over time, making the choice of estrogen replacement therapy less confusing. The choice must be individualized, and benefits versus risks must be weighed carefully by a well-informed patient in consultation with her health care provider. —*Matthew Berria*

See also Arteriosclerosis; Beauty; Bone changes and disorders; Breast cancer; Cancer; *Change: Women, Aging, and the Menopause, The*; Cholesterol; Fractures and broken bones; Heart attacks; Heart disease; Menopause; Osteoporosis; Reproductive changes, disabilities, and dysfunctions; Skin changes and disorders; Strokes; Women and aging; Wrinkles.

FOR FURTHER INFORMATION:

Carey, Charles F., Hans H. Lee, and Keith F. Woeltje, eds. *The Washington Manual of Medical Therapeutics.* 29th ed. Philadelphia: Lippincott-Raven, 1998.

Fitzgerald, Paul A. "Endocrinology." In *Current Medical Diagnosis and Treatment,* edited by Lawrence M. Tierney, Jr., Stephen J. McPhee, and Maxine A. Papadakis. 38th ed. Stamford, Conn.: Appleton and Lange, 1999.

"Menopause: A Guide to Smart Choices." *Consumer Reports* 50 (January, 1999).

Smith, Kristen E., and Howard L. Judd. "Menopause and Postmenopause." In *Current Obstetric and Gynecologic Diagnosis and Treatment,* edited by Alan H. DeCherney and Martin L. Pernoll. 8th ed. Stamford, Conn.: Appleton and Lange, 1994.

EUTHANASIA

RELEVANT ISSUES: Death, family, health and medicine, law, values

SIGNIFICANCE: With the continuing development of the technological means to keep elderly, terminally ill patients alive, euthanasia has become an increasingly important and volatile issue

Medical technology has made it possible to maintain or prolong life through machines that can keep the heart beating, the blood circulating, and the lungs functioning, even when there is little or no hope of recovery. Such technological advances have often made it difficult to determine just when a person is "dead."

Death has been defined by various criteria, including when the heart and respiration cease (traditional definition), when all electrical activity in the brain ceases (whole-brain death), when all higher brain functions are lost (irreversible coma), and when there is loss of the ability to perform actions necessary or essential to personal identity, such as reasoning, interacting with others, and making choices (loss of personhood). How these concepts are specifically applied, and by whom, are matters of debate. If death is circumvented through medical intervention that prevents completion of what has been termed the "dying trajectory," or if a person's dying is extended or unbearably painful, euthanasia presents an alternative.

FORMS OF EUTHANASIA

"Euthanasia" is a word derived from Greek meaning "the good death." It is often referred to as "mercy killing," a reference to an active form of euthanasia that implies a deliberate intervention to end a patient's life when the patient is terminally ill or in unbearable pain. Passive euthanasia, however, simply means withholding the treatment that keeps the patient alive, including life support, and allowing the patient to die. Assisted suicide occurs when physicians, family members, or friends provide the means or comply with a patient's instructions for assistance to end his or her life. In addition to these concepts, other considerations include whether the decision is voluntary (the patient requests the discontinuation of treatment), nonvoluntary (the patient is unable to make his or her own decision), or involuntary (the patient does not wish to cease treatment); how and under what conditions the decision is made; and who makes it.

Although active euthanasia is against the law and assisted suicide, made prominent by Jack Kevorkian, is hotly debated, passive euthanasia has long been accepted by society and employed by physicians. This acceptance has been reinforced through the movement for patients' rights to refuse treatment as embodied in advance directives, such as living wills and the durable power of attorney for health care. A living will can take various forms depending on whether it is written by a legal professional, written by an individual, or issued by an organization; in all cases, however, the text is generally similar. The individual, before the fact of incapacitation, seeks to ensure that under specific conditions, such as when the medical prognosis states that there is no hope of recovery from an illness or condition, extraordinary treatment will not be used to keep the patient alive. Even a living will, however, does not guarantee that a patient's wishes will be respected. Some states have laws that contain strict requirements for withdrawal of treatment. It is also not always clear whether artificial feeding and hydration are to be considered medical treatments or ordinary maintenance care.

Durable power of attorney for health care is a legal document through which the individual appoints a surrogate decision maker in the event that the patient is no longer able to make his or her own decision. This document is considered by many legal experts to be stronger and more flexible than the living will, since it names an advocate who may legally represent the wishes of the patient. Even so, the advocate may be unavailable or unable to represent the patient at the time that it becomes necessary.

By 1999, most states had passed "right-to-die" acts stating the conditions under which treatment may be withheld from an individual. The first case that brought the problem into focus was that of a young woman named Karen Quinlan. In 1975, Quinlan lapsed into a coma from causes never completely determined and was placed on life support. Three and a half months later, her condition was pronounced hopeless by her physician; her family, with support of their priest and physicians, agreed to take her off the respirator. One doctor then changed his mind, and a long legal battle ensued. More than ten months passed before the court finally ruled that if the physicians agreed that Quinlan would never recover or emerge from

the coma, the respirator could be disconnected. When the respirator was removed, Quinlan continued to breathe. It was not until ten years later, having been placed in a nursing home in a vegetative state, that she died at age thirty-one.

In 1990, a young woman named Nancy Cruzan suffered irreversible brain damage in an automobile accident. The U.S. Supreme Court upheld the right of a competent patient to refuse treatment, including artificial nutrition and hydration. Since the patient was not on a respirator, the issue was whether being fed through a tube is "extraordinary treatment." The Court stated that artificial nutrition and hydration may be discontinued if it is determined that the patient would wish it. They also endorsed the use of advance directives. However, the ruling allowed individual states to require high standards in determining whether the actions of a surrogate decision maker actually reflect the wishes of the patient. The ruling also left procedural issues to be determined by the states. This decision reflects the concern over abuse when patients are incompetent or when decisions do not conform with their wishes.

ISSUES FOR THE ELDERLY

As a consequence of the baby-boom generation reaching retirement age, the number of individuals over sixty-five years of age was expected to grow to more than 22 percent of the U.S. population by the year 2050. The percentage of people eighty-five years of age and over was also expected to grow, from 1.3 percent in 1990 to 5.1 percent by 2050. Such a large population of elderly people will further increase the importance of questions concerning the use of technology to extend life, the high cost of medical care, patients' wishes concerning their own treatment, and euthanasia itself.

In the light of financial insolvency or expense to family and society, many elderly people are concerned that policy decisions might be made that will deny medical care or that will place pressure on elderly patients to refuse care. As the elderly population grows, pressures to withhold care may increase as well. Ethicists have suggested that it may be necessary for society to determine priorities for care and treatment based upon various criteria, including age. Many elderly people are also concerned, however, that in some cases their right to make the decision to discontinue care, for whatever reason, may also be undermined. This may occur because of family opposition or physician noncooperation in respecting the wishes of the patient, even when the patient is judged to be of sound mind.

Mental competency, particularly in the case of the elderly, is another important issue. A decision to refuse treatment or end one's life generally requires that the individual be of sound mind and legally competent. Since many elderly people, especially those eighty-five years or older, may often be labeled "forgetful" or "senile," the question of their competency is a delicate one. Such dilemmas may be solved, in part, through the implementation of improved advance directives.

Dr. Jack Kevorkian leaves a Michigan police station in 1998 with some of his euthanasia devices that had been seized after an assisted suicide. (AP Photo/Richard Sheinwald)

PERSONAL AUTONOMY AND SUICIDE

The strong American value of personal autonomy and fear of being involuntarily subjected to an extended period of pain and dying have essentially driven the acceptance of passive euthanasia and the more controversial alternatives such as physician-assisted suicide. The desire for personal control is exemplified in the Patient Self-Determination Act (PSDA), which went into effect in 1991. Hospitals, nursing homes, and other health care facilities are required by law to advise all admitted patients of their right to refuse medical treatment and inform them that they may sign advance directives.

In spite of this law—and in spite of the fact that opinion polls have revealed that most American adults would not want to be kept on life support if there was no hope of recovery—few people, including those over sixty-five years of age, have completed advance directives. Part of the explanation for this may lie in the fact that physicians themselves remain ambivalent about advance directives. Although they generally tend to favor allowing patients to make their own decisions about such treatment, few physicians actually discuss these issues with their patients. In addition, it has been shown that doctors often disregard such directives and provide care against their patients' wishes. The PSDA, then, is often not sufficient to guarantee that a patient's wishes will be honored. Other reasons for not signing an advance directive may include the possibility of changing one's mind, the idea that there may be unforeseen circumstances, or the tendency to avoid the topic of death and dying in general.

The continuing debate concerning the use of both passive and active euthanasia in cases of terminal illness and the prospect of publicly supported physician-assisted suicide have caused physicians to rethink the issue of care at the end of life. Since physicians generally reject such acts as physician-assisted suicide and view them as morally and ethically wrong, the question of the responsibility of physicians to their dying patients has become more pressing.

The suicide rate among the elderly began to increase during the 1980's; by the 1990's, 17 to 25 percent of all suicides were committed by those aged sixty-five or older. Most people who seek to end their lives do so because of unbearable or unceasing pain. Physicians have been trained not only to fight to preserve life but also to be cautious in prescribing pain medications that might result in addiction or hasten the patient's death. Doctors recognize that much more could be done to ease suffering and that the argument against addiction has no substance and little meaning when dealing with a terminal patient. By doing more to reassure patients, to respect their rights to refuse extraordinary care, and to ease pain and suffering, it is suggested that far fewer patients would choose to commit suicide with or without the physician's assistance.

The Hospice Movement

For those individuals who choose to refuse treatment and wish to die without medical intervention, hospice provides support and care. Begun in England in the late 1960's, the modern hospice movement promotes the philosophy that dying patients and their families should receive love and support and that patients should remain in their own homes when possible. Patients receive necessary medical maintenance care, including pain medication, but no medical intervention to prolong their dying. Hospice personnel attempt to provide the maximum quality of life possible for patient and family.

Physicians, many of whom rejected the idea of refusal of care and acceptance of death, were initially nonsupportive of the idea and practice of the hospice alternative. An increasing number of physicians, however, have begun to recognize the value of advance directives and legal issues involved in patients' rights and have become more supportive of hospice. Right-to-die legislation does not force the physician to withhold treatment from a patient if the patient refuses it, and the physician may feel morally bound not to do so. However, the physician, in most cases, must then find another physician who is willing to abide by the patient's wishes. —*Martha Oehmke Loustaunau*

See also Death and dying; Death anxiety; Durable power of attorney; Health care; Hospice; Living wills; Medications; Suicide; Terminal illness.

For Further Information:

Arras, John D., and Bonnie Steinbock. *Ethical Issues in Modern Medicine.* 5th ed. Mountain View, Calif.: Mayfield, 1998. Part 2, "Defining Death, Forgoing Life-Sustaining Treatment, and Euthanasia," contains a series of articles addressing such issues as defining death, competency, advance directives, and physician-assisted suicide. Includes cases and commentary.

Hoefler, James M., with Brian E. Kamoie. *Deathright: Culture, Medicine, Politics, and the Right to Die.* Boulder, Colo.: Westview Press, 1994. Explores related social, cultural, and legal issues involving euthanasia in the United States.

Roberts, Carolyn S., and Martha Gorman. *Euthanasia: A Reference Handbook.* Santa Barbara, Calif.: ABC-Clio, 1996. Addresses various definitions and moral perspectives; includes information on assisted suicide.

Thornton, James E., and Earl R. Winkler, eds. *Ethics and Aging: The Right to Live, The Right to Die.* Vancouver: University of British Columbia Press, 1988. This volume deals with issues of self-determination and incorporates multidisciplinary viewpoints on involvement of the elderly in policy and research that affect them. A bibliography on aging and ethics is included.

Urofsky, Melvin, and Philip E. Urofsky, *The Right to Die.* Vols. 1 and 2. New York: Garland, 1996. An anthology of scholarly articles covering laws and legislation, as well as moral and ethical issues, surrounding the right to die.

Executive Order 11141

Date: Signed into law on February 12, 1964
Relevant issues: Economics, law, work
Significance: This executive order established the first formal federal prohibition on certain kinds of age discrimination and set the political and legal stage for further governmental support for equal opportunity for aging persons

In March, 1963, as part of the struggle to achieve civil rights legislation, President John F. Kennedy issued a memorandum reaffirming the federal government's policy of hiring and promoting employees on the basis of merit alone and assuring that older people are not discriminated against on the basis of age. After President Kennedy's death, President Lyndon B. Johnson continued the civil rights struggle. On February 12, 1964, just three months after becoming president, Johnson issued Executive Order 11141, *Declaring a Public Policy Against Discrimination on the Basis of Age*. The order prohibited age discrimination in employment by federal contractors and subcontractors. Firms performing contract work for the United States government were prohibited from discriminating in hiring, promoting, or discharging employees on the basis of age unless pursuant to a statutory requirement or retirement plan.

Although limited in scope to federal contractors—at that time there was no statutory authority for a more extensive order—President Johnson's order was significant because it ensured that the moral and political power of the government would work against age discrimination. There was an immense amount of federal contracting, and many older people were promoted, hired, or retained in their jobs longer than they would have been without the order. Many remained employed on projects other than those contracted by the federal government. The order and its associated regulations also provided Congress with a model for dealing with age discrimination when civil rights acts were later passed. Age discrimination prohibitions were later applied to all public and private employment that the federal government had the power to reach.   —*Robert Jacobs*

See also Advocacy; Age discrimination; Age Discrimination Act of 1975; Age Discrimination in Employment Act of 1967; Employment; Politics.

EXERCISE AND FITNESS

RELEVANT ISSUES: Biology, health and medicine

SIGNIFICANCE: Regular exercise contributes to successful aging by enabling older adults to maintain an independent lifestyle while reducing the risks associated with cardiovascular disease, hypertension, osteoporosis, and sarcopenia

The physiological deterioration commonly associated with aging is not entirely caused by the aging process; it is also caused by the physical inactivity that often accompanies aging. In the United States, it has been reported that adults over age fifty are the most sedentary members of the population. By the year 2030, it has been predicted that 22 percent of the population will be over age sixty-

five. Increased physical activity is a frequently suggested mechanism for reducing the rising health care costs that accompany cardiovascular disease and deterioration of the musculoskeletal system. Even so, 50 percent of men and 70 percent of women over age sixty-five are not participating in enough regular exercise to have a sufficient impact on their health.

Four general components collectively represent physical fitness: cardiorespiratory endurance (aerobic capacity), anaerobic power, muscular strength and endurance, and body composition. All these components are susceptible to decline with aging; however, the magnitude of this decline is dependent upon the extent of physical inactivity and other health factors.

AEROBIC CAPACITY

Aerobic capacity refers to the body's ability to maximally transport and utilize oxygen to the cells (maximal volume of oxygen consumed, or VO_2max). The body requires a higher volume of oxygen (VO_2) to sustain increased magnitudes of exercise. Aerobic capacity declines with aging because of a cumulative effect of age-related functional changes in the heart as well as muscle mass loss caused by disuse or disease. The higher the VO_2max value (measured in milliliters of oxygen used per kilogram of body weight per minute, or ml/kg/min), the greater the person's aerobic capacity, or aerobic fitness. A higher aerobic capacity will allow an individual to exercise more comfortably and will also permit the older individual to complete activities of daily living without fatigue. Thus, functional ability is improved when aerobic fitness is improved.

Up to age thirty, VO_2max declines about 1 percent per year. Once adults reach middle age, the loss of VO_2max is accelerated unless regular aerobic exercise is undertaken. Between forty-five and fifty-five years of age, VO_2max will be lost at a rate of 9 to 15 percent. Other accelerated losses occur between the ages of sixty-five to seventy-five and from seventy-five to eighty-five years of age. However, regular participation in aerobic exercise can slow or even reverse this decline. When middle-aged or older individuals participate regularly in aerobic exercise, they can expect a 10 to 25 percent improvement in VO_2max. This can mean the difference between being functionally impaired, on one hand, and gaining back independent-living skills and sports participation, on the other. Research reports on sixty-year-old endurance athletes have shown their VO₂max values to be above the values for some twenty-year-olds. For men over fifty years of age, "good" VO₂max values would be above 35 ml/kg/min; good VO₂max values for women over fifty would be above 29 ml/kg/min. VO₂max values below 20 ml/kg/min for either gender would indicate severe functional impairment.

Individuals can have their aerobic capacities determined with an exercise stress test administered by a team of medical professionals, including a cardiologist, a nurse, and an exercise physiologist. An aerobic exercise training program that elicits 50 to 70 percent of one's VO₂max would be sufficient to improve an older individual's aerobic capacity. Examples of aerobic exercise are walking, swimming, cycling, skiing, and dancing. Exercise of moderate intensity—enough to cause an increase in breathing and heart rate but not so much that it prevents one from being able to carry on a conversation—is sufficient for most people to gain health benefits. The experience of pain is a cue to stop exercise and reevaluate the exercise intensity level.

The Cardiovascular and Respiratory Systems

The primary purpose of the cardiovascular and respiratory or pulmonary systems (also referred to collectively as the cardiopulmonary or cardio-respiratory system) is to deliver oxygen and nutrients to the tissues while removing carbon dioxide and waste products from the tissues.

With aging, lung tissue loses elasticity, the chest wall becomes more rigid, and respiratory muscle strength is lost. This causes a loss of ventilatory (breathing) efficiency, making the mechanics of breathing harder for the aged. With exercise, the demand for more oxygen requires more frequent and deeper breaths. Since the aged pulmonary system is compromised, pulmonary ventilation is decreased during maximal exercise as well as during recovery after exercise. Even with aging limitations, in the absence of pulmonary disease, the resting tissues still have an adequate oxygen supply to carry out daily functional and recreational activities. The oxygen deficit and higher respiratory work is not noticed until vigorous exercise puts a

demand on the system for more oxygen, challenging the ventilatory capacity of the lungs. Although the total amount of blood flow increases as aerobic capacity increases, this does not result in an improvement in gaseous diffusion in the aged. In fact, gas exchange of oxygen and carbon dioxide in the tissues decreases with aging, and exercise training appears to have little impact on this function. On the other hand, forced vital capacity (FVC), the maximum amount of air that can be expelled after a maximal inhalation, is one of the few pulmonary volumes influenced by both aging and exercise training. With aging, FVC declines approximately 4 to 5 percent per decade in the average individual. However, research studies that tracked aerobically trained individuals over twenty or more years found that their FVCs at age forty-five were the same as their FVCs at age twenty. This maintenance may be because of the mechanical stressing of the respiratory muscles afforded by regular aerobic exercise.

As with the pulmonary system, resting cardiovascular function experiences only moderate changes, whereas the cardiovascular response during exercise declines substantially with aging. The major reason that maximal aerobic capacity declines with aging is because of the decrease in maximal heart rate. Maximal heart rate (the highest heart rate attainable) declines approximately 6 percent per decade. Using the mathematical formula to estimate maximal heart rate (220 minus age equals heart rate in beats per minute), it can be seen that the estimated maximal heart rate of a seventy-year-old (150 beats per minute) is significantly less than that of a twenty-year-old (200 beats per minute). Heart rate is under the control of both the parasympathetic and sympathetic nervous systems. The parasympathetic nervous system is responsible for keeping the heart rate lower at rest. The sympathetic nervous system takes over during exercise so that heart rate can be increased in order to meet the increased oxygen demand. The decline in maximal heart rate is caused by the aging heart becoming less sensitive to sympathetic nervous system stimulation, thereby decreasing the heart's maximal contractile capabilities. This results in the inability of the heart to attain the higher maximal values that were possible during youth. No amount of exercise training can alter this. Submaximal exercise is also more strenuous for an older adult. Exercise sessions that were once easy during youth cause higher heart rates and longer recovery times when one is older. This reflects the heightened need of the aging heart to work harder in order to meet the increased oxygen demands of the exercising tissues.

Regular exercise participation lowers resting heart rate (the number of times the heart beats per minute) and improves stroke volume (the volume of blood ejected with each beat of the heart) in both the young and the old. Even though cardiac contractility and total blood volume in older individuals is less and the ventricular walls are less compliant, regular aerobic exercise training increases total blood volume and tone of the peripheral vessels, thereby reducing vascular resistance and increasing the volume of blood flow back to the heart. This enables the heart to eject more blood with each beat. In aerobically trained individuals, stroke volume is improved not only during exercise but also at rest. The lower resting heart rates commonly seen in trained individuals is partially caused by the improved stroke volume. Since the heart is able to deliver more blood with each beat of the heart, the heart does not need to work as hard to deliver oxygen. In addition, regular aerobic exercise enhances the heart's parasympathetic activity. Therefore, the combined effect of improved parasympathetic activity and improved stroke volume explains the bradycardia (a heart rate below 60 beats per minute) commonly observed in healthy, aerobically trained individuals.

Even though the cardiovascular parameters that determine aerobic fitness all decline with the aging process, participation in regular aerobic exercise has been shown to improve maximal stroke volume and cardiac output (the volume of blood pumped by the heart each minute, equal to heart rate minus stroke volume) by as much as 25 percent. Maximal cardiac output is increased because of the increase in stroke volume, since maximal heart rate does not increase. The types of exercise training employed, as well as the person's initial level of fitness, influences the magnitudes of these increases. Aerobic exercise, not strength training, is the type of exercise required to improve cardiovascular function. Those who are more severely deconditioned will be able to accomplish greater gains simply because they have more room for improvement.

Aerobic Exercise and Heat

Exercising in the heat places additional demands on the cardiovascular system for both young and old; however, there is no consensus as to whether thermoregulatory demands are heightened in the older individual. There is no difference in internal temperature between the young and old when exercising in the heat, nor is heat acclimatization any different. Some research has shown that cardiac outputs are lower during exercise in the heat in older individuals in comparison to younger individuals, perhaps because of greater exercise-induced reductions in plasma volume. Other research suggests that well-conditioned older and younger men have similar thermoregulatory responses. Therefore, physical deconditioning and lack of generalized heat acclimatization, rather than the aging process per se, are most likely the causes for the decreased thermoregulatory responses often observed in the aged.

The standard recommendation for exercising in the heat is to reduce the exercise intensity when the air temperature exceeds 80 degrees Fahrenheit and the relative humidity exceeds 80 percent. To compensate for fluid loss from sweating, water should be drunk before, during, and after exercising in the heat. A general rule of thumb is to drink 6 to 8 ounces of water every 15 to 30 minutes whether one feels thirsty or not. This is especially relevant for older adults who often have a blunted thirst sensation.

Anaerobic Power

Converse to aerobic capacity, anaerobic power is not dependent upon the replenishment of oxygen to the cells. The fuel source used to power anaerobic movement is retrieved from energy stores located within the cell. Quick, explosive movements characterize anaerobic activities. In most athletic events, the ability to generate anaerobic power will have a direct effect upon athletic success. It is also important in daily living when one encounters an emergency situation demanding a quick, powerful response. A few examples of anaerobic activities include sprinting, throwing the discus, and lifting heavy objects.

The sports-related "anaerobic response" includes a sharp rise in lactic acid accumulation in the muscles and blood, a sharp increase in pulmonary ventilation, and a drop in the blood pH, giving rise to a more acidic state. Lactic acid accumulates with high-intensity or maximal exercise because of a combination of an increased production rate and a reduced rate of removal. The recruitment of fast-twitch muscle fibers (those fibers responsible for performing quick, explosive movements) also triggers the production of lactic acid. In addition, the need for more oxygen at maximal exercise stimulates the metabolic pathways to speed up. This results in an increase in glycolysis. Glycolysis is the energy pathway responsible for the initial breakdown of blood glucose (blood sugar) so that energy (adenosine triphosphate, or ATP) can be created to perform work. At the end of glycolysis, if enough oxygen is not available, excess lactic acid will be formed. An abundance of lactic acid quickly causes muscle fatigue, and exercise soon stops.

Data on aging suggest that anaerobic power, mechanical power, and mechanical capacity peak by age forty, then decline thereafter. Several factors may explain this decline. First, older adults have reduced blood glucose stores (glycogen) in the muscle tissue, which results in a decrease in glycolysis. A decrease in glycolysis will decrease energy production. Second, with aging, fewer fast-twitch muscle fibers are available because of atrophy (shrinkage from disuse). Third, the enzyme lactate dehydrogenase (LDH), which is responsible for lactic acid production when fast-twitch muscle fibers are activated, decreases with aging. Even though the anaerobic processes decline with aging, participation in anaerobic-type activities is still possible as long as the health and fitness status of the older adult is carefully considered.

THE NERVOUS AND MUSCULOSKELETAL SYSTEMS

With aging, the nervous system is unable to receive, process, and transmit messages as quickly as it did in youth. The clinical outcome is slower reaction and movement times. This is an important issue, as many aspects of functional independence require an individual to be able to react quickly in certain situations to prevent potential injury, such as when driving a car or regaining one's balance to prevent a fall. Older individuals who exercise regularly have demonstrated better reaction times, balance, and coordination in comparison to their sedentary peers. Research investigating older adults who play tennis regularly has demonstrated that active older adults can maintain and perhaps improve their motor skills with continued use. Blood flow to the brain also increases during exercise. Short-term, immediate improvements in performance of memory tasks have been demonstrated immediately following aerobic exercise. Whether there is a long-term increase in cerebral blood flow because of regular exercise participation is a question subject to continued research.

Beginning in middle age, muscular strength declines because of a combination of factors, such as muscle mass loss, decreased motor unit activation, and a decreased ability of the muscles to contract forcefully. This decline is selective as well, with some muscle groups losing substantially more strength than others. For instance, leg and trunk muscle strength appears to decline at a faster rate than arm strength. The decline in muscle mass occurs in phases. From twenty-five to fifty years of age, only about 10 percent of muscle mass is lost. However, by

---

Exercise Guidelines for Older Adults

Aerobic Training:
Minimum of 3 days a week, working up to 5-6 days a week
20 to 40 minutes per session
Moderate intensity (one should be able to talk at same time)
Adapt the program to individual needs
Perform weightbearing activities, if possible

Strength Training:
2 or 3 times a week, with 24 to 48 hours of rest between sessions
Exercise all the muscle groups at 50% to 70% of maximum ability
Complete 8 to 12 repetitions for each muscle group targeted
Gradually increase the weight intensity
Never hold the breath
Include flexibility and balance exercises
Step 1: Use own body weight as resistance, no external devices used
Step 2: Try toning with rubber exercise bands
Step 3: Add wrist and ankle weights
Step 4: Use handheld weights (if no hypertension or heart problems)
Step 5: Try strength training machines

Membership in a gym can motivate some middle-aged people to combat the physical declines that accompany aging, such as shifts in body composition and bone loss. (James L. Shaffer)

age eighty, almost 40 percent of muscle mass is lost because of atrophy. This "wasting away" of muscle tissue commonly seen in the elderly is known as sarcopenia. Weakened respiratory muscles will result in limited aerobic capabilities. Weakened lower-extremity muscles give rise to balance problems and increased risk for falls. Insufficient strength to carry out activities of daily living or functional tasks results in a loss of independent living. Although the age-related loss of muscle mass and strength cannot be totally eliminated, it can be reduced. Aging does not impair the ability of skeletal muscles to respond to exercise training.

Progressive strength training programs have demonstrated that older adults can achieve gains in muscle mass (hypertrophy) and muscle strength similar to what has been observed in young individuals.

Exercise has been shown to be beneficial in reducing bone mass loss (osteoporosis). Both weight-bearing aerobic training and strength training have been found to be beneficial in improving bone mass. However, the modest improvements shown to occur with bone mass because of exercise conditioning is not great enough to prevent a fracture caused by a fall. Rather, exercise training will help to reduce the risk of falls by strengthening the ambulatory musculature. Research studies indicate that aerobic training and strength training improve neuromuscular functioning, gait, and balance, all of which are important variables in the risk profile for falls.

Psychosocial Benefits of Exercise

Psychological well-being includes components such as self-esteem, self-efficacy, depression, and anxiety. The majority of research studies investigating these factors in older individuals agree that participation in regular exercise is associated with improved psychological well-being. The benefits are greater and more consistent if the individual participates in an exercise program for at least ten weeks. Either aerobic training or strength training will work well, but very light or very vigorous exercise is not as effective as moderate-intensity exercise.

It is often cited that older individuals benefit from group activities—group interactions alleviate feelings of loneliness often encountered with aging. While this may be true for some, home-based exercise may be preferable to the class setting for certain groups of older adults. Many older adults remain very active and are unable to fit a regularly scheduled exercise class into their own tight schedule. Others are unable to get to the exercise site because of transportation problems or physical disabilities but are still capable of performing some type of exercise or physical activity at home. A safe, moderately paced home program would better meet their needs.

Risk Factors for Heart Disease and Diabetes

It has been demonstrated that participation in regular exercise can assist with weight management and body-fat reduction, lower blood pressure for those with mild hypertension (elevated blood pressure), reduce blood triglyceride and low-density lipoproteins (LDL, or "bad cholesterol"), and improve high-density lipoprotein levels (HDL, or "good cholesterol"). Both aerobic and strength training programs can promote a loss of calories and therefore reduce fat deposits and encourage muscle maintenance or growth throughout the life span. However, only aerobic training has been proven to be effective in improving the lipoprotein profiles and lowering blood pressure in older individuals.

The risk of glucose intolerance increases as one ages because of insulin resistance. "Glucose intolerance" is a

Elderly individuals may find low-impact exercise, such as swimming, to be a safer and easier way to stay fit. (Ben Klaffke)

term used to describe the body's inability to regulate its glucose (blood sugar) level. This causes the blood glucose level to be chronically elevated, which can lead to diabetes. Insulin is a hormone that helps to regulate blood glucose levels. It is released when the blood glucose levels are elevated, such as after eating a meal or during high-intensity exercise. Therefore, the role of insulin is to reduce the blood glucose level. However, sometimes the body cannot utilize its insulin properly. This creates a condition known as insulin resistance. The result is an overload of blood glucose in the system, which again predisposes the individual to diabetes. Physical inactivity and obesity compound the problem. Regular participation in either aerobic exercise or strength training have been shown to be equally effective for improving glucose balance and the body's ability to use insulin in older adults.

MEDICATIONS AND THE PERCEPTION OF EXERCISE INTENSITY

Older adults often take several different types of medications to treat a variety of health problems. Of all the medications, beta-blockers are among the most widely prescribed. Beta-blockers are used to treat hypertension, anxiety, and heart disease. As the name suggests, these drugs block beta-receptors in the sympathetic nervous system. Among other functions, beta receptors stimulate the heart to contract and directly influence heart rate. If this action is blocked, the heart rate response will be lowered, an action necessary to reduce the workload of a diseased heart. Beta-blockers can also cause vasodilation of blood vessels, an action important for controlling hypertension. However, if an individual is going to exercise and needs to maintain his or her exercise level in the "moderate" range, heart rate will not be able to be used as an intensity index because the heart rate response will be altered by the drug. Therefore, a person will need to regulate exercise intensity based upon his or her perception of how hard the exercise feels. Perceived exertion has been shown to closely reflect the workload of the heart. The simplest advice that can be given to individuals for keeping track of exercise intensity level is the instruction to be able to "walk and talk at the same time." This eliminates the need to take heart rate measurements during exercise.

EXERCISE BENEFITS, RISKS, AND GUIDELINES

There are many exercise options available for the older adult, depending on specific goals and health status. Even though exercise is associated with a variety of health benefits, it is also associated with such health risks as worsening existing medical problems, muscle and joint injuries, and, in some cases, heart attack. Therefore, exercise programs should be designed to maximize the benefits and minimize the potential risks.

Regardless of age, the Report of the Surgeon General recommends that everyone should participate in moderate exercise for at least thirty minutes on all or most days of the week for optimal health and fitness. This should be accomplished gradually. If one's goal is to improve aerobic fitness, blood pressure, cholesterol level, mood, or glucose tolerance or to reduce body fat, moderate aerobic exercise should be done at least three times per week. This requires activities that are rhythmic in nature, involve the use of larger muscle groups, and can be sustained for at least fifteen to twenty continuous minutes. If the goal is to increase muscle mass, muscular endurance, or strength, then a well-rounded strength-training program should be done twice per week, with each session followed by at least one day of rest. If the goal is to maintain or improve bone mass, either weight-bearing aerobic exercise or resistance training could be used. The ideal exercise program includes both aerobic training and strength training.

A healthy older individual can begin a light to moderate exercise program without the need for a medical examination or clinical exercise test. However, if the individual has risk factors for heart disease, is taking medications, or has any medical concerns, he or she should consult with a physician to determine a safe level of exercise participation.

—*Bonita L. Marks*

See also Balance disorders; Cholesterol; Diabetes; Fractures and broken bones; Heart changes and disorders; Hypertension; Medications; Mobility problems; Osteoporosis; Reaction time; Respiratory changes and disorders; Safety issues; Sarcopenia; Sports participation; Temperature regulation and sensitivity.

FOR FURTHER INFORMATION:

American College of Sports Medicine. *ACSM Fitness Book*. Edited by Susan M. Puhl, Madeline

Paternostro-Bayles, and Barry Franklin. 2d ed. Champaign, Ill.: Human Kinetics, 1998. A basic book written by academic and clinical professionals intended to guide adults who wish to begin a low-intensity exercise program.

Ettinger, Walter H., Brenda S. Mitchell, and Steven N. Blair. *Fitness After Fifty*. St. Louis: Beverly Cracom, 1996. A "how-to" book written by experts in the field of aging and epidemiology for middle-aged and older individuals desiring to become physically active.

Hurley, Ben F., and James M. Hagberg. "Optimizing Health in Older Persons: Aerobic or Strength Training?" In *Exercise and Sport Science Reviews*, edited by John O. Hollszy. American College of Sports Medicine Series 26. Baltimore: Williams & Wilkins, 1998. This chapter in a collection of exercise-related papers reviews the facts known about the effects of aerobic exercise and strength training on the physiological processes in the older adult.

Plowman, Sharon A., and Denise L. Smith. *Exercise Physiology for Health, Fitness, and Performance*. Boston: Allyn & Bacon, 1997. An undergraduate textbook in exercise physiology with a clinical perspective and unique integration of the aging response to exercise.

Powers, Scott K., and Edward T. Howley. *Exercise Physiology: Theory and Application to Fitness and Performance*. 3d ed. Chicago: Brown & Benchmark, 1997. An excellent upper-level undergraduate or lower-level graduate textbook on the physiology of exercise.

Rowe, John W., and Robert L. Kahn. *Successful Aging*. New York: Pantheon Books, 1998. A summary of research results dedicated to determining the effects of aging on the body and maximizing health in older individuals; written for the layperson by renowned gerontologists.

Spirduso, Waneen W. *Physical Dimensions of Aging*. Champaign, Ill.: Human Kinetics, 1995. A comprehensive textbook addressing all of the physiological aspects of the aging individual.

U.S. Department of Health and Human Services. *Physical Activity and Health: Report of the Surgeon General, Physical Activity and Health*. Atlanta: United States Department of Health and Human Services, 1996. A key report issued by the U.S. government regarding the extent and health outcomes of physical inactivity in the United States; includes suggestions for promoting increased physical activity for all Americans.

Van Norman, Kay. *Exercise Programming for Older Adults*. Champaign, Ill.: Human Kinetics, 1995. A practical handbook aimed at the practitioner for developing and supervising exercise programs for older adults.

Westcott, Wayne L., and Thomas R. Baechle. *Strength Training Past Fifty*. Champaign, Ill.: Human Kinetics, 1998. An excellent layperson's guide for safe and effective strength training written by leaders in the field of strength and conditioning.

EXTENDED CARE FOR THE ELDERLY. *See* **LONG-TERM CARE FOR THE ELDERLY.**

EYE DISEASE. *See* **VISION CHANGES AND DISORDERS.**

FACE LIFTS

RELEVANT ISSUES: Health and medicine, psychology, values, work
SIGNIFICANCE: The maintenance of a youthful appearance is important to many individuals in midlife and the later years, and face lifts hold the answer for some people

The term "face lift," as used by the general public, seems to include all methods of improving the appearance of the face by surgical and nonsurgical procedures. The difference between skin resurfacing and face lifts can cause confusion. Resurfacing is designed to change the texture of skin by removing the top layers and restructuring the deeper layers. Resurfacing is good at diminishing fine lines (called rhytids) or wrinkles, although a small amount of tightening does occur. Face lifts are designed to tighten loose skin through a surgical procedure. The most common sites needing improvement are around the mouth and eyes, the neck, and the jowls. Fine lines may be improved, but the primary purpose is tightening of the skin.

HOW AGING CHANGES THE SKIN

As an individual ages, many things happen to the body's largest organ, the skin. These changes occur all over the body, inside it as well, but the face and hands are where changes are witnessed every day. Faces and hands are exposed constantly to the sun and to weather. Sunlight accelerates changes to the skin, but it also has effects of its own. Before the invention of sunscreen, many people swam and played sports unprotected under the hot sun, and some even basted their bodies with baby oil mixed with iodine. At the time, such activities were considered healthy, but it is now known that sun damage is cumulative. The worst problems manifest themselves later in life. Sun damage is most marked in those with fair skin and blue eyes; blondes and redheads are especially vulnerable.

Aging tends to thin the skin while damage from sunlight thickens the outer layer (the epidermis). The elastic fibers in the skin are damaged. Premalignant and malignant cells may appear, causing skin cancer. Sunscreen should be a daily habit. Even prematurely aged skin can be improved by the use of sunscreen.

The three main changes in the skin caused by aging are thinning (atrophy), loss of elasticity, and loss of adherence of the skin to the deeper tissues. These effects plus gravity cause sagging. Exaggeration of normal facial features may develop as a subtle sign of aging. Lengthening of the earlobes, drooping of the tip of the nose, lowering of the brow, and increased fat pads below the chin and in the fold between the nose and lip can occur. Some may have drooping (ptosis) of the chin (sometimes called a witch's chin), which creates a tired look. Loose skin around the eyes is not the only cause of a baggy appearance. Small fat pads herniate from around the eye itself and come to rest beneath the skin, emphasizing the skin's laxity. Some people inherit a dark coloration around the eye, making the defects more noticeable.

THE HISTORY OF PLASTIC SURGERY

Although no surgery can reverse the changes of aging, cosmetic surgery can help improve appearance. Ever-improving technology has made face lift surgery affordable and less painful with a shorter recovery period.

Plastic surgery has been practiced longer than most people realize. The founder of plastic surgery was Gaspare Tagliacozzi, who stated in 1597, "We restore, repair and make whole parts which nature hath given, but which fortune hath taken away." Modern plastic surgery came to light with World War I. This new kind of war produced very severe injuries. Military surgeons contributed much to the rehabilitation of deformed faces and

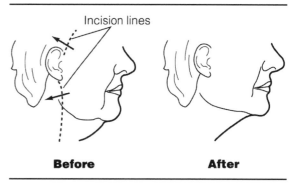

A face lift involves the excision and tightening of sagging skin on the face, which smoothes wrinkles and provides a more youthful profile. The results are temporary, however, because of permanent changes in aging skin. (Hans & Cassidy, Inc.)

bodies. After World War II, the discoveries of sulfa drugs and penicillin produced valuable tools against infection, enabling surgeons to conduct long and difficult surgeries. Infection was, and still is, every surgeon's enemy.

Cosmetic surgery evolved as a new surgical specialty with the goal of restoring normal appearance as well as youth and beauty. In the book *Consultation with a Plastic Surgeon* (1975), the authors state:

> With rejuvenation created by the plastic surgeon's face lift, there is a resurgence of physical activity, a renewed vigor in vocation, a revived interest in social activities, and "another chance" for those whose happiness was abruptly threatened by the loss of a mate. Psychological stimulation is probably the explanation.

REJUVENATION VS. REFINEMENT

Many procedures are available for those individuals who wish to gain a better balance between the way they look and feel. The following procedures are used for facial rejuvenation: dermabrasion, chemical peel, laser resurfacing, face lift (rhytidectomy), eyelid surgery (blepharoplasty), eyebrow and forehead rejuvenation, and chin and neck fat removal. The following procedures are used for refinement of facial features: nose job (rhinoplasty), ear pinback or reshaping (otoplasty), contour alterations of the face, chin alterations (genioplasty), contour alteration of the jaw (orthognathic surgery), and hair restoration (for both men and women).

The face lift surgical procedure may be performed under local or general anesthesia. Incisions are placed in natural creases in front of the ear and extended upward to the hairline. For women, sometimes the incision is taken inside the middle third of the ear behind the protruding cartilage (the tragus). This location is less common for men because the procedure can pull hair-bearing skin onto the ear. Incisions can also go downward, around to the back of the ear, and just below the posterior hairline (behind the ear). A small incision under the chin may also be necessary. Skin and muscle tissues are then separated from the deeper tissue. The skin is pulled tighter, excess skin is cut away, and very fine sutures are used to close the incisions. Liposuction to remove fat from under the chin (submental region), cheeks, or from the fold between the nose and mouth may be performed at the same time as the face lift or as a separate procedure.

In many cases, bandages are applied to the head and sides of the face and left in place for several days. Some sutures are removed five to six days after surgery, the rest at ten days postoperatively. Swelling and bruising usually diminish in three weeks. In most patients, makeup can be worn within a week after surgery. The healing period is harder for men, as few choose to wear makeup to hide the redness and bruising. The effects of face lift surgery generally last seven to ten years. Results depend on such variable factors as skin type, the amount of tightening necessary, subsequent weight gain or loss, the extent of sun damage, and the general health of the patient.

Prices in the United States for surgical and nonsurgical procedures vary depending on a number of factors and area of the country. Some estimates, as of 1999, gathered from several sources and averaged, are listed in the accompanying table.

Average Prices for Various Cosmetic Procedures, 1999

Hair transplant	$1,500-$5,000
Skin resurfacing (laser, peel, sanding)	$2,000-$2,500
Liposuction	$2,000-$2,500 per area
Ear pinback (otoplasty)	$2,750
Eyelid tightening (blepharoplasty)	$3,000
Forehead lift	$3,000
Nose job (rhinoplasty)	$3,250
Face lift (rhytidectomy)	$4,500

POSSIBLE COMPLICATIONS

Several complications must be considered in face lift surgery in addition to the possibility of infection. The most common complication is damage to the sensory nerves. Permanent numbness is usually the result of damage to the greater auricular nerve, which supplies feeling to the lower part of the ear. Permanent numbness and/or discomfort can persist in this area. The incidence of nerve injury after a face lift ranges from one in two hundred to one in fifty cases. Damage to the facial nerve, which supplies movement to the face, occurs in about 1 percent of face lift surgeries. Weakness of the facial nerve may not be noticed for some time because of swelling and bruising in the first few weeks after surgery. Facial nerve weakness exhibits the same symptoms. Surgery to repair the facial nerve is possible. About 95 percent of facial nerve damage cases show a complete return of function within a year.

Face lift surgery is tailored to meet the needs of each individual. Physicians advise their patients to read, plan, ask questions, and discuss openly what is wanted. A plastic surgeon should be chosen carefully.

NONSURGICAL OPTIONS

Nonsurgical commonsense methods to improve the effects of aging skin are avoiding the sun, abstaining from smoking, and maintaining a healthy lifestyle with proper diet and exercise. In addition to good skin care, nonsurgical methods are available to improve the appearance of aging skin. Daily applications of Retin A (tretinoin) improve skin texture. A physician may use injections of collagen and fat to disguise fine lines. Botox (*botulinum* toxin) injections into the muscle around the face relax the harsh lines and improve the appearance of wrinkles.

Both surgical and nonsurgical procedures have their place. Nonsurgical procedures are often the choice for older people who cannot have surgery for medical reasons or for those who have had previous face lift surgery and need only "freshening up." Any decision should be discussed with a physician and proper preparation made. The right choice is very important.   —*Virginiae Blackmon*

See also Age spots; Aging process; Antiaging treatments; Beauty; Cosmetic surgery; Fat deposition; Obesity; Premature aging; Skin cancer; Skin changes and disorders; Weight loss and gain; Wrinkles.

FOR FURTHER INFORMATION:

Cocke, William N., Jr., Richard H. McShane, and John S. Silverton. *Essentials of Plastic Surgery.* Boston: Little, Brown, 1979. A medical text of surgical procedures, with diagrams and pictures.

Decker, Ralph M., and Victor Royce Syracuse. *Consultation with a Plastic Surgeon.* Chicago: Nelson-Hall, 1975. Questions and answers covering everything a person would ask about face lifts and other plastic surgery.

Grabb, William C., and James Walter Smith. *Grabb and Smith's Plastic Surgery.* 5th ed. Philadelphia: Lippincott-Raven, 1997. A medical text of cosmetic surgical procedures with diagrams and pictures.

Hales, Dianne. "If You Want a Tuck or a Lift." *Parade: The Sunday Newspaper Magazine,* June 29, 1999. A general discussion of cosmetic surgery.

FALLEN ARCHES

RELEVANT ISSUES: Biology, health and medicine

SIGNIFICANCE: As individuals age, the arches of their feet often lose strength and flatten, a condition that sometimes causes pain and may affect other parts of the body

The main supportive structure of a foot is its arch. If the arch loses strength, the bony framework begins to collapse, the arch "falls" and the foot flattens. Similar to a sagging bridge, the weakness in the middle strains the joints at both ends of the foot. Fallen arches, or flatfeet, are most commonly found in overweight women who are middle aged or older. The condition is often associated with hypertension, obesity, diabetes, previous trauma, exposure to steroids, and rheumatologic ailments. However, an individual who does not have any of these predisposing factors may still develop fallen arches.

Symptoms may include pain along the inside of the ankle, often accompanied with swelling. This may develop over a period of months or even years. In some cases, the progressive flattening of the foot's arch may be observed. Eventually, those affected will not be able to walk for extended periods of time without experiencing significant pain. Fallen arches may also affect other parts of the body, causing fatigue, pain, or stiffness in the ankles, knees, hips, or lower back. If not treated, fallen arches may lead to arthritis, a source of significant disability.

Treatment may involve the use of custom orthotics that are placed inside the shoe to readjust the weight-bearing position of the foot. Anti-inflammatory medication, such as aspirin, may temporarily relieve pain caused by fallen arches. If fallen arches cause chronic pain, surgery may be required to realign the bones or to support the tendon structures in the foot.   —*Alvin K. Benson*

See also Arthritis; Bone changes and disorders; Diabetes; Foot disorders; Hammertoes; Hypertension; Mobility problems; Obesity.

FAMILY RELATIONSHIPS

RELEVANT ISSUES: Demographics, economics, family, sociology

SIGNIFICANCE: Increasing longevity has brought greater complexity to modern families, which include more generations and longer relationships than ever before

With increased longevity, family relationships have become both more complex and more enduring. At the end of the twentieth century, four-generation and even five-generation families were not uncommon, and with longer life comes longer lifelong relationships, such as marriage. Advanced age presents many families with the challenge of caring for the very old, often at a time when adolescent children also require attention and care. The stress of caregiving can, in some cases, result in abuse of the elderly family member. Today's aging families operate in a complex society and may confront legal considerations around issues related to illness and death.

MULTIPLE GENERATIONS IN CHANGING TIMES

One popular myth holds that in colonial America, intergenerational relationships among European immigrants were intimate and warm—that extended families chose to live together in love and harmony and that elders were universally revered. The reality of these relationships, as described by Carol Haber in her book *Beyond Sixty-Five: The Dilemma of Old Age in America's Past* (1983), was quite different. Grandparents enjoyed authority by virtue of their control of the family's land holdings, and many used that authority to control decisions that had a profound impact on their children's lives. So, for example, it was not unusual for the elder of the family to determine who and when an adult child would marry. Adults who rebelled from parental authority risked losing their inheritance and hence their livelihood—the land.

Although the European settlers tend to dominate scholarship on colonial America, two other groups merit consideration: Africans, who were kidnapped and brought to the continent as slaves, and American Indians, who had come to the continent centuries prior to the Europeans.

Even the brutal conditions of slavery did not wipe out intergenerational relations among African slaves. Slave marriage lacked legal sanction in most areas, but many couples established long-term bonds with immediate family and extended kin. These bonds sometimes did not require blood relationships. When children were separated from all blood relatives, they were often raised by unrelated adults. Slave children were taught to refer to adult slaves as "aunt" or "uncle." This established so-called fictive kinship relations, in which elders assumed the authority and responsibilities of blood relations. These ties enabled slaves to survive poverty, overwork, disease, and physical abuse, and they did not interfere with strong emotional ties to blood relations. For decades after the end of the Civil War, newspapers in the South ran lists of former slaves trying to reunite with their spouses and children.

The Indian tribes of North America varied tremendously in their intergenerational relations. Some, like the Cheyenne, were patrilineal, with land-use rights and identification flowing through fathers. Others, like the Pueblo, were matrilineal. In these groups identification and inheritance came from mothers. Tribes also varied in their treatment of grandparents. Among the Omaha, for example, elders enjoyed tremendous power and authority over younger generations. Honor for the elderly, however, did not preclude abandonment or euthanasia when times were hard.

INTERGENERATIONAL RELATIONS IN MODERN TIMES

Intergenerational relationships in Colonial America were not only tremendously varied but also rare. Few adults—whether European, African American, or American Indian—survived to advanced age. As a result, few families consisted of more than one or two generations. Yet today, multigenerational families are increasingly common. As Gunhild Hagestad pointed out, increased longevity has produced greater "life overlaps" among generations.

By the late twentieth century, there were more than fifty-eight million grandparents in the United States, ranging in age from 30 to 110. Nearly half

The relationship between elders and their adult children can become closer over time as aging brings shared losses and increased financial or physical dependency. (Jim Whitmer)

of them were under the age of 60. Indeed, the most common age for first becoming a grandparent is 49 to 51 years for women and 51 to 53 years for men. With teenage pregnancies, some adults become grandparents in their thirties. These individuals hardly conform to the stereotyped notion of gray-haired grandparents who spend their days waiting for their children to call.

The role of grandparents has changed considerably since colonial times, from distant authority figures to their children to playmates and companions of grandchildren. Most grandparents today may not live with their adult children. Instead, they maintain what some scholars have termed "intimacy at a distance," with separate households but a good deal of contact and support.

Several researchers have attempted to describe types of grandparents. In these studies a central theme is tremendous diversity in individual ap-

proaches to a somewhat ill-defined role. The best-known work of this type was published by Bernice Neugarten and K. Weinstein in 1964. In what is now considered a classic study, these authors identified five grandparenting styles: formal, fun-seekers, surrogate parents, reservoirs of family wisdom, and distant family figures. Another well-known model was developed by Helen Q. Kivnick. Instead of describing styles and putting grandparents into single categories, Kivnick described five dimensions of grandparenting and rated individuals along each dimension. These included centrality, valued elder, immortality through clan, reinvolvement with personal past, and indulgence.

Sociologists have identified a variety of societal functions that can be filled by grandparents. They transmit the family heritage, provide role models for their grandchildren, serve as nurturers, devote time to listening to their grandchildren and engaging in unstructured activities, mediate parent-child conflicts, act as buffers between parents and children, and support and care for grandchildren when parents are in crisis.

There may be gender differences in individual approaches to grandparenting. Contemporary researchers have reported that traditional gender roles also extend to grandparents, with grandmothers reporting more emotional contact with children and grandparents being more likely to offer advice or instruction. Neugarten and Weinstein reported that grandmothers were more likely to serve as surrogate parents, while grandfathers served as fonts of family wisdom. Hagestad examined topics of conversation and concluded that grandmothers were more likely to discuss interpersonal relationships with children, while grandfathers were more likely to talk about work, education, and money. It is unclear whether these gender differences will hold for future generations.

Grandparents often contribute to the healthy development of their grandchildren. Their role is significantly affected when parents divorce. In the United States and Canada, growing numbers of grandparents have pursued legal remedies to secure visitation rights to their grandchildren. Indeed, associations have been organized in both countries to address this issue. Parents seeking divorce can ensure that grandparents' visitation rights will be respected by stipulating them in divorce agreements. Some states have enacted legislation to protect grandparents' visitation rights.

In addition to divorce, parental crises such as illness, death, and substance abuse may change the role of grandparents. A growing number have found themselves assuming responsibility for raising their grandchildren, with or without obtaining legal custody of the children. In the United States an estimated 3.4 million children live with their grandparents and in at least a third of these homes grandparents have primary responsibility for the children. An estimated 44 percent of grandparents spend one hundred or more hours per year caring for their grandchildren. Among African Americans, the proportion of grandparents providing custodial care is roughly three times that among whites.

Custodial grandparents often face challenges that include securing access to financial assistance, health care coverage, social services, and educa-

tion. Often public programs require that grandparents assume legal custody of the children. Yet securing legal custody may force grandparents to demonstrate that their own children are unfit parents, a potentially brutal situation. A few organizations, such as the American Association of Retired Persons (AARP), have established support groups and resource centers for grandparents taking care of their grandchildren.

LIFELONG RELATIONSHIPS

While it is popular to bemoan contemporary rates of divorce, few acknowledge that increased longevity has placed tremendous demands on modern marriage. During the colonial era, when few lived beyond the age of forty, a man might expect to lose at least one wife (possibly more) in childbirth. So, while the mean age at marriage was young (generally in the teens), marriages by and large did not last for more than a couple of decades. They ended, not by divorce, but by death—usually that of the wife. In the late twentieth century, an estimated one in five married couples could expect to celebrate their golden (fiftieth) wedding anniversary.

If they are to last "until death do us part," marriages must endure for decades longer than in previous eras. As a result, modern marriages must adapt to a wide variety of personal, economic, and social changes. Numerous researchers have joined the lay public in attempting to describe universal trends in marital satisfaction over the life of a marriage. Two main trajectories have been proposed. In the first, high levels of satisfaction are associated with the honeymoon phase and the remaining years of marriage see a steady decline in happiness. The second theory postulates an initial period of high satisfaction, which declines during child rearing only to rise steadily during later years. Neither of these theories has been conclusively demonstrated, as researchers have seldom had the opportunity (or the stamina) to interview couples regularly over the duration of a fifty-year marriage. Such research, if conducted, is likely to reveal that patterns of marital satisfaction are as distinctive as the individuals in the marriage.

LATE-LIFE MARRIAGES

Growing numbers of older adults remarry and find themselves in relationships that can be extremely satisfying but that bear little resemblance to marriages of young adulthood or middle age. Among the complications of late-life marriages are the presence of stepchildren and possibly stepgrandchildren on one or both sides. Adult children of an older bride or groom may experience conflicting emotions: on one hand, feeling gratified that their parent has found a partner, and on the other, feeling concerned that their inheritance and relationships will be threatened in the process. Many older couples use prenuptial agreements to ensure the marriage will not jeopardize inheritance. Women entering into late-life marriages often expect to assume caregiving responsibilities for their (typically older) spouses. Indeed, some find this expectation is a deterrent to late-life marriage. Older women are considerably less likely than older men to remarry, however, simply because fewer men than women survive to advanced ages.

Physical changes associated with the aging process can affect the sexual dimension of marriage. Attitudes toward sex are often linked to cohorts, so studies conducted on individuals who are currently aged may have limited relevance to future generations of elderly. General findings from these studies have suggested an overall decline in sexual activity in advanced age, with the most significant drop observed in individuals over the age of seventy-five. Older men generally report more interest in sex than older women. Men are also likely to report having sex more frequently than women. While most older adults report a decline in sexual activity it is important to note that some couples experience increased activity in old age. This has been attributed to more leisure, fewer children in the home, and less worry about pregnancy.

The most definitive studies that addressed sexuality among older adults were the Duke Longitudinal Studies, reported by Erdman Palmore. Like most researchers in this area, Palmore reported what is known as an interest-activity gap, particularly among men. That is, interest in sex exceeded the frequency of sexual activity. Nonetheless, among even the oldest respondents in the study (aged seventy to seventy-five), one-third of both men and women reported that they had stable patterns of sexual activity. Among couples who reported diminished sexual activity, the most com-

mon reason was health difficulties experienced by the husband. These couples often reported that compensatory forms of intimacy such as holding hands, sitting close together, and conversation can take the place of sex.

WIDOWHOOD

While in colonial times men might have expected to become widowed, in modern times, the loss of a spouse is a more common experience for women. Women have longer life expectancies than men. In addition, most women marry older men. These two factors combine to make widowhood a "normative" transition for women.

The transition may be expected, but it is seldom easy. Modern widowhood typically occurs late in life and disrupts well-established patterns of behavior. Apart from the grief caused by loss of a partner, widowhood places new responsibilities and demands on the bereaved. Gender differences in adaptation have been observed among surviving spouses. Typically, women who are bereaved report that they confront new challenges relating to financial management, home and car maintenance, and some types of decision-making—all realms traditionally managed by husbands. Women also experience loss of income with bereavement. In the United States, Social Security benefits usually decline by one-third when a spouse dies. This reduction can result in impoverishment of the surviving spouse. So widowhood is one of the most common precursors of poverty for American women.

In contrast, men often report that they face unfamiliar household tasks and that they lack the skills to maintain their social networks. Most older men rely on their wives for emotional support and companionship. Wives typically plan and orchestrate social activities on behalf of older couples. Indeed, while women often maintain extensive social networks, many older men rely exclusively on their wives for companionship. So the loss of a wife can place a man at risk of severe isolation, and even suicide.

While family members and friends are often available for consolation shortly after the death, they are seldom aware of a widow's need for long-term support and concern. Widows often report that the most difficult period for them occurs not immediately following their loss but months later, when family members expect them to "get on with life." Organizations that serve the elderly, such as AARP, offer support groups for widows that can be of assistance.

FAMILY CARE, FAMILY ABUSE

There is some difference of opinion about the extent to which family members should be held responsible for meeting the needs of dependent elders. On one hand, theorists as such as Eugene Litwak have argued that the family is the best structure for meeting personal (idiosyncratic) needs. Policymakers typically prefer that the family serve as the first line of defense against the disabilities of age. Cost-containment pressures on public support programs for the elderly (such as Medicare and Medicaid in the United States) place great demands on families. Yet many elderly prefer professional care over the embarrassment of asking family members for help. Because most women work, family resources to care for the elderly may be severely limited.

Both government and families must accommodate this tension. Families provide as much care as they can—some have estimated that families provide 80 percent of the care received by the elderly in the United States. Government entities provide what support is possible. In emerging trends, businesses are now facing the need to accommodate employees' responsibility for elder care, and nonprofit organizations are organizing supportive services for family caregivers. Nonetheless, the experience of caring for a frail or dying elder can take a tremendous toll on everyone involved.

The overwhelming demands involved in meeting the physical needs of a frail elder can either strengthen or destroy other family bonds. Caregivers often experience a cycle of resentment and guilt. The demands of caregiving deprive them of privacy, rest, and even health, generating a natural feeling of anger or resentment. Then, reminded of the sacrifices their parents made while raising them, a caregiver can move into the guilt cycle. The presence of children can further complicate the caregiving scenario, as adults struggle to meet the needs of both generations. Individuals in this situation have been termed the "sandwich generation," squeezed by the vulnerabilities of both parents and offspring. Meanwhile, their elderly parents often experience their own emotional roller coasters—living through the embarrassment and

pain of severe dependence on children they meant only to nurture. Yet some caregivers report tremendous rewards, such as time spent with a beloved parent, greater communication, an opportunity to return the care provided during childhood, and the sense of doing something that is right.

Changes in health coverage and financing have increased the demands on family caregivers. In the United States, the "prospective payment system" has resulted in elders being released from hospitals "quicker and sicker." They go home to spouses or adult children who must provide more intensive health care than ever before. A burgeoning home health industry provides professional assistance to families able to pay for their services.

ELDER ABUSE

Increased dependence on family care has placed growing numbers of elders in situations with high risk of abuse. Most family violence is intergenerational, and reports of elder abuse have increased in recent years. It is unclear, however, whether the rate of elder abuse has actually risen or increased awareness has led to higher reporting rates. It is clear that elder abuse, like child abuse, typically involves the presence of a dependent and vulnerable victim. Abuse is much more common among families that are stressed by conditions such as unemployment or caregiving. Yet it is important to remember that abuse is by no means common among caregiving families.

Unlike child abuse, with elder abuse the state cannot step in and assume custody of the victim. When the victim is a legally competent adult, professionals must rely on the victim's willingness to report incidents and pursue legal remedies. Older parents are often reluctant to admit that their children are abusive. So cases of elder abuse, even when detected, often arise in circumstances that preclude effective intervention.

LEGAL ISSUES AFFECTING THE ELDERLY AND THEIR FAMILIES

Distinct aspects of old age as a time of life often present legal issues for families. Perhaps the most common of these are issues related to illness and death.

In the United States, the main source of funding for health care of the aged is Medicare. As growing numbers of families are learning, Medicare provides only limited coverage for long-term care in nursing homes. As a result, many frail elders are required to "spend down" in order to become eligible for Medicaid coverage of their nursing home care. Because Medicaid is a means-tested program designed to meet the health needs of low-income Americans, the net effect of spending down may be to impoverish the surviving spouse and dissipate the family inheritance.

Other health-related considerations relate to advance directives, such as the durable power of attorney or living will. These are vehicles through which adults can determine what care they will receive in the event of incapacity. The durable power of attorney can be used to designate an individual who will make decisions on behalf of the individual. A living will specifies which life-sustaining procedures will be applied or withheld under circumstances in which the patient is unable to communicate his or her wishes. While the legal standing of these instruments has become more clear in recent years, their greatest value probably lies in their use as a vehicle for communicating older adults' preferences to their loved ones.

Physical or cognitive decline may also lead to involuntary legal action designed to establish that an older adult is not competent to care for himself or herself. Two procedures apply in this situation: guardianship and conservatorship. In guardianship proceedings, a court determines that the individual is not legally competent and appoints a guardian to be responsible for the well-being or the financial affairs of the ward or both. Sometimes separate guardians will be used, with one assuming responsibility for the person's well-being and another managing the finances. Conservatorship is similar in that it involves a court procedure with right of appeal. In this case, the court grants the conservator only the power to manage property, not to care for the personal affairs of the ward. Conservatorships can be used to preserve a vulnerable elder's personal freedom while preventing waste or dissipation of assets through fraud or mismanagement. Both guardianship and conservatorship can be extremely painful for the elderly and their families, particularly when the procedure is disputed.

Inheritance is often used as a way of rewarding family members for care. Transferring property upon death is more complicated than it may at first appear, so individuals with sizeable estates are well advised to seek legal counsel. A will is a formal device for transferring property. Wills typically involve probate and must comply with technical rules to be valid. A will can be changed at any time, and so is more flexible than a gift. Trusts are also used to transfer property. Trusts involve three persons, the person giving away property (the grantor), the person or legal entity who will take care of the property for a time (the trustee), and the person or persons who will benefit from the gift (beneficiaries). A living trust is revocable. That is, the grantor can change its provisions.

SUMMARY

Ethel Shanas once referred to the elderly and their families as "the new pioneers." The term is an apt one. Never before have humans enjoyed such longevity, and never before have families faced the challenges and opportunities presented by growing numbers of older members. In the United States some have attempted to argue that the growth of the elderly population will create "age wars," that the interests of children conflict with those of their grandparents and resources devoted to the elderly are stolen from the young. This argument ignores the importance of family ties, suggesting that people identify more closely with their age peers than with other generations in their family.

Clearly, the growth of the aging population has changed modern family relationships. Longevity affords the opportunity for family members to be close as adults over an extended period. The presence of more adults in families might enhance the quality of life for children, even as elder care supplants child care as a role expectation for women.

—*Amanda Smith Barusch*

See also Absenteeism; Adopted grandparents; African Americans; American Indians; Asian Americans; Biological clock; Caregiving; Childlessness; Children of Aging Parents; Cohabitation; Death of a child; Death of parents; Divorce; Dual-income couples; Durable power of attorney; Elder abuse; Empty nest syndrome; Estates and inheritance; Filial responsibility; Full nest; Gay men and lesbians; Grandparenthood; Great-grandparenthood; Grief; *Having Our Say: The Delany Sisters' First One Hundred Years*; Health care; Living wills; Long-term care for the elderly; Marriage; Medicare; Men and aging; Midlife crisis; Multigenerational households; Neglect; Neugarten, Bernice; Parenthood; Pets; Remarriage; Sandwich generation; Sexuality; Sibling relationships; Single parenthood; Singlehood; Skipped-generation parenting; Stepfamilies; Trusts; Widows and widowers; Wills and bequests; Women and aging.

FOR FURTHER INFORMATION:

Brubaker, T. H. *Family Relationships in Later Life.* Newbury Park, Calif.: Sage Publications, 1983. This book presents research on diverse relationships of the elderly, including those with spouses, adult children, and siblings. It also discusses practice and policy implications of the research presented.

Cherlin, Andrew J., and Frank F. Furstenberg. *The New American Grandparent: A Place in the Family, a Life Apart.* New York: Basic Books, 1986. Based on interviews with hundreds of grandparents, this book examines how the role of grandparenting is experienced in modern families.

Haber, Carol. *Beyond Sixty-Five: The Dilemma of Old Age in America's Past.* New York: Cambridge University Press, 1983. Careful examination of the status of the elderly in colonial and postcolonial America effectively counters the "myth of a golden age," when the elderly were universally respected. Also examines the changing role of elders as life expectancy extended the period when adults were not raising dependent children.

Mintz, S., and S. Kellogg. *Domestic Revolutions: A Social History of Domestic Family Life.* New York: Free Press, 1987. Presents a detailed review of the values that have influenced family life in the United States from the arrival of the Mayflower to the present and argues that modern families are characterized by their diversity and lack unified ideals or standards.

Neugarten, Bernice, and K. Weinstein. "The Changing American Grandparent." In *Journal of Marriage and the Family* 26 (1964). The authors describe grandparenting styles and provide examples.

Shanas, Ethel, and Marvin B. Sussman, eds. *Family, Bureaucracy, and the Elderly.* Durham, N.C.: Duke University Press, 1977. This classic work examines the relationship between public bureaucracies and the elderly and their families. It includes chapters of both theoretical and practical significance and should be required reading for anyone interested in the aging and their families.

Stroebe, M. S., W. Stroebe, and R. O. Hansson, eds. *Handbook of Bereavement: Theory, Research, and Intervention.* Cambridge, England: Cambridge University Press, 1997. This book offers a comprehensive review of scientific knowledge on the consequences of losing a loved one through death. It addresses theoretical approaches, physiological changes associated with loss, and normal and pathological grief.

FAT DEPOSITION

RELEVANT ISSUES: Health and medicine
SIGNIFICANCE: Body composition with relation to fat changes as people age, with significant implications for health

In adult males who are not obese, fat tissue comprises about 10 to 15 percent of the total body mass, while in females, fat comprises about 20 percent of body mass. Fat is the reservoir of calories for the body's emergency energy needs. A normal and expected part of the aging process is that the relative amounts of water and fat in the body change, with an increase in the total amount of body fat and a decrease in the total amount of water. Lean body mass, especially muscle mass, also decreases. At the same time, the layer of fat immediately under the skin thins.

These bodily changes have important implications for the health of older persons. Changes in the way the fat is distributed in the body are important. Health care providers commonly use the waist-to-hip ratio to indicate fat distribution. If this ratio is greater than 1.0 in men or 0.8 in women, these individuals have an increased risk of cardiovascular disease. Another common way of expressing this is the "apple and pear" analogy. People with increased fat around the waistline (apples) are at greater risk for heart disease than people with increased fat around the hips (pears).

Another health implication of changes in body fat involves prescription and nonprescription drugs. Most drugs are soluble either in water or in fat and are dependent on these elements for distribution throughout the body. Health care providers must change the dosages of prescription drugs to avoid either undertreatment or overdose in an older person, depending on the solubility of the drug. Finally, the layer of fat under the skin serves to both protect the internal structures of the body and provide warmth. As this layer thins, older people have increased difficulty in avoiding trauma to underlying structures and in keeping warm.

—*Rebecca Lovell Scott*

See also Cosmetic surgery; Heart disease; Medications; Nutrition; Obesity; Sarcopenia; Skin changes and disorders; Temperature regulation and sensitivity; Weight loss and gain.

FILIAL RESPONSIBILITY

RELEVANT ISSUES: Culture, family, values

SIGNIFICANCE: With the advent of modern medicine, people live longer, posing the question of who is responsible for parents' physical, emotional, and financial needs when traditional roles are reversed and parents become like children

Filial responsibility is the responsibility of children to their parents. As advances in medicine since the early years of the twentieth century have made it possible for humans to live longer, healthier lives, a social problem has arisen. Persons who approached fifty years of age during the 1990's likely have two living parents. These parents, who are often seventy years old or older, may already be under custodial care. If they do not already receive custodial care, they certainly may require it as they age.

For society the question arises as to how this care is to be provided and by whom. Historically, filial responsibility traditionally devolved upon women who raised their families, worked in the home, and cared for aging parents who were part of the household or lived nearby. However, in the late twentieth century multigenerational households became increasingly rare. Young adults in the fast-growing economies of developing nations moved away from rural areas to larger population centers, leaving their aging parents behind to fend for themselves. Twentieth century women joined the workforce in increasing numbers, leaving no one at home to care for elderly parents.

As members of the baby-boom generation, persons born between 1946 and 1964, approached middle age in the late twentieth century, elder care replaced child care as the primary concern of families, both monetarily and practically. Caring for aging parents is not new. However, combining elder care, child care, and careers outside the home has created a new level of responsibility for adults, especially for women, in their middle years. In the late 1990's demographic studies showed that individuals in the workforce were more likely to have living parents than they were to have dependent children. In the United States these same demographic trends began to indicate that "gray panthers" outnumbered "young lions."

In other parts of the world, care of the elderly has been legislated. Chinese law, for example, requires that adult children support their parents. If the children are dead, their children are required to care for their grandparents. Failure to comply can result in prison sentences. Similar legal statutes exist in Morocco, Tunisia, Japan, and Singapore. However, in the Republic of Georgia, parents who do not fulfill their parental duties can be legally denied the financial support of their adult children. In the late twentieth century, with the human life span increasing, adult children found it necessary to develop plans for elder care that acknowledge the wisdom and value of their aging parents while providing for their parents' possible need for long-term care. —*Barbara C. Stanley*

See also Abandonment; Caregiving; Children of Aging Parents; Cultural views of aging; Family relationships; Life expectancy; Long-term care for the elderly; Multigenerational households; Sandwich generation.

FILMS

RELEVANT ISSUES: Media, sociology

SIGNIFICANCE: In the United States, images of the elderly in films have reflected broader social changes and trends but have defined stereotypical images, positive and negative attributes, and roles for the elderly in society. As the population ages, however, filmmakers may pay greater attention to the diversity among the elderly and to their viewing habits

Popular film images are reflections of a culture's attitudes, beliefs, and standards as well as projections of desired realities. Whether accurate descriptions of daily living, or wishful thinking on the part of filmmakers, films tell stories that are eagerly received by consumers. To the extent that consumers digest such material as truth, rather than fiction, the depictions laid forth in film can be influential in the development and maintenance of stereotypes.

Public awareness about aging and the impact of baby boomers has grown tremendously. At the end of the twentieth century, baby boomers were dealing with aging parents and associated caregiving and lifestyle issues, as well as planning for their own retirement and later life. This growing awareness increased the demand for accurate information about aging.

Images of the elderly are transmitted in a variety of ways—through the family, in the workplace, between groups of friends, and through film and other media. Films have the potential of providing children with their first exposure to people in old age. What they see on the screen, therefore, can have an impact on their attitudes and ultimate treatment of the elderly. With the growth of the older population, considerable public concern has arisen over the issue of portrayal of aging and the aged in the media, as it is generally accepted that mass media have strong social and psychological effects on viewers. It has been argued that films are one of the clearest and most accessible representations of the past, present, and future of American society. Because of this concern, a number of advocacy organizations have formed to address the quality of films dealing with diversity and related issues. The Research Retirement Foundation sponsored the National Media OWL Awards to encourage productions that break down traditional stereotypes of aging. Their mission is to recognize and encourage high-quality films about aging.

Gwen Verdon and Don Ameche in a scene from the film Cocoon. *(Archive Photos)*

A HISTORY OF FILMS FEATURING AGING THEMES

Films have always featured representations of older people and interpretations of the aging experience, although the number of them has been small. A historical examination of some of the most popular films reveals startling parallels between their themes and changes occurring in society. While the portrayal of aging in films has followed social trends, the presentations of aging have tended to be simplistic and stereotypical. When they do appear, elderly men are far more likely to be shown as powerful, active, and productive. Women generally appear as passive and in a supportive role to men. Also, older men and women tend to be portrayed in one of two extremes—as wealthy and in good health or as deprived and suffering.

In the early twentieth century, Americans were experiencing changes in the family caused by industrialization and urbanization. As the extended family structure was replaced by the smaller, more mobile nuclear family, the assumption was that older people would be left behind and neglected as their children moved to follow their work. Two popular silent films were stories of helpless maternal sacrifice. *Over the Hill* (1920) told the story of a hardworking mother who ends up scrubbing floors in a poorhouse because her thankless children are too preoccupied with their own lives to care for her. In 1928, *Four Sons* depicted a homebound German mother who loses her children one by one through war and emigration. *Tugboat Annie*, a talking film released in 1934, was a story of extreme maternal sacrifice.

In 1937, *Make Way for Tomorrow* moved away from the maternal sacrifice theme to tell the story of a devoted elderly couple forced to separate and live with their children. For the first time in film, elderly characters were treated on the screen as people with identities of their own first and parental figures second. The couple was defined by their love for each other; however, while the film showered enormous sympathy on these characters, stereotypical faults were also presented. They were intrusive, set in their ways, and a genuine burden on the younger generation suddenly forced to provide shelter for them. The 1940's and 1950's presented simple, stereotypical roles for elderly men and women. Older men were presented as cantankerous old codgers, sharp-eyed or snake-tongued. Older women were presented as matriarchs with quavery voices and firm, no-nonsense gazes. With the generational and ideological divisions typical of the 1960's, filmmakers portrayed the elderly in active and contributory roles. *The Last Angry Man* (1959) presented an old, overworked, tired, but unbending slum doctor. John Wayne often depicted hardheaded geezers in rawhide, a symbol of completeness and wisdom, in films such as *Rooster Cogburn* (1975).

During the 1970's, the United States as a whole was in pursuit of youth. Therefore, the most popular elderly characters in films were those who could portray youthful behavior and spunk. Helen Hayes was popular in *Airport* (1970) as a feisty stowaway. In *Harold and Maude* (1971), Ruth Gordon played a zesty seventy-nine-year-old who steals cars, smokes pot, and befriends a rich teenager obsessed with suicide who decides he wants to marry her. The film is ultimately uplifting. Gordon earned a cultlike following for her character's childlike defiance and hedonistic behaviors.

In the late 1970's and early 1980's, with the women's movement at its height, women of all ages began to complain that the male-dominated silver screen seemed incapable of treating women realistically. This was definitely true of the elderly in film. In real life, wives tend to outlive their hus-

bands, but the most popular films about aging focused, almost without exception, on the lives of elderly widowers. The 1970 film version of the play *I Never Sang for My Father* portrayed a widower's relationship with his son. *Harry and Tonto* (1974) showed a widower driving across the country in a quest for a new life.

A study of films released over more than five decades demonstrates the perpetuation of both ageist and sexist stereotypes. Research reveals ageist stereotypes, in general, to be prevalent across the decades. For the most part, older individuals of both genders have been portrayed as less friendly, having less romantic activity, and as enjoying fewer positive outcomes than younger characters by the end of the film. Older women are often cast in a particularly negative light. Compared to older men, older women have been presented as less friendly, less intelligent, less good, possessing less wealth, and being less attractive. Ageist stereotypes are also evident in the conspicuous absence of older individuals in most popular films and particularly the absence of older women as lead characters.

Little scholarship directly compares ageist depictions of men and women in films. E. W. Markson and C. A. Taylor found a particularly striking bias in the ages of Academy Award nominees and winners for actors and actresses from 1927 through 1990. In the sixty-three years of awards for Best Actress and Best Actor, only 27 percent of female winners were over the age of thirty-nine, as compared to 67 percent of male winners. The authors concluded that in films, a woman is considered "older" by the time she is thirty-five and a man may experience continued demand on the silver screen well past the age of forty.

In a study of film up until the 1980's, Doris Bazzini and others found that compared to men, women of all ages were underrepresented. This was particularly the case for women over the age of thirty-five. Approximately 80 percent of characters over the age of thirty-five were male, leaving only 20 percent as female. The discrepancy between male and female characters under the age of thirty-five was much less pronounced, with 46 percent of these characters being women and 54 percent being men.

The film that turned the tide in the portrayal of the elderly and elderly women in particular was the 1981 film version of the play *On Golden Pond* because it parted from the familiar images of the old that had been presented for decades. Instead, it told the story of a woman (played by Katharine Hepburn) who is warmhearted, quick-witted, and yet whimsical enough to exchange birdcalls with the loons on the lake and sufficiently tough to keep family ties from unraveling. She is also a champion swimmer, speedboat pilot, and firewood carrier. Her husband, on the other hand, is incorrigibly stubborn and irrepressibly self-assured while his emaciated frame in motion is the touching embodiment of human frailty and mortality.

After *On Golden Pond*, films about the elderly were more realistic and had a wider variety of themes related to aging. The theme of aging as a journey of self-revelation was prominent in the film versions of such plays as *The Trip to Bountiful* and *Driving Miss Daisy*, made in 1985 and 1989, respectively. In other films, older people play the lead roles and the plots center on sympathetically drawn characters who deal with the realities of aging or cope with intergenerational relationships. In *Dad* (1989), a middle-aged man who has put all of his energies into his career suddenly finds himself responsible for the care of his aging father. As he learns to adjust his priorities to incorporate his new responsibilities, he is rewarded by seeing his seemingly dying father suddenly exhibit a renewed energy for life. In *Grumpy Old Men* (1993), the theme is two feuding neighbors whose longstanding rivalry escalates when they fall in love with the same woman. This film calls into question stereotypes of the aged as inactive, disengaged, and uninterested in sex. *Fried Green Tomatoes* (1991), adapted from Fannie Flagg's novel, illustrates the development of a friendship between a middle-aged woman and an old woman in a nursing home. Their friendship results in the younger woman learning the history of the town and gaining a sense of personal power and self-worth from hearing about a strong woman who lived there in the past. This film suggests a positive role for the elderly as oral historians.

Strangers in Good Company (1990) presented an eclectic group of seven elderly women and a young female bus driver stranded in the remote Canadian countryside. As they gather materials for food and shelter and await a rescue, each woman tells about her life, her fears, and her memories. This film provides the viewers with the knowledge that each one of these women, like every woman growing old, has a past, still might tell an occasional off-color joke, has survival skills, and is an important and interesting human being, not simply an old woman whose clothes are slightly out of date or whose songs recall the past.

While the images of elderly in film are becoming more diverse and more positive, they still fall short of reality. Elderly women are presented as commanding and powerful but essentially separate from men. Older men are presented with younger female characters who are secondary to the men. In real life, many elderly people, especially women, are poor; the older they are, the greater the likelihood of being poor. In film, family in the blood sense is almost totally left out; in reality, most elderly still live in, struggle with, and enjoy a blood-family context.

Patrick McKee and Jennifer McLerran argue that while many American films have had aging themes, contemporary film watchers, with their bias toward youth and fear of old age, have a blindness to old age that accompanies them to the theater. The Western bias toward youth is the source of the struggle that American filmmakers face in the portrayal of the aging process in films.

FILM-VIEWING HABITS OF THE ELDERLY

The motion-picture industry will have to adapt to the needs of an aging population to be successful. Filmgoers are getting older, and aging baby boomers make up an increasing part of the first-run audience. The Motion Picture Association of America reported that between 1981 and 1992, the percentage of filmgoers aged sixteen to twenty dropped by approximately 10 percent while attendance of forty to forty-nine-year-olds increased by 10 percent.

Older adults are attracted to a greater mix of films than are teenagers. They appreciate films with adult themes and selectively attend those that appear to be popular, entertaining, and original. Older adults are also attracted to family films. They accompany young children to motion pictures and appreciate the music, acting, story lines, and animation. The film industry reported that older adults contributed to the success of such animated films as *Beauty and the Beast* (1991) and *Aladdin* (1992) and such live-action family films as *Hook* (1991) and *Home Alone* (1990).

Additional research is needed that considers more diverse groups of elderly and their film preferences. Filmmakers should recognize the growing number of elderly people with greater amounts of leisure time and direct themes toward their interests as well as the interests of younger people. —Peggy Shifflett

See also Advertising; Ageism; *All About Eve*; *Autobiography of Miss Jane Pittman, The*; Baby boomers; *Cocoon*; Communication; Cultural views of aging; *Driving Miss Daisy*; *Grumpy Old Men*; *Harold and Maude*; *Harry and Tonto*; *I Never Sang for My Father*; *On Golden Pond*; *Robin and Marian*; *Shootist, The*; Stereotypes; *Sunset Boulevard*; Television; *Trip to Bountiful, The*; *Wild Strawberries*; *Woman's Tale, A*.

FOR FURTHER INFORMATION:

Bazzini, Doris, et al. "The Aging Woman in Popular Film: Underrepresented, Unattractive, Unfriendly, and Unintelligent." *Sex Roles: A Journal of Research* 36, nos. 7-8 (1997). This article presents a study of one hundred top-grossing motion pictures spanning from the 1940's through the 1980's.

George, Diana. "Semi-Documentary/Semi-Fiction: An Examination of Genre in *Strangers in Good Company*." *Journal of Film and Video* 46, no. 4 (Winter, 1995). This article discusses how *Strangers in Good Company* reveals the lives of women that normally remain hidden in the folds of aging skin and the drape of loose-fitting "old lady" clothing.

Harvey, Stephen. "Coming of Age in Film." *American Film* 7 (December, 1981). This article traces the images of aging in film from 1920 to 1980.

McKee, Patrick, and Jennifer McLerran. "The Old Prospector: *The Treasure of the Sierra Madre* as Exemplar of Old Age in Popular Film." *International Journal of Aging and Human Development* 40, no. 1 (1995). This article examines gerontological themes in this classic popular film.

Markson, E. W., and C. A. Taylor. "Real Versus Reel World: Older Women and the Academy Awards." *Women and Therapy* 14 (1993). This article presents a study of gender differences in Academy Award winners over the history of filmmaking.

Pampel, Fred, Dan Fost, and Sharon O'Mally. "Marketing the Movies." *American Demographics* 16, no. 3 (1994). This article argues that the motion-picture industry will have to adapt to the needs of the aging population to be successful in the future.

Schickel, Richard. "Mind Slips: Remembering and Disremembering Movies." *Film Comment* 34, no. 5 (1998). Proposes that the history of films is becoming increasingly complicated.

Sontag, Susan. "A Century of Cinema." *Parnassus: Poetry in Review* 22, nos. 1-2 (1997). Sontag claims that films today are not as great as they once were and are made for commercial purposes.

FITNESS. *See* EXERCISE AND FITNESS.

FLU. *See* INFLUENZA.

FOOT DISORDERS

RELEVANT ISSUES: Health and medicine
SIGNIFICANCE: Increased care must be taken near the end of the life span to prevent or correct problems associated with such foot disorders as flat feet, neuromas, Achilles tendinitis, plantar fascitis, and heel spurs

Each foot contains twenty-six bones, including fourteen phalanges (toe bones), five metatarsals (instep bones), and seven tarsals (ankle bones). The thirty-three joints in each foot are stabilized by more than a hundred ligaments, with their movements governed by nineteen muscles and their tendons. All these structures must work together in precise harmony during gait. When the delicate biomechanical action of one or both feet is upset and compensatory movements are made, abnormal compensations and pain often occur.

It is estimated that the average American takes approximately nine thousand steps per day and walks the equivalent of three and a half times around the equator in a lifetime. Recreational and competitive sports enthusiasts who previously had well-functioning feet often develop foot health problems at around age fifty, by which time the average foot has ambulated more than seventy-five thousand miles. Even less-active people in midlife and later are prone to foot disorders that can have serious consequences for mobility, even loss of the ability for independent living.

FLATFEET AND NEUROMAS
Chronic foot problems are often caused by excessive pronation (rotation of the midtarsal me-

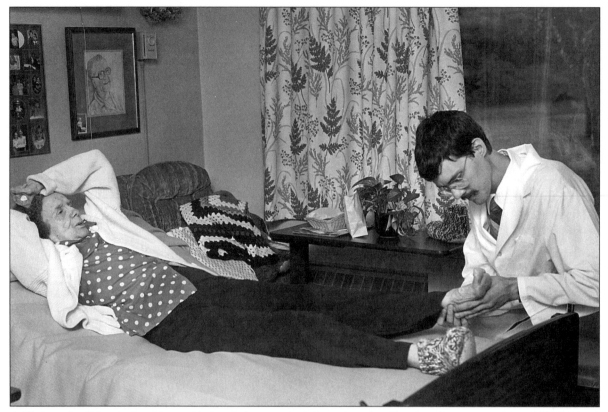

A lifetime of walking and problems with circulation can result in various foot disorders that compromise mobility in the elderly. (James L. Shaffer)

dial bones inward when walking, so that the foot comes down on its inner margin) of the rearfoot at the subtalor joint between the heel bone (calcaneus) and the wedge-shaped talus bone directly above it. Also called overpronation or fallen arches, flatfeet involve a flattening of the medial longitudinal arch, resulting in the middle of the ankle joint rolling in toward the midline of the body and a calcaneus that often appears to turn out laterally when viewed from the back. The big toe may also point up more than it should during weightbearing, causing the medial part of the foot to be more unstable. Calluses may build up under the second or third toes, indicating a lack of propulsion during the toe-off phase of running.

A neuroma, essentially a benign tumor of the nerves, involves the classic signs of aching, burning, numbness, and shooting sensations in the forefoot, often occurring during the latter half of prolonged activities. Excessive foot pronation is often the culprit, as rotation of the metatarsal heads tends to pinch the nerve running between the third and fourth toes. Chronic pinching inflames and enlarges the nerve sheath, causing increasing pain as the enlarged sheath becomes squeezed even more.

CHRONIC HEEL PROBLEMS

The most common disorder of the heel is plantar fascitis, evidenced by pain and fatigue on the sole, arch swelling, and inflammation of dense fibrous connective tissue called fascia on the plantar (bottom) surface of the foot. When the foot flattens and becomes unstable during stance, the plantar fascia stretches excessively, possibly even pulling away from its attachment onto the calcaneus. The discomfort is particularly evident while pushing off with the toes, as this motion further stretches the inflamed fascia. When fascia begins to tear away from the bone, the bone often attempts to compensate by laying down more calcium and creating more bone, thus forming a heel spur that can been seen on an X ray. Plantar fascitis and heel spurs that go untreated often cause an alteration in stride mechanics, with these additional compensatory actions causing even more damage.

MUSCLE AND TENDON INJURIES

The Achilles tendon connects the calcaneus to both the lateral and medial heads of the gastrocnemius muscle (which crosses the knee, ankle, and subtalor joints) and the soleus (an important balance muscle underneath the gastrocnemius that does not cross the knee). Nagging inflammation of the Achilles tendon often takes months to heal, with the biggest contributor to chronic tendinitis being ignoring the pain and continuing heavy activity during its early stages. The Achilles tendon is not protected by a true tendon sheath as are many other tendons, and it does not possess a rich blood supply to enhance healing. It is highly recommended that, if the Achilles tendon is feeling sore, one should reduce activities that aggravate it immediately. Sudden increases in exercise level and movement up and down hills greatly aggravate Achilles tendon problems.

Some runners attempt to combat chronic Achilles tendinitis by wearing excessive heel cushioning such as huge air-filled soles, but this action may actually increase the ongoing damage. Wearing shoes that provide inappropriately large shock absorption causes the heel to sink lower as the shoe attenuates the shock, thus rapidly stretching the already-tender tendon more than necessary with every step. Prolonged, gentle stretches to both the calves and the hamstrings are important prior to any lower extremity workout; repeated, short, and bouncy stretches, however, are the primary cause of tendinitis.

SHOE SELECTION

Distance walking and running for people of all ages is best done in shoes designed predominantly for forward running, whereas court sport shoes (such as tennis shoes) are designed more to provide stability during lateral movements in addition to forward movement. Court sport shoes generally do not have enough heel elevation to make them effective running shoes. Running shoes have a slightly elevated heel to reduce stress to the Achilles tendon, although this design does reduce lateral stability and can contribute to ankle sprains. The feet of distance runners generally come into contact with the ground heel first for a majority of the race, until the sprint to the finish, and are thus designed appropriately. Shoes for sprinting are constructed for more forefoot contact upon footstrike.

The useful life of athletic shoes is approximately 350 to 550 miles, depending greatly on the ground surface. Shoes should be purchased at the end of the average day because the feet will be somewhat larger. The heel counter should be vertical, and pressing down vertically with the end of a pencil in the middle of the heel can determine shoe stability. The area of highest flexibility of a running shoe should occur approximately 40 percent of the way from the toe of the shoe to the heel.

ORTHOTIC INSERTS AND HEEL LIFTS

Orthotic inserts placed within the shoe can be made of soft, semiflexible, or rigid material. They can be customized via computer-aided construction or with casts made of each foot. Orthotic inserts improve function and efficiency of foot motion by keeping the subtalar joint in neutral at midstance and balancing the rear part of the foot to both the forefoot and the ground. Orthotics are often specifically designed to prevent the foot from excessive pronation during midstance and to maintain stability so the foot can function as a rigid lever during push-off. An orthotic device only exerts its influence when the foot comes into contact with the ground, and often, but not always, creates an arch within the foot. Orthotic inserts can be designed to support or restrict range of motion in specific foot joints, dissipate body weight over a larger contact area and thus decrease shearing force on the bottom of the foot, redistribute weightbearing to stronger parts of the foot, and eliminate contact on weaker areas. Semiflexible orthotics, constructed from rubber, plastic, or leather, are generally first used to determine if the expense of individualized computer-constructed orthotics is necessary.

Heel lifts essentially bring the ground up to the foot and save the individual from having to compensate continually by slapping the foot to the ground. They are effective in alleviating a variety of orthopedic problems, including leg length discrepancies and loss of the fat pad beneath the heel. Leg length discrepancies should be corrected gradually by increasing the heel lift height over several months. Instantly overcorrecting foot problems will quickly redistribute the weight of the body over a relatively smaller and weaker area of the foot and possibly cause more problems than before.

Diagnosis and Treatment

Foot abnormalities can only be diagnosed specifically during a clinical evaluation by a physician, physical therapist, or podiatrist. Most active older adults do not make the effort to see a physician or physical therapist for foot problems until knee pain develops. Examination of the feet and also shoes worn for at least 300 miles can help identify many foot disorders. The skin of the foot should be thick in areas where an increase in weight-bearing normally occurs, such as the heel, the lateral border, and just medial to the base of the first and fifth toes at the metatarsal heads. Bunion deformities are common in older women who wear dress shoes with high heels and pointed toes. Shoes worn by flatfooted individuals will generally have broken medial counters, whereas persons with toe-in gait will cause excessive wear on the shoe's lateral sole. The absence of a significant crease across the forefoot area indicates a reduction in toe-off at the end of stance phase.

Rehabilitation after even a relatively minor foot injury caused by either overuse or trauma can become a long and frustrating process if not conducted properly. Balance, coordination, strength, and overall posture during various types of movements are the major focus of clinical treatment. Foot pain can often be alleviated at home by superficial heat and cold application, stretching the muscles and fascia, and stimulating the feet using various types of massage. —*Daniel G. Graetzer*

See also Bone changes and disorders; Bunions; Canes and walkers; Exercise and fitness; Fallen arches; Fractures and broken bones; Hammertoes; Mobility problems; Sports participation; Wheelchair use.

For Further Information:

Hertling, Darlene, and Randolph M. Kessler. *Management of Common Musculoskeletal Disorders: Physical Therapy Principles and Methods.* Philadelphia: Lippincott, 1996. An often-referenced physical

therapist text on the evaluation and treatment of orthopedic disorders.

Magee, David J. *Orthopaedic Physical Therapy Assessment.* Philadelphia: W. B. Saunders, 1997. Discusses physical therapy assessment and treatment of various orthopedic conditions effecting the middle aged and elderly.

Forced retirement

Relevant issues: Economics, work
Significance: As baby boomers approach retirement age, mandatory retirement based on age has come under increasing attack

The issue of whether legislation supporting mandatory retirement should exist has been exacerbated by the growing number of elderly people within Western societies. A study of data from the United States, West Germany, Great Britain, and Australia revealed that attitudes toward retirement differ sharply according to country, with the Americans most strongly opposed to mandatory retirement and the Britons most accepting of it. Measures of political ideology are significant predictors of attitudes toward compulsory retirement; that is, acceptance of government intervention in various areas of the labor market is positively related to the acceptance of government regulation of retirement age.

Several studies on retirement have reported that compared to people not yet retired, recent retirees exhibit lower income, more physical and mental illness, lower self-esteem, and less life satisfaction. These findings, however, have been challenged by longitudinal studies using data from large samples that claim to show that the way individuals adapt and cope following retirement is largely predicted by how they adapted and coped before retirement. The main thing that does change for most people when they retire may well be the amount of discretionary time they have. As the opportunities and responsibilities of work are abandoned with retirement, new opportunities and responsibilities for decision making appear.

Planning is needed for retirement, particularly for some of the business aspects of retirement, such as career changes and possible job searches, financial management, housing, health management, and legal arrangements. Leisure and volunteer activities may also require systematic information and assessment. As the average life span has increased, retired people have become healthier and more capable of living independent and productive lives. A growing number of people believe that it is economically, socially, politically, and culturally imperative that older people continue to make contributions to society and that retirement should be seen as a transition from one activity to another rather than a withdrawal from useful, productive living.

LABOR PROBLEMS

Many economists, government officials, and industrial leaders, fearing an impending labor shortage, believe that the trends of early retirement should be reversed. Many also believe that the cost to society of supporting huge numbers of people who are no longer working is too great. The fact that fewer younger workers are paying into Social Security, while more older workers are drawing money out, has raised concerns about the health of the Social Security program and has added to the pressure to create incentives to keep people in the workforce.

Despite the increased recognition of the value of older workers, many have faced major adjustments in their career plans. Midlife and older workers have been especially vulnerable in three main areas: losing their jobs unexpectedly, retiring earlier than planned, and staying in positions no longer challenging to them. In the 1980's, people in the over-fifty age group were hard hit by layoffs. It is estimated that 20 percent of workers between fifty-five and fifty-nine years of age who leave the workforce do so unwillingly; of this population, 18 million people have stated that they want to work or to get a better job.

Legislation has made mandatory retirement illegal in most sectors of the American workforce. However, it has been relatively easy for employers to get around these laws, and many have sought to do so because of intense economic pressures. During the 1960's, the retirement age dropped from sixty-five to sixty-two years old. However, the affordability of retirement has changed because of changes in pay, pensions, and saving rates. A Harris Poll found that 76 percent of retirees would like to be working and that 86 percent opposed mandatory retirement. Another Harris Poll found that life satisfaction among sixty-five year olds was sig-

nificantly higher for those who were employed than for those who chose to retire early and then decided they had made a mistake.

Mature workers who stay in their jobs do not escape from the implications of the trends already discussed. A decrease in the number of middle-management jobs has meant less chance for promotion. Many mature employees who remain in organizations feel that they have reached a plateau, often at a much earlier age than they had planned. For many, this has produced feelings of burnout and anxiety about their future security.

AGE STEREOTYPES

Although it may be officially denied, many older workers have been victims of age stereotypes and age discrimination. This is based on the attitudes toward aging that exist in the United States, as well as on financial realities. Bias toward hiring and retaining younger workers, while squeezing out mature employees, often exists because of a pervasive youth culture and the feeling that young people are more flexible and comfortable with technology. In addition, cutting older workers can be attractive since their salaries tend to be higher than those of younger workers. Health benefit costs are also a consideration.

In October of 1996, the U.S. Congress passed amendments to the Age Discrimination in Employment Act of 1967 that allow cities to force police officers and firefighters to retire at age fifty-five. Many of these older workers have valuable experience and can serve ably for many more years. Such legislation has created renewed interest in redefining retirement criteria in terms of a functional age concept that would give attention to individual variability in the maintenance and development of behavioral competence.

Although inflation has forced many older people to find part-time employment or to continue working past their anticipated retirement age, stereotypes of aging may hinder the acceptance of older people in the workplace. It is particularly important to assess attitudes toward the elderly in the working-class population, which will be the first to feel the impact of increased numbers of older workers in the labor force. Since very young workers and retired people who seek employment are both competing for the same low-status jobs, it is also important to assess the attitudes of young people toward the elderly in the labor force. Studies have indicated that there are significant differences in perceptions between male and female subjects and between high school students and adults. In general, students, more than working adults, consider older workers to have poor coordination, to be prone to accidents, and to have problems learning new methods. Students also tend to think that older workers are overpaid, frequently absent because of illness, and too costly for employers.

The increased life span means that retirement can last for fifteen to twenty years or longer, during which three additional subtransitions may occur: onset of sickness and disability, institutionalization, and widowhood. The growing trend of early retirement causes a further extension of the retirement period through earlier entry into this role by relatively young elderly people, widening the gap between retirement and traditional concepts of old age. Some researchers have found that many people experience conflicting role expectations and strain after early retirement. It has been suggested that three distinct stages emerge during the extended retirement period: preaging (early) retirement, active (engaged) retirement, and passive (stabilized) retirement, each with its own characteristics and needs. These developments require long-range planning, with individuals and society adjusting to specific situations and needs as they arise.

Preparing for retirement can sometimes be problematic since it means that one is aging and moving into another life cycle change. The impact of retirement on older citizens is frequently neglected in the counseling arena. In American youth-oriented society, it is hard to get people to discuss the need for providing counseling services for the millions of people who are considering retirement. A preretirement counselor must be trained as a counselor plus understand what a person will face in retirement. Limited counseling is given to retirees by most employers, but it usually only concerns pensions. —*Jane Cross Norman*

See also Age discrimination; Age Discrimination in Employment Act of 1967; Early retirement; Employment; Job loss; *Johnson v. Mayor and City Council of Baltimore*; *Massachusetts Board of Retirement v. Murgia*; Retirement; Retirement planning; Social Security; Stereotypes; *Vance v. Bradley*.

FOR FURTHER INFORMATION:
Chandler, John. "Mandatory Retirement and Justice." *Social Theory and Practice* 22, no. 1 (Spring, 1996): 35-46.
Gall, T. L., D. R. Evans, and J. Howard. "The Retirement Adjustment Process: Changes in the Well-Being of Male Retirees Across Time." *Journals of Gerontology Series B—Psychological Sciences and Social Sciences* 52B, no. 3 (1997): 110-117.
Gillin, C. T., and Thomas R. Klassen. "Age Discrimination and Early Retirement Policies: A Comparison of Labor Market Regulation in Canada and the United States." *Journal of Aging and Social Policy* 7, no. 1 (Winter, 1995): 85-102.
Hayward, M. D., S. Friedman, and H. Chen. "Career Trajectories and Older Men's Retirement." *Journals of Gerontology Series B—Psychological Sciences and Social Sciences* 53B, no. 2 (1998): S91-103.
Levine, Martin. *Age Discrimination and the Mandatory Retirement Controversy.* Baltimore: The Johns Hopkins University Press, 1988.
Miller, Tom, and William H. Smith. "Should Public-Safety Officers Be Subject to Mandatory Retirement?" *CQ Researcher* 7, no. 29 (August 1, 1997): 689.
Ozawa, M. N., and Y. Lum. "Economic Satisfaction Among American Retirees." *Journal of Gerontological Social Work* 27, no. 4 (1997): 21-40.
Quadagno, Jill S., and Melissa Hardy. "Regulating Retirement Through the Age Discrimination in Employment Act." *Research on Aging* 13, no. 4 (December, 1991): 470-475.
Reis, Myrna, and Dolores P. Gold. "Retirement, Personality, and Life Satisfaction: A Review and Two Models." *Journal of Applied Gerontology* 12, no. 2 (1993): 261-282.
Shultz, Kenneth S., Kelly R. Morton, and Joelle R. Weckerle. "The Influence of Push and Pull Factors on Voluntary and Involuntary Early Retirees' Retirement Decision and Adjustment." *Journal of Vocational Behavior* 53, no. 1 (1998): 45-57.

FORGETFULNESS

RELEVANT ISSUES: Biology, health and medicine, psychology

SIGNIFICANCE: Age-related forgetfulness or memory loss varies from the normal to significant impairment; despite forgetfulness, it is still possible for older adults to learn new information and to retain and control previously learned material, although it may take longer to do so

Many older persons become anxious when they forget things previously learned. When they complain of forgetfulness, older adults are typically referring to a decline in their ability to recall recent events. They complain of difficulty recalling the names of acquaintances, family members, and dates of events that will occur in the near future. They complain that as they get older it takes them longer to remember. Older adults say their most frequent memory lapse is not being able to recall a word that was on the "tip of the tongue." What is most worrisome to them is forgetting where they had placed an object, failing to do something they should have done, or forgetting something someone had told them.

Many older adults fear that forgetfulness is a sign of a brain disease called dementia. Dementia seriously affects a person's ability to perform daily activities. The symptoms of this disease include severe memory loss, impaired thinking, and altered personality. Other signs of dementia are asking the same question repeatedly, becoming lost in familiar places, being unable to follow directions, being disoriented, losing track of time, and neglecting personal health, hygiene, and safety. Dementing illnesses are usually categorized by their suspected causes, including degenerative, vascular, infectious, toxic, or metabolic. Dementia affects less than 10 percent of people who are older than sixty-five, but increases to between 15 and 20 percent by the time they reach age eighty-five.

Alzheimer's is one such degenerative disease. With an estimated four million Americans exhibiting the symptoms, Alzheimer's disease is the most common form of dementia and the fourth leading cause of death in the United States. Alzheimer's disease and stroke-induced dementia are irreversible. The earliest symptoms of the disease include progressive forgetfulness, reminders that do not help patients with recall, and a decline in reasoning skills. Approximately 10 percent of people in the United States over the age of sixty-five suffer from Alzheimer's disease and as many as 50 percent of people over the age of eighty-five suffer from the disease. Amnesia, a still rarer memory disorder, leaves patients unable to learn or recall any new information.

To older adults, significant forgetfulness—whatever the cause—represents a threat to independence and their ability to think clearly. While many people report they forget things, research confirms that significant forgetfulness is not an inevitable consequence of aging. Surveys of older people show that as many as 20 percent of adults over age eighty-five report they have never had significant trouble with their memory.

Empirical research indicates that temporary lapses in memory become increasingly common as people age. Some types of memory decline faster than others. For example, substantial losses occur in the working memory of older adults. Working memory refers to the ability of the mind to hold information, manipulate and reorganize it, and combine it with new information. Research, however, indicates most people will not develop significant memory impairment as they age. People's ability to remember autobiographical material, for example, does not normally decline with age. Although age-related forgetfulness may cause older adults to take longer to absorb new information, they are just as capable as younger people to retain and recall it. In fact, vocabulary and reasoning skills often improve as a person ages.

BIOLOGICAL FACTORS

The root causes of age-associated forgetfulness are largely biological—a decline in the efficiency of cortical processing in the brain. Psychological and sociological factors may also lead to a decline in mental energy or attention span. Forgetfulness that is greater than expected in healthy aging can often be treated medically. Age-related forgetfulness is usually not accompanied by other thinking impairments and is not severe enough to grossly interfere with daily living and be linked to dementia.

Evidence suggests that memory loss associated with aging may be linked to a gene malfunction. Age-related memory disorders may be due to cardiovascular disease, poor vision and hearing, fatigue, depression, infections, or medication side effects. Other common causes of memory disorders are strokes (which are blockages or bleeding in the blood vessels in the brain), thyroid disease, and vitamin B_{12} deficiency. Untreated high blood pressure (hypertension) can also cause mild memory impairment and lengthen recall time.

Another contributor to cognitive decline is the fact that the brain gradually begins to shrink as early as age forty—especially in the frontal regions that play a critical role in remembering. Brain mass steadily shrinks as people enter their sixties and seventies, at approximately 5 to 10 percent per decade. Research done by the National Institute on Aging shows that the most dramatic memory decline does not occur until about age seventy. A significant loss of neurons in the regions of the brain responsible for memory—the hippocampus and forebrain—probably contributes to age-related memory difficulties. The forebrain delivers the critical neurotransmitter acetylcholine to the hippocampus and many regions of the cerebral cortex.

Such psychological factors as stress may even make people forgetful. High concentrations of cortisol, a hormone released by the adrenal glands in response to danger, threat, and aggravation, correlate with higher levels of forgetfulness.

What Causes Forgetfulness?

The oldest and most common explanation for forgetting is decay. The decay theory holds that if unused, memory traces will vanish. In the 1880's, German psychologist Hermann Ebbinghaus developed the "curve of forgetting," which illustrates just how rapidly memory decays. People forget 80 percent of what they have learned after one month of having learned it. According to an alternative theory of forgetting, the interference theory, memories do not so much disappear as lose themselves in the crowd of memories. As people age and their experiences multiply, they tend to become neglectfully absentminded. The interference theory holds that a lack of a precise cue to trigger recall of the memory causes the forgetting. Still another theory holds that age-related memory loss is behavioral, brought on by negative cultural stereotypes rather than by physical deterioration.

People who believe memory inevitably declines with age tend to believe that trying to do something about the problem is futile. Adherents say it is virtually impossible to compensate for age-related memory loss. It is important to remember that age-related memory deficits are accompanied by general cognitive slowing. Thus, age-related memory loss is considered normal.

The degree to which memory is lost can be a function of good health, intellectual stimulation, daily activity, and a positive attitude. Research indicates it is possible to do something about forgetfulness. However, no magic wand exists to make age-related forgetfulness better. Scientists have been searching to find drugs (called "smart drugs") to boost memory. Sugar, for example, enhances memory by fueling the active neurons in the brain, which require high quantities of blood sugar. By the late 1990's, little or no strong evidence showed substances such as ginkgo, choline, or lecithin improve memory. Staying physically fit and problem-solving mental activity also contribute to managing age-related memory loss.

Older adults use an array of strategies to enhance or improve memory. The more effective tools and techniques for the older adult require the user to pay close attention and be organized. They rely on memory retrieval cues such as an image, a number, a word, a sentence, an acronym, a face, an auditory signal, or a smell. External memory aides include reminders from other people, to-do lists, address books, alarms and timers, strings around the finger, calendars, and appointment books. Another useful memory aid involves repeating a new acquaintance's name several times during a conversation.

Evidence points to the fact that to be successful, forgetful older adults must invest themselves in compensating for age-related memory loss. They must be motivated, have a positive attitude, and be willing to put in the effort it will take to manage their forgetfulness.

Age may make older people more forgetful, but it has little or no effect on the ability to think. Most people remain both alert and able as they age, although it may take them longer to remember things. Older people are less likely to have major memory problems if they believe in themselves and work to improve their recall. Indeed, older people's perception of themselves—their self-confidence—can be improved. Older people who use their minds are not as likely to lose them, or at least not as fast.

—Fred Buchstein

See also Aging process; Alzheimer's Association; Alzheimer's disease; Brain changes and disorders; Caregiving; Dementia; Memory changes and loss; Mental impairment; Psychiatry, geriatric.

FOR FURTHER INFORMATION:

Baddeley, Alan D. *Your Memory: A User's Guide.* 2d ed. London: PRION, 1993.

Baddeley, Alan D., Barbara A. Wilson, and Fraser N. Watts. *Handbook of Memory Disorders.* Chichester, England: John Wiley & Sons, 1995.

Perlmutter, Marion, and Elizabeth Hall. *Adult Development and Aging.* 2d ed. New York: John Wiley & Sons, 1992.

Rupp, Rebecca. *Committed to Memory: How We Remember and Why We Forget.* New York: Crown, 1998.

Schacter, Daniel L. *Searching for Memory: The Brain, the Mind, and the Past.* New York: Basic Books, 1996.

Williams, Mark E. *The American Geriatric Society's Complete Guide to Aging and Health.* New York: Harmony Books, 1995.

FOUNTAIN OF AGE, THE

AUTHOR: Betty Friedan

DATE: Published in 1993

RELEVANT ISSUES: Culture, media, values, work

SIGNIFICANCE: An extended argument against media and cultural images of older people as pitiable or invisible, this book claims aging can bring new levels of self-discovery and accomplishment

In *The Fountain of Age,* Betty Friedan, whose *The Feminine Mystique* (1963) is often credited with launching the modern women's movement, indicts modern attitudes toward the aging as destructive. Like her first book, this one was inspired by personal traumas. She opens by describing the shock of her sixtieth birthday, when younger friends acted as if she were crossing into a foreboding, miserable land of exile.

Friedan comments that she began to search for media images of older people. These were relatively rare, even though the median age of Americans is rising. Virtually all the older women shown were either celebrities or appeared to be under forty. Gerontology seemed preoccupied with nursing homes and dire disabilities, and older patients were always assumed to need "guidance" about how to live their lives. Finding these phenomena at odds with the reality of the age-group peers she knew, the author decided to study aging in America.

Noted feminist Betty Friedan, the author of The Fountain of Age. (Courtesy of Betty Friedan)

Subsequent chapters discuss societal denial of age, the idea of aging as inevitable decline, the paradoxes of retirement law and work practices, and possible reasons that women live longer than men. The book looks at institutions such as total-care retirement communities and Leisure World. Friedan argues that these "solutions" to the aging "problem" are ultimately unsatisfactory; they are created with commercial goals foremost, and they wall off residents from the larger world. Friedan gives a hopeful picture of the hospice movement and pleads for more measures to keep disabled elderly people in their homes whenever possible.

Friedan portrays many older Americans as living happy lives with verve and purpose. Those with medical problems carry on by making minor changes in their routines. For a satisfactory transit to this state, however, it is necessary to move beyond prevailing social values about success, masculinity and femininity, and age-appropriate behavior. Friedan's major finding is that "only self-chosen purposes, projects, and ties . . . are important beyond midlife." Once these are claimed, she shows, either paid employment or unpaid pursuits can be fulfilling.

Reviewers criticized the book's focus on affluent and relatively healthy elders. Most aging Americans cannot give house parties on Mexican beaches or go white-water rafting, as Friedan and her friends do. However, the larger point about community and mutual help is also made with scenes from a Florida trailer park and from an apartment court where poor elderly widows live.

Although a significant work, *The Fountain of Age* failed to have the high impact of Friedan's feminist manifesto. Its length (671 pages) and plodding style may help account for this. Moreover, its message seemed to be one American society was not ready to hear. The advance wave of baby boomers had not reached fifty when the book was published, and the forces Friedan resists, from media fantasies of perpetual youth to the nursing home industry, continued to wield economic and cultural power.　　　　　　　*—Emily Alward*

See also Advertising; Ageism; Cultural views of aging; Films; Nursing and convalescent homes; Stereotypes; Television; Women and aging.

401K PLANS

RELEVANT ISSUES: Economics, family, law, work
SIGNIFICANCE: 401K plans allow employees to establish company-sponsored pretax retirement accounts for greater earnings potential

401K plans, also known as salary reduction plans, are retirement investment programs that allow a percentage of an employee's pretax salary to be deducted and placed into a company-sponsored investment plan. Created by Congress in 1978 in an effort to provide an incentive for Americans to save more for retirement, 401K plans offer a number of advantages to participants. All earnings placed into 401K plans are deducted from gross earnings, reducing an individual's taxable income, and all money invested continues to grow tax-free until withdrawn. Many employers match the employee's contributions to 401K plans. In many instances, contributions are also exempt from state and local taxes. There is a set maximum limit, adjusted annually for inflation, that can be placed into a 401K; in 1998, the maximum annual amount an individual could invest in a 401K was $10,000. Nonprofit employers were allowed to begin offering employee 401Ks in 1997.

Employers are 401K plan sponsors and set guidelines and limitations for employee participation. Most employers limit participation to full-time employees who have been working for the company more than one year. Some allow employees to contribute immediately, but others require a six-month or one-year probationary period before giving employee eligibility or matching employee contributions. By law, all money contributed by the employee is immediately 100 percent vested, but the employer may place vesting requirements on matching contributions.

Financial advisers encourage employees to participate in 401K plans when possible. In most instances, the investor has considerable flexibility over how 401K funds are invested; often, almost all of the standard options available to anyone opening a brokerage account are available to the 401K participant. The specific opportunities available to employees depend on the plan offered by the company. Municipal bond funds, money-market funds, foreign bond funds, global funds, international funds, and individual stocks may be purchased depending on the specifics of the plan.

As with almost every other retirement plan offering pretax salary investment, government regulations discourage investors from early withdrawals by leveling a 10 percent penalty. 401K contributions may not be distributed to individuals who have not reached the age of fifty-nine and a half. Funds may be distributed in extreme cases where there is a demonstrated need. Loans from 401K funds are allowed by the vast majority of programs, but usually for a maximum of five years. Failure to repay 401K loans within the specified period is considered equivalent to a withdrawal from the account, resulting in a 10 percent penalty and taxes due on the outstanding balance.

　　　　　　　—Donald C. Simmons, Jr.

See also Early retirement; Income sources; Individual retirement accounts (IRAs); Retirement; Retirement planning.

FRACTURES AND BROKEN BONES

RELEVANT ISSUES: Health and medicine
SIGNIFICANCE: Fractures can occur at any age, but older people are at greater risk for certain types of fractures and often have an increased recovery time

A fracture is a break in the continuity of a bone. Fractures can occur at any age, but there are certain causes and types of fractures that are more common in older people. Internal and external factors influence the development of a fracture. The internal factors include the strength of the bone and whether it is affected by disease. For example, osteoporosis, which is common in the elderly, makes the bone thin and fragile and more likely to break with minimal trauma. External factors include the type of trauma that occurs. In the elderly, falls are the major cause of trauma leading to fractures.

Fractures may be complete or incomplete. Complete fractures involve a break across the entire section of the bone. In incomplete fractures, the break occurs in only a part of the bone. Open, or compound, fractures involve a break in the bone as well as a break in the skin, with an increased risk of acquiring an infection in the wound. In closed, or simple, fractures, the bone is broken but does not pierce the skin. Fractures that occur with minimal but repeated stress on a bone, such as in running, are called stress fractures. Fractures that occur in diseased bones are referred to as "pathologic." Fractures are also named according to the bone affected, such as the femur (thigh bone), humerus (upper arm bone), or vertebra (back bone).

Broken bones begin to heal as soon as they are injured. Bleeding from the blood vessels inside the bone occurs first. Then a clot forms, which later develops into a callus. The callus serves as a bridge or framework in which new bone cells begin to develop. The length of time for complete healing varies with the age of the person and the type of bone injured. In general, older people take longer to heal.

Fractures in Older Adults

Older people are at special risk for certain types of fractures, including those of the wrist, upper arm, and ankle. Hip fractures frequently occur as a result of injury caused by falls; complications may lead to additional problems and even death. The number of hip fractures that occur each year is expected to increase as the baby-boom population ages. Crush or compression fractures in the backbone may occur with minimal trauma and are related to weakening of the bone because of osteoporosis. The presence of osteoporosis increases the risk of fractures in women after the menopause, as well as in elderly men.

Many factors increase the risk of accidental injury in the elderly. Older adults with mental impairment or other health problems affecting their balance are more likely to fall. The chance of falls increases with the use of tranquilizers and medications to lower blood pressure, and also increases in people who are poorly nourished or do not exercise regularly. Decreases in both mobility and independence that accompany fractures lessen the individual's quality of life. The medical costs related to fractures measure in the billions of dollars each year.

Treatment of Fractures

Prompt recognition and treatment of a fracture increases the likelihood of a better outcome for healing. One of the most common signs of a broken bone is pain in the affected part. The ability to use the injured part may or may not be affected. If a bone in the arm or leg is broken, swelling will become noticeable in the painful area. The extremity may appear abnormal in shape or position because of the break in the normal alignment of the bone. Some fractures do not displace the bones, so the extremity may not appear abnormal except for swelling.

The immediate treatment of fractures involves measures to protect the injured part and person from further injury. If a fracture is suspected after a fall, the most important concern is to watch for signs of shock, including pale, cool, and moist skin. The person may become light-headed or may seem less alert. If these signs are present, it will be necessary to call for emergency assistance; the injured person should remain quiet and should not be moved.

A fractured body part should not be moved. Attempts to put the part back into normal position may cause further injury and pain. If a broken bone is suspected, the injured part should not be used. Ice may be applied to reduce swelling and discomfort. If the suspected fracture is in an arm or a leg, the extremity should be elevated to reduce swelling. People with suspected fractures should be examined by a health professional who can confirm the diagnosis with specialized testing, such as X rays or bone scans.

Fractures must be treated to restore correct position and function of the affected part. A physician who specializes in broken bones is called an orthopedic surgeon or an orthopedist. The physician can diagnose the fracture and determine the best method for treatment. The fractured bone must be properly aligned for proper healing. The physician will return the bone to its normal position if necessary. The bone must be immobilized to prevent movement while healing occurs. Methods of immobilizing the bone include casts, which may be made of plaster or fiberglass. Some fractures may require surgery to insert different types of metal devices into the bone to stabilize the fracture. The healing time varies according to the type of fracture and the age of the individual. Older people generally require a longer time to heal. Rehabilitation after a fracture may involve physical or occupational therapy to help the individual regain maximum function of the affected part.

PREVENTION OF FRACTURES

Prevention of fractures is extremely important for older people. The development of osteoporosis is one of the major factors related to fractures in the elderly. Measures that may be taken to reduce the effect of this disease include regular weightbearing exercise such as walking, dancing, or stair climbing; sufficient calcium intake; and avoiding smoking. Screening tests are available that measure the density of the bone. Medications and hormones may be ordered by the health care provider for those who are particularly at risk for osteoporosis.

The consequences of falls and fractures in the older population are significant. Measures to reduce the chance of falls include safety precautions in the home. The chance of tripping may be reduced by applying nonskid backing to throw rugs and keeping electrical cords or other small objects out of walking areas. The more medications a person takes, the greater the chance that he or she may experience side effects that may affect balance or judgment. Individuals should be aware of these side effects and exercise caution when moving about. The physician should be informed about these side effects to see if changes in the medication could be made. —*Bobbie Siler*

See also Bone changes and disorders; Exercise and fitness; Foot disorders; Hip replacement; Injuries among the elderly; Osteoporosis; Safety issues; Smoking.

FOR FURTHER INFORMATION:

American Academy of Orthopedic Surgeons, Public Information, Patient Education Brochures. http://www.aaos.org/wordhtml/home2. htm

Horan, Michael Arthur, and Rod A. Little, eds. *Injury in the Aging.* New York: Cambridge University Press, 1998.

Preventing Falls and Fractures. Bethesda, Md.: U.S. Department of Health and Human Services, Public Health Service, National Institutes of Health, National Institute on Aging, 1998.

Siegel, Irwin M. *All About Bone: An Owner's Manual.* New York: Demos Medical Publishing, 1998.

FRAUD AGAINST THE ELDERLY

RELEVANT ISSUES: Economics, law, psychology, sociology

SIGNIFICANCE: Although people sixty-five years of age and older make up only 12.5 percent of the population of the United States, they are the victims in more than 35 percent of the cases involving fraud

Perpetrators of consumer fraud frequently target the elderly because they are viewed as an accessible group who often live alone. When living alone, the elderly individual is unable to discuss with others questionable deals and offers. Consequently, the older person can often be persuaded to follow suggestions to pursue fraudulent endeavors. Since many elderly people are retired, they tend to spend more time in the home than younger adults do. This increases the likelihood that individuals promoting fraudulent schemes will be able to contact them.

Senior citizens as a group are typically a trusting and polite population. Rather than abruptly cutting off another individual when speaking, they will often permit the other person to finish a presentation. A one-on-one interaction between a person focused on committing fraud and a victim enhances the probability of the successful completion of the task. This allows the con artist an opportunity to charm and persuade a targeted elderly person. With the availability of cash or liquid assets, older adults are often unable to reflect on immediate events until much later, after they have released funds.

Fraud against the elderly is an ongoing problem that is predicted to increase in severity with the aging of the population. The number of people over age sixty-five grew dramatically during the 1980's and 1990's and was expected to continue to increase dramatically during the first few decades of the twenty-first century. It was estimated that by 2010 there would be twice as many Americans over age eighty-five as there were in 1990. By 2030, it is likely that one in five Americans will be over age sixty-five and that there will be more elderly people in the United States than individuals under eighteen. In the late 1990's, the United States government estimated that there were eight hundred active "bunco" or fraud scams targeting senior citizens. These scams involve such activities as deceptive sales pitches for living trusts; low-risk, high-yield investment schemes; unneeded home improvements; and unnecessary automobile repairs.

HEALTH FRAUD

The elderly population has a high incidence of chronic health problems. The combination of the increasing number of elderly people, their accessibility, and chronic health problems makes them attractive targets to those who commit health fraud. It has been estimated in a report by the U.S. House of Representatives that elderly Americans spend $10 billion per year on questionable or fraudulent health products or services. The elderly comprise approximately 60 percent of all health care fraud victims. Because of the numerous health care needs of older people, they are susceptible to fraudulent claims of miracle cures and tonics for promoting good health.

Since arthritis symptoms tend to come and go, older people easily attribute relief from symptoms to fraudulent remedies. Arthritis sufferers have paid excessive amounts for bottled seawater, New Zealand green-lipped mussel shell extracts, and Chinese "herbal" medicines that do not contain any herbs. Cancer clinics that advertise miracle cures using unscientific treatments such as laetrile or mineral therapy target the vulnerable elderly

"Nellie," the eighty-year-old victim of a scam that she reported to the Crimes Against Retired and Elderly (CARE) police unit, speaks at the meeting of a support group for similar victims in 1995. (AP Photo/Nanine Hartzenbusch)

cancer patient. Sexual aids and aphrodisiacs, substitutes for hearing aids, antiaging compounds, baldness remedies, body-toning devices, weight-loss schemes, and potions to improve vitality are all repeatedly presented to the elderly consumer, accompanied with exorbitant claims of effectiveness.

A number of red flags that typically signal health fraud have been identified by consumer protection groups. Such warning signals include promises of quick and dramatic cures, extensive advertisement of the product using testimonials, the utilization of imprecise and nonmedical language, appeals to the emotions rather then rationality, the declaration that a single product cures many ills, and the inclusion of criticisms of the medical and nutritional sciences in advertising materials.

SOCIAL SECURITY FRAUD

Since older adults are often dependent upon Social Security income, they can be targeted for fraudulent schemes using the suggestion that these benefits may be in jeopardy. They may receive official-looking letters that trick the reader into believing that a government agency is associated with the solicitation. Such letters attempt to convince the readers that their donations are needed to help protect Social Security benefits. The American Association of Retired Persons (AARP) warns that such mailings seek fees for services already provided by the Social Security Administration or by local advocacy organizations. The letters may also sell "required" items such as laminated Social Security cards, conduct sweepstakes to entice older citizens to purchase other unnecessary services, or state that a failure to contribute will eliminate lobbying that would prevent Social Security cutbacks.

TELEMARKETING FRAUD

The commission of fraud through telemarketing operations has grown into a major concern. The Federal Bureau of Investigation (FBI) has estimated that up to fourteen thousand telemarketing operations in the United States annually bilk citizens of $40 billion. One-third of the fraudulent telephone "boiler rooms" exclusively target older adults. According to the AARP, 56 percent of the telemarketing fraud victims are over age fifty. Fraudulent telemarketers maintain a "mooch list" that contains the names of likely victims for their scams. Most elderly fraud victims do not make the connection between illegal telemarketing and criminal activity. Typically, they do not associate the person on the phone with someone who is trying to steal their money. Many older adults may evaluate the caller as a "nice young man or woman" who is simply trying to make an honest living. They may view the caller as a college student working his or her way through school. Even if the telemarketer begins using a hard sell, the older adult often believes that the caller is an ambitious person trying to set a good sales record or receive a bonus. Once they realize that they have not received their money's worth after a telemarketing fraud, many senior citizens remain reluctant to admit that they have been cheated or robbed.

The AARP has identified a number of typical telemarketing fraud solicitations targeting older adults. Contests and sweepstakes are a major category of telemarketing fraud. One popular pitch focuses on prize promotions. The elderly person will hear the exciting phrase, "You have won a valuable prize." Following this enthusiastic greeting, the promoter will demand several hundred dollars to cover shipping and handling costs, to prepay taxes, or to make a "refundable" deposit of good will. Often the "winner" is required to provide a credit card or checking account number as a way to establish eligibility for the prize. (Even legitimate sweepstakes can be misleading in their claims; some mailings cause elderly individuals to believe that they have won millions of dollars.)

Another common telemarketing pitch directed toward the elderly offers products that are being sold at "below wholesale." The telemarketer will emphasize that the low cost is available for a short period of time; it is usually the final day of the sale. Inevitably, the merchandise is actually being sold for a price that is higher than normal retail. A similar offer combines bargain prices with the promise that portions of the payments are being passed on to charitable endeavors. In the "one-in-four" prize gimmick, the caller promises that the person has won one of four expensive-sounding prizes. In order to determine which prize the person has won, the elderly individual must donate a certain amount of money to a charitable-sounding campaign. The "one-in-four" scam is a way for a fraudulent telemarketer to sell things for grossly inflated prices. One of the expensive-sounding prizes is actually of little monetary value, and it is the object "won" by the elderly person for the donation.

It has become quite common for elderly people to receive phone calls from counterfeit charities. These callers present themselves as representatives of organizations associated with police or fire-fighter benevolent associations. The scam artists have established these "associations" as a means to take advantage of the feelings of civic responsibility held by many senior citizens. A related scam involving the selling of magazine subscriptions cheats elderly consumers out of tens of thousands of dollars each year. Special handling fees far exceed the standard subscription rates for the magazines. The telemarketing of the magazine subscriptions often is accompanied with promises of phony prizes, contests, and sweepstakes. Even elderly people who refuse a subscription may receive threats and be badgered into paying bogus bills.

Senior citizens can have a difficult time with a caller who is convincing. They may be reluctant to hang up. The scam artist may become very friendly on the phone or use bullying tactics that intimidate the elderly person. Elderly people may receive up to twenty solicitations each day from callers trying to perpetrate a fraud. This continual barrage of calls can eventually wear down the defenses of the elderly person. Even after elderly people have been victimized by a fraudulent telemarketer, they may fall prey to the "recovery scam." A number of "reloaders" call victims from the mooch lists and promise to recover previous losses.

The National Fraud Information Center (NFIC) suggests that elderly people need to know a number of facts concerning telemarketing fraud. Congress passed the Telephone Consumer Protection Act in 1991 as a protection to the consumer. Senior citizens must realize that illegal telemarketing is a crime that is perpetrated by criminals. The tone of voice used by the telemarketer is not an effective way to determine the legitimacy of the call. Legitimate companies do not pressure people into sending money immediately. It is illegal for contest or sweepstakes promoters to require payment to enter or claim a prize. It is illegal for a telemarketer to call if a person has requested not to be contacted. Calling times are restricted to between the hours of 8 A.M. and 9 P.M. Legitimate telemarketers may not lie about any information, including facts about the goods or services they are marketing. Also, telemarketers may not withdraw money from a checking account without specific verifiable authorization.

Friends and relatives of elderly people should be sensitive to warning signals that often indicate victimization by fraudulent telemarketers. Since the names of victims appear on mooch lists, they begin to receive more mail offering free prizes. Frequent visits by couriers or the presence of courier receipts lying around a home is a troublesome sign. Many fraudulent telemarketers use courier services as a means to commit the elderly person to immediately send money to them. If a senior citizen is spending large amounts of time in phone conversations and is secretive about the nature of the calls, another red flag should be raised.

INVESTMENT FRAUD

It has become apparent that some stockbrokers and financial planners are using abusive practices when contacting elderly investors. The North American Securities Administrators Association (NASAA) issued this warning in special testimony before the United States Senate Special Committee on Aging. The NASAA found that although many elderly people have significant financial investments, they do not spend a large amount of time learning about the language or theory behind financial matters. This gap between having investments and having the knowledge of what might constitute sound investing actions puts many of them at risk of being victimized by perpetrators of investment fraud. Many senior citizens attempt to increase their income by seeking higher returns on their principal. Unfortunately, they may fall victim to fraudulent promises of "safe" high-yielding investments that may, in fact, lead to the loss of principal. Scam artists will usually prey upon the fears of elderly citizens. During the sales pitch, they suggest to the target that he or she will likely outlive their financial resources or lose everything because of a catastrophic illness or hospitalization.

Many elderly investors not only trust unscrupulous investment planners with the initial financial decisions but also fail to monitor the progress of the investments. This can lead to excessive or unauthorized trading of investments as a way to increase commissions for the unscrupulous broker.

Fraudulent investment planners often make it difficult for the elderly investor to retrieve funds once the investment has been made. Elderly people will be pressured to "roll over" nonexistent profits into new investments that promise even higher rates of return.

The elderly are often embarrassed by their poor judgment in making faulty investments. This leads to a zone of safety for the unscrupulous financial planner. Some elderly people have reported that they fear public scrutiny of their participation in fraudulent investment scams because it may lead to loss of independence. Con artists are aware that elderly people fear the possibility that they would be declared incompetent and forced into an institution. Scam investment planners entice the elderly to increase investments as a means to recover lost funds. The unscrupulous broker may promise to make good on the original funds that were lost and generate new income beyond what was originally promised. This is termed taking a "second bite" out of the elderly citizen. The end result is further financial losses for the victim.

Internet fraud is promising to become a major source of concern. Hundreds of on-line investment newsletters have appeared on the Internet. Anyone can reach tens of thousands of potential fraud victims by building a Web site, posting a message on an on-line bulletin board, sending mass e-mails, or entering live chat rooms. As elderly people increase the time they spend on the Internet, investment scam artists will be there to entice them with promises of high yields and low risk.

FRAUD INFORMATION RESOURCES

The NFIC is operated by the private, nonprofit National Consumers League, which was founded in 1899. The organization promotes research, education, and consumer advocacy. The NFIC was established in 1992 as a response to the increasing incidence and negative impact of fraud on the elderly population. The organization provides special tips for seniors concerning identification of the danger signs for telemarketing fraud. It also provides resources to help elderly victims of fraud contact appropriate enforcement agencies. The Elder Fraud Project is a formal component of the NFIC that provides specific materials designed to prevent telemarketing fraud on the elderly.

—*Frank J. Prerost*

See also Consumer issues; Health care; Loneliness; Poverty; Scams and con artists; Social Security.

FOR FURTHER INFORMATION:

Breckler, Rosemary. *If You're Over Fifty You Are the Target!* San Leandro, Calif.: Bristol, 1991. This book provides practical advice about all of the various types of scams targeting senior citizens.

Bruni, Frank, and Elinor Burkett. *Consumer Terrorism: How to Get Satisfaction When You're Being Ripped Off.* New York: HarperPerennial, 1997. This book explains how the consumer can take aggressive action to ensure that businesses do not engage in fraudulent practices. It includes a number of useful phone numbers and addresses that can be used to combat fraud.

Cheney, Walter. *The Second Fifty Years: A Reference Manual for Senior Citizens.* New York: Paragon House, 1992. This is an oversized book with large-sized print that contains information on fraud and advice for seniors as consumers.

Engel, Peter. *Scam! Shams, Stings, and Shady Business Practices, and How You Can Avoid Them.* New York: St. Martin's Griffin, 1996. Engel presents a number of real-life cases of fraud. Suggestions on how to avoid becoming a victim of fraud are interspersed throughout the book.

Lieberman, Marc. *Your Rights as a Consumer: Legal Tips for Savvy Purchasing of Goods, Services, and Credit.* Hawthorne, N.J.: Career Press, 1994. The book contains a good chapter on consumer fraud and the elderly with a focus on health and medical scams.

FREE RADICAL THEORY OF AGING

RELEVANT ISSUES: Biology, health and medicine

SIGNIFICANCE: Free radicals are naturally produced, reactive molecules that damage cellular components; long-term accumulation of this damage may explain the aging process

Free radicals are oxygen-containing molecules that have taken on additional electrons during chemical reactions that occur during normal cellular processes, such as mitochondrial electron transport, enzymatic processes involving oxygen (particularly oxidases or oxygenases), peroxisome activity (which breaks down cellular toxins), and other aerobic processes. Because of these "extra" electrons, free radicals are unstable and therefore highly reactive. Cells normally produce enzymes that routinely convert free radicals to a less reactive form. However, while they exist, free radicals can damage other molecules, particularly lipids, proteins, and deoxyribonucleic acid (DNA). Although a number of substances can eliminate free radicals and help to repair the damage done by them, such substances cannot be completely effective. It is believed that the gradual accumulation of free radical damage in cells contributes to certain diseases, particularly cancer, and to aging.

Why would a biological system that continually produces such damaging substances originally evolve? Presumably, because life originated when there was a much lower percentage of atmospheric oxygen than there is today, free radical production in primitive cells occurred at a lower rate. With the evolution of photosynthetic organisms that produce oxygen, the subsequent rise of atmospheric oxygen levels, and the establishment of aerobic cellular respiration as a prevalent source of cellular energy, the production of cellular radicals increased. It has even been suggested that free radical reactions, initiated by ionizing radiation in the prebiotic atmosphere, may have formed many of the organic chemicals needed for living systems and may have contributed to the origin of life itself. Because of the role of radicals in causing DNA mutations, radical reactions may also have contributed to the evolution of life by producing new genetic variants.

RADICAL DAMAGE AND PROTECTIVE MECHANISMS

Denham Harman first proposed the free radical theory of aging in 1956, after the discovery of the existence of free radicals in living cells and of their effects on cellular molecules. The theory states that the biological changes associated with the aging process are partially or completely a result of long-term damage to cellular components through reactions with free radicals. The theory is consistent with observations that the aging process can be affected by environmental changes (such as diet or exposure to radiation) and modified by genetic factors, since either of these can affect the production of radicals or the efficiency of repair to radical damage.

It is clear that the action of free radicals can lead to problems for cells, since the cell produces several enzymes to remove free radicals. For example, the superoxide radical is formed during a number of cellular processes. Superoxide can be "dismutated" by the enzyme superoxide dismutase, producing oxygen and peroxide. Peroxide, in turn, is converted to oxygen and water by the enzyme catalase or is degraded by peroxidases. Other substances called antioxidants are believed to aid in minimizing damage by radicals. These substances do not directly react with radicals but inhibit the damage done by radicals to other molecules. Because vitamins C and E have antioxidant properties, they are often recommended as either dietary supplements or ingredients in foods as part of an "antiaging" diet. In addition to antioxidants, some dietary substances are "radical scavengers," which directly remove radicals. Ethanol, the type of alcohol found in alcoholic beverages, is a radical scavenger, leading to suggestions that a moderate intake of alcohol is somewhat beneficial.

Sometimes, both superoxide and peroxide can react with each other before enzymes can eliminate them. This is called the Haber-Weis reaction, and its products are oxygen, the hydroxide ion, and the hydroxyl radical. The hydroxyl radical is much more reactive than either superoxide or peroxide and can cause more extensive damage. For example, it can cause DNA-DNA or DNA-protein cross-linking. Cross-linking is the formation of irreversible connections between molecules, which drastically impairs their functions. Action of the hydroxyl radical could presumably burden cells with DNA damage, impaired enzymatic activity, or the inability to divide. While all of these effects could result in the gradual deterioration associated with aging, there is no clear demonstration that cross-linked molecules in cells increase with age.

Free radicals also damage lipids, particularly polyunsaturated fatty acids. Such reactions often produce malonaldehyde, which can cause further damage by cross-linking to proteins. One possible product of protein-malonaldehyde cross-linkage is lipofuscin, a pigment that is known to increase with age. It may be that some lipids work in conjunction with antioxidants to protect cells from radical damage by acting as "targets" for radicals. Lipotuscin, an oxidized proteolipid, may serve this purpose and is known to accumulate in tissues with age. Proteins can also be oxidized by radicals, and there is evidence that cellular protein oxidization occurs, increases with age, and may contribute to a number of degenerative diseases associated with aging, including cancer and brain dysfunction.

RADICALS AND DNA MUTATIONS

The direct effects of radicals on DNA may have the most serious consequences, since DNA contains information that directs the activity of other cellular molecules. Radicals can cause mutations in genes in specific cells, leading to impaired functioning of those cells. It may be that aging at the cellular level is a result of damage not only to molecules themselves but also to genes that direct the manufacture or processing of those molecules. Since most cells are somatic (as opposed to germ cells, which are responsible for the formation of reproductive cells), such changes are not usually inherited but are maintained in individual cells and their descendants.

As with other molecules, several types of DNA repair enzymes, or endonucleases, routinely locate and correct DNA damage, but sometimes the correction mechanism can result in a point mutation. Also, sometimes the damage is not repaired before cell division so that some of the cell's descendants carry mutations. Oxidative damage to DNA has been measured, and it increases with metabolic rate, which is directly related to the production of free radicals. There is some evidence that levels of oxidative damage to DNA are associated with decreased life span and increased rate of cancer with age.

EVIDENCE FOR THE THEORY

It is not clear whether the damage to cellular molecules occurs mainly as a result of an increase in free radical production with age, a decrease in protective mechanisms with age, a combination of the two, or a combination of these and other factors. However, there are a number of lines of evidence that suggest that the free radical theory of aging is at least plausible.

Ionizing radiation is known to cause both direct damage to DNA and the formation of free radicals, so it is not surprising that exposure to ionizing radiation appears to accelerate aging. Such exposure reduces life span, increases the physical deterioration associated with aging, and increases susceptibility to diseases associated with aging. Because radicals are generated by radiation, it is difficult to separate the effects of the radiation itself from the effects of radicals alone. However, there are some biological differences between the separate effects that may allow the direct effects of radical damage to DNA, and the rate of its repair, to be measured.

In addition to the possible benefits of dietary antioxidants and radical scavengers, there is some evidence that low-calorie diets have beneficial effects on both cancer and aging. Specifically, calorie-restricted diets appear to result in better DNA repair, better maintenance of natural antioxidant defenses with increasing age, and increased average and maximum life spans. Also, restriction of certain dietary proteins that contain amino acids that are easily oxidized by radicals may increase life span.

Other lines of evidence are suggestive, though not conclusive. In comparisons of mammalian species, the average life span decreases as the basal metabolic rate increases. This observation is consistent with the idea that life span decreases because of free radical damage, since a higher metabolism generates more radicals. Also, autoimmune and immune deficiency diseases tend to be more prevalent in advanced age, and certain cells responsible for immunity are known to suffer more from radical damage with increasing age than other cells. In addition to these diseases and cancer, other age-associated diseases may result, in part, from radical accumulation. These include hypertension, atherosclerosis, and amyloidosis.

While it is by no means certain that the complex changes associated with the aging process can be attributed entirely to cellular changes induced directly or indirectly by reactions with free radicals, it is clear that they play an important role.

—*Stephen T. Kilpatrick*

See also Aging: Biological, psychological, and sociocultural perspectives; Aging process; Antiaging treatments; Antioxidants; Caloric restriction; Cross-linkage theory of aging; Genetics; Nutrition; Vitamins and minerals; Weight loss and gain.

FOR FURTHER INFORMATION:

Finch, Caleb E., and Leonard Hayflick, eds. *Handbook of the Biology of Aging*. New York: Van Nostrand Reinhold, 1977.

Halliwell, Barry, and Okezie I. Aruoma, eds. *DNA and Free Radicals.* New York: Ellis Horwood, 1993.

Maddox, George L., et al., eds. *The Encyclopedia of Aging.* 2d ed. New York: Springer, 1995.

Moody, Harry R. *Aging: Concepts and Controversies.* Thousand Oaks, Calif.: Pine Forge Press, 1994.

Poli, G., E. Albano, and M. U. Dianzani, eds. *Free Radicals: From Basic Science to Medicine.* Boston: Birkhäuser Verlag, 1993.

FRIENDSHIP

RELEVANT ISSUES: Culture, media, psychology, recreation, sociology, values

SIGNIFICANCE: The patterns, functions, and social conditions of friendship among older individuals, and the personal and social impact of friendship on them, are increasingly being studied by sociologists in an effort to understand and assess the psychological and physical well-being of a growing elderly population

Stereotypical views of the elderly often portray old age as a period of life characterized chiefly by loss of roles and relationships. Such loss undeniably does occur. However, studies of the elderly in a variety of life situations reveal that people from middle age to "old" old age do have rich and rewarding relationships and friendships, some carried over from previous stages of their lives and others acquired in contexts related to their current living conditions and lifestyles.

PATTERNS AND FUNCTIONS OF FRIENDSHIP AMONG THE ELDERLY

Friendship differs from primary ties such as those of family in several ways. Some sociologists point to the element of choice and absence of legal processes for both creating or dropping friendships. Friendships can be based on common status, values, or goals. As in all stages of life, older adult friendships can serve several specific purposes. They can satisfy an individual's need for enjoyment, understanding, respect, equality, and affection; they can compensate for the loss or unavailability of family members; and they can assist in many practical ways as well. Thus, later-life friendships are both affectional and instrumental. One researcher found that older individuals may have different types of friendships based on differ-

ing needs. Long-term friends may fulfill permanent needs, such as those associated with religion or ethnic group. Intermediate-term friends may be related to more easily changed factors, such as marital status or occupation. Short-term friendships are formed to satisfy an individual's immediate requirements.

Patterns of friendship among older people can also vary according to individual personality differences and class structures. It has been found that some middle-class elderly may have access to and therefore prefer friendships beyond their immediate residential area. Other middle-class individuals desire more friends, but physical isolation or lack of social skills prevents the formation of new friendships. Many working-class elderly, on the other hand, show complete satisfaction with family and exhibit no desire for further relationships, while others may be satisfied with neighbors as friends. In all classes, insatiable friendship-seekers may exist. These individuals constantly seek to increase their circle of acquaintances but do not necessarily form deep relationships. Depending on personal characteristics, some people are acquisitive throughout life where making friends is concerned, while others may find it difficult to replace friends made in earlier life because of high expectations and standards of friendship.

The loss of roles at work and within the family, physical changes and health issues, diminished income, and relocation can place severe strains on friendship, especially among the oldest of the old, who have been found to be the most vulnerable to factors leading to decline of friendship. However, while the frequency of contact with friends and even the nature of friendship may change with advancing age, often the skills that individuals acquire earlier in life to make and nourish friendships affect their ability to undertake new friendships and maintain older ones as they encounter the changing circumstances of life.

FACTORS INFLUENCING OLDER ADULT FRIENDSHIPS

Older adults experience transitions, change, and loss in both the roles they play in life and the contacts and relationships they have with family and friends. Research shows that although there is considerable diversity in friendship patterns and choices, a variety of factors may influence the num-

Women are more likely than men to keep longtime friends and make new ones in old age. (Jim Whitmer)

ber of friends elderly people have, the ways in which they maintain previous friendships and forge new ones, and the type of activities in which they engage with friends in their social networks.

Residence and proximity can affect the ability of older adults to maintain and build friendships. Relocation and mobility often involve separation from friends and can affect frequency of contact with friends one leaves behind, although many elders report keeping friendships alive through phone calls, letters, and some technological means of communication. Where one lives is also important. In age-homogeneous communities or in neighborhoods and apartment buildings where there is a concentration of 50 percent or more older adults, local friendship networks among the aging are more likely to exist.

Some evidence has been found for differing friendship patterns in rural and urban areas. In rural communities, a wider circle of friends may exist, and greater numbers of rural elderly report at least one close friend. Activities shared with friends in rural settings include home entertainment, out-

door recreation, and vacation visits. Urban friends participate together in celebrations, commercial recreation, drop-in visits, and vacations.

Types of helping behaviors among friends can also vary according to rural or urban residence, with gender and marital status also playing a part. Elderly rural married men receive and give more help with car care, finances, decision making, transportation, and shopping, while urban married men help with household and yard care and repairs. Older rural married women provide and receive more help with health care, shopping, and transportation, while older urban married women help most with transportation. Rural widows provide friends with practical help, including car care, decision making, housekeeping, household repairs, health care, shopping, transportation, and yard work. Urban widows are more likely to offer comfort and psychological support.

Income plays a part in activities and recreation available to older adults and may affect rural and urban friendships differently. Home and outdoor recreation with friends occurs more frequently among lower-middle-class rural elderly, while drop-in visits and shopping together are more prevalent among older adults in urban areas. Commercial recreation is more common among older urban friends than among rural ones, regardless of income level. However, this may be a consequence of the greater availability of commercial entertainment in urban locations.

Evidence exists that the form and nature of friendship can be affected by gender, and this remains true in later life. Some studies show that women find friendship more meaningful than men do and that women tend to have more friends as confidants and sources of support in old age. The emotional well-being of some older single women has been associated with the number of friends who are both geographically and affectively close to them.

Men and women approach relationships differently, and this is reflected in the quality of their friendships, especially with members of their own sex. Women report looking for more intimate and confiding relationships, and these they often find with other women. In one study, single women between the ages of sixty-five and the mid-nineties acknowledged the importance of initiating and nurturing new friendships with women, both because of lifelong habits and because of a statistical likelihood of living the rest of their lives among other women. Men's friendships with other men are often based on similar interests and shared activities. Men are more likely to expect intimacy in relationships with women, especially with their spouses.

Gender and marital status reveal differing patterns of friendship among men and women. Married couples are reported to interact as couples with friends and family, although women spend more time with these people when their husbands are not present than men do in the absence of their wives. In retirement communities, older married couples spend less time with friends than married couples who live in other types of communities.

In the past, retirement was more likely to have an impact on men than on women in terms of friendship. Friendships based primarily on work situations and contacts might be more likely to fade after retirement. This was found to be especially true for working-class men. Moreover, friendships nourished in social conditions requiring a certain income level, such as fitness clubs, political parties, or recreational societies, may also erode because of diminishing means after retirement. On the other hand, men who are not affected by considerable income decline, or by the loss of male friends through illness or death, have the opportunity to enlarge their circle of friends. The relationship-building skills that many individuals, both men and women, gain during their working years can assist them in building friendships after retirement.

Women tend to live longer than men; moreover, because they are often younger or of the same age as their spouses, they tend to experience widowhood more and for a longer period of time than men do. Social isolation can occur when contemporaries do not experience similar role losses. Friendships made during married life may end when a person is single again, although autonomous friendships that have been established during life as a couple and that continue into single or widowed life are often helpful in adjusting to a person's altered status. When men are widowed, they may have a smaller pool of male friends among whom to seek social and emotional support than women, who are likely to find larger numbers of widows sharing similar experiences. However, there is evidence that younger widows feel more isolated owing to a greater number of married couples in society, while older widows are more able to find friends among a larger pool of elderly widows. This element carries into the different stages of aging as well: Women widowed in their sixties, or in relatively early old age, have a more difficult time making friends or socializing with them than women widowed in their seventies.

Like those of older men, older women's friendships, especially in widowhood, are affected by material circumstances, especially if the women are dependent on their husbands' pensions. Studies show that working-class widows have fewer opportunities to socialize, and have fewer friends, than upper-class or middle-class widows. Lack of transportation can be one factor inhibiting social experiences with friends; fear of going out at night in urban areas can be another.

The health of older adults is another factor which may have consequences for friendship. In age-homogeneous communities, illness or physical handicaps may serve as a resource and basis for friendship, a factor that may be especially crucial for frail elderly persons. Closer friendship networks have been found to exist in such conditions, with helping behaviors more evident and status differences less evident than in other elderly residential situations.

Researchers in several countries, including Great Britain, France, and the United States, report that the existence of ties of friendship can affect the health and well-being of aging adults. Older adults identify loneliness as one of their greatest fears and a source of increased feelings of insecurity and vulnerability. As may be expected, individuals who are separated, divorced, or widowed report more loneliness than those who are married or cohabiting. When the primary support network is composed chiefly of kin, with few or no friends, a greater sense of loneliness is experienced. Although children and families are very important in warding off isolation, some older adults

At any age, friendships among men are often based on shared activities or interests. After retirement, their opportunities for social interaction can decline markedly. (James L. Shaffer)

have reported friendships, especially long-term friendships, as being more critical for their sense of well-being and life satisfaction than their relationships with adult children. Women especially report that in the middle and later years, they may begin to think of close friends as extended family.

People who have strong relationships with friends and family may suffer fewer illnesses and have a lower death rate, while individuals with poor social bonds have been found to have a higher mortality rate. There is some evidence that these factors have similar effects in old age.

FRIENDSHIP AND CAREGIVING

In the 1990's, thirty-four million Americans were sixty-five years or older, and about 17 percent of these elders needed some help with daily activities. As America's population ages, different caregiving relationships and styles continue to emerge. In the 1980's, about seven million households needed to provide care for a family member. In the 1990's, more than twenty-two million households provided some form of care. According to the National Alliance for Caregiving, the caregivers are not only relatives but also unpaid friends and neighbors. Although caregiving is involved, new friendships are formed, old ones deepen, and help is often reciprocal in both tangible and intangible ways. Such help with care by friends and volunteers in many cases allows elderly people to remain in their homes rather than relocating to retirement or nursing homes.

Whether in caregiving capacities or as support groups, friends, relatives, and communities can provide practical assistance and emotional support. Networks such as Share the Care provide help to sick friends and neighbors. Support and self-help groups such as Just Friends have also been formed in numerous communities. Various links to support networks are also found on the Internet.

THE ELDERLY, FRIENDSHIP, AND THE MEDIA

Traditionally, the media and the entertainment industry have not focused much on the middle-aged and elderly, or on the friendships of older adults. In the 1980's and 1990's, a handful of films and television shows did portray people in their "golden years," most of them active and several of them living with friends. However, the proportion of such productions was small, and the range of individuals covered was limited in terms of age span, class, health, and other aspects of diversity.

One area where friendships involving the elderly have been increasingly depicted is in children's literature, although here, too, the proportion is small. The friendships portrayed can be nonfamilial and are often intergenerational and intercultural, reflecting situations in which learning and support are reciprocal. In such stories, both young and old are typically valued as individuals. The proliferation of such literature acknowledges, in at least one media-related field, the crucial nature of friendships at all stages of human life. —*Nillofur Zobairi*

See also Caregiving; Communication; Family relationships; Films; Housing; Independent living; Leisure activities; Loneliness; Men and aging; Nursing and convalescent homes; Relocation; Retirement communities; Social ties; Television; Transportation issues; Widows and widowers; Women and aging.

FOR FURTHER INFORMATION:

Adams, Rebecca G., and Rosemary Blieszner. *Older Adult Friendship.* Newbury Park, Calif.: Sage Publications, 1989. Reviews and discusses various aspects of friendship. Examines forms of friendship, related problems, and the impact of social status on friendships of the elderly.

Ade-Ridder, Linda, and Charles B. Hennon, eds. *Lifestyles of the Elderly: Diversity in Relationships, Health, and Caregiving.* New York: Human Sciences Press, 1989. Presents research on diverse lifestyles of older adults, marriage, friends and family, the relationship of health and quality of life, and issues of caregiving.

Brown, Arnold. *The Social Processes of Aging and Old Age.* Englewood Cliffs, N.J.: Prentice Hall, 1990. Discusses age-related processes influencing social change.

Dykstra, Pearl. *Next of (Non)Kin: The Importance of Primary Relationships for Older Adults' Well-Being.* Amsterdam: Swets & Zeitlinger, 1990. Discusses loneliness and social networks in old age.

France, David. "The New Compassion." *Modern Maturity* 40, no. 3 (May/June, 1997). Explores the increase of new types of friendships created as new types of caregiving situations emerge for older Americans.

Pratt, Michael W., and Joan E. Norris. *The Social Psychology of Aging: A Cognitive Perspective.* Oxford, England: Blackwell, 1994. Discusses friendship styles, models of attachment, and the role of friendship in the social cognitive functioning of older adults.

FULL MEASURE: MODERN SHORT STORIES ON AGING

EDITOR: Dorothy Sennett
DATE: Published in 1988
RELEVANT ISSUES: Media, psychology
SIGNIFICANCE: By providing a collection of short stories with sympathetic elderly characters, this anthology addresses the concerns of the aged and denies many stereotypes associated with aging

Full Measure consists of twenty-three stories by noted authors that feature ten women and fourteen men ranging from the ages of sixty to ninety-one as significant characters. All the stories originally appeared in English and were published in the years spanning 1948 and 1985.

Some of the stories belie stereotypes associated with aging. "Leaving the Yellow House," by Saul Bellow, highlights a seventy-two-year-old woman's desire for independence. "Gunnar's Sword," by Carol Bly, shows an eighty-two-year-old woman who organizes activities for her nursing home. "Old-Age Pensioners," by Frank O'Connor, pits a seventy-six-year-old man against an eighty-one-year-old man in a rowing race. "Suttee," by Louis Auchincloss, concerns a recent widow's discovery that even at the age of sixty-seven, she is found very attractive by a younger man.

Many stories address the concerns of elderly people, such as loneliness, lack of sympathy from others, funeral arrangements, living arrangements, and senility. "Tea with Mrs. Bittell," by V. S. Pritchett, shows a seventy-year-old woman inviting a younger man to tea so as to have company. "Sleep It Off, Lady," by Jean Rhys, has a seventy-year-old woman fail at convincing her neighbors that her rat problem is real. "The Resurrection Man," by Wallace E. Knight, presents the image of a man carrying out his own death and burial with the help of dynamite. Several stories mention the problems that middle-aged children have in dealing with the question of whether their parents should live in a nursing home or with them. Senility is presented as a worry to otherwise active elderly people, who fret self-consciously about how they appear to others. —*Rose Secrest*

See also Ageism; Death and dying; Family relationships; Literature; Loneliness; Mental impairment; Sexuality; Stereotypes.

FULL NEST

RELEVANT ISSUES: Economics, family, values, work
SIGNIFICANCE: The full nest, in which adult children live with their parents, reverses America's long-held cultural assumption that successful adulthood depends on independence, and also creates new challenges for middle-aged and older parents

At a time when millions of Americans are leaving the parental nest determined to gain their independence, large numbers of grown children are continuing to live with or are moving back in with their parents. Perceived by psychologists as "failed adults," these single adults, aged eighteen to thirty-four, see living at home as the best option while attending college, looking for work, or coping with a major life change, such as divorce. American culture has tended to predicate the idea of success upon separation from family, which makes remaining at home or returning home seem a violation of a natural way of life and therefore forces many parents to rethink the idea of family.

In general, American society prizes independence and appears to put less stock in family closeness than European countries. Encouraged to leave home for psychological and material growth, America's young people disengage themselves from family togetherness, avoid prolonged parent-child relationships, and, if affluent or well educated, seem less likely to return to the nest or even take their elderly parents into their homes.

PROBLEM AREAS

Not all middle-aged or older parents are capable of coping with their grown children in the nest. Some have declined to allow them to stay or return, refusing to attempt such coexistence. For those who open their doors to their adult children,

the experience is, at best, challenging. Issues involving space or territory almost immediately become sensitive, especially if some family members lack consideration for other members. Endless wrangles can erupt about small but annoying differences in sleeping, eating, and housekeeping habits. Conflicts can arise over towels on the bathroom floor, late-night phone calls that wake up the rest of the household, the disrupting volume of a radio or stereo, or food that disappears from the refrigerator. Borrowing possessions or a car can impose burdens on parents that require considerable sacrifice. Small irritations, such as messy rooms, friends, or late hours, can grow until stress affects the parents' marital relationship.

One of the more volatile areas for both parents and adult children is money. Parents are sometimes confronted with adult children who cannot or will not pay room and board or who need help with either paying their own bills or obtaining a loan for a car. Some parents are reluctant to ask their children for money, some insist they want none, and some seethe with resentment because they feel their adult children are taking advantage of them. Money problems can arise through insensitivity and ignorance—the children never knowing or inquiring about the state of the family's finances and the parents' ability to absorb the extra cost of their living at home. Some nesting children are incapable of filing income tax returns with the Internal Revenue Service or are woefully inept at budgeting. Parents who feel obligated to help their children achieve financial responsibility must weigh their options carefully. Should they give financial aid freely, or should they lend their children money with a precise pay-back schedule? Would cosigning a bank loan for the adult child be more appropriate? Although each situation may require a different solution, many money problems can be alleviated by talking directly with the adult children about the financial situation and the parents' expectations from them.

Many parents are devastated by their children's lifestyles or find it difficult to allow their adult children the freedom to make choices contrary to their own inclinations. While they realize that the pressures on young people are not the same that they experienced in their growing-up years, many middle-aged and older parents are shocked at modern attitudes toward authority, work responsibilities, sexual freedom, and drug use. Some of the most loving parents have clearly announced to their young adults what standards are acceptable in their home. Probably the most difficult aspect of the nesting adult's lifestyle for some parents is allowing sexual freedom for the offspring under the parents' roof. While some parents become apoplectic at the thought of sexual activity occurring in the nesting person's bedroom, others maintain that what occurs there is none of their business.

BENEFITS

At a time when many middle-aged parents long for respite from the rigors of child rearing, they must also worry if they are hindering their children's growth. While young adults seek independence and parents also seek it for them, progress largely depends upon the people involved. Children who readily adopt their parents' views without question or who appear aimless or uncertain about their own identity tend to live at home longer. Parents who are authoritarian and mostly continue to see their children as their property demand total obedience as long as they are under the parents' roof. Permissive parents who coddle children are no more effective than authoritarian ones in helping them become independent persons. Parents who see their young adults as adults (even if they are not)—who do not insist on giving money, cars, free room and board, or advice—tend to benefit their children more in their transition to independence.

Adult children often remain at home or return for reasons deeper than finances. If children eighteen or older need security, confidence building, growing up, or maturity, parents can utilize their time at home to help them become independent. Nesters are often encouraged to make decisions and take responsibility for them. In addition to helping out with rent and utilities, adult children are often encouraged to help with household chores. One way to ensure the success of this endeavor is to be very specific about who does what. Posting a work sheet in a conspicuous place that lists individual responsibilities works well for many families. Some children have less free time than younger siblings, and conscientious parents usually take this fact into consideration.

Because many young people living at home are in a state of transition or growth, which, in turn, causes tension or pressure for the parents, communication between the two is extremely important. Relating to the state of mind of family members can, in some instances, initiate freer communication among all involved. Circumstantial problems involving decisions about school, work, or social life can overwhelm young adults living at home and create communication breakdown. Coping with the attitudes of returning children who resent the rights and freedom of younger siblings places additional pressure on parents, which, to avoid festering resentments and the destruction of good feelings, necessitates open communication among all family members.

Criticism from friends can cause parents to begin to have negative thoughts about their own nesting children and, at a deeper level, anxieties about the dictates of society. Society's emphasis on individual success, along with the disparaging remarks that suggest the child's failure, can easily cause the parents to doubt the wisdom of their own decision. One way parents can avoid making the situation at home more difficult is to choose how they will react. By pointing out the benefits of nesting, they will reinforce their commitment to their children and refuse to allow others to set policy for their family.

Despite the frustration and turmoil that adult children living at home can beget, there are also surprising rewards to be found. Family interests expand through the reports of the progress of the nesting son, daughter, or grandchild at school or work. Families can enjoy activities together, thereby lessening the strain of living in close quarters. Family members provide support and encouragement for each other and build relationships as one adult to another. Some parents are actually surprised that they have much in common with their adult children and can relate to them as individuals. The full nest can provide parents with frequently missed opportunities to enjoy their adult children.

—*Mary Hurd*

See also Communication; Empty nest syndrome; Family relationships; Multigenerational households; Parenthood.

FOR FURTHER INFORMATION:

Baskerville, Dawn M. "Grown but Not Gone." *Essence* 29, no. 3 (July, 1998).
Boo, Katherine. "Grow Up, Twenty-Somethings:

You *Can* Go Home Again." *The Washington Monthly* 24 (April, 1992).

Jacoby, Susan. "Look Who's Living in My House." *Good Housekeeping* 227, no. 201 (July, 1998).

Levinson, David, ed. *Encyclopedia of Marriage and the Family.* New York: Simon & Schuster/Macmillan, 1995.

O'Kane, Monica Lauen. *Living With Adult Children.* St. Paul, Minn.: Diction Books, 1981.

White, J. M. *Dynamics of Family Development: A Theoretical Perspective.* New York: Guilford Press, 1991.

FUNERALS

RELEVANT ISSUES: Culture, death, family, religion

SIGNIFICANCE: The funeral is a multifaceted experience through which family and friends of the deceased are able to realize the meaning of the death, dispose of the body of the deceased in a sanitary manner, and initiate the grieving process, which in turn leads to a period of mourning

The funeral, the roots of which have been traced to ancient Egyptian culture, is the final event in the life cycle of an individual. This concept is universally recognized as societies practice rituals of how to care for the body of the deceased. While one may die at any age, the concept of death is most often anticipated as one moves through the aging process. A traditional funeral is initiated at the time that the body of the deceased is removed from the place of death and concludes with the committal of the body to its final resting place. The traditional process is marked by processions as the body is moved and accompanied to a place of preparing it for viewing (such as embalming or cosmetic services), to the place where the funeral service will be held, and to the place of committal, which is generally a cemetery plot or mausoleum. The term "funeral" derives from the Latin word *funeralis*, meaning "torchlight procession," and connotes the presence of the body of the deceased throughout the process. Having the body of the

Funerals can be an important element of the grieving process, allowing friends and loved ones to express their feelings and gather support from one another. Increasing age often brings multiple losses, resulting in "bereavement overload" for elders who do not have an adequate support network. (James L. Shaffer)

deceased on view helps mourners to accept the reality and finality of the separation from the deceased. Not viewing the body of the deceased may give rise to a sense of denial that the death has actually occurred.

Alternatives to a funeral include a memorial service, a formal ceremony during which the body of the deceased is not present; an immediate burial, during which the body of the deceased is present but there is no viewing or formal ceremony other than a graveside service; and a direct cremation, in which without viewing or ceremony the human remains are reduced to ashes through burning.

FAMILY PARTICIPATION

During the earlier years of the 1900's, it was customary for the family to be an integral part of the funeral process when the aged person died at home. The funeral arrangements, including the preparing of the body of the deceased for viewing, were completed by family and community friends. However, changes related to society, changes to family structure, and mobility of family members have contributed to the transition from funerals being held in the home of the deceased to being held in professional funeral homes. With this change, the family and friends of the deceased have become more removed from the process. It is more likely that the aged will die in a hospital, nursing home, or other facility than at home and that funeral arrangements will be made long-distance. The funeral director has become the primary person to orchestrate the mechanics of the funeral, which has become more commercialized with "custom packages." While family may still be involved in choosing specific funeral merchandise (for example, coffins or vaults), they may no longer have the privilege or responsibility to care for the body of the deceased. Depending upon state laws, family members may not be allowed to care for their own dead. For example, in the state of Indiana, a statute identifies the funeral director as the only one to whom a permit may be granted for disposition of a dead body.

In addition to caring for the body of the deceased, the funeral director is also taking more responsibility for caring for the surviving family members. Meeting the needs of the grieving family has also been recognized by various religious groups, as is evidenced by the International Commission on English in the Liturgy's *Order of Christian Funerals* (1989), which was implemented throughout the Roman Catholic Church in the United States on November 2, 1989. This publication directs a shift from the mechanics of funeral rites focusing on the deceased to ministering to the bereaved by the community.

PREARRANGED FUNERALS

Many of the aging population consider prearranged funerals. Erik H. Erikson, whose concept of human psychosocial development spanned birth to death in eight stages, viewed the aged in the last stage of life as dealing with the developmental crisis of integrity versus despair. Integrity is the product of being able to review one's life and find that it has had meaning, with a sense of contentment as both the happy and sad times have been integrated; this aging individual is able to anticipate and even accept the coming of death. On the other hand, the aging individual who has reviewed the events of life with regret and has a sense of fear when considering impending death is found to be in a state of despair. Depending on how the aging person views his or her life, funeral arrangements may either be considered as a celebration of that life or as a means of dismissing an unfulfilled life of disappointments. By prearranging a funeral in either of these situations, the aging person may be assured of having a funeral conducted according to his or her desires and will lessen the decision-making responsibilities of survivors during the grieving period.

The aging person who has attained integrity may even enjoy the experience of planning his or her funeral and find some humor in it when presented with such decisions as whether to purchase a coffin with an inner-spring mattress or an adjustable headrest. Some may choose to have visual mementos, such as photographs and videotapes, as part of the viewing or funeral service; others may choose mementos to reflect their occupation or hobbies. Songs and readings present additional areas in which choices may be made to celebrate one's life. The ultimate desire is to plan for a personal, yet cost-effective, funeral. It is easier for surviving family members to feel comfortable with burying the deceased in a less-expensive coffin or vault if that is what was chosen prior to the time of death by the deceased. The aging individual whose developmental crisis has resulted in a state of despair might choose to have a more subdued funeral. In either case, it is important that details of the prearranged funeral are shared with those who will survive and have the responsibility of implementing those wishes.

Information for funeral planning may be obtained from the Funeral and Memorial Societies of America in Egg Harbor, Wisconsin; the National Funeral Directors Association in Milwaukee, Wisconsin; the Federal Trade Commission located in Washington, D.C.; or the American Association of Retired Persons (AARP) in Long Beach, California.

CUSTOMS AND RELIGION

Many funerals are influenced by the customs and religious beliefs that the deceased practiced during life. The aging process may act as a catalyst for one to recapture the meaning of life through his or her customs and religion. For the Irish, the funeral process is a time of both merrymaking in celebration of the most important event within one's individual life cycle and a time of sorrow, which may be as much for the survivors not being released from this life as well as for the loss of the deceased. At an Irish wake, storytelling, laughter, drinking, and eating are the norm. Such activities may also be found at the funerals of aged American Indians, whose lives are celebrated as they once again become one with nature. Ethnic groups, such as Mexican Americans, Lebanese Americans, and Cape Verdeans, tend to have displays of emotion at viewings and funerals.

In addition to cultural customs that influence the funeral process, religious beliefs also shape the form the funeral may take. For example, the Jewish funeral emphasizes simplicity and focuses on the immediacy of burying the dead, which for the traditional Jewish community is done within twenty-four hours of death. Muslims also generally conduct funerals for their dead within a day's time after death. Although there is a wide range of funeral types among Protestant religions, they are generally held two to three days after the death with a focus on celebrating the life of the deceased and affirming the transition to an afterlife. The Roman Catholic funeral is often incorporated into a larger mass service and tends to be of a more formal nature.

As society continues to change and modifications are evident in customs and religious practice, it is expected that how the aging process and funerals are perceived will also undergo change in order to meet the needs of those who are anticipating death and the needs of the bereaved survivors.

—*Matilda E. Casler*

See also Cultural views of aging; Death and dying; Death anxiety; Death of a child; Death of parents; Grief; Life insurance; Religion; Terminal illness; Widows and widowers.

FOR FURTHER INFORMATION:

Astor, Bart. "Facing the Inevitable." In *Baby Boomer's Guide to Caring for Aging Parents*. New York: Macmillan Spectrum, 1998.

Barnard, Charles N. "Shop Before You Drop." *Modern Maturity* 39, no. 4 (July/August, 1996).

Carlson, Lisa. *Caring for the Dead: Your Final Act of Love*. Hinesburg, Vt.: Upper Access, 1998.

Habenstein, Robert W., and William M. Lamers. *The History of American Funeral Directing*. Detroit: Omnigraphics, 1990.

Magida, Arthur J., ed. *How to Be a Perfect Stranger: A Guide to Etiquette in Other People's Religious Ceremonies*. Woodstock, Vt.: Jewish Lights, 1996.

GASTROINTESTINAL CHANGES AND DISORDERS

RELEVANT ISSUES: Biology, health and medicine

SIGNIFICANCE: The incidence of gastrointestinal disorders increases with age; such disorders usually present more severe complications in the elderly

The gastrointestinal tract is also known as the digestive system or the alimentary canal. Food is taken in through the mouth, and undigested remains pass out through the anus. Digestion is the mechanical and chemical processes by which food is broken down into smaller molecules; the nutrients thus obtained are used by the body for energy, growth, and repair. The primary features of the digestive tract are the mouth, the oral cavity, the pharynx, the esophagus, the stomach, the small intestine, and the large intestine, or colon. In addition to the main tract, there are several important accessory organs or glands that assist in the process of digestion: the salivary glands, the gallbladder, the liver, and the pancreas.

The process of chemical digestion begins in the mouth. However, the mechanical breakdown of food by the teeth is probably of greater significance. It is easy to appreciate how diseased or missing teeth, diseased gums, or ill-fitting dentures may lead to a loss of the pleasures of eating. The tongue contains taste buds, also important for appreciating the quality of food.

Partially processed food passes from the mouth, through the esophagus, and to the stomach. Food remains in the stomach for only three to five hours; little chemical digestion takes place there. Most digestion takes place in the small intestine, where nutrients are absorbed into the capillaries and lymph vessels. The small intestine receives bile (produced in the liver) from the gallbladder and strong digestive enzymes from the pancreas to assist in breaking down food into smaller components. The stomach and small intestine are not normally affected by digestive enzymes because they secrete a protective layer of mucus.

From the small intestine, food passes into the large intestine, where no further digestion or absorption of food takes place; however, water is absorbed there, and billions of bacteria produce valuable vitamins from the undigested material. The undigested remains and wastes pass out through the anus. Although the digestive processes generally become less efficient with age, the gastrointestinal tract functions quite well unless there are specific age-related disorders, such as cancer, ulcers, periodontal disease, gastritis, diverticulitis, and constipation.

CHANGES WITH NORMAL AGING

As people age, changes are seen in virtually every organ system of the body; the gastrointestinal tract is no exception. From a clinical point of view, it is critical to distinguish those changes that may be a result of normal aging from those that are caused by a disease or pathological process. In many situations, it is especially difficult to delineate these two types of changes in the gastrointestinal tract. Although there are some exceptions, acute or sudden changes in the functioning of a part of the gastrointestinal system are likely to be caused by a disease process, whereas a chronic or slow change is more likely to be caused by a change associated with normal aging. It is also critical to understand how the effects of aging themselves may lead to diseases or pathological processes.

Beginning in the mouth, the most significant change with age is the apparent decrease in the number of taste buds. Even if, as some evidence indicates, changes in taste perception are not caused by an actual decrease in the number of taste buds but rather a decline in their sensitivity, the net result can have devastating consequences. Altered taste perception may not only lead to a decline in the pleasures of eating but may also cause a person to change his or her diet and possibly lead to a severe case of malnutrition. The decline in taste sensitivity may also be exacerbated by certain medications taken for other conditions or diseases. Also affecting the pleasure of eating is the condition known as "dry mouth," or xerostomia. A reduced secretion of saliva may be age-related and can also be caused by low levels of water intake or frequent breathing through the mouth.

Food passing through the gastrointestinal tract is likely to take longer in elderly people than in younger people. There is an overall loss of muscle tone and strength along the gut, and the overall process of digestion may not be as efficient. Movement of partially digested food through the esophagus may be slowed as a result of muscle tone loss, so delays in emptying may occur. Similar problems may be encountered in the stomach, which shows a reduction in the number of gastric cells and a consequent decline in the production of hydrochloric acid and digestive enzymes. Such problems, however, may not actually be a part of normal aging, as there is some evidence that the changes are associated with an inflammation of the stomach mucosa, a condition known as atrophic gastritis. Atrophic gastritis causes a loss of gastric and mucosal cells and a decline in the production of hydrochloric acid and pepsin. Pepsin—the only digestive enzyme produced in the stomach—acts in the beginning stages of the digestion of proteins. Although there is a decline in the amounts of pepsin in middle age, it does not appear to decline further in healthy people after the age of sixty. Smoking, as well as the use of many drugs, including alcohol and aspirin, may also contribute to chronic gastric problems.

In addition to being the site for most chemical digestion, the small intestine also serves as the primary organ for absorption of the end products of digestion; fortunately, the functions of the small intestine show little impairment with aging. Among the few effects of aging seen in the small intestine is the inefficient absorption of nutrients, particularly incomplete digestion of fats. The absorption of digested proteins and carbohydrates is little affected. After age sixty, decreases in the absorption of iron, zinc, calcium, and vitamins B_1, B_{12}, and D are common. By age eighty, most people are likely to have a reduced absorption of most of these substances. Usually, if the diet is good, reduced absorption does not lead to other problems. However, as many people age, their diets become less than adequate, and vitamin, iron, and calcium deficiencies may develop.

The large intestine shows few changes with aging. As is true of the rest of the gastrointestinal tract, however, movements are slowed down in the large intestine. The main effect of this slowing is that feces remain in the colon longer, more water is absorbed, and the feces become firmer, possibly leading to constipation. In many cases, the problem can be managed effectively by an adequate fluid intake and exercise.

The other primary structures associated with the gastrointestinal tract—the liver, the gallbladder, and the pancreas—usually continue to function well into old age. The liver has amazing abilities to replace lost cells by regeneration. However, regenerative powers decrease after adulthood, and the size of the liver is much reduced after sixty years of age. The shrinking of the liver can cause a decrease in enzymatic activity, leading to a reduced ability to remove chemical toxins from the blood. Also, drugs taken for therapeutic purposes may not be metabolized as quickly, reducing their effectiveness. In most cases, however, the liver retains enough reserve capacity to function normally.

AGE-RELATED DISORDERS

Gastrointestinal disorders are not unique to the elderly, but many of the disorders show an increased incidence with aging. Among such disorders are periodontal disease, hiatal hernia, peptic ulcers, pernicious anemia, duodenal ulcers, colorectal and pancreatic cancer, gallstones, constipation, and fecal incontinence. In addition, the clinical symptoms are likely to be more severe in the elderly than in younger persons.

Disorders of the mouth are likely to have more severe consequences than the initial condition might indicate. By the time people have reached age sixty-five, over one-third have lost all of their teeth. There is a tendency for the gums to recede, making it easier for bacteria to establish at the base of the tooth. Plaque is formed around the bacteria, and the gums become inflamed. The inflamed condition and the persistent presence of plaque cause periodontal disease. Eventually, the support for the tooth weakens, and the tooth falls out. Loss of teeth or ill-fitting dentures can have a major impact on dietary practices, possibly leading to malnutrition.

Herniation of a part of the stomach through the diaphragm occurs in over two-thirds of adults over seventy years old. In most cases, the condition does not cause any symptoms. In some cases, however, the hernia can lead to difficulty in swallowing (dysphagia) or a backflow of gastric juices into the esophagus (reflux esophagitis). The latter condition can cause a regurgitation of the gastric contents into the mouth and may produce a heartburn that, in more severe cases, resembles a heart attack. Certain foods and drinks, such as coffee and chocolate, may worsen the condition.

Diverticulosis is a condition that occurs when the wall of the large intestine herniates. The deep outpocketings, known as diverticula, produce a thickening in the wall of the intestine with a narrow opening. Although the incidence of diverticulosis is common in older people, over three-fourths of the people do not have any symptoms. There is a tendency for bacteria and fecal matter to become trapped in the pouches, causing an inflammation, known as diverticulitis, to occur. Symptoms include abdominal pain, diarrhea, fever, constipation, and bleeding. Treatment may include antibiotics to control the bacterial infection and increasing the amount of fiber in the diet. In extreme cases, surgery may be used to remove affected parts of the large intestine.

Peptic ulcers occur in the stomach (gastric peptic ulcer) or the beginning section of the small intestine called the duodenum (duodenal peptic ulcer). If, for some reason, the acid and digestive enzymes in the gastrointestinal tract cause the stomach lining cells to die and erode away, an ulcer may be formed. Ulcers occur at all ages but are slightly more common in people age forty-five to sixty-four.

Many medications, especially those containing anti-inflammatory steroids, can result in damage to the lining of the wall of the stomach and lead to an ulcer. Aspirin, which does not contain steroids, also may increase the risk of a gastric peptic ulcer. The most serious risk from a peptic ulcer is bleeding, which may cause death. The problems associated with bleeding tend to be worse in the elderly than in younger adults with ulcers. Ulcers can also lead to an actual perforation of the stomach wall, resulting in the gastric contents of the stomach escaping into the abdominal cavity.

It used to be thought that ulcers were caused by stress and diet-related factors. It is apparent, however, that a bacterium, *Helicobacter pylori*, is related to the development of gastric and duodenal ulcers. The infection rate of gastric *H. pylori* is higher in people sixty to eighty years of age and older, and the specific effects of the infection on gastric physiology and the development of ulcers in the elder are still not clear. Treatment options for ulcers include dietary modifications, medications, and, if necessary, surgery.

Older adults frequently have vitamin and mineral deficiencies because of dietary changes and problems in absorption. Interesting effects may be seen as a result of a deficiency in vitamin B_{12}, which may lead to neurological disturbances, in-

cluding depression and even anorexia. Most cases of B_{12} deficiency in the elderly are not caused by problems in the diet; they are more likely to be caused by problems of absorption in the small intestine. Deficiencies usually can be treated effectively with injections of the vitamin. High-fiber diets or laxatives, used by many older adults to combat constipation, can increase problems of poor vitamin and mineral absorption. Factors that decrease the time available for absorption in the intestine, such as laxatives, may lead to inefficient mineral absorption.

Constipation is one of the most common conditions among aging people. Many factors may contribute to the retention of feces in the lower portion of the large intestine. Retention that causes a noticeable decrease in the frequency of bowel movements should be of concern. In addition, the longer the feces are retained, the dryer they become; in such cases, excessive strain may be needed for elimination. Among the elderly, constipation may be a result of lack of exercise and a decrease in normal activity and movement, inadequate fluid intake, poor diet (including inadequate fiber intake), and certain prescription and over-the-counter drugs. Laxatives taken to improve the situation may, at times, worsen the condition.

Cancers or carcinomas can occur in any part of the gastrointestinal tract from the mouth to the rectum, including the accessory digestive glands. In general, the incidence of cancer increases with age and is thought of as a disease primarily of middle and late life, although there are cancers of childhood and early adulthood. Cancers of the esophagus often invade surrounding tissues, including the respiratory system. Men are more likely than women to develop cancer of the esophagus, and the great majority of people have a five-year survival rate. Cancer of the stomach also has a high mortality rate, primarily because of metastasis to other organs. Colon cancer ranks behind only lung cancer and breast cancer as a cause of death overall and is a major cause of death among the aged. In general, treatments for cancer include radiation therapy, chemotherapy, and surgery.

—*Donald J. Nash*

See also Aging: Biological, psychological, and sociocultural perspectives; Aging process; Cancer; Dental disorders; Malnutrition; Nutrition; Sensory changes; Vitamins and minerals.

FOR FURTHER INFORMATION:

Costin, Carolyn. *The Eating Disorders Sourcebook.* Los Angeles: Lowell House, 1996. The author is a recovering anorexic and professional on eating disorders. Symptoms and therapies of various disorders are described.

Dashe, Alfred M. *The Man's Health Sourcebook.* Los Angeles: Lowell House, 1996. Each chapter provides information on different body systems in an interesting and informative style.

Dollinger, Malin, and Ernest H. Rosenbaum. *Everyone's Guide to Cancer Therapy.* Toronto: Summerville House, 1998. Useful material is given on the causes of cancer, how it spreads, and different treatment options.

Saxon, Sue V., and Mary Jean Etten. *Physical Change and Aging.* 3d ed. New York: Tiresias, 1994. This basic text covers the physical, psychological, and social aspects of aging.

Silverman, H. M. *The Pill Book.* New York: Bantam Books, 1996. Over 1,500 of the most commonly prescribed drugs are included. Special attention is given to food and other drug interactions.

GAY MEN AND LESBIANS

RELEVANT ISSUES: Culture, demographics, family, marriage and dating, values

SIGNIFICANCE: The older gay and lesbian population is often ignored or stereotyped; more research is needed on this segment of older adults

As the population of older adults increases, so does the diversity of individuals in late life. An often-ignored group of older individuals is gay men and lesbian women. There are several reasons that this group has been termed by some academics as the "invisible elderly." Homosexuality is an issue that makes many people in all age groups uncomfortable to consider or discuss. In addition, older adults suffer from many damaging stereotypes, especially about their sexual desires and behaviors. Therefore, older adults who are gay and lesbian have the combined disadvantage of being a member of a sexual minority in later life. The outcome is that this group is ignored and discounted by both younger cohorts of gay men and lesbian women and the overall social culture.

Just as the older population in general is diverse, so is the population of older gay men and lesbian women. Even though both men and women are lumped together here, the experience of either gender may be very different from the other. In older lesbian couples, for example, there may be a dual economic disadvantage compared to gay men, as women's wages tend to be lower across the life span. Conversely, men tend to have shorter life expectancies than women, which may create critical issues for male partners if both are in poor health in late life.

Other aspects of diversity are found within the older homosexual population. One is the point in life at which the individual determined that she or he is homosexual. Some older adults may have lived their entire lives being gay or lesbian. Others may have come to this realization during the adulthood years. Some of these individuals chose to continue a heterosexual lifestyle for various reasons—from a desire to preserve their marriage, for the sake of their children, or out of fear of abandonment by their families. Therefore, even within this group, the experience of being gay or lesbian can be vastly different for various individuals.

DESCRIPTION OF THE POPULATION

Because of the invisibility of the population, difficulty exists in arriving at an accurate number of older gay men and lesbian women. Figures about this older group are unreliable, as many people are reluctant to be identified as homosexual. In addition, measurement bias often hinders accurate population estimates. For example, questions about marital status rarely include a category that reflects same-sex partnering. Gay men and lesbians with partners are forced to choose between responding that they are "married" or "single." Neither of these categories accurately reflects their relationship status.

In addition, older adults may fear being identified as gay or lesbian as a result of their experience of living during historically oppressive times. The feeling of gay pride that exists in younger generations is less present in older cohorts who lived much of their lives prior to advances in civil liberties for same-sex couples. For these various reasons, it is extremely difficult to gauge accurately the number of people in the older cohort who are homosexual. With these caveats in mind, the estimated number of older gay men and lesbian women in the United States in 1999 was probably somewhere between 1.75 and 3.5 million.

Gay veterans from World War II march in front of the White House in 1993 in support of gay rights in the military.
(Reuters/Vidal Medina/Archive Photos)

An important aspect of describing this population is understanding the social context that was experienced by the current older cohort. In general, social behaviors toward homosexuals were at least unaccepting, and most probably quite hostile. During McCarthyism, for example, homosexuality was viewed as being "subversive" and un-American. The American Psychiatric Association labeled homosexuality as a psychiatric disorder in earlier decades. As these attitudes demonstrate, homosexuality was considered a danger and a pathological condition during the formative years of many in the current cohort of older adults.

The real beginning of the gay pride movement started in 1969 with the Stonewall Inn riots. This event took place at a gay bar in New York City called the Stonewall Inn when customers resisted the usual discriminatory practices and harassment by the city police department. While this event was a watershed for gay and lesbian rights and activism, it took place only after many in the current older cohort had experienced years of oppression and discrimination. The cohort of older adults may carry vivid memories of abuse, ridicule, and rejection that are the determining experiences of how they define cultural attitudes toward homosexuality.

FAMILY AND FRIENDS

One of the most damaging myths about older gay men and lesbian women is that they are lonely, isolated, and have few social contacts. In fact, older homosexuals may have been married at one time and have adult children and grandchildren. Like older heterosexuals, gay and lesbian older adults are often involved in long-term relationships that are loving and supportive. In addition, siblings who became distant following the declaration of the homosexuality by a brother or sister may decide that the issue is less important than preserving family bonds as they face advancing age. Reconciliations and reconnecting can take place when the developmental issues of later life cause a reprioritization of relationship issues.

Close friendships are often formed within gay and lesbian social networks as a way to create support systems that buffer feelings of difference and unacceptance in society. These "families of choice" are often long-lasting relationships that promote a sense of kinship and belonging. Such surrogate family systems are especially salient as support systems for individuals whose blood relations rejected them because of their sexual orientation.

Although partnership and friendship relations have functional value for older gay men and lesbians, often no legal rights are connected to them. Older same-sex couples do not receive health, financial, or social protections equivalent to legally married couples. After the death of a significant other, for example, the living partner is not entitled to any protection over property that is not jointly owned or legally identified (for example, specified in a will). Regardless of how close or distant the biological family has been, these "legal family members" have rights over the estate. This vulnerability extends to other areas, such as the lack of decision-making power in health or medical areas, the receiving of benefits such as pensions or annuities, and the joint filing of income tax returns.

Organizations and Affiliations

Just as groups have been formed to provide opportunities and assistance for the older population in general, some programs have been formed specifically for older adults who are gay and lesbian. It is important to note that there is still a paucity of these organizations and that they tend to exist in more progressive, urban locations. Unfortunately, too many members of this segment of the older population have limited options to socialize with others who have the same sexual orientation.

Probably the earliest group, Senior Aging in a Gay Environment (SAGE) is based in New York City. This organization was founded in 1977 to provide homebound services for older gay men and lesbian women. Since then, it has expanded dramatically and includes social, educational, and advocacy activities. In 1992, SAGE held a national conference to plan for similar organizations across the country. As a result, several communities have sponsored programs to promote involve-

ment and services to gay and lesbian older adults, including locations in both the United States and Canada.

Additional programs and research have been initiated to assist and provide greater understanding about this group of older adults. Services that have specific outreach to homosexual elders include Gay and Lesbian—An Older Way (GLOW) in Philadelphia and Emerald Community Outreach to Lesbians/Gay Seniors (ECOLS) in Oregon. Advocacy groups have also been formed, including the Lavender Panthers, Old Lesbian Organizing Committee (OLOC), and the Stonewall Union Task Force on Lesbian and Gay Aging. Research and scholarship have generated interest and study groups in gerontology organizations. For example, the American Society on Aging has an interest group on lesbian and gay issues that publishes a newsletter on related topics called *Outword*. While these types of organizations are not present in all communities and organizations, the number dramatically increased in the 1980's and 1990's.

Summary

The older population contains a broad diversity of individuals, including those who are gay and lesbian. Historically, this group has been "invisible" and its unique needs and resources have not been understood. Civil rights have been expanding for members in same-sex families, which has increased the number of service and advocacy groups. As the cohort of younger gay men and lesbian women ages, it can be expected that even more programs, legislation, and research will be enacted for this group of older adults.

—*Nancy P. Kropf*

See also American Society on Aging; Cohabitation; Friendship; *Look Me in the Eye: Old Women, Aging, and Ageism*; Marriage; Sexuality; Single parenthood; Singlehood.

For Further Information:

Adelman, M. "Stigma, Gay Lifestyles, and Adjustment to Aging: A Study of Later-Life Gay Men and Lesbians." *Journal of Homosexuality* 20, nos. 3 and 4 (October and November, 1990).

Duberman, M., M. Vicinus, and G. Chauncy, eds. *Hidden from History: Reclaiming the Gay and Lesbian Past*. New York: Meridian, 1990.

Kimmel, D. C. "The Families of Older Gays and Lesbians." *Generations* 17 (1992).

Lee, J. A., ed. *Gay Midlife and Maturity*. New York: Harrington Press, 1991.

Mallon, G. P., ed. *Foundations of Social Work Practice with Lesbian and Gay Persons*. New York: Harrington Press, 1998.

National Association for Lesbian and Gay Gerontology. *Lesbian and Gay Aging Resource Guide*. San Francisco: Author, 1993.

Weston, K. *Families We Choose: Lesbians, Gays, Kinship*. New York: Columbia University Press, 1991.

Woodman, N. J., ed. *Lesbian and Gay Lifestyles: A Guide for Counseling and Education*. New York: Irvington, 1992.

GENETICS

RELEVANT ISSUES: Biology, health and medicine

SIGNIFICANCE: In the light of modern science and medicine, it has become apparent that the roots of aging lie in genes; therefore, the genetic changes that take place during aging are the source of the major theories of aging currently being proposed

Biologists have long suspected that the mechanisms of aging would never be understood fully until a better understanding of genetics was obtained. As genetic information has exploded, a number of theories of aging have emerged. Each of these theories has focused on a different aspect of the genetic changes observed in aging cells and organisms. Animal models, from simple organisms such as *Tetrahymena* (a single-celled, ciliated protozoan) and *Caenorhabditis* (a nematode worm) to more complex organisms like *Drosophila* (fruit fly) and mice, have been used extensively in efforts to understand the genetics of aging. The study of mammalian cells in culture and the genetic analysis of human progeroid syndromes (that is, premature aging syndromes) such as Werner's syndrome and diseases of old age such as Alzheimer's disease have also improved the understanding of aging. From these data, several theories of aging have been proposed.

GENETIC CHANGES OBSERVED IN AGING CELLS

Most of the changes thus far observed represent some kind of degeneration or loss of function.

Many comparisons between cells from younger and older individuals have shown that more mutations are consistently present in older cells. In fact, older cells seem to show greater genetic instability in general, leading to chromosome deletions, inversions, and other defects. As these errors accumulate, the cell cycle slows down, decreasing the ability for cells to proliferate rapidly. These genetic problems are partly a result of a gradual accumulation of mutations, but the appearance of new mutations seems to accelerate with age due to an apparent reduced effectiveness of deoxyribonucleic acid (DNA) repair mechanisms.

Numerous mutations and deletions have been found in mitochondrial DNA (mtDNA), a circular DNA molecule found in mitochondria. Because mtDNA includes many of the genes important in cellular respiration, which produces most of the adenosine triphosphate (ATP) required by cells, such mutations often lead to inefficient energy production. The appearance of abnormally shaped mitochondria and a significant reduction in cellular respiration efficiency are common traits of older cells. Muscle fibers, in particular, are affected and may be a primary reason for loss of muscle mass and strength during aging.

Cells that are artificially cultured have been shown to undergo a predictable number of cell divisions before finally becoming senescent, a state where the cells simply persist and cease dividing. This phenomenon was first established by Leonard Hayflick in the early 1960's when he found that human fibroblast cells would divide up to about fifty times and no more. This phenomenon is now called the Hayflick limit. The number of divisions possible varies depending on the type of cell, the original age of the cell, and the species of organism from which the original cell was derived. It is particularly relevant that a fibroblast cell from a fetus will easily approach the fifty-division limit, whereas a fibroblast cell from an adult over age fifty may be capable of only a few divisions before reaching senescence.

The underlying genetic explanation for the Hayflick limit appears to involve regions near the ends of chromosomes called telomeres. Telomeres are composed of thousands of copies of a repetitive DNA sequence and are a required part of the ends of chromosomes due to certain limitations in the process of DNA replication. Each time a cell divides, it must replicate all of the chromosomes. The process of replication inevitably leads to loss of a portion of each telomere, so that with each new cell division the telomeres get shorter. When the telomeres get to a certain critical length, DNA replication seems to no longer be possible, and the cell enters senescence. Although the above correlation is fairly consistent with most studies, the mechanism whereby a cell knows it has reached the limit is unknown. Experiments where telomeres have been lengthened in older cells have resulted in cells that continue dividing beyond their typical limit. An enzyme called telomerase, abundant in many kinds of cancer cells, has been found to increase the length of telomeres, accounting in part for the immortal nature of these cells. Telomerase is not present in most normal cells, but recently geneticists have been able to cause cells to express the telomerase gene, causing them to become immortal, like cancer cells, without the other detrimental traits of cancer cells.

A result of the above genetic changes in aging humans is that illnesses of all kinds are more common. This is due in part because the immune system seems to function more slowly and less efficiently with age. Other diseases, like cancer, are a direct result of the relentless accumulation of mutations. Cancers generally develop after a series of mutations or chromosomal rearrangements have occurred that cause the mutation of or inappropriate expression of proto-oncogenes. Proto-oncogenes are normal genes that are involved in regulating the cell cycle and often are responsible for moving the cell forward toward mitosis (cell division). Mutations in proto-oncogenes transform them into oncogenes (cancer cells), which results in uncontrolled cell division, along with the other traits displayed by cancer cells. Overexpression of proto-oncogenes can have much the same effect. Another class of genes, called tumor suppressor genes, have the opposite effect and are involved in slowing down or stopping cells from actively dividing. Mutations in tumor suppressor genes can destroy their regulatory function, thus releasing cells to divide uncontrollably. Because problems with several proto-oncogenes and tumor suppressor genes are generally required for cancer to develop, cancer tends to be more common in older age when more mutations have accumulated.

PROGEROID SYNDROMES AS MODELS OF AGING

Several progeroid syndromes have been studied closely in hopes of finding clues to the underlying genetic mechanisms of aging. Although such studies are useful, they are limited in the sense that they only display some of the characteristics of aging. Also, because they are typically due to a single mutant gene, they represent a gross simplification of the aging process. Recent genetic analyses have identified the specific genetic defects for some of the progeroid syndromes, but often this has only led to more questions.

Down syndrome is the most common progeroid syndrome and is usually caused by possession of an extra copy of chromosome 21 (also called trisomy 21). Affected individuals display rapid aging for a number of traits such as atherosclerosis and cataracts, although the severity of the effects varies greatly. The most notable progeroid symptom is the development of Alzheimer's disease-like changes in the brain such as senile plaques and neurofibrillary tangles. One of the genes sometimes involved in Alzheimer's disease is located on chromosome 21, possibly accounting for the common symptoms. Because Down syndrome occurs in some individuals who are trisomic for only a portion of chromosome 21 (resulting in familial Down syndrome), it is probable that the symptoms are the result of only a small number of genes. A few rare individuals who are trisomic for all but a small portion of chromosome 21 lack the characteristic facial features and mental deficiencies, suggesting that as little as overexpression of a single gene (caused by possession of one more copy than normal) may be responsible for the main progeroid symptoms of Down syndrome.

Huntington's disease is one of the classic progeroid syndromes that is sometimes classified as a "late-onset" disease. It is caused by a single dominant gene. The first symptoms usually appear sometime in middle age (although they sometimes appear even in the early twenties), with death occurring within fifteen years. The most striking symptom, uncontrollable jerky movements, is due to degeneration of neurons. Memory loss and dementia eventually follow. Other signs of premature aging such as diabetes mellitus, brittle bones, weight loss, and pale, wrinkled skin may appear even earlier in the progression of the disease. The gene responsible for Huntington's disease has been isolated, cloned, and sequenced, but how it causes the disease symptoms is still unknown.

Werner's syndrome is a very rare autosomal recessive disease. The primary symptoms are severe atherosclerosis and a high incidence of cancer, including some unusual sarcomas and connective tissue cancers. Other degenerative changes include premature graying, muscle atrophy, osteoporosis, cataracts, and calcification of heart valves and soft tissues. Death, usually by atherosclerosis, often occurs by fifty or sixty years of age. The gene responsible for Werner's syndrome has been isolated and encodes a DNA helicase (called WRN DNA helicase), an enzyme that is involved in helping DNA strands to separate during the process of replication. The faulty enzyme is believed to cause the process of replication to stall at the replication fork, the place where DNA replication is actively taking place, which leads to a higher than normal mutation rate in the DNA, although more work is needed to be sure of its mechanism.

Hutchinson-Gilford progeria shows even more rapid and pronounced premature aging. Effects begin even in early childhood with balding, loss of subcutaneous fat, and skin wrinkling, especially noticeable in the facial features. Later, bone loss and atherosclerosis appear, and most affected individuals die before the age of twenty-five. The genetic inheritance pattern for Hutchinson-Gilford progeria is still debated, but evidence suggests it may be due to a very rare autosomal dominant gene. Nothing is known about the gene involved, but evidence suggests it may represent a defect in a DNA repair system.

Cockayne syndrome, another very rare autosomal recessive defect, displays loss of subcutaneous fat, skin photosensitivity (especially to ultraviolet, or UV, light), and neurodegeneration. Age of death can vary, but seems to center around forty years of age. The specific genetic defect is known and involves the action of a few different proteins. At the molecular level, the major problems all relate to some aspect of transcription, the making of messenger ribonucleic acid (mRNA) from the DNA template, which can also affect some aspects of DNA repair. Another somewhat less rare autosomal recessive defect is ataxia telangiectasia. It displays a whole suite of premature aging symptoms, including neurodegeneration, immunodefi-

ciency, graying, skin wrinkling, and cancer, especially leukemias and lymphomas. Death usually occurs between forty and fifty years of age. The specific defect is known to be loss of a protein kinase, an enzyme that normally adds phosphate groups to other proteins. In this case, kinase appears to be involved in regulating the cell cycle, and its loss causes shortening of telomeres and defects in the repair of double-stranded breaks in DNA. One of the proteins it appears to normally phosphorylate is p53, a tumor suppressor gene whose loss is often associated with various forms of cancer.

Although the genes involved in the various progeroid syndromes are varied, they do seem to fall into some common functional types. Most have something to do with DNA replication, transcription, or repair. Other genes are involved in control of some part of the cell cycle. Although many other genes remain to be discovered, they will likely also be involved with DNA or the cell cycle in some way. Based on many of the common symptoms of aging, these findings are not too surprising.

GENETIC MODELS OF AGING

The increasing understanding of molecular genetics has prompted biologists to propose a number of models of aging. Each of the models is consistent with some aspect of cellular genetics, but none of the models, as yet, is consistent with all evidence. Some biologists have suggested that a combination of several models may be required to adequately explain the process of aging. In many ways, understanding of the genetic causes of aging is in its infancy, and geneticists are still unable to agree on even the probable number of genes involved in aging. Even the extent to which genes control aging at all has been debated. Early studies based on correlations between time of death of parents and offspring or on the age of death of twins suggested that genes accounted for 40 to 70 percent of the heritability of longevity. More recent research on twins has suggested that genes may only account for 35 percent or less of the observed variability in longevity, and for twins reared apart the genetic effects appear to be even less.

Initially a smaller genetic component to longevity seems hopeful, because it would open the door to increasing longevity by environmental modifications (for example, diet or drug therapy). Although history supports this idea, to an extent, as seen by the significantly longer average life spans today over any time in the past, there are also limits to longevity. A typical upper limit for human life span, according to many gerontologists, appears to be approximately 120, and though genetics may not be the primary cause for the variation in human longevity, genetics could be the dominant reason why people do not typically live beyond 120. This is not to say that science will not be able to increase average life spans beyond 120, but it does suggest that the limits may not be far beyond it. Of course, the eventual hope is that geneticists will learn how genetics determines the upper limit and develop ways to genetically engineer humans for greater longevity. Such possibilities are currently well beyond reach and verge on science fiction.

Genetic theories of aging can be classified as either genome-based or mutation-based. Genome-based theories include the classic idea that longevity is programmed, as well as some evolution-based theories such as antagonistic pleiotropy, first proposed by George C. Williams, and the disposable soma theory. Mutation-based theories are based on the simple concept that genetic systems gradually fall apart from "wear and tear." The differences among mutation-based theories generally involve the causes of the mutations and the particular genetic systems involved. Even though genome-based and mutation-based theories seem to be distinct, there is actually some overlap. For example, the antagonistic pleiotropy theory (a genome-based theory) predicts that selection will "weed out" lethal mutations whose effects are felt during the reproductive years, but that later in life lethal mutations will accumulate (a mutation-based theory) because selection has no effect after the reproductive years.

GENOME-BASED THEORIES OF AGING

The oldest genome-based theory of aging, sometimes called programmed senescence, suggested that life span is genetically determined. In other words, cells (and by extrapolation, the entire organism) live for a genetically predetermined length of time. The passing of time is measured by some kind of cellular clock and when the predetermined time is reached, cells go into a self-destruct sequence that eventually causes the death of the organism. Evidence for this model comes from the discovery that animal cells, when grown in culture, are only able to divide a limited number of times, the so-called Hayflick limit discussed above, and then they senesce and eventually die. Further evidence comes from developmental studies where it has been discovered that some cells die spontaneously in a process called apoptosis. A process similar to apoptosis could be responsible for cell death at old age. The existence of a cellular clock is consistent with the discovery that telomeres shorten as cells age.

In spite of the consistency of the experimental evidence, this model fails on theoretical grounds. Programmed senescence, as for any complex biological process, would be required to have evolved by natural selection, but natural selection can only act on traits that are expressed during the reproductive years. Because senescence happens after the reproductive years, it cannot have developed by natural selection. In addition, even if natural selection could have been involved, what advantage would programmed senescence have for a species?

Because of the hurdles presented by natural selection, the preferred alternative genome-based theory is called antagonistic pleiotropy. "Pleiotropy" is a standard genetic term used to describe the multiple effects that many genes have. For example, the mutant gene responsible for cystic fibrosis causes clogging of the lungs, sterility, and excessive salt in perspiration, among other symptoms, and is therefore said to display pleiotropy. In the antagonistic pleiotropy theory, genes that increase the chances of survival before and during the reproductive years are detrimental in the postreproductive years. Because natural selection has no effect on genes after reproduction, these detrimental effects are not "weeded" out of the population. There is some physiological support for this in that sex hormones, which are required for reproduction earlier in life, cause negative effects later in life, such as osteoporosis in women and increased cancer risks in both sexes.

The disposable soma theory is similar, but is based on a broader physiological base. It has been noted that there is a strong negative correlation among a broad range of species between metabolic rate and longevity. In general, the higher the average metabolic rate, the shorter lived the species. In addition, the need to reproduce usually results in a higher metabolic rate during the reproductive years than in later years. The price for this high early metabolic rate is that systems burn out sooner. This theory is not entirely genome-based, but also has a mutation-based component. Data on mutation rates seem to show a high correlation between high metabolic rate and high mutation rate.

One of the by-products of metabolism is the production of free oxygen radicals, single oxygen atoms with an unpaired electron. These free radicals are highly reactive and not only cause destruction of proteins and other molecules, but also cause mutations in DNA. So the high metabolic rate during the reproductive years causes a high incidence of damaging DNA mutations which lead to many of the diseases of old age. After reproduction, natural selection has no use for the body anymore, so it gradually falls apart as the mutations build up. Unfortunately, all attempts so far to assay the extent of the mutations produced have led to the conclusion that not enough mutations exist to be the sole cause of the changes observed in aging.

MUTATION-BASED THEORIES OF AGING

The basic premise of all the mutation-based theories of aging is that the buildup of mutations eventually leads to senescence and death, the ultimate cause being cancer or the breakdown of a critical system. The major support for these kinds of theories comes from a number of recent studies that have found a larger number of genetic mutations in elderly individuals than in younger individuals, the same pattern being observed even when the same individual is assayed at different ages. The differences among the various mutation-based theories have to do with what causes the mutations and what kinds of DNA are primarily affected. As mentioned above, the disposable soma theory also relies, in part, on mutation-based theories.

The most general mutation-based theory is the somatic mutation/DNA damage theory, which relies on background radiation and other mutagens in the environment as the cause of mutations. Over time, the buildup of these mutations begins to cause failure of critical biochemical pathways and eventually causes death. This theory is consistent with experimental evidence from the irradiation of laboratory animals. Irradiation causes DNA

damage, which, if not repaired, leads to mutations. The higher the dose of radiation, the more mutations result. It has also been noted that there is some correlation between the efficiency of DNA repair and life span. Further support comes from observations of individuals with more serious DNA repair deficiencies, such as those affected by xeroderma pigmentosum. Individuals with xeroderma pigmentosum have almost no ability to repair the type of DNA damage caused by exposure to UV light, and as a result they develop skin cancer very easily, which typically leads to death.

The major flaw in this theory is that it predicts that senescence should be a random process, which it is not. A related theory called error catastrophe also predicts that mutations will build up over time, eventually leading to death, but it suffers from the same flaw. Elderly individuals do seem to possess greater amounts of abnormal proteins, but that does not mean that they must be the ultimate cause of death.

The free radical theory of aging is more promising and is probably one of the most familiar theories to the general public. This theory has also received much more attention from researchers. The primary culprit in this theory is oxygen free radicals, which are highly reactive and cause damage to proteins, DNA, and RNA. Free radicals are a natural by-product of many cellular reactions and most specifically of the reactions involved in respiration. In fact, the higher the metabolic rate, the more free radicals will likely be produced. Although this theory also involves a random process, it is a more consistent and predictable process, and through time it can potentially build on itself, causing accelerated DNA damage with greater age.

Significant attention has focused on mtDNA. Because free radicals are produced in greater abundance in respiration, which takes place primarily in the mitochondria, mtDNA should show more mutations than nuclear DNA. In addition, as DNA damage occurs, the biochemical pathways involved in respiration should become less efficient, which would theoretically lead to even greater numbers of free radicals being produced, which would, in turn, cause more damage. This kind of positive feedback cycle would eventually reach a point where the cells could not produce enough energy to meet their needs and they would senesce. Assays of mtDNA have shown a greater number of mutations in the elderly, and it is a well-known phenomenon that mitochondria are less efficient in the elderly. Muscle weakness is one of the symptoms of these changes.

The free radical theory has some appeal, in the sense that ingestion of increased amounts of antioxidants in the diet would be expected to reduce the number of free radicals and thus potentially delay aging. Although antioxidants have been used in this way for some time, no significant increase in life span has been observed, although it does appear that cancer incidence may be reduced.

FROM THEORY TO PRACTICE

Many of the genetic theories of aging are intriguing and even seem to be consistent with experimental evidence from many sources, but none of them adequately addresses longevity at the organismal level. Although telomeres shorten with age in individual cells, cells continue to divide into old age, and humans do not seem to die because all, or most, of their cells are no longer able to divide. Cells from older individuals do have more mutations than cells from younger individuals, but the number of mutations observed does not seem adequate to account for the large suite of problems present in old age. Mitochondria, on average, do function more poorly in older individuals and their mtDNA does display a larger number of mutations, but many mitochondria remain high functioning and appear to be adequate to sustain life.

Essentially, geneticists have opened a crack in the door to a better understanding of the causes of aging, and the theories presented here are probably correct in part, but much more research is needed to sharpen the understanding of this process. The hope of geneticists, and of society in general, is to learn how to increase longevity. Presently, it seems all that is possible is to help a larger number of people approach the practical limit of 120 years through lifestyle modification and medical intervention. Going significantly beyond 120 years is probably a genetic problem that will not be solved for some time.

—*Bryan Ness*

See also Aging: Biological, psychological, and sociocultural perspectives; Aging process; Antiaging treatments; Antioxidants; Cancer; Free radical theory of aging; Longevity research; Premature aging.

FOR FURTHER INFORMATION:

Austad, Steven N. *Why We Age: What Science Is Discovering About the Body's Journey Throughout Life.* New York: John Wiley & Sons, 1997. A review of the latest biological research and theories of aging, including an assessment of the oldest attainable age for humans.

De Gray, Aubrey D. N. J. "A Proposed Refinement of the Mitochondrial Free Radical Theory of Aging." *BioEssays* 19, no. 2 (February, 1997).

Finch, Caleb E. *Longevity, Senescence, and the Genome.* Chicago: University of Chicago Press, 1990. A comprehensive overview of the finer details of the genetic aspects of aging, focusing especially on the molecular level and aimed at more educated readers.

Knight, Joseph A. "The Process and Theories of Aging." *Annals of Clinical and Laboratory Science* 25, no. 1 (January, 1995). An overview of genetic theories of aging, presenting evidence that the genome-based and free radical theories are most consistent with recent research.

Lewis, Ricki. "Telomere Tales." *Bioscience* 48, no. 12 (December, 1998). An overview of some of the latest molecular research that supports the telomere shortening model of cellular aging.

Martin, George M. "The Genetics of Aging." *Hospital Practice* 32, no. 2 (February, 1997). Presents an evolution-based theory of aging with supporting evidence from some of the progeroid syndromes and other molecular data from molecular biology.

Medina, John J. *The Clock of Ages: Why We Age—How We Age—Winding Back the Clock.* New York: Cambridge University Press, 1996. A book written especially for the general public with no biology background. Covers aging on a system-by-system basis and includes a large section on the genetics of aging.

Ricklefs, Robert E., and Caleb E. Finch. *Aging: A Natural History.* New York: W. H. Freeman, 1995. A good general introduction to the biology of aging by two biologists who specialize in aging research.

GERIATRICS AND GERONTOLOGY

RELEVANT ISSUES: Health and medicine, psychology, sociology

SIGNIFICANCE: Gerontology is the study of normal aspects of aging, from maturity to old age; geriatrics is the study and treatment of pathological aspects of aging

Aging is the result of the interaction of biological, psychological, social, and environmental forces. Myths and musing about aging have been of great interest to people from the time humans first recorded their thoughts. However, the systematic study of aging has only begun to occur within the past two hundred years. Geriatrics and gerontology, as professions, are even newer, having first gained notice in the 1950's.

TWO INTERRELATED FIELDS

Geriatrics and gerontology are rapidly growing fields. One reason for this is because of population changes. There are more older people alive now than at any other time in history, and more older people are living longer. Where once it was uncommon to know of people who were in their eighties and nineties, it is now more common to see people this age living in the community and living well. In fact, most older people live independently. At the end of the twentieth century, only 5 percent of people over age sixty-five lived in nursing homes or institutions. Also, changes in birthrates and advances in medical technology have influenced the age composition of American society. While the number of children born to a family may be decreasing, the infant mortality rate has declined, and life-saving technology has increased.

Geriatrics is the study and treatment of pathological aspects of aging. Aging is looked at in terms of decline and pathology. This field of study tends to use a medical or biological model of aging. In fact, geriatrics is narrowly defined as a subdivision of medicine that focuses on the care of the older adult and diseases of old age. While geriatrics as a field of study tends to be narrowly focused on medical or biological processes, geriatrics as a profession uses a broader perspective that encompasses psychosocial, economic, historical, and physiological factors. Knowledge related to biological, biomedical, behavioral, and social aspects of aging is applied to the prevention, diagnosis, treatment, and care of older persons. Thus, geriatrics is concerned with two primary processes: clinical assessment and medical management to identify and correct health problems, and functional assessment to determine how the independence of the

older adult can be maintained or maximized by using appropriate human, mechanical, and environmental manipulations.

Gerontology is the study of the aging process from maturity to old age, as well as the study of older adults as a special population. Whereas geriatrics is pathology-oriented, gerontology covers the entire scope of the aging process. It covers both normal aging and pathological aging. Thus, in one sense, geriatrics is a component of gerontology.

Three primary disciplines dominate gerontology. The biological approach to aging includes studies of all kinds of animals, including humans. This perspective is concerned with longevity and with what leads to death. The psychological approach to aging focuses on the individual and those relationships that impact the individual's life. The individual is considered in terms of his or her life span, rather than at one particular point in time. Geriatric psychology is also interested in the aging mind—how perception, memory, emotions, and mental capacities change over time and across an individual's life span. The sociological approach examines the structure of society. This perspective investigates how norms and values influence how an individual perceives and reacts to the aging process.

There are four basic themes that apply to geriatrics and gerontology: inevitability and human choice, normal aging versus disease, slowing, and interdisciplinary work. Some aspects of aging are unavoidable. People grow old and eventually die. Although individuals cannot control the rate of aging or markedly postpone the time of death, they can influence both of these things through diet, exercise, lifestyle, and medical technology. Normal aging versus disease is critical in understanding human aging. As an individual ages, there is increased vulnerability to disease and disability. However, there are enormous differences among older adults, with some being very healthy and some being very sick and frail. Slowing seems to be a universal change with age. Many behavioral changes that occur with age can be explained in terms of slowing of the central nervous system. Finally, geriatrics and gerontology are interdisciplinary. Aging cannot be fully understood in the context of a single discipline. Biology, psychology, sociology, and environment all influence human aging.

Another important difference between geriatrics and gerontology lies in how the two fields emerged. The field of gerontology has developed from a broad scientific research base, while the field of geriatrics has developed from an applied or practical base. Geriatrics emerged as a discipline because the presentation and course of illness in old age differs from that found in the rest of the population. This is caused, in part, by the effects of the aging process on the individual. Health problems in older adults present themselves differently than in younger adults. The presenting problem is often not as distinct as with a younger patient because older patients are more likely to have multiple health concerns. Additionally, many signs and symptoms of illness are not produced directly by the disease but instead by the body's response to the insult caused by the disease. Since one of the hallmarks of aging is a reduced response to stress, the stress of having a disease can change the intensity of illness signs and symptoms.

HISTORY OF GERONTOLOGY

Sixteenth and seventeenth century English philosopher Sir Francis Bacon was one of the earliest people to consider aging to be a legitimate area of science. Before this, aging was considered to be an element of religion. Bacon advocated using systematic observations to discover underlying laws that governed behavior. He believed that by studying the processes of aging in an orderly manner, the causes of aging might be discovered. Bacon thought that poor hygiene practices made people age faster. He was one of the first scientists to hypothesize a cause for the aging process that could be controlled by humans and that was set apart from the will of God.

Benjamin Franklin also conducted scientific research on aging. He was interested in rejuvenation and increasing the life span. Franklin hypothesized that lightning could be used to bring dead animals and humans back to life because the electricity in lightning had a stimulating effect. His experiments were not successful.

While Bacon and Franklin stimulated scientific experiments and research on aging, nineteenth century Belgian scientist Adolphe Quételet is considered to be the first gerontologist. Quételet was a mathematician who created some major statistical tools and developed concepts that reshaped thoughts about human behavior. Perhaps his most important concept was the idea of the average—a point around which extremes were distributed. His idea was that there was a continuum of levels of an ability, and the continuum was distributed around the average on a bell-shaped curve. Quételet used this idea to collect data on a variety of human abilities, such as hand strength, body weight, death rates and birthrates, and professional productivity at different ages.

Various aspects of the aging process began to be studied scientifically around 1900. These studies represented beginning attempts by biologists to describe and explain how to modify the aging process. Psychological studies of aging also began. Intelligence testing, which originated in France as a way to predict academic achievement in children, was first used in the United States to predict success in the military during World War I.

During the 1940's, several basic concepts of gerontology were developed, and gerontology began to be recognized as an independent and important field. One concept was that problems of aging are complex and can be best understood in an interdisciplinary context. A second concept was that aging resulted from the interaction of biological predisposition and the environment. As the number of individuals over age sixty-five dramatically increased from 1900 through 1940, there was an increasing recognition of the social consequences of an aging population. This led to an increased need for basic information about both normal and pathological aging.

Gerontology as a profession and as a field of study exploded during the 1940's and 1950's. In 1940, the surgeon general appointed a national advisory committee to assist in the development of a gerontology unit within the National Institutes of Health (NIH). This resulted in the creation of the National Institute on Aging (NIA) in 1974. The Gerontological Society of America was founded in 1945 and continues to promote the scientific study of aging. Its purpose is to promote research in aging and to disseminate gerontological research knowledge to researchers, practitioners, and decision and opinion makers. In 1946, the first International Congress of Gerontology was convened as a forum for the exchange of research ideas and scientific evidence about aging and the aging process.

RESEARCH IN GERIATRICS AND GERONTOLOGY

Knowledge about aging and late life has come from scientific studies of the processes associated with aging and from studies of mature and older adults. These studies have been conducted from a multidisciplinary perspective and have produced applications, techniques, and programs designed to benefit older adults.

One of the major contributions of geriatrics and gerontology has been the development of sophisticated research strategies that are sensitive to the developmental patterns of individuals and to sociohistorical times. Research generally takes two forms. It can either describe an aging phenomenon or attempt to manipulate a factor thought to cause aging. A great deal of aging research uses a cross-sectional research design, where an older group is compared to a younger group in an attempt to explain age differences. For example, one strong and persisting research finding is that older people demonstrate slower reaction times than younger people. Some aging research seeks to explain how people or organisms change over time as they age. This type of research uses a longitudinal research design, where the same group of people (or organisms) is measured at several times. This type of research design has established that personality traits do not fluctuate dramatically over the life course.

A problem with these two types of research designs is that they confuse age with generational differences and time of measurement. The cross-sectional research design can explain age differences but cannot tell if those differences are caused by aging or generational differences. The longitudinal research design can explain age changes but cannot tell if those changes are caused by aging or time of measurement. For this reason, K. Warner Schaie developed the concept of sequential research design, which combines cross-sectional and longitudinal research designs by following several groups of people of different ages and generations over several times of measurement. Sequential research can be expensive and time-consuming to conduct but can separate aging effects from generational effects and time-of-measurement effects.

When conducting research in geriatrics and gerontology, one must consider ethical issues. Researchers may be able to identify some of the causes of aging; when these causes are harmful, the potential for intervening and changing the course of aging exists. However, the right of the individual to be protected from physical or psychological harm must be considered. Research subjects can only participate in research voluntarily. It is unethical to misinform research subjects about the nature of the research or the potential risks involved in participating. To protect the rights of research subjects, the federal government and research institutions require approval of all research projects.

GERIATRICS AND GERONTOLOGY AS PROFESSIONS

Both geriatrics and gerontology rely on a scientist-practitioner model as professions. Basic and applied research on the aging process is used to develop new ways to care for and treat older adults. Gerontology, therefore, is a science because it includes many aspects of other scientific disciplines, such as reliance on the scientific method and experiments to gain knowledge. However, gerontology and geriatrics go beyond traditional science by applying scientific knowledge to practical care.

Because the field of gerontology draws from many disciplines, it can be difficult to describe exactly who is a gerontologist. Besides professionals who have formal educational training in geriatrics and gerontology, all people become interested in the aging process as they grow old themselves. Professional roles in gerontology and geriatrics cover a broad spectrum of activities, ranging from basic biological and social sciences, to applied practical knowledge derived from biology, medicine, and social sciences, to common experience.

Because life expectancy increased so dramatically during the twentieth century, most Americans will live to be old and will be old for a long time. U.S. Census data indicated that the average life expectancy for people born in 1980 was seventy years for men and seventy-seven years for women. For people already aged sixty-five in 1980, however, life expectancy was almost eighty years for men and nearly eighty-four years for women. If old age is defined as beginning at age sixty-five, then most people will be old for many years. Further increases in life expectancy are predicted for the future.

—Linda M. Dougherty

See also Aging: Biological, psychological, and sociocultural perspectives; Aging process; Gerontological Society of America; Life expectancy; Longevity research; National Institute on Aging; Neugarten, Bernice; Psychiatry, geriatric.

FOR FURTHER INFORMATION:

Hayslip, Bert, Jr., and Paul E. Panek. *Adult Development and Aging*. Philadelphia: Harper & Row, 1989. This textbook examines basic and applied issues of adult development and aging.

Hillier, Susan, and Georgia M. Barrow. *Aging, the Individual, and Society*. 7th ed. Belmont, Calif.: Wadsworth, 1999. An introductory textbook presenting a multidisciplinary perspective of aging using scientific, professional, and popular literature.

Kane, Robert L., Joseph G. Ouslander, and Itamar B. Abrass. *Essentials of Clinical Geriatrics*. New York: McGraw-Hill Information Services, 1989. This book is a practical guide for those who provide health care to older adults.

Schaie, K. Warner, and Sherry L. Willis. *Adult Development and Aging*. 4th ed. New York: Harper-Collins College Publishers, 1996. The authors examine the major psychological issues involved in adult development and aging.

Woodruff-Pak, Diana. *Psychology and Aging*. Englewood Cliffs, N.J.: Prentice Hall, 1988. Although the focus of this book is on the psychology of aging, biological and social sciences perspectives are also included.

GERONTOLOGICAL SOCIETY OF AMERICA

DATE: Founded in 1945

RELEVANT ISSUES: Biology, law, psychology, sociology

SIGNIFICANCE: The Gerontological Society of America promotes high-quality, multidisciplinary scientific study of the process of aging

The Gerontological Society of America (GSA) was established in 1945 to promote the scientific study of aging, to encourage exchanges among researchers and practitioners from various disciplines related to gerontology, and to foster the use of gerontological research in forming public policy. The founders of the GSA were pioneers in establishing gerontology as a legitimate area of research. Since then, GSA members have worked to dispel the myths of the frail and dependent aged and have attacked the scientific, medical, and po-

litical barriers to the attainment of a healthier and more productive aging population.

The primary activity of the GSA in its early years was the establishment of a journal on aging. In January, 1946, the founders published the first issue of the *Journal of Gerontology*, the first, and for many years the only, journal on gerontological research in the United States. In June, 1954, the GSA began publication of the *Newsletter of the Gerontological Society*, which carried news about the society, its members, and its activities. In 1961, another journal, *Gerontologist*, was established by the GSA.

The *Journal of Gerontology* was reorganized in 1988 into four distinct journals, each with its own editor and editorial board, but they were still issued under one cover. *Gerontologist* evolved into a journal about applied research and analysis of aging, including social policy, program development, and service delivery. In 1995, the *Journal of Gerontology* was split into two covers, with the biological and medical sciences under one cover and the psychological and social sciences under the other. In addition, in 1995, the GSA added another publication, the *Public Policy and Aging Report*. This report, a quarterly policy newsletter, examines policy issues associated with the aging society. The publication is targeted to those outside the academic and traditional aging communities.

Although the journals on aging are the GSA's most visible products, its most visible activity is its annual scientific meeting. This meeting showcases the vibrancy and the extent of research on aging and is the oldest and largest gathering devoted to gerontological research. At the 1995 meeting in Los Angeles, over 3,300 researchers were present.

The GSA successfully advocated the creation of a Gerontological Study Section at the U.S. Public Health Service in the late 1940's, and it was a principal player in the development and organization of the 1971 White House Conference on Aging. The GSA was also influential in the establishment of the National Institute on Aging (NIA) in 1974. Several members of the GSA became founding members of NIA's National Advisory Council.

Until the mid-1990's, the study of aging primarily focused on older white people. The GSA has encouraged more quality research on minority aging, has increased the number of minority researchers, and has expanded the participation of minority members in the GSA leadership. In 1994, the GSA established the National Academy on Aging as a freestanding public policy institute. The academy's mission is to promote education, research, and public understanding of the well-being of present and future elderly people. —*Alvin K. Benson*

See also Aging process; Geriatrics and gerontology; National Institute on Aging.

GERONTOLOGY. *See* GERIATRICS AND GERONTOLOGY.

GIN GAME, THE

AUTHOR: D. L. Coburn
DATE: Produced in 1976, published in 1977
RELEVANT ISSUES: Culture, economics, family, recreation
SIGNIFICANCE: This Pulitzer Prize-winning tragicomic play depicts how boring, undignified, lonely, regretful, and desperate life can be for older adults on welfare in a culture that prizes youth, utility, financial success, perfection, and winning

The play opens revealing the solitary, disheveled, bathrobe-clad figure of Weller Martin, seated and playing (and cheating at) solitaire at a card table on the shabby sun porch of the Bentley Home for the Aged. Weller's game is interrupted when carelessly groomed Fonsia Dorsey, a new arrival at the home, seeks solitude on the porch. It is visitors day at the home, but neither Weller nor Fonsia has any visitors. Weller introduces himself and talks Fonsia into playing gin rummy, a game she has not played but which he thinks takes great skill and at which he fancies himself an expert. He eagerly offers to teach her.

While playing gin, they lament the conditions at the nursing home: meaningless and insulting leisure activities, condescending and underpaid staff members who steal from them, minimal space for personal belongings, fellow residents who cease to think or feel, unappetizing food that promotes diarrhea, quack doctors, and decrepit conditions. Meanwhile, Fonsia steadily wins at cards to the initial amusement of Weller (who claims beginner's luck) and then to his consternation.

The play unfolds through successive meetings and inevitable gin rummy rematches between the now-well-groomed Weller and Fonsia. Their initial companionability motivates self-disclosure during the games: health problems, divorces, failed business attempts, questionable ethics in business, failed family relationships, children, how bad luck operated in life, how society failed them, and plausible reasons for the lack of visitors. As Fonsia's winning streak continues and Weller's consternation turns to open hostility and bullying, however, the facades are stripped from each character. Raw emotion and truth are laid bare—the truth of why they have no visitors, of why they are at the nursing home, and of missed opportunities and regret in their lives. —*Patricia I. Hogan*

See also Abandonment; Friendship; Leisure activities; Literature; Loneliness; Nursing and convalescent homes; Poverty; Social ties.

GLAUCOMA

RELEVANT ISSUES: Health and medicine
SIGNIFICANCE: Glaucoma, which primarily affects those over the age of forty, is a buildup of fluid pressure inside the eyeball; excess pressure

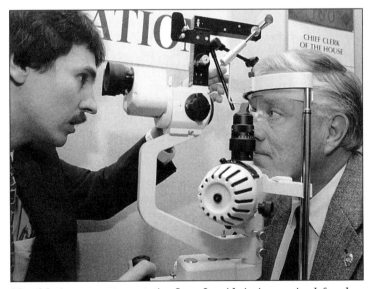

New Mexico state representative Jerry Lee Alwin is examined for glaucoma in 1998. Free screenings were offered to the elderly. (AP Photo/ Michael Pahos)

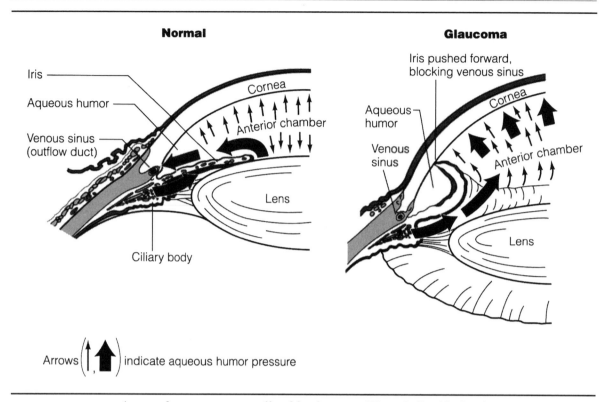

Normal

Iris

Aqueous humor

Venous sinus
(outflow duct)

Cornea

Anterior chamber

Lens

Ciliary body

Glaucoma

Iris pushed forward,
blocking venous sinus

Aqueous
humor

Venous
sinus

Cornea

Anterior chamber

Lens

Arrows indicate aqueous humor pressure

A normal eye versus an eye affected by glaucoma. (Hans & Cassidy, Inc.)

damages the optic nerve fibers at the back of the eye, causing a gradual loss of peripheral vision and eventual blindness if untreated

The front of the eyeball has a transparent, tough outer skin called the cornea. Inside the eye is the lens that focuses light rays onto the retina. Between the cornea and the lens is a layer of aqueous (watery) fluid. This fluid brings nourishment to the cells of the cornea that cannot be fed by blood vessels. Fresh fluid is produced continuously and later drains out through a small duct in the corner of the eye. If the duct becomes obstructed, the outflow is inhibited, resulting in an abnormal rise of fluid pressure called glaucoma. The extra stress can damage the bundle of nerve fibers that connect the eye to the brain. Outer nerve fibers are affected first, causing a gradual narrowing of the field of view. A person can still see straight ahead but not toward the sides. When the cone of forward vision has narrowed to less than 20 degrees (called tunnel vision), the person is considered legally blind. Without medical treatment, glaucoma

eventually results in total blindness. In the United States, about two million people, primarily those over the age of forty, suffer from the effects of glaucoma.

In the early stages, glaucoma is a disease without noticeable symptoms. Diagnosis by an optometrist is needed. During an eye examination, the doctor uses a mechanical device called a tonometer to detect abnormal pressure in the eye by making momentary contact with the cornea. Then the peripheral (side) vision is checked by having a patient look straight ahead while a small light source is moved to various angles on the two sides. Finally, the doctor can look into the interior of the eye with an ophthalmoscope. The bundle of optic nerve fibers exits from the rear of the eyeball at a place called the optic disk, which is normally flat. If the outer fibers have deteriorated because of glaucoma, the disk develops a curved surface, a condition known as "cupping."

If glaucoma is present, it is treated first with eye drops or ointments, and later with surgery if necessary. The goal is to relieve excess pressure by improving the drainage path for fluid. One type of eye drop constricts the pupil of the eye toward the middle, giving the drainage duct at the edge a larger opening. The drops usually have to be applied several times per day. Another drug, taken orally, is a diuretic that helps to remove fluid from the eyeball. If these treatments do not work, surgery may be necessary. For eye surgery, lasers have largely replaced handheld scalpels. The laser beam can make a tiny hole through which fluid will pass. One surgical procedure is to enlarge the drainage duct. Another procedure is to cut into the edge of the iris if the path toward the drainage duct is obstructed. *—Hans G. Graetzer*

See also Cataracts; Macular degeneration; Nearsightedness; Reading glasses; Vision changes and disorders.

GOLDEN GIRLS, THE

CAST: Beatrice Arthur, Rue McClanahan, Betty White, Estelle Getty

DATE: Aired from 1985 to 1992

RELEVANT ISSUES: Culture, media

SIGNIFICANCE: This television series presented aging in a positive manner by chronicling the active lives of four older women

The Golden Girls was a thirty-minute situation comedy that aired on the National Broadcasting Company (NBC) network from 1985 to 1992. The 180 episodes featured four women enjoying their "golden years" of retirement or semiretirement while sharing a home in Miami Beach, Florida. There were four main characters. Dorothy (played by Beatrice Arthur) was an outspoken divorced woman. Rose (Betty White) was a soft-spoken widow given to comedic misinterpretations of almost every situation or conversation. Blanche (Rue McClanahan), also a widow, was a sexy Southern belle from Georgia often obsessed with her looks and her numerous personal relationships. Sophia (Estelle Getty), a widow and Dorothy's mother, told stories about her native country of Sicily. She enjoyed shocking her roommates and viewers with her dry sense of humor.

The show stands out as one of the few that presented aging, particularly the aging of women, in a positive light. The characters were shown enjoying retirement or semiretirement through work, volunteerism, community involvement, and per-

sonal relationships. Most of the episodes focused on the daily events in their lives.

Until *The Golden Girls*, many of the popular television shows presented women over fifty only as sideline characters—someone's grandmother or neighbor—to the main characters. In this series, the women were the stars and were shown as the type of people so many women over fifty really are—active, vital human beings.

The popular series won ten Emmy Awards, including Best Comedy twice. Each of the leading actresses won Emmys either as Best Actress or as Best Supporting Actress. *—Sherri Ward Massey*

See also Friendship; Sexuality; Social ties; Television; Women and aging.

GOUT

RELEVANT ISSUES: Health and medicine

SIGNIFICANCE: Gout is a form of inflammatory arthritis caused by deposits of uric acid crystals in the joints that leads to significant short-term disability

Gout was first described by Hippocrates in the fifth century B.C.; because of its association with certain rich foods, it has been known as the "king of diseases and the disease of kings." This disease is caused by a sustained increase in the level of uric acid in the blood greater than or equal to 7 milligrams per deciliter. Gout can be manifested by recurrent attacks of acute arthritis, tophi (deposits of uric acid crystals in and around joints), renal (kidney) disease, and uric acid kidney stones. The peak age of onset for men is forty to fifty years of age, while for women it is greater than sixty years. The male-to-female distribution is somewhere between two to one and seven to one. The incidence rate is estimated to be from 1.0 to 3.0 per 1,000 for men and 0.2 per 1,000 for women. The overall prevalence is about 5.0 to 28.0 per 1,000 for men and 1.0 to 6.0 per 1,000 for women.

Uric acid is the normal end-product of the breakdown of nucleic acids. Gout occurs when there is sustained increase in the production of uric acid or decreased elimination of uric acid by the kidneys. Some causes of uric acid overproduction include alcohol consumption, a diet high in purine (from anchovies, sardines, sweetbreads, kidney, or liver), chemotherapy, trauma, surgery, and some blood diseases such as leukemia and polycythemia. Decreased excretion of uric acid by the kidneys may occur as a result of diuretic (water pills) use, diminished kidney function, and thyroid disease.

Gout results from the deposition of uric acid crystals in the tissues of and around joints. Acute gout most commonly starts in the base of the great toe with swelling, redness, warmth, and pain so severe that the weight of bedsheets hurts. Over time, the attacks of gout occur more frequently, become longer in duration, and involve more joints. Chronic gout may develop over ten or more years of acute intermittent gout and can lead to crippled and deformed joints, kidney stones, persistent pain, and the development of tophi. Gout is diagnosed by identifying uric acid crystals in joint fluid or in a tophus.

Several medications are available to treat acute gout, including colchicine, corticosteroids, and nonsteroidal anti-inflammatory drugs (NSAIDs). Corticosteroids are frequently used in the elderly because these individuals often cannot tolerate the other medications as a result of diminished kidney function or illnesses that increase the risk of adverse reactions. After the acute attack of gout resolves, diet modification, a drug regimen, and lifestyle changes may be suggested to decrease the frequency of acute attacks. For people with recurrent or chronic gout, medications to lower the blood uric acid level to less than 5 milligrams per deciliter may be prescribed. Allopurinol is the drug of choice for people with uric acid overproduction, tophus formation, decreased kidney function, or uric acid kidney stones; the dose is adjusted based on a person's kidney function. Many older people with recurrent attacks of gout have diminished kidney function and are given allopurinol. Probencid and sulfinpurazone are some of the medications available to lower the serum uric acid level for people who underexcrete uric acid and have good kidney function.
—*Meika A. Fang*

See also Arthritis; Gastrointestinal changes and disorders; Malnutrition; Nutrition; Urinary disorders.

GRANDPARENTHOOD

RELEVANT ISSUES: Demographics, family, sociology

SIGNIFICANCE: Increases in health, longevity, and complexity in family structures and roles have produced new opportunities and new stresses for grandparents

With the first of the huge baby-boom generation reaching the fifty-year-old mark in 1996, interest in aging and the roles of the aged rose. The role of grandparent has taken on a greater emphasis in the lives of middle-aged and older adults. Grandparenthood changed dramatically during

---

Excerpt from the Declaration by Congress of 1995 as the "Year of the Grandparent"

Whereas grandparents bring a tremendous amount of love and power for good into the lives of their grandchildren;

Whereas grandparents, in partnership with parents, help deepen every child's roots and strengthen every child's wings so that every child may soar into adulthood with a glad heart and a confident spirit;

Whereas grandparents are a strong and important voice in support of the happiness and well-being of children;

Whereas grandparents often serve as the primary caregivers for their grandchildren, providing a stable and supportive home environment;

Whereas grandparents should be acknowledged for the important role they play within families, and for the many and varied contributions they make to enhance and further the value of the family and family traditions;

Whereas public awareness of and appreciation for the contributions of grandparents should be strengthened;

Whereas grandparents should be encouraged to continue as a vital force in the shaping of American families today and into the future;

Whereas the Nation acknowledges the contributions of grandparents by celebrating National Grandparents Day each September; and

Whereas there should be a year-long national celebration of grandparents and grandparenting;

Now, therefore, be it

Resolved by the Senate and House of Representatives of the United States of America in Congress assembled, that 1995 is designated the "Year of the Grandparent" . . .

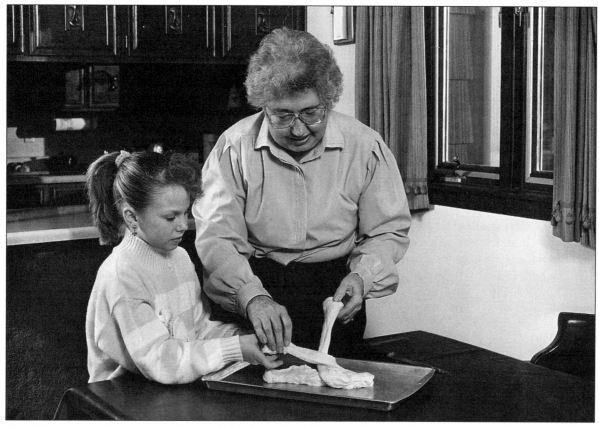

Grandparents often have the experience and the time to hand down traditions and teach important skills to younger generations. (James L. Shaffer)

the last several decades of the twentieth century because of developments in health technology, as well as increases in life expectancy, geographic mobility, and divorce and remarriage rates.

There is much diversity among grandparents. According to the U.S. Census Bureau, grandparents can range in age from thirty to over one hundred. Most first become grandparents between ages forty-five and fifty-three and can spend as many as thirty to fifty years in that role. These statistics do away with the stereotype of a very old and gray grandparent in a rocking chair. Because of increased health technology, America's elderly are living longer, healthier lives during which they remain active and vital. As the baby boomers age, more people will experience the grandparent role than ever before. Longer lives and improved health, along with financial stability, have also made geographic mobility possible for retirees. Higher divorce and remarriage rates have in-

creased the complexity of intergenerational relationships. Grandparenthood has been impacted by all of these changes.

HEALTH AND LONGEVITY

In the early twentieth century, most people did not live long enough to see their grandchildren. More than three-quarters of adults can now expect to become grandparents. While increasing life expectancy has resulted in more generations in extended families, decreasing fertility has resulted in smaller nuclear families. In *Handbook of Aging and the Social Sciences* (1996), by R. H. Binstock and L. K. George, the American extended family is described as changing from a pyramid shape, with larger numbers of young people at the base, to a bean-pole shape. There are now more three-, four-, and five-generation families with fewer members in each generation. With fewer members within the nuclear family, intergenerational family members may take on added importance. Older adults have more opportunity to know their grandchildren not only as infants and young children but also as adolescents, young adults, and possibly parents.

In the past, grandparents played the role of the "family watchdog." They passed on family heritage, acted as family mediators and advocates for grandchildren, and provided emotional support. The grandparent role may be an ambiguous one for older adults who did not have grandparents after whom they can model themselves.

GRANDPARENT STYLES

In 1964, Bernice Neugarten and K. Weinstein identified five styles of grandparenting. A study in 1986 by Andrew J. Cherlin and Frank Furstenberg identified only three. These styles have been combined to identify five typical styles: remote, advisory, companionate, involved, and surrogate parent. These styles are only typologies. Some grandparents adopt a combination of styles at different times in their lives or with different grandchildren. Older grandparents and those in poor health tend to adopt the remote or advisory styles, while younger grandparents, who tend to be in better health, are more likely to opt for the companionate style.

In a 1998 research article for the periodical *Family Relations*, Karen Fingerman recognized the importance of considering the other side of the duo in the grandparent-grandchild relationship. The age, personality, and health of the grandchild also affect the style that the grandparent adopts with that grandchild. Younger children may bring out the playful side of a grandparent. Personality conflicts between grandparent and grandchild may result in the grandparent adopting a more advisory or remote style, at least with that particular child. Grandchildren that are described by grandparents as "worrisome" or "irritating" fatigue grandparents more, resulting in a more remote grandparenting style. The psychological and physical health needs of the child also affect the grandparent-grandchild relationship, as such needs may limit the type of contact a grandparent can have with the grandchild. In *Of Human Bonding* (1990), Alice and Peter Rossi point out that the relationship between grandparents and their adult children or children-in-law (that is, the grandchild's

parents) plays a crucial role in the involvement of grandparents in the lives of the grandchildren. Parents, especially mothers, act as gatekeepers to their children. If the relationship between parent and grandparent has been fraught with conflict, the parent may not allow the grandparent to be closely involved with the child.

Remote grandparents may be benevolent but distant. They may be emotionally remote or remote because of geographic distance. Geographic distance between grandparents and grandchildren occurs often in the United States. Geographic mobility is often a career necessity for young and middle-aged adults. Increases in health, longevity, and financial well-being also mean that grandparents may travel more or retire to warmer climates. This can result in the adoption of a remote style of grandparenting. Remote grandparents have only occasional contact with their grandchildren, usually on holidays or birthdays. Their relationship with their grandchildren is more formal and reserved than friendly. Since retirement communities serve to limit in-person contact with grandchildren, grandparents who choose to live in retirement communities may also be remote grandparents. Older grandparents and great-grandparents are even more likely to adopt the remote style because of age, health, and geographic distance.

The second grandparenting style is the advisory style. Those grandparents who serve as reservoirs of family wisdom often dispense advice, skills, money, or other resources to their grandchildren. An example is a grandmother teaching her granddaughter how to knit. This type of grandparent is more involved than the remote grandparent but not as involved as the companionate grandparent.

The companionate style seems to be emerging as the most common grandparent style. These grandparents want to be a companion of their grandchild. They adopt a fun-seeking style, playing with their grandchildren, taking them on fun outings to the park or the zoo, and inviting them to be part of their leisure activity. This type of grandparent does not want to be a disciplinarian or a parent. That stage of their life is over, and they are happy to enjoy their grandchildren. Taken to an extreme, this type of grandparent may tend to overindulge, or "spoil," the grandchild, believing that this is his or her "job" as a grandparent.

Involved grandparents see their grandchildren as often as the companionate grandparent, but they are more involved in helping to raise the grandchild. They exert authority over their grandchild, expecting obedience. They may be the daytime caregiver of their grandchild. Involved grandparents may be part of a three-generation household, sometimes residing in their adult child's home or sometimes living in a home that their adult child has moved back into, bringing the grandchildren with him or her. This type of grandparent role may be adopted out of necessity to help their child, who may be a single parent. This style is adopted more often among grandmothers who are young, are of ethnic minority status, and have a lower income. In some cases, the involved grandparent becomes so involved that he or she becomes the surrogate parent of the grandchild.

The surrogate parent style of grandparenting is more likely to be adopted by ethnic minority grandmothers. The grandparent who becomes a surrogate parent usually does so because of disturbed family relations in the grandchild's nuclear family. This family form increased over 40 percent in the 1990's and is projected to continue to grow, according to Maximiliane E. Szinovácz in the *Handbook on Grandparenthood* (1998). This type of grandparent style may be the result of substance abuse, either drugs or alcohol, by the parent of the grandchild. Surrogate parenthood by grandparents might also be caused by violence in the grandchild's family or abandonment by the parent.

The social, emotional, and financial costs suffered by the surrogate parent grandparent can be overwhelming. The financial burden can be great if the grandparent takes on the primary care of a grandchild. Health care, food, and clothing for the child are expensive. Caretaking grandparents can collect welfare benefits for their grandchildren in some cases. Legally, they may also be able to collect child support from the parents. Emotionally, grandparents serving as surrogate parents may struggle because of guilt feelings or resentment over what their own child has done. Guilt feelings may result because the grandparent may feel he or she did a poor job of parenting the now-wayward adult child. Resentment may be experienced because of the financial and social burdens that are placed on them. Socially, surrogate parent grandparents may suffer because they must consider the needs of their grandchildren before they can engage socially. Social activities must include the grandchild, or a baby-sitter must be hired. If a surrogate grandparent is married, the reentrance of children into the home will also affect the marital relationship.

As many adult children delay childbearing until their thirties or forties, grandparenthood may come later in life than for previous generations. (James L. Shaffer)

GENDER AND ETHNICITY

Just as there are age differences in grandparenting style, there are also gender differences. Grandmothers are more likely than grandfathers to view the grandparent role as one that is more central to their self-concept. They are more likely to look forward to the onset of this role, provided it comes "on time" and not earlier. Grandmothers are more likely to be involved than are grandfathers. Grandfathers are more likely to adopt the remote or advisory style. Grandmothers, especially maternal grandmothers, are most likely to be the favored grandparent. This follows from the importance of their role as grandmother and from the likelihood that their daughter, the mother of the grandchild, is the gatekeeper to the child. Grandparents also tend to prefer grandchildren who are the same gender as they.

Ethnic differences in grandparenting styles are also recognized. The grandparent role tends to be more central for African Americans, Asian Americans, and Latinos than for Caucasian Americans. These ethnic groups are more likely to live near their grandchildren, perhaps in the same household. Minority grandparents tend to see their grandchildren as the future. In *Older Men's Lives* (1994), Edward Thompson argues that, as ethnic minority members become acculturated, the extended family ties are weakened. Cultural values of the third and fourth generation change as they become "Americanized." Studies also show that if a grandchild speaks the native tongue of the grandparent, there will be more contact between them.

DIVORCE AND REMARRIAGE

The structure of American families has undergone great changes as a result of trends in divorce and remarriage. The grandparent-grandchild relationship is altered by divorce. The divorcing parents are the middle generation, which mediates the relationship between grandparent and grandchild. This relationship may be weakened or enhanced as a result of the divorce.

In 90 percent of divorce cases, the mother is granted physical custody of the children. Divorce may actually serve to strengthen the relationship between the grandchild and the maternal grandparents, as the grandparents step in to offer social and financial support. However, many times divorce acts to weaken the bond between child and father; therefore, the relationship between the grandchild and the paternal grandparents is also weakened. This can be devastating to grandparents if they have been very involved with their grandchild. The custodial parent, usually the mother, can prevent the paternal grandparents from visiting. A good relationship with one's former daughter-in-law may be the key for continuing a relationship with grandchildren. If conflict between the mother and father is involved, children may feel the need to take sides and generalize the feelings for the parent to the grandparent.

All fifty states have enacted grandparent rights legislation that gives grandparents the right to go to court for visitation rights. If provisions for visiting grandparents were made prior to divorce, visitation is generally permitted after divorce. However, grandparent visitation rights are not guaranteed. Judges may rule in what they perceive to be in the best interest of the child.

Parental remarriage may result in "step" relationships, including the relationship between stepgrandparents and stepgrandchildren. The role of stepgrandparent is even more ambiguous than the role of grandparent. Research in this area is lacking. Several possibilities may occur. First, and most optimistic, is that the new complex family arrangement will provide an untapped resource for stepgrandparents, especially if stepgrandchildren are young at the beginning of the step relationship and live nearby. The intergenerational bond that develops may be just as strong as any intergenerational biological bond. A second possibility is that stepgrandparents will value the role of biological grandparent higher and display a remote or advisory style toward stepgrandchildren. Last, stepgrandparents may not be considered to be as important as the "real" grandparents and may not be given the opportunity to bond with stepgrandchildren.

Grandparenthood carries important meaning for some grandparents, but not for others. The grandchild can be seen in a variety of ways, from a biological tie to the future to a young companion that brings out the playful side of the grandparent. Degree and type of involvement also vary with age, health, gender, race, personality, and geographic distance between the grandparent and grandchild. Evidence suggests that in the United States, grandparenthood is an enjoyable role for most grandparents but not necessarily a primary role. For many middle-aged and older grandparents, work and marriage roles are more central to their identity.

—*Naomi J. Larsen*

See also Adopted grandparents; African Americans; Asian Americans; Caregiving; Divorce; Family relationships; Great-grandparenthood; Latinos; Leisure activities; Multigenerational households; Neugarten, Bernice; Parenthood; Remarriage; Skipped-generation parenting; Stepfamilies; Wisdom.

FOR FURTHER INFORMATION:

Binstock, R. H., and L. K. George, eds. *Handbook of Aging and the Social Sciences.* 4th ed. San Diego:

Academic Press, 1996. A comprehensive reference source examining issues pertinent to social aspects of aging.

Cherlin, Andrew J., and Frank F. Furstenberg. *The New American Grandparent: A Place in the Family, a Life Apart.* Cambridge, Mass.: Harvard University Press, 1992. The authors examine grandparent-grandchild relationships.

Fingerman, Karen. "The Good, the Bad, and the Worrisome: Emotional Complexities in Grandparents' Experiences with Individual Grandchildren." *Family Relations* 47, no. 4 (October, 1998). Fingerman provides the results of research on the impact of grandchild characteristics on the grandparent-grandchild relationship.

Neugarten, Bernice, and K. Weinstein. "The Changing American Grandparent." *Journal of Marriage and the Family* 26 (1964). The authors describe grandparenting styles and provide examples.

Rossi, Alice, and Peter Rossi. *Of Human Bonding: Parent-Child Relations Across the Life Course.* New York: Aldine de Gruyter, 1990. This life-course analysis of family development focuses on the social dynamics among family members.

Szinovácz, Maximiliane E. *Handbook on Grandparenthood.* Westport, Conn.: Greenwood Press, 1998. This comprehensive sourcebook on grandparenthood focuses on variations in grandparenthood experience, intergenerational dynamics, and interventions in grandparenting.

Thompson, Edward H. *Older Men's Lives.* Thousand Oaks, Calif.: Sage Publications, 1994. Part of a series on research on men and masculinities. The emphasis is on social and psychological aspects of aged men in the United States.

GRANDPARENTS RAISING GRANDCHILDREN. *See* SKIPPED-GENERATION PARENTING.

GRAY HAIR

RELEVANT ISSUES: Biology, health and medicine

SIGNIFICANCE: Gray hair is a natural by-product of aging; for some, gray hair symbolizes maturity, while for others, it only signifies the aging process

Hair color is produced by tiny pigment cells in hair follicles called melanocytes. Each melanocyte has long, armlike extensions that carry the pigment granules known as melanin to the hair cells. In the course of a lifetime, the production of pigment-forming enzymes drops, and the activity of the melanocytes in each follicle begins to wane, resulting in gray hair. Each individual's melanocyte clock is different, but in Caucasians the reduction of melanocyte activity usually occurs earlier than in other ethnic groups. On the average, graying starts at age thirty-four in Caucasians, in the late thirties in Asians, and at age forty-four in African Americans.

Pigment loss starts at the root, with some strands of hair gradually fading in color, while others may grow in gray or white. Initial graying can be accelerated by hyperthyroidism, anemia, autoimmune disease, severe stress, or vitamin B_{12} deficiency. Disorders of skin pigmentation, such as vitiligo, can also result in the loss of hair pigmentation.

Once gray hair begins to appear, the rate at which it progresses over the rest of the head depends entirely upon each individual. It does not appear to be a function of the original hair color or texture, ethnic background, or the condition of the scalp. By age fifty, 50 percent of Caucasians are significantly gray. As hair loses its pigment, it often gets drier, resulting in coarser, wirier hair.

For some individuals, gray hair is a symbol of maturity, while for others it is an embarrassing sign associated with the aging process. In most cases, graying can be readily masked if so desired. Effective chemical and vegetable rinses and dyes are available.   —*Alvin K. Benson*

See also Aging: Biological, psychological, and sociocultural perspectives; Aging process; Hair loss and baldness; Skin changes and disorders.

GRAY PANTHERS

DATE: Founded in 1970

RELEVANT ISSUES: Economics, health and medicine, law, work

SIGNIFICANCE: Members of the Gray Panthers protest age discrimination, strive to alter cultural perception of age in the United States, and defend the rights of the elderly through legislative lobbying

Founded in 1970, the Gray Panthers is an intergenerational organization that counters ageism and seeks social reform. Maggie Kuhn, a charismatic, outspoken humanitarian, was perhaps the best-known Gray Panther. She and several friends organized the group in Philadelphia when they were forced to retire at age sixty-five. While protesting the Vietnam War with college students, they decided to unite activists of all ages. Kuhn emphasized that the Gray Panthers was not a gray lobby but a coalition of generations interested in improving and protecting the quality of life.

Kuhn disliked how society segregated age groups. "Life is a continuum: only we—in our stupidity and blindness—have chopped it up into little pieces that we keep separate," Kuhn complained. She recommended intergenerational housing, and the Gray Panthers sponsors National Housing Resource Centers to match roommates. The organization also targets social injustices such as mandatory retirement. Lobbying efforts have influenced such legislation as the 1978 amendment to the Age Discrimination in Employment Act of 1967, which increased age limits for retirement. The Gray Panthers was the first group to secure national reform of nursing homes, exposing substandard conditions, negligence, and profiteering in "Nursing Homes: A Citizen's Action Guide" (1977). As a result, the U.S. Senate established regulations to improve inspections.

Health care is a major concern of the Gray Panthers. Stressing that many physicians misunderstand and disregard their elderly patients, the Gray Panthers compiles directories of doctors who accept Medicare assignments. The Gray Panthers' Healthy Block program encourages residents of the same neighborhoods to study disease prevention together. Nutrition and the cost of eating for the elderly are also of concern to the Gray Panthers. In 1982, the Gray Panthers convinced the U.S. Food and Drug Administration (FDA) to regulate the hearing aid industry. Other Gray Panther issues include the effect of the economy on the elderly, pension reform, and problems the elderly encounter in financing energy to heat and cool their homes.

The Gray Panthers strives to eliminate stereotypical thinking about both young and old people. Group members work to counter the myth that the elderly are helpless and dependent. The Gray Panthers' National Media Watch Project seeks more accurate portrayals of the elderly in advertising and entertainment. In September, 1985, the Gray Panthers opened an office in Washington, D.C., so members could lobby to save programs that are at risk, including Social Security. *The Gray Panther Manual* outlines ways that members can achieve legislative goals. The Gray Panthers also supports several other causes, such as nuclear disarmament and civil rights.

Membership in the Gray Panthers peaked at 80,000 in the 1980's. Approximately 40 percent of members are under fifty, with one-third less than thirty-five years old. Members of the Gray Panthers belong to local networks, state groups, and the national chapter. Before she died in 1995, Kuhn contributed an article to the Gray Panther newsletter *The Network* urging increased commitment. The essay concluded with the group's motto, We Are Age and Youth in Action.   —*Elizabeth D. Schafer*

See also Advertising; Advocacy; Age discrimination; Forced retirement; Health care; Hearing aids; Housing; Kuhn, Maggie; Medicare; *No Stone Unturned: The Life and Times of Maggie Kuhn*; Nursing and convalescent homes; Nutrition; Politics.

GRAYING OF AMERICA

RELEVANT ISSUES: Demographics, economics, sociology

SIGNIFICANCE: This phrase refers specifically to the aging of the U.S. population

The proportion of older people in the United States will increase from 2 percent in 1790 to a projected 22 percent in 2030. This "graying of America" is not about individual aging, although individuals clearly do age. Rather, it is about societal aging, or the broad changes that occur in a society that is undergoing this shift.

Population aging is the result of the three basic demographic processes: fertility, mortality, and migration. Migration plays a minor role in comparison to the other two processes and can essentially be ignored as a factor in the United States. Mortality is thought by most people to be the most important component, and it does play a role, but in fact fertility is primarily responsible for the increase in the older population.

High fertility in a country is associated with a "young" population. Fertility, however, declined in the United States until 1945, when the "baby boom" occurred. This decline was associated with an increase in the median age of the population, from sixteen years in 1800 to twenty-nine years in 1940. The baby boom added a large number of young people, and these people will increase the older population. Then fertility went back down, and so the median age started to increase again; it was thirty-three in 1990.

Mortality also declined during this period (from 1800 to 1945), but the major declines in mortality were among the young. This had the effect of increasing the young population, which would later become old. After 1945, improvements in mortality were increasingly concentrated in the older age groups. More people were living to the older years and living longer once they were there.

Therefore, the major increase in the over sixty-five age group, the so-called graying of America, is mainly the result of changes in fertility.

—*David Redburn*

See also Aging: Historical perspective; Baby boomers; Childlessness; Demographics; Life expectancy; Longevity research.

GREAT-GRANDPARENTHOOD

RELEVANT ISSUES: Family, marriage and dating, values

SIGNIFICANCE: As people live longer, families are now extending to four or more generations, making great-grandparenthood a reality for many parents in this generation

With advances in health care in the twentieth century, people are living longer and are in better health than ever before. Infant deaths have decreased, and children are surviving infancy and childhood, as children's diseases have almost been eradicated. Emphasis on nutrition and preventive health care has resulted in longer, healthier life spans. The baby boomers, a large cohort of people born in the 1940's and 1950's, married at an early age and became grandparents in their forties or fifties. This placed their parents in a great-grandparent role at the age of sixty or seventy.

At the end of the twentieth century, it was estimated that over 16 percent of families had four or more living generations. In general, the trend toward larger families has declined with the advent of better birth control measures and changing lifestyles. By the late twentieth century, many women chose to have their families later in life or to re-main child-free. This shift may again make great-grandparenthood a rarity.

ROLES

The role of the great-grandparent is not easily defined, as a healthy great-grandparent was a new phenomenon of the late twentieth century. In the past, great-grandparents were very old and frail, leaving few sturdy role models for future generations. Today, they are people in their sixties, seventies, or eighties who are healthy and busy with their own lives. On the brink of retirement or retired for many years, they have established a lifestyle that may be active or quiet, as suits their needs and personalities.

For some people, becoming a great-grandparent is a reward for living so long. They appreciate the continuation of the family, see family traits in the children, and take delight in watching them grow.

One research report stated that great-grandparents had an influence on older grandchildren's religious, educational, and family values. This was especially true if they lived in geographic proximity to the family. Geographic proximity, however, is not a criterion for a relationship among family members. With the advent of better mass communication, families can stay connected if they choose. The great-grandparent role may be determined by the relationship between generations in the family. If there is conflict between generations, family loyalty may dictate that the conflict be carried over from generation to generation and therefore may exclude great-grandparents from family functions. In families that have been closely connected throughout the elder's life span, there may be a close relationship between child and great-grandparent. If there have been divorces in or disruption between the generations, the great-grandparent may be able to assume the role of family peacemaker or may be alienated from the family.

Affiliation is often affected by the ethnicity of the family. Some examples of this are the respect for the elderly implicit in the family values of Asian American and American Indian families. African American families value extended kinship ties and have a strong sense of family obligation. Latino families have a strong commitment to all generations. Differences in ethnic perspectives among

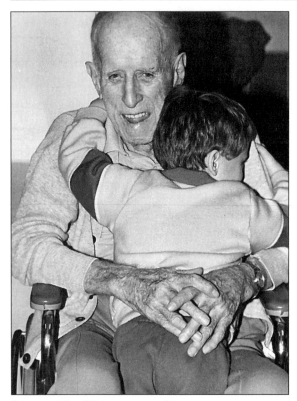

Increases in life expectancy have meant more great-grandparents, although decreases in the number of children have resulted in fewer great-grandchildren. (James L. Shaffer)

generations can lead to conflict as younger members become acculturated into the American way of life. Elders can be a source of ethnic information and role modeling regarding family values and religious traditions or be saddened by the loss of ethnic identity in the younger generation.

The socioeconomic status of family members affects intergenerational relationships in several ways. If the grandparent generation is still working, the great-grandparent may become the caregiver to the great-grandchild generation. If the great-grandparent is not financially solvent, this caregiving may present an opportunity to assist with income or may become a burden if no financial support is available.

CAREGIVING

Great-grandparents may become caregivers to their great-grandchildren when, through unplanned pregnancy, divorce, death, illness, or neglect, the parents are not able to care for their own children and the grandparents are still in the workforce. This may be a day-to-day task or a full-time commitment. For some great-grandparents, the role of caregiver may be a way to stay involved in the family and may be a welcome change from a quiet daily existence. For the very frail elder, children in small doses may be appreciated.

There are many changes in child-rearing practices that need to be negotiated between active parents and a great-grandparent. Although infants still need to be fed and diapers changed, there is a difference between what is acceptable today and what the great-grandparent did forty or fifty years ago with his or her own child. Changes in the areas of feeding and toilet training may cause criticism and conflict. If parents are still the primary caregivers, rules and boundaries set by parents need to be respected and cooperation between the generations is needed if the child is to grow and prosper. If parenting styles are not reasonably consistent, the child will sense this at an early age and promote chaos in all households.

As great-grandchildren get older, elders may be astonished at the different clothing styles, language, and lifestyles they observe. This may become a source of intense family conflict if criticism becomes a way of communicating. Open communication and the ability to negotiate differences are the keys to coparenting and caregiving.

Although most caregivers are women, men too may be involved, as men are living longer and marriages or remarriages may still be intact. Great-grandfathers may be happily involved in the children's lives and may enjoy the children most of the time. They too, however, may resent the intrusion of a small child's needs after a recently child-free lifestyle and find the lack of time to follow their own schedule disruptive.

For elders, setting boundaries on what they can and cannot do may be hard to accomplish. Saying no to a grandchild in need of assistance with his or her own child may be difficult for the elder. The communication between the generations may start out as open and loving and become polite, restrained, or angry as caregiving needs increase or energy decreases.

It takes a lot of energy to raise a young child, and if the caregiving is full time, it may become physically burdensome for the great-grandparent.

Although good health in the elder generation is more common today, some of this is due to better medical intervention and maintenance medication. The presence of medication taken by great-grandparents, if inadvertently taken by the child, may prove fatal. As the great-grandparent has had a child-free environment for many years, safety hazards for infants and toddlers may be rampant in the elder's home.

Rearranging a household, putting away precious items, and becoming mindful of safety hazards are all issues to be taken into account if young children are to join a great-grandparent's household, even on a part-time basis.

CONCLUSIONS

Great-grandparenthood has been an increased phenomenon of the late twentieth century due to the advent of better health care and increased longevity. The role of the great-grandparent varies from being a remote figurehead, to being a family sage and historian, to being an active caregiver. Although there have been few role models for great-grandparenthood, each family defines the role from its family model—which may be close or distant, intact or separated, geographically near or far—and from the needs of the extended family as life continues. The role is further defined by the family's ethnic, cultural, and generational differences.   —*Carolyn L. Scholz*

See also African Americans; American Indians; Asian Americans; Baby boomers; Cultural views of aging; Demographics; Family relationships; Grandparenthood; Latinos; Multigenerational households; Parenthood; Skipped-generation parenting.

FOR FURTHER INFORMATION:

Barrow, Georgia M., and Susan Hillier. *Aging, the Individual, and Society.* 7th ed. Belmont, Calif.: Wadsworth, 1999.

Cherlin, Andrew J., and Frank F. Furstenberg, Jr. *The New American Grandparent: A Place in the Family, a Life Apart.* New York: Basic Books, 1986.

Papalia, Diane E., Cameron J. Camp, and Ruth Duskin Feldman. *Adult Development and Aging.* New York: McGraw-Hill, 1996.

Roberto, Karen A., and Renee Robbe Skoglund. "Interactions with Grandparents and Great-Grandparents: A Comparison of Activities, Influences, and Relationships." *International Journal of Aging and Human Development* 43, no. 2 (September, 1996).

Rossi, Alice S., and Peter H. Rossi. *Of Human Bonding: Parent-Child Relations Across the Life Course.* New York: Aldine de Gruyter, 1990.

Shanas, Ethel. "Old Parents and Middle-Aged Children: The Four- and Five-Generation Family." *Journal of Geriatric Psychiatry* 17, no. 1 (1984).

Strong, Bryan, Christine DeVault, and Barbara W. Sayad. *The Marriage and Family Experience.* 7th ed. Belmont, Calif.: Wadsworth, 1998.

Szinovácz, Maximiliane E. "Grandparents Today: A Demographic Profile." *The Gerontologist* 38, no. 1 (February, 1998).

GREETING CARDS

RELEVANT ISSUES: Culture, media
SIGNIFICANCE: Greeting cards are an expression of the sentiment the sender has for the recipient; the portrayal of aging in greeting cards can either reflect or influence attitudes toward growing older

Greeting cards are a culturally sanctioned way of expressing sentiment: feelings of goodness, affection, tenderness, admiration, sympathy, and compassion. It is especially true in American society that sentimentality—the grouping of these sentiments and the context in which they are expressed, appreciated, and understood—while often objectionable in other forms, is communicated in an acceptable manner through greeting cards. Attitudes can, therefore, be shaped by or reflected in greeting cards. Society's attitudes toward aging are especially recognized in birthday cards.

One frequent channel for the expression of sentiment in greeting cards is humor. Emotional issues are more easily dealt with in a humorous context. For example, gerontophobia (the fear of aging) is expressed through humor, such as over-the-hill or rest-in-peace themes. Greeting card text allows the recipient to laugh at a sentiment, such as fear of aging, which may or may not be held by the sender. Moreover, humorous greeting cards may allow both the sender and the recipient to laugh together over a shared experience, such as growing older together.

Birthday cards for the elderly are not restricted to the humorous genre. Other cards marketed for older individuals have a floral motif. Coincidentally, flowers are also the preferred theme for sympathy cards. Thus, many greeting cards make an indirect connection between aging and death. This association both strengthens and reflects a cultural fear of aging.

Greeting cards present other attitudes toward aging, often based on myths of aging. One myth is that there is a generation gap creating a war between the young and the old. Texts from greeting cards often pit one generation against the other— for example, "Don't hate me because I'm beautiful. Hate me because I am younger than you." Greeting cards often focus on the disabilities of aging as though loss were a necessary part of growing older, such as loss of sensation (hearing, vision, touch, smell, or taste) and bladder control. Other issues addressed in greeting cards include irritation at elderly drivers, the inevitability of digestive irregularity, and the stereotype of the grumpy old person.

Society infantilizes a group of people when it treats them like children, placing that group in a subordinate position in relation to other groups. Greeting cards infantilize the elderly by giving them the characteristics of children, such as gumming food or slobbering. Other childlike attributes given to the elderly in greeting cards include references to incontinence or temper tantrums and depictions of older people wearing party hats and holding balloons.

Some companies have recognized the need for more diverse images of aging in greeting cards. One company produces a line of cards and other products celebrating the accomplishments of a long life. —*Elizabeth McGhee Nelson*

See also Advertising; Ageism; Aging: Biological, psychological, and sociocultural perspectives; Consumer issues; Cultural views of aging; Death and dying; Death anxiety; Humor; Over the hill; Stereotypes.

GRIEF

RELEVANT ISSUES: Death, family, health and medicine, psychology, work

SIGNIFICANCE: Loss and bereavement among aging adults are the precipitants for grief reactions, which may result in psychological difficulties or growth in later life

Grief is an emotional reaction that follows the loss of someone or something of great value. In older age, individuals may encounter the death of relatives and friends, declining health, and changes in social roles. All of these have the potential to affect the older adult's psychological stability, self-esteem, and status in his or her family and community.

Grief is more intense than sadness; it involves emotional, psychological, and physiological processes. A spouse who survives a lifelong partner after a long illness often feels a combination of fatigue, relief, and loneliness. Physical symptoms, such as lack of energy and a sensation of hollowness in the chest or stomach, are common. Typical behaviors among grieving older people include sleep and appetite disturbances, social withdrawal, crying, and absent-minded behavior.

Colin Murray Parkes's research during the last quarter of the twentieth century was critical to the understanding of grief. The third edition of his classic book, *Bereavement: Studies of Grief in Adult Life*, was published in 1996 with additional sections on aging. Parkes's four phases of grieving formed the conceptual base upon which subsequent authors relied and elaborated. These phases are numbness, shock, disbelief; yearning and pining; disorganization and despair; and reorganized behavior and reinvestment.

Until the mid-1990's, the prevailing view of grief was that it was a condition from which one could recover by resolving painful feelings. The phrase "stages of grief" was widely interpreted as a linear process through which an individual should proceed with the goal of cure. An alternative view, held by Polly Young-Eisendrath as the thesis of her book *The Resilient Spirit* (1996), emphasizes the growth potential of the grief experience and people's ability to change positively in response to loss. This model is based on the belief that suffering is a part of the human condition out of which emerges new meaning. The ability to thrive, not just survive, after having encountered some significant loss or adversity is called resilience. Older people vary greatly in how they cope with losses in later life. Those who possess resilience are more likely to reengage in new learning and find meaning in spite of losses.

EXPRESSING GRIEF

Expressing grief with support from others is essential for psychological well-being. It is important to grieving persons to have their feelings validated and their pain acknowledged. Families tend to be intolerant of expressed distress in their loved ones; it is natural for children and parents to seek relief for the sufferer, even when the grieving person is best helped by crying or talking about the loss. Comments such as "you are doing fine" or "it could have been worse" are well meaning but not comforting to the older adult who has sustained a major loss.

Family members sometimes urge an elderly relative to get out of the house and socialize prematurely, before the person feels ready to do so. This complicates the assessment of professional counselors who are called upon to determine if the person is experiencing a normal grief reaction or is clinically depressed. In some instances, the family may need support to tolerate the open expression of grief in others.

Normal and Abnormal Grief

Feelings of overwhelming sadness are common in grief reactions; however, older people are particularly vulnerable to depression and other pathological conditions. Studies have shown an increased risk of death and disability for older persons who have recently sustained the loss of a loved one. Many of the classic symptoms of clinical depression (tearfulness, poor concentration, changes in sleep or appetite) may be present in a grieving individual. When symptoms persist for many months with no improvement or when they are accompanied by feelings of hopelessness or thoughts of dying, treatment for depression may be necessary. After performing an evaluation, a qualified mental health professional might recommend a combination of medication and psychotherapy.

Complicated grief, another abnormal reaction, refers to a set of behaviors characterized by unwillingness to accept a death or loss; being in a stunned or disbelieving state; or having constant thoughts about a deceased person. Researchers have found that antidepressant drugs have little effect on complicated grief, which usually lasts longer than depression.

It is not unusual for widows and widowers who are survivors of long marriages to report seeing or hearing their deceased spouse. This phenomenon can be initially soothing but may become disturbing and symptomatic of complicated grief if it pre-vents an individual from moving on in his or her life. A dramatic example of this condition occurs in Hume Cronyn and Susan Cooper's play *Foxfire* (1982), in which the protagonist, Annie Nations, staunchly refuses to move out of her remote farmhouse in the Georgia mountains despite her son's pleading. She converses and argues daily with her husband, Hector, who has been dead for five years and is buried on the property. Her experience of his presence is both a comfort and a burden, as it assuages her loneliness but confines her to the house. She even feels guilty when she leaves for an evening to see her son give a concert in town. When Annie realizes that her son and grandchildren need her more than Hector, she stops hearing his voice, decides to sell the farm, and reinvests in a new life with her family.

Older Women and Grief

After an extensive review of the literature on older women and grief, N. Jane McCandless and Frances P. Connor proposed that pathological grief reactions in older women may be influenced by much earlier losses that are unique to females. Biological events such as miscarriages, health-related trauma (such as a mastectomy), and developmental losses (such as loss of a parenting role) may complicate the grief process in women by intensifying their reactions to recent losses. Thus, a grieving widow who is evidencing symptoms of depression or complicated grief could be mourning earlier, perhaps unacknowledged, losses. McCandless and Connor suggest that a complete biopsychosocial history should be obtained when trying to determine if an older woman's grief is affected by past events.

A large number of women entered or returned to the workforce in response to the feminist movement of the 1960's; health care professionals in the 1990's encountered an increasing number of older women who were grieving the loss of their jobs. Until then, depression related to retirement was almost exclusively a male phenomenon. Older women typically experienced the empty nest syndrome when their last child left home, diminishing their role as mother and homemaker. The latter half of the twentieth century spawned a cohort of aging women who joined their male counterparts in dealing with the loss of financial and social status associated with their careers.

OTHER STRESSORS

Moving, either by choice or necessity, is another source of stress and grief in older age. Retirement, the death of a significant other, or medical problems might require relocating to a more restrictive or less expensive living situation. Even under the best circumstances, such as a voluntary move to a warm climate, older people will grieve the loss of familiar possessions and surroundings. If the change results in less independence, such as a move to an in-law apartment in a child's home or an assisted-living facility, the relocation may compound and prolong grieving.

During periods of grieving, family, religious, and social networks (including peer and self-help groups) can provide solace and support. In addition to emotional support, older people often need help with concrete tasks, such as house maintenance, financial management, and legal issues. The enormity of dealing with these, especially if they have been the responsibility of a deceased spouse or family member, can be just as stressful as the loss itself. When failing health or the death of a loved one results in a significant change in a person's financial or social status, reorganization and reinvestment are more challenging. In later life, grief is intensified by multiple losses associated with changes in lifestyle.
                                        —*Susan L. Sandel*

See also Death and dying; Death of a child; Death of parents; Depression; Empty nest syndrome; Funerals; Psychiatry, geriatric; Relocation; Remarriage; Retirement; Widows and widowers; Women and aging.

FOR FURTHER INFORMATION:

Felber, Marta. *Grief Expressed When a Mate Dies*. West Fork, Ark.: Lifewords, 1997.

James, John W., and Frank Cherry. *The Grief Recovery Handbook*. New York: Harper & Row, 1988.

McCandless, N. Jane, and Frances P. Connor. "Older Women and Grief: A New Direction for Research." *Journal of Women and Aging* 9, no. 3 (1997).

Parkes, Colin Murray. *Bereavement: Studies of Grief in Adult Life*. 3d ed. London: Routledge, 1996.

Prigerson, H. G., et al. "Complicated Grief and Bereavement-Related Depression as Distinct Disorders: Preliminary Validation in Elderly Bereaved Spouses." *American Journal of Psychiatry* 152, no. 1 (January, 1995).

Worden, J. William. *Grief Counseling and Grief Therapy: A Handbook for the Mental Health Practitioner*. New York: Springer, 1972.

Young-Eisendrath, Polly. *The Resilient Spirit*. Reading, Mass.: Addison-Wesley, 1996.

GROWING OLD IN AMERICA

AUTHOR: David Hackett Fischer
DATE: Published in 1977
RELEVANT ISSUES: Culture, family, values
SIGNIFICANCE: Fischer produced the first scholarly history examining how American attitudes toward old age changed from the colonial period to the 1970's

In *Growing Old in America* (1977), David Hackett Fischer extensively documented his thesis concerning the way attitudes toward the aged shifted drastically over time. Fischer asserted that in the seventeenth and early eighteenth centuries, age conferred authority and that most old people, other than paupers and slaves, were treated with deference and respect. From 1770 to 1820, changing cultural values, inspired by the social revolutions in America and France, emphasized progress and youthfulness. The result was a reversal in attitudes toward the aged; the authority of the elderly weakened, and Americans began to celebrate youth and to fear growing old. A second transition occurred in the twentieth century as reformers viewed old age as a social problem requiring government action, which eventually led to the enactment of Social Security and Medicare.

Fischer cited specific evidence to support his thesis. In early American churches, people were seated by age, with the seats of highest honor being assigned to the oldest, not the richest, inhabitants. The practice ended in various churches between 1775 and 1836, often being replaced by an auction method of selling seats that favored wealth. In early American families, it was common for one child to receive the same first name as a grandparent, but this practice declined after 1800. Eighteenth century American censuses showed that people identified themselves as older than they actually were; a disproportionate number of people said they were thirty or forty rather than twenty-nine or thirty-nine. However, U.S. censuses from 1850 to the 1970's showed an opposite tendency: Those claiming to be twenty-nine or thirty-nine far outnumbered those aged thirty or forty. Descriptions of elderly people in literary works became increasingly negative during the nineteenth century, and the old were frequently described as decrepit and dependent. Mandatory retirement did not exist in America until the 1770's, but in the twentieth century it became a normal way to ensure that the elderly were removed from active participation in life.

Publication of Fischer's book encouraged other historians to engage in research on aging and to challenge various aspects of his interpretation. Historians of the colonial period sketched a far more ambiguous picture than Fischer, arguing that the prestige of the elderly depended on their ability to retain control of property, especially land, rather than upon their length of life. Many who accepted Fischer's thesis that denigration replaced respectful treatment of the elderly during the nineteenth century objected to his dates. Some researchers insisted that positive attitudes toward the old continued through the 1860's. Historians who favored economic interpretations of history rejected Fischer's assertion that cultural beliefs determined the social worth of aged individuals; they considered changing attitudes to be a consequence of the rise of industrial capitalism and dated the shift in views regarding the elderly to the years after the Civil War.   —*Milton Berman*

See also Aging: Historical perspective; Cultural views of aging; Forced retirement.

GRUMPY OLD MEN

DIRECTOR: Donald Petrie
CAST: Jack Lemmon, Walter Matthau, Ann-Margret, Burgess Meredith, Daryl Hannah
DATE: Released in 1993
RELEVANT ISSUES: Culture, media

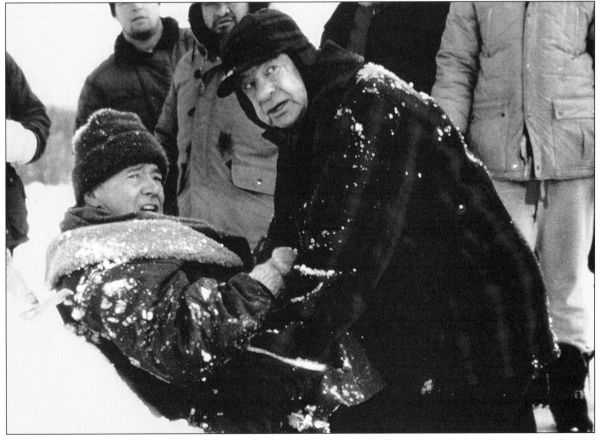

Jack Lemmon (left) and Walter Matthau fight each other in a scene from the film Grumpy Old Men. *(Warner Bros./ Fotos International/Archive Photos)*

Significance: This delightful comedic film featuring two older men examines a lifelong rivalry, intergenerational relationships, and family

John Gustafson (portrayed by Jack Lemmon) and Max Goldman (Walter Matthau), friends since boyhood, continually trade insults and irritate each other with pranks and practical jokes. Both lead solitary lives, playing chess or watching television. Now retired and in their later years, the two men are next-door neighbors. Friends and family are tolerant of and amused by their abrasive relationship.

The story begins during winter, when ice fishing is a popular sport in Wabasha, Minnesota. Both men are trying to catch the big, elusive 40-pound muskie. An attractive widow named Ariel (Ann-Margret) moves into the neighborhood. She brings new zest into the mundane lives of John and Max. She somewhat scandalizes them with her wild snowmobile rides, use of a sauna, and interest in nude art. The men have never seen anything like her. The competition shifts to Ariel, proving that the quest for romance exists at any age. When John and Max were young men, they competed for May, who became John's wife. Now the two widowers are in another race for the same woman. Max was a television repairman before his retirement, while John and Ariel have more in common, as both were educators.

As parents, John and Max give advice to their children, wanting to help ease their path in life. John encourages his daughter Melanie (Daryl Hannah) to leave her husband because he is not providing a stable relationship while trying to "find" himself. John's father (Burgess Meredith) in turn offers him advice on courting Ariel.

John soon faces adversity in the guise of the Internal Revenue Service. He is about to lose his home for nonpayment of income taxes from miscalculation of health benefits. Max joins ranks and covers for him. Rather than lose his friendship with Max, John rejects Ariel. The stress of his daughter's disintegrating marriage, the loss of Ariel, and the impending loss of his home contribute to John's heart attack. During his recovery, however, he and Ariel are reconciled, and they later marry.

Grumpy Old Men is full of sage comments. This film demonstrates that each generation has a part to play in the continuity of family. Long-standing friendship influences behavior, and family and friends support one another in good times as well as bad. It was followed by a sequel, *Grumpier Old Men* (1995).
—*Phyllis J. Reeder*

See also Family relationships; Films; Friendship; Humor; Marriage; Men and aging; Multigenerational households; Sexuality; Stereotypes.

HAIR LOSS AND BALDNESS

RELEVANT ISSUES: Biology, culture, health and medicine

SIGNIFICANCE: For many men, hair loss and eventually some degree of baldness are a natural part of the aging process; various methods have been tried to hide, halt, or even reverse this symbol of increasing age

Since biblical times, and perhaps before, a full head of hair on a man was considered a symbol of strength and masculinity. The story of Samson relates his great physical strength to the length and thickness of his hair. When his hair was cut by his captors, Samson was reduced to a weakling. When his hair grew back, Samson's strength was restored. In modern times, hair loss is still associated with a perceived loss of masculinity and desirability for older men.

In 1999, more than thirty million men in the United States were bald or going bald, mostly from the condition known as androgenetic alopecia, or male pattern baldness. This condition usually starts with a receding hairline at the forehead and temples and often is accompanied by a hairless spot at the crown of the head—the "monk's tonsure." Finally, the hairless areas join over the skull until the individual is left only with a fringe over the ears and collar.

Nearly all male pattern baldness is hereditary and is passed on by both the male as well as the female line. As the name suggests, it affects mostly men, although some older women undergo a general thinning of scalp hair with actual bald spots. Male pattern baldness usually begins at puberty or the early twenties, although it may not make an appearance until the forties. By middle age, the degree of baldness is usually known.

THE NATURE OF HAIR AND TYPES OF HAIR LOSS

Hair is an accessory organ of the skin and consists primarily of two parts: the hair shaft, which protrudes above the skin surface, and the root, which lies below the skin. The hair follicle surrounds the root and it is here, in the follicle, where blood vessels provide nourishment for the growing hair. The hair shaft—which is combed, brushed, pomaded, shampooed, dyed, and "nourished" by a variety of nostrums—is a thread of keratinized cells, dead material similar to fingernails and toenails.

The average number of human scalp hairs is between 100,000 and 150,000. Individual scalp hairs may persist for three to five years and then are shed in a cycle that includes growth, a resting stage, shedding, and another growth period. Balding occurs when the number of hairs shed in the cycle exceeds the number that grow.

Dermatologists, medical specialists in the study and treatment of diseases of the skin, recognize three main forms of alopecia, or baldness. Alopecia areata refers to the loss of hair in patches that vary in size; although it usually affects the scalp, hair loss may involve the beard or other body hair. If the follicles are not compromised, regrowth of the hair usually occurs. Alopecia totalis occurs when all the scalp hair is lost and the scalp remains totally bare, smooth, and shiny. Other body hair such as the eyebrows, pubic hair, and beard usually is not involved. Alopecia universalis is the most extreme form of hair loss. Not only is the scalp hair lost, but the pubic hair, underarm hair, eyebrows, and leg and arm hair is lost as well. The affected individuals undergo both the psychological trauma of the hair loss and the physical trauma of the loss of the protective qualities of the hair. Perspiration that usually is trapped by the eyebrows may now trickle directly into the eyes. Dust, pollen, and other airborne particles freely enter the nasal passages in the absence of nose hair.

GENETICS AND BALDNESS

About 95 percent of male pattern baldness is genetic in nature. It appears to run in families on either the mother's or the father's side. As has long been suspected, the tendency toward this condition is influenced by the male sex hormone, testosterone. Testosterone is produced by the primary male sex glands, the testes. The hormone is responsible for the secondary sexual characteristics in males, including facial hair, a deepened voice, and a more robust body build. Testosterone begins to exert its influence at puberty, the time of sexual maturation. It is not the testosterone itself that is the culprit in androgenetic alopecia; it is its derivative, dihydrotestosterone (DHT). As testosterone circulates through the blood, it is converted by an enzyme to DHT, which attaches to hair follicle cells. If there is a large amount of DHT, the follicles begin sprouting hair that is progressively thinner in diameter. Finally, the follicles no longer pro-

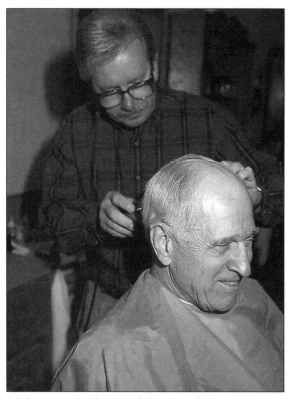

Male pattern baldness and the natural thinning that occurs with age result in significant baldness for many older men. (Ben Klaffke)

duce hair and in turn waste away. It is the production of more or less amounts of the enzyme, and thus DHT, not the production of testosterone, that determines the retention or loss of an individual's head of hair.

Many false ideas have evolved to explain what today is recognized as androgenetic baldness. It is not caused, for example, by poor blood supply to the scalp. Thus, standing on one's head or vigorously massaging the scalp to increase blood flow will not restore a full head of hair, nor will the application of stimulating (or irritating) potions. Except in rare instances, vitamin deficiency is not involved, and megadoses of vitamins and minerals will have little if any effect on restoring the receding hairline. Loss of hair is not related to clogged hair follicles, and neither vigorous brushing nor expensive shampoos will bring it back. Wearing a hat, especially a tight one, will not contribute to baldness. Conversely, wearing a hat to protect the scalp from the sun's rays will not help either. (How-

ever, wearing a hat outdoors in sunlight will protect the scalp from the development of skin cancers and in cold weather will keep the wearer warm by reducing the loss of body heat through the scalp and its profusion of blood vessels.)

BALDNESS COVER-UPS AND SURGICAL RESTORATION

Some steps can be taken by the balding individual. One alternative is to do nothing about the hair loss and to accept the inevitable as a natural part of the aging process. Some men allow one side of the hair that remains in the fringe to grow long and fashion it in a variety of loops and swirls over the balding center of the scalp. A variation of accepting the inevitable is to remove the remaining hair by shaving the entire scalp. Another option is to buy and wear a hairpiece (toupee) or a wig. A good one is expensive, however, and regardless of how much is paid for it, a hairpiece is detectable in bright light or when the wearer is in close proximity to others.

A number of surgical techniques have been developed to put hair on the balding scalp. One technique is hair weaving, in which anchoring stitches are sewn into the bald scalp and new hair is woven and knotted into the anchors. In the hands of a skilled technician, hair weaving can be a satisfactory prosthesis. The wearer can swim, shower, shampoo, blow dry and style, as well as be windblown, almost as though the hair was his own natural growth. Periodic tightening of the knots is required, however, and there is always the danger of irritation or infection from the anchoring stitches.

Hair transplantation has worked well for some men. In this technique, skin plugs containing dense hair from the back or sides of the individual's head are transplanted into prepared holes in the bald areas. The success of the procedure depends greatly on the skill of the physician. A skillful surgeon can achieve a natural-looking hairline and a fair-to-good coverage of hair if the donor sites are good. The procedure may take many weeks to months, depending on the area of scalp to be covered. Not all hair transplants "take," and there is also the danger of infection. Women usually are not good candidates for hair transplantation because their hair loss is diffuse, involving almost the entire scalp. Thus, good donor sites generally are not available.

A more radical approach to covering the balding scalp with the individual's own hair is scalp reduction surgery. This involves removing a large section of the hairless scalp and stitching the edges together. The looseness and stretch of the human scalp makes this technique possible. Another radical surgical procedure is one in which a flap of hair-bearing scalp is moved from the sides or back of the head to replace a section of hairless scalp. Unfortunately, the flap technique involves bleeding, infection, and scarring.

REGROWING HAIR

Over the centuries, the search for a "cure" for baldness has involved the use of a variety of exotic devices and substances. The devices included a metal skullcap that could operate as an air-pressure helmet. Alternate compression and decompression of the air in the cap was supposed to massage the wearer's scalp and thus increase the flow of blood to the hair roots to produce a luxurious growth of hair. A variety of plant compounds and animal body products, when vigorously massaged into the balding scalp, similarly were supposed to restore the lost hair. None of these accomplished anything more than to enrich the maker and seller of the product.

The search for a magic bullet to cure male pattern baldness and restore a healthy head of hair to the afflicted individual seemed to have ended with the development and availability of minoxidil (Rogaine). This prescription drug had been developed and prescribed for high blood pressure (hypertension). Researchers discovered that a lotion form of the drug applied to the scalp grew some hair in some men.

Clinical trials of a 2 percent solution of minoxidil among a group of men nineteen to forty-nine years of age with varying degrees of male pattern baldness produced varying results. Approximately 26 percent of the men reported moderate-to-dense regrowth of hair. This is compared to 11 percent of the men of the control group who applied only the liquid part of the solution minus the active ingredient. About 33 percent of the men achieved what was considered minimal regrowth of hair, while 31 percent of the control group also achieved minimal regrowth of hair. In each group, the experimental and the control, a sizeable portion of men experienced no regrowth of hair, either with the drug or with the placebo.

The lotion is available in a 2 percent solution form without a prescription. It must be applied twice daily for at least four months before any new hair growth can be expected. If no new hair develops after one year, the user is advised to stop applying the product and consult a physician. The product works best on men under fifty years of age with bald spots no larger than 3 to 5 inches in diameter. Once favorable results are obtained, the user must continue to apply the lotion or the new hair will be lost.

Some cautions are associated with the use of minoxidil. It should not be used if there is no family history of hair loss, if the individual is less than eighteen years old, or if scalp irritation is present. Users should consult their physicians if they experience chest pain, rapid heartbeat, dizziness or fainting, or swelling of the feet or hands. Clearly, the magic bullet has not yet been found.

—*Albert C. Jensen*

See also Aging process; Beauty; Men and aging; Middle age; Midlife crisis.

FOR FURTHER INFORMATION:

Hanover, Larry. "Hair Replacement: What Works, What Doesn't." *FDA Consumer* 31 (April, 1997). Discusses the use of minoxidil, surgical techniques such as transplants, and cover-ups, including wigs and toupees.

Mayhew, John. *Hair Techniques and Alternatives to Baldness.* New York: Oweni Trado-Medic Books, 1963. A review of hair dressing, care and hygiene of the hair, and alternatives to baldness, including transplantation.

Sadick, Neil S., and Donald C. Richardson. *Your Hair and Helping to Keep It.* Yonkers, N.Y.: Consumer Reports Books, 1991. An authoritative review of baldness, its causes, and what to do about it. Includes a discussion of human hair growth and hair care.

SerVaas, Cory. "Early Male Pattern Baldness." *Saturday Evening Post* 266 (March/April, 1996). In a question-and-answer format, SerVaas offers four suggestions for coping with this condition, including wait and see, application of minoxidil, surgery (including transplantation), and, if necessary, a hairpiece.

Thompson, Wendy, and Jerry Shapiro. *Alopecia Areata: Understanding and Coping with Hair Loss.* Baltimore: The Johns Hopkins University Press,

1996. Provides a guide to the diagnosis and treatment of hair loss with reliable information from two medical professionals.

HAMMERTOES

RELEVANT ISSUES: Health and medicine

SIGNIFICANCE: Hammertoes are common among the elderly; the condition can lead to pain, infection, and ulceration of the skin on the top of the toe

A hammertoe is one that is bent permanently at the joint nearest to the foot. The closely related term "clawtoe" denotes a toe that is bent at both joints. Hammertoes and clawtoes can occur in one or more of the four smaller toes on each foot, with the second toe being the most common site for these deformities. Hammertoes and clawtoes are thought to be caused by muscle imbalance, contraction of the tendons, and enlargement of the toe joints. Although anyone can develop these conditions, they are felt to be caused primarily by wearing high heels or shoes that are too tight. It is common for people to develop painful corns and calluses in association with these conditions, particularly on the top or on the tip of the toe where it is most likely to rub against the shoe. Furthermore, people with hammertoes or clawtoes may experience considerable pain if the toe gets inflamed and may also develop skin ulcers from the rubbing of their shoes against the bent toe. These ulcers can become infected and develop abnormal channels to the skin surface called sinus tracts. These conditions may also cause significant problems with walking for the affected individual.

Treatment of hammertoes or clawtoes depends on the severity of the condition and whether there are secondary complications such as corns or ulcers. The simplest treatment is to change to shoes with broad toes and soft soles that cushion the foot and to avoid wearing high heels and shoes that pinch the toes. Accompanied by excellent foot care such as callus and corn removal, this may be all that is required to prevent pain and irritation of the toes. In cases that are more advanced, various inserts can be added to the shoes. These include metatarsal bars, orthotics, and other devices. A metatarsal bar supports the ball of the foot, spreading the pressure normally put on this area over a greater part of the foot. Orthotics are spe-

cially molded plastic devices that serve much the same purpose. In some cases, podiatrists (foot doctors) or orthopedists recommend toe caps, padded sleeves that help prevent friction between the toe and the shoe. In a few cases, it may be necessary to cut the tendons in the toe or to perform arthroplasty (repair of the joint itself) to provide relief. —*Rebecca Lovell Scott*

See also Bone changes and disorders; Corns and calluses; Foot disorders; Mobility problems; Skin changes and disorders.

HANDICAPS. *See* DISABILITIES.

HAROLD AND MAUDE

DIRECTOR: Hal Ashby

CAST: Ruth Gordon, Bud Cort

DATE: Released in 1971

RELEVANT ISSUES: Death, values

SIGNIFICANCE: This film examines intergenerational friendships and the rights to choose who and how one loves and one's time and manner of death

Directed by Hal Ashby with music by Cat Stevens, this classic dark comedy celebrates the relationship that a seventy-nine-year-old woman initiates with an eighteen-year-old young man who takes pleasure in staging fake suicides and attending funerals. Observing Harold (Bud Cort) at many of the same funerals that she attends, Maude (Ruth Gordon) takes him on as a special project, as the recipient of her last gift—the gift of listening to the rhythms of life.

This is, in large part, a film about listening. Harold is not listened to by his mother, and Harold does not listen closely to Maude when they first meet. He misses what she tells him about her own plans for death and dying, but he takes an interest in her wild, bright energy. Within the space of a week, he becomes an accomplice to Maude's cosmic dance of connection. Harold breathes, eats, and sleeps differently as he comes to hear the voices of the world around him. Maude directs his gaze to the beauty of living, opening him to risk and adventure, cultivating his stunted sense of play.

Seeing Harold evolve and change is one of Maude's final joys, because her choice is to die at age eighty. What begins as Maude's eightieth birthday celebration, with Harold's intention to pro-

Bud Cort and Ruth Gordon in a scene from the film Harold and Maude. *(Archive Photos)*

pose marriage, changes into his tragic loss of what he most loves, despite his efforts to intervene. Maude's death forces Harold to choose—"to go and love some more"—and to surrender his love of the idea of death to the joys of life.

—*C. Turner Steckline*

See also Death and dying; Death anxiety; Films; Friendship; Humor; Sexuality; Suicide; Wisdom.

HARRY AND TONTO

DIRECTOR: Paul Mazursky

CAST: Art Carney, Ellen Burstyn, Larry Hagman, Geraldine Fitzgerald

DATE: Released in 1974

RELEVANT ISSUES: Culture, family, values

SIGNIFICANCE: In this film, a free-spirited senior citizen who has few attachments, a sense of adventure, and broad tolerance for the variety of human lifestyles embarks on a cross-country journey to find new experiences

Harry (Art Carney) is an elderly widower who is supposed to vacate his New York apartment because the building is being razed to make way for a new development. He is an obstinate tenant who has to be forcibly evicted by the police. Accompanied by his most cherished possession, a cat named Tonto, he moves in with his son and family. This arrangement does not last long, however, because tensions develop with his daughter-in-law and two grown grandsons who are trying to "find" themselves while still living at home. Harry decides to visit his daughter in Chicago and then his son in Los Angeles, traveling by bus and car and hitchhiking.

The appeal of the film is in the variety of unique characters he meets along the way, such as an Indian medicine man who relieves his arthritis, a runaway teenage girl headed to a commune, a hooker going to Las Vegas, a health foods salesman, and a woman who feeds neighborhood cats. One poignant scene is his visit to a nursing home to look up a girlfriend from fifty years ago; her memory is failing, but she remembers how to dance with him. Another emotional moment comes when he goes to a morgue to identify the body of an elderly friend. Harry finds meaning for his life not from his past accomplishments or his family but from the encounters with interesting characters along his life journey.

Carney won the 1975 Academy Award for Best Actor for his portrayal of Harry.

—*Hans G. Graetzer*

See also Family relationships; Films; Friendship; Vacations and travel.

HAVING OUR SAY: THE DELANY SISTERS' FIRST ONE HUNDRED YEARS

AUTHORS: Sarah Delany and A. Elizabeth Delany
DATE: Published in 1993
RELEVANT ISSUES: Family, race and ethnicity, work
SIGNIFICANCE: *Having Our Say* is the memoir of two African American sisters who were both more than one century old when it was published

Sarah Louise ("Sadie") and Annie Elizabeth ("Bessie") Delany were born in North Carolina in 1889 and 1891, respectively. Their parents were members of the black elite in the city of Raleigh. Their father was the first black Episcopal bishop in the United States, and their mother was a schoolteacher. Sadie, Bessie, and their eight siblings all earned college degrees. After teaching in North Carolina for a few years, the Delany sisters joined many other southern African Americans during the Great Northern Migration by relocating to the black community of Harlem in New York City during the 1910's.

Sadie earned bachelor's and master's degrees from Columbia University and taught home economics in New York schools until she retired in 1960. Bessie received a dentistry degree from Columbia, becoming the second African American woman licensed to practice that profession in New York State. She retired in 1950.

Neither of the Delany sisters ever married, and they always lived together after migrating to New York. Other family members also moved to Harlem, and the sisters were able to maintain close ties with them. Their mutual support—and that of their relatives—helped them cope with the physical and economic difficulties they faced as they grew older and their income shrank to that available from Social Security, Sadie's pension, and their savings.

In 1991, a reporter for *The New York Times*, Amy Hill Hearth, wrote an article on the Delanys a few days after they turned 102 and 100 years old. Reader response led Hearth to record an oral history that was published in 1993 as *Having Our Say: The Delany Sisters' First One Hundred Years*. While the Delanys recount incidences of prejudice they experienced, famous people they encountered, and generally interesting events that occurred in their lives, much of their autobiography is about growing old and learning to deal with decreased physical and economic resources.

Key to their longevity was maintaining lifestyles that were as active as possible. They exercised on a regular basis, closely monitored their diets, and performed as many household chores as practicable. They abandoned such activities as driving only when necessity required them to do so. They also kept up with current events by listening to news shows on radio and television, reading newspapers, and voting in every election. They visited neighbors, went shopping, attended church, and cultivated a flower and vegetable garden. In short, they refused to allow old age to prevent their participation in normal life activities. Bessie Delany died in 1995, and Sadie Delany died in 1999.

—*Roger D. Hardaway*

See also African Americans; Centenarians; Family relationships; Sibling relationships.

HEALTH CARE

RELEVANT ISSUES: Demographics, economics, health and medicine
SIGNIFICANCE: Health care for the older adult is a major source of concern for the older person, care providers (family and health care professionals), and the government

More people in the United States are living longer. Advances in medicine, technology, and health care now allow healthier young and middle years. Consequently, poor health is now compressed into the later years of life. Older individuals' perception of their health status frequently influences their decision to obtain health care services.

An individual's perception about his or her health is frequently associated with health-related practices. A major stereotype associated with aging is that illness and functional impairment are to be expected and accepted. Older people may feel both healthy and ill. They may have a chronic disease, such as diabetes, but have it under control with treatment and be coping and functioning very well. Perception of one's health is evaluated in comparison with one's peers. An individual may experience some limitation in activities, through aging changes or health problems, but still perceive his or her health as better than that of peers. In a 1995 survey, 28.3 percent of older persons assessed their health as fair or poor.

Some of the diseases and health problems of the elderly are preventable, and many can be postponed with appropriate health care. Nevertheless, as compared to other groups, the elderly have significantly more diseases and disabilities, have more visits to physicians, spend more days in hospitals, take more medications, and spend more on health care. The coordination between acute care and chronic care is poor.

The medical specialty of geriatrics was developed to address elderly health care needs. The majority of the health care expenses are borne by federal or state programs, Medicare or Medicaid, or by personal out-of-pocket payments. Family and friends provide most at-home and long-term care. Due to the high costs incurred, there is a move toward using managed care as a means of controlling health care costs for older people.

The Need for Health Care Services

The American Association of Retired Persons' *A Profile of Older Americans: 1998* (1999) gives basic demographic facts and projections that show that Americans aged sixty-five and older account for 34.1 million people, or almost 13 percent of the population. The baby boomers, those Americans born between 1946 and 1964, begin turning sixty-five in 2011. By the middle of the twenty-first century, one in five Americans will be sixty-five. By 2030, the sixty-five and older population is projected to be 20 percent.

The older population is frequently divided into three segments: the young-old (those sixty-five to seventy-four), the middle-old (those seventy-five to eighty-four), and the old-old (those eighty-five and older). Persons aged eighty-five and over are considered the fastest growing segment of the aging population. In 1990, the old-old were only 10.3 percent of the older population but were projected to be over 13 percent by the year 2000.

The elderly frequently have the occurrence of two or more diseases at the same time, with multiple symptoms affecting several body systems. The most commonly occurring problems in those over age sixty-five focus on eight conditions: arthritis, hypertension, heart disease, hearing impairments, cataracts, orthopedic impairments, sinusitis, and diabetes. Impairments in vision and hearing are more common in each consecutively older age group. Injury rates are higher after age eighty-five, and disability rises markedly in the presence of multiple diseases and increases gradually with age.

In 1995, over one-third (37.2 percent) of older persons reported they were functionally limited in their activities by chronic conditions, and more than half (52.5 percent) reported having at least one disability. As suggested by these comparisons and studies, the age-specific prevalence of many acute and long-term chronic diseases and other disabling conditions rises proportionately among populations in their late seventies and in their eighties.

Types and Use of Health Care Services

Compared with other age groups, older adults are the heaviest users of health services. The rates of care utilization increase substantially at older ages within the elderly population. The use of health care services is greatly influenced by access to services and reimbursement. Once a person turns sixty-five and is eligible for Medicare, an increase in physician contacts and increased utilization of hospitals is seen. Correspondingly, as dental care is poorly covered under Medicare, there is a decrease seen in dental care obtained.

The use of physician services by persons sixty-five and over shows an increase with age. In aggregate, persons of all ages averaged 5.2 visits to a physician a year in the late 1990's, while older persons averaged 11.1 visits.

Hospitals provide acute and intensive care for individuals. The care may be needed for a new disease, increase in severity of a chronic condition, accident, or serious injury. Persons aged sixty-five and over account for 49 percent of the days of care provided in acute care hospitals. Their average length of stay is nearly two days longer than that of the population in general, 7.1 days for older people compared to only 5.4 days for people under sixty-five. Those aged eighty-five and older use hospitals at a rate that is 12 percent higher than those aged sixty-five to seventy-four.

A nursing home is an extended care facility for persons who need medical attention of the type and complexity not requiring hospitalization. Nursing homes provide twenty-four-hour nursing supervision, rehabilitation, activity, and social services. Some nursing homes offer specialized units for patients with dementia, chronic ventilator support, or head injuries. Some facilities provide subacute units for patients who are not as medically stable as patients in the typical nursing home setting or who are finishing rehabilitation prior to returning home. It is estimated that 43 percent of persons reaching the age of sixty-five can expect to spend time, short-stay or long-term, in a nursing home before they die. The rate of nursing home use increases with older age within the elderly population. In 1999, about 1 percent of those aged sixty-five to seventy-four were in nursing homes, in comparison with 15 percent of persons aged eighty-five and older. It was estimated that about 4 percent of all persons sixty-five years and older were in nursing homes at any given moment.

A similar pattern of increasing need for health care assistance holds true among older persons living in the community. Community-based care encompasses a wide range of medical, home care, homemaking, and social services. These agencies work with older people and their families, if available, to allow individuals to remain in their own homes. Home health care services are provided by a certified agency using an interdisciplinary team to meet the needs of the patient. Services are provided in out-of-hospital settings such as private homes, boarding homes, hospice centers, shelters, and so on. Caregivers include professional and practical nurses, nursing assistants, physical, occupational and speech therapists, social services, and other professionals as needed. Home care has been considered more desirable than institutional care, but reimbursement for home health care services is limited.

Studies have found that friends and relatives provide about 80 percent of home care. The majority (65 percent) of older persons live in a family

Beginning or maintaining trusting relationships with physicians or other health care professionals is vital to obtaining quality medical treatment in the later years. (James L. Shaffer)

setting, and about 31 percent live alone. These family- and friend-provided services and support allow the majority of older individuals to live in the community.

The proportion of individuals who, because of functional limitations, need home health services from paid professionals or from their families or friends rises from 7.7 percent in the sixty-five- to seventy-four-year-old category to 26.6 percent in the group aged eighty-five and over.

In general, older persons tend to use the wide range of available health care goods and services at higher rates than younger population groupings. Persons sixty-five years and older use medical equipment and supplies at twice the rate of younger persons; they also use prescription drugs and vision and hearing aids at slightly higher rates.

Health for older adults is a complex interaction of physical, functional, and psychosocial factors. Medical management cannot be compartmentalized when there is the coexistence of several problems. Health problems can be magnified by difficulties in other areas such as psychological distress or economic hardship. Medical care and hospital stays alone cannot solve all the health care needs of the older population—health care encompasses more. It includes working closely with social services, patients, and family to make sure the person is in a suitable residential setting, has adequate resources to meet his or her needs, and is receiving appropriate support and community services. With multiple health care settings, services, and organizations providing care, it is very easy for duplication of services or loss of coordination and fragmentation to occur.

Preventive care for the elderly has not been as prominent in health care services as it could be. In 1999, the only direct preventive services paid for under Medicare were influenza immunizations and limited payments for mammograms. The direction of preventive attention to older persons has been shown to produce positive health effects. Actions toward getting older people to stop smoking or to exercise more and early detection of problems such as depression or correctable causes of disability can do much to improve the quality of life for older people. Comprehensive geriatric assessments and interventions have been shown to reduce mortality and improve functioning, and there is evidence to suggest that the incidence of

and complications from falls can be reduced by appropriate exercise and training programs.

COST, FINANCING, AND REIMBURSEMENT

Much of the public discussion about health care is linked to concerns about rising health care costs. In the mid-1980's, persons sixty-five years of age and older accounted for about a third of all the health care expenditures in the United States; this amounted to about $120 billion. In addition, relatives and friends provided a substantial amount of health care services and support that cannot be easily quantified as expenditures.

The creation of Medicare and Medicaid in 1965 increased the access to health care for Americans aged sixty-five and over. Medicare coverage is divided into two parts. Part A, or Hospital Insurance, is available without a premium and covers the costs of hospital care, brief stays in nursing homes, and some home health care. Part B, or Supplemental Medical Insurance, covers the costs of physician services and related costs such as laboratory tests, specialized services, and some durable medical equipment. Part B is an option for the older person and is obtained by monthly premium payments. Medicare does not cover some items that are important to adequate health care, such as medications outside of a hospital stay, eyeglasses, or hearing aides.

In the 1990's, over 33.1 million persons, or four out of every five Americans aged sixty-five and over, were enrolled in Medicare. The average payment in 1995 for health and medical services, per episode, was $15,074. This makes Medicare the biggest single source of payment for health care in the United States.

Medicaid is a federal-state welfare program designed to cover the health costs of those who cannot otherwise afford it. Not originally intended to meet the health needs of older persons, it does, however, contain a provision that extends coverage to those of frail health who are in poverty or at near-poverty level. Medicaid pays for most services not covered under Medicare, and thus nursing home care and medications become major Medicaid items. Over eleven million older people received services under the Medicaid program in 1995.

Medicare pays 40 percent of older persons' health care costs; other government programs, in-

Some seniors have taken to the streets to press for better health care for older Americans. This group advocates a universal single-payer plan in a 1999 protest. (AP Photo/Kuni)

cluding Medicaid, pay for another 18 percent. Older persons themselves pay 42 percent of their aggregate care by direct out-of-pocket expenditures, Medicare premiums, and private insurance premiums.

Originally, the emphasis of the Medicare program was universal health care for all Americans over age sixty-five. As access improved, however, the costs expanded far beyond anticipated projections. In the 1980's, the federal government limited Medicare reimbursements to hospitals by implementing a prospective payment system (PPS). Diagnosis-related groups (DRGs) that paid a fixed rate were developed and implemented. The rate was set on the basis of the patient's primary diagnosis and other modifying factors instead of the length of the hospital stay and the services received by the patient. This had a large impact on hospital finances and subsequent lengths of stay. An outgrowth of this was an increase in after-hospital or community-based care. There was also an increase in the use of nursing homes and home health, and expanded interest in developing outpatient, ambulatory, and subacute care alternatives.

The apparent success of PPS in controlling Medicare hospital costs led to interest in expanding this idea to other aspects of care under Medicare reimbursement. The late 1990's saw PPS measures put into place in the nursing home and home health industries as a way to contain those rising costs.

Medicare is exploring managed care as a way to reduce health care costs. Several Medicare managed care model programs are being piloted. These programs provide the equivalent of Medicare services without premiums, deductibles, or copayments, and they cover a broad range of services including both acute and chronic care at a capitated, or negotiated, cost-efficient fee to Medicare.

HEALTH CARE ISSUES

The need for health care of the elderly in the twenty-first century will be determined by their numbers and health. Demographic projections indicate that the number and proportion of elderly will continue to grow. Health services will be particularly important for elderly women and minorities, many of whom will be among those least able to pay for it. In the late 1990's, by age eighty-five and older, there were 248 women for every 100 men. Minority populations are projected to increase to 25 percent of the elderly population in 2030, up from 15 percent in 1997. There will be a need for culturally relevant low-cost coordinated health care. Chronic illness patterns with chance of disability will also increase.

Geriatrics is the medical specialty of care to frail older persons. It has been a branch of medicine for over seventy years but has only begun to make an impression and receive recognition in the last two decades. Geriatricians are the physicians trained to meet these needs. Although no one can project how many geriatricians will be needed in the future, the number entering the specialty yearly is small. To assist primary care physicians in meeting the needs of their aging patients, increasing geriatric content appears to be the way to update their educational preparation. An alternative would be to utilize geriatric nurse practitioners as primary care providers in managing the care of frail older persons in various settings.

Innovations in health care technology will continue to increase and improve, permitting more care of the elderly outside of the hospital. These advances have allowed care to be moved into the physician's office, the nursing home, and the patient's home. There has been a rapid increase in the number of outpatient services and day treatment centers available in the last few years. High-tech equipment, such as ventilators, monitors, dialysis, and infusers, has become almost commonplace in the nursing home and home setting. Personal computers in the home with modems connected to telephone lines will permit practice-linked clinical support and education of the family to upgrade the quality of home care. The access to portable computer-based patient records should improve the continuity of care given to patients as they move through different sites to obtain care.

A proactive stance of preventing disease and disability and teaching people how to adopt healthier lifestyles could be successful for the older population. A report from the Institute of Medicine, *Healthy People 2000: Citizens Chart the Course*, advocates expanding preventive services through health promotion, screening, and prevention. New programs could lead to healthier lifestyles, and early recognition and control of diseases would delay or prevent illnesses and disabilities. These services would promote more independent living for older people and increase their quality of life.

Health care services for older persons are undergoing continuous transitions. Several issues require active attention as the system evolves. The cost of Medicare has received repeated focus. This spending has grown more rapidly than any other component of health care and is the most sensitive to changing demographic patterns. With the aging of the baby boomers and increasing old-old within the older population, Medicare's solvency has been questioned. New policies and methods will need to be examined and implemented if the United States is to continue to provide health care to those aged sixty-five and over.

Vastly expanded and integrated community, home health, and social services are needed. Programs of coordinated long-term care that provides a full array of seamless services for persons in their homes or in community settings need to be put into place. New programs are needed to recognize and acknowledge the services provided by family and friends. Long-term facilities will always be needed for patients who cannot be safely managed at home or who require monitoring and care around the clock. The challenge will be to finance, link, and integrate acute care and community-based long-term care services in a cost-effective manner.

When looking into the future, one can be relatively confident that medical treatment and prevention programs will improve. Change will continue to occur in the organization, financing, and delivery methods of health care in the years ahead. However, comparisons among older age groups suggest that no matter how the health care arena evolves, the changing age structure within the older population itself will have a substantial impact on the needs, the amount of care, and the increased resources necessary. To be successful in meeting the needs of the future, Americans need to consider ways to redesign health and social systems to have the programs to care for much larger groups of elderly in the years ahead. The decisions made for the future will have tremendous implications for the overall well-being of older adults, their families, the health care professionals who serve them, and society as a whole.

—Beverley E. Holland

See also Caregiving; Geriatrics and gerontology; Home services; Hospitalization; Illnesses among the elderly; Immunizations and boosters; Injuries among the elderly; Long-term care for the elderly; Medical insurance; Medicare; Nursing and convalescent homes; Poverty.

FOR FURTHER INFORMATION:
American Association of Retired Persons. *A Profile of Older Americans: 1998.* Washington, D.C.: Author, 1999. Brochure providing current demographics of the older American.

"Health Care: Organization, Use, and Financing." In *The Encyclopedia of Aging,* edited by George Maddox. New York: Springer, 1987. Discusses the current status of elderly health care.

Institute of Medicine. *Healthy People 2000: Citizens Chart the Course.* Washington, D.C.: National Academy Press, 1990. Discussion of programs to help meet the health promotion, protection, and preventive health services goals and objectives for the elderly in the year 2000.

Jahnigen, Dennis, and Robert Binstock. "Economic and Clinical Realities: Health Care for Elderly People." In *Too Old for Health Care?,* edited by Binstock and Stephen Post. Baltimore: The Johns Hopkins University Press, 1991. Essay discussing the cost of health care for the older person and the clinical implications economic policy changes could have.

Kane, Robert, and Bruce Friedman. "Health Care and Services." In *Encyclopedia of Gerontology,* edited by James Birren. Vol. 1. San Diego: Academic Press, 1996. Discusses health care services, coverage, and managed care issues affecting the elderly.

Lewis, Carole. *Aging: The Health Care Challenge.* 3d ed. Philadelphia: F. A. Davis, 1996. Provides an interdisciplinary approach to assessment and rehabilitative management of problems of the elderly.

Mundinger, M. "Advanced-Practice Nursing—Good Medicine for Physicians?" *New England Journal of Medicine* 330 (1994). Discusses the use of nurse practitioners as primary health care providers.

HEALTH INSURANCE. *See* **MEDICAL INSURANCE.**

HEARING AIDS

RELEVANT ISSUES: Health and medicine

SIGNIFICANCE: The improvement in hearing aid technology has enabled many people over sixty-five years of age who exhibit hearing loss to show dramatic improvements in their hearing capabilities

In the United States, about 10 percent of the population have some degree of hearing loss. Hearing loss tends to worsen with aging, and, as the proportion of people living past sixty-five years of age increases, so will the percentage of those who develop hearing loss.

The magnitude of the change can be seen in the statistics of aging in the United States. In 1950, there were more than twelve million people over sixty-five years of age (8.1 percent of the population); this number (and percentage) increased dramatically during the second half of the twentieth century and is predicted to reach more than fifty million (17 percent) by the year 2020. This striking change in population structure has profound implications for the treatment of health conditions—including hearing loss—among the elderly. The causes of hearing loss are many and must be pinpointed in individual cases before any treatment can be initiated.

TYPES OF HEARING LOSS

There are three general types of hearing loss, classified according to what structures of the ear may be involved. All types of hearing loss are not equally amenable to improvements with the use of hearing aids. In conductive hearing loss, changes have occurred in the outer and middle ear. Sensorineural hearing loss involves the inner ear. In the third type, damage involves both conductive and sensorineural aspects, resulting in a mixed loss. It is not unusual to find the mixed type of hearing loss among the elderly.

The causes of the different types of hearing loss are varied. In some cases of conductive damage, the loss may be caused by an infection and may be effectively treated by medication. Surgery may be recommended in those cases where the hearing loss is a result of a problem in the middle ear. In the condition known as otosclerosis, a bony growth forms at the base of the stapes and prevents the proper movement of the small, bony ossicles in the middle ear so that normal transmission of the sound wave cannot occur. Otosclerosis is the most common cause of conductive deafness in adults. The condition can usually be corrected by surgically removing the stapes and replacing it with a plastic or metal device.

Hearing aids may be of considerable benefit to most people who have sensorineural hearing loss. However, people with severe sensorineural hearing loss (commonly known as nerve deafness) who do not gain any benefit from hearing aids may use cochlear implants, which allow the auditory nerve to be directly stimulated.

Presbycusis, or age-related deafness, is the most common cause of sensorineural hearing loss among those individuals sixty-five years of age and older. By the age of sixty-five, nearly 20 percent of the population suffers from presbycusis, which results from changes in the inner ear and in the auditory nerve. The inner ear contains hair cells that are, in fact, nerve cells that respond to stimuli, including sound vibrations.

At birth, there are twenty thousand to thirty thousand hair cells in the ear; as they gradually wear out and die during the course of a lifetime, people experience a loss of their ability to hear high-pitched sounds. A person might have difficulty hearing all the words produced by some women and children. Since individuals suffering from presbycusis have trouble hearing only certain things from certain people, they may not be aware of the deterioration in hearing and may not realize that the situation might be improved through use of a hearing aid. The loss of hearing also may affect a person's ears unequally. If the imbalance is severe enough, a person may experience difficulty in localizing sound, which may lead to disorientation.

This condition tends to get progressively worse with age, and certain families are at higher risk than others. Factors that contribute to presbycusis are many, and it is difficult to determine how these factors interact with those "normal" changes that accompany aging. Without a doubt, occupational noise and other everyday noises are major contributors to presbycusis. There is wide variation in the rate of decline in hearing among individuals as they age.

TYPES OF HEARING AIDS

Hearing aids fall into four general types: those worn on the body, those that are part of an eyeglass frame, those worn behind the ear, and those worn in the ear. Some types are effective only for mild hearing loss, whereas other models may be required for more severe hearing impairments. Continued advances in technology have increased the ability of hearing aids to help improve even severe hearing loss. The different types of hearing aids are not used in equal numbers. Relatively few people use the body-worn type or the eyeglass unit. Used somewhat more frequently is the behind-the-ear aid. However, the majority of hearing-impaired

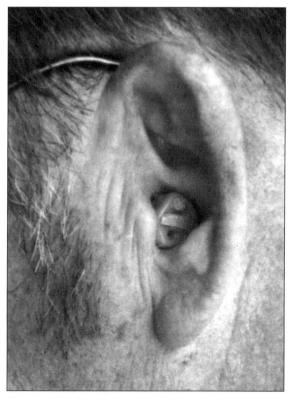

Hearing aids have become both better and smaller. Many can be worn inside the ear and are difficult to detect at first glance. (James L. Shaffer)

people use some form of the in-the-ear type. Like any product, the useful life of a hearing aid will vary, but they should last, on the average, four to five years.

All hearing aids function in a similar manner. A battery furnishes the operational power source. The size of the battery depends on the size of the aid and the amount of power required to carry out its specific function. The life of a battery is related to the length of time the aid is used and the power needs of the hearing aid. Zinc-air batteries usually maintain performance until they go completely dead, whereas other types, such as mercury batteries, tend to weaken before they are entirely drained. Batteries may last three weeks or less, and it is prudent to always have a supply on hand.

Hearing aids work by picking up sound waves with a microphone and converting them into electrical energy. An amplifier unit controls the volume by increasing the strength of the electrical energy. The receiver then converts the electrical signal back into sound waves. One final, but critical, component of the behind-the-ear hearing aid, the body aid, and the eyeglass aid is the earmold, which connects the hearing aid to the ear. Earmolds must be fitted or molded to individual ears. Since the earmold governs the amount and quality of the sound that passes from the aid into the ear, it not only must match the physical characteristics of each ear but also must be chosen on the basis of the type of hearing loss. Once a person begins to wear a hearing aid, it is essential that hearing and the hearing aid be checked regularly. The checkup usually includes an examination of the earmold, since the shape and size of the ear may change over time. A hearing aid is an extremely sensitive instrument that must be carefully adjusted for the individual who is using it.

THE INVISIBLE HANDICAP

Although the nature and cause of an individual's hearing loss may have been determined and a proper hearing aid may have been decided upon, it does not necessarily mean that a person's hearing problem has been solved. Hearing loss is often referred to as the "invisible handicap." Many people are slow to recognize that their hearing is deteriorating, others are slow to do anything about it, and many go into a period of denial. Individuals may have problems adjusting to wearing hearing aids because they feel embarrassed or do not want to "stand out." Learning to hear with hearing aids also requires a period of adjustment. However, once a hearing-impaired person has overcome these obstacles, a return to a near-normal life, with all its personal and social benefits, follows. In her book *How to Survive Hearing Loss* (1989), Charlotte Himber provides a useful personal account of her experience with her own hearing loss.

—Donald J. Nash

See also Aging process; Communication; Disabilities; Hearing loss; Sensory changes.

FOR FURTHER INFORMATION:

American Association of Retired Persons. *A Report on Hearing Aids: User Perspectives and Concerns.* Washington, D.C.: Author, 1993.

Dugan, Marcia P. *Keys to Living with Hearing Loss.* New York: Barron's Educational Service, 1997.

Himber, Charlotte. *How to Survive Hearing Loss.* Washington, D.C.: Gallaudet University Press, 1989.

Pope, Anne. *Solutions, Skills, and Sources for Hard of Hearing People.* New York: Dorling Kindersley, 1997.

Wayner, Donna A. *Hear What You've Been Missing.* Minneapolis: Chronimed, 1998.

_____. *The Hearing Aid Handbook: User's Guide for Adults.* Washington, D.C.: Gallaudet University Press, 1990.

HEARING LOSS

RELEVANT ISSUES: Biology, health and medicine, sociology

SIGNIFICANCE: Hearing loss is the most common sensory loss experienced by older adults. Approximately 28 to 55 percent of this group have hearing loss, with men experiencing the problem twice as often as women

Hearing loss has increasingly become a concern of the medical community and society in general with the growth of the older adult population. The most rapid increase in this population is predicted from 2005 to 2030, as the baby-boom generation reaches age sixty-five. Hearing loss will be a major concern of this age group.

Hearing loss interferes with the perception of a person's own voice and that of others, thereby creating behavioral and social disabilities. These conditions may lead to social withdrawal and isolation. A person with hearing loss is no longer able to enjoy the sounds of favorite music, a bird singing on a spring day, or the whispered words "I love you." Hearing loss takes its toll by robbing a person of such simple pleasures of life.

The causes of hearing loss are many, although three major factors enhance the progression of this loss with advanced age: exposure to noise, previous middle-ear disease, and vascular disease. The different effects of aging on the hearing mechanism also play a role in hearing loss. These effects may include atrophy and disappearance of cells in the inner ear, reduction of cells in the auditory areas of the cortex, and calcification of membranes in the inner ear.

How Do Humans Hear?

For a better understanding of the function of hearing, an overall review of the ear is helpful. There are three parts of the ear: the external ear, the middle ear, and the inner ear. The external ear consists of the pinna, external auditory canal, and tympanic membrane (eardrum). The tympanic membrane separates the external and middle ear. The middle ear consists of the ossicular chain. Three tiny bones (the malleus, incus, and stapes) extend from the tympanic membrane to the fenestra vestibuli. The middle ear conducts sound vibrations from the outer and middle ear to the central hearing structures in the inner ear. The inner ear is made up of a bony labyrinth that mainly consists of the semicircular canals, vestibule, and cochlea. At the base of the cochlear duct is the organ of Corti, with its sensitive hair cells. The cochlea is the essential organ of the auditory system. Sound waves travel through the ear by two pathways: air conduction and bone conduction. In air conduction, sound waves travel in the air through the external and middle ear to the inner ear. In bone conduction, sound waves travel through the bone to the inner ear. Vibrations transmitted through air and bone stimulate nerve impulses in the inner ear. The cochlear branch of the acoustic nerve (the eighth cranial nerve) transmits these vibrations to the auditory area of the cerebral cortex, where the temporal lobe of the brain interprets the sound.

The sound waves that travel through the ear have two main characteristics, frequency and amplitude. Frequency is related to the pitch of a sound and is measured by the number of vibrations or cycles per second. The higher the vibration frequency, the higher the perceived pitch. Hertz (Hz) is the unit of measurement to denote cycles per second. Amplitude is related to the loudness of a sound. The greater the intensity with which a sound strikes the eardrum, the louder the tone. The unit of measurement for intensity of sound is decibels (dB).

Among the offenders to hearing are radio headphones, lawn mowers, diesel trucks, and rock music. A single very loud noise can damage the middle ear. A broken eardrum can occur at 160 decibels at 1,000 hertz. Also, continuous noise over 80 to 85 decibels can cause harm. Normal conversation is measured at 60 decibels. A noisy restaurant, a vacuum cleaner, an electric shaver, and a screaming child are 80 to 85 decibels. Louder everyday noises include a blow-dryer (100 decibels), a subway train (100 decibels), and a car horn (110 decibels). Anyone exposed to noise in the 80 decibel range should wear hearing protection.

Types of Hearing Loss

There are basically two types of hearing loss: conductive hearing loss and sensorineural hearing loss. Conductive hearing loss results from interference with sound vibration through the external and middle ear. In other words, the sound cannot get to the inner ear. In some conductive hearing loss, if the sound amplitude is increased enough, the person is able to hear. Possible causes include impacted or large amounts of cerumen (wax), foreign bodies, otitis media, rheumatoid arthritis, and otosclerosis (in which the stapes becomes fixed to the oval window of the cochlea).

Wax buildup is a common and treatable cause of conduction hearing loss. There have been reports that as much as 25 percent of nursing home residents have impacted cerumen. Older adults can be taught how to remove the wax. Cerumenex (prescription only) and debrox (sold without a prescription) can be used as directed, followed by lavage to remove the wax and residual medication. Some authorities recommend the installation of mineral oil into the ear canal for twenty-four hours, followed by lavage with one part hydrogen peroxide to three parts water at room temperature.

Sensorineural loss means disease anywhere from the organ of Corti to the brain. The result is high-tone hearing loss because it is the hair cells in the basal turn of the organ of Corti that are sensitive to high tones. Presbycusis is the sensorineural hearing loss caused by aging of the inner ear. The onset of presbycusis may begin anytime from the third to the sixth decade of life, depending on type. Presbycusis affects 60 percent of individuals over age sixty-five in the United States. Older adults suffering from these disturbances show distinct and differing audiograms, which are used clinically to diagnose types of impairment. The standard type of presbycusis with hearing loss at high hertz is often associated with sensory and neural presbycusis. There are four types of presbycusis: sensory, neural, metabolic, and cochlear conductive.

The elderly first start to lose hearing in the high-frequency range. High-frequency consonants and sibilants become harder to recognize—for example, *f, g, l, t, s* and *ch, sh, th.* In presbycusis, high-frequency sounds become unintelligible. Understanding spoken words depends largely on the clear perception of high-frequency consonants rather than low-frequency vowel sounds. This is why words starting with the above letters or combinations become unintelligible. For example, the sentence "The light snow froze on the ground like shimmering chintz" may be unrecognizable. Many times, older adults have both conduction and sensorineural frequency losses. The precise nature of the defect requires help from a specialist and the use of sophisticated audiometric testing.

Another common hearing problem in the elderly is tinnitus (ringing in the ears). Medications such as aspirin, aminoglycoside antibiotics, and diuretics can cause toxic effects to the hair cells of the organ of Corti, thereby resulting in sensorineural hearing loss. Tinnitus, an internal noise generated within the hearing system, occurs in many types of hearing disorders at all ages but is reported more frequently in the elderly. Perhaps the elderly cannot block out these unusual sounds, while the young can do so. Tinnitus affects seven million people, of which 10 to 37 percent are elderly. The sound is generally increased pitched with sensorineural loss and low pitched with conductive hearing loss. However, tinnitus may be present with or without hearing loss. Tinnitus does not usually awaken affected people, nor does it interfere with pleasurable activities. Older adults can attempt to alleviate the condition through biofeedback or by disguising the sound. Soft radio music or other distracting sounds may be helpful.

TREATMENT AND PREVENTION

There are many treatments for hearing loss; depending on the type of loss, some work better than others. For example, with conductive hearing loss, if the cause is excessive wax buildup, the results may be remarkable when the wax is removed. For both types of hearing loss, simple measures can be used to facilitate better communication. One of these techniques is always facing people with hearing loss directly when speaking to them. The older adult can then observe lip movement, facial expression, and body language.

Advances in hearing aid technology have allowed many seniors to remain independent and active despite hearing losses. (Marilyn Nolt)

Using simple, short sentences or phrases and speaking slowly and in a low voice can be helpful. Loudness can be irritating, whereas a low voice enables people to hear lower frequencies, which usually can be heard more easily.

Although hearing aids may help certain types of hearing loss, many older people do not use them. There are various reasons for this phenomenon. Hearing aid use may be associated with getting older. In addition, hearing loss may be seen as a normal and inevitable event for older people; therefore, treatment is not sought. The cost of purchasing a hearing aid is also a concern. In 1999, on average, a hearing aid cost $2,500 or more, and Medicare did not provide reimbursements for hearing aids. The hearing aid itself can create problems for the user. A person wearing such a device for the first time needs to go through an adjustment period. Some older adults do not give themselves enough time to get used to the hearing aid. Some hearing aids have been known to cause irritation to the external ear. Also, the increased humidity within the external auditory canal can cause the infection otitis externa.

There are basically three kinds of hearing aids: the body type, the behind-the-ear type, and the in-the-ear type. The body type resembles a handheld amplifier with a wire that attaches to an earpiece. The behind-the-ear type is worn behind and in the ear. A person with poor eyesight and rheumatoid arthritis would probably benefit from the body type or behind-the-ear type of hearing aid. These types are easier to see and handle because of the larger size. The in-the-ear hearing aid is worn completely in the ear canal. The in-the-ear devices are small, cosmetically more acceptable, but more difficult to manipulate. The selection often depends on the wearer's personal preference, vision capabilities, and manual dexterity.

Older adults need to have realistic expectations about their hearing aids. Sounds and voices are made louder, not clearer. The wearer usually takes a while to get used to the background noise. The user must be encouraged to continue using the hearing aid during this initial period. Face-to-face conversation and lip reading may still be necessary to make sounds more intelligible. Greatest satisfaction is achieved with hearing aids if hearing loss is between 55 and 80 decibels. There is only partial benefit if the loss is greater than 80 decibels.

Attitude is also key. One well-adjusted patient said that his hearing loss made him more aware of the world. He appreciated the sounds that some people would find annoying, like a dripping faucet. Wearing two body-type hearing aids, one in each ear, he comically said he was listening to the ball game on two stations. When asked how he felt about his hearing loss, he responded, "unlike other people, when I get tired of listening to sounds all day, I just turn off my hearing aids and tune out."

Hearing loss can occur, and be prevented, at all ages. Following some simple guidelines can preserve hearing well into old age: keeping loud noises to a minimum, wearing protective hearing gear, seeking professional help when an ear infection is suspected, taking the full course of antibiotics if they are prescribed for an ear infection, and not putting anything "smaller than an elbow" in the ear.

Several organizations can help the hearing-impaired. The American Academy of Otolaryngology, Head, and Neck Surgery, based in Alexandria, Virginia, offers information about hearing, head, and neck disorders and diseases. Its telephone number is (703) 836-4444. The Cochlear Implant Club International (CICI) educates the public about implants, gives referrals to medical centers that perform implants, and steers patients to other self-help groups and resources. Its address is 5335 Wisconsin Ave. N.W., Suite 440, Washington, D.C. 20015. The telephone number is (202) 895-2781, and the organization's Web site is www.cici.org.

—*Janet Mahoney*

See also Aging process; Communication; Disabilities; Hearing aids; Sensory changes.

FOR FURTHER INFORMATION:

Carmen, Richard, ed. *The Consumer Handbook on Hearing Loss and Hearing Aids: A Bridge to Healing.* Sedona, Ariz.: Auricle Ink, 1998. This book has received rave reviews within the hearing profession. A consumer author for more than twenty years, clinical audiologist Richard Carmen brings together the most renowned audiologists, scientists, physicians, thinkers, and experts in the field. A wide range of topics is discussed, including the emotions involved in hearing loss, where and how to find help, self-assessment for those who do not yet admit a loss, and effective transition from hearing loss to hearing aids.

Craine, Michael. *Hear Well Again.* Chapel Hill, N.C.: Professional Press, 1999. An easy-to-read, comprehensive review of hearing aid technology, hearing health care, and solutions to alleviate hearing problems.

"Facts About Hearing Disorders." *Hearing Statistics and Key Facts.* http://www.betterhearing.org/demograp.htm. This Web site offers statistics on key facts about hearing disorders. The percentages of hearing loss in children, adults, and older adults are discussed. Presents facts about conditions associated with hearing loss, such as presbycusis and tinnitus.

Gallo, J. J., W. Reichel, and L. M. Andersen. *Handbook of Geriatric Assessment.* 3d ed. Gaithersburg, Mass.: Aspen, 1999. Emphasizes material that has practical application in primary care settings in order to encourage a multidimensional approach for the care of the aged.

International Hearing Society. "Hearing Aid Tips." http://www.hearingihs.org/aid/htm. This Web site offers tips about the types, use, and care of hearing aids.

Lichtenstein, M. J. "Hearing and Visual Impairments." *Clinical Geriatric Medicine* 8, no. 1 (1992): 173-182. This article offers useful information about both hearing and visual impairments.

Matteson, M., E. S. McConnell, and A. D. Linton. *Gerontological Nursing: Concepts and Practice.* 2d ed. Philadelphia.: W. B. Saunders, 1997. This book contains literature in nursing, medicine, and social science in relation to the aging population. Describes the aging process across the health care continuum from wellness to illness. Physiological and psychological aspects of aging are discussed, as well as the assessment of and practice in all settings using the nursing process.

Paterson, J. "What You Need to Know About Hearing Loss." *USA Weekend,* November 21-23, 1997. An article that gives valuable insight into the topic of hearing loss. Included is a self-quiz about hearing loss.

Shelp, S. G. "Your Patient Is Deaf, Now What?" *RN* 60, no. 2 (1997): 37-41. This article illustrates the use of American Sign Language (ASL). Includes a comprehensive Signed English Dictionary that represents both ASL—the national language of the deaf in the United States—and manually signed English, another type of sign language that resembles ASL but has a structure similar to written or spoken English.

Timiras, P. S., ed. *Physiological Basis of Aging and Geriatrics.* 2d ed. Boca Raton, Fla.: CRC Press, 1994. Contributors discuss the biology of aging. Old age is viewed as being a dynamic process. Reports of studies of cellular and molecular events throughout the life span.

HEART ATTACKS

RELEVANT ISSUES: Death, health and medicine

SIGNIFICANCE: The leading cause of death in the United States among older people is diseases of the heart, with over one-third of a million dying annually from heart attacks

People can do many things to reduce their risk of having a heart attack. Understanding coronary artery disease and how to slow its progression can result in a longer, healthier life.

HEART DISEASE

The long process that results in a heart attack is called coronary artery disease or heart disease. Heart disease begins early in life, as early as preadolescence in some people. Cholesterol deposits begin to form in the arteries. A common location for these plaques is in the first few centimeters of the arteries around the heart. As the deposits grow thicker, blood flow becomes restricted. A heart attack, or myocardial infarction, usually begins with the formation of a blood clot (thrombus) in the narrowed part of the artery. If the blood clot becomes large enough, blood flow can cease. The area of heart muscle that receives its blood from the blocked artery fails to get enough oxygen. If blood flow is not restored to the muscle soon, the muscle tissue will die and will no longer be able to pump blood. The severity of the heart attack depends on the size and location of the area that ultimately dies.

Additionally, when the oxygen supply to the heart muscle is low, there is a greater risk of sudden cardiac death. This complication occurs when the heart begins to beat rapidly and disorderly, called ventricular fibrillation. During ventricular fibrillation, the heart does not pump blood and then goes into cardiac arrest. Without immediate medical attention, the person dies quickly.

UNCONTROLLABLE RISK FACTORS FOR HEART DISEASE

Many factors increase a person's risk for coronary artery disease and heart attacks. Some of these risk factors are controllable, and some are not. For example, age is a risk factor that cannot be controlled. As people get older, the chances of suffering from coronary artery disease and having a heart attack increase.

Genetics, or a family history of heart disease, is another uncontrollable risk factor. People who have had a parent, grandparent, or sibling who experienced a heart attack at an early age are more likely to have a heart attack themselves. Several other risk factors are related to genetics, such as high blood pressure (hypertension), high blood cholesterol, or high blood triglycerides. These conditions can be influenced to some extent through lifestyle choices, but they are not completely controllable in people who have a genetic predisposition to them.

Another uncontrollable risk factor is gender.

Men are more likely to have a heart attack than women are. The lower risk for women evens out, however, after the menopause. It is believed that female hormones, principally estrogen, have a protective effect against fat deposits on the arterial walls and assist in maintaining a positive blood lipid profile.

CONTROLLABLE RISK FACTORS FOR HEART DISEASE

It is important for individuals to know their risk level and attempt to change the factors over which they have some control. There are four major controllable risk factors—high blood pressure, high blood cholesterol, tobacco use, and physical inactivity—as well as several other important risk factors.

Blood pressure is the force that the blood exerts against the arterial walls. A blood pressure reading is given as two numbers. The systolic pressure is the pressure when the heart is contracting, and the diastolic pressure is the pressure when the heart is

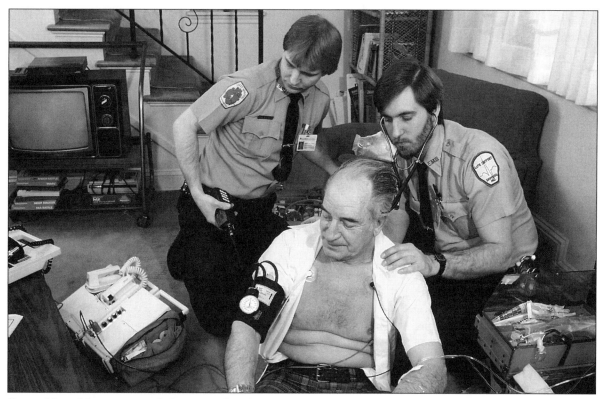

Recognition of the symptoms of a heart attack and quick medical response can increase the chances of survival with minimal permanent damage. (Digital Stock)

resting. Both are measured in millimeters of mercury. A systolic pressure of 140 or higher or a diastolic pressure of 90 or higher would be considered high blood pressure (hypertension) and a risk factor for heart attacks.

Blood cholesterol levels are measured in milligrams of cholesterol per deciliter of blood. The higher the cholesterol level, the higher the risk for a heart attack. An ideal level is below 200 milligrams per deciliter. People with levels of 240 milligrams per deciliter have twice the risk of a heart attack. Another determinant for risk is the type of cholesterol in the blood. High-density lipoproteins (HDLs) are considered "good cholesterol" because they carry cholesterol to the liver, where it can be removed from the body. People with low levels of HDLs, below 35 milligrams per deciliter, have a higher risk for a heart attack than people with higher levels.

Use of tobacco products, particularly cigarette smoking, is a major health risk for the heart. The contents of tobacco can damage the walls of arteries, making it easier for cholesterol deposits to form. Additionally, tobacco can decrease the level of HDLs and promote the formation of blood clots. All these complications significantly increase the risk of having a heart attack.

Lack of sufficient physical exercise also increases the risk. People who exercise regularly have lower blood cholesterol and triglyceride levels, higher HDL levels, and a lower incidence of obesity. These positive effects of exercise reduce the chances of having a heart attack and increase the chances of surviving one.

Several other controllable risk factors are evident. Individuals who suffer from diabetes are at greater risk because the disease causes irregularities in blood cholesterol levels that accelerate the deposition of fat on the arterial walls. Obese individuals are at a greater risk of heart attacks because they typically have higher blood cholesterol and triglyceride levels, lower HDL levels, higher blood pressures, and a higher incidence of diabetes. In addition, individuals with higher stress levels are more likely to suffer heart attacks than individuals with lower stress levels.

Many lifestyle habits can be modified to reduce the risks of coronary artery disease and heart attacks. Although not all risk factors can be controlled, the overall risk can be reduced.

REDUCING THE CHANCE OF HEART ATTACK

The best way people can reduce their risk for having a heart attack is to make lifestyle changes that reduce the likelihood of heart disease. In some cases, such changes involve stopping destructive behaviors; in other cases, they involve adopting healthy behaviors.

To control hypertension, people need to have their blood pressure checked regularly. The chance of developing high blood pressure increases with age. If blood pressure is checked on a regular basis, unsafe levels are more likely to be detected early and appropriate medications prescribed. Maintaining proper body weight and abstaining from drinking large amounts of alcohol can minimize hypertension. Reducing the amount of salt or sodium in the diet can also help to reduce blood pressure.

Controlling blood cholesterol levels is primarily achieved by changing the diet. Saturated fats and cholesterol contribute to the deposition of cholesterol on the blood vessel walls. Reducing total fat, especially fat from animal sources such as meat, eggs, and dairy products, reduces the risk for having a heart attack. It is also helpful to increase the HDL levels in the blood by getting more exercise, reducing body weight, and stopping the use of tobacco products if necessary.

Since tobacco is habit-forming, it is not reasonable to smoke in moderation. Cessation is the only logical option. For people who smoke or use other forms of tobacco, quitting is the best way to reduce the chances of a heart attack.

Individuals who are physically inactive can reduce their risk of heart attack by starting a regular exercise program. People need to focus on activities that are aerobic in nature, including walking, running, biking, swimming, aerobic dancing, and using aerobic equipment such as stair climbers. These activities all use large muscle groups and can be performed continuously for twenty or more minutes. To obtain the benefits of exercise, people should participate in one or more of these activities for thirty to forty minutes, three to four times per week. All individuals should consult a physician prior to initiating an exercise program.

Reducing body weight involves two activities. First, the number of calories consumed must be decreased; this can be done by reducing the amount of food eaten, especially foods high in sugar and fat. Second, the number of calories burned must be increased; this can be done by introducing or increasing regular exercise. Although one of these activities alone can help take off weight, the best results for weight loss and the corresponding reduction in heart attack risk are obtained with a combination of the two.

Controlling stress can also help reduce the risk for a heart attack. This factor is compounded by the fact that many individuals who are under significant stress deal with it by smoking and/or over-eating. Practicing relaxation techniques and time management are better methods for dealing with stress.

WARNING SIGNS OF A HEART ATTACK

A major problem with heart attacks is that many people think they are having indigestion when they are actually experiencing heart pains, or angina. Therefore, they do not seek medical attention for the pain soon enough, and the delay in treatment results in more severe problems or even death. A heart attack causes a pressure or squeezing pain, typically in the center of the chest and lasting more than a few minutes. The pain may spread to the shoulders, neck, arms, or jaw. It is frequently accompanied by light-headedness, sweating, nausea, shortness of breath, or fainting. However, not all these signs take place in every attack, and some signs may come and go.

When someone is experiencing the signs of a heart attack, it is important to get medical help quickly. The sooner a person can get to a hospital, the faster blood clot-dissolving drugs can be administered. This quick treatment minimizes the health complications of a heart attack and saves lives.

CLINICAL DIAGNOSIS

In the hospital, the diagnosis of a heart attack is made by considering the following three factors: the patient's history, signs, and symptoms; the changes in the patient's electrocardiogram (ECG or EKG); and the level of certain enzymes in the blood. In addition to observing the signs and symptoms of a heart attack, listening to the heart with a stethoscope can identify changes in sounds indicative of an attack.

Electrocardiography is the process of measuring the electrical activity of the heart. Obvious

Pain Associated with Heart Attack

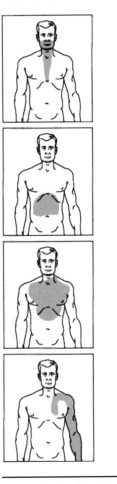

Pain radiating up into jaw and through to back.

Pain felt in upper abdomen.

Pressure in the central chest area from mild to severe.

Pain radiating down left arm; may cause sensation of weakness in the arm.

(Hans & Cassidy, Inc.)

wave changes are noticed when the heart tissue is damaged and oxygen supply is low. An ECG is a very useful and easy test, but it is not always conclusive. Therefore, a blood test is also performed to look for specific enzymes in the serum. When a heart attack occurs and the heart muscle is damaged, these enzymes are released from the muscle cells into the blood. Two major enzymes found in the blood with heart attacks are creatine kinase and lactate dehydrogenase.

TREATMENT OF A HEART ATTACK

When a patient is diagnosed with a heart attack, three areas of treatment are needed: pain relief, reduction or easing of the workload on the heart, and dissolution of the blood clot or clots. The first two approaches are interrelated, since helping the heart to work easier will help reduce the pain. One method to achieve this aim is rest. Rest also provides the medical personnel with an opportunity to collect information and administer other treatments to reduce the strain on the patient's heart. Nitroglycerin and related drugs reduce the workload of the heart and reduce pain. The class of drugs known as beta-blockers also helps reduce workload. Aspirin is typically given to help break down blood clots and to reduce their tendency to form. Anticoagulant drugs are also used for this reason. In general, all these treatments help minimize heart damage and reduce pain.

Thrombolytic therapy is an important treatment for breaking up blood clots before they do more damage to the heart muscle. Early treatment with these clot-busting drugs, such as streptokinase and TPA (or tPA), results in the blood clots being dissolved and thus restores blood flow to the heart muscle. If these drugs are given soon enough, heart damage may be avoided almost entirely.

REHABILITATION

The recovery process after a heart attack involves two components. First, a program is developed to strengthen the heart and prepare the body for normal day-to-day activities. Second, lifestyle modification is used to decrease the chances of another heart attack.

The program developed to strengthen the heart involves regular, strenuous exercise. Phase I cardiac rehabilitation begins in the hospital. Patients begin by sitting up in bed and eventually taking short walks down the hall. These sessions are under the direct supervision of a health care professional. Possibly before discharge and certainly after discharge, the patient graduates to a phase II program. Generally, these programs are operated in a hospital and involve closely monitored exercise on treadmills, stationary bikes, and other aerobic equipment. The patient's ECGs and blood pressure are monitored continually to ensure safe exercise. Phase III programs are less restrictive. Patients typically exercise in community facilities and monitor the intensity of their own workouts by checking their pulses. Professional supervision is provided, but individual attention is reduced when compared with the previous phases of the program.

The other component of cardiac rehabilitation is lifestyle management. Unhealthy habits that were risk factors are identified for change. Intervention programs are developed to modify risky behaviors and ultimately reduce the risk of having another heart attack.

With proper medical care and lifestyle habits, many heart attacks can be avoided. People must take control of their own health. They must develop healthy habits early in life to avoid the pain and suffering of heart attacks later in life.

—Bradley R. A. Wilson

See also Arteriosclerosis; Cholesterol; Diabetes; Exercise and fitness; Heart changes and disorders; Heart disease; Hospitalization; Hypertension; Nutrition; Obesity; Smoking; Stress and coping skills; Strokes.

FOR FURTHER INFORMATION:

American Heart Association. "Controlling Your Risk Factors for Heart Attack." Dallas: Author, 1993. This small booklet tells how individuals can reduce their heart attack risk.

Perlmutter, Cathy. "Do Your Heart Good." *Prevention* 49 (February, 1997). Contains a personal assessment for evaluating the risk of heart disease.

_____. "The Heart of the Matter." *Prevention* 50 (February, 1998). Discusses the risk factors for heart disease.

Schwade, Steve. "Heart Healthy: Can Vitamins Disarm a Hidden Villain?" *Prevention* 46 (July, 1994). Evaluates the role of vitamins in reducing the risk of heart attacks.

Smith, Marion Roach. "How to Talk Your Way out of a Heart Attack." *Prevention* 44 (June, 1992). Uses communication to reduce the chances of having a heart attack.

HEART CHANGES AND DISORDERS

RELEVANT ISSUES: Biology, health and medicine

SIGNIFICANCE: Even in a healthy individual, subtle changes occur in heart structure and function with age. Age continues to be one of the most significant predictors of cardiovascular events such as stroke, heart attack, or coronary heart disease

The human heart is actually two pumps responsible for supplying all the cells of the body with oxygen and nutrients through the circulation of blood. The heart is divided into four chambers, left and right atria and left and right ventricles. The atria receive the blood into the heart from veins, and the ventricles pump blood away from the heart through arteries. The right ventricle pumps blood to the lungs, where red blood cells exchange carbon dioxide (a cellular waste product) with oxygen (which is necessary for cellular activity). The freshly oxygenated blood returns from the lungs to the left atrium. It will be pumped out by the left ventricle through the aorta and eventually to all the cells and tissues of the body. The frequency and regularity of the pumping is regulated by a biological pacemaker in the heart, a patch of heart cells called the sinus node. The heart is protected by a tough sac called the pericardium. Fluid in the pericardium keeps the heart lubricated, and the energy-requiring cardiac cells of the heart are supplied with oxygen and nutrients from blood that flows through the coronary arteries.

With age, the muscles of the heart become stiffer and therefore do not relax as much between contractions, leading to less efficient pumping. The heart may not pump as strongly, and it is less able to respond to signals from the nervous system, such as adrenaline, to increase heart rate or strength of contraction. Because of the natural tendency of vessel walls to become harder and less elastic, even without complicating fatty blockages, older individuals often experience a type of high blood pressure called isolated systolic hypertension. Also, the reflex that maintains blood pressure when a person moves from a lying or sitting position to standing becomes slower. Sometimes, older individuals experience dizziness if they change positions rapidly because of this slower reflex. By themselves, these changes in the biology of the heart usually do not result in disease. Combined with other risk factors such as high total cholesterol or obesity, however, these changes place the older person at greater risk for heart disease.

Risk Factors for Cardiovascular Disease

Age continues to be the strongest predictor of many cardiovascular diseases. Along with physical changes in the heart itself, many of the other risk factors for cardiovascular disease become more of a concern as a person ages. For example, blood cholesterol levels greater than 200 milligrams per deciliter in any individual increase risk for heart disease. As a person ages, the levels of total cholesterol, fats (triglycerides), and low-density lipoprotein (LDL), or "bad," cholesterol increase. These lipid components of the blood are major players in the formation of sclerotic plaques or blockages in arteries. Furthermore, the levels of high-density lipoprotein (HDL), or protective or "good," cholesterol decrease. In women, total cholesterol will rise after the menopause until age sixty or sixty-five; a woman at this age will have higher cholesterol levels than a comparably healthy man of the same age.

As a person ages, the body's requirement for calories decreases. Extra calories in the diet are converted by the body into fat, leading to increased blood lipid levels and weight gain. High blood lipid levels and unhealthy weight are risk factors for cardiovascular disease. The blood lipids contribute to the narrowing and blockage of the arteries, and the additional weight places an extra load on the heart. As weight increases, fat tissues grow. The cells of these tissues must be supplied with nutrients from the blood like all other body tissues. Tiny capillaries grow into the expanding fat tissues, and this new growth forces the heart to pump blood to a greater area. The heart must work harder.

Hypertension, or high blood pressure, is another risk factor that slowly increases with age. Blood pressure measures the force with which the heart has to pump blood; it is a measure of how hard the heart is working. Blood pressure measurements consist of two numbers: the systolic pressure, the force that the heart exerts when the left ventricle contracts to send blood throughout the body, and the diastolic pressure, the resting pressure. These numbers are reported as a fraction, with the systolic number on the top and the diastolic number on the bottom. Blood pressure naturally rises as a person ages. In infants, blood pressure is often 70/50, but in a young adult, a normal reading is 120/80. For middle-aged and older adults, any reading over 140/90 is considered high.

Another age-related disease, adult-onset (type II) diabetes mellitus, is a risk factor for heart disease. This disease usually manifests itself after age forty. With diabetes, the body is unable to respond to normal levels of the hormone insulin. Because of the lack of response to the hormone, more insulin is circulated in the blood. (Indeed, many diabetics take medications that serve to increase circulating insulin.) Insulin is involved not only in regulating blood sugar levels but also in stimulating higher blood pressure and increasing cholesterol deposition in the arteries. Both of these effects are themselves risk factors for cardiovascular disease.

Lack of exercise contributes to heart disease risk by leading to increased weight and increased levels of blood cholesterol and fats. Any person who has a family history of heart disease is also at increased risk. In women, loss of the protective effects of estrogen after the menopause greatly increases the risk of cardiovascular problems.

AGE-RELATED CARDIOVASCULAR CHANGES AND PROBLEMS

Around age sixty, some people experience a phenomenon called brady-tachy syndrome. In this condition, periods of extremely rapid heartbeats (tachycardia) alternate with periods of slow heartbeats (bradycardia) because the sinus node is unable to regulate heart rate properly. Many people

with this syndrome are unaware of it and live normal, productive lives. In severe cases, this syndrome can be treated with medications but often requires a pacemaker to regulate heartbeat.

Isolated systolic hypertension is a particular kind of high blood pressure often experienced by individuals age sixty-five to seventy. Isolated systolic hypertension is characterized by a high systolic reading, greater than 160, accompanied by a diastolic reading of 90 or below. This hypertension is as much a risk factor in heart disease as the more common kinds of hypertension.

After age fifty-five, the chance of a man having a stroke will double with each decade of life. Strokes are defined as any disturbance in brain function that is caused by either the blockage or the rupture of a blood vessel supplying the brain, and brain damage from strokes is often permanent. Annually, 1 percent of the U.S. population aged sixty-five to seventy-four will suffer strokes.

Coronary artery disease generally affects men over age forty-five and women over age fifty-five. In

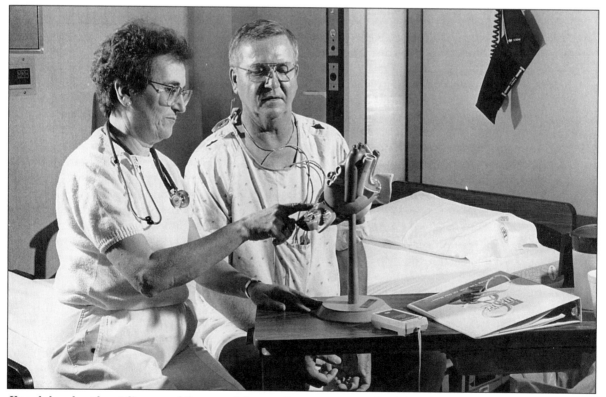

Knowledge about heart disease and the normal changes that accompany aging is invaluable throughout life but particularly in middle age, when the risk for heart disorders increases significantly. (James L. Shaffer)

coronary artery disease, the arteries that supply blood to muscle cells of the heart become blocked, or sclerosed. This blockage results in the failure to supply heart cells with oxygen and other nutrients. As a result, the cardiac cells are not able to function properly and heart attacks ensue. Coronary artery disease is treated with bypass surgery, in which blood to the heart cells is rerouted around the blocked arteries through vessels placed by the surgeon.

PREVENTION OF AGE-RELATED CORONARY PROBLEMS

A healthy lifestyle is the single most important factor in preventing cardiovascular disease. A diet that is low in total cholesterol, total fat, and saturated fat and high in fiber will lower blood lipid levels by at least 5 percent and decrease a person's risk of developing cardiovascular problems. The risk of coronary heart disease decreases 2 percent for every 1 percent decrease in blood cholesterol.

Exercise is another important component in lowering cardiovascular disease risk, particularly in elderly people who have decreased their overall activities. There is no need to enroll in a strenuous, athletic-level exercise program in order to decrease one's risk of heart disease. Regular, moderate exercise will help to stimulate the production of HDL and decrease circulating fats. Exercise also acts to decrease weight and reduce stress, two factors that contribute to heart disease risk. Elderly individuals who exercise should start at a slower pace and increase the intensity of their exercise program very slowly. They should also select low-impact activities to protect fragile bones and joints. Consultation with a physician before starting a new exercise program is recommended.

—P. Michele Arduengo

See also Aging process; Arteriosclerosis; Cholesterol; Diabetes; Exercise and fitness; Fat deposition; Heart attacks; Heart disease; Hypertension; Malnutrition; Nutrition; Obesity; Strokes; Weight loss and gain.

FOR FURTHER INFORMATION:

American Heart Association. http://www.american heart.org.

National Heart, Lung, and Blood Institute. *Live Healthier, Live Longer.* Washington, D.C.: National Institutes of Health, 1996.

_____. *Stay Young at Heart Program.* Washington, D.C.: National Institutes of Health, 1994.

Notelovitz, Morris, and Diana Tonnessen. *The Essential Heart Book for Women.* New York: St. Martin's Press, 1996.

Zaret, Barry L., Marvin Moser, Lawrence S. Cohen, and Genell J. Subak, eds. *Yale University School of Medicine Heart Book.* New York: William Morrow, 1992.

HEART DISEASE

RELEVANT ISSUES: Health and medicine
SIGNIFICANCE: Heart disease is the number-one killer of older people in the United States

Cardiovascular disease (CVD) is the leading cause of death in the United States, accounting for nearly half of the mortality rate in 1995. CVD can affect any aspect of the cardiovascular system, including the heart and blood vessels. Major forms of CVD include high blood pressure (hypertension), congenital heart disease, coronary artery disease (heart disease), peripheral vascular disease, stroke, rheumatic heart disease, and atherosclerosis. The most predominant form of CVD is coronary artery disease, which causes a narrowing of the coronary arteries that supply the heart with nutrients.

The heart, like all other muscles and organs in the body, needs a constant blood supply. The muscle layer of the heart (the myocardium) is not nourished by the blood being pumped to other parts of the body. Blood is supplied to the myocardium through the coronary artery system. If a portion of the heart does not receive adequate blood, it begins to die.

As heart disease causes the arteries to close, chest pain called angina pectoris can occur during times of excitement or physical exertion. A heart attack (myocardial infarction) occurs when the blood supply to part of the heart is blocked. This is typically brought about when a blood clot forms in a narrowed coronary artery. The first indication of a heart attack may be one of several warning signals: uncomfortable pressure, fullness, squeezing, or pain in the center of the chest lasting two minutes or more; pain that spreads to the shoulders, neck, or arms; or severe pain, dizziness, fainting, sweating, nausea, or shortness of breath. Sharp, stabbing twinges of pain are usually not signals of a heart attack.

Since the 1950's, research has been conducted in an effort to determine the basic cause of heart disease. Large populations have been studied over long periods, with their living habits and medical records assessed in relation to the incidence of heart disease. These studies have helped identify how heart disease develops and what factors predispose one to this disease. Risk factors which lead to its development can be classified into major and minor categories, with the major factors having much more influence on disease risk.

MAJOR RISK FACTORS

Smoking is the number-one cause of heart disease. Individuals who smoke have a 2.5 times greater-than-average risk of developing this disease. Although cancer is the disease that typically is associated with smoking, smokers are much more likely to die of heart disease than of cancer. A close relationship exists between the development of heart disease and smoking. This means that the more one smokes, the greater the risk. Someone who smokes one pack per day has twice the risk of a nonsmoker, while someone who smokes two packs per day has three times the risk.

It is easy to understand why smoking has such an impact on the development of heart disease. As smoke enters the alveoli of the lungs, carbon monoxide competes with oxygen to be carried into the blood. The hemoglobin portion of a red blood cell is the oxygen-carrying component. Even though hemoglobin likes oxygen and picks it up for transport to the necessary organs and muscles, it also likes carbon monoxide. In fact, hemoglobin likes carbon monoxide better than oxygen and attaches itself to carbon monoxide when it is present, therefore ignoring oxygen. This reduces the amount of oxygen in the blood and forces the heart to pump much more blood in order for adequate oxygen to be delivered.

Hypertension (high blood pressure), which is considered a type of cardiovascular disease, is also a major risk factor for developing heart disease. A systolic blood pressure consistently elevated above 140 millimeters of mercury or a diastolic blood pressure above 90 millimeters of mercury constitutes hypertension. As with smoking, heart disease has a close relationship with hypertension—the higher the blood pressure, the greater the risk for heart disease. Control of hypertension depends to a large extent on the cause. Some of the causes of hypertension are stress, obesity, and lack of exercise. Thus, control methods may include learning how to control stress, beginning a weight loss plan, and starting an exercise program. Hypertension has been called the "silent killer," a statement which enforces the fact that individuals have no way of knowing their blood pressure unless they have it checked. An individual should monitor his or her blood pressure on a regular basis.

Hypercholesterolemia is a technical name for having too much fat (lipids) in the blood. Blood lipids are responsible for the buildup of plaque on the walls of arteries. The higher an individual's blood lipids or fats, the greater his or her risk for heart disease.

The accompanying table includes the normal and abnormal values for blood lipids. Blood lipids include cholesterols and triglycerides. Cholesterol can be broken down into subfractions that include low-density lipoproteins (LDLs), very low-density lipoproteins (VLDLs), and high-density lipoproteins (HDLs). These subfractions are very important in determining an individual's risk of heart disease. In simple terms, LDLs have a low density of protein and a high density of fat, while the opposite is true for HDLs (high protein content, low fat). Not all cholesterol is bad. In fact, the higher the level of HDL cholesterols, the lower the risk for heart disease. Evidence suggests that HDL levels are a better predictor of heart disease than total cholesterol. People with low total cholesterol (less than 200 milligrams per deciliter) and also low HDL cholesterol (less than 40 milligrams per deciliter) may have heart disease risk that is three times greater than that of people with high total cholesterol but good HDL levels. HDL cholesterol acts as a scavenger, removing cholesterol from the body and preventing plaque from forming in the arteries. LDL cholesterol releases cholesterol which may penetrate the lining of the artery wall and cause the formation of plaques. Many authorities suggest that the ratio between total cholesterol and HDL cholesterol is the strongest indicator of potential heart disease. A total cholesterol-to-HDL ratio of 3.5 or lower is excellent for men, and 3.0 or lower is excellent for women.

Triglycerides are also a blood lipid that, if elevated, can lead to heart disease. Triglyceride levels below 150 milligrams per deciliter are considered to be excellent, with levels above 500 considered moderate-to-high in risk.

Blood lipids can be altered by changes made in an individual's lifestyle. Starting an aerobic exercise program is an excellent way to increase HDL cholesterol and to lower LDL cholesterol and triglycerides. Research suggests that an aerobic exercise program that expends 1,000 calories per week (for example, ten miles of walking or jogging) at moderate intensity is required to produce blood lipid changes. Greater changes occur with greater caloric expenditure.

Dietary adjustments are another way to alter blood lipids. Total cholesterol, LDL cholesterol, triglycerides, and even HDL cholesterol can be improved through proper nutritional practices. The American Heart Association publishes dietary recommendations for the treatment of hypercholesterolemia. These recommendations include a fat intake below 30 percent of total calorie consumption, with not more than one-third of these calories coming from saturated fat. Since saturated fat has the greatest influence on the production of cholesterol, limiting its intake is the most important dietary control. Monounsaturated fats, such as canola oil or olive oil, should make up one-third or more of fat calories, since these oils may raise HDL levels. Polyunsaturated fats, which may help lower total cholesterol without reducing HDL cholesterol, should account for up to one-third of the total fat calories consumed.

In addition to lowering fat consumption, the National Cholesterol Education Program (NCEP) recommends limiting dietary cholesterol to under 300 milligrams per day, which is about the amount of cholesterol found in one large egg.

In 1993, the American Heart Association identified a sedentary lifestyle as a major risk factor for heart disease. Lack of physical activity is on par with smoking, hypertension, and high cholesterol and triglyceride levels as a major factor in determining heart disease risk. When compared to other major risk factors, lack of physical activity affects more of the population than the others combined. Roughly 60 percent of the U.S. population

Risk Profile of Lipid and Lipoprotein Concentrations (No Other Risk Factors Present)

	Total Cholesterol (mg/dl)	LDL Cholesterol (mg/dl)	HDL Cholesterol (mg/dl)	Triglycerides (mg/dl)
High risk	≥245	≥190	≤36	≥1,000
Moderate risk	221-244	160-189	35-44	500-999
Mild risk	201-220	130-159	45-54	250-499
Average risk	182-200	100-129	55-64	151-249
Low risk	<182	<100	≥65	≤150

is at risk because of physical inactivity. This makes lack of exercise the most changeable of all the risk factors. As little as ninety minutes per week of mild exercise is reported to reduce heart disease risk significantly. Exercise may include walking, gardening, or cycling.

Obesity is considered to be 10 percent above the ideal fat percentage. Excess body fat places a strain on the cardiovascular system, creating a much less efficient heart. Although obesity is recognized as an independent risk factor for heart disease, the risk attributed to obesity may actually be caused by other risk factors that are usually associated with excessive body fat. Risk factors such as high blood pressure, high blood lipid levels, and diabetes improve with a decrease in body fat.

An increase in daily physical activity, which includes participation in both aerobic and strength-training programs, and a moderate reduction in caloric intake cause a significant reduction in percent body fat.

MINOR RISK FACTORS

Diabetes mellitus (commonly called diabetes) is a condition in which blood glucose (sugar) is inhibited from entering the cell. This condition is created because the pancreas either stops producing insulin or does not produce enough insulin to meet the body's needs or because the body cannot use insulin. As a result, blood glucose absorption by the cells is low, leading to high blood glucose levels. Long-term complications involving the eyes, kidneys, nerves, and blood vessels result from this condition. The risk of heart disease is quite high in the diabetic population. Over 80 percent of diabetics die of heart disease.

Blood glucose levels above 120 milligrams per deciliter are considered to be a sign of diabetes and should be brought to the attention of a physician. Values between 121 and 159 milligrams per deciliter are considered to be borderline high, while values above 160 milligrams per deciliter are high. Other signs and symptoms of diabetes include excessive urination, excessive thirst, unsatisfied hunger, weight loss, cessation of growth among the young, irritability, and drowsiness.

When individuals are subjected to stressful conditions, they experience an increase in catecholamines (stress hormones), which in turn elevates heart rate, blood pressure, and blood glucose levels. This is commonly referred to as the fight-or-flight response because the body is preparing to either fight or flee. If the person takes action, either fights or flees, the catecholamines are metabolized and the body returns to its normal state. However, if a person is under constant stress because of the death of a relative or friend, loss of employment, marital troubles, or any other of a number of circumstances, catecholamine levels stay elevated and so do blood pressure, heart rate, and blood glucose.

Individuals who are unable to relax have a constant stress applied to the cardiovascular system. Eventually, this strain could lead to heart disease. Developing day-to-day coping skills and the ability to deal with work and social stressors are important ingredients to a healthy life. Exercise is one of the best ways to relieve the symptoms of stress. When an individual exercises, the body metabolizes excess catecholamines and the cardiovascular system is able to return to its normal state.

Cardiovascular disease is the leading killer of both men and women. However, death rates are three times higher for men than for women during the middle decades of life. Even at younger ages, women are not as prone to heart disease as men are. After age fifty-five, however, this disparity drops dramatically. Moreover, when heart attacks occur in women, they are more deadly than for men: 39 percent of women who have heart attacks die within a year, compared to 31 percent of men. After age sixty-five, this disparity grows, because women who have heart attacks are twice as likely to die as men are.

Levels of HDL cholesterol are the protective factors causing younger women to be at lower risk for heart disease. HDL helps clear the arteries of disease-causing plaque, thus lowering heart disease risk. Because of high estrogen levels, women naturally produce about 20 percent more HDL cholesterol than men do. After the menopause, estrogen levels decrease, causing a drop in HDL. Consequently, women experience a greater risk for heart disease. Estrogen replacement therapy after the menopause can help maintain HDL levels; with supplemental estrogen, however, comes a higher risk for cancer. It is always advisable for women who are considering estrogen supplementation to visit with a physician.

Even though heredity plays a role in the development of heart disease, the role is much less than most people think. People with a family history of heart disease are more likely to develop disease than people with no family history, but it is not clear why this is the case. Most people think that it is obvious—genetics is the reason—but to date, no gene has been identified as a carrier of heart disease. The saying that people turn into their parents is probably true and may be the answer to why heredity plays a role. It should be remembered, however, that most people inherit a lifestyle from their parents. If the parents are sedentary, then it is more than likely that their children are too. In addition, people develop a taste for the foods that they eat as youths. If the family meals consist of high-fat, high-calorie foods, then these foods are the choice of the children as they grow into adults.

Persons with a family history of heart disease need to monitor the other risk factors closely. Maybe more important, these people need to examine the lifestyle of their family members who have suffered from heart disease and make lifestyle modifications to reduce their risk.

As a person becomes older, the risk of heart disease increases. Other factors such as less physical activity, obesity, and poor nutrition may be partly responsible for this increased risk with aging. Evidence demonstrates that a fit individual at age fifty, sixty, or even seventy is at a lower risk for heart disease than unfit individuals of younger years. It is important to think in terms of physiological age instead of chronological age when determining heart disease risk. Risk factor management and positive lifestyle habits are the best means for slowing down physiological aging.

African American men and women are at greater risk for heart disease. African Americans are almost one-third more likely to have high blood pressure compared to Americans of Caucasian ancestry. Latinos are also more likely to have high blood pressure and to suffer from other forms of heart disease. Historically, Asian Americans have exhibited lower rates of heart disease than Caucasian Americans. Data show, however, that heart disease is on the rise in this population, presumably owing to their adoption of the American lifestyle.

SUMMARY

All the major risk factors for heart disease are controllable. A person with a family history of heart disease is not doomed to develop the disease as well. Preventive medicine is the key to reducing the development of heart disease. It is evident that lifestyle habits largely determine susceptibility. Most physicians agree that eating a healthy diet low in fat and high in complex carbohydrates, exercising regularly, quitting smoking, maintaining proper body composition, and developing effective ways to handle stress does more to improve health than anything medicine could do. Heart disease is typically caused by a neglect in lifestyle, which can be reversed. What is required is a commitment to develop habits that contribute to total well-being.

—*Gary L. Oden*

See also African Americans; Cholesterol; Diabetes; Exercise and fitness; Heart attacks; Heart changes and disorders; Hypertension; Latinos; Nutrition; Obesity; Smoking; Stress and coping skills; Strokes; Weight loss and gain.

FOR FURTHER INFORMATION:

American Heart Association. *Heart and Stroke Facts.* Dallas: Author, 1996. A collection of statistics focusing on cardiovascular disease.

Fahey, T. D., P. M. Insel, and W. T. Roth. *Fit and Well: Core Concepts and Labs in Physical Fitness and Wellness.* 2d ed. Mountain View, Calif.: Mayfield, 1997. A textbook focusing on healthy lifestyle choices.

Hoeger, W. K., and S. A. Hoeger. *Lifetime Physical Fitness and Wellness: A Personalized Program.* 5th ed. Englewood, Colo.: Morton, 1998. This textbook concentrates on health and fitness topics.

Hyman, W. V., et al. *Fitness for Living.* Dubuque, Iowa: Kendall/Hunt, 1999. A textbook focusing on the role of exercise and nutrition in disease prevention.

Nieman, D. C. *Fitness and Sports Medicine: A Health-Related Approach.* 3d ed. Palo Alto, Calif.: Bull, 1995. This textbook focuses on cardiovascular disease risk factors and how to modify heart disease risk.

HIGH BLOOD PRESSURE. *See* HYPERTENSION.

HIP REPLACEMENT

RELEVANT ISSUES: Health and medicine
SIGNIFICANCE: Total hip replacement is one of the most common elective surgical procedures chosen by adults over the age of sixty-five

Total hip replacement is one of the most common surgical interventions that older adults face. The American Academy of Orthopedic Surgeons estimates that more than 120,000 hip replacement surgeries are performed in the United States each year. The average age of the patient who undergoes hip replacement surgery is sixty-seven years, while 67 percent of total hip replacements are performed on individuals age sixty-five or older. Approximately 60 percent of hip replacement surgeries are performed on women.

REASONS FOR HIP REPLACEMENT

The most common reason for hip replacement surgery is the decline in efficiency of the hip joint that often results from osteoarthritis. Osteoarthritis is a common form of arthritis that causes joint and bone deterioration, which may lead to the wearing down of cartilage and cause the underlying bones to rub against each other. This may result in severe pain and stiffness in the affected areas. Other conditions that may lead to the need for hip replacement include rheumatoid arthritis (a chronic inflammation of the joints), avascular necrosis (loss of bone caused by insufficient blood supply), and injury.

Generally, physicians may be more inclined to choose less invasive techniques such as physical therapy, medication, or walking aids before resorting to surgery. In some cases, exercise programs may help reduce hip pain. In addition, if preliminary treatment does not improve the patient's condition, doctors may use corrective surgery that is not as invasive as hip replacement. However, when these efforts do not reduce pain or increase mobility, hip replacement may be the best option. In addition, the age of the patient may be an important factor in the decision to replace the hip. The majority of hip replacements are performed on individuals over the age of sixty-five. One of the reasons for this is that the activity level of older adults is lower than that of younger adults, therefore reducing the concern that the new hip will wear out or fail. However, technological advances have improved the quality of the artificial hip, making hip replacement surgery a more likely intervention for younger adults as well.

TOTAL HIP REPLACEMENT SURGERY

Generally, a candidate for total hip replacement surgery (THR) possesses a hip that has worn out from arthritis, falls, or other conditions. The hip consists of a ball-and-socket joint where the head of the femur (thigh bone) fits into the hip socket, or acetabulum. In a normal hip, this arrangement provides for a relatively wide range of motion. For some older adults, however, deterioration caused by arthritis and other conditions reduces the effectiveness of this arrangement, compromising the integrity of the hip socket or the femoral head. This state can lead to extreme discomfort.

Total hip replacement may provide the best long-term relief for these symptoms. Total hip replacement involves the removal of diseased bone

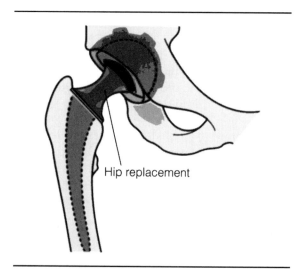

Hip replacement

The hip joint can be replaced by a metal or plastic ball-and-socket prosthesis when disease or injury is too extensive to repair the existing joint. (Hans & Cassidy, Inc.)

tissue and the replacement of that tissue with prostheses (artificial devices used to replace missing body parts). Usually, both the femoral head and hip socket are replaced. The femoral head is replaced with a metal ball that is attached to a metal stem and placed into the hollow marrow space of the femur. The hip socket is lined with a plastic socket. Other materials have been used effectively as hip replacements.

In some cases, the surgeon will use cement to bond the artificial parts of the new hip to the bone tissue. This approach has been the traditional method of ensuring that the artificial parts hold. One problem with this method is that over time, cemented hip replacements may lose their bond with the bone tissue. This may result in the need for an additional surgery. However, a cementless hip replacement has been developed. This approach includes a prosthesis that is porous so that bone tissue may grow into the metal pores and keep the prosthesis in place.

Both procedures have strengths and weaknesses. In general, recovery time may be shorter with cemented prostheses since one does not have to wait for bone growth to attach to the artificial prostheses. However, the potential for long-term deterioration of the replaced hip must be considered. A cemented hip generally lasts about fifteen years. With this in mind, physicians may be more likely to use a cemented prosthesis for patients over the age of seventy. Cementless hip replacement may be more advisable for younger and more active patients. Some physicians have used a combination of approaches, known as a "hybrid" or "mixed" hip. This combination relies on an uncemented socket and a cemented femoral head.

COMPLICATIONS AND RECOVERY

Total hip replacements are generally quite successful, with about 96 percent of surgeries proceeding without complications. In rare instances, however, complications occur, including blood clots and infections during surgery, and hip dislocation or bone fracture after surgery. In addition, in some cases, bone grafts may be used to assist in the restoration of bone defects. In these instances, bone may be obtained from the pelvis or the discarded head of the femur. Other postoperative complications may include some pain and stiffness.

Patients recovering from total hip replacement

usually remain in the hospital up to ten days if there are no complications. However, physical therapists may initiate therapy as soon as the day after surgery. Physical therapy involves the use of exercises that will improve recovery. Many patients are able to sit on the edge of their bed, stand, and even walk with assistance as early as two days after surgery. Patients must remember that their artificial hip may not provide the same full range of motion as an undiseased hip. Physical therapists teach patients how to perform daily activities without placing an undue burden on their new hips. This may require learning a new method of sitting, standing, and performing other activities.

While many factors may affect recovery time, full recovery from surgery may take up to six months. At that point, many patients enjoy such activities as walking and swimming. Doctors and physical therapists may discourage patients from participating in such high-impact activities as jogging or playing tennis, which may burden the new hip. Despite these restrictions, many patients are able to perform normal activities without pain and discomfort. Nonetheless, people who have undergone hip replacement surgery are advised to consult with their doctor about proper exercise and activity levels.　　　　　　　—*H. David Smith*

See also Arthritis; Bone changes and disorders; Canes and walkers; Mobility problems.

FOR FURTHER INFORMATION:

Baron, John A., Jane Barrett, Jeffrey Katz, and Matthew H. Liang. "Total Hip Arthroplasty: Use and Select Complication in the U.S. Medicare Population." *The American Journal of Public Health* 86, no. 1 (January, 1996).

Best, A. J., D. Fender, W. M. Harper, A. W. McCaskie, K. Oliver, and P. J. Gregg. "Current Practice in Primary Total Hip Replacement: Results from the National Hip Replacement Project." *Annals of the Royal College of Surgeons of England* 80, no. 5 (1998).

Bucholz, Robert, and Joseph A. Buckwalter. "Orthopedic Surgery." *JAMA: The Journal of the American Medical Association* 275, no. 23 (June 19, 1996).

Callaghan, John J. "A Seventy-Six-Year-Old Woman Considering Total Hip Replacement." *JAMA: The Journal of the American Medical Association* 276, no. 6 (August 14, 1996).

Duffey, Timothy P., Elliott Hershman, Richard A. Sanders, and Lori D. Talarico. "Investigating the Subtle and Obvious Causes of Hip Pain." *Patient Care* 31, no. 18 (November 15, 1997).

Dunkin, Mary Anne. "Hip Replacement Surgery." *Arthritis Today* 12, no. 2 (March/April, 1998).

Finerman, Gerald A. M. *Total Hip Arthroplasty Outcomes.* New York: Churchill Livingstone, 1998.

Hubers, Michael J., Constantine A. Toumbis, Sam Nasser, Lawrence Pottenger, and John Callaghan. "Informing Patients About Total Hip Replacement." *JAMA: The Journal of the American Medical Association* 276, no. 23 (December 18, 1996).

MacWilliam, Cynthia H., Marianne U. Yood, James J. Verner, Bruce D. McCarthy, and Richard E. Ward. "Patient-Related Risk Factors That Predict Poor Outcome After Total Hip Replacement." *Health Services Research* 31, no. 5 (December, 1996).

Orbell, Sheila, Arthur Espley, Marie Johnston, and David Rowley. "Health Benefits of Joint Replacement Surgery for Patients with Osteoarthritis: Prospective Evaluation Using Independent Assessments in Scotland." *Journal of Epidemiology & Community Health* 52, no. 9 (1998).

HISPANIC AMERICANS. *See* **LATINOS.**

HOME OWNERSHIP

RELEVANT ISSUES: Economics, family, sociology
SIGNIFICANCE: Racial identity and life events such as change in marital status, degree of economic success, number of children, income, and employment history may all be determining factors affecting home ownership in the later years, since all these factors may be reflected in the equity that resides in the home

Equity is a resource that may be managed to enable the older person to spend his or her later years in greater comfort. Home ownership enables the older citizen to provide for his or her senior years, to feel emotionally secure in a changing world, and to leave a legacy to loved ones. Psychological well-being is an important aspect of home ownership, as is economic self-sufficiency. Yet, many older citizens, although homeowners, live on the edge of poverty.

BACKGROUND

If the American Dream can in any way be quantified, it must certainly be through the possibility, and for many people the reality, of owning one's own home. This dream goes back to the founding of the United States, as well as of other countries on the American continent. The earliest settlers were often persons disenfranchised in their country of origin, and the new possibility of acquiring land and a home—whether through homesteading, cash payment, or inheritance—was one of the features of the New World that promised a decent living and a secure future.

Over time, and with the gradually increasing value of real estate, new options and new burdens have accompanied the original vision of home ownership, the chief of these being the long-term mortgage. While for many younger persons, the decision and financial obligations involved in the buying of a home are daunting at best, for the older citizen who owns a home, the advantages of owning real property are considerable. This fact is reflected in the constantly accelerating rates of home ownership for persons over sixty-five during the second half of the twentieth century, when the rate of home ownership slowly but steadily increased in spite of fluctuations in cost of living, increases in the cost of real estate, and demographic changes. In fact, demographic changes such as projections of increasing numbers of immigrants, many of whom were denied the American Dream of home ownership in their countries of origin, may bring increased numbers of older citizens into the homeowner category once they are able to realize this dream. It is also the case that neighborhoods in which most of the residents are homeowners are likely to be more desirable places to live from the standpoint of safety and convenience.

THE MONETARY ANGLE

It is a truism that owning real estate, particularly a home, is a hedge against inflation. Mortgages at a fixed interest rate, particularly a low rate, mean that housing costs remain stable, even when all other living costs may rise. For those elderly persons who purchased a home during their working years, this often means that by the time they retire, they pay much less for living in the family home than they would pay for comparable rental housing. For those persons fortunate enough to have paid off a mortgage, this cost may be limited to property tax, utilities, and maintenance. Since even a modest house may represent considerable monetary value, a person living in such a situation may seem to be in an enviable position.

It is also often the case, however, that older retired workers have an income greatly reduced from that previously enjoyed during their working life. Therefore, the retired or older citizen may live in a house that is really beyond his or her means in terms of the overall cost of living and may find that other desires, such as travel and social expenditures, must be forgone.

Various options exist for managing this situation. One option is to sell the house, invest the proceeds, and use that money as a form of income. This option has been enhanced by changes in the capital gains taxation structure, which allows for the sheltering of profit from the sale of a principal residence from capital gains tax. The drawback of selling the home, however, is that it removes what may be the older person's greatest equity resource from any future use. On a practical level, however, many older homeowners may decide to sell a house that has suddenly become bigger than they need, purchase a smaller one, and use the profit to finance other goals. Another financial stratagem that has become available to older homeowners is the reverse mortgage, which allows the older person to continue living in the family home for as long as wished while drawing upon the equity over time. This financial instrument was instituted in the 1980's for homeowners over sixty-two years of age. Although repayment is not required until the homeowner no longer occupies the home, this could easily mean that no value would remain in the home at that point. Other options might include sharing the home with former family members, returning children, or acquaintances needing temporary or permanent shelter. This may be of particular benefit for older persons who require care or need help in maintenance of the home.

THE PSYCHOLOGICAL ANGLE

The common-law tenet that "A man's home is his castle" is more than an outworn legal maxim. For many people, and particularly the elderly, the most important factor about continuing to be a

Ownership of a house can provide seniors with a base for a home business in their retirement years. (James L. Shaffer)

homeowner is a psychological and sociological one. While a younger person may enjoy the freedom of feeling geographically unattached, with increasing age often comes a desire for greater permanence, particularly in relation to place. The Irish poet William Butler Yeats described this as the desire for a "dear, perpetual place," a refuge that does not seem so affected by the inevitable changes that life brings.

When one adds to this preference for "aging in place" the memories that accumulate in the course of many years spent in a house, perhaps surrounded by loving family members or friends, pets, and acquaintances, the prospect of leaving to live in an alien space can be quite chilling. These are personal considerations that may outweigh some imagined financial advantage or tax break. It is not

surprising then that statistical studies of homeowner attitudes reveal a decided preference for home ownership among older persons, who are understandably reluctant to uproot themselves.

A further psychological factor that affects home ownership among the elderly is simply fear of the unknown, which may be considerable for someone who has lived as a homeowner in a particular neighborhood for many years. The feeling that one is in control of one's own environment, particularly in the United States, depends to a great extent on the same factors that are also operative in home ownership: the ability to suit one's surroundings to one's own liking, the feeling of autonomy that comes with living in a neighborhood that has become familiar, or the freedom to make choices about living arrangements.

FAMILY MATTERS

It is not uncommon for American families to disperse once the children leave home. It is also not unusual, however, for children to have concerns about the housing and welfare of their parents in their later years or even to have some unexpected housing needs themselves. Concern about elderly parents is often reflected in decisions about home ownership because of problems of mobility, medical care of ailing elders, or the high costs of alternative care. All these factors enter into the consideration of whether continued home ownership is the best solution to the housing of older family members. The sheer number of older Americans in the baby-boom generation reaching retirement age and beyond guarantees that this situation will persist for the foreseeable future.

Added to this situation is the desire of many older persons with families to leave the fruits of their efforts to their loved ones. With ownership of the family home representing a large portion of the inheritable property of many older persons, this is a matter that becomes of material concern and affects the upcoming generation as well.

—Gloria Fulton

See also Caregiving; Empty nest syndrome; Estates and inheritance; Family relationships; Full nest; Home services; Housing; Income sources; Independent living; Multigenerational households; Nursing and convalescent homes; Retirement planning; Safety issues.

FOR FURTHER INFORMATION:

Carlin, Vivian F. *Can Mom Live Alone? Practical Advice on Helping Aging Parents Stay in Their Own Home.* Lexington, Mass.: Lexington Books, 1991.

Gold, Margaret. *Guide to Housing Alternatives for Older Citizens.* Mount Vernon, N.Y.: Consumer Reports Books, 1985.

Johnson, James A. *Showing America a New Way Home: Expanding Opportunities for Home Ownership.* San Francisco: Jossey-Bass, 1996.

Katsura, Harold M., Raymond J. Struyk, and Sandra J. Newman. *Housing for the Elderly in 2010: Projections and Policy Options.* Washington, D.C.: Urban Institute Press, 1989.

Low, Setha M., and Erve Chambers, eds. *Housing, Culture, and Design: A Comparative Perspective.* Philadelphia: University of Pennsylvania Press, 1989.

HOME SERVICES

RELEVANT ISSUES: Family, health and medicine, sociology

SIGNIFICANCE: Home services include many things, such as home maintenance, shopping, companions, equipment, skilled nursing visits, physical therapy, and hospice care; these services are offered in a variety of ways, both public and private

The advantages to assisting the older adult to stay in his or her own home are many. There are obvious benefits to the individual's own independence and sense of well-being. Less obvious are benefits to the community, such as the economic benefits from taxes being paid and shopping in local businesses. The older adult is usually a law-abiding person who contributes to the stability of a neighborhood. Society benefits when nursing home placement is delayed because of the expenses incurred. Often, older adults need only a few services to keep them in their own homes.

One common way older adults receive home services is from family members. This works well in an extended family arrangement, but many times this system is inadequate and the caregiver experiences fatigue and frustration. Systems to support family caregivers are slow in coming and have many needs to address. The basic maintenance and custodial supports that can assist people to meet their goal of living at home as they age are many times unavailable or unaffordable. Several volunteer programs have developed to fill the gap that older adults and their families experience.

Three such programs are the Healthy Seniors Project, Interfaith Volunteer Caregivers, and the Living at Home/Block Nurse Program. These programs were chosen because they function in several areas of the United States and each represents a slightly different approach to care of the older adult.

The Healthy Seniors Project is a neighborhood-based nurse case-management model. There are award-winning sites in Arizona, Illinois, New York, and Minnesota. This project is a partnership between community-health nurses and an established health care facility. They work together to establish health care services in a specific neighborhood to serve the Medicare population. The community is involved through volunteer recruitment and training. Some services are included that Medicare does not reimburse, such as wellness care, respite care, custodial and maintenance services, and friendly visits and phone calls.

The National Federation of Interfaith Volunteer Caregivers coordinated the start of Interfaith Volunteer Caregivers all over the United States. A toll-free call to headquarters in Kingston, New York, will provide any "church" group (regardless of religion) with the information, support, and material needed to start its own program. Members of the church volunteer to be partnered with a person needing help. Services are provided to all age groups, without regard to insurance, religion, or specific need. The primary focus is support services (lawn work, baby-sitting, transportation, shopping), but when health care professionals are among the volunteers, they do participate in some direct care activities.

The Living at Home/Block Nurse Program starts with a steering committee from within the community whose members discuss and define the needs and capabilities of the community. The focus is to provide the coordinated care that would meet the individual needs of each older adult in the designated "block" (community). This typically includes social support, health education, prevention-oriented intervention, support for daily living needs, and custodial and maintenance care. This essential care is provided regardless of insurance coverage or the ability to pay. Enhancing the ability of the family to meet the needs of its own members and organizing community support when the family is not available are the cornerstones of the Living at Home/ Block Nurse Program. This program is funded by local fundraisers, local donations, grants, and some government funding where available.

Churches may provide some in-home services to their members. Large churches often have a person dedicated to community outreach programs. Nonmembers may find that a local church might be able to provide leads on individuals in the community who provide sitter or domestic service in homes, although reference checks are the responsibility of the person doing the hiring. If there is a college or university in the area, its social work or nursing department can be a source for temporary help (nursing or social work students could make good temporary hired help). These departments might also be able to give referrals to other area agencies.

HOME HEALTH SERVICES

Private and public home health agencies are abundant. They provide health care services that are paid for by insurance carriers, state-funded reimbursement plans, and Medicare. In order to receive services, the older adult with Medicare or one of the Medicare options usually must require skilled services (a nurse with a license, physical therapy, speech or occupational therapy); require services intermittently (visits are about one hour each and usually not more than once a day, many times less often); be homebound (leave the home seldomly, only for medical purposes and with much difficulty); and have the services ordered by a physician.

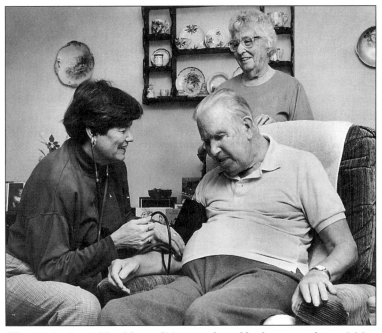

The monitoring of health conditions such as blood pressure by a visiting nurse is an example of an invaluable home service. (James L. Shaffer)

The services available through a home health agency are subject to change depending upon the latest federal regulations governing reimbursement. The most common reasons for home health services include education regarding new medications or a new diagnosis, dressing changes, diabetic care, severe cardiac or respiratory problems, and physical therapy following a stroke, fracture, or joint replacement.

Depression is prevalent among older adults. Psychiatric nursing care is available through many home health agencies when the other criteria for services are met. There are home health agencies that specialize in one specific type of care, such as psychiatric, ventilator-dependent, cardiac, or acquired immunodeficiency syndrome (AIDS) patients. The nurse or therapist in the home may make a referral for a home visit from a social worker. This is usually related to financial issues or the need for services that the home health agency cannot provide. Some home health agencies, especially those affiliated with church-related institutions, will provide chaplain visits, although there would likely be no reimbursement for such a visit.

While home health care patients are receiving skilled care, they may also be eligible for a home health aide to meet personal hygiene needs. This service may include bathing, shampoo, shaving, changing linen, and tidying the bedroom, bath, and kitchen area. The aide visits average between one to two hours and may be as often as daily for a person who is confined to bed. When the skilled need (services of a nurse or therapist) no longer exists, the aide visits cease also, regardless of continued personal hygiene needs.

HOSPICE CARE

Hospice care is a Medicare benefit and is also provided by many of the health maintenance organizations (HMOs). The National Hospice Organization (NHO) has developed general guidelines which direct and explain the services provided by most reputable hospice organizations. NHO guidelines directly affecting the client include palliative care (may include comfort measures up to and including surgical procedures) to all terminally ill people and their families with a focus on keeping terminally ill persons in their homes as long as possible; coordination of trained professionals and volunteers working together to meet the physiologic, psychologic, social, spiritual, and economic needs of the patient and family through illness and bereavement (this may be intermittent or continuous care); work with the physician for an individualized plan of care (may provide patient advocates to facilitate medical care); and availability of care twenty-four hours a day, seven days a week without interruption even if the care setting changes (it is possible to be admitted to a hospital and still maintain hospice status; rules for this type of admission include no curative treatment).

Hospice care provides pain control, needed physical maintenance, and the opportunity to die at home but not alone. The family is supported during the dying process and continues to receive supportive services after the death of a loved one. Life and death are made as meaningful and humane as possible.

PUBLIC SERVICES

Most communities have an organization dedicated to the needs of older adults. The services provided vary but often include transportation, home cleaning, and meals-on-wheels. These services are provided by volunteers and paid employees with money from grants and the government. Funding may vary year to year and therefore affect the services provided.

The local public hospital can furnish information about the services it provides, which may include home services. Public health departments differ considerably in the services they provide. Many times, home health care services are available, but some public health departments concentrate their efforts on women and children. Some public health departments will make home visits only in a crisis situation.

PRIVATE HOME SERVICES

There are agencies that specialize in providing home services not covered any other way; for example, all-night or all-day sitters, private duty nurses, or extended respite care. These agencies are listed in the phone book under "nurses." They may or may not be connected with a home health agency. It is wise to ask for references and check with the Better Business Bureau before hiring in-home help through such an agency. There are many well-managed, reputable agencies available.

Home delivery of goods is a service that home-bound older adults need. Many pharmacies and most medical supply companies will deliver to a home. Grocery stores are also beginning to deliver. Catalog and on-line shopping present other ways to receive goods at home. Beauticians, barbers, and massage therapists are available for in-home service.

IN-HOME EQUIPMENT

In many cases, all older adults need to maintain independence in their own home is specialized equipment. This can range from a bedside commode to supplemental oxygen obtainable from a durable medical equipment (DME) company. Needed equipment is often covered by Medicare or the HMO options. A physician's order and documented need are required. Some items require special testing. For example, to obtain oxygen for home use, the oxygen in the blood must be below a certain level before the expense will be covered. If a client is receiving home health services, that agency can facilitate obtaining needed equipment.

Besides the obvious equipment such as wheelchairs, shower chairs, walkers, and hospital beds, there are types of equipment for more specialized use. For example, sometimes a very simple alteration in eating utensils or scoopdishes can make a person able to feed himself or herself again. There are devices to enable a person to dress independently, such as a button hook, zipper pull, dressing stick, hip sock aide, and reacher.

SERVICES BY SPECIFIC ORGANIZATIONS

There are special-interest organizations that provide goods and services for in-home use. Lighthouse for the Blind will provide books on tape for the blind or when holding a book or turning pages is impossible. Many of these groups maintain Web sites that can be accessed easily through most search engines. The local library can assist in this referral also. The Arthritis Foundation operates chapters in many cities. They provide education, equipment, and services and can be found in the phone book. Any time there is a specific medical diagnosis, it is wise to look for an organization whose primary goal is devoted to that problem. The local library or the social worker department in the local hospital will be able to assist with a list of services specific to a given community. Many cit-

ies have published manuals of groups in the area, including the services they provide, addresses and phone numbers, and fees for service.

The challenge of finding needed services is great. If older adults do not have family members or very close friends to help in the search process, it can be overwhelming to an already compromised individual. People without families would be well advised to develop an extended family of friends within their neighborhood or "church" family before a dire need arises.

—*Penny Wolfe Moore*

See also Canes and walkers; Caregiving; Communication; Disabilities; Friendship; Health care; Home ownership; Hospice; Housing; Independent living; Meals-on-wheels programs; Medicare; Psychiatry, geriatric; Religion; Transportation issues; Wheelchair use.

FOR FURTHER INFORMATION:

Able, E., and M. Nelson. *Circles of Care: Work and Identity in Women's Lives.* Albany: State University of New York Press, 1990. Discusses family caregiving in a sensitive and compassionate way; very supportive reading for caregivers.

Brickner, Philip, ed. *Geriatric Home Health Care: The Collaboration of Physicians, Nurses, and Social Workers.* New York: Springer, 1997. A general text covering many aspects of in-home care of the older adult.

Ferrini, Armeda, and Rebecca Ferrini. *Health in the Later Years.* Dubuque, Iowa: Brown and Benchmark, 1993. Discusses the expected changes in the aging process, possible complications, and suggested interventions, including in-home services that may be needed.

Kellogg Foundation. *Timely Opportunities: What Works in Community Care for the Elderly.* Battle Creek, Mich.: EPI Printing, 1995. A collection of reports from groups that provide services to the older adult including phone numbers, addresses, and other pertinent contact information.

Mason, Diana, and Judith Leavitt. *Policy and Politics in Nursing and Health Care.* Philadelphia: W. B. Saunders, 1998. Covers all the political and government issues that contribute to the in-home services that are and are not available.

Sulmasy, Daniel, and Joanne Lynn. "End-of-Life Care." *Journal of the American Medical Association*

277, no. 23 (June, 1997). Reports the current condition of end-of-life care, including resources and recommended actions for improvement.

HOMELESSNESS

RELEVANT ISSUES: Demographics, family, health and medicine, sociology

SIGNIFICANCE: The growing problem of homelessness among older adults is a significant national issue, which until very recently received little attention

Homelessness has become one of the most prevalent problems in the United States, and indeed, the world. According to researchers, however, to many, "homelessness" is a term that conjures up a distant and misunderstood issue. Nevertheless, homelessness is a reality in nearly every large city in America.

PROBLEM OF HOMELESSNESS AMONG THE ELDERLY

Many among the growing homeless population are older adults who, prior to the 1980's, have been largely ignored by public social service agencies. Gerontologists attribute this lack of attention to the problems and identification of the homeless to misconceptions and stereotypes about the older homeless as a group. Yet older adults are increasingly vulnerable to homelessness due to the declining availability of affordable housing as well as to increased poverty among specific segments of the elderly population. Findings from a 1996 study released by the United States Department of Housing and Urban Development revealed that of the 5.3 million households experiencing "worst case housing needs," 1.2 million were headed by an elderly person. Additionally, almost half of the low-income elderly renters who receive no public assistance were identified as having the "worst case housing needs."

Moreover, the proportion of older adults in the homeless population has been reported by some studies as between 2.5 percent and 19.4 percent for persons in the fifty-five- to sixty-year-old age group. Other studies that traditionally included only elderly men over the age of sixty-five note the percent of elderly homeless as 3 percent of the general homeless population. Since persons over sixty-five years of age make up 12 percent of the national population, there are fewer older-aged homeless than there should be. Three reasons account for this shortage of homeless persons over age sixty-five: Homeless persons may only rarely survive to age sixty-five; the homeless over sixty-five are undercounted because of their reluctance to stay in shelters; and Medicare and Social Security entitlements become available to people once they turn sixty-five. Despite variances in the numbers recorded for the population of the elderly, among them are those who have recently become homeless, some who have lived on the street most of their adult lives, and others who are in danger of becoming homeless due to housing displacement. Overall, the proportion of older persons among the homeless population has declined over the last twenty years, but their absolute number has grown.

CHARACTERISTICS OF THE ELDERLY HOMELESS

Many of the elderly homeless have problems similar to those in the general low-income elderly population: inability to work because of physical conditions and chronic health and dental problems. Still others have experienced domestic violence or abuse, are substance abusers, or suffer from mental illnesses, especially elderly women who are homeless. Impoverished, single, middle-aged women without children or disabilities are also among the ranks of the older homeless adults. This group of homeless women are members of the newly emerging group of older adults who have fallen through the cracks of the social welfare system. These women do not qualify for public assistance for a number of reasons. Some are unable to maintain jobs because of their lack of skills or because of disabilities, yet the disabilities are not severe enough to qualify them for public benefits; and some are single without children or disabilities and thus do not qualify for subsidized housing.

Elderly homeless men are more likely to abuse drugs or be long-term alcoholics who started drinking early in life but survived despite associated medical and social complications. Some continue to drink, while others fall victim to medical complications of alcoholism. Some in the general elderly homeless population are "skid row bums" as well as alcoholics, drug addicts, and people who have not planned for old age, but some do not fit into these categories. Rather, they are individuals who because of loss of job, divorce, death of a spouse, or other reasons find themselves unable to maintain their independence in traditional housing on a continual basis. Some of the elderly homeless also work; however, their paychecks are inadequate to cover the spiraling cost of room rent or other housing. Since the 1980's, minorities and women have become a disproportionate segment of the homeless.

INATTENTION TO THE ELDERLY HOMELESS PROBLEM

In the late 1990's, as a group, older Americans occupied 21 percent of the country's 88 million residential dwellings. They also made up two out of every five low-income households nationwide. Increasingly, the elderly are being forced to move from the cheap single rooms that they once called home. Most of these elderly are entitled to Social Security benefits, but even the benefits are inadequate to cover housing costs. Further complicating the problem is the fact that some homeless older persons are unaware of their eligibility for public assistance and face even greater difficulties getting through the bureaucratic web and acquiring their benefits. A 1990 study by the National Law Center on Homelessness and Poverty found that in some parts of the United States, less than 10 percent of eligible homeless persons receive Social Security. With less financial resources to pay for food, health care, and medical costs, the elderly are especially vulnerable to homelessness.

Moreover, older adults who are homeless often find shelters and programs inadequate to accommodate their needs. The shelters usually provide for short-term stays based on the assumption that job-training programs and other types of assistance will enable homeless patrons to leave the shelters and move on into better situations. Poor health or mental disabilities prevent most older homeless persons from qualifying for training programs. Further, the lack of stable environments or other related complications prevent the elderly from obtaining needed assistance. The homeless problem is exacerbated even more due to the lack of social service programs available to those in their early fifties. The middle-aged older homeless are therefore often left to survive as best they can, especially unskilled alcoholics and the mentally ill.

Several factors contributed to the lack of attention to the issues of elderly homeless in the past.

First, the elderly homeless were viewed as responsible for their own condition or situation. Second, due to hearing problems, mental illnesses, and chronic health problems, older persons were viewed as difficult clients and thus shunned or brushed aside. Priority for limited financial resources and assistance was often diverted to younger, single homeless persons and homeless families with children because they were perceived as being more salvageable. As the population of homeless grows, agencies that service the elderly have begun to give some significance to their needs and problems.

RESPONSE TO ELDERLY HOMELESSNESS

Many of the federal programs designed to ease the misery of homeless people and lift them out of poverty were either cut or failed to keep pace with the cost of living during the 1980's. Likewise, unsubsidized low-rent housing declined as many "single room occupancy" (SROs) hotels were torn down in numerous large cities across the nation.

Alcoholism, poverty, mental impairment, and lack of social support are among the causes of homelessness for the elderly. (James L. Shaffer)

These SROs traditionally provided cheap rental housing for many in the elderly homeless population.

The housing crisis, together with major federal budget cuts in programs designed to assist the homeless, motivated many segments of society to respond to the homeless problem. In 1993, Henry Cisneros, secretary of the Department of Housing and Urban Development (HUD), unveiled a model program to end homelessness in large cities. The program recognized that homelessness was broader than previous studies acknowledged. State and local agencies, volunteer organizations, and coalitions from private and religious sectors developed additional initiatives to combat the homeless problem.

Among the programs implemented to assist the elderly homeless were Project Rescue in New York City and the Senior Reach Program in Chicago. Project Rescue serves older homeless adults with basic needs and health, depression, and alcohol abuse problems, as well as providing legal assistance to elderly persons at risk of being evicted. The Chicago Senior Reach Program provides resettlement for older adults, many of whom are distrustful of shelters and clinics.

Homelessness is not a new problem, but the extensiveness of homelessness exceeds anything experienced in this country in the last half-century. The last major outbreak occurred as a consequence of the worst economic crisis in American history; the current condition exists amid national prosperity. The homeless of today suffer a more severe form of housing deprivation than did the homeless of twenty or thirty years ago. Elderly homeless persons face additional perils of chronic health problems and mental illnesses. To prevent more elderly persons from becoming homeless, more low-income housing, income supplements, and health care services to support independent living must be provided. For older adults who are already homeless, comprehensive outreach health and social services must be implemented and special assistance given to help access public assistance programs. Elderly homeless persons also need sufficient incomes and affordable housing and health care to remain adequately housed.

—*Shirley Rhodes Nealy*

See also Alcoholism; Disabilities; Divorce; Home ownership; Housing; Job loss; Malnutrition; Mental impairment; Poverty; Singlehood; Widows and widowers.

FOR FURTHER INFORMATION:

Brickner, Philip W., Linda K. Scharer, Barbara Conanan, Marianne Savarese, and Brian Scanlan, eds. *Under the Safety Net: The Health and Social Welfare of the Homeless in the United States.* New York: W. W. Norton, 1990.

Butler, Sandra S. *Middle-Aged, Female, and Homeless: The Stories of a Forgotten Group.* New York: Garland, 1994.

Coates, Robert C. *A Street Is Not a Home.* New York: Prometheus Books, 1990.

Ladner, Susan. "The Elderly Homeless." In *Homelessness: A National Perspective,* edited by Marjorie Robertson and Milton Greenblatt. New York: Plenum Press, 1992.

Margolis, Richard J. *Risking Old Age in America.* Boulder, Colo.: Westview Press, 1990.

O'Connell, James J., Jean Summerfield, and F. Russell Kellogg. "The Homeless Elderly." In *Under the Safety Net: The Health and Social Welfare of the Homeless in the United States,* edited by Philip W. Brickner et al. New York: W. W. Norton, 1990.

Rich, Diane W., Thomas Rich, and Larry Mullins. *Old and Homeless—Double Jeopardy: An Overview of Practice and Policies.* Westport, Conn.: Auburn House, 1995.

Ropers, Richard H. *The Invisible Homeless: A New Urban Ecology.* Cedar City, Utah: Human Sciences Press, 1988.

HORMONE REPLACEMENT THERAPY. *See* **ESTROGEN REPLACEMENT THERAPY.**

HOSPICE

RELEVANT ISSUES: Death, family, health and medicine, sociology

SIGNIFICANCE: Hospice care is a holistic approach to caring for the dying and their families by addressing their physical, emotional, and spiritual needs

Hospice is a philosophy of care directed toward persons who are dying. Hospice care uses a family-oriented holistic approach to assist these individuals in making the transition from life to death in a manner that preserves their dignity and comfort.

This approach, as Elisabeth Kübler-Ross would say, allows dying patients "to live until they die." Hospice care encourages patients to participate fully in determining the type of care that is most appropriate for their comfort. By creating a secure and caring community sensitive to the needs of the dying and their families and by providing palliative care that relieves patients of the distressing symptoms of their disease, hospice care can aid the dying in preparing mentally as well as spiritually for their impending death.

Unlike traditional health care, where the patient is viewed as the client, hospice care with its holistic emphasis treats the family unit as the client. There are usually specific areas of stress for the families of the dying. In addition to the stress of caring for the physical needs of the dying, family members often feel tremendous pressure maintaining their own roles and responsibilities within the family itself. The conflict of caring for their own nuclear families while caring for dying relatives places a huge strain on everyone involved and can be a source of anxiety and guilt for the patient as well. Another area of stress experienced by family members involves concern for themselves, that is, having to put their own lives on hold, keeping from getting physically run down, dealing with their newly acquired time constraints, and viewing themselves as isolated from friends and family. Compounding this is the guilt that many caregivers feel over not caring for the dying relative as well or as patiently as they might, or secretly wishing for the caregiving experience to reach an end.

Due to the holistic nature of the care provided, the hospice team is actually an interdisciplinary team composed of physicians, nurses, psychological and social workers, pastoral counselors, and trained volunteers. This medically supervised team meets weekly to decide on how best to provide physical, emotional, and spiritual support for dying patients and to assist the surviving family members in the subsequent grieving process.

This type of care can be administered in three different ways. It can be home health-agency based, delivered in the patient's own home. It can be dispensed in an institution devoted solely to hospice care. It can even be administered in traditional medical facilities (such as hospitals) that allot a certain amount of space (perhaps a wing or floor, or even a certain number of beds) to this type of care. Fewer than 20 percent of hospices are totally independent and have no affiliation with one or more hospitals.

PRINCIPLES

Hospice care attempts to enhance the quality of dying patients' final days by providing them with as much comfort as possible. It is predicated on the belief that death is a natural process with which humans should not interfere. The principles of hospice care, therefore, revolve around alleviating the anxieties and physical suffering that can be associated with the dying process, and not prolonging the dying process by using invasive medical techniques. Hospice care is also based on the assertion that dying patients have certain rights that must be respected. These rights include a right to absent themselves from social responsibilities and commitments, a right to be cared for, and the right to continued respect and status. The following seven principles are basic components of hospice care.

The first principle is highly personalized and holistic care of the dying, which includes treating dying patients emotionally and spiritually as well as physically. This interpersonal support, known as bonding, helps patients in their final days to live as fully and as comfortably as possible, while retaining their dignity, autonomy, and individual self-worth in a safe and secure environment. This one-on-one attention involves what can be called therapeutic communication. Knowing that someone has heard, that someone understands and is concerned can be profoundly healing.

Another principle is treating pain aggressively. To this end, hospice care advocates the use of narcotics at a dosage that will alleviate suffering while, at the same time, enable patients to maintain a desired level of alertness. Efforts are made to employ the least invasive routes to administer these drugs (usually orally, if possible). In addition, pain medication is administered before the pain begins, thus alleviating the anxiety of patients waiting for pain to return. Since it has been shown that fear of pain often increases the pain itself, this type of aggressive pain management gives dying patients more time and energy to respond to family members and friends and to work through the emotional and spiritual stages of dying. This dispensation of pain medication before the pain actually occurs, however, has proven to be perhaps the most controversial element in hospice care, with some critics charging that the dying are being turned into drug addicts.

A third principle is the participation of families in caring for the dying. Family members are trained by hospice nurses to care for the dying patients and even to dispense pain medication. The aim is to prevent the patients from suffering isolation or feeling as if they are surrounded by strangers. Participation in care also helps to sustain the patients' and the families' sense of autonomy.

The fourth principle is familiarity of surroundings. Whenever possible, it is the goal of hospice care to keep dying patients at home. This eliminates the necessity of the dying to spend their final days in an institutionalized setting, isolated from family and friends when they need them the most. It is estimated that close to 90 percent of all hospice care days are spent in patients' own homes. When this is not possible and patients must enter institutional settings, rules are relaxed so that their rooms can be decorated or arranged in such a way as to replicate the patients' home surroundings. Visiting rules are suspended when possible, and visits by family members, children, and sometimes even pets are encouraged.

The fifth principle is emotional and spiritual support for the family caregivers. Hospice volunteers are specially trained to use listening and communicative techniques with family members and to provide them with emotional support both during and after the patient's death. In addition, because the care is holistic, the caregivers' physical needs are attended to (for example, respite is provided for exhausted caregivers), as are their emotional and spiritual needs. This spiritual support applies to people of all faith backgrounds, as impending death tends to put faith into a perspective where particular creeds and denominational structures assume less significance. In attending to this spiritual dimension, the hospice team is respectful of all religious traditions while realizing that death and bereavement have the ability to both strengthen and weaken faith.

The sixth principle is having hospice services available twenty-four hours a day, seven days a week. Because of its reliance on the assistance of trained volunteers, round-the-clock support is available to patients and their families.

The seventh principle is bereavement counseling for the survivors. At the time of death, the hospice team is available to help families take care of tasks such as planning the funeral and probating the will. In the weeks after the death, hospice volunteers offer their support to surviving family members in dealing with their loss and grief and the various phases of the bereavement process, always aware of the fact that not all bereaved need or want formal interventions.

History

The term "hospice" comes from the Latin *hospitia*, meaning "places of welcome." The earliest documented example of hospice care dates to the fourth century, when a Roman woman named Fabiola apparently used her own wealth to care for the sick and dying. In medieval times, the Catholic Church established inns for poor wayfarers and pilgrims traveling to religious shrines in search of miraculous cures for their illnesses. Such "rest homes," usually run by religious orders, provided both lodging and nursing care, since the medieval view was that the sick, dying, and needy were all travelers on a journey. This attitude also reflects the medieval notion that true hospitality included care of the mind and spirit as well as of the body. During the Protestant Reformation, when monasteries were forcibly closed, the concepts of hospice and hospital became distinct. Care of the sick and dying was now considered a public duty rather than a religious or private one, and many former hospices were turned into state-run hospitals.

The first in-patient hospice establishment of modern times (specifically called "hospice") was founded by Mary Aitkenhead and the Irish Sisters of Charity under her leadership in the 1870's in Dublin, Ireland. Cicely Saunders, a physician at St. Joseph's Hospice in London, which was founded by the English Sisters of Charity in 1908, began to adapt the ancient concept of hospice to modern palliative techniques. While there, Saunders became extremely close to a Holocaust survivor who was dying of cancer. She found that she shared his dream of establishing a place that would meet the needs of the dying. Using the money he bequeathed her at his death as a starting point, Saunders raised additional funds and opened St. Christopher's Hospice in Sydenham, outside London, in 1967. Originally it housed only cancer patients, but with the financial support of contracts with the National Health Service in England and private donations, it later expanded to meet the needs of all the dying. In fact, no patient was ever refused because of inability to pay. St. Christopher's served as a model for the hospices to be built later in other parts of the world.

Even though hospice care did not originate with Cicely Saunders, she is usually credited with founding the first modern hospice, since she introduced the concept of dispensing narcotics at regular intervals in order to preempt the pain of the dying. She was also the first to identify the need to address other, nonphysical sources of pain for dying patients.

Two years after St. Christopher's Hospice was opened, Kübler-Ross wrote *On Death and Dying*, which validated the hospice movement by relating stories of the dying and their wishes as to how they would be treated. In 1974, the United States opened its first hospice, Hospice, Inc. (later called the Connecticut Hospice), in New Haven, Connecticut. Within the next twenty-five years, over three thousand hospice programs would be implemented in the United States. In Canada, the first "palliative care" unit (as hospices are referred to in Canada) was opened in 1975 by Dr. Balfour M. Mount at the Royal Victoria Hospital in Montreal. This is considered to be the first hospital-based hospice in North America.

COST

Because of hospice care's reliance on heavily trained volunteers and contributions, and because death is seen as a natural process that should not be prolonged by invasive and expensive medical techniques, hospice care is much less costly than traditional acute care facilities. Because hospice care is a philosophy of care rather than a specific facility, though, legislation to provide monetary support for hospice patients took a great deal of time to be approved. In 1982, the U.S. Congress finally added hospice care as a Medicare benefit. In 1986, it was made a permanent benefit. Medicare requires, however, that there be a prognosis of six months or less for the patient to live. Hospice care is also reimbursable by many private insurance companies.

The National Hospice Organization (NHO) originated in 1977 in the United States as a re-source for the many groups across the country who needed assistance in establishing hospice programs in their own communities. The purpose of this organization is to provide information about hospice care to the public, to establish conduits so that information may be exchanged between hospice groups, and to maintain agreed-upon standards for developing hospices around the country. The NHO publishes *Guide to the Nation's Hospices* on an annual basis.   —*Mara Kelly-Zukowski*

See also Death and dying; Death of a child; Death of parents; Euthanasia; Family relationships; Funerals; Grief; Health care; Hospitalization; Kübler-Ross, Elisabeth; Medicare; Religion; Terminal illness; Widows and widowers.

FOR FURTHER INFORMATION:

Buckingham, Robert W. *The Handbook of Hospice Care.* New York: Prometheus Books, 1996. Covers the history and philosophy of hospice care while providing practical information as to its cost, how to find hospice programs in your own community, and how to manage grief. Focuses on two target populations for hospice care: children and AIDS victims.

Byock, Ira. *Dying Well: The Prospect for Growth at the End of Life.* New York: Riverhead Books, 1997. President of the American Academy of Hospice and Palliative Medicine at the time he wrote this book, Dr. Byock uses the personal stories of his patients to show the best ways to die. Provides information for the families of the dying who wish to make their loved ones' final days as comfortable and meaningful as possible.

Corr, Charles A., and Donna M. Corr, eds. *Hospice Care: Principles and Practice.* New York: Springer, 1983. A collection of salient essays on hospice care addressing issues ranging from the needs of the dying to the stress associated with caregiving to the terminally ill. Contributors include Cicely Saunders, physicians, hospice directors, psychologists, and chaplains.

Kübler-Ross, Elisabeth. *On Death and Dying.* New York: Macmillan, 1969. Landmark work which outlines the psychological stages of dying and the deficiencies in modern medicine's ability to care for dying patients in an appropriate manner.

Kutscher, Austin H., and Samuel C. Klagsbrun et al. *Hospice U.S.A.* New York: Columbia University Press, 1983. In addition to essays on the history and principles of hospice care, this book contains a few more unusual entries, such as essays dealing with senior citizens as hospice volunteers, the role of humor and laughter in quality of life and of care, and preserving sexuality and privacy in the dying.

Lattanzi-Licht, Marcia, John J. Mahoney, and Galen W. Miller. *The Hospice Choice: In Pursuit of a Peaceful Death.* New York: Simon & Schuster, 1998. Definitive resource from the National Hospice Organization. Provides practical information such as range of hospice services, methods of payment, and so on. Intersperses stories of families who have received hospice care with a thorough explanation of its history, principles, and benefits. Provides personal accounts of hospice nurses and volunteers with discussion of psychological and emotional responses to life-threatening illnesses.

Munley, Anne. *The Hospice Alternative: A New Context for Death and Dying.* New York: Basic Books,

1983. Examines hospice care from the perspective of its relationship to American society and gives accounts of hospice patients, family members, and caregivers in their day-to-day experience.

HOSPITALIZATION

RELEVANT ISSUES: Health and medicine

SIGNIFICANCE: The elderly are substantial users of inpatient hospital services. The number of hospital admissions for individuals sixty-five and over rises significantly with increasing age

In 1996, those aged sixty-five and over accounted for 38 percent of the admissions to nonfederal, acute care hospitals. Those aged forty-five through sixty-four accounted for 20 percent of all admissions. The average length of stay (ALOS) was 5.3 days for people forty-five through sixty-four and 6.5 days for those sixty-five and over. Although the major portion of inpatient services is provided in acute care community hospitals, elderly patients

Average Length of Stay in Non-Federal, Short Stay Hospitals

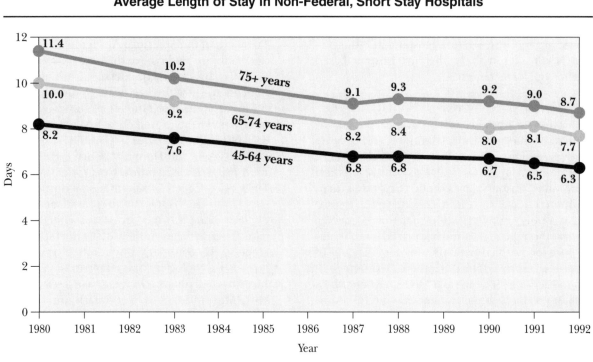

Source: Centers for Disease Control and Prevention, National Center for Health Statistics, National Hospital Discharge Survey.

Hospital Discharge Rates for Non-Federal, Short Stay Hospitals

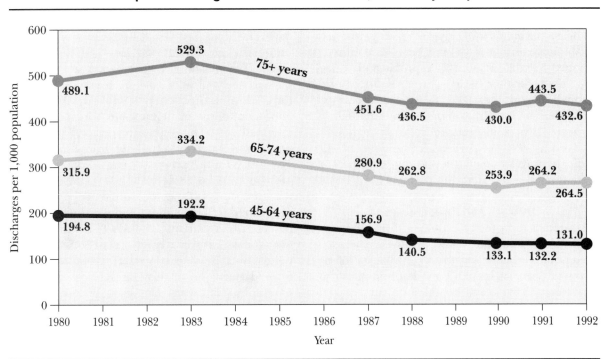

Source: Centers for Disease Control and Prevention, National Center for Health Statistics, National Hospital Discharge Survey.

may also receive inpatient services in hospitals operated by the Department of Veterans Affairs or in proprietary facilities such as psychiatric hospitals.

Approximately 97 percent of all hospital care in the United States is financed by third parties. The vast majority of Americans over the age of sixty-five (33.4 million people in 1996) had hospital insurance through the Medicare program. According to data compiled by the Health Care Financing Administration (HCFA), the administrative agency for the Medicare program, the largest component of national health expenditure is hospital care. Inpatient hospital care for beneficiaries resulted in costs to the Medicare program of $79.9 billion in 1996.

Cost and Payments

Medicare pays most short-stay hospitalization under a prospective payment system (PPS) in which hospitals are reimbursed for services according to the diagnosis-related group (DRG) to which the patient is assigned. The DRG system is used to clas-sify patients based on their principal diagnosis and other patient data, such as comorbidity or coexisting conditions. Medicare has set a fixed, preestablished amount of payment for each DRG based on the average cost of resources needed to treat a patient with that particular diagnosis.

The PPS was instituted as a means of containing costs for hospital services by replacing the cost-plus payment system. Since the hospital is paid a fixed amount for each patient stay, the incentive is for the hospital to reduce the average length of stay per inpatient episode. The PPS has been effective in reducing the growth of short-stay hospitalization by providing financial incentives to shift services from inpatient to outpatient settings, to provide services in a more efficient manner, and to reduce the length of stay. These measures were effective in reducing the ALOS from 8.8 days in 1990 to 6.5 days in 1996 and reducing the portion of Medicare payments for inpatient services to 47.8 percent in the same year (from a high of 69.7 percent in 1974).

Approximately 7 million Medicare recipients were hospitalized in 1996, representing 23.1 percent of all people enrolled and 79.1 percent of all Medicare payments for the year. Yearly payments for Medicare enrollees who had been hospitalized averaged $18,925, which was approximately thirteen times higher than payments for non-hospitalized enrollees. One factor that accounts for the higher costs is that in the last months of life, Medicare services, including hospital usage, intensify. During 1996, 6.4 percent (1.9 million) of all Medicare enrollees died; they accounted for 20.5 percent of all yearly Medicare payments.

DISEASES AND PROCEDURES

Hospitalization for an elderly individual commonly occurs because of acute illness, such as pneumonia; because of the exacerbation of a chronic illness, such as an episode of pulmonary edema caused by chronic heart failure; for a major operative procedure, such as coronary artery bypass surgery; because of injury, such as a fracture; or for complex diagnostic procedures, such as an endoscopy.

The most frequent diagnostic category resulting in short-stay hospitalization for Medicare beneficiaries in 1996 was heart disease. These patients made up 20 percent of all Medicare hospitalizations—accounting for 23.7 percent of all payments—and had an ALOS of 5.6 days with an average cost of $7,893 per hospital stay. Related conditions include chest pain (angina), with an ALOS of 2.3 days; cardiac arrhythmia and conduction disorder, with an average cost per episode of $4,548; and coronary artery bypass surgery, with an average cost of $51,583 per patient.

The second most common diagnostic category was cerebrovascular disease (stroke), accounting for 5.7 percent of all hospitalizations and 4.9 percent of all payments. The ALOS for this group was 6.0 days, and payments averaged $5,945 per patient. Pneumonia was the third most frequent cause of hospitalization, accounting for 5.6 percent of discharges, resulting in 5.2 percent of all payments, and having an ALOS of 7.4 days. Malignant neoplasms (cancers), the fourth leading cause of hospitalization, with 5.5 percent of all Medicare discharges affected, resulted in an ALOS of 7.9 days and accounted for 7.5 percent of all payments. The fifth-leading condition resulting in

hospitalization was fractures, which accounted for 3.7 percent of all Medicare hospitalizations and 3.9 percent of all payments, with an ALOS of 6.6 days. The highest ALOS, at 14.9 days, was hospitalization for rehabilitative services.

Of all Medicare payments, 74 percent were applied to hospitalizations involving a medical procedure. The most frequent procedure in 1996 was an endoscopy of the small intestines, which may have included a tissue biopsy, performed on 330,035 patients, or 4.9 percent of all Medicare admissions. The ALOS for this procedure was 6.7 days, and the average cost was $4,648. Cardiac catheterization was the second most common medical procedure performed on hospitalized patients, involving 4.4 percent of all patients. The ALOS for this group was 4.7 days, with an average cost of $5,882 per patient. Other medical procedures commonly performed during hospitalization were computed tomography (CT) scan, diagnostic ultrasound, and respiratory therapy.

In 1996, the rate per 1,000 population for inpatient procedures was 62.9 in the fifteen through forty-five age group, 77.2 in the forty-five through sixty-four age group, and 196.5 for the sixty-five and over age group.

ADVERSE REACTIONS

Longer and more frequent hospitalizations place the elderly patient at higher risk for iatrogenic complications (those accidentally induced by the physician), nosocomial infections (those acquired in the hospital), and falls. The most frequently encountered problem in hospitalized elderly is an adverse drug reaction. The elderly are especially prone to adverse drug reactions because of age-related changes in body composition and function, resulting in altered ability to absorb, metabolize, and excrete medications. Elderly patients frequently require a number of medications (polypharmacy) to control multiple health problems, and additions to and changes in the medication regimen are common during hospitalization.

Functional decline of the elderly person is a common problem leading to hospitalization, and deterioration in function can be worsened during hospitalization. Factors that contribute to a decline in functional level are the disease process itself, medical procedures and treatments, and deconditioning caused by restricted activity. Patients most likely to experience reduced functional ability during hospitalization are those who are older, those with cognitive impairments, and those who exhibited functional losses prior to hospitalization. Early recognition and intervention can decrease the likelihood of functional losses during and after hospitalization.

Delirium or confusion develops in many hospitalized elderly. The development of delirium can have multiple causes, such as drug reactions, sepsis, or the disruption caused by hospitalization. Rapid identification and treatment of the cause is essential to prevent permanent impairment. Elderly patients are more likely to develop respiratory tract infections as a result of immobility, decreased immunity, and decreased respiratory function. They are also more susceptible to urinary tract infections caused by urinary stasis or the use of indwelling catheters. Age-related skin and circulatory changes often increase the older patient's risk of developing pressure ulcers. Pressure, or decubital, ulcers (commonly called bed sores)

are more likely to develop in patients who are immobile, incontinent, febrile, or malnourished, or in those who have poor circulation. Special attention to the skin care of the hospitalized elderly is important in preventing skin breakdown.

Visitation by family members and friends plays a therapeutic role in the patient's recovery. Interacting with familiar people helps keep the patient mentally alert and oriented, decreases the sense of loneliness, and increases motivation. Because of the special needs of elderly hospitalized patients, a team approach to treatment is suggested. Involvement by physical therapists, nutritionists, pharmacists, and social workers, as well as nurses and physicians, can be beneficial in promoting rapid and maximum recovery.

ADVANCE DIRECTIVES

The federal Patient Self-Determination Act, which went into effect on December 1, 1991, dictates that all Medicare providers, including hospitals, must have policies and procedures in place that ensure that all patients receive information

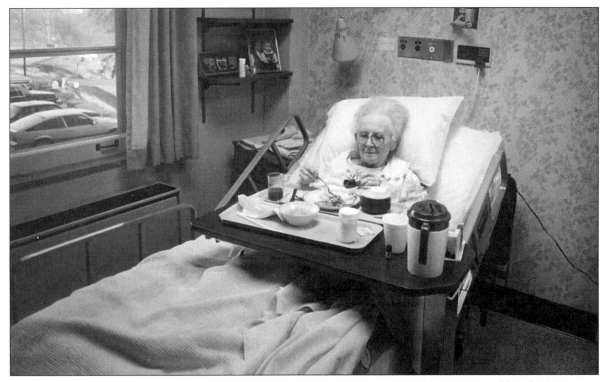

Hospitalization can have both drawbacks (social isolation, the possibility of acquired infections) and benefits (proper rest and nutrition, constant medical care). (James L. Shaffer)

about advance directives at the time of admission. Advance directives, such as "do not resuscitate" orders or living wills, allow competent people to extend their right of self-determination regarding health care into the future. Such directives ensure that the patient's decisions regarding the acceptance or rejection of particular types of treatment will be respected should the patient become incompetent. At admission, patients should be asked whether they have an advance directive, and, if they do, it should be included in the medical record. Advance directives are especially important for elderly patients, since they are more prone to cognitive impairments caused by illness.

—*Roberta Tierney*

See also Cancer; Fractures and broken bones; Heart attacks; Heart disease; Illnesses among the elderly; Injuries among the elderly; Living wills; Medical insurance; Medicare; Medications; Mental impairment; Pneumonia; Strokes; Urinary disorders.

FOR FURTHER INFORMATION:

Graves, Edmund J., and Maria F. Owings. "1996 Summary: National Hospital Discharge Survey." In *Data: Vital and Health Statistics of the Centers for Disease Control and Prevention/National Center for Health Statistics.* Hyattsville, Md.: U.S. Department of Health and Human Services, Public Health Service, Centers for Disease Control and Prevention, National Center for Health Statistics, 1998.

Health Care Financing Administration. *Health Care Financing Review: Statistical Supplement.* Baltimore, Md.: U.S. Department of Health and Human Services, 1998.

Holmes, H. Nancy, ed. *Mastering Geriatric Care.* Springhouse, Pa.: Springhouse, 1997.

Luggen, Ann Schmidt, ed. *National Gerontological Nursing Association Core Curriculum for Gerontological Nursing.* St. Louis: Mosby, 1996.

Owings, Maria F., and Lola Jean Kozak. "Ambulatory and Inpatient Procedures in the United States, 1996." In *Data: Vital and Health Statistics of the Centers for Disease Control and Prevention/National Center for Health Statistics.* Hyattsville, Md.: U.S. Department of Health and Human Services, Public Health Service, Centers for Disease Control and Prevention, National Center for Health Statistics, 1998.

HOUSING

RELEVANT ISSUES: Demographics, economics, family, sociology

SIGNIFICANCE: Housing becomes a critical part of self-identity with increasing age, since it not only reflects career success, life choices, and familial circumstance but also has implications for future security, physical and mental health, and well-being

Persons entering retirement or older persons who have suddenly found themselves on their own due to loss or absence of family, economic difficulties, or physical hardship may find themselves making housing decisions that help them to cope with, or at least minimize, changed circumstances.

A TIME OF CHOICE

Housing needs change with increasing age, and not always in expected ways. A family group may be formed, endure years of economic, social, and personal crisis, and then, seemingly without warning, disband, leaving the elderly family founders alone in a house echoing with memories. The years of retirement that had been anticipated as a time of personal exploration, freedom, and leisure may become encumbered by unexpected illness or disability. Lives lived at the brink of economic hardship may be suddenly imploded—by job loss, forced early retirement, or physical incapacity—leaving the older worker with no nest egg beyond a Social Security pension inadequate for more than the most austere living style. Persons who have faced adversity or discrimination during their working years may find that this situation does not change, and may even worsen, with increasing age. Altered family circumstances such as illness, divorce, and death may also dictate choices in housing arrangements.

On the other hand, housing needs may change in very positive ways. Seniors released from daily familial obligations may experience the exhilaration of being able to choose new housing options from numerous possibilities: caravanning with groups of like-minded enthusiasts in a variety of mobile shelters, establishment in retirement communities designed with the needs of the older person in mind, or adventurous experiments in multigenerational living. Other options might include turning the family home into a home-based business enterprise, opening up a bed and breakfast inn, sharing living quarters with family members or other relatives, or even hitting the road, gypsy-style, leaving behind "no known address." Perhaps the feeling of having earned a well-deserved retirement offers a chance to take up new hobbies and ventures in familiar territory. All these new or changed circumstances bring up a host of choices to be made.

The housing challenges that confront the older citizen may be considered as threats or opportunities, depending partly on how they are viewed but also on the ability of the persons involved to respond to them. For many older persons who have achieved economic independence, the decision about where, with whom, and how to live may offer liberation from former responsibilities. On the other hand, for many persons facing old age, housing choices may seem to confine the older person to a restricted universe in which there is little choice. A number of factors affect how these choices are made, including health, physical and emotional makeup, family support systems, financial condition, intellectual interests, and general outlook on life.

Issues that emerge for seniors contemplating housing possibilities after retirement and into old age have a great deal to do with earlier life choices. The older person who already has a home, who has raised a family and made lifelong friends, may prefer to stay in the home as he or she grows older, welcoming returning family members, hosting visiting friends, and enjoying the fruits of economic security and success. This is not an infrequent choice. Numerous studies reveal that the majority of older persons would actually prefer to stay in the family home. In many cases, this is a viable option. If the home is paid for, the expense of maintaining it may be significantly less than finding a smaller house or apartment to rent, since these are costs that are constantly rising. Even for those who have ongoing house payments, options such as renting living space to students, younger workers, family members, or other older persons may make economic sense. Such financial instruments as refinancing to lower mortgage payments or taking out a reverse mortgage to recoup home equity are additional options. Here, the personal preference of the person affected, and his or her ability to make flexible decisions, is a crucial factor.

LIFESTYLES

Just as there is no typical child, teenager, young worker, or middle-aged person, older persons too have a wide variety of lifestyles and housing preferences. The choice of what kind of housing is the best fit for an aging person should reflect the lifestyle that seems most in keeping with that individual's own preference and physical adaptability. Most older persons would prefer a housing choice that enables them to continue the lifestyle they have developed over time. On the other hand, some might prefer to try a different housing option.

Such variables as health, family ties, marital status, financial condition, economic resources, and even political persuasion all enter into the decision about housing. Although the majority of older persons might prefer to remain in the family home, even they might not want to spend the remainder of their lives at home alone. Women, in particular, often find themselves alone in later life, having raised their children and lost their husbands through divorce or death, and perhaps have insufficient financial resources to continue the upkeep on a house that may suddenly seem too large. Such persons often decide to sell the house and make other arrangements. Some decide to live with children or other relatives, while others might prefer a footloose life of travel and independence. Still others might want to join a social organization and perhaps find another life partner. Older couples often decide to see the world together, perhaps in a motor home or other recreational vehicle (RV). A variety of options, from RV campers to mobile home parks, might meet the needs of the newly peripatetic. Still others decide to have the best of both worlds, spending part of the year in the family home and the remainder of the year in a vacation or second home in another location.

SNOW BIRDS

Older people from the northern regions often migrate to milder climates in the south for the winter. Florida, for example, has based a great deal of its statewide social and economic decision making on its ability to lure the "snow birds" of the northern states to its warm shores. Many smaller and medium-sized cities in Florida cater to the needs of the aging, with social organizations, churches, clubs, and community services designed with the

Housing facilities designed for elders offer important peer contact and activities. (James L. Shaffer)

older resident in mind. In planning for a future in which the number of older citizens will be much greater than at present, it is instructive to consider how Florida, where more than 25 percent of the population is over sixty, has addressed this situation. On the one hand, the influx of large numbers of wealthy retirees has brought unprecedented affluence to the state, while on the other, the increasing needs of the elderly for health and other services have caused social inequities to develop. For some older persons, Florida seems to be the ideal solution to their housing problems, since the sunny climate, social ambiance, and tax structure are all designed to attract the elderly. For others, however, the social setting that caters to the elderly does not provide the variety that they feel is essential.

Among older people who want to retire in a place where their money will go as far as possible, many consider spending their postretirement years abroad. Americans flock to Mexico and other of the less-affluent countries, where they often find the combination of lower living expenses, cheaper housing, and a more relaxed social environment attractive. Some popular periodicals feature articles on places that promise great benefits to the leisure class of senior citizens who are in the market for new living accommodations. Such features as climate, a favorable tax structure, easy availability of transportation, abundance of social and community programs, and varied cultural offerings can be important to older citizens who may live on a fixed income, need to use public transportation, or want to become involved in community life. For these people, a number of housing choices exist, from bringing a mobile home or RV to staying in a pension, renting a villa, or buying a house. Often older persons in these locations seek out others of their own nationality, in order to feel more at home in unfamiliar surroundings.

HOUSING ALTERNATIVES

For many persons, the later years become an ideal time to try out social experiments that interested them in their youth. The concepts of communal living and cohousing, for example, have a great deal of appeal to many aging baby boomers who have always believed in various types of social experimentation and who want in their later years to take advantage of their greater maturity and life experience to try new ways of sharing lifestyles with others of similar interest. A number of highly successful communal efforts of this kind have been made, often seeking to create a utopian social milieu in which persons of all ages feel welcome and secure. Notable examples of such intentional communities include the Findhorn community in Scotland, with its tradition of ecological and spiritual self-sustenance, the Twin Oaks community in rural Virginia, and the New Age Sirius community in Amherst, Massachusetts. Typical of a great number of these large intentional communities is the philosophy of making all age groups equally welcome. In many ways, these "new" communities replicate an earlier age, in which the extended family lived together on shared property and was responsible for the well-being of all its members. In other areas of the world, the multigenerational family model is looked upon as the normal pattern for housing the elderly in a rural setting. In many agricultural communities in Europe and elsewhere, the older and younger generations all live together, with the younger members of the family providing the farm labor, while the older family members provide cooking, child care, and knowledge.

Other successful examples of multigenerational living accommodations are afforded by numerous nonprofit organizations, particularly in medium and large urban areas. The object of these housing ventures is to create an environment that is friendly to the elderly, but that takes advantage of support that can be provided by other age groups, college students, for example.

Older persons in city settings also often share housing on a private or independent basis, either out of economic necessity or to alleviate feelings of loneliness or alienation. The popular television program *The Golden Girls* featured one variation on this theme, but many other possibilities exist. A frequent occurrence in university and college communities, for example, is the renting of rooms in houses owned by older citizens to students, a form of small business that is profitable to the homeowners and helpful to the student population. This can be of particular benefit to older people who want to maintain some connection with the upcoming generation after their own children are grown. If supplemental income is not the primary objective, living space may be traded for home and garden maintenance, food preparation, transportation, or other services.

Some older persons may prefer to spend their later years with other senior citizens who are similar to themselves in interests, socioeconomic status, age, sex, or educational level. For many of these people, a retirement community that is planned and marketed to their age or income group might be the preferred housing choice. These can range from retirement communities that are designed to appeal to older persons who prefer to live with their peers but who are able to take care of most of their needs, to congregate housing projects, often called life care facilities, which are designed to provide health care assistance to elderly residents, including those who are less able to look after themselves.

The latter may become of increasing importance as projections of population growth into the twenty-first century prove to be accurate. According to these projections, the percentage of persons over sixty-five will nearly double between 1995 and 2050, while the percentage of persons aged eighty-five and over will nearly quadruple, and those over one hundred will become a measurable statistic for the first time in history. This fact, in conjunction with the increasing number of householders living alone, will have great implications for the managed care facilities of the short- to long-term future. In the course of the twentieth century, the life expectancy at birth in the United States nearly doubled. Although it is questionable whether a similar increase in longevity will characterize the twenty-first century, the results of this dramatic change in life span will inevitably have major social implications for housing far into the twenty-first century.

Some housing facilities are designed with the needs of the very frail elderly in mind, in order that the elderly needing assistance with daily tasks be able to get help in a positive living environment. The style of accommodation for this type of housing can range from modest to quite luxurious, depending on the economic status of the occupants. Managed care options vary greatly in quality and cost, as do the capabilities of the elderly that inhabit them. Although many very elderly people require only assistance on occasion, elderly Alzheimer's disease patients and other invalids require almost constant attention.

THE ECONOMIC IMPERATIVE

Some housing alternatives are driven more by economic necessity than choice. Many older workers, for a variety of reasons, have only meager economic resources in their later years. These people often subsist on inadequate Social Security income. Many of them can expect little or no assistance from family and have little in the way of savings. In most cases, these persons are not homeowners, or, if so, they have little equity in their homes. Often, these older persons would need to seek rental housing.

For these senior citizens, some kind of government-subsidized housing is a frequent recourse, since the portion of the rent that the tenant pays is dependent on income, with the government supplying the balance. Public housing was begun as the U.S. Housing Act of 1937 and was designed to serve as temporary housing for the unemployed, but it has instead been viewed by many, including many older citizens, as a permanent solution to their housing needs. This type of housing is often located in inner cities or rural areas, which may not be the ideal locations for older citizens. For example, 12 percent of public housing in the United States is in New York City. Funding for public housing, and whether it should be centrally or locally administered, is a further issue affecting housing resources for the elderly, since many of the poorest frail elderly have virtually no income. The benefits of this type of housing include low cost, proximity to city centers, and convenience. Availability is a further issue, however, since there is seldom enough housing of this type to meet demand. In some of the larger cities, safety may also be a concern. The quality of subsidized housing ranges from excellent to minimal, but is usually better than the substandard housing that may be the only other option for the economically disadvantaged.

For those homeowners who do have substantial equity in their homes but insufficient cash flow to meet their monthly expenses, investigating reverse mortgage options might be advisable. Free information and referrals on these mortgages, in which equity is gradually deducted from the house in return for access to money, with the repayment delayed until after the present owner dies or sells the home, are available from the Housing and Urban Development (HUD) Administration. There is also a list of HUD-approved counseling agencies on the Internet at http://www.hud.gov.

Many housing issues become matters of public policy, with legislation introduced to protect the interest of older citizens. For example, legislators voiced many concerns about the lack of public housing options for older Americans following the Reagan administration of the 1980's, during which market-driven considerations dominated. For example, many lending institutions that specialized in reverse mortgages charged fees in excess of those charged for other types of lending instruments for real estate. This resulted in legislation being introduced to modify this practice. Unfortunately, such legislative remedies often become foci of partisan politics, which may delay much-needed housing legislation in being passed. Other public policy issues relate to welfare reform, which attempts to address one problem, that of welfare for unemployed people of working age, but which then might militate against the aged, many of whom live in subsidized housing but are too old or frail to work.

ELDERLY MINORITIES

The American Housing Survey, conducted by the United States Census Bureau, and studies by other agencies have shown that, statistically, elderly African Americans and Latinos, whether renters or homeowners, are more likely to live in substandard housing than are other Americans, with African Americans faring worse in that regard than Latinos. Many elderly American Indians also live in substandard housing, although this problem is associated with the wider problem of housing for American Indians on government reservations.

The issue of minority housing and its deficiencies brings up a host of social and health issues, since older persons are more likely to suffer from discrimination and extreme poverty than younger persons and are less able to adjust to it. Demographic data project a relative increase in the numbers of African American and Latino elderly into the future, which makes addressing their housing needs of primary importance in planning public policy. Complicating factors for this population include frequency of health problems, less stable societal and family structures, and fewer cultural opportunities.

INTERNATIONAL ASPECTS

Housing of the elderly is an issue that is international in dimension, since changes in social structure, demographics, and even economics are an increasingly worldwide phenomenon. Just as the selection of a place to live for older people is not restricted to their country of origin, solutions to the housing problem are also not restricted geographically. A number of countries have devised answers to the elderly housing dilemma, including some that can be adopted on a global level.

A frequent concern of the aging is that they not be a burden to their children or families. However, some assisted-living housing options are quite expensive and beyond the means of the individual. An option that some families are increasingly choosing originated in Australia and is known there by the name "granny flat." This is a type of detached dwelling that can be quickly assembled and then removed if no longer needed. It may resemble a mobile home or may be attached to the main house. This type of housing is called echo housing in some communities, while others call this type of subsidiary housing a mother-in-law unit. Increasingly, forward-looking communities are modifying zoning laws in order to permit construction of this type of housing in residential neighborhoods. It has the virtue of permitting independent living while allowing caring family members to be available in case assistance or simply proximity is desired.

Among the most forward-looking Europeans in the matter of housing the elderly have been the Scandinavians. Sweden, in particular, has been a pioneer in building communities for a mixture of older and younger citizens at public expense. In these communities, cooking is centralized, household chores and the upkeep of the community is shared, but each resident has private space as well. Germany, on the other hand, has instigated some programs that promote the exchange of large homes owned by older citizens for smaller apartments, with the government paying the moving costs.

Worldwide, women have been among the greatest leaders and innovators in the movement to make housing for the elderly more humane and individual. Perhaps this is in part due to the greater longevity of women, but it may also be attributed to women's greater empathy for the discomforts of age. Women in particular have been among the most active in establishing communities for shared living for the elderly that are comfortable, affordable, and appealing.

A key factor in the study of the housing preferences of elderly people that is sometimes overlooked is the intense emotional attachment to a particular place that can develop over a lifetime. The concept of "aging in place" recognizes the importance of sentimental values in planning and providing housing for older citizens. The psychological dimension of housing is perhaps more significant for the elderly than for any other group, since a lifetime of memories associated with a place may be among their most prized possessions.

—*Gloria Fulton*

See also African Americans; American Indians; Home ownership; Home services; Income sources; Independent living; Laguna Woods, California; Latinos; Multigenerational households; Older Americans Act of 1965; Relocation; Retirement communities; Vacations and travel; Women and aging.

FOR FURTHER INFORMATION:

Golant, S. M. *Housing America's Elderly: Many Possibilities, Few Choices.* Newbury Park, Calif.: Sage Publications, 1992. This study focuses on problems of elderly minorities in finding adequate housing.

Gold, Margaret. *Guide to Housing Alternatives for Older Citizens.* Mount Vernon, N.Y.: Consumer Reports Books, 1985. A guide from the Consumers Union of the United States focusing on housing choices for older persons and the concomitant decisions and actions that need to be carried out for each choice.

Heumann, Leonard F., and Duncan P. Boldy, eds. *Aging in Place with Dignity: International Solutions Relating to the Low-Income and Frail Elderly.*

Westport, Conn.: Praeger, 1993. A collection of essays on providing humane care for the frail elderly, often in their own homes.

Jaffe, Dale J., ed. *Shared Housing for the Elderly*. New York: Greenwood Press, 1989. A collection of essays that discuss and illustrate shared housing alternatives in North America for the aging.

Katsura, Harold M., Raymond J. Struyk, and Sandra J. Newman. *Housing for the Elderly in 2010: Projections and Policy Options*. Washington, D.C.: Urban Institute Press, 1989. A report from the Urban Institute that projects elder housing needs and resources into the immediate to short-term future and shows the social impacts of various alternatives.

Porcino, Jane. *Living Longer, Living Better: Adventures in Community Housing for Those in the Second Half of Life*. New York: Continuum, 1991. An upbeat look at a variety of shared housing and other alternatives for older persons.

Regnier, Victor, Jennifer Hamilton, and Suzie Yatabe. *Assisted Living for the Aged and Frail: Innovations in Design, Management, and Financing*. New York: Columbia University Press, 1995. An overview of housing choices that should be made for the frail elderly who need help in finding suitable living accommodations.

Scott, Terrence J., and Robert F. Maziarka. *Elderly Housing Options*. Chicago: Pluribus Press, 1987. Gives a developer's perspective of planning for housing of the aged.

Stroud, Hubert B. *The Promise of Paradise: Recreational and Retirement Communities in the United States Since 1950*. Baltimore: The Johns Hopkins University Press, 1995. A survey of land development projects for the elderly in the last half-century.

Sumichrast, Michael, Ronald G. Shafer, and Marika Sumichrast. *Planning Your Retirement Housing*. Glenview, Ill.: Scott, Foresman, 1984. A broad-based guide, published by the American Association of Retired Persons, the leading retirees association in the United States. Emphasizes planning housing choices before retirement and gives a wide variety of possibilities, along with useful, practical information.

Tilson, David, ed. *Aging in Place: Supporting the Frail Elderly in Residential Environments*. Glenview, Ill.: Scott, Foresman, 1990. A collection of residential care options for the frail elderly.

HUMOR

RELEVANT ISSUES: Health and medicine, psychology, sociology

SIGNIFICANCE: The relationship between humor and aging well is being explored by professionals interested in the aging process

The benefits of humor for all people, and especially the elderly, have increasingly become a topic of research in medicine and psychology. The results confirm that laughter makes people healthier and helps them control pain and manage stress.

Much has been written concerning the benefits of laughter and having a sense of humor. In his 1979 best-seller *Anatomy of an Illness*, Norman Cousins proclaimed that laughter had helped speed up his recovery from a serious disease. William F. Fry, professor emeritus of psychiatry at Stanford University, studied humor and its effect on the human body. He notes that laughter increases heart rate and hormone production, improves muscle tone and circulation, and helps move nutrients and oxygen along to the body's tissues. According to Fry, a good laugh is similar to an aerobic workout. Other researchers have indicated that a sense of humor is a significant characteristic of executives and those in leadership roles in business, while others have espoused the power of a sense of humor in enhancing a person's mental well-being and social status. All suggest that a sense of humor is one of the most important characteristics that a person can possess.

THE HISTORY OF HUMOR

The origin of the word "humor" is a Latin word meaning "liquid," "fluid," or "moisture." In ancient Greece, a person's temperament was thought to be controlled by four humors (fluids). When in proper balance, a person was in good humor. Too much of one of the fluids produced moods: irritable if yellow bile was disproportionate, gloomy if black bile predominated, sluggish if phlegm was too abundant, and sanguine if an individual had an oversupply of blood. A person possessing an excess of one of the fluids came to be known as a "humorist." The prescription for controlling bad temperament caused by excessive "humors" was laughter.

Throughout history, scholars and philosophers have studied humor and why people laugh, with philosophers being the first laughter critics. Plato described laughter as something to be avoided, and Aristotle believed people used it too much. Christians of the Middle Ages considered laughter and play contradictory with their values, and the Pilgrims in America thought that humor and laughter were low forms of behavior and contradictory to Christian sobriety. The Bible, however, refers to laughter and humor. The Old Testament has twenty-nine references to humor, many in the book of Proverbs. An often-quoted passage from Ecclesiastes 3:4 is, "To everything there is a season, and a time to every purpose under heaven; a time to weep, a time to laugh; a time to mourn, and a time to dance."

Over the centuries, views of humor and what makes people laugh have changed. These views have included everything from wit and buffoonery to mocking and jesting. Another view—using humor appropriately in social situations and using it creatively in thinking and writing—examines a more cognitive aspect of what makes people laugh. Through it all seems to have remained the idea that humor is something that is ludicrous, incongruous, abnormal, and out of the ordinary. A contemporary view of humor is that whereas humor is characterized by making people laugh, it is not necessarily jokes, stories, and anecdotes but rather an attitude.

STRATEGIES FOR PEOPLE WORKING WITH THE ELDERLY

Professionals in medicine, health care, education, nutrition, social work, religion, and fitness/wellness who work with the elderly have long understood the benefits of laughter to this population. Many elderly find themselves with chronic pain and chronic stressors related to the aging process. Humor and laughter can help control pain by distracting attention from pain, reducing tension, changing one's expectations and outlook on a situation, and increasing the production of endorphins, the body's natural painkillers. Laughter also has the ability to cause muscles suddenly to go limp, a great value in the treatment of stress.

Those who work with older people can employ simple strategies to make humor a part of their own lives and their caring attitude toward the elderly. They can adopt a playful frame of mind and not take themselves too seriously. They can look for the lighter, brighter side of situations. They can laugh at themselves, thus enabling others to laugh with them. They can make a humor first-aid kit containing stories, anecdotes, cartoons, and jokes to be shared on bulletin boards, in newsletters, in presentations, and on a one-on-one basis. They can laugh with others, not at them. They can make others laugh by letting one's own natural sense of humor emerge. They can listen and look for humor in their surroundings: in church bulletins, in newsletters, on television, in magazines and journals, and in daily life experiences. They can build a humor support group by gathering together people who share the same sense of humor, especially in the workplace. They can let a sense of humor get them through embarrassing moments

Keeping a sense of humor across the life span can actually maintain good health. (James L. Shaffer)

and enable them to accept problems that have no immediate solutions. Finally, they can get the "maximum requirement" of humor; the average person laughs fifteen times per day.

For professionals who want to get serious about laughing, an organization founded by Joel Goodman is available. The Humor Project at 110 Spring Street, Saratoga Springs, NY 12866 (518-587-8770) provides workshops, a speakers' bureau, and seminars for people who wish to use humor as a positive force in their work. It also supplies a free information packet on the positive power of humor.

SOURCES OF HUMOR AND INSPIRATION FOR OLDER PEOPLE

Sources of humor abound in society. Humor appears in almost every facet of daily living. Popular publications such as *Reader's Digest* are resources of humor on numerous topics. Television supplies many weekly series of situation comedies. Books such as those by Erma Bombeck and Dave Barry portray American life in a humorous fashion. Comments from comedians George Burns, Andy Rooney, Phyllis Diller, and Joan Rivers often bring laughter to the older generation, as much of their humor is about growing old. Technology provides sources of humor through the Internet and electronic mail. Newspaper cartoons are an excellent source of humor about growing old and life situations related to the aging process. Some comic strips appreciated by older readers are *Peanuts, Pickles, Garfield, Frank and Ernest, Dennis the Menace, Crankshaft, Shoe,* and *Family Circle.* Films are also sources of humor, information, and inspiration. For example, the 1998 film *Patch Adams,* starring Robin Williams, tells the true story of a doctor who used laughter as a healing force with his patients.

The elderly are bombarded with information concerning exercise as a key factor and positive lifestyle change that can help combat and slow down many chronic disabilities of aging. Yet, many elderly find adhering to an exercise program difficult. Humorous one-liners, used appropriately, can make light of health and exercise situations that elders might prefer to ignore. Some examples of short quips are as follows: Erma Bombeck on exercise—"The only reason I would take up jogging is so I could hear heavy breathing again"; Joan Rivers on exercise—"If God wanted us to bend over, He would put diamonds on the floor"; and

George Burns on nutrition—"I want nothing to do with natural foods. At my age, I need all the preservatives I can get." Burns created a "Don't List" of things that may not make people live longer but that make life seem longer: "Don't smoke, don't drink, don't gamble, don't eat salt, don't eat sugar, don't overeat, don't undereat, don't play around."

CONCLUSION

The relationship between humor and the healing process and other health benefits is well documented. The relationship between humor and aging well is being explored by professionals interested in the aging process. One area of interest is the role of humor in assisting the elderly in their perceived control of life situations or in their personal control. Simply understanding the multidimensional nature of humor, however, is a challenge. Whereas humor is associated with creativity, social cohesion, and relief from stress, it can also be hostile, aggressive, or demeaning. Training and encouraging older people to use positive humor in their lives may allow them to remain involved in society and in relationships with family and friends. Perhaps it can enable them to take advantage of the possibilities and choices that exist and thus promote and facilitate aging well.   —*Gail Clark*

See also Advertising; Communication; Depression; Films; Friendship; *Golden Girls, The;* Greeting cards; *Grumpy Old Men; Harold and Maude;* Internet; Literature; Social ties; Stereotypes; Stress and coping skills; Successful aging; Television; *You're Only Old Once!*

FOR FURTHER INFORMATION:

Cousins, Norman. *Anatomy of an Illness.* New York: W. W. Norton, 1979.

"Divine Comedy." *The University of California, Berkeley Wellness Letter* 8, no. 11 (August, 1992).

Doskoch, Peter. "Happily Ever Laughter." *Psychology Today* 29, no. 4 (July/August, 1996).

Fry, William F. "Humor, Physiology, and Aging." In *Humor and Aging,* edited by L. Nahemon et al. San Diego: Academic Press, 1986.

Haig, Robin A. *The Anatomy of Humor.* Springfield, Ill.: Charles C Thomas, 1988.

Solomon, Jennifer C. "Humor and Aging Well: A Laughing Matter or a Matter of Laughing?" *American Behavioral Scientist* 39, no. 3 (January, 1996).

HUNDRED-YEAR-OLDS. *See*
CENTENARIANS.

HYPERTENSION

RELEVANT ISSUES: Health and medicine
SIGNIFICANCE: The incidence of high blood pressure, or hypertension, increases with age; it is known as the "silent killer" because it has no obvious symptoms

In 1994, it was estimated that 50 million Americans had hypertension. This number represented nearly 20 percent of the American population. A major concern for the prevalence of hypertension is its relationship to other serious diseases, such as stroke, coronary artery disease, congestive heart failure, renal (kidney) failure, and peripheral vascular disease.

High blood pressure that is not controlled by medication or lifestyle can damage the body. The higher the blood pressure, the harder the heart must work to pump blood throughout the body. When the heart has to work harder, the heart muscle gets larger, or hypertrophies. An enlarged heart can work well at first, but as it gets larger, it does not function efficiently and begins to fail. Additionally, arteries get harder and less elastic with age. Having high blood pressure accelerates this process, resulting in further degradations in heart function.

A serious concern of high blood pressure is the increased potential for a stroke, which has been the leading cause of disability in the United States. A stroke occurs when a blood vessel in the brain becomes clogged or bursts. The brain tissue that gets its blood from the affected vessel is deprived

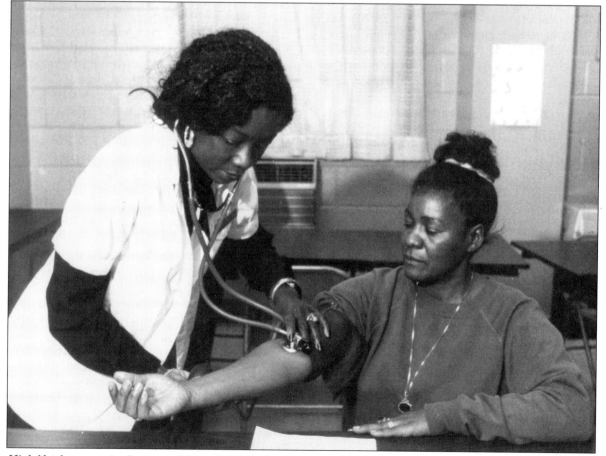

High blood pressure is often termed "the silent killer" because it can be detected only through screening. Postmenopausal women and African Americans are at risk for hypertension. (Frances M. Roberts)

of oxygen and begins to die within minutes. The death of the brain tissue can cause paralysis, loss of vision, difficulty talking or hearing, or, in extreme cases, death.

Another complication of hypertension is related to the kidneys. When systolic pressures get high, small blood vessels in the kidneys can rupture and bleed. Over time, this can destroy kidney cells, resulting in impaired function and higher blood pressure. In order to make the kidneys filter blood effectively after the damage, the body must increase the blood pressure, further complicating the health of the whole body. In the extreme cases, this process results in the need for kidney dialysis, which is very costly and a burden for the individuals involved. Blood vessel ruptures can cause complications with the eyes as well. High pressures can damage the eye's retina tissues. In many cases, it can cause blindness.

Hypertension is a major health problem by itself. When left untreated, it can complicate and contribute to many other health problems. Therefore, individuals must be screened periodically and make the necessary lifestyle modifications to minimize their risk of this disease.

DIAGNOSIS OF HYPERTENSION

Because no symptoms are felt by individuals with hypertension, it is important to have one's blood pressure checked periodically by a qualified person. Blood pressure is measured by a sphygmomanometer (blood pressure cuff) and a stethoscope. The cuff is wrapped around the upper arm and filled with air to compress the brachial artery. The pressure is slowly released while the health practitioner listens for blood flow through the stethoscope. When the pulsating blood is first heard, the systolic blood pressure is recorded. After the pulsating sound stops, the diastolic blood pressure is recorded. All values are measured in millimeters of mercury. Systolic blood pressure indicates the pressure the blood exerts against the blood vessel walls when the heart is contracting. A value of 140 millimeters or higher would be considered high blood pressure. In general, the greater the value is over 140, the more severe the hypertension. Diastolic blood pressure is the pressure the blood exerts against the blood vessel walls when the heart is at rest (between beats). A value of 90 millimeters or higher denotes high blood

pressure. As with the systolic blood pressure, the greater the value is over 90, the more severe the hypertension.

Although there are two different measures for blood pressure, only one of them has to be elevated to be diagnosed as hypertension. Diastolic and systolic blood pressures are highly correlated to one another. Additionally, both are correlated with cardiovascular disease when considered alone and when combined. Generally, the risks of complications are higher for elevated systolic blood pressure than for elevated diastolic blood pressure. An important factor to understand is that blood pressure fluctuates greatly over the course of a day. Therefore, one random reading that happens to be high should not immediately be used to diagnose hypertension. High values at rest on two or more days are required to make an accurate diagnosis.

RISK FACTORS FOR HYPERTENSION

Conditions that increase an individual's likelihood of having a disease are called risk factors. There are several risk factors for high blood pressure. Some risk factors are controllable, while others are uncontrollable. Three risk factors have been identified that cannot be controlled. Heredity is one: Individuals from families with a history of high blood pressure, strokes, or heart attacks are more likely to have high blood pressure. Age is another uncontrollable risk factor: Individuals over the age of thirty-five are more likely to have hypertension than younger individuals. Ethnic background has also been found to be an uncontrollable risk factor: African Americans, Puerto Ricans, Mexican Americans, and Cuban Americans are more likely to have high blood pressure than European Americans.

Fortunately, there are several risk factors that can be controlled. Individuals who are overweight are more likely to have high blood pressure. Also, individuals who consume more than one alcoholic drink per day are at a higher risk. Some individuals are sensitive to sodium (a major component of table salt). These individuals are more likely to have hypertension if they consume too much salt or other sodium-containing products. It has also been found that women who use some types of birth control pills are more likely to develop high blood pressure. Lack of exercise is another risk factor that can be controlled. Proper aerobic exercise has been found to decrease blood pressure.

Risk factors indicate the likelihood for health problems. Not having any risk factors is no guarantee of good health. Therefore, medical experts urge all individuals to have their blood pressure checked at least annually (and more often if risk factors are present) to be sure the "silent killer" is not present.

LIFESTYLE MANAGEMENT OF HYPERTENSION

Based on the risk factors identified for high blood pressure, there are several activities that can decrease the likelihood of having hypertension. It is recommended that individuals maintain a proper weight and that overweight individuals implement a reduced-calorie diet. All individuals can benefit from regular exercise. Continuous, vigorous activities are best. Besides developing a stronger cardiovascular system, it can also help people lose weight. These exercises should be done three to four days per week. Long, steady walks can be as good as running for many people.

Other controllable activities include using an alternative to birth control pills, decreasing or discontinuing the consumption of alcoholic beverages, and reducing the intake of sodium. For individuals who have been diagnosed with hypertension, strict adherence to the medication regimen is critical. High blood pressure medication works by getting rid of excess body fluids and sodium, opening up narrowed blood vessels, or preventing blood vessels from narrowing or constricting. It can lower the pressures substantially if taken as directed by a physician. A major problem exists with individuals forgetting or skipping doses and trading medicines with family and friends. It is critical that blood pressure medications be taken exactly as directed and other lifestyle modification recommendations are followed.

A lifestyle habit that indirectly affects hypertension is smoking. Although smoking contributes no known, long-term risk, it does cause immediate, short-term increases in blood pressure. This can complicate an elevated blood pressure by pushing it even higher. Additionally, smoking has been found to increase the risk of coronary artery disease and stroke. Both of these major health problems are related to and complicated by hypertension.

Hypertension can have serious negative effects on health. This disease can affect individuals at any age, but its incidence increases with age. Fortunately, proper lifestyle habits can significantly improve the chances of avoiding hypertension. It is important that people implement positive lifestyle habits early in life rather than waiting until after the problems develop later in life.

—*Bradley R. A. Wilson*

See also Alcoholism; Death and dying; Exercise and fitness; Heart attacks; Heart changes and disorders; Heart disease; Illnesses among the elderly; Nutrition; Smoking; Strokes.

FOR FURTHER INFORMATION:

American Heart Association. *About High Blood Pressure.* Dallas: Author, 1995.

_____. *Human Blood Pressure Determination by Sphygmomanometry.* Dallas: Author, 1994.

_____. *Sodium and Blood Pressure.* Dallas: Author, 1996.

Delaney, Lisa. "The Ultimate High-Blood-Pressure Prevention Plan." *Prevention* 45 (November, 1993).

Smith, Susan C. "Take Control of High Blood Pressure in Two Weeks." *Prevention* 50 (September, 1998).

I NEVER SANG FOR MY FATHER

AUTHOR: Robert Anderson

DATE: Produced and published in 1968

RELEVANT ISSUES: Culture, family, sociology, values

SIGNIFICANCE: This play addresses the problem of how children must come to terms with how to relate to their aging parents

Robert Anderson's best-known play, *Tea and Sympathy* (1953), analyzes the relationship between an older woman and a young troubled student. *I Never Sang for My Father,* which was made into a film in 1970 and a television drama in 1984, is also a play about an intergenerational relationship, this time a strained attempt at understanding between a son and his aging father.

The opening scene clearly establishes the loving attachment of the mother and son and the love-hate connection between the father and son. Tom Garrison, the father, is a self-made and self-centered man who, although eighty years old and failing in health, still insists on being in control. When Mrs. Garrison dies, Gene attempts to connect with his father and at one point admits that he feels more open toward his father than ever be-

fore. His father, in turn, remembers that Gene used to sing to his mother but never sang for his father—he always seemed to finish just as his father entered the room. Gene's offer to find a place for his father near him and his future wife in California, however, is met with obstinate resistance, and the two relapse into their strained relationship.

Tom is hospitalized while visiting Gene, slowly lapses into senility, and dies. Gene never discovers whether he loved his father or his father loved him. Although advised that he should accept the sadness of the situation, Gene's last words in the play are "still, when I hear the word Father. . . . It matters."

—*Robert L. Patterson*

See also Death and dying; Death of parents; Family relationships; Grief; Literature; Parenthood.

ILLNESSES AMONG THE ELDERLY

RELEVANT ISSUES: Biology, health and medicine

SIGNIFICANCE: Many diseases appear with greater frequency, greater severity, and greater resultant functional impairment in older individuals than in younger groups

Physical and intellectual performance reach their peaks between the ages of twenty and thirty, followed by more or less rapid deterioration during the life span of the individual. Substantial reserve potentials are built into human physiological functions, including the cardiovascular, pulmonary, and musculoskeletal systems. These reserves decrease with time. Illnesses and diseases may subtract from these functions; the lesser reserves of older individuals may result in a greater lessening of the ability to perform than would have occurred at an earlier age. The problems of older individuals can be compounded by the occurrence of multiple disorders, by atypical presentations, and by the withholding of important complaints and information, making diagnosis and treatment more difficult. What may be tolerated in youth may be lethal in old age.

Robert Anderson, the author of I Never Sang for My Father. *(Museum of the City of New York/Archive Photos)*

INFECTIOUS DISEASES

Older individuals are particularly vulnerable to attacks by the influenza viruses and by the pneumococcus, an organism associated with pneumonia. Although symptoms may vary, influenza is characterized by fever, aches, pains, and prostration. Susceptibility to secondary infections, particularly of the lungs, is greatly increased. Both influenza and pneumococcal infections can, to a substantial degree, be prevented through the timely administration of vaccines that, unfortunately, do not provide complete immunity. Influenza vaccines are designed each year to protect against the most prevalent strains. These vary from year to year so that administration of the vaccine must be done yearly. Pneumococcal vaccines protect against only twenty-three of the most prevalent serotypes (there are more than eighty). The effectiveness of the vaccines is limited in older individuals because the immune responses tend to diminish with age. Influenza vaccine is recommended for all adults. Pneumococcal vaccine is strongly recommended for all people age sixty-five and over, with a repeat every five years. This has become particularly important because of the emergence of pneumococcal strains resistant to most of the usual antibiotics.

Although the incidence of tuberculosis declined markedly during the twentieth century, the disease remains a threat to older individuals, particularly to those with diminished immune responses. Easy fatigability, chronic cough, low-grade fever, and anemia are among the signs of tuberculosis. Early diagnosis can make a cure possible, but here again the emergence of resistant strains makes appropriate treatment more difficult. Legionnaires' disease, a relatively recently recognized pulmonary disease, is another significant threat to older individuals. Many so-called childhood diseases are now preventable with vaccines, but the immune response achieved in childhood is not always maintained. Emergence of these diseases in later life has occurred.

The increased mobility of older generations, be it by automobile, cruise ship, or airplane, can bring them into areas that are the habitat of the pathogens for malaria, Rocky Mountain spotted fever, babesiosis, ehrlichiosis, tularemia, yellow fever, cholera, Lyme disease, and the plague. Vaccines or chemoprophylaxis are available for some.

Avoidance may be the only available protection for others. Physicians and public health authorities should be consulted, particularly if travel is contemplated to areas of infestation by pathogen vectors, such as ticks, or to the tropics.

THE CARDIOVASCULAR SYSTEM

Some individuals maintain essentially normal, although diminished, cardiac function as they age and as their cardiac reserve diminishes. Others, less fortunate, develop disorders of the heart's rhythm or an inability to maintain a level of activity satisfactory for an enjoyable life. In still others, musculoskeletal problems may limit their physical activities so that declining cardiac function is not noticed.

Among the more frequent problems of rate and rhythm are bradycardia (reduction of pulse to below sixty beats per minute) and skipped beats. Their appearance should be brought to the attention of a physician, as should other irregularities of rhythm. Shortness of breath on exertion, a change in exercise tolerance, feelings of heaviness or oppression, and precordial pain are frequent signals of cardiac problems mediated by inadequacy of the blood supply to heart muscle.

Both large and small blood vessels can show changes with age. Atherosclerosis, the deposition of fatty substances on the interior walls of blood vessels, spares neither. The aorta, the main blood vessel from the heart, may be so damaged by atherosclerosis that the strength of its wall decreases, causing it to enlarge and form an aneurysm, or a saccular distension. Blood may leak into its wall and beyond, and it may suddenly rupture, causing a massive loss of blood, or it may compress arteries vital to organs, such as the kidneys. Decrease of the effective cross section of blood vessels can be caused by deposition of cholesterol, growth of plaques and calcification, and, not infrequently, occlusion by formation of clots on the plaques. This sequence can occur in the carotid arteries, which are major routes for bringing blood to the brain. Occasionally, small clots can detach and lodge in the brain, causing transient ischemic attacks (TIAs), essentially miniature strokes. Decreased pulsations of the carotid arteries can be felt but tested only one side at a time, and murmurs can often be heard through a stethoscope. In such an event, a physician's attention should be

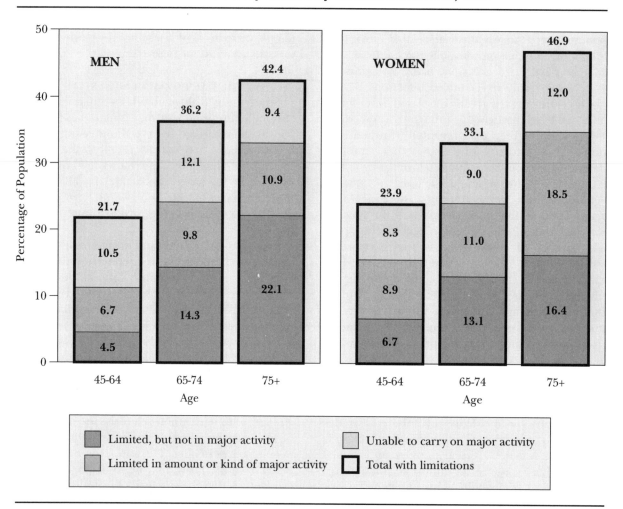

Limitation of Activity Caused by Chronic Conditions, 1992

Note: Data based on household interviews of a sample of the civilian noninstitutionalized population.
Source: Centers for Disease Control and Prevention, National Health Interview Survey.

sought. Similar changes can occur in the arteries to the kidneys, but such changes are reflected by the development of hypertension and the accumulation of waste products in the blood.

The coronary vessels supply the blood required by the heart. If they are diseased, the blood flow through them may be adequate at rest but inadequate during exertion. Atherosclerosis of these vessels, occasionally found in young individuals, increases markedly with age. The gradual decrease of the cross section of these vessels by cholesterol deposition causes the breakdown of the continuity of the cellular lining (the endothelium), offer-

ing the opportunity for the formation of clots, which may completely block the circulation to an important part of the heart. The precordial sensations of heaviness or the dull ache felt with limitation of blood flow may eventually become severe pain and suggest the death of some muscle tissue, which, if extensive enough, can cause sudden death. When the changes in the blood vessels are more gradual, heart function deteriorates more slowly and, depending on which chamber of the heart is more affected, can lead to different symptoms. The right ventricle pumps blood through the lungs to the left side of the heart. The more dominant features of right-sided failure are swellings of the ankles and legs, sometimes extending to the abdomen because of fluid retention. In left ventricular failure, shortness of breath on exertion or on lying flat (orthopnea) are more prominent symptoms.

Small-vessel disease from atherosclerosis is frequent in diabetes mellitus and can also occur from the deposition of proteinlike materials, as in amyloid disease. The decrease of the lumen of the vessels results in increases of blood flow inadequate to meet the demands of exercise. The result is pain in the muscles and the need to rest before continuing the exercise (intermittent claudication). Severe blood flow restriction can result in the death of tissue, gangrene, and the need for amputation. Early and appropriate attention may arrest this deterioration.

Underlying much of these and other cardiocirculatory problems is the tendency for more and more cholesterol to be deposited in the walls of arteries as individuals age. Paying earlier attention to reducing cholesterol intake from the diet and, if necessary, reducing cholesterol synthesis by the liver will increase the chances of reducing the levels of cholesterol in the blood. Those with a family history of early cardiac problems or elevated cholesterol levels may particularly benefit from such preventive measures.

THE GASTROINTESTINAL SYSTEM

One of the more common disorders of gastrointestinal function in the aging process is difficulty in swallowing food and, in some instances, even liquids. This may result from neurological problems with a decreased motility of the esophagus, from obstruction because of scarring from an old injury, from a growth or malignancy, or from psychological problems. In the latter case, the swallowing difficulty is apt to be episodic, while the others are more likely to be unremitting and to increase in severity with time. Ulcers in the stomach, at the pylorus, and in the duodenum are common and may bleed. This can be marked by regurgitation of blood or by black stools. Benign ulcers are often caused by the microorganism *Helicobacter pylori*, which can he eradicated by appropriate antibiotics, resulting in the cure of the ulcer. In the stomach in particular, malignancies may present as ulcers; in such cases, direct examination of the

lesion and a biopsy are essential. More benign disorders can also occur, such as the decrease in acid production and resultant poor digestion. Such disorders may signal the presence of an underlying pernicious anemia.

The gallbladder, which stores bile produced by the liver and discharges it into the gastrointestinal tract and thus aids digestion, can be the site of infections, of stone formation, and, more rarely, of malignancies. Gallbladder attacks, as in acute cholecystitis (inflammation and infection of the gallbladder), more frequent in women but not sparing of men, occur about midlife and later. Symptoms include tenderness and severe pain in the region of the liver that may radiate to the back, chills and fever, and jaundice (if stones have blocked the ducts leading from the gallbladder to the duodenum). Fever suggests an infection. In younger individuals, such symptoms can lead to early diagnosis and intervention. In older individuals, the symptoms and signs may be lacking, and diagnosis may be delayed. Many individuals have stones in their gallbladders and manifest neither symptoms nor disease.

The pancreas, which discharges insulin and bile by way of a common duct into the duodenum, plays an essential role in digestion. Lack of insulin results in diabetes mellitus. The latter disorder occurs frequently in older individuals as adult-onset diabetes (type II) and may require dietary control, the use of agents to lower the blood glucose, or the administration of insulin. Diabetes is often accompanied by circulatory problems because of associated small-vessel disease.

Inflammatory diseases of the small intestine include regional enteritis (Crohn's disease), which occurs mainly in younger people but has significant persistent residual effects from scarring. The large bowel (the colon) can be the site of similar inflammatory changes often referred to as ulcerative colitis, more usual in younger individuals but sometimes requiring colostomies, which can be a problem as the patients age. Quite common in older individuals is diverticulosis, outpocketings of the colon that can become infected and cause diverticulitis, which is occasionally accompanied by perforation and infection of the abdominal cavity. Large-bowel polyps are more frequent with age and may be the site of malignancies. Colon cancer often presents with rectal bleeding in men and obstruction in women. If detected early, the prognosis is excellent. However, hemorrhoids are probably the most common cause of rectal bleeding.

RESPIRATORY, KIDNEY, AND URINARY PROBLEMS

Cigarette smoking is a major risk factor in diseases of the respiratory tract. Smoking is a major cause of cancers in the nasopharyngeal passages and lungs, usually after many years so that the incidence increases greatly with aging. In addition, the natural decline in respiratory functions from age twenty on is accelerated in smokers and is often associated with chronic obstructive pulmonary disease and emphysema. Susceptible individuals who smoke cigarettes may become oxygen-dependent respiratory cripples by age sixty and die within a few years, while nonsmokers may live comfortably to eighty and beyond. Malignancies unrelated to smoking can also occur as individuals age. Periodic medical checkups with respect to pulmonary functions are appropriate, but chest X rays have not been found to be very effective because their resolution is not sufficient to detect the earliest stages of malignancies. However, new, more effective technologies are being developed.

Kidney function declines with age so that, despite a substantial reserve in youth, the capacity of the kidneys to excrete waste and other products decreases. Adjustments must be made in the dosages of medications excreted by the kidneys, and the blood levels may have to be monitored closely. Excretion of urine, which is mostly water, is not affected unless there is disease of the heart, liver, kidneys, or lower urinary tract. Hypertrophy (enlargement) of the prostate can markedly affect the process of urination (dribbling, decrease in the force of the stream, or urinary retention). The hypertrophy may be benign or the result of a malignancy. Prostate cancer may occur in nearly 80 percent of the male population by the time the age of eighty has been reached. Systematic and regular rectal examinations, along with the prostate-specific antigen (PSA) test, provide the basis for early detection. Surgical procedures, local radiation, and, in case of spread, chemotherapeutic agents can be used, in most cases quite successfully.

Both sexes can develop renal (kidney) stones (calculi), which often produce extraordinary flank pain, requiring narcotics for control. The stones may pass spontaneously or may need to be broken up by ultrasonic radiation (lithotripsy). Surgical intervention is sometimes necessary. The stones can result from metabolic abnormalities or, more usually, from infection; the latter is often not suspected, particularly in older women. The frequency of stones and of urinary tract infections, whether of the bladder or of the kidneys, increases with age, as does urinary incontinence, a cause of major embarrassment to many older individuals.

Chronic infection of the kidneys (pyelonephritis) is often unsuspected but frequent in those who have had lower urinary tract infections, incompetent sphincters, or obstruction to the flow of urine, as occurs in prostate enlargement. Small-vessel disease, such as occurs in diabetes mellitus and in lupus, is often associated with hypertension and the appearance of red cells and protein in the urine.

THE CENTRAL NERVOUS SYSTEM

The brain also suffers declines of function with aging. These are often related to a decrease in brain tissue, which can result in a condition called normal-pressure hydrocephalus, in which loss of brain tissue allows more water to accumulate in the brain. The blood flow to the brain may decrease or may not increase during stimulation to the extent seen in younger individuals. Symptoms include memory loss, attention lapses, increased caution in voluntary movements, and prolonged reaction times (of concern while driving). These individuals, in general, continue most of their mental and physical activities, which may serve to maintain the essential blood flow to the brain. Continuation of intellectual activity after retirement may be helpful in slowing the natural decay process.

More disturbing, more profound, and more rapidly progressing are the changes seen in Alzheimer's disease, which causes defects in memory (both recent and remote), difficulty in recognizing errors, reduction in attention span, decrease of coordination, limitations in abilities of self-care and, distressing to all, nonrecognition of close family members. The patient's awareness of the deterioration is not always lost. One estimate is that about one-half of the population over eighty-five has Alzheimer's disease and that a total of nearly 2 million Americans are so affected. The disease occurs more frequently in women than in men and often manifests itself at a younger age. A family history of the disease puts the individual at higher risk than those who do not have such a history. The disease is associated with the occurrence in the brain of neurofibrillary tangles and the deposition of the protein beta amyloid. These abnormalities are under intensive study, and some means have been proposed that may prevent or even reverse their occurrence. Alzheimer's disease, a major problem for its victims, is also a major problem for society because of the costs of the care that must be provided by families or in nursing homes or other institutions.

Among the other major abnormalities of the brain that occur with increasing frequency with age is, in addition to the damage related to carotid artery changes, blockage of blood vessels by clots that form in the brain or that are brought there by the circulation. These produce infarcts, areas without blood flow in which the tissue is dead. Similar damage can be produced by rupture of blood vessels and hemorrhage into the brain substance. Small defects in the walls of cerebral arteries produce aneurysms, which may rupture, particularly when there is hypertension, and become a source of hemorrhages. Small infarcts and hemorrhages may have mainly transient effects, while large ones may lead to strokes, which often cause major losses of control (paralyses), speech (aphasia), or cognition. Death may occur.

Other losses of central nervous system function that occur with age include those of hearing and smell (more common in males). Loss of vision may occur because of cataracts, macular degeneration, and retinal detachment or hemorrhages. The latter frequently occur with uncontrolled hypertension. Parkinson's disease, manifested by uncontrollable tremors and a peculiar, rigid gait, imposes further limitations on physical activities.

MUSCULOSKELETAL PROBLEMS AND OTHER THREATS

Some degree of osteoarthritis occurs in practically all older and aging individuals. Fingers and toes, as well as major joints (such as knees and hips), may be affected. Pain and limitation of motion are common, and analgesics (painkillers) are often necessary. The deformities often limit activities and motion, sometimes severely. Medications and surgical procedures can provide relief from pain and a return to full activity. Osteoporosis (bone loss), which can lead to fractures of long bones and collapse of vertebrae, is most common in postmenopausal women and is largely preventable.

Breast cancer in women and prostate cancer in men remain major problems, in spite of earlier detection and improvements in treatment. Lung cancers in women are increasing in relation to the increase in cigarette smoking. Liver malignancies associated with hepatitis C infections are on the increase and are likely to be a major problem later in life because of the long latent period. Brain tumors, as well as pancreatic and renal carcinomas, increase with increasing life spans, as do skin cancers and leukemias.

Menopause in women and the decrease in sexual performance in men are indicators of decreases of endocrine functions in aging. The thyroid may provide fewer hormones than needed. Because of declines in activity, possibly related to blood flow changes, the endocrine responses to stresses may be blunted, and older individuals may become more vulnerable to environmental stresses. Limited physical abilities may be accompanied by mental impairment and an underlying chronic disease. The need to escape from an overheated environment may not be recognized, and heat stroke may result. Cold, with a drop of body temperature, blunts mentation and slows physical activity. Unprotected older individuals may not recognize and respond to environmental extremes and may not survive situations that are easily tolerated by younger people.

—*Francis P. Chinard*

See also Alzheimer's disease; Arteriosclerosis; Arthritis; Bone changes and disorders; Brain changes and disorders; Breast cancer; Breast changes and disorders; Cancer; Cataracts; Cholesterol; Dementia; Dental disorders; Diabetes; Emphysema; Gastrointestinal changes and disorders; Glaucoma; Gout; Health care; Heart attacks; Heart changes and disorders; Heart disease; Hypertension; Immunizations and boosters; Influenza; Macular degeneration; Medications; Memory changes and loss; Menopause; Multiple sclerosis; Osteoporosis; Parkinson's disease; Pneumonia; Prostate cancer; Prostate enlargement; Respiratory changes and disorders; Sarcopenia; Sensory changes; Smoking; Stones; Strokes; Temperature regulation and sensitivity; Terminal illness; Thyroid disorders; Urinary disorders; Varicose veins; Vision changes and disorders; Weight loss and gain.

FOR FURTHER INFORMATION:

Abrams, W. B., et al., eds. *The Merck Manual of Geriatrics.* 2d ed. Whitehouse Station, N.J.: Merck Research Laboratories, 1995. A convenient repository of useful information in an easily handheld format. Accurate and concise.

Bennett, J. C., and F. Plum, eds. *Cecil Textbook of Medicine.* 12th ed. Philadelphia: W. B. Saunders, 1996. One of the several standard textbooks of medicine with excellent sections on geriatric medicine.

Cassel, C. K., et al., eds. *Geriatric Medicine.* 3d ed. New York: Springer, 1997. Easier to read than but not as extensive as most specialized texts on the subject.

Dale, D. C., and D. D. Federman. *Scientific American Medicine.* New York: Scientific American, 1999. A loose-leaf, frequently updated textbook of medicine with several useful, clearly written sections on aging and geriatrics; includes information on dosages of medications in relation to age.

Fauci, A. S., et al., eds. *Harrison's Principles of Internal Medicine.* 14th ed. New York: McGraw-Hill, 1998. Contains several well-documented chapters on aging and associated illnesses.

Hazzard, W. R., et al., eds. *Principles of Geriatric Medicine and Gerontology.* 4th ed. New York: McGraw-Hill, 1999. An excellent and in-depth text.

Tallis, R., et al., eds. *Brocklehurst's Textbook of Geriatric Medicine and Gerontology.* 5th ed. New York: Churchill Livingstone, 1998. A thoroughly revised textbook with comprehensive presentations.

Wallace, R. B., et al., eds. *Maxcy-Rosenau-Last Public Health and Preventive Medicine.* 14th ed. Stamford, Conn.: Appleton & Lange, 1998. Contains several chapters that deal with preventive and public health aspects of geriatrics and aging.

IMMUNIZATIONS AND BOOSTERS

RELEVANT ISSUES: Health and medicine

SIGNIFICANCE: Routine immunization of older adults can reduce the risk of complications and death from some of the common infections against which vaccines are available

As age increases, the body's ability to counter infections successfully is reduced, which results in increased rates of complications and death. Pneumonia and influenza are among the leading causes of death in the elderly against which effective vaccines are available. Data suggest, however, that immunizations are underused in the elderly even though many infections and death can be prevented by the proper use of these vaccines. Some of the common reasons for underutilization include practitioners' limited knowledge of specific recommendations, poor documentation of vaccination records, inadequate reimbursement, patients' reluctance or refusal to be vaccinated, and poorly developed and insufficiently promoted programs for immunizing adults.

The use of routine vaccination in the elderly not only decreases complications and death but also is highly cost effective. Each vaccine is administered according to its own guidelines, depending on the length of time that the immunity lasts or depending on the frequency with which the offending organism changes its properties, thus requiring new vaccine. Some of these vaccines require periodic boosters, which are added doses of vaccines to amplify the immune response of the body. Based on the current guidelines, all older persons should be vaccinated against influenza, pneumococcal pneumonia, tetanus, and diphtheria, of which the latter two are usually combined into one vaccine.

INFLUENZA

Influenza, which is commonly referred to as flu, begins with fever, sore throat, dry cough, and muscle aches, and usually lasts less than a week. It is caused by a virus. There is currently no treatment for this disease. It is associated with ten thousand to forty thousand excess deaths annually, and 80 to 90 percent of those deaths are among those over sixty-five years of age. Because of this high rate of complication in the elderly, it is important that all elderly persons should receive yearly influenza vaccine unless it is contraindicated. The vaccine is 40 to 80 percent effective in preventing illness in the elderly, and even if they get the disease, the vaccine will reduce the rates of complication and death. It must be given each year because the virus that causes influenza changes its protein components each year, making the previous vaccine ineffective. The vaccine is manufactured based on the predictions of the most likely viruses to circulate during the upcoming influenza season.

Influenza vaccine cannot cause the disease, as is commonly believed, since it is made from inactive virus. It is given in the muscles of the upper arm in 0.5 milliliter doses and should ideally be given in mid-September; however, it can be given any time until mid-December. The vaccine causes antibody production against the influenza virus and it takes about two to four weeks to reach protective levels. It is important that older persons should be vaccinated in the fall so that the body can produce sufficient antibody levels in time for the influenza season, which begins in early winter. Generally the vaccine is quite safe, but it may cause low-grade fever, muscle aches, and fatigue that lasts for one to two days. Persons with known allergies to egg products should not be given the vaccine because the viruses used to make the vaccine are grown in eggs. A person who can eat eggs without complications can receive influenza vaccine without the risk of severe allergic reaction.

PNEUMOCOCCAL PNEUMONIA

The most common cause of pneumonia is caused by bacteria called pneumococci. It results in fever, chills, cough, phlegm, shortness of breath, weakness, and lethargy. Patients generally appear ill, and unless treated with appropriate antibiotics in a timely manner, they may have serious complications including death. It is responsible for an estimated forty thousand deaths per year in the United States, with rates highest among the elderly. Despite the high rates of complications, only about 14 percent of those over sixty-five years have received the pneumococcal vaccine.

The vaccine is effective in about two-thirds of the adult population but is somewhat less effective in the elderly. The pneumococcal vaccine, which is also called pneumovax, contains materials from the twenty-three types of pneumococcal bacteria that cause 88 percent of pneumococcal infections. It is given in the muscles of the upper arm in the dose of 0.5 milliliter, and every adult over the age of sixty-five should be vaccinated at least once. It can be given at the same time as influenza vaccine. Most healthy adults develop protection within two to three weeks of vaccination. Older individuals and persons with impaired immune systems may

have a blunted response. In most cases, the protection lasts for at least five years after vaccination.

There is some controversy about routine revaccination. However, those with kidney disease or kidney transplantation and those who lack a spleen should receive a booster dose six years later. These individuals have declining antibody levels that put them at greater risk of fatal pneumonia. Side effects of pneumococcal vaccine include soreness and redness at the site of injection. Fever and muscle aches are rare and occur in less than 1 percent of patients. There are no contraindications for pneumococcal vaccine.

TETANUS AND DIPHTHERIA

The conditions tetanus and diphtheria are discussed together because the vaccine is usually given as a combination. Tetanus is caused by the bacteria called *Clostridium tetani*. Spores of this organism, which are present in the soil, enter through a wound and, in an unimmunized individual, cause tetanus. The patient usually has slight pain and tingling at the site of wound followed by muscle spasms throughout the body. Most cases occur in those over the age of sixty and almost exclusively in persons who are unimmunized or inadequately immunized, or whose history of immunization is unknown. About 40 percent of the patients who develop tetanus die from this disease.

Diphtheria is caused by *Corynebacterium diphtheriae*, which usually attacks the respiratory system. It causes runny nose, sore throat, fever, and fatigue and can cause serious heart and nervous system complications unless treated adequately with appropriate antibiotics. Since most physicians have not seen a case of diphtheria, they rarely think of this as an adult disease. The few cases that occur each year are in unimmunized patients. As many as 84 percent of those over the age of sixty lack adequate immunity to diphtheria.

The vaccine for tetanus and diphtheria is available as a combination; the majority of individuals receive these shots as part of their childhood immunization. Those adults who have not received tetanus-diphtheria vaccine during childhood should complete a series of three vaccinations. They are usually given in the muscles of the upper arm in the dose of 0.5 milliliter. The second dose should be given one to two months after the first, and the third dose six to twelve months after the second. Every individual, regardless of whether he or she received immunization during childhood or adulthood, should receive a booster dose every ten years. It is recommended that a dose of tetanus-diphtheria vaccine be repeated every time there is an injury unless the last booster dose was less than five years ago. Almost all older persons develop protective levels of antibodies after completing the initial three doses of the vaccine. The duration of protective levels is somewhat reduced in older persons, and therefore it is important that they receive booster doses every ten years or at the time of injury if the last booster dose was less than five years ago. Side effects are mild and include soreness and redness at the site of injection. The only contraindication to the tetanus-diphtheria vaccine is a serious allergic reaction at the time of the last dose.

SPECIAL SITUATIONS

In addition to the above vaccines, older individuals may need additional vaccines depending on their level of risk, which is based on their lifestyle, preexisting diseases, occupation, or travel. These include hepatitis A and B, measles, mumps, rubella, and chicken pox vaccines. It is important to carefully review the immunization history for persons planning to travel outside the United States. Depending on the area to which they are traveling and the presence of diseases in those regions, they may require poliomyelitis, typhoid fever, cholera, Japanese encephalitis, meningococcus, or rabies vaccines. —*Shawkat Dhanani*

See also Health care; Illnesses among the elderly; Influenza; Medications; Pneumonia; Vacations and travel.

FOR FURTHER INFORMATION:

Bentley, David W. "Vaccinations." *Clinics in Geriatric Medicine* 8, no. 4 (November, 1992).

DiGuiseppi, Carolyn, David Atkins, and Steven H. Woolf, eds. *Guide to Clinical Preventive Services: Report of the U.S. Preventive Services Task Force.* 2d ed. Baltimore: Williams & Wilkins, 1996.

Gleich, Gerald S. "Health Maintenance and Prevention in the Elderly." *Primary Care: Clinics in Office Practice* 22, no. 4 (December, 1995).

Harward, Mary P. "Preventive Health for the Elderly: Role of Vaccination." *Journal of the Florida Medical Association* 79, no. 10 (October, 1992).

Long, Jennifer, and Kay Kyllonen. "Adult Vaccinations: A Short Review." *Cleveland Clinic Journal of Medicine* 64, no. 6 (June, 1997).

Plichta, Anna M. "Immunization: Protecting Older Patients from Infectious Disease." *Geriatrics* 51, no. 9 (September, 1996).

IMPOTENCE

RELEVANT ISSUES: Biology, health and medicine, psychology

SIGNIFICANCE: Impotence affects approximately 35 percent of all men between the ages of forty and seventy; however, it occurs most often in men older than age sixty-five

Healthy and satisfying sexual function is an important issue for all men, particularly for those in older age groups. Sexual relationships provide self-esteem, emotional gratification, interpersonal closeness, and intimacy. Sex between loving partners enhances emotional bonding and serves as both a sensory stimulant and a soothing tranquilizer. It offers a form of mild exercise and provides a gentle release of physical and mental tension.

AGING AND SEXUAL PHYSIOLOGY

Sexual physiology changes with age. Some older men experience less turgid erections, less forceful ejaculations, and a longer refractory period, which simply means that at certain times a man may have sexual relations without a firm erection and sometimes without ejaculation. As a man grows older, his sexual response cycle may begin to slow down. At age sixty, a man may not have an erection as hard or as lasting as he did at age twenty-five. However, most men tend to equate their satisfactory sexual functioning with their ability to achieve and maintain penile erection during sexual intercourse. For them, erection difficulties often carry the implication of sexual failure and result in excessive anxiety, depression, and, in some cases, marital disharmony. The man may feel that by not having adequate control over his erection, he is letting his partner down. There may also be an internalized fear that any impairment of erection would ultimately result in a loss of sexual relationship.

It is not unusual for many men to experience an isolated erection problem at some time in their lives. For others, it may happen more frequently. It is only when the inability to respond naturally to one's partner becomes a recurring problem that a man is considered to be suffering from a treatable sexual disorder called erectile dysfunction, commonly known as impotence. Impotence thus is the consistent inability to achieve and maintain penile erection sufficient for satisfactory sexual intercourse.

Impotence is a widespread condition, shared by approximately 30 million men in the United States. Data from a male aging study conducted in 1999 revealed that 34.8 percent of men aged forty to seventy years suffered from moderate to complete erectile dysfunction. A 1994 study found that 50 percent of men over age forty had experienced the problem to some degree. The trend seems to stem from several factors including some men's high or exaggerated expectations about their sexual performance and the increase in life expectancy, which substantially increases the population of men who encounter age-related barriers to their erectile

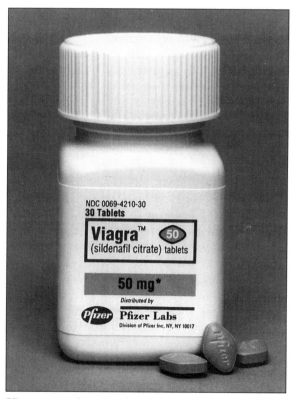

Viagra created a stir when it was introduced in 1998. Many older men who had experienced sexual dysfunction for years were able to achieve adequate erections after taking this drug. (Reuters/HO/Archive Photos)

functioning. The prevalence of erectile dysfunction has been shown to triple between the ages of forty and seventy; however, fewer than 1 percent of affected men seek professional treatment. Sexuality is an area that suffers from a considerable lack of information, particularly for older people. Many elderly men consider matters relating to sexual problems a taboo subject and are often reluctant to discuss their concerns with their friends, caretakers, and health care providers. Some mistakenly believe that sexual difficulties are a normal part of aging and have learned to accept them as a way of life.

Of all the male sexual dysfunctions, impotence is often considered the most traumatic; it makes a man feel personally inadequate and "less of a man." The word "impotent" comes from Latin and literally means "without power." The implication is that a man is powerless as a lover without an erection. Erectile difficulties thus deeply affect the masculine self-concept. In behavioral terms, impotence merely means that a man's penis is not cooperating in an intimate encounter. Emotionally, however, it may carry the implication for the man that he is inept in every area of male endeavor. Many older men do not seek treatment because of a deep sense of shame and embarrassment.

THE PHYSIOLOGY OF ERECTION

The anatomy of the penis provides for rapid engorgement with blood, an increase in size, and the development of rigidity. Erection involves increased arterial blood flow to the penis, resulting in penile engorgement and decreased venous outflow from the organ, a process regulated by the autonomic nervous system. Erection begins with sensory and mental stimulation. Impulses from the brain and local nerves cause the penile muscles to relax, allowing blood to flow in and create the pressure necessary for the penis to expand. The surrounding membrane helps trap the blood, thereby sustaining the penile erection. Erection is reversed when muscles in the penis contract, stopping the inflow of blood and opening the outflow channels. Erection thus requires a sequence of events involving nerve impulses in the brain, spinal column, and the area around the penis, and appropriate responses in muscles, fibrous tissues, arteries, and veins. Impotence can occur when one or more of these events are disrupted.

It is not unusual for a man occasionally to be unable to achieve or maintain an erection because of minor factors such as fatigue, stress, or alcohol or drug use. Sometimes, men tend to become heavily preoccupied with other aspects of their lives. They get distracted by small day-to-day problems or may feel somewhat distant from their partners. This may adversely affect their sexual arousal and penile erection. However, such occasional lapses do not constitute impotence. A man is said to be suffering from impotence only when the psychophysiological arousal, erotic sensations, and the subjective feelings of being "turned on" are chronically diminished or are mostly absent.

Aging does not cause impotence. Although the incidence of erectile disorders increases with age, the problem is not an inevitable part of aging. Impotence can be triggered by physical causes, such as disease, injury, or drug side effects. Any disorder that impairs blood flow in the penis has the potential to cause impotence. Erectile capacity can also be destroyed by a spinal cord injury in the precise region of the lower spine where erectile function is controlled. Damage to arteries, smooth muscles, and fibrous tissues, often as a result of disease, is the most common cause of impotence. Diseases such as diabetes, kidney disease, chronic alcoholism, multiple sclerosis, and vascular disease can affect erectile function. Prostate surgery can sometimes injure nerves and arteries near the penis, causing impotence. Injury to the penis, spinal cord, prostate, bladder, or pelvis can lead to impotence by harming nerves, smooth muscles, arteries, and fibrous tissues of the corpora cavernosa. Many common medicines produce impotence as a side effect. These include blood pressure drugs, antihistamines, antidepressants, appetite suppressants, and certain drugs used to treat ulcers. Factors such as chronic smoking can result in the narrowing of arteries and veins, thus constricting and reducing the normal blood flow to the penile area during the arousal stage. In some cases, hormonal abnormalities, such as insufficient testosterone, can contribute to erectile difficulties.

Psychological factors—such as stress, anxiety, guilt, depression, low self-esteem, and fear of sexual failure—can contribute significantly to or increase the incidence of impotence. They can also become associated as secondary responses to the erectile failures caused by other organic or physiological factors. Impotence was once considered to be a largely psychological problem. However, advances in diagnosis have confirmed that organic factors, such as diabetes or hypertension, present significant independent risk for erectile dysfunction. The field of medicine has many tools at its disposal, such as Doppler ultrasound, which can measure penile vascular blood flow, and sleep-related erection studies, which noninvasively examine erectile physiology. Psychological difficulties often coexist with physiological causes and symptoms of impotence. Some of the physical factors that contribute to impotence are behaviorally based. Smoking, poor diet, and lack of exercise all can lead to the vascular problems or diseases that can result in impotence. Even medically based factors can create relationship problems between sexual partners that further aggravate the situation.

A man's general health is an important factor. Those who exercise regularly, watch what they eat, make healthy communication a priority, and discuss sexual issues with their partners generally maintain good sexual functioning even in their advancing years. Also, sexual activity is a physiological function that tends to deteriorate if not regularly exercised. It is particularly fragile in the elderly. Sexual vitality is a function of being in better health, exercising regularly, and engaging in sexual activity on a regular basis. Sexually inactive men, irrespective of their age, tend to report higher rates of erectile dysfunction.

ASSESSMENT

Medical, psychological, and sexual histories can help define the degree and nature of impotence. A medical history can identify diseases that generally lead to impotence. A history of use of prescription drugs, over-the-counter drugs, and illegal drugs can suggest a chemical cause. A physical examination can give clues for systematic problems. For example, if the penis does not respond as expected to certain touching, a problem in the nervous system may be a cause. Abnormal secondary sex characteristics, such as hair pattern, can point to hormonal problems, which would mean the endocrine system is involved. A circulatory problem might be indicated by, for example, an aneurysm in the abdomen. Unusual characteristics of the penis itself could suggest the root of impotence. For example, bending of the penis during erection could be the result of Peyronie's disease. Laboratory tests for systematic diseases include blood counts, urinalyses, lipid profiles, and measurement of creatinine and liver enzymes. Measurement of testosterone in the blood can yield information about problems with the endocrine system.

Measuring erections that occur during sleep (nocturnal penile tumescence) can help rule out certain psychological causes of impotence. Healthy men have involuntary erections during sleep. If nocturnal erections do not occur, then the cause of impotence is likely to be physical rather than psychological. A psychosocial examination, using an interview and questionnaire, may reveal psychological factors. An interview with the man's sexual partner may shed important light on the interpersonal expectations and perceptions encountered during sexual intercourse.

TREATMENT

The treatment for impotence may include psychotherapy, sex therapy, vacuum devices, oral drugs, locally injected drugs, surgically implanted devices, and, in rare cases, surgery involving veins and arteries. Up until the 1980's, erectile dysfunction was considered to be dichotomous: It was either psychogenic or organic. Patients with psychogenic erectile difficulties were referred to psychologists and sex therapists, whereas general medical practitioners and urologists mostly treated those with physiological deficiencies and medical problems. Men with testosterone insufficiency received hormone replacement, and those with untreatable organic conditions were offered penile prostheses. Psychologists and sex therapists concentrated their efforts on assessing the psychosocial origins of impotence, offering therapy to men or couples with primarily psychological dysfunctions and treating the relationship problems and psychological aftereffects of organic conditions.

During the 1980's, medical professionals began to realize that in the case of impotence, psychological and medical factors often overlap and contribute to each other. A newer interactive paradigm more accurately focuses upon the interaction among organic causes, psychosocial factors, relationship problems, and fluctuating influences of medication, lifestyle, mood, and disease. Following this paradigm, the ideal treatment team is made up of a psychologist, a sex therapist, a primary care physician, and a urologist.

Treatment for impotence generally proceeds from the least invasive to the most invasive. This starts with a complete physical examination and evaluation, followed by replacement or reduction of medications that may have a potential adverse effect on sexual arousal and erection. Psychotherapy and sex therapy can identify and treat possible depression, anxiety disorder, and relationship difficulties. Other treatment options may include vacuum devices, oral drugs, locally injected drugs, and surgically implanted devices. In rare cases, surgery involving veins and arteries may also be considered.

Drugs for treating impotence can be taken orally, injected directly into the penis, or inserted into the urethra at the tip of the penis. Oral testosterone can reduce impotence in some men with low levels of natural testosterone. Many men gain potency by injecting drugs into the penis, causing it to be engorged with blood. Drugs such as papaverine hydrochloride and Caverject (alprostadil) widen the blood vessels. However, the use of these drugs can, in some cases, cause priapism (persistent erection), which may at times require a visit to the doctor's office or an emergency room. Rubbing nitroglycerin (a muscle relaxant) on the surface of the penis can sometimes enhance erection. Injecting a pellet of alprostadil about 1 inch deep into the urethra can also cause an erection that may last up to one hour. However, some users have complained of pain in the penis, the testicle, and the area between the penis and the rectum. Vacuum devices cause erection by creating a partial vacuum around the penis, which draws blood into the penis and allows it to be engorged. An elastic band is then placed around the base of the penis to prevent blood outflow from the expanded penis.

The introduction of Viagra (sildenafil) during the late 1990's represented a turning point in the treatment of sexual dysfunction. Taken orally one hour before intercourse, it relaxes smooth muscles in the penis during sexual stimulation, allowing increased blood flow and a solid penile erection. While Viagra improves the response to sexual stimulation, it does not trigger an automatic erection as injections do. Psychologically based impotence is treated using techniques that decrease anxiety associated with intercourse. The patient's partner is encouraged to participate in these techniques, which are aimed at developing greater intimacy and providing gradually increasing stimulation. These techniques can also help relieve anxiety when physical impotence is being treated.

THE IMPORTANCE OF RELATIONSHIPS

Social scientists have long been interested in ascertaining how aging men and their partners adapt to changes in their sexual relationships. More than one-half of older people say that sex is better than at age twenty-five. They attribute this to practice. With experience, one becomes more comfortable with one's body, sexuality, and the partner. For those recovering from impotence, relational therapy is an important ingredient. Even after the "hydraulics" of the penis are fixed, there remains the man's psychological reaction to the medical disorder and the problems it can cause in the relationship. Addressing only the genital component of sexual dysfunction does not always guarantee satisfactory resolution of relational difficulties prompted by impotence. Impotence treatment, by centering only on a man's ability to engage in intercourse, may ignore interpersonal aspects of sexuality and overlook the female partner's role in a sexual relationship. In the case of the elderly, the emotional bonds that are built up over the years are far more important to sexuality than physical gratification. A warm, loving relationship is often the best aphrodisiac a couple can have.

—*Tulsi B. Saral*

See also Medications; Men and aging; Reproductive changes, disabilities, and dysfunctions; Sexuality; Smoking; Stress and coping skills.

FOR FURTHER INFORMATION:

Butler, Robert N., and Myrna I. Lewis. *Love and Sex After Sixty*. New York: Harper & Row, 1988. The authors explore medical, psychological, and social aspects of sexual problems experienced by men and women over the age of sixty; they also examine the role of loving relationships in later life.

Felstein, Ivor. *Sex in Later Life*. Middlesex, England: Penguin Books, 1973. Presents a new perspective on the sexual lives of the elderly in a lively and entertaining manner. Includes many personal case histories.

Purvis, Kenneth. *The Male Sexual Machine: An Owner's Manual*. New York: St. Martin's Press,

1992. Purvis provides accurate explanations of male sexual anatomy, functions, and health; he discusses issues ranging from the chemistry of sexual desire to male impotence in an easy-to-read style.

Wagner, Gorm, and Richard Green. *Impotence: Physiological, Psychological, Surgical Diagnosis and Treatment*. New York: Plenum Press, 1981. Presents case vignettes illustrating psychogenic and organic factors underlying impotence and examines treatment strategies appropriate for each of the two categories.

Wagner, Gorm, and Helen Singer Kaplan. *The New Injection Treatment for Impotence: Medical and Psychological Aspects*. New York: Brunner/Mazel, 1993. A highly informative and clear description of medical and psychological aspects of injection treatment for impotence. The book discusses the effects of aging on human sexual behavior and describes the combined use of sex therapy and injection therapy for certain cases of psychogenic impotence.

IN FULL FLOWER: AGING WOMEN, POWER, AND SEXUALITY

AUTHOR: Lois W. Banner

DATE: Published in 1992

RELEVANT ISSUES: Demographics, economics, marriage and dating, values

SIGNIFICANCE: Banner's book examines the ways in which women's sexuality and power have been interconnected with aging from ancient times to the twentieth century

In Full Flower: Aging Women, Power, and Sexuality was Lois W. Banner's fourth published work. In the introduction, she acknowledges that her inspiration for the book came from her own personal experience with aging and relationships. This inspiration was nurtured by her interest in feminist spirituality and prepatriarchal goddesses. The work's strength and relevance to the present come from her involvement in the fields of women's studies and history. She describes her purpose in writing the book as that of celebrating aging and unconventionality. Throughout *In Full Flower*, Banner examines changes in the way that aging women have viewed themselves and in the way that aging women have been viewed by others from ancient Greek and Roman times to the twentieth century.

The book's title suggests a variation on the typical use of flower imagery to describe women's beauty. Banner suggests an image of aging more aligned with abundance, richness of color and texture, and continued blooming rather than with the loss of beauty or decay, as in the seventeenth century description of menopause as the "end of flowers."

Two topics are interconnected throughout *In Full Flower*: repeating cycles of attitudes toward aging woman, and the incidence of age-disparate relationships or associations between older women and young men. Banner contends that repeating cycles of attitudes toward aging women can be grouped in such a way that periods of freedom are usually followed by periods of repression.

According to Banner, age-disparate relationships and society's attitude toward them are influenced by demographics, economics, beliefs about physiology, and understanding of psychology. To support the demographic argument, she contends that when there are more men than women, younger men seek relationships with older women. From the economic perspective, Banner argues that, historically, young men seem more likely to seek relationships with older women when older women have an increased possibility for accumulated wealth and higher social status. She claims that this was true during the medieval period and suggests that it may have been true again during the last decades of the twentieth century.

Banner discusses the menopause as one of the physiological factors influencing how women are viewed by society. She explains that the menopause has been viewed as providing positive attributes at some times in history, while at other times it has been viewed as providing negative attributes. The impact of psychology on the lives of older women is illustrated by several examples throughout the book, including gender equivalency resulting from widowhood during the late medieval period and the nineteenth century view of older women as being more spiritual than sexual.

Banner acknowledges that most of *In Full Flower* is viewed from the European American perspective. However, she does suggest that exploration of experiences of women of other ethnicities might create new levels of understanding, awareness, and power for all aging women in the United States. —*Janet C. Benavente*

See also Beauty; Menopause; Sexuality; Women and aging.

INCOME SOURCES

RELEVANT ISSUES: Economics, family, law, work

SIGNIFICANCE: As people grow older, their ability to earn income from work decreases, while their medical expenses increase, threatening to reduce their well-being and independence

During their middle years, people's chief source of income is the wages and salaries they receive from employment. In any given year, family incomes tend to be highest for families whose head is in his or her fifties. Although age sixty-five has often been viewed as a "normal" retirement age, by the 1990's a large proportion of working Americans retired earlier. Social Security benefits can be claimed from age sixty-two (though at a reduced rate), and the same is true for many private pensions. Some continue to work well into their elderly years, but many either cannot work or choose not to. Many choose to retire on public and private pensions. Others leave work for reasons of health or because they are laid off or cannot find suitable employment. Laws prohibiting compulsory retirement have widened people's choices.

There is wide diversity in the income status of the elderly. In 1995, the median income (one-half of families higher, one-half lower) of elderly households (households with at least one person aged sixty-five or over) was about $19,400. However, the median was only $14,000 for those aged eighty-five or over. The median for married couples was $30,000, but for unmarried people only $13,000. About 22 percent of elderly households

Proportion of Age Group Employed for July, 1998

Age	Men	Women	Total
50-54	87.5%	71.9%	79.5%
55-59	78.4%	59.3%	68.4%
60-64	55.1%	37.0%	45.6%
65-69	29.0%	17.5%	22.8%
70-74	16.3%	8.9%	12.2%
75+	7.9%	2.7%	4.7%

Source: Employment and Earnings, August, 1998, p. 19.

had incomes less than $10,000, while 14 percent had incomes of $50,000 or more. The proportion of the elderly falling below the poverty line was actually less than for the rest of the population. While 14 percent of the total population were classed as poor in 1995, only 11 percent of the elderly were so classed.

INCOME FROM WORK

The employment rate for all families drops by more than 10 percentage points between the fifty to fifty-four and fifty-five to fifty-nine age groups. This phasing into retirement is also reflected in the fact that families headed by people aged fifty-five to sixty-four received an average of 28 percent of their income from sources other than work. Wages, salaries, and self-employment income constituted about one-third of the income of elderly households in 1995, and such incomes were received by about one-third of such households. Laws against compulsory retirement have made it easier for people in well-paid professions to continue working beyond age sixty-five. However, people with more physically demanding jobs are often worn out by age sixty-five or earlier. Although the law prohibits discrimination against the elderly in employment, this is more effective against discrimination in layoffs than against discrimination in hiring. However, part-time work or self-employment are often options for the elderly.

In 1996, about 17 percent of men over sixty-five and 9 percent of women over sixty-five participated in the labor force. Between 1970 and 1997, life expectancy for people aged sixty-five increased by about two years. As medical science and healthier lifestyles increase people's expected life span, the proportion of life spent in retirement also increases. Income from work makes a big difference for the poverty status of the elderly. Elderly households living in poverty received only 6 percent of their income from work, and only 9 percent of such households received such income.

INCOME FROM SOCIAL SECURITY

In 1995, 92 percent of elderly households received income from Social Security (or railroad retirement, financed by a similar federal program). Such income constituted about one-third of the income of these elderly families. Social Security has undoubtedly lifted many elderly above the poverty line, although 19 percent of the elderly poor do not receive Social Security benefits. In 1994, it was estimated that if no Social Security benefits were paid, 54 percent of elderly families would have been in poverty.

People must qualify for Social Security benefits by working in covered employment and paying Social Security tax for at least forty quarters (three-month periods). An eligible person can begin receiving retirement income at age sixty-two, but the benefits are larger if the individual waits longer. Disabled people can begin receiving benefits at a lower age. Surviving dependents of a deceased eligible person can receive benefits; most widows of covered workers receive benefits even if they did not work themselves. Benefits are indexed for inflation and rise each year by the same percentage as the consumer price index. Workers who received higher incomes when working usually receive higher benefits upon retirement. However, benefits for lower-wage workers tend to be a larger proportion of their previous wage income. In 1995, the average monthly payment was about $700 for individuals and $1,200 for couples. People receiving Social Security benefits are also covered by Medicare, under which the federal government pays for a substantial proportion of the medical expenses of the elderly. However, this does not cover most prescription drugs or long-term custodial care.

One controversial feature of Social Security is the provision that workers who continue to work past the normal retirement age of sixty-five lose one dollar of Social Security benefit for every three dollars of income they receive from work, beyond a threshold level. (From age seventy, there is no such loss of benefits.) Critics argue that if this penalty were removed or reduced, more people would continue to work. This might benefit them psychologically, enable them to accumulate more savings, and raise national productivity. As expected life spans increase, legislation connected with Social Security benefits may shift the "normal" retirement age upward.

PENSIONS AND PROPERTY INCOME

In 1995, about 43 percent of elderly households received income from some sort of private pension, usually one provided by an employer. Typically, individuals qualify by working a certain number of

Sources of Income in Retirement

These excerpts are from a survey by the Pew Research Center for the People and the Press on "Public Attentiveness to Social Security and Medicare." Results are based on telephone interviews conducted under the direction of Princeton Survey Research Associates. The survey was among a nationwide sample of 1,002 adults, 18 years of age or older, during the period October 29-November 9, 1997. For results based on the total sample, the sampling error is plus or minus 3 percentage points.

Q: Please tell me how much you think each of the following will help you have enough money during your old age. Do you think (INSERT) will help you a lot, some, only a little, or not at all?

	A lot	Some	Only a little	Not at all	Don't know/Refused
Social Security	18	30	34	17	1
Your own savings and investments	44	29	16	9	2
The retirement benefits from a job	30	33	19	16	2
An inheritance	15	19	21	43	2
Money from your children or other family members	5	14	22	57	2

Q: (IF NOT RETIRED/DISABLED) Which single source of income do you expect will provide for MOST of your living expenses when you are older? Is it . . . (IF RETIRED/DISABLED) Which single source of income provides for most of your living expenses? Is it . . .

Percentage of total		Not retired/disabled	Retired/disabled
22	Social Security?	17	45
39	Your own savings or investments?	44	17
23	Your company's pension plan (or your spouse's plan)?	22	26
8	Income from a job?	9	4
3	Some other source?	3	3
*	Do not ever plan to retire	*	0
5	Don't know/Refused	5	5
100%		100%	100%
	Number of respondents	(811)	(191)

years for the employer and by contributing a certain proportion (most often one-half) of the pension costs. Most such pensions are managed by insurance companies or other financial institutions. In the best programs, individual workers are vested—that is, they have a property right in the pension that they retain even if they leave that employer long before retirement. However, workers who leave for another job may receive their vested pension property in a lump sum, and many do not hold on to the money in retirement assets.

Pension rights are unevenly divided among elderly households. Many employers do not offer pension programs. If they do, some workers choose not to participate. The percentage of all workers participating in pension plans was 46 percent in 1979 and 44 percent in 1993. Changes in taxes and other regulations have led many firms to substitute other types of programs. For instance, 401K plans (named for the provision in the tax code) are generally voluntary plans for employees to put a limited proportion of their pay into securities investments, with the employer matching some of this. The employer is not committed to any market value for the assets or the retirement income they may yield.

Because women have lower pay levels and are generally employed for a shorter time, their pensions tend to be lower. In 1991, male pension recipients averaged $859 per month, while female recipients averaged only $481.

In 1995, pension income constituted 15 percent of the income of elderly households. However, only 7 percent of the poverty-class elderly received such pensions, which made up only 3 percent of their income. Of all elderly households, 69 percent received some income from interest or dividends. However, the amounts were often not very large, and such income was only about 15 percent of their total income. While 30 percent of the elderly poor received such income, it constituted only 3 percent of their total income.

Ownership of the stocks, bonds, and savings assets that yield such incomes is also uneven among elderly households. In 1992, the median net worth for families headed by a person aged sixty-five to seventy-four was $104,000, much of which typically reflected ownership of a home. The median value of financial assets for this group was only about $30,000. For many households, these funds are held in such conservative forms as savings deposits or certificates of deposit (CDs). Assuming average yields of about 5 percent, assets worth $30,000 would yield $1,500 of income per year. Families headed by a person aged seventy-five or older had only $20,000 median financial assets, representing annual income of only $1,000. Clearly, families with net worth above the median received most of the income from interest and dividends.

Owners of financial assets have the opportunity to spend the capital value as well as the income, or they can use assets as collateral for loans. Besides the desire for investment income, families accumulate financial wealth as protection against emergencies and in order to transmit wealth to their heirs.

Tax provisions affect saving for these types of retirement income. Workers' payroll deductions for pension fund contributions are normally tax deferred: Income taxes will come due when the retirement income is paid. At times, the government has permitted limited amounts of private savings to be tax-deferred when put into individual retirement accounts (IRAs). In contrast, the money taken out of individual paychecks for Social Security tax is not tax-exempt or tax-deferred, and Social Security benefits are subject to a partial tax. Tax deferment typically benefits individuals in the upper half of the income distribution.

The types of income already discussed provided 96 percent of the income of elderly households in 1995. Much of the remainder came from government transfer payments, particularly means-tested (eligibility is limited to people with low incomes, unlike Social Security retirement benefits) payments aimed at alleviating poverty.

POVERTY AMONG THE ELDERLY

In times past, few elderly people received enough income from work or ownership of property to live comfortably on their own. Many had to live with their grown children. By the 1990's, however, only about 10 percent of the elderly were poor. In 1995, the incidence of poverty was slightly higher than average for African American men (15 percent) and Latino men (16 percent), but much higher for African American women (31 percent) and Latino women (29 percent). More than 20 percent of all elderly women living alone or heading a household were living in poverty. Since women tend to outlive men, a large (and increasing) proportion of women over sixty-five are widows. A significant number did not spend many years in paid employment and thus did not accumulate any wealth or pension rights. If they do not marry, they have little or no eligibility for Social Security. However, divorced women are now eligible for benefits based on the former husband's income.

About 78 percent of the income of the elderly poor came from either Social Security (67 percent) or various government transfer payments specifically targeting the poor (11 percent). Among the latter were Aid to Families with Dependent Children (AFDC), Supplemental Security Income (SSI), general assistance, and veterans benefits. All of these are means-tested.

At retirement, many individuals can expect to live another twenty years or more. It is therefore important that their income sources do not dwindle and that they are protected against inflation. Social Security benefits and many private pensions are paid as lifetime annuities, with payments based on actuarial calculations of expected life span. Some individuals will die sooner and receive fewer monthly payments, while others will live longer and receive more. Social Security benefits are indexed for inflation. The closest counterparts in private pensions and private financial assets are annuities based on investments in corporate stocks. Stock prices rise an average of 10 percent per year. Stock-based annuities (such as those offered by the College Retirement Equities Fund, or CREF) registered impressive increases in values in the 1980's and 1990's. In any case, annuities offered by private financial firms provide a basis for people to consume the capital value of their assets gradually over time without having to worry that they will run out.

In the late 1990's, there were proposals to reform the Social Security system by investing some of the funds in corporate stocks. However, stock prices have been unstable, and one cannot assume they will continue to rise in the future as in the past. Home ownership also provides protection against inflation. Furthermore, the value of the home can be used as a basis for borrowing.

—*Paul B. Trescott*

See also Age discrimination; Employment; Forced retirement; 401K plans; Home ownership; Individual retirement accounts (IRAs); Pensions; Poverty; Retirement; Social Security; Women and aging.

FOR FURTHER INFORMATION:

Darnay, Arsen J., ed. *Statistical Record of Older Americans.* Washington, D.C.: Gale Research, 1994. The editors have been ingenious in finding a vast variety of statistical reflections of the condition of the elderly.

Ferguson, Karen, and Kate Blackwell. *Pensions in Crisis: Why the System Is Failing America and How You Can Protect Your Future.* New York: Arcade, 1995. The authors investigate the failure of the pension system and offer advice on how to prepare for retirement.

Manheimer, Ronald J., ed. *Older Americans Almanac.* Washington, D.C.: Gale Research, 1994. This comprehensive survey (more than eight hundred pages) has sizable sections on employment and retirement, and on the financial aspects of aging.

Radner, Daniel B. "Incomes of the Elderly and Non-elderly, 1967-92." *Social Security Bulletin* 58, no. 4 (Winter, 1995). Presents valuable data on the evolution of different types of income for different age groups over time.

Rappaport, Anna M., and Sylvester J. Schieber. *Demography and Retirement: The Twenty-first Century.* Westport, Conn.: Praeger, 1993. These symposium papers look at the future prospects for the economics and finance of aging and retirement.

Rejda, George E. *Social Insurance and Economic Security.* 6th ed. Upper Saddle River, N.J.: Prentice Hall, 1999. Rejda gives extensive coverage to economic conditions and problems of elderly persons, as well as to Social Security and other relevant programs.

Sass, Steven A. *The Promise of Private Pensions.* Cambridge, Mass.: Harvard University Press, 1997. This scholarly history provides a good overview of changes in pension programs and their regulation in the 1980's and 1990's.

Williamson, Robert C., Alice Duffy Rinehart, and Thomas O. Blank. *Early Retirement: Promises and Pitfalls.* New York: Plenum Press, 1992. Based on questionnaires and interviews, this study looks at the emotional and financial aspects of the experience with early retirement.

INCONTINENCE

RELEVANT ISSUES: Health and medicine

SIGNIFICANCE: Incontinence, the inability to control evacuative functions, affects 30 percent of community-dwelling elderly and 53 percent of the homebound elderly; the condition has important physical, psychological, social, and economic consequences

Urinary incontinence is the second leading cause of early institutionalization of the elderly and is twice as common in women as in men. According to researchers in 1994, the annual cost in the United States of providing care for community-dwelling urinary incontinence sufferers was estimated to be $11 billion, while the cost of providing care for those of the nursing home population was another $5 billion.

A TREATABLE PROBLEM

Fewer than one-half of the 13 million Americans with urinary incontinence have been evaluated or treated. One of the unanswered questions about urinary incontinence is why, given the high prevalence of incontinence, so few people report it and seek treatment. One reason may be that individuals, believing that incontinence is a normal aging-related condition, believe that they can manage urinary incontinence effectively on their own.

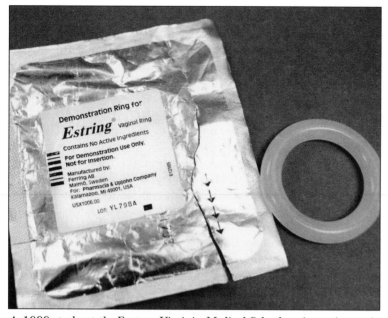

A 1999 study at the Eastern Virginia Medical School on incontinence in women used a device called a vaginal ring. (AP Photo/Gary C. Knapp)

water from the blood. Tiny tubes called ureters connect the kidneys to the bladder, which is located under the pelvic bone. The bladder is like a muscular holding tank that is capable of storing 8 to 16 ounces of urine and, in some cases, much more. The bladder empties to the outside of the body through the urethra. This muscle has sturdy internal and external sphincters that keep the bladder tightly closed until it reaches capacity. When the bladder is full, it sends a signal to the brain. This signal is translated as an urge to urinate. When a cognitively alert person reaches an appropriate place to void, the sphincter muscle is relaxed, the bladder contracts, and urine is released into the urethra.

When a person reports such symptoms as urgent, painful, and frequent urination, along with frequent night toileting, many health professionals fail to evaluate the problem because of the myths associated with urinary incontinence and the lack of knowledge regarding solutions. A persistent myth is that urinary incontinence is a normal occurrence of aging often associated with mental incompetence. The inability to control urine is unpleasant and distressing. One major consequence is that untreated incontinence often becomes progressively worse. Secondary problems, such as rashes, decubitus ulcers, and skin and urinary tract infections, can also occur. Psychological consequences, such as embarrassment, loss of self-esteem, social isolation, and even depression, are common.

Studies have demonstrated that as many as 80 percent of urinary incontinent patients can be cured or significantly improved. Even incurable problems can be effectively managed to reduce complications, anxiety, and stress. When treatment is not completely successful, management can help make the problem more livable.

The urinary tract begins with the two kidneys, one on each side of the spinal column, midway in the back. They filter chemical wastes and excess

TYPES OF INCONTINENCE

Urinary incontinence has many definitions. The *American Heritage Dictionary* defines it as being "incapable of controlling the excretory functions." *Taber's Cyclopedic Medical Dictionary* (1997) defines it as "the inability to retain urine, semen, or feces because of a loss of sphincter control, or cerebral or spinal lesions." The Agency for Health Care Policy and Research (AHCPR) guidelines define urinary incontinence is an "involuntary loss of urine which is sufficient to be a problem." The four basic types of urinary incontinence are stress, urge, overflow, and functional.

Stress incontinence is apparent by the involuntary loss of small to moderate amounts of urine when pressure is placed on the pelvic floor, as when one coughs, sneezes, or laughs. It is caused by weak supporting pelvic muscles, estrogen deficiency, and obesity. This form of incontinence is common in women as they age, particularly those who have had several pregnancies, and men who have had prostrate surgery. It may be caused by congenital weakness of the sphincter or acquired after exposure to radiation, trauma, or a sacral cord lesion. It is common to leak continuously or with minimal exertion. Behavioral approaches, such as habit training and pelvic muscle exercises, are useful in improving some stress incontinence; surgery may be needed in some situations.

A sudden loss of moderate to large amounts of urine is characteristic of urge incontinence. Urge incontinence is the most common type, affecting an estimated 65 percent of all cases. It results from irritation or spasms of the bladder wall because of urinary tract infections, prostate enlargement, diverticulitis, or tumors of the bladder or pelvic region. Urge incontinence may also be caused by bladder stones, fecal impaction, stroke, dementia, suprasacral injury, and Parkinson's disease. Highly spiced foods, artificial sweeteners, coffee (even decaffeinated), tea, cola, wine, chocolate, and medicines that contain caffeine may cause bladder irritation. Treatment of infections can correct the problem in some people with this form of incontinence. Since the person notes a sudden urge to urinate but is unable to reach the toilet in time, behavioral approaches, such as habit training, prompted voiding, and bladder retraining, can improve continence for some cases.

A failure of the bladder muscles to contract or of the muscles around the urethra to relax causes retention of an excessive amount of urine in the bladder and, consequently, overflow incontinence. The main symptom of overflow incontinence is frequent or constant leaking (dribbling) of small amounts of urine. Bladder neck obstructions from an enlarged prostate, fecal impaction, or urethral stricture can be associated with overflow incontinence. Habit training can be used to completely empty the bladder.

Functional incontinence is caused by factors outside the urinary tract. This occurs when the function of the lower urinary tract is intact but other factors, such as impaired mobility, impaired cognition, and environmental barriers, result in incontinence. This may be as simple as being unable to get to the bathroom in time because of arthritis. People with cognitive impairments, such as Alzheimer's disease, may be unable to understand the need to void, may be unfamiliar with the location of the bathroom, or may no longer remember the function of the toilet itself.

A THREE-PART EXAMINATION

In order to determine the type of urinary incontinence from which the patient suffers, a comprehensive examination is necessary. The basic evaluation includes three parts: a patient history, a physical examination, and urinalysis. The use of both prescription and nonprescription medications, herbs, and vitamin supplements is also reviewed. Close attention is paid to the patient's symptoms and such characteristics the frequency and timing of continent and incontinent episodes, as well as the amount voided during each episode. These questions can be answered with the help of a voiding diary that is kept for several days, preferably one to two weeks. This diary can provide useful clues to the underlying cause of urinary incontinence and helps gauge the severity of the problem and what treatment options are best.

A complete physical examination often includes an evaluation of the environment and social factors. Important considerations include how far the individual must walk to the toilet or whether he or she understands instructions or has the physical ability to undress well enough to go to the bathroom unassisted. These types of considerations would help with a diagnosis of functional urinary incontinence.

The third part of the examination is the laboratory study of the urine itself. Analysis of the different cells, sediment, color, specific gravity, and presence or absence of bacteria are suggestive of the cause of urinary incontinence. Older adults can have an infection without experiencing the fever, chills, and pain that are common among younger patients. The amount of postvoid urine or residual in the bladder is also important to know. This can be tested either by scanning the bladder with a noninvasive pelvic ultrasound or by catheterization, in which a sterile tube is inserted into the bladder to drain it.

MANAGING INCONTINENCE

AHCPR guidelines designate three treatment categories for urinary incontinence: behavioral, pharmacologic, and surgical. The least invasive and least dangerous technique, the behavioral one, is usually tried first. A number of behavioral techniques are available. Habit training is used for urge incontinence. The goal is to get the person to ignore the urge to void and to train the bladder to tolerate larger volumes of urine without urgency. The person is encouraged to gradually, consciously extend the time between voidings. This approach can sometimes be used with cognitively impaired people as well. Like habit training, bladder training also emphasizes scheduled voiding, but it also involves a substantial retraining effort through education and positive reinforcement, using booklets and other teaching aids.

Using exercise to strengthen the pelvic muscles, which are frequently weakened by childbirth, extreme obesity, or the menopause, is another behavioral technique that can work for women. Kegel exercises involve squeezing and relaxing the pelvic muscles. Squeezing the muscles helps keep the urethra closed until it is time to void. Upon reaching the toilet, the woman can relax the muscles surrounding the urethra and allow it to open. At that point, the bladder contracts and forces urine out through the urethra. It has been documented that sixty to eighty Kegel exercises daily, done properly, can reduce significantly or even eliminate stress incontinence. Improvement can be seen within three weeks to nine months, with most women noting some progress by the end of the eighth week. To make sure women are contracting the right muscle, they are told to constrict the anus as if holding back stool or to try to stop and start the stream while urinating in the toilet. However, doing Kegel exercises routinely during urination can damage the urethra.

Biofeedback helps ensure that the woman is doing the contractions correctly and is a good complement to Kegel exercises. The perineometer, a device used for biofeedback, has a manometer attached to a probe that can be inserted into the vagina. Vaginal cones can also help strengthen the pelvic floor. When one is inserted, wide end first, and it begins to slip out, the pelvic floor contracts to retain it. The woman holds the cone in place for fifteen minutes, twice per day. In time, she will be able to progress to heavier cones. In several studies, approximately 70 percent of the women using the cones reported significant improvement in their stress incontinence. Although the cones work faster than Kegel exercises, some women may be reluctant to use them.

Depending on the type of urinary incontinence, behavioral techniques are not always successful, and the person may need to be referred for pharmacologic treatment. Urge incontinence caused by detrusor muscle instability and stress incontinence caused by urethral sphincter insufficiency may both be helped with medications. In posthysterectomy or postmenopausal women, stress incontinence may be treated with estrogen replacement therapy.

If pharmacologic treatment is not appropriate, or if it fails, surgery may be recommended. Guidelines state that surgery may be necessary to return the bladder neck to its proper position in women with stress incontinence, to remove tissue that is causing a blockage, to support or replace severely weakened pelvic muscles, or to enlarge a small bladder to hold more urine. Before undergoing surgery to correct urinary incontinence, the patient should understand the procedure, its risks and benefits, and the expected outcome.

SUPPORTIVE DEVICES

Once all the alternative approaches to resolving incontinence have been explored and exhausted, supportive devices—including intermittent, indwelling, and external (condom) catheters; penile clamps; pessaries; and absorbent pads and undergarments—may be considered.

Performing self-catheterization intermittently may help people with overflow incontinence caused by an inoperable obstruction or other detrusor muscle problems. The caregivers and the involved individual must be both physically and psychologically able to insert a clean catheter tube into the bladder every three to six hours. When done properly, this procedure can be performed at home without any increased risk of infection. Only those with untreatable urinary retention should leave the catheter in place. Using an indwelling catheter for longer than two to four weeks greatly increases the risk of chronic bacteria in the urine and urinary tract infections.

Men may be able to use external collection systems, or condom catheters, which are best for short-term use because of skin irritation. Men with chronic obstruction are advised not to use condom catheters. Urine-collecting devices are also available for women but are not as satisfactory, causing redness and perineal itching. As a temporary solution for males with stress incontinence that is caused by inadequate sphincter contraction, a penile clamp may be an option. The clamp must be removed every three hours to empty the bladder. Improper use can lead to penile and urethral erosion, penile swelling, pain, and obstruction.

Women who have pelvic prolapse with or without urinary incontinence can obtain temporary relief by means of a pessary, a doughnut-shaped rubber or silicone device that is inserted into the vagina. The pessary may help frail, elderly women who have no other treatment options. A specially trained physician or nurse fits and inserts the pessary, then monitors it frequently. A misused or neglected pessary can lead to ulceration of the vagina and fistulas.

There is a growing trend to make use of absorbent pads and pants, largely because urinary incontinence is so often dismissed rather than treated. Although absorbent garments help people feel more secure about their incontinence, the AHCPR recommends that the person's level of disability, preference, gender, and type and severity of incontinence be taken into account before absorbent products are used. Before choosing a product, the person and caregivers must consider the amount of urine voided per incontinent episode, the type of clothing the person usually wears, manual dexterity, and financial means. Regardless of which absorbent products are chosen, people are advised that they must maintain proper hygiene and change the garment or pad frequently to prevent urinary tract infections and skin problems.

Urinary incontinence affects people of all age groups, especially those in the geriatric population. An overwhelming number are women. In fact, it has been estimated that one-half of all adult women suffer from loss of bladder control at some time in their lives. Yet the number of women and men who fail to seek treatment for urinary incontinence is surprisingly high. Many people think loss of bladder control is a normal part of growing old. Still others think urinary incontinence is just something one must live with. The truth is that urinary incontinence is not caused by aging. Usually, it is brought on by specific changes in the body function that result from infection, hormonal changes, diseases, pregnancy, or the use of certain medications. In most cases, it can be controlled or cured. Left untreated, however, urinary incontinence can make life miserable. It can increase the chance of skin irritation and the risk of developing bedsores, and it often leads to social isolation and personal frustration.   —*Maxine M. McCue*

See also Men and aging; Prostate enlargement; Urinary disorders; Women and aging.

FOR FURTHER INFORMATION:

Agency for Health Care Policy and Research (AHCPR). http://www.ahcpr.gov/clinic. For free information on incontinence, see the on-line publications *Helping People with Incontinence: Caregiver Guide* (96-0683) and *ALERT for Directors of Nursing* (96-0063).

Kennedy, K. L., C. P. Steidle, and T. M. Letizia. "Urinary Incontinence: The Basics." *Ostomy/Wound Management* 41, no. 7 (August, 1995). A review of stress, urge, and overflow incontinence, and the various types of treatments available for urinary incontinence.

Luft, Janis, and Amy Vriheas-Nichols. "Identifying the Risk Factors for Developing Incontinence: Can We Modify Individual Risk?" *Geriatric Nursing* 19, no. 2 (March/April, 1998). Reviews various literature on risk factors.

Mondoux, Linda C. "Patients Won't Ask." *RN* 57, no. 2 (February, 1994). Mondoux describes new treatment guidelines.

National Association for Continence (NAFC). http://www/nafc.org. This organization offers a resource guide, a continence referral service, audiovisuals, newsletters, and other publications about incontinence.

National Kidney and Urologic Diseases Information Clearinghouse. http://www.niddk.nih.gov. This Web site includes the on-line publication "Let's Talk About Bladder Control for Women." Free consumer and health care provider kits are available, with booklets explaining the symptoms, types, and causes of poor bladder control, as well as treatment options.

Newman, D. K., J. Wallace, N. Blackwood, and C. Spencer. "Promoting Healthy Bladder Habits for Seniors." *Ostomy/Wound Management* 42, no. 10 (November/December, 1996). Describes the development, implementation, and results of a health promotion project called Dry Expectations, aimed at providing incontinence education in the community.

INDEPENDENT LIVING

RELEVANT ISSUES: Family, sociology, work

SIGNIFICANCE: Independent living is designed to help keep individuals in their homes supported by other-directed or self-directed activities; such arrangements are sought out by individuals and families as alternatives to nursing homes

Cultural myths surround the concept of independence. It may be viewed as a state of mind rather than a reality of living. Living at home without the intervention of others may be a better alternative than being forced to live in an unfamiliar setting. Care must be exercised to determine the appropriateness of an independent-living situation. Appropriateness can be determined by examining the concerns of the individual and family member. A professional skilled in independent-living alternatives and community resources is often required to assist in the decision-making process.

SOCIETAL PERSPECTIVES

Less than 5 percent of households in the United States contain an elder parent who is the head of that household. Typically, generations do not continue to live together in households once children achieve a level of independence. Three (or more) generations of a family living together is highly atypical. Most elderly individuals who might be eligible to live independently feel living with their adult children is not desirable.

Although most children feel that responsibility for the quality of life of aged parents lies with them, the majority of elderly individuals do not assign such responsibility to their offspring. Self-reliance, independence, and autonomy are highly valued by members of the elderly population. As the social, safety, and recreation needs of elderly persons are decreasingly met within neighborhoods, pressures to relinquish ownership of their home may increase. In such circumstances social forces rather than personal inclination will motivate individuals to sell their house and relocate. Adjustment and psychological well-being are dependent upon the entire living environment or the total atmosphere in which the individual functions or dwells.

Independence and self-reliance are highly praised values in U.S. society. Most individuals are taught that dependency is a sign of weakness, a lack of character, or even a sickness. This societal pressure may work to maintain an independent-living situation for the wrong reasons.

OWNERSHIP TRENDS

The percentage rate of home ownership from 1980 to 1990 for those over sixty-five years of age shows an increase in all age groups. These statistics reflect both better health (enabling individuals to live in their own homes longer) and a better financial situation (enabling them to afford a home of their own). The National Affordable Housing Act of 1990 has some provisions to help older homeowners. For instance, a home equity provision allows use of home equity to make home repairs.

To allow elders to remain in their original homes, some states provide property tax relief by not taxing property after the owner has attained a certain age. When the older person dies, the tax bill is deducted from the estate.

LIVING ENVIRONMENTS

Being able to view one's immediate surroundings from the windows or doors is an important part of an independent-living environment. As aging continues, this visual surveillance zone increases in importance. Redirecting Medicaid dollars toward at-home programs could be one way to help secure both physical safety and visual surveillance

One of the crucial activities of daily living used to measure independence is the ability to prepare food. (James L. Shaffer)

zones. Also, through the Older Americans Act, the federal government funds a number of multipurpose senior centers for the elderly. Spending time at these centers can be an alternative means of addressing the safety issues and concerns that surface when the visual surveillance zone decreases to an uncomfortable level.

Due to declining physical and mental functioning of elderly members, families sometimes do reach a point where someone must stay at home with a person to assist in an independent-living situation. When a family member is that person, a choice to retire early and to provide needed care in order to minimize nursing and custodial expenses may be made. There are several trade-offs to consider in this decision. If a family member elects early retirement, later financial security may be compromised because a reduction in the years available to work and build up retirement benefits takes place.

Also, the individual might give up a lifestyle that includes friendships of coworkers and increased breadth of interest that comes from employment situations. Often the individual who is in declining physical and mental condition will require nursing home care and the family member living at home is left in a situation with less retirement income and the need to develop new relationships and interests.

HOME SERVICES

Home services to encourage independent living include home-delivered meals, transportation, shopping and escort services, home chore services, friendly visiting, telephone reassurance, and community agencies assisting individuals to remain living independently. Chore services around the home include help with major housecleaning, yard work, and minor home repairs.

Congregate housing complexes provide special apartment environments that provide a supportive environment. Typically, residents have their own apartments. Meals might be provided in a central location as well as providing a variety of services such as laundry, housekeeping, and personal care. Alternative dining arrangements are also available.

Friendly visitors are nonmedical attendants who provide companionship and time-limited supervision. Home-delivered meals (known as meals-on-wheels) provide hot, nutritious meals delivered to an individual's home, usually at lunch. The person delivering the meals also performs an important social role. Home health aides provide personal care and basic health care. The amount of time home health aides are available can vary from twenty-four hours a day to a few hours a week. Finally, a personal emergency response system can be initiated, which when activated places a call for help to an emergency response center. The transmitter is generally worn around the neck or on the wrist. *—Daniel L. Yazak*

See also Caregiving; Children of Aging Parents; Family relationships; Health care; Home ownership; Home services; Housing; Meals-on-wheels programs; Multigenerational households; Nursing and convalescent homes; Retirement communities; Safety issues.

FOR FURTHER INFORMATION:
Barrow, Georgia M. "Living Environments." In *Aging, the Individual, and Society.* 5th ed. St. Paul, Minn.: West, 1992.
Harris, Diana K. *Sociology of Aging.* 2d ed. New York: Harper & Row, 1990.
Herr, John J., and John H. Weakland. *Counseling Elders and Their Families.* New York: Springer, 1979.
Hooyman, Nancy R., and H. Asuman Kiyak. *Social Gerontology: A Multidisciplinary Perspective.* 5th ed. New York: Allyn & Bacon, 1999.
McKenzie, Sheila C. *Aging and Old Age.* Glenville, Ill.: Scott, Foresman, 1980.
Mettler, Molly, and Donald W. Kemper. *Healthwise for Life.* Boise, Idaho: Healthwise, 1992.
Myers, Jane E. *Infusing Gerontological Counseling into Counselor Preparation.* Alexandria, Va.: American Association for Counseling and Development, 1989.

INDIVIDUAL RETIREMENT ACCOUNTS (IRAs)

RELEVANT ISSUES: Economics, work
SIGNIFICANCE: Individual retirement accounts (IRAs) can help provide a more comfortable and secure financial future for aging Americans

The Employee Retirement Income Security Act (ERISA) of 1974 was enacted to protect employee pension rights. It specified certain conditions that a pension plan in the private sector must meet and also made some provision for workers whose employers did not have pension plans. These individuals were encouraged to save for retirement by opening individual retirement accounts (IRAs), which provided tax-sheltered retirement savings. For federal tax purposes, taxpayers could deduct the annual amount deposited to the IRA from their gross incomes for the year. Income tax would be deferred on the deposit and on the earnings of the account until withdrawal. The popularity of this retirement vehicle lies in its simplicity and its benefits.

Under President Ronald Reagan's 1981 tax revisions, the rules were changed to allow any person to open an IRA. Withdrawals before the age of fifty-nine years and six months became generally subject to a penalty tax of 10 percent, and withdrawals had to begin when the account holder reached the age of seventy years and six months. The Tax Reform Act of 1986 limited tax deferrals on IRA contributions to those whose incomes fell below $25,000 for single people and $40,000 for married couples filing joint income-tax returns.

Individuals may establish an IRA account with tax-deferred contributions of $2,000 annually. For an individual with a nonworking spouse who files a joint return, $2,250 may be contributed to an IRA, and this money can be split into two different IRA accounts, one for each spouse. The only stipulation is that the amount contributed to any one account may not exceed $2,000. Any individual covered under another retirement plan is not permitted tax deferrals on the contributions. However, all earnings in the IRA are tax-deferred.

Almost any debt or equity security can be held by the IRA. However, investment brokers and firms typically do not recommend investment in speculative stocks, bonds, or aggressive mutual funds. IRA contributions may not be invested in collectibles, including coins, stamps, rugs, or artwork, with the exception of new gold and silver coins that are issued by the United States government. If any part of an IRA is used to purchase collectibles, that amount is immediately taxed as a premature distribution.

If after reaching the age of seventy years and six months, an individual does not withdraw a sufficient amount annually from an IRA, the Internal Revenue Service (IRS) levies a 50 percent tax on the insufficient withdrawal. The IRS does not want older people leaving their money in an IRA that earns tax-deferred savings. Since at the age of seventy years and six months a man has a life expectancy of twelve years, the IRS requires that one-twelfth of the IRA be withdrawn.

When it comes time for payout, there are two choices. The one almost always chosen is a monthly payout. The individual only pays tax on the annual IRA payout, which is taxed as ordinary income. The alternative is a lump sum payout. However, the IRS taxes the entire lump sum distribution at that time as ordinary income.

In 1998, the federal government introduced a new form of IRA, the Roth IRA. This variant allowed individuals to make contributions out of aftertax dollars (rather than having taxes deferred, as in conventional IRAs), but with all distributions from the accounts being free of taxation; that is, all earnings would be tax-free even though the initial contribution had been taxed. In addition, these accounts have no minimum required distribution and no maximum age at which contributions can be made. Individuals can make a total of $2,000 in qualified contributions to the two types of IRA in each calendar year. The law allowed for "rollovers" of traditional IRAs into the new Roth IRAs.   —*Alvin K. Benson*

See also Employment; 401K plans; Income sources; Pensions; Retirement; Retirement planning.

INFERTILITY

RELEVANT ISSUES: Biology, health and medicine, marriage and dating

SIGNIFICANCE: Aging is accompanied by a progressive decline in the reproductive production of gametes, particularly in women at the menopause, but also in men because of various physiological conditions

As people age, their cells accumulate damage. Although reproductive cells receive greater protection, at least for a time, these germ-line cells ultimately succumb to age-related damage as well, thereby contributing to infertility. The term "infertility" refers to the inability of a couple to conceive a child after at least one year of frequent, unprotected sexual activity together. The lack of fertility can exist in the reproductive physiology of the man, the woman, or both.

Infertility is often confused with the term "impotence," the failure of the male penis to achieve or maintain erection for sexual intercourse. Whereas impotence certainly contributes to infertility and is caused by many of the same factors, infertility involves many different problems with the male and female reproductive physiologies that ultimately prevent the fusion of sperm and egg to form a new individual.

GAMETOGENESIS

Eggs in the female ovaries and sperm in the male testicle are formed by a common process called meiosis, or reduction division. Adult somatic cells are diploid, meaning that they have two copies of each chromosome per cell. Germ-line cells (sperm and egg cells) are haploid, meaning that they have one copy of each chromosome per cell. In humans, the diploid chromosome number in the somatic cells is forty-six, or a pair for each of twenty-three chromosomes. Prior to meiosis in germ-line cells, the deoxyribonucleic acid (DNA) of every chromosome is copied, doubling the chromosome number to ninety-two. When meiosis starts, this single cell proceeds through a series of two meiotic divisions to yield four haploid cells, each containing twenty-three chromosomes.

In the female ovary, one of every four haploid cells produced by meiosis actually becomes an egg. The other three cells degenerate. Egg-producing meiosis is called oogenesis, and through this process an average woman produces about five hundred eggs in her lifetime. A woman's eggs will begin meiosis in her ovaries while she is still a fetus. The eggs are maintained in a suspended, meiotic state for several decades. Beginning at puberty, one egg completes meiosis and becomes ready for possible fertilization once per lunar cycle (about twenty-eight days). These cycles, called menstruation, continue until the menopause (usually by the age of fifty to fifty-five), when the cycles stop permanently.

In the male testicle, sperm are produced continuously throughout the man's life, beginning at puberty. All four haploid cells from each meiosis become fully functional sperm by a process called spermatogenesis. Beyond meiosis, this process compacts each cell, which grows a mitochondrion-rich midpiece for energy production and a long flagellum for propulsion of the sperm. A man's two testicles can produce over one hundred million sperm in just a few days. Sperm production can be maintained at relatively high levels even into later life, although the numbers of sperm decline steadily past age fifty. Furthermore, average worldwide male sperm production across the life span appears to have declined since the 1950's, possibly because of environmental exposure to industrial chemicals.

The meiotic halving of the chromosome number from forty-six to twenty-three in oogenesis and in spermatogenesis has one critical goal: sexual reproduction, in which one haploid sperm carrying twenty-three chromosomes fuses with one haploid egg carrying twenty-three chromosomes. The resulting diploid cell, called a zygote, with forty-six chromosomes, will give rise to all the adult somatic cells of a new individual person.

FEMALE PHYSIOLOGY AND INFERTILITY

Among the major contributors to female infertility are tumors of the reproductive tract, hormonal imbalances, reproductive tract inflammation, ovulation irregularities, increased cervical mucus, persistent infections and sexually transmitted diseases, the menopause, and exposure to certain drugs and environmental chemicals.

The woman's reproductive tract contains two ovaries, each surrounded by an ovarian follicle where one egg completes meiosis about halfway through each menstrual cycle. Under the influence of hormones secreted by the pituitary gland, the follicle completes an egg's oogenesis and then ruptures to release the mature egg into the Fallopian tube. The egg is moved slowly down the few inches of the Fallopian tube by tiny cilia over the course of several days. The egg has a life span of about two days, after which it will die if it is not fertilized. If sexual intercourse occurs and a sperm fertilizes the egg in the Fallopian tube, the resulting zygote begins dividing and implants itself in the endometrium, the nerve- and blood-rich lining of the uterus. The early embryo releases human chorionic gonadotropin, a hormone that stimulates the mother's ovaries to produce the steroid hormone progesterone, whose critical function is to maintain the thick endometrial lining to support the embryo and to maintain the pregnancy. If the egg is not fertilized or if the ovaries do not produce enough progesterone, the endometrium and its contents will be discharged out of the woman's vagina; she will experience menstrual bleeding, and her body will then reset a new cycle to prepare another egg.

Tumors, including both benign cysts and malignant cancers, of the Fallopian tubes and uterus can block both egg and sperm transport, thus causing infertility. Such blockages can be detected by a special X-ray analysis called uterosalpingography.

Hormonal imbalances in the woman's endocrine glands, particularly the pituitary gland and the hypothalamus in the brain, can cause infertility. The pituitary gland releases follicle-stimulating hormone (FSH) and luteinizing hormone (LH), which are essential for egg preparation and release during the menstrual cycle. The hypothalamus controls bodily rhythms and many endocrine glands, including the pituitary. The ovaries produce the steroid hormones estrogen and progesterone, which make a pregnancy possible by building and maintaining the endometrium. Imbalances in any of these hormones would make conception or the maintenance of a pregnancy impossible.

Inflammation of the endometrium or Fallopian tubes can impede both egg and sperm movement. Ovulation irregularities can disrupt or inhibit egg release and can result from a variety of factors, including psychological stress, hormonal imbalances, and exposure to certain drugs and environmental chemicals. Increased mucus and acidic secretions in the cervix and vagina can slow or kill many sperm.

Infections of the female reproductive tract, especially sexually transmitted diseases, can cause infertility and even permanent sterility. Bacteria (such as *Escherichia coli*, a normal inhabitant of the large intestine) and yeast (such as *Candida albicans*) can irritate and inflame the vagina and other parts of the female reproductive tract. Both of the sexually transmitted bacteria *Chlamydia trachomatis* and *Neisseria gonorrhoeae* can cause pelvic inflammatory disease, a condition characterized by pain and severe discomfort in the lower abdominal-pelvic region of the body. Both chlamydia and gonorrhea can inflame the Fallopian tubes, creating difficulty in achieving conception.

Untreated gonorrhea can cause severe accumulation of Fallopian scar tissue that may permanently block the tubes, resulting in sterility. Among sexually transmitted viruses, herpes simplex II, or genital herpes, affects about one out of every five Americans and may contribute to both cervical cancer and sterility. Many individuals infected with genital herpes are unaware of their infection, and the sores in the reproductive tract are highly contagious.

The menopause is the permanent shutdown of the ovaries, usually occurring between ages fifty and fifty-five in most women. Decreasing bodily estrogen levels following the menopause can cause loss of sexual desire in many, but not all, women. The menstrual cycles end, and the linings of the uterus and vagina become

Common Causes of Female Infertility

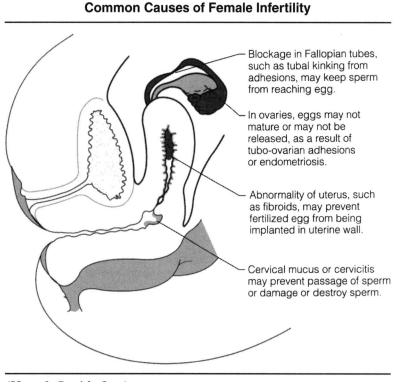

Blockage in Fallopian tubes, such as tubal kinking from adhesions, may keep sperm from reaching egg.

In ovaries, eggs may not mature or may not be released, as a result of tubo-ovarian adhesions or endometriosis.

Abnormality of uterus, such as fibroids, may prevent fertilized egg from being implanted in uterine wall.

Cervical mucus or cervicitis may prevent passage of sperm or damage or destroy sperm.

(Hans & Cassidy, Inc.)

drier, shrinking because of the lack of hormonal stimulation from the pituitary gland and the ovaries. The menopause can sometimes occur prematurely before the age of forty.

Finally, drugs and environmental chemicals that can cause infertility include organic solvents, such as benzene, toluene, and xylene; pharmaceuticals, such as alkylating agents, cimetidine, diethylstilbestrol, and salicylazosulfapyridine; metals, such as boron, cadmium, lead, and mercury; marijuana; alcohol; and tobacco. The heavy use of insecticides on food crops, exposure to chemicals, and improper use of medications can increase the chances of infertility. These drugs and chemicals have similar effects upon the male reproductive system.

MALE PHYSIOLOGY AND INFERTILITY

Major contributors to female infertility that also contribute to male infertility include hormonal imbalances of the hypothalamus and pituitary glands, tumors of the reproductive tract, drugs and environmental chemicals, and infectious and sexually transmitted diseases. Infertility factors that are unique to male physiology include abnormal sperm development, autoimmune disease, damage to the testicles, and the effect of wearing tight-fitting clothing around the scrotum.

A major feature of the male reproductive system is the descent of the two testicles out of the pelvic cavity into the scrotum, a pouch of skin located immediately posterior to the man's penis. This anatomical arrangement is critical to sperm survival because the scrotum keeps the sperm at a temperature about 3 to 4 degrees Celsius cooler than body temperature (37 degrees Celsius), which would kill the sperm. Surrounding each testicle is the epididymis, a follicle-like structure that can store hundreds of millions of sperm. Within the epididymis, specialized nurse cells surround and protect the sperm from attack by the man's own immune system cells.

During sexual intercourse and ejaculation, over one hundred million sperm are rapidly forced from the two epididymi into the vas deferens, two tubes several inches long that coil up into the pelvic cavity and then down to meet at the urethra. In this region, the seminal vesicle, the bulbourethral gland, and the prostate gland release sugar-rich semen to the sperm. The semen protects the sperm and supplies sugar to the sperm mitochondria for

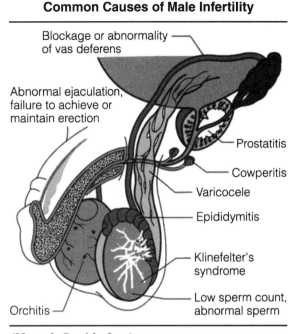

Common Causes of Male Infertility

Blockage or abnormality of vas deferens

Abnormal ejaculation, failure to achieve or maintain erection

Prostatitis

Cowperitis

Varicocele

Epididymitis

Klinefelter's syndrome

Low sperm count, abnormal sperm

Orchitis

(Hans & Cassidy, Inc.)

propulsion of their flagella. The sperm-semen ejaculate exits the man's erect penis through the urethra.

Hormonal imbalances in the hypothalamus or in the pituitary gland hormones can lead to underdeveloped testicles or low sperm count. Simultaneously, low testosterone production by the testicles would inhibit sperm production as well. Tumors, both benign and malignant, can block sperm flow or affect critical production sites. Testicular cancer severely reduces sperm production. Likewise, prostate cancer affects semen production. Surgery for prostate cancer can lead to erectile dysfunction, also known as male impotence. Furthermore, chemotherapy and radiation therapy kill sperm.

Drugs and environmental chemicals that generate infertility in the female reproductive system also can make men infertile. Sexually transmitted gonorrhea can make men sterile. The herpes simplex II virus can produce pus in the urethral tract, which comes from painful sores in the tract. These sores, which can spread the virus to a sexual partner, make urination and erection difficult.

Abnormal sperm development, termed germ-cell dysplasia, in the testicle can produce sperm that are too large, that have abnormal flagella, or that have multiple flagella. Such sperm have considerable motility problems and never reach the egg during intercourse. Autoimmune disorders can damage and destroy many sperm when hyperactive immune-system cells penetrate the protective nurse cells and attack the haploid sperm. Injuries to the testicles caused by severe blows, disease, or surgery can seriously impair the production of sperm. Also, wearing tight clothing can hold the testicles near body temperature, thus killing sperm.

Treating Infertility

Infertility can be a serious emotional issue for couples desiring to have children. A variety of unpredictable, uncontrollable factors in either or both partners may cause of infertility. Facing the reality of infertility involves each partner working with the other and with the family physician, who may suggest several techniques for attacking the condition. Older couples may find discussing sexual matters with a physician to be difficult. However, the basic human sexual drive is important to people, and most physicians are prepared to work with couples facing infertility.

Several assisted reproduction techniques may be used to help couples to conceive. When a woman is infertile, a willing surrogate mother can be artificially inseminated with her mate's donated sperm, carry the child to birth, and then give up the child to the couple. There are occasional legal problems with this approach when the surrogate mother wishes to keep the child. With improving technology, an embryo transfer procedure from the surrogate mother to the infertile woman's uterus may help to alleviate these problems in the future.

When the man is infertile, the woman can be artificially inseminated with sperm from an anonymous donor male. This widespread procedure relies upon the ease of freezing donated sperm in sperm banks for long periods of time. In the case of male impotence, certain medications, such as Viagra, are promising treatments for erectile dysfunction.

A difficult but increasingly viable procedure is in vitro fertilization, in which injected hormones are used to hyperstimulate a woman's ovaries to develop and release eggs. The eggs are collected from the woman's ovary by an instrument called a laparoscope, fertilized by the man's sperm in a culture dish, allowed to grow, and then surgically implanted into the woman's uterus. A modification of this procedure called gamete intrafallopian transfer involves using the laparoscope to reinsert the artificially fertilized eggs into the Fallopian tubes for natural passage and implantation into the uterus.

Finally, many infertile couples choose adoption. Even with the strict confidentiality involved in this approach, legal cases exist in which the biological parents have wished to reclaim the children that they had previously put up for adoption. Nevertheless, adoption is a humane, popular option that has been chosen by tens of thousands of infertile couples.

—*David W. Hollar, Jr.*

See also Biological clock; Childlessness; Impotence; Men and aging; Menopause; Parenthood; Prostate cancer; Reproductive changes, disabilities, and dysfunctions; Sexuality; Women and aging.

For Further Information:

Aiman, James, ed. *Infertility: Diagnosis and Management.* New York: Springer-Verlag, 1984. This work includes numerous contributions from experts on infertility, including chapters on pituitary disorders and environmental agents affecting fertility.

Gaudin, Anthony J., and Kenneth C. Jones. *Human Anatomy and Physiology.* San Diego: Harcourt Brace Jovanovich, 1989. This premedical textbook includes chapters on female and male reproductive systems, diseases, and disorders.

Marieb, Elaine. *Human Anatomy and Physiology.* 4th ed. Menlo Park, Calif.: Benjamin/Cummings, 1998. This comprehensive premedical textbook contains chapters on reproduction and development with a good discussion of infertility treatments.

Stanton, Annette L., and Christine Dunkel-Schetter, eds. *Infertility: Perspectives from Stress and Coping Research.* New York: Plenum Press, 1991. This compilation of infertility studies examines both the causes of infertility and methods for helping infertile couples emotionally.

Starr, Cecie, and Ralph Taggart. *Biology: The Unity and Diversity of Life.* 8th ed. Belmont, Calif.: Wadsworth, 1998. This popular, comprehensive introductory biology textbook includes two chapters on reproduction and development, as well as detailed information on sexually transmitted diseases and agents that affect fertility.

Winston, Robert M. L. *What We Know About Infertility: Diagnosis and Treatment Alternatives*. New York: Free Press, 1987. This book identifies various causes of infertility and presents techniques for helping infertile couples to conceive.

INFLUENZA

RELEVANT ISSUES: Health and medicine

SIGNIFICANCE: Influenza is a common illness that annually causes a significant number of deaths among the elderly; effective prevention and treatment methods are underutilized

Influenza is a respiratory infection caused by the influenza virus. Although many viral illnesses are commonly referred to as influenza, or "the flu," true influenza has a characteristic set of symptoms. Influenza is characterized by muscle aches (myalgias), fever (up to 39.4 degrees Celsius or 103 degrees Fahrenheit), cough, pain behind the eyes, laryngitis, and headache. Gastrointestinal symptoms such as nausea or diarrhea are generally not associated with true influenza. Periods of weakness and depression may be associated with influenza, and bacterial pneumonia may follow it. Influenza usually lasts from three to seven days, and most cases in the United States occur from late December through March.

CAUSE AND SPREAD

The term "influenza" was derived four hundred years ago from an Italian word for "influenced by the stars." This term was coined because of the seasonality of influenza; it was thought that influenza epidemics were influenced by the alignments of certain stars and planets. The influenza virus is spread via exhaled droplets or hand-to-hand contact. There are three strains of influenza viruses: A, B, and C. Strains A and B account for the majority of cases of severe influenza; strain C usually produces a mild form of the disease. Influenza can be deadly. It causes thousands of deaths annually in the United States, primarily among the elderly and people with chronic illnesses.

A drastic change in the structure of the influenza virus can cause a widespread outbreak, called a pandemic. The most-famous influenza pandemic was the Spanish flu of 1918-1919, which killed about twenty-two million people worldwide. Other worldwide influenza outbreaks include the Asian flu of 1957 and the Hong Kong flu of 1968. Influenza can also be found in other animals, including birds and pigs. In 1976, an outbreak of a virus found in pigs which was similar to the deadly Spanish flu virus caused U.S. health officials to vaccinate people against the "swine flu" virus. After several vaccine recipients contracted a rare nerve disorder called Guillain-Barré syndrome, the vaccine program was canceled. The feared "swine flu" pandemic never materialized.

PREVENTION AND TREATMENT

Prevention of influenza includes appropriate use of an influenza vaccine, good handwashing techniques, and cough control to prevent the spread of the virus via aerosol droplets. A bout of influenza confers temporary immunity, but only against the specific virus that caused the infection. An influenza vaccine is 70 to 90 percent effective in providing immunity for six months or longer. The A and B strains of the influenza viruses undergo periodic changes in their genetic structure, mandating annual changes in the influenza vaccine (flu shot).

Annually, manufacturers develop vaccines to protect against the three types of influenza most likely to be found during the current "flu season." The vaccine is recommended for people over the age of sixty-five, those people with chronic illnesses, and "essential" people—firefighters, police officers, and health care professionals. The purpose of the vaccination program is to protect those at greatest risk of death during an influenza outbreak (the elderly and ill) and to protect vital services (fire, police, and medical services).

Influenza vaccine generally becomes available in every October or November, confers immunity in two weeks, and can be given any time during the flu season. Side effects, which are relatively uncommon, are usually mild fever and mild muscle aches. Even though the influenza vaccine and associated medications could prevent hundreds or thousands of deaths in the United States each year, it is estimated that fewer than 50 percent of the susceptible population is protected by either vaccine or medication.

Treatment includes proper amounts of fluids, analgesics for pain relief, and bed rest. For people who contract influenza A, amantadine (Symmetrel) or rimantidine (Fluradine) can be used to shorten and decrease the severity of symptoms. These drugs can also be given during the flu season to those who cannot take the vaccine because of allergy, in order to give some protection from influenza A.

—*Paul M. Paulman*

See also Health care; Hospitalization; Illnesses among the elderly; Immunizations and boosters.

FOR FURTHER INFORMATION:

Barker, William H., Hannah Borisute, and Christopher Cox. "A Study of the Impact of Influenza on the Functional Status of Frail Older People." In *What to Do About Flu*, edited by the National Institute on Aging. Bethesda, Md.: U.S. Department of Health and Human Services, Public Health Service, National Institutes of Health, 1994.

Krug, Robert M., ed. *The Influenza Viruses*. New York: Plenum Press, 1989.

Nicholson, Karl G., Robert G. Webster, and Alan J. Hay, eds. *Textbook of Influenza*. Malden, Mass.: Blackwell Science, 1998.

Peters, S. "Flu Prevention and Management: Strategies for the Elderly." *Advance for Nurse Practitioners* 5, no. 10 (October, 1997): 57-59.

Simonsen, Lone. "The Impact of Influenza Epidemics on Mortality: Introducing a Severity Index." *American Journal of Public Health* 87, no. 12 (December, 1997): 1944-1950.

Taylor, Robert B., ed. *Family Medicine: Principles and Practice*. 5th ed. New York: Springer, 1998.

Van Hartesveldt, Fred R., ed. *The 1918-1919 Pandemic of Influenza: The Urban Impact on the Western World*. Lewiston, N.Y.: E. Mellen Press, 1992.

INHERITANCE. *See* ESTATES AND INHERITANCE.

INJURIES AMONG THE ELDERLY

RELEVANT ISSUES: Health and medicine

SIGNIFICANCE: As people age, they tend to become more prone to injuries; such injuries often constitute a threat to the elderly person's health and functional abilities

Accidents are the seventh leading cause of death in people over the age of sixty-five and the fifth leading cause of death in those over the age of eighty-five. When such accidents do not result in death, they may lead to serious threats to the person's health and functional abilities. Because elderly people often fear a recurrence of injury, accidents may cause a decrease in physical and social activity, as well as a loss of confidence.

INJURIES FROM FALLING

Falls are the most frequent cause of injury among the elderly. Those people over eighty years of age have a mortality rate from falls eight times greater than people sixty years of age. Falls are the major risk factor for hip fractures; approximately 200,000 hip fractures occur each year in the United States, 12 to 20 percent of which lead to death. Only one-fourth of older adults who sustain a hip fracture fully recover. Elderly people who suffer from osteoporosis have a greater chance of sustaining fractures of the hips, wrist, pelvis, and lumbar vertebra. The loss of skin elasticity and subcutaneous tissue that generally accompanies aging can also lead to bruising and skin tears.

Although most falls occur when a person is descending a stairway, they may be caused by numerous factors in the home, including unstable furniture, loose floor coverings, poor lighting in hallways and bathrooms, clutter, pets, and slick substances on the floor, such as polish, ice, water, or grease. The use of certain medications may also cause the elderly to fall. Some diuretics, sedatives, antibiotics, antidepressants, and antipsychotics can cause drowsiness, confusion, or dizziness. Physical changes that accompany the aging process can also make people more susceptible to sustaining injuries from falls. Vision and hearing may become impaired, leading to changes in perception. Reflexes may become slower. Vertigo and syncope episodes may cause falls. Mental changes, such as depression and inattention, can also cause falls in the elderly.

Medical experts advise elderly people to take precautions against falls. People who do not have good balance are often advised to wear shoes with a soft sole and a low, broad heel. High heels, loose-fitting slippers, or socks without shoes on stairs or waxed floors should be avoided. In addition, tennis shoes that have good traction can cause people to trip. Elderly people with poor night vision can use bedside lamps or night-lights in case they have to get up in the middle of the night. Those prone to dizziness are advised to stand up slowly to avoid vertigo. Keeping the thermostat at 65 degrees Fahrenheit or above at night can help people avoid the drowsiness that tends to accompany prolonged exposure to cold temperatures.

Another way to prevent falls is to keep walkways free of clutter and to keep electrical and phone cords out of the way. Low furniture can be positioned so it is not an obstacle to people when walking. White paint or white strips on the edges of steps can help elderly people see them better. The risk of falls in the kitchen can be minimized by placing frequently used items in accessible cupboards to avoid reaching, bending, or stooping, and by covering tile or linoleum floors with nonskid wax. In the bathroom, grab bars can be installed on the wall by the tub, shower, and toilet, while nonskid mats or adhesive strips can be placed on all surfaces that can get wet and slippery.

Exercise can also help minimize the risk of injury from falls. Such activities as walking, gardening, and housework can improve gait, posture, and balance. Weight-bearing exercise, such as walking, helps prevent loss of bone mass, as well as stiffness and loss of muscle tone. Lifting small weights can prevent loss of muscle tone and help strengthen hand grip, both of which are important for holding on to railings and properly executing such tasks as getting up from chairs.

Elderly people who fear falling may decrease their activity level, which causes their muscles to deteriorate even more. The fear of falling can also make them clinically depressed, which often shortens their attention span and makes them more likely to fall. This is especially true if they have fallen before and have sustained an injury or fracture.

POISONING AND CHOKING

Decreases in visual acuity may make some elderly people susceptible to taking poison that might be on a shelf or in the medicine cabinet, especially the wrong medication. Because of the poor eyesight, they may use something in their eyes for eye drop medication when in reality it is some other type of fluid that can damage the eyes or cause blindness.

The elderly need to take special care during the recovery process after an injury because their bones and tissues do not heal as quickly or completely as in younger individuals. (PhotoDisc)

Decreases in the sense of smell and taste may lead people to eat spoiled food or inhale toxic fumes from substances in the home. Decreased gag and swallowing reflex may lead to choking, which can be fatal for someone who lives alone and dies before help arrives. Poorly fitted dentures, poor dental hygiene, or other factors that make chewing difficult may also increase the risk of choking.

BURNS AND INJURIES FROM EXTREME HEAT AND COLD

Burns account for 8 percent of the accidental deaths among the elderly. Burn injuries are most commonly caused by scalds from hot baths, showers, or fluids on the stove; flames from the ignition of clothing or flammable liquids; and house fires. A large percentage of fires started by elderly people are caused by the use of electrical equipment for cooking and heating and by careless smoking. The danger posed by fire is even greater among those elderly people who have a decreased sense of smell and therefore cannot detect smoke or the odor of leaking gas.

Elderly people are often susceptible to temperature extremes. Those without air conditioning may be overcome by heat during the summer months. Diminished sense of thirst may lead to dehydration. In the winter, some elderly people may not be able to afford to heat their homes properly. Low body temperatures can lead to hypothermia, particularly among those who do not eat well enough to provide the energy necessary for the body to stay warm. The problem is exacerbated by the fact that aging reduces the body's percentage of subcutaneous tissue, which helps keep the body warm.

TRAFFIC ACCIDENTS AND CRIME

Approximately 25 percent of accidental deaths in people over sixty-five years of age are from motor vehicle accidents. Among the physiological changes that increase the risk of accidents are poor depth perception, decreased response time, sensory impairment, and alterations in musculoskeletal, nervous, and cardiovascular systems. Despite these changes, many elderly people continue to drive in order to maintain a certain degree of independence. Traffic injuries may also be sustained by pedestrians who step off the curb into traffic, often because they do not see well or hear the cars. Declining perceptions may decrease a person's ability to judge the speed and distance of approaching traffic.

The elderly are more likely to be attacked by strangers than other age groups. The reason is their vulnerability. Many poor elderly people depend on public transportation and live in high-crime neighborhoods. Many lack the physical strength to defend themselves, while others suffer from poor eyesight and may not be able to identify their attacker. An attack can cause physical damage—such as broken bones, heart and respiratory failure, or head injuries—and can also cause serious damage to pride and self-esteem. Victims may become so fearful of another attack that they will not leave their homes, even to buy food or get medical care. —*Mitzie L. Bryant*

See also Back disorders; Balance disorders; Bunions; Canes and walkers; Disabilities; Driving; Exercise and fitness; Fallen arches; Foot disorders; Fractures and broken bones; Hammertoes; Hip replacement; Hospitalization; Medications; Mobility problems; Osteoporosis; Reaction time; Safety issues; Sensory changes; Sports participation; Temperature regulation and sensitivity; Violent crime against the elderly; Vision changes and disorders; Wheelchair use.

FOR FURTHER INFORMATION:

Barrow, Georgia M. *Aging, the Individual, and Society.* 6th ed. St. Paul, Minn.: West, 1996. Barrow discusses demographics, the effect aging has on society, and the influence aging has on the health of the individual.

Burkes, Mary M., and Mary B. Walsh. *Gerontologic Nursing.* 2d ed. St. Louis: Mosby, 1997. The authors discuss problems of the elderly, along with causes and prevention.

DeWit, Susan C. *Keanes Essentials of Medical-Surgical Nursing.* 3d ed. Philadelphia: W. B. Saunders, 1992. DeWit provides information on fractures, accidents, and burns in the elderly and how to prevent them.

Murray, Ruth B., and Judith P. Zenter. *Health Assessment and Promotion Strategies Through the Life Span.* 6th ed. Stamford, Conn.: Appleton & Lange, 1997. Provides insight on contributing factors and prevention of injuries in the elderly.

Rosdahl, Caroline Bunker. *Textbook of Basic Nursing.* 6th ed. Philadelphia: J. B. Lippincott, 1995. Discusses the normal physical signs of aging that can be associated with and contribute to injuries.

Solomon, Jacqueline. "Osteoporosis: When Supports Weaken." *RN* 61 (May, 1998). Solomon provides useful information on a condition of the bone common among the aged that causes fractures and weak muscles.

Walker, Bonnie L. "Preventing Falls." *RN* 61 (May, 1998). Walker discusses the likelihood of falls in the elderly and how to keep the risk at a minimum.

AGING

LIST OF ENTRIES BY CATEGORY

CULTURAL ISSUES

Advertising
African Americans
Ageism
American Indians
Asian Americans
Baby boomers
Beauty
Communication
Cultural views of aging
Films
Gay men and lesbians
Grandparenthood
Great-grandparenthood
Greeting cards
Internet
Jewish services for the elderly
Latinos
Leisure activities
Maturity
Men and aging
Middle age
National Asian Pacific Center on Aging
National Caucus and Center on Black Aged
National Hispanic Council on Aging
Old age
Over the hill
Parenthood
Religion
Stereotypes
Television
Women and aging

DEATH AND DYING

Acquired immunodeficiency syndrome (AIDS)
Breast cancer
Cancer
Cocoon
Death and dying
Death anxiety
Death of a child
Death of parents
Depression
Durable power of attorney
Estates and inheritance
Euthanasia
Funerals
Grief

Harold and Maude
Heart attacks
Hospice
I Never Sang for My Father
"Jilting of Granny Weatherall, The"
Kübler-Ross, Elisabeth
Life expectancy
Living wills
Memento Mori
Pets
Prostate cancer
Psychiatry, geriatric
Remarriage
Robin and Marian
Shootist, The
Stress and coping skills
Strokes
Suicide
Tell Me a Riddle
Terminal illness
Trusts
Widows and widowers
Wills and bequests
Woman's Tale, A

EMPLOYMENT ISSUES

Absenteeism
Adult education
Age discrimination
Age Discrimination Act of 1975
Age Discrimination in Employment Act of 1967
Americans with Disabilities Act
Dual-income couples
Early retirement
Employment
Executive Order 11141
Forced retirement
Job loss
Johnson v. Mayor and City Council of Baltimore
Massachusetts Board of Retirement v. Murgia
Matlock
Mentoring
Murder, She Wrote
Older Americans Act of 1965
Older Workers Benefit Protection Act
Retired Senior Volunteer Program (RSVP)
Retirement
Retirement planning

Dental disorders
Dentures
Depression
Diabetes
Disabilities
Durable power of attorney
Emphysema
Estrogen replacement therapy
Euthanasia
Exercise and fitness
Face lifts
Fallen arches
Fat deposition
Foot disorders
Forgetfulness
Fractures and broken bones
Free radical theory of aging
Gastrointestinal changes and disorders
Genetics
Geriatrics and gerontology
Glaucoma
Gout
Gray hair
Hair loss and baldness
Hammertoes
Health care
Hearing aids
Hearing loss
Heart attacks
Heart changes
Heart disease
Hip replacement
Hospice
Hospitalization
Hypertension
Illnesses among the elderly
Immunizations and boosters
Impotence
Incontinence
Infertility
Influenza
Injuries among the elderly
Kyphosis
Life expectancy
Living wills
Long-term care for the elderly
Longevity research
Macular degeneration
Malnutrition
Medical insurance

Medicare
Medications
Memory changes and loss
Menopause
Mental impairment
Mobility problems
Multiple sclerosis
Nearsightedness
Nutrition
Obesity
Osteoporosis
Overmedication
Parkinson's disease
Pneumonia
Premature aging
Prostate cancer
Prostate enlargement
Reaction time
Reading glasses
Reproductive changes, disabilities, and
    dysfunctions
Respiratory changes
Rhinophyma
Safety issues
Sarcopenia
Sensory changes
Skin cancer
Skin changes and disorders
Sleep changes and disturbances
Smoking
Stones
Strokes
Temperature regulation and sensitivity
Terminal illness
Thyroid disorders
Urinary disorders
Varicose veins
Vision changes and disorders
Vitamins and minerals
Weight loss and gain
Wheelchair use
Wrinkles

HOUSING ISSUES

Age discrimination
Empty nest syndrome
Full nest
Home services
Homelessness
Housing

Virtues of Aging, The
Why Survive? Being Old in America

Television
Golden Girls, The
Matlock
Murder, She Wrote
Television

MEN'S ISSUES
Aging process
Cancer
Cultural views of aging
Death and dying
Divorce
Early retirement
Employment
Erikson, Erik H.
Genetics
Grumpy Old Men
Harry and Tonto
Heart attacks
Heart changes and disorders
Heart disease
Home ownership
Hypertension
I Never Sang for My Father
Impotence
King Lear
Life expectancy
Longevity research
Marriage
Matlock
Men and aging
Middle age
Midlife crisis
Old age
Old Man and the Sea, The
Pensions
Prostate cancer
Prostate enlargement
Remarriage
Reproductive changes, disabilities, and
    dysfunctions
Retirement
Rhinophyma
Sexuality
Smoking
Sports participation
Stress and coping skills

Strokes
Urinary disorders
Widows and widowers
Wild Strawberries

ORGANIZATIONS AND PROGRAMS
Adult Protective Services
Alzheimer's Association
American Association of Retired Persons (AARP)
American Society on Aging
Center for the Study of Aging
Children of Aging Parents
Gerontological Society of America
Gray Panthers
Jewish services for the elderly
Little Brothers-Friends of the Elderly
Meals-on-wheels programs
Medicare
National Asian Pacific Center on Aging
National Caucus and Center on Black Aged
National Council of Senior Citizens
National Council on the Aging
National Hispanic Council on Aging
National Institute on Aging
Older Women's League (OWL)
Retired Senior Volunteer Program (RSVP)
Social Security

PEOPLE
Erikson, Erik H.
Kübler-Ross, Elisabeth
Kuhn, Maggie
Neugarten, Bernice
Sarton, May
Sheehy, Gail

PSYCHOLOGICAL ISSUES
Alzheimer's disease
Beauty
Biological clock
Creativity
Death and dying
Death anxiety
Death of a child
Death of parents
Dementia
Depression
Empty nest syndrome
Forgetfulness
Full nest

Grief
Hospice
Humor
Loneliness
Maturity
Memory changes and loss
Mental impairment
Midlife crisis
Over the hill
Personality changes
Psychiatry, geriatric
Sexuality
Stereotypes
Stress and coping skills
Successful aging
Suicide
Widows and widowers
Wisdom

SOCIAL ISSUES

Abandonment
Advertising
Advocacy
African Americans
Age discrimination
Ageism
Aging: Biological, psychological, and
    sociocultural perspectives
Aging: Historical perspective
American Indians
Asian Americans
Baby boomers
Caregiving
Centenarians
Communication
Consumer issues
Demographics
Driving
Elder abuse
Films
Friendship
Funerals
Geriatrics and gerontology
Graying of America
Greeting cards
Home services
Homelessness
Hospice
Housing
Humor

Independent living
Internet
Laguna Woods, California
Latinos
Leisure activities
Life expectancy
Long-term care for the elderly
Longevity research
Men and aging
Middle age
Neglect
Nursing and convalescent homes
Old age
Pets
Politics
Relocation
Retirement communities
Senior citizen centers
Social ties
Sports participation
Television
Townsend movement
Transportation issues
Vacations and travel
Violent crime against the elderly
Voting patterns
Women and aging

WOMEN'S ISSUES

Ageism
Aging Experience: Diversity and Commonality Across
    Cultures, The
All About Eve
Beauty
Breast cancer
Breast changes and disorders
Caregiving
Cosmetic surgery
Cultural views of aging
Demographics
Divorce
Dual-income couples
Employment
Empty nest syndrome
Estrogen replacement therapy
Face lifts
Family relationships
Fountain of Age, The
Golden Girls, The
In Full Flower: Aging Women, Power, and Sexuality